GHOSTS: LIFE AND
DEATH IN NORTH INDIA

RUTH S. FREED

Research Associate, Department of Anthropology
American Museum of Natural History

STANLEY A. FREED

Curator, Department of Anthropology
American Museum of Natural History

ANTHROPOLOGICAL PAPERS OF

THE AMERICAN MUSEUM OF NATURAL HISTORY

Number 72, 396 pages, 10 figures

Issued September 7, 1993

ISSN 0065-9452

ISBN 0-295-97303-X

CONTENTS

ABSTRACT 8
INTRODUCTION 8
   Acknowledgments 10
Chapter 1: The Village Setting 11
Chapter 2: Basis for the Study of Ghost Beliefs 15
   Definitions of Ghost Illness, Ghost Possession, and Poltergeist Attack 17
Chapter 3: Fieldwork, Techniques, and Problems 18
Chapter 4: Brief History of the Delhi Region 21
Chapter 5: Causes of Death 24
   War and Other Turbulence 25
   Famine 26
   Disease 28
Chapter 6: Deaths of Females and the Favored Status of Males 32
   Biomedical Differences 33
   Sati 34
   Female Infanticide 37
   Female Feticide 41
   Dowry and Other Murders, and Suicides 43
   Infant and Maternal Mortality 43
Chapter 7: Health Culture 44
   Prevedic Age 45
   Vedic Age 46
   Ayurveda 46
      Laws of Manu and Hereditary Diseases 49
      The Arya Samaj 49
   Islamic Period 49
   Western Influences 51
Chapter 8: Ideology: Sanatan Dharma, Arya Samaj, Eclecticism 54
Chapter 9: Ideological Interviews 58
   Life, Death, Soul 61
   Action, Rebirth, Release 63
Chapter 10: Fruit of Action, Fate, Discipline 70
   Believers and Nonbelievers 72
   Fence Sitter's Ambivalence 72
   Jat Viewpoints 74
   Discussion in a Chamar *Baithak* 74
   Jat Children 76
Chapter 11: Ghosthood 80
   Ancient Traditions 80
   Pan-Indic Beliefs 81
   Village Terms for Ghosts 82
   Becoming a Ghost 84
Chapter 12: Merchant, Muslim, Priest 86

Old Priest's Autobiography 86
The Legend of Merchant and Muslim Ghost 89
Merchant's Descendants 91
Dead Issue 92
Death of Old Priest 93
Raconteur, His Brothers, and Their Families 95
The Families of Progenitor and Gentle Soul 98
Chapter 13: Old Fever 103
Fever, Old Fever, Tuberculosis 103
Two Branches of Old Fever 104
Senior Branch 104
    Politico 106
    The Tuberculosis Scourge 107
    Troubled 109
Junior Branch 113
    Deaths of Little Boy and Scapegoat 114
    Old Codger, Barker, and Mrs. Barker 115
    Reformer and Family 118
    Curmudgeon, Cattleman, Soldier, and Families 120
A Group Discussion 122
Comparison of the Merchant-Muslim-Priest and Old-Fever Lineages 125
Chapter 14: Death of Children 126
Pregnancy, Deaths of Infants and Children, and Ghosts 126
Death: Terms, Times, Causes, and Cases 127
Sad Memories 131
The Ghost of Cat Woman 131
Death on Mother Sixth 132
The Medical Childbirth Survey 132
Two Tragic Deaths 133
Daughter-in-Law vs. Mother-in-Law 133
A Ghost Took My Son 134
The Ghost of Whose Daughter 141
The Boy Had To Die 144
Chapter 15: Death of Adults 148
Homicides 148
Case Histories: Murders and Manslaughter 149
    Tippler's First Wife 150
    Little Bride 156
    Illusion's Death 159
    Brother vs. Brother 162
    Jats vs. Brahmans 164
    Chamars vs. Chamars 166
Case Histories: Suicides and Questionable Deaths 167
    Rule of Authority 168
    Breakdown and His Three Wives 170

    Murder Or Suicide 170
    An Attempted Murder Or Suicide.. 172
    A Maternity Death 172
  Discussion... 173
Chapter 16: The Headless Sweeper in a Line of Hereditary Exorcists.......... 176
  The Beheaded 178
  Old Survivor 180
  Lord of Ghosts... 182
    Life and Family History 182
    Techniques for Curing the Evil Eye and Ghost Possession 182
    Family Jealousies and Sorcery 184
    Jealousy, Paranoia, and Folie à Deux 187
  Finale... 189
Chapter 17: Illusionist, a Self-Selected Exorcist 190
  Early History 190
  Learning to be an Exorcist 194
  Illusionist's Curing and Interviewing Techniques 196
  Illusionist's Patients 199
  Illusionist as Exorcist 201
  Comments.. 202
Chapter 18: The Health Network 203
  Brahmans as Exorcists and Curers 204
  A Jat *Vaid* and Miscellaneous Curers.................................. 206
  Nai Barbers: Technician, Dresser, and Practitioner of Popular Pharmaceutical
    Medicine 206
  Chamars as Bhagats and Users of Bhagats 207
  Mullahs from Palam.. 208
  Villagers as Exorcists and Exorcism 208
Chapter 19: Three Wives and Four Husbands 211
  Honesty and Moneylender 212
  Old Soldier 215
  Manipulator and Family 217
  Close Mouth, Fomenter, and Driven Mad 220
  Forthright's Marriage 222
  Mrs. Manipulator and Children 223
  Mrs. Manipulator's Possessions 225
  Manipulator's Daughters 226
  College Man, City Girl, and Tricky.................................... 227
  City Girl's Possessions 229
  Group Session 232
Chapter 20: First and Second Wives.. 235
  The Bairagis: Fearful, Handsome, and Delicate Flower 235
  The Lohar Blacksmiths: Sorrowful and Difficult 241
  The Potters and The Lady.. 246
  Summation 249

Chapter 21: Breakup of Old Brahman Lane 251
  The Joint Family of the Three Brothers...................................... 251
  Withdrawn's Possessions in 1959 254
  The Lineage of Old Grandfather 257
  Relocation of Members of Joint Family of Senior, Withdrawn, and Junior 258
  Mrs. Doctor John, Polio, and Karma 260
  Gabbler and Student Doctor... 262
  Withdrawn's Interview.. 264
  New Brahman Lane 268
  Mrs. Earnest 268
  Beauty 270
  Comments.. 271
Chapter 22: Ghost Attacks and Possessions of Jats 273
  Widows, Patriarchs, Twins 274
    Resourceful, Only Heir, and Matriarch 274
    The Benevolents 275
    The Patriarchs 275
    Beloved 276
    Mrs. Patriarch and the Health Opinion Survey 277
    Pragmatic and Morning Star... 278
    Possible Disease Factors in Patriarch's Family......................... 281
  Farmer.. 282
  Little Goddess 289
  Summary of Jat Cases 290
Chapter 23: Hairless, Haunted, Immature... 291
  Immature's Possessions 291
  Immature and Sita 297
  Hairless and Haunted 300
  Haunted... 301
Chapter 24: Ghost Possessions in the Four Stages of the Life Cycle 305
  Stage 1: Survival in Childhood 306
  Stage 2: Coping with Coming of Age 307
  Stage 3: Midlife Crises 308
  Stage 4: The Wear and Tear of Age 309
Chapter 25: Conclusion 310
REFERENCES.. 315
APPENDIX I: DISEASE... 330
  Introduction 330
  History.. 331
  Discoveries 332
  Descriptions 338
APPENDIX II: SACRED HINDU TEXTS 347
APPENDIX III: KINSHIP CHARTS 352
  Introduction 352
  Coding 353

Connected Charts for Merchant, Muslim, Priest 354
    Chart 1.1: Merchant, Muslim, Priest: Ancestral Generations 354
    Chart 1.2: Merchant, Muslim, Priest: Raconteur, His Brothers, Their Families,
        and Descendants 355
    Chart 1.3: Merchant, Muslim, Priest: Progenitor, Gentle Soul, Their Families,
        and Descendants 355
    Chart 1.4: Merchant, Muslim, Priest: Dead Issue, End of a Line of Descent 356
Connected Charts for Old Fever 356
    Chart 2.1: Old Fever: Ancestral Generations 357
    Chart 2.2: Old Fever: Senior Branch of Lineage 357
    Chart 2.3: Old Fever: Junior Branch of Lineage 358
    Chart 3: A Ghost Took My Son 359
    Chart 4: The Newcomers.. 359
    Chart 5: The Headless Sweeper in a Line of Hereditary Exorcists 360
    Chart 6: Three Wives and Four Husbands 361
    Chart 7: The Bairagis: Watchman, Fearful, Handsome, and Delicate Flower 361
    Chart 8: The Lohar Blacksmiths: Sorrowful and Difficult 362
    Chart 9: The Potters and the Lady 362
    Chart 10.1: Breakup of Old Brahman Lane: Lineage of the Three Brothers
        and Old Bachelor 363
    Chart 10.2: Breakup of Old Brahman Lane: Lineage of Old Grandfather 364
    Chart 11: Widows, Patriarchs, Twins 365
    Chart 12: Hairless, Haunted, Immature.. 366
APPENDIX IV: MAPS 367
    Map 1: Properties of the Two Lineages in 1958–59: Old Fever and
        Merchant, Muslim, Priest 367
    Map 2: Properties of the Two Lineages in 1977–78: Old Fever and
        Merchant, Muslim, Priest 368
    Map 3: Dwelling of Truthful and Teacher Described in "A Ghost Took My Son" .. 369
    Map 4: Crossroads, Pond, Cremation Grounds, Buildings, and Other Places
        Associated with Ghosts 370
APPENDIX V: CALENDRIC EVENTS 373
APPENDIX VI: THE HEALTH OPINION SURVEY (HOS) 377
APPENDIX VII: DAILY TEMPERATURES, MARCH–APRIL 1978 379
INDEX AND GLOSSARY 380
TABLES

    Table 1: Population of Shanti Nagar by Caste in 1958–59 and 1977–78 13
    Table 2: Births and Deaths of Children, Jan. 1958–June 1959 130
    Table 3: Yearly Cycle of Calendric Events 374
    Table 4: Health Opinion Survey (HOS) Selected Scores........................ 378

FIGURES

    1. Village street 13
    2. Subzi Mandi 14

  3. Cremation 78

  4. Ancestor shrine 90

  5. Guga Pir 98

  6. Hoi Mata 132

  7. Village well.. 167

  8. Brahman woman making offerings 193

  9. Exorcism... 198

10. Altar design 224

The cover depicts Yama, God of Death, in his fearful form with dark green skin and glowing red eyes riding a black buffalo and accompanied by his two four-eyed dogs. He wears a crown of flames and carries a mace with a death's-head carved on it and a noose for seizing his victims' souls and carrying them away.

ABSTRACT

This monograph is the ninth of a series devoted to the description and analysis of life in Shanti Nagar, a village in the Union Territory of Delhi. Our research is based on holistic fieldwork carried out in 1957–59 and 1977–1978. Previous monographs, all published in the *Anthropological Papers of the American Museum of Natural History*, have dealt with social organization, economics, rites of passage, fertility and sterilization, elections, sickness and health, enculturation and education, and ghosts in the context of a woman's psychomedical case history. The present monograph places ghost illness, ghost possession, and poltergeist attacks in an historical, psychological, ecological, medical, ideological, and holistic ethnographic context. A descriptive and comparative case-study method is central to the analysis. Among the ghost-related topics that are covered are beliefs; causes; gender, age and caste distribution; sectarian differences (the Arya Samaj vs. Sanatan Dharma); and the recruitment, training, and methods of exorcists and curers.

INTRODUCTION

Our first analysis of ghost beliefs in Shanti Nagar (S. Freed and R. Freed, 1964) was based on four cases that we recorded in 1958–59. We were able greatly to expand our database during our second trip owing to an epidemic of ghost possession that took place in 1977–78. Moreover, during that trip we obtained a long finely detailed psychomedical case history of a Chamar Leatherworker woman, one of whose possessions we observed in 1958–59. For a number of years, she suffered from ghost possession and later, from fits. This case history was the basis of our second publication dealing at length with ghosts and possession (R. Freed and S. Freed, 1985). In the 1964 article, we identified the Chamar woman by the pseudonym Daya. The pseudonym of Sita was used for the same woman in the 1985 monograph and is retained in the present study. The current monograph is our most comprehensive analysis of ghost beliefs and their historical, mythological, social, economic, medical, and psychological concomitants. It is based on thousands of pages of fieldnotes buttressed by extensive library research, especially about ghost beliefs, alternate states of consciousness, and stress, and a careful reexamination of village terms regarding ghosts. For us as anthropologists, this research has been an enriching exploration of human behavior.

Some place names and geographical expressions have changed in recent decades. The new spelling of Dhaka, instead of Dacca, is now well established. Varanasi, sometimes called Kashi by the villagers, has replaced Benares or its variants, i.e., Banaras. In the older literature, Punjab was frequently preceded by the definite article, as "in the Punjab." Modern usage drops the article, thus "in Punjab." We have compromised, tending to use the article when writing of pre-Independence India and dropping it when the reference is to modern times. We use the older Rajputana instead of Rajasthan in appropriate historical context.

Delhi includes two cities, Old Delhi and New Delhi, and also can mean Delhi Union Territory in some contexts. We use the phrase, "City of Delhi," to refer to the undifferentiated city as distinct from the union territory or region of Delhi. Old Delhi and New Delhi are used when greater precision is appropriate.

Throughout this monograph it has been necessary to use a sprinkling of Hindi words. Only those words which are not in Webster's Unabridged Dictionary (Gove, 1986) are italicized. We generally use the English "s" at the end of an italicized word to form the plural.

To mask the identity of individuals and yet emphasize the importance of individuals in culture, we have given them pseudonyms. In this text we have chosen English pseudonyms (with the exception of the Indian pseudonyms of Sita and her cousin, Taraka) to make it easier for a non-Indian reader to remember the principal characters than would be the case with the two other common styles of pseudonyms: replacement of the true name by another Indian name or by initials. Many pseudonyms identify a characteristic of an individual, for example, occupation. We have tried to avoid pseudonyms that are inappropriately pejorative. However, some individuals are characterized by behavior or personality traits that are generally known. In such cases, we sometimes base a pseudonym on the behavior, for example, "Tippler" for a notorious drinker. Such pseudonyms do not compromise anonymity since the behavior is not unique. Tippler was not the only drinker. Where the same pseudonym is applicable to more than one person, we use a roman numeral with the pseudonym: examples, Buddhist I, Buddhist II, Atheist I, Atheist II. The Index and Glossary lists all the pseudonyms with their gender and caste.

Appendices provide fuller information on subjects that cannot be elaborated in the text. Because footnotes or endnotes would become repetitive, we have not used them. Instead, we have organized a number of subjects, which otherwise would require lengthy explanations in the text, into appendices. The appendices are generally aimed at supplying information for readers not familiar with special subjects. Some examples are: Disease (Append. I), Sacred Hindu Texts (Append. II), and Calendric Events (Append. V). Throughout the text they are referred to as above in parentheses or brackets, the latter when within a quotation, for example [Append. II].

Ghost illness, ghost possession, and poltergeist attacks are manifestations of the belief in ghosts. Karma (action), one of the major concepts of Hinduism, is basic to the belief in ghosts, for whether one's soul becomes a wandering ghost is determined principally by the sum of the soul's good and bad actions in past lives. Life and death are related to karma. The index of ghost illness is Fever, conceived of as a supernatural being, for the belief is that Fever is brought by a ghost who tries to seize the soul of the victim. If the ghost is successful, the person dies. However, instead of having ghost illness, individuals may suffer ghost possession wherein ghosts speak from them and cause them to go through dissociative states. On recovery the victim does not remember the possession. A poltergeist upsets the dwelling and/or workplace of the victim who is aware of the attack, in contrast to the amnesia that follows ghost possession. For ghost illness, ghost possession, and a poltergeist attack, the treatment is exorcism of the ghost.

During fieldwork in 1958–59 and 1977–78, we gathered data on ghost beliefs and also interviewed followers of the Arya Samaj, a reform sect of Hinduism, who generally do not believe in ghosts. During the second field trip, numerous events upset the villagers. Typhoid and malaria epidemics contributed to an epidemic of ghost possession and also to a poltergeist attack, which brought the phenomena forcefully to our attention and led us to gather as much information as possible, especially concerning specific case histories that substantiate attacks and illustrate ghost beliefs. Our notes from both trips contain considerable data concerning village beliefs about ghosts, exorcists, other curers, and case histories of individuals who were believed to have died from ghost illness or who suffered ghost possessions or poltergeist attacks.

Our treatment of the subject of ghosts uses a descriptive and comparative case-study method. Analysis takes several forms. Functional analysis places the phenomena into ethnographic context showing the relationships of ghost illness, ghost possession, and poltergeist attack to, for example, family life. Historical analysis relates ghost illness and ghost possession to such traumatic regional and national events as famines, the plague and influenza epidemics, and the relation of ghost beliefs to Hindu ideology and the sacred texts of Hinduism. Ghost illness is analyzed in the context of curing practices and theories of medicine: Ayurveda (the ancient Hindu art and science of medicine), Western medicine (allopathy), homeopathy, Unani (Greek), and popular pharmaceutical medicine with emphasis on the first two. Analysis of ghost phenomena draws on psychological and biological concepts, especially the research that deals with dissociative states like ghost possession. Some Indian regional differences concerning ghost beliefs and illness are noted. We describe comparable phenomena in other countries in order to provide a broader geographical and phenomenological dimension.

This combination of descriptive and analytical methods grew from the holistic approach to fieldwork that we have practiced for over 30 years. It leads to a deeper understanding of human behavior than do more narrow, problem-focused studies. We admire and have used the latter when relevant and appreciate the possibility that their methodological rigor might confirm relationships that are suggested by studies such as ours. For example, the relationship of "stress" to ghost possessions might be investigated by comparing individuals who suffer ghost possessions with a control group of individuals living under comparable stress who do not. Such a study would have considerable value, but for it to escape the pitfalls that accompany a narrow focus, it would have to be presented against the background of the kind of study offered in this monograph.

ACKNOWLEDGMENTS

We thank the Social Science Research Council and the National Science Foundation for supporting our fieldwork in 1957–59; and the American Institute for Indian Studies and the Indo-U.S. Sub-Commission for Education and Culture, the Indo-American Fellowship Program for fellowships that supported our work in 1977–78.

During our fieldwork in India in the 1950s and 1970s, we were aided by many individuals and organizations. Their indispensable assistance and hospitality are acknowledged with thanks in S. Freed and R. Freed (1976: 28–29) for the work in the 1950s and in S. Freed and R. Freed (1982: 200–201; 1985: 232) for the 1970s.

We thank Geraldine Santoro for her invaluable library research, Laila Williamson for her assistance with proofreading and checking details, Patricia Bramwell who typed the first annotated draft, the late Nicholas Amorosi, Donald McGranaghan, and Diana M. Salles for drawing the figures, charts and maps, Salles for her drawing of Yama that graces the cover, William H. Weinstein for computer assistance, Manjit Chawla Misra for compiling the index, and Brenda Jones for suggestions and copy editing.

In particular, we extend our heartfelt thanks for the comments, criticisms, and suggestions given by the prepublication reviewers: Dr. James M. Freeman, Professor of Anthropology, San Jose State University; and Dr. Helen E. Ullrich, Anthropologist and Psychiatrist, School of Medicine, Tulane University.

Finally, we thank the people of Shanti Nagar for admitting us to their village and for treating us with unfailing kindness and hospitality. Nothing would have been possible without their acceptance and cooperation. That we were able to take their darshan for two long periods is one of our fondest memories.

CHAPTER 1: THE VILLAGE SETTING

In a search for a village to study in the fall of 1957, we became acquainted with the Delhi region. The monsoon season had already passed so the area was dry and dusty. As we traveled around on different days from village to village by bus or jeep, the dust from the Grand Trunk Road, side lanes, and the countryside whirled around us. Villages sometimes appeared to be located on mounds or tumuli formed from the remains of ancient inhabitants' dwellings and the cremation and burial grounds located near them. Interspersed in the rural and urban regions are ruins of medieval caravansarais (camps with hunting lodges for travelers erected by the Moghul emperors). In and around the twin cities of Old and New Delhi are the ruins of seven ancient cities (Steel, 1929: 31; Spate, 1954: 490–493; Gazetteer Unit, Delhi Adm., 1976: 41). The ruins and dusty countryside brought to mind the millions of Hindus and Muslims who for centuries had died, been cremated or buried, and whose ashes had turned to dust. Later, from April to the end of June before the monsoon, the full impact of the dust came with the *loo*, a hot wind, which made daily life unpleasant.

An excerpt from a Punjabi poem entitled "Life in the Desert" depicts the *loo* as it affected wanderers in the Indo-Gangetic Plain, the Punjab, and the Thar Desert (Usborne, 1905: 5):

> We came; the dust-storm brought us. Who knows where the dust was born?
> Behind the curtains of Heaven and the skirts of the silver morn.
> We go where the dust-storm whirls us; loose leaves blown one by one.
> Through the light towards the shadows of evening down the tracks of the sloping sun.
> We are blown of the dust that is many and we rest in the dust that is one.

This study of ghosts was not a planned project for the field trips of 1958–59, and 1977–78. However, it reveals the value of long-term, holistic ethnography, which includes the study of culture, society, biology, psychology, ecology, history, and individuals within a community (Foster et al., 1979; Colson, 1984; Skinner, 1984). The thrust of our first field trip was to gain a comprehensive understanding of the culture and to learn about cultural change within the holistic framework. During both field trips, we heard about ghosts, sometimes in the context of Hinduism and eclectic beliefs, sometimes in connection with specific events, such as illness caused by a ghost (hereafter called ghost illness) and possession by a ghost, and more often randomly when people mentioned individuals who had died and were believed to have become ghosts. Prior to and during our 1977–78 fieldwork, several events increased stress so that village life became more unpredictable than usual (Sapolsky, 1988: 42). The frequency of ghost possession rose. One poltergeist attack occurred, and we learned of another, which took place before 1977. The correlation with stressful events led to a concentrated effort to learn as much as possible about ghost beliefs, ghost possession, ghost illness, poltergeists, and the ghosts said to be haunting the village.

A most stressful factor in 1977–78 was the resurgence of malaria; another source of stress was an epidemic of typhoid. After an effective governmental campaign using powerful insecticides had almost eliminated malaria in the Delhi region in the early 1960s, by 1965 it was on the rise. Anopheles mosquitoes had developed resistance to insecticides. Increased irrigation from tubewells and canals resulted in more standing water in the fields as potential breeding sites for mosquitoes. The explosive growth of handpumps in the village added to the surface water. From 1974 to 1978, malaria was present in epidemic proportions. The years 1977 and 1978 marked the highest incidence of malaria in the Delhi region to that date (W. Peters, 1975; Sarkad, 1975; Pattanayak and Roy, 1980: 1, 5–6, table 1). The Delhi region suffered greatly from a prolonged monsoon in 1977, which left so much water that in flying over the region toward the end of November about two to three months after the monsoon, we still saw large flooded areas. The monsoon helped to cause the typhoid epidemic, damaged crops, and contributed to the increase in malaria. *The Indian Express* (April 19, 1978: 3) reported that "Delhi citizens are in for a worst form of malaria epidemic this year. . . . As many as 33,296 positive cases of malaria have been detected . . . from January to March this year as against only 5389 cases for the corresponding period last year."

In addition to the malaria and typhoid epidemics, other sources of stress marked the late 1970s. A number of villagers had died during 1977, and their ghosts were believed to linger around the village and cremation grounds during the year of mourning. Further, in 1974 a Jat man had been murdered, and a woman of the same lineage was either murdered or committed suicide in the spring of 1977. In 1976 an eight-year-old girl drowned in the village pond. The ghosts of these dead and other ghosts from past times were part of the ghost epidemic in March–April 1978.

Contributing greatly to stress was the Emergency Period proclaimed by Prime Minister Indira Gandhi which began in 1975 and ended in 1977. It featured a coercive sterilization program which aroused a strong popular reaction. The campaign placed many people, especially government employees, under intense pressure to undergo sterilization themselves or to have their wives sterilized (S. Freed and R. Freed, 1985a: 246–248). Complicating village life further, in February–March, 1978 two hailstorms in the village damaged crops, and a tornado struck near the main campus of Delhi University, located northwest of Old Delhi. It frightened people in the region. The village population had increased by 66 percent in 20 years and was crowding the village (S. Freed and R. Freed, 1985a: 238–239, tables 1 and 2). All these stress factors heightened the villagers' awareness of the ghosts believed to be lingering around the village and cremation grounds. It was in these circumstances that a number of individuals suffered ghost possessions and one man, a poltergeist attack.

Shanti Nagar conforms to a type of village, common in northern India, often described as nucleated. The houses are crowded together, sometimes sharing one or more walls with adjacent houses. The compact habitation site is bordered by undivided village common land. Beyond this tract lie the cultivated fields. The shared architecture and geographic arrangements of nucleated villages are matched by similarities of culture patterns concerning domains such as caste, family life, ceremony, and economy. As the population of Shanti Nagar has grown, the habitation site has been expanded, but not very much, at the expense of the common land.

Throughout this study individuals are identified by caste. Representatives of 13 castes lived in Shanti Nagar in the 1950s; 14 castes, in the 1970s. Table 1 gives the population of Shanti Nagar by caste both in the 1950s and the 1970s. We have tried to reflect the ghost beliefs of almost all castes, but castes with few members do not receive as much attention as the most populous ones.

In the interval between our two periods of research in Shanti Nagar in the 1950s and 1970s, a number of social and economic trends had become more firmly established or newly introduced: the educational level rose dramatically; health services improved; there was a substantial increase in salaried urban occupations; a few women worked for salaries outside the home; the technological level of agriculture was considerably higher especially due to tractors and tubewells; the villagers were deeply involved in markets outside Shanti Nagar, owing to the construction of an immense vegetable market just north of Delhi and within easy reach of the farmers of Shanti Nagar; electricity was introduced; radios were commonplace; there were a few television sets and automobiles; and newspapers were delivered daily. The village had a somewhat different appearance: it was larger to accommodate the increased population, and houses made of dried chunks of mud, which were common in 1958, had almost entirely been replaced by structures of brick. The village was more modern, better informed, and more prosperous in 1977–78 than in 1958–59. Despite such changes, many cultural values, chiefly in the domain of family life, kinship, ideology, and proper conduct (dharma), persisted relatively unchanged. A detailed description of the village as it was in the 1950s, and to some extent in the 1970s, may be found in a series of monographs that have appeared in the 1970s and 1980s (S.

Fig. 1.   Village street in 1958. Mud huts like the one near the two dogs were common then but had been replaced by brick houses by 1978.

Freed and R. Freed, 1976, 1978, 1985a, 1987; R. Freed and S. Freed, 1979, 1980, 1981, 1985).

In 1958, Shanti Nagar was located about 11 mi (18 km) northwest by road from the city limits of Delhi, a distance which has decreased slightly since that time due to the gradual spread of the city. Several villages are situated between Delhi and Shanti Nagar. Travel between Shanti Nagar and Delhi was relatively easy in 1958. Except for about 1 mi (1.6 km) the road to Delhi was paved. A bus made four round trips daily; during the rainy season, the bus traveled only to the end of the paved road and passengers had to complete the journey on foot through flooded fields. By 1977, the paved road had been extended to Shanti Nagar, and bus service was more convenient.

Although Shanti Nagar is located close enough to Delhi to make it possible for many men to hold urban jobs and commute daily,

TABLE 1

Population of Shanti Nagar by Caste in 1958–59 and 1977–78

Caste	1958–59	1977–78
Bairagi Mendicant	27	48
Baniya Merchant	6	13
Brahman Priest	187	319
Chamar Leatherworker	98	188
Chhipi Dyer	5	7
Chuhra Sweeper	96	140
Gola Potter	58	125
Jat Farmer	260	385
Jhinvar Watercarrier	13	21
Khati Carpenter	0	3
Lohar Blacksmith	11	23
Mahar Potter	3	1
Mali Gardener	10	7
Nai Barber	25	44
TOTAL	799	1324

Fig. 2.   Subzi Mandi, the Delhi vegetable market, 1978. Delhi is the commercial center for scores of nearby villages. Farmers make frequent trips to Subzi Mandi to sell vegetables, especially tomatoes as here shown.

agriculture is still the principal occupation. Men often combine more than one occupation, frequently farming and urban employment. Most women also have several principal occupations: agricultural work, raising children, and housework.

The population totaled 799 persons in 1958–59, of whom 392 were females and 407 were males; in 1977–78 there were 629 females and 695 males, for a total of 1324 persons. Thus, in the 19.5 years between our two village censuses, the population had increased by 65.7 percent. There were 110 families in 1958–59 and 176 in 1977–78.

CHAPTER 2: BASIS FOR THE STUDY
OF GHOST BELIEFS

Life and death are inseparable. There is no life without death, no
death without life. (Daniélou, 1964: 272)

Ghosts of the dead haunted and still haunt Shanti Nagar. A major belief among the villagers is that the soul of a person becomes a ghost at death and continues as a ghost for a time based on the sum of the soul's actions in past lives. Thus, ghosts are linked with the souls of the dead and are entwined with life and death. The fear of death and anxiety about becoming a ghost persist among villagers and are reinforced by a long history of many deaths, a relatively short life expectancy through centuries, and an ideological perspective about life and death deriving from Hindu beliefs about the soul (atman), the soul's actions (karma), and ghosts causing death.

Understanding the complex of ghost beliefs requires information of impressive scope. Because we studied Shanti Nagar from a holistic point of view, we had considerable information that was later to prove critical in our analysis. Such data as the record of daily events, censuses of families, genealogies of patrilineages, details about the lives and personalities of individuals and families, and surveys on various subjects were invaluable. Much of the information about ghosts collected both in the 1950s and 1970s was elicited in many open-ended, explorative interviews on miscellaneous subjects recorded verbatim as much as possible.

The ideology of the villagers is important. They claim to be an all-Hindu village although interviews and a review of the field-notes reveal heterogeneous beliefs about ghosts and other supernatural beings, primarily based on Hinduism but with influences from Islam. Two villagers claim to be Buddhists; three profess to be atheists. Although a number of villagers claim to be non-believers in ghosts, the majority of villagers believe in them. To understand how supernatural beliefs are linked to persons who died and are believed to have become ghosts, an overview of the villagers' ideology, including thoughts about life and death, is necessary.

Interviews with villagers about Hindu beliefs concerning ghosts and other supernatural beings include statements on individual, cultural, biological, ecological, psychological, and past aspects of village life. A special effort has been made to reflect individual villagers' views by quoting them.

The villagers provided data from the 19th and 20th centuries when many changes took place. These changes affected ghost beliefs primarily through reform cults of Hinduism in the last part of the 19th and early 20th centuries. In the 20th century, the gradual education of a largely nonliterate population, the introduction of governmental medical services, a modernization of and emphasis on Ayurveda, the spread of popular pharmaceutical medicine applied by indigenous curers, and influences from the mass media brought additional changes. Despite these changes, by the late 1970s ancient beliefs about illness, death, and ghosts persisted along with a conglomeration of curing practices, including Western medicine. Although villagers knew the modern names of some diseases and how to treat them, little biological knowledge and its relation to disease and death had yet become part of village culture. Furthermore, most villagers were not aware of how the psychological connection between stressful conditions, difficult personal relationships both between the living and between the living and the dead, and a cultural tradition of ghost beliefs might haunt them in the forms of ghost illness and possession. The intimate village setting where most families have lived for generations fosters the belief in ghosts and the persistence of ghost tales about past inhabitants, especially relatives and neighbors. The setting is coupled with the belief that ghosts cause illness and death.

The belief that ghosts cause ghost illness and death derives from ancient Hindu texts regarding the origin of Fever, who is identified in the texts as a supernatural being. The great god Shiva plays the main role in the tales which derive from Vedic texts, the Mahabharata, and the Puranas, concerning Daksha, Shiva, and Fever. Rudra was the Vedic equivalent of Shiva; the later name of Shiva came from "shiva," used in the Vedas as an epithet of Rudra, which means auspicious (Daniélou, 1964: 188). Ancient Hindu texts show many aspects and names for Shiva, symbolic of his various powers. He sends disease; drives it away; is known as the First Physician; Bhairava, The Destroyer; Bhutesvara, Lord of Ghosts; and Hara, Death, The Remover. These names appear in the Vedas, Brahmanas, Upanishads, Mahabharata, and some of the Puranas (Append. II: Sacred Hindu Texts). One example is the Linga Purana (Dowson, 1950: 117, 296–300; Daniélou, 1964: 188–198).

Doniger O'Flaherty (1980: 132, 154, 162, 272–275), citing the Rig-Veda, Atharva-Veda, as well as other Vedic texts, then the later Mahabharata, and a number of Puranic texts, traced the events and motifs from the earlier Hindu texts which led to the following tale in the Puranas. As Hara, Shiva is identified with disease and death and his messenger is Fever. As Hara-Shiva, he quarreled with Daksha, Ritual Skill, because Daksha would not allow him to participate in the sacrificial rituals with the other deities. Sati, Daksha's daughter and Shiva's wife, then destroyed herself in the fire of her anger. In retaliation Hara-Shiva sent a monster to cut off Daksha's head, and Shiva began destroying the ritual sacrifices. He was so angry that a drop of sweat fell from his forehead, which first became a fire and then a short, red-eyed and red-bearded man named Fever. Brahma, the Creator and Daksha's father, on behalf of himself and the other deities was afraid that Fever would wander the earth uncurbed so he told Shiva that the deities would let him participate in the sacrifices if he curbed Fever. Shiva then restored Daksha by allowing him to have the head of the first animal he encountered, a goat. Thereafter, goats became the sacrificial animals. Furthermore, instead of allowing Fever to bring illness and death without limits to animals and humans in the whole world, Shiva curbed him to limited parts of the world.

Based on these sources and our fieldwork, it is our theory that the tales about Hara-Shiva and his messenger, Fever, had the effect of establishing the connection between illness as Fever and the belief that Fever signals illness brought by a ghost, for villagers associated ghost illness with Fever. The Khanna study of the 1950s in Punjab also found that deaths from disease were recorded as due to Fever (Wyon and Gordon, 1971: 173). The persistence of Fever as an index of ghost illness and the identification of illness by the word Fever in village lore is comparable to the finding that before the introduction of Western medicine in the 19th century disease in most of the world was identified as fever. For example, Tuchman (1988: 195) noted that in colonial America "Eight out of ten deaths in the 18th century were ascribed to 'fever'." (Dowson 1950: 76–79, 298; Daniélou 1964: 189, 196–197, 320–322; Imperato 1983: 34; Append. II: Sacred Hindu Texts.)

Because disease and subsequent death may strike one person and not another in ways which the survivors, relatives, and friends close to the deceased may not understand, they may ask, "Why did this happen to him, and why did the other survive?" They find the answer in their ideology. For example, if two teen-aged, reasonably healthy brothers fall ill and only one dies, people might wonder why one brother died but not the other. A villager would say that he had Fever, an index of ghost illness, and died before his allotted time due to the sum of his actions in his present and past lives. Some people might add that the surviving brother, who also had Fever, may have had the will to live, but such a statement would be tempered by the observation that his soul may have had more advantageous past actions than the soul of the brother who died.

This study shows how ghost beliefs persist in Shanti Nagar where so many inexplicable and tragic deaths occurred in the past and still do. In all probability ghost beliefs will endure despite the worldwide spread of scientific knowledge, for there will always be unexplained, differential susceptibilities to causes of disease and death. Throughout the world people have cultural traditions regarding the connections of illness, life, and death on the one hand, and animistic beliefs in the soul, a deity or deities, and other supernatural beings, such as ghosts on the other (Tylor, 1958: 10). Furthermore, despite scientific knowledge and cures for biologically caused diseases, new causes arise, and sometimes iatric cures lead to death (Illich, 1976).

Because disease and death are linked to ghost beliefs, cultural attitudes and practices about health, illness, and death are an essential part of this study. The cases of ghost illness and death as described by villagers are compared with ancient Hindu beliefs, Ayurvedic medical theories, and Western medicine when sufficient information exists to warrant the comparisons.

DEFINITIONS OF GHOST ILLNESS, GHOST POSSESSION, AND POLTERGEIST ATTACK

Since the phrases "ghost illness," "ghost possession," and "poltergeist attack" are used in this study, they are here defined symptomatically and separately in village terms. However, they share one trait in common, which is that a ghost tries to take the soul of its victim. Two phrases are used: bhut *grasth* (ghost-possessed) and bhut *lagna* (attacked by a ghost). The main index of ghost illness is Fever. Sometimes a voice may come from a person with Fever who is delirious, and the voice may occur in children and adults but not in infants who have not yet learned to speak. The voice is identified as the ghost trying to take the soul of the person who is ill. Other symptoms are convulsions and body movements indicating pain and discomfort; choking or difficult breathing, interpreted as a death rattle because a ghost is trying to take the victim's soul; and in the case of an infant, incessant crying.

Ghost possession is dramatic. The victim may fear a ghost and see it. Then the ghost is believed to enter the individual and is identified by its voice speaking from the victim. In both ghost illness and possession, villagers often say that the voice coming from the victim is "talking nonsense." Ghost possession is also characterized by alternate mental states, which psychiatrists designate as dissociative states. A range of mental states and behavior is associated with ghost possession from total unconsciousness to various stages of semiconsciousness with a voice or voices

speaking from the possessed. These voices are identified as ghosts trying to take the victim's soul. In these states, victims walk or run around and ghostly voices speak from them (Ludwig, 1966: 226–227; West, 1975: 300; Tart, 1979; R. Prince, 1982a: 303–316; R. Freed and S. Freed, 1985: 111–113). Afterward victims have amnesia for their behavior during possessions. While they are possessed, victims may try to run to a well, pond, the railroad tracks, or a fire, interpreted by spectators as suicide attempts caused by the ghost or ghosts trying to gain the victims' souls.

In psychiatric parlance, ghost possession may be classified as a Dissociative Disorder, or if a somatic complaint or physical disorder is involved as a Somatoform-Conversion Dissociative Disorder (Am. Psych. Assn., DSM-III, 1980: 241–249; 253–260). These terms are not known in the village, but the villagers distinguish between ghost illness and ghost possession by the two types of behavior described above. Ghost attacks by a poltergeist differ from ghost possession because the ghost does not enter and speak from the victim and the victim does not have amnesia for a poltergeist attack. A poltergeist is noisy and disturbs households and workplaces (Gove, 1986: 1756). The distinction made by villagers between ghost possession and a poltergeist is that in possession the ghost enters the victim to seize the soul. The poltergeist attacks the victim for the same purpose but does not enter or speak from the victim.

This study shows that beliefs about ghosts are linked with village ideology deriving primarily from Hinduism, a principal doctrine of which is that the fruit of one's actions in the lives of a soul's rebirths determines whether a soul (atman) will be reborn, will be released from the round of rebirths, or will become a wandering ghost. Because the soul, atman, includes in its meaning the concept of self, and because it is all that remains of the dead person after cremation, it becomes a ghost under specific circumstances. Therefore, for those who believe in ghosts, see them, hear them, or are troubled by them, whatever they may experience may reflect the self of a dead person, i.e., the individual's personality, appearance, and life history before becoming a ghost.

This study is a village prose epic about ghosts and the lives and deaths of villagers in Shanti Nagar in the 19th and 20th centuries. The tales in the form of case histories are best read as a series of family, caste, and community stories and events. In form and emphasis it is a holistic anthropological study.

Narration is the best way to present episodes in the lives of individuals and families which are effectively dramas, each one with a beginning and end. Such detailed descriptions convey both the variety and the constant themes of the phenomena. Description is augmented by pointing out historical, communal, familial, and individual concomitants not apparent in a specific episode. Researchers using this material in their own comparative studies will find full description more useful than a compact presentation in which case material is reduced to and analyzed in terms of a few categories, which may not be the ones of interest in other studies. Compact presentation is useful as a summary of full presentation but not as a substitute. Because an ethnographic study can never be duplicated as can many experiments of bench science, full description is the key component.

CHAPTER 3: FIELDWORK, TECHNIQUES, AND PROBLEMS

From fieldwork with the Washoe Indians before going to India in 1957, we were aware that life in different societies is seldom if ever idyllic, as is sometimes assumed by anthropologists embarked on their first field experience in a strange culture. Konner (1987a) has reviewed the literature about anthropologists who expected to find a paradise or idyllic society. He mentioned a number of anthropologists who started from this basis, including Margaret Mead in her study of adolescent girls in Samoa and his own initial work among the !Kung of South Africa. However, he as well as other anthropologists, Mead among them, were soon disillusioned. When we sat in on Mead's fieldwork seminar at Columbia University, she told about a student who went into the field with this idyllic concept. When he began his fieldwork, he suffered extreme culture shock and had to be hospitalized. Because of our previous experience, we were not surprised to find that human behavior in Shanti Nagar ranged from commendable to greedy, violent, and murderous.

However, all behavior has to be evaluated in terms of the ideology of the villagers. Context and nuance share the scene with absolute criteria. In North India, villagers judge actions and intentions primarily on whether they conform to dharma, ethical or proper behavior, but dharma varies from caste to caste, lineage to lineage, and family to family. Channa (1984: 160–164) stated that for Indians the words *pun* for good actions and *pap* for bad actions are well known but many situations arise which are either ambiguous or difficult to judge. Villagers resolve ambiguities to some extent by referring to circumstances. They note that a man killed someone but that in the circumstances he had little choice. We briefly make this point about value judgments because some anthropologists go into the field today with the intention of intervening in the lives of their hosts. We have always avoided that approach. We were there to learn from our hosts, not to meddle.

Our living and working arrangements in Shanti Nagar and our field techniques have been described in previous publications, so no more than a summary is needed here. In brief, observation of activities was a major technique from the beginning to the end of our work, as were open-ended exploratory interviews to establish rapport as well as to obtain information. They often were recorded as close to verbatim as possible. Some of them appear in this text to show how the villagers speak and think. Interviews became more focused as fieldwork progressed and information gradually accumulated. Many interviews were group sessions or were conducted in a group setting, which took place in informants' houses, our living quarters, a courtyard, a caste compound, or the fields. We began to collect census data as soon as the villagers grew accustomed to us and we could move about the village without attracting too much attention. The census data proved invaluable as a basis for planning interviews and understanding what informants told us. Toward the end of the fieldwork, we used surveys, such as the Health Opinion Survey (Append. VI). Rapport was not a problem. We were well-known in the village, and most villagers enjoyed talking to us. We and our assistants were almost never refused an interview, although some people avoided specific topics (S. Freed and R. Freed, 1976: 17–28; R. Freed and S. Freed, 1985: 106–107).

As for the ghost project in particular, a review of the fieldnotes recalled subtle and specific problems encountered in interviews. It was at times quite difficult to obtain information about the dead, particularly from mothers of dead infants. If mothers talked about infants or young children who had died, they tended to do so toward the end of their childbearing years or in old age. More rarely, young women might do so when under great stress from the repeated deaths of infants, but there are exceptions, as will be seen in the cases of "A Ghost Took My Son" and "The Boy Had to Die" (Chap. 14). Surviving members of a family in which a dead person was believed to have become a ghost were reluctant to mention the deceased's name for fear the ghost would trouble them. In discussions of dead wives believed to have become ghosts, their names were almost never spoken because of the fear that they had become ghosts malevolent toward their husband's new wife and her children, or toward a pregnant woman. More distant relatives, daughters-in-law, for example, and close neighbors might identify ghosts by family or lineage, but did not name them, especially if their deaths may have been or were believed to have been caused by other persons, or because they died of a disease, such as tuberculosis, which the family did not want to be widely known. Not mentioning the names of the dead for fear

that they would appear as ghosts seems widespread in the world (Krappe, 1964: 293).

The custom throughout the region of using kinship and fictive kinship terms instead of names as terms of address and reference may have arisen long ago to protect the living from ghosts (cf. S. Freed, 1963a; S. Freed and R. Freed, 1976: 148–149). Neither wife nor husband referred to a spouse by name. The names of infants and small children similarly were seldom used. Infants might not be given names immediately after birth or might have their names changed because it was believed that late naming and name changes would protect children from attacks by female ghosts who died in childbirth and who wanted to take the souls of children, including their own. Temple (1883: 76) found in the Punjab that every Hindu had two names, one that was bestowed at the casting of the horoscope, and the other by which the individual was known for life. The real or birth name was not used, only the other name, with which no ceremony was connected. In Shanti Nagar the horoscope or real name was provided by a priest between the sixth to tenth day from birth, depending on caste affiliation.

Small children and infants were enumerated in census data, but if a name was given for an infant or small child, it was not the real name because of the fear that a ghost might seize the child's soul. If deaths of infants and children took place before our fieldwork in the 1950s or the children were born and died between the two field trips, information about them and their names was often difficult or impossible to trace. Adult males, even those who died before we began our work or who were born and died in the 1950s–1970s interval, were generally identified in patrilineal genealogies. Males who died without issue were believed to have become ghosts, and males and females who died before experiencing the satisfactions of adult life were likewise believed to have become ghosts. Through persistent efforts, it was possible to identify many of the dead by family and lineage. Old people, who believed they would soon die and were reconciled to death, were sometimes more willing to talk about ghosts than younger persons, but they used kinship terms instead of names. To identify the ghost of a married woman, the informant would refer to her, for example, as the wife of Krishna Gopal. If the ghost was the soul of a dead infant or child, the ghost would be alluded to as the son or daughter of Krishna Gopal, or the son or daughter of Krishna Gopal's wife, a system of referral known as teknonymy (Hunter and Whitten, 1976: 184).

Men provided the names of male ancestors when reciting their genealogies. In this patrilineal, male-dominated society, men wanted to perpetuate the names of their dead male consanguines and tended to dub them ancestral ghosts (pitris) even when they were ordinary ghosts (bhuts). Men, who were familiar with their own lines of descent, could recite the litanies of their dead male consanguines. No one recited a litany of female ancestors, for as Maine (1963: 145) stated, "In Hindoo law . . . kinship is entirely agnatic and . . . in Hindoo genealogies the names of women are generally . . . omitted altogether." Although a fair number of males professed not to fear ghosts or believe in them, the liturgical recitations of the names of ancestors may have been a subconscious way of warding off their ghosts, a ritual whereby they propitiated their male ancestral ghosts through pride in being able to remember them.

Because of fear and beliefs about ghosts, it was sometimes difficult to trace a ghost's family line, but in most cases the ghosts were associated with a specific family history. The best sources of information about ghosts and their victims were daughters-in-law or persons outside the immediate family, either more distant relatives in the patrilineage, members of the same caste, or neighbors. The exception to the reluctance of family members to discuss ghosts was an ancestral male ghost, a pitri, regarded as somewhat of a family and household godling, *devata*. Once the linkage of a ghost to a family or patrilineage was obtained, it was then possible to use the censuses, genealogies, family histories, and other clues from interviews to clarify the position of the deceased in the society and to determine the reasons why the dead person was believed to have become a ghost or to have become the victim of a ghost.

Children, who knew us well because they often visited us, sometimes in small groups, provided worthwhile information about their beliefs and disbeliefs in ghosts. For example, a group of Jat children was regularly in and out of our quarters, heard us ask questions, and saw us write down the answers. As a result, they told us what they, too, thought. The children interviewed ranged from five to 13 years of age, but those in the five-to-six age range seldom provided much information. One family, trying to please us, coached a son to answer according to what the family members thought he should say. We could easily see that the boy was upset and did not want to be interviewed, so we did not interview him.

CHAPTER 4: BRIEF HISTORY OF THE DELHI REGION

Ghost beliefs in Shanti Nagar have been perpetuated in the historical context of the Delhi region, whose tumultuous history has inevitably affected the lives of the villagers. The epidemics and wars that led to many untimely deaths and the various medical traditions that form village health culture are all part of the regional history that has to be taken into account in order to understand ghost beliefs. Moreover, many tales of the beloved Mahabharata took place in and near the region. Villagers are quite familiar with these tales. Indian classical literature contributes to village ideology which in turn is basic to ghost beliefs. The brief history of the Delhi region that is outlined in chapters 4 and 5 and emphasizes the principal causes of death in the 19th and 20th centuries helps to fill out our understanding of the cultural, cognitive, and psychological environment of the villagers of Shanti Nagar.

The cities of Old Delhi and New Delhi, are often collectively called Delhi or, more often in newspaper datelines, New Delhi. New Delhi is the capital of India. The two cities and the surrounding region form a federal district now known as the Union Territory of Delhi. The Union Territory of Delhi, studded with the remains of ruined cities, ranks as one of the more ancient urban sites in the world. The earliest city was the legendary Indraprastha of the Mahabharata, built by the Pandavas (five brothers, heroes of the Mahabharata) along the bank of the Yamuna River (van Buitenen, 1980: 9–10). The Pandavas received the Kandava tract where Indraprastha was located from their blind uncle, Dhritarashtra, who wanted to prevent their claiming the succession at Hastinapura where their cousins, the Kauravas, were in power. Van Buitenen stated that the Mahabharata was composed and added to through time but that the main events, including the building and occupation of Indraprastha, took place around the ninth to eighth centuries B.C. (van Buitenen, 1980: xiv–xv, 8, 9, fn. 12, 11, fn. 2l). He commented, based on meager data, "neither a single author nor a single date can be assigned to the great epic." (van Buitenen, 1980: xxiii). Despite this statement, van Bui-

tenen (1980: xxv) postulated that the date of the Mahabharata is "not too far removed from the eighth or ninth century B. C." Basham (1954: 39) dated the events of the epic to the 9th century B.C. The Gazetteer Unit, Delhi Adm. (1976: 41–42) affirmed that Dhritarashtra gave the Kandava tract to the Pandavas but noted that Cunningham, an archaeologist, fixed the founding of Indraprastha in the 15th century B.C. Although Doniger O'Flaherty (1980: 11) dated the Mahabharata from ca. 300 B.C. to A.D. 300, these dates refer to the writing of the text but not to the events portrayed. Later cities located on the site of Indraprastha bore different names and their locations shifted, but the urban tradition in the area has been continuous (Append. II: Sacred Hindu Texts: Mahabharata).

The name Delhi goes back to the first century B.C. It derived from a leader of a Rajput clan in the Haryana region, who called his capital Dillika. The name was given prominence by Ptolemy, the mathematician, astronomer, and geographer from Alexandria, who visited India in the second century A.D. and mapped it, including Delhi. He identified the city as Daedala (Gole, 1983: 26). Ptolemy's map was used until the 16th and 17th centuries, when other cartographers mapped India, correcting Ptolemy's errors and using a variety of spellings to identify Delhi, such as Dilli, Delli, Delly, and Dely (Balfour, 1885: 1: 904–907; Steel, 1929: 31, 219–221; Harris and Levey, 1975: 2238; Gazetteer Unit, Delhi Adm., 1976: 1, 41–43; Gole, 1983: 26, 58, 60, 65).

Delhi was under Hindu rule until A.D. 1193 when Muhammad Ghori (Muhammad of Ghor or Ghur) defeated Prithvi Raj. From then until the early years of the 19th century Delhi was ruled by Muslims. Shahjahan ascended the throne in 1628 and then restored what is today the present Old Delhi region to its former glory by building his capital, Shahjahanabad, there. Construction began in 1638 and was completed in 1648 (Gazetteer Unit, Delhi Adm., 1976: 57). The centuries of Islamic influence in the region are reflected in animistic beliefs, compatible with Hindu beliefs about ghosts and exorcism as well as Unani and Unani Prophetic medical theories, partially derived from the Greeks. The British introduced their version of Christianity and, gradually, Western medicine, as it began to develop at the end of the 18th century (Append. I: Discoveries). Christianity was introduced in India before the end of the third century. The Portuguese, who dominated ocean trade-routes in the 16th century, established Christianity wherever they settled (Moreland and Chatterjee, 1957: 83, 200–202). In North India and Bengal, Islam and Christianity have influenced Hinduism with the founding of the monotheistic reform sects of the Brahmo Samaj and the Arya Samaj. The Arya Samaj, which came to Shanti Nagar in 1923, holds that there is only one god, as do Islam and Christianity. The sect excludes all other supernaturals, including ghosts. It is prominent in the Jat caste in Shanti Nagar (Bürgel, 1976; K. W. Jones, 1976: 24, 27–29, Chap. 2).

Flora Annie Steel (1847–1929), who lived from 1867 to 1898 in the Punjab and Delhi District, in retrospect and prophecy commented on her last visit to the City of Delhi. She wrote:

I am told that now these desert brick sands about the Kutb [Kutab Minar] are covered by a fine city, that has cost Heaven only knows how much gold to build. Well, I think it is rather a rash experiment. It only adds one more to the many cities that have risen and fallen there. Delhi has an ill name. No dynasty that has chosen it as its capital has survived long. It may well be, therefore, that it may see India given Dominion status; and in its turn Dominion status may fade into the Independence of many States, for that India can ever exist as a homogeneous entity appears to me impossible.

However, at this time [1898] the memories of the place were too strong for aught else; there was a ghost at every turn (Steel, 1929: 221).

Several stories are told regarding the settlement of the Delhi region, two of which mention land grants in the rural area and pertain to Shanti Nagar. One story concerns the grandson of the last Hindu ruler, Prithvi Raj. One day while hunting, he saw some Jat

women who had come to the pond for water. A man came out of a nearby village leading a buffalo calf by a rope when suddenly the animal broke free. The man and a number of people chased after the calf, which crossed the path of a Jat woman. She put her foot on the trailing rope and stood fast until the pursuers caught the animal. The grandson of Prithvi Raj so admired her fortitude that, although she was already married and he was a Kshatriya, which ranked above the Jats, he arranged to marry her. The couple then had three sons who settled the Delhi and Rohtak Districts of the Punjab.

The second story claims that about A.D. 700 some Gaur Brahmans came from Bengal to Delhi. The king was taken with their learning and piety and they became his constant companions. One day while hunting, they came to a region which so pleased the Brahmans that the king granted them 52,000 bighas (4386 hectares) of jungle land, which took the name of Bawana, later corrupted to Bowana. It is within this region that Shanti Nagar is located. The two stories are intended to verify the ancient right of settlement in the region by Brahmans and Jats, who still are major landowners throughout what is today the Union Territory of Delhi (Wood and Maconachie, 1882: 86–87, 98). The Brahmans in Shanti Nagar are Gaur Brahmans. The two castes differ somewhat in matters of ideology, the Brahmans following a more traditional form of Hinduism, Sanatan Dharma, while many Jats are followers of the Arya Samaj.

Villagers recited several stories about the founding of Shanti Nagar. The gist of these stories is that Brahmans and Jats split off from a nearby village, having received a grant of land from the Moghul ruler, Iradat Khan. According to different stories, this split occurred 550, 750, or 900 years ago. A former lambardar (a village revenue official) stated in 1958 that evidence in the land records office placed the date at about A.D. 1208.

Jats seem to have the stronger claim to being the first settlers and state that they invited the Brahmans to serve them as priests. Both castes are still very competitive and each claims to have arrived first (S. Freed and R. Freed, 1976: 51, 53–54). People of other castes have settled in the village over the years, so that now some 14 castes are represented. The Jats and Brahmans own almost all the village land, but the Jats own much more land than the Brahmans. The Jats have the largest population of the village castes and are the strongest economically, making them dominant.

In 1958, a Brahman elder told the following story of the Brahman-Jat settlement:

Originally a large nearby village consisted of Brahmans and Baniyas. Then one Brahman family had a Jat servant. The Brahman family eventually gave him some land and he brought his family to the village. Later he gave a feast and killed all the Brahmans except one girl who was visiting her parents in their village and was pregnant. After the killing of the Brahmans, the Jats fell ill with leprosy and were rotting away. They were told that in order to be cured, they had to return the land to one of the original Brahman owners so they called the girl back from her parents' village and gave her some land. All the Brahmans in this village are descended from that girl's son. The Jats originally came from Bara Basa beyond Panipat in the Rohtak District of the Punjab.

A number of castes, including Jats, told similar origin stories (Crooke, 1896: 1: 261–262; 3: 25, 33). Despite the above story, it was well known that some Brahmans came to the village later than others and from different parts of the region. In the 1930s the last of the Brahman settlers, a small group, came from Chiragh Delhi, which lies to the south of New Delhi.

Although the British East India Company was present in India prior to the 17th century, the penetration into the north and northwestern portions of the subcontinent came about in the 19th century. In 1803, General Lake captured Delhi and brought the Moghul Emperor Shah Alam II under British control. Thereafter the city became the frontier capital of Great Britain in India. It and surrounding territory were governed by the First Resident and Chief Commissioner of Delhi (Gazetteer Unit, Delhi Adm., 1976: 76–77).

After the Mutiny of 1857, Delhi and its regional territory became the Delhi District and was annexed to the newly formed Punjab. The rule of the East India Company was transferred to the viceroy of the British Crown. In 1877 when Queen Victoria became Empress of India and the British Empire, a durbar (elaborate formal reception of Indian dignitaries) was celebrated in Delhi. After another durbar held in the presence of King-Emperor George V, December 12, 1911, he proclaimed that the capital of India was to be transferred from Calcutta to Delhi. The Delhi tahsil was separated from the Delhi District of the Punjab and became part of Delhi Province as of January 1, 1912. The government buildings were located in the Old Civil Lines to the north of Old Delhi. Setting the capital of India in Delhi gratified both Hindus, because of ancient legends going back to the founding of Indraprastha, one of the events in the Mahabharata, and also Muslims because Delhi was the seat of the Moghul Empire. New Delhi, due to delays caused by World War I, did not formally become the administrative center of Delhi and India until 1930. The partition of India into India and Pakistan and Indian Independence from British rule took place in August 1947. What was formerly the Province of Delhi became part of Delhi State (1952), which later became the Union Territory of Delhi in 1956 (Leasor, 1957: 23; Moreland and Chatterjee, 1957: 442; van den Dungen, 1972: 113, 345; Harris and Levey, 1975: 1325; Gazetteer Unit, Delhi Adm., 1976: 2–4, 95, 96, 97).

Delhi is situated on the historical invasion route into northern India, a location which guarantees a complex history of conquest and the associated influence of diverse cultures. After the conquest of Delhi in 1193, it was burned by Timur in 1398, occupied by Babar in 1526, sacked by Nadir in 1739, taken by Mahrattas in 1758, captured by the British in 1803, recovered by the British in 1857, and returned to Indian secular rule in 1947, accompanied by an enormous influx of Hindu and Sikh refugees from the part of the Punjab that came under Pakistani control (Balfour, 1885, 1: 905). Major differences exist between North and South India and there are subregional differences within both areas. India is famous for its history of invasions, linguistic diversity, and various cultures of Hindus, Jains, Buddhists, Muslims, Sikhs, Parsees, and Christians, reflecting different ideologies, which include multiple supernatural beings such as ghosts.

CHAPTER 5: CAUSES OF DEATH

The high mortality rates and general lack of knowledge regarding the causes of death perpetuated the Hindu beliefs in ghosts, ghost illness, ghost possessions, attacks by poltergeists, and ghosts taking the souls of people who died untimely deaths. The causes of death were war and other turbulence, famine, disease, poor delivery practices at birth, female infanticide, Sati, murder, suicide, and accident. They often resulted in individuals dying early in life, who then were believed to become ghosts. War and other turbulence, famine, and disease are discussed first, followed by the other causes. The many deaths from endemic and epidemic diseases are linked to souls that become lingering and often malevolent ghosts.

The population of India at the time of Alexander the Great's invasion (327 B.C.) has been estimated at 140 million. Thereafter the population decreased due to famine, disease, war and other turbulence, as well as practices favoring male offspring. The decline lasted until sometime between A.D. 1600 and 1800. In 1800, India's population was an estimated 125 million. It then slowly rose during the 19th century. The first national census taken in 1871–1872 showed that the population had risen to about 250 million. Until 1921, growth was slow, but thereafter with the gradual control of disease and famine the population expanded more rapidly, increasing from 251 million in 1921 to 684 million in 1981 (Wyon and Gordon, 1971: 55–56; Visaria and Visaria, 1981: 1729, table 2).

Due to untimely deaths from war and other turbulence, famine, epidemics, and many other causes, human life expectancy in India was short. An average life expectancy of no more than 30 years persisted into the 20th century. India still lags behind the West with regard to average life expectancy. Readers who have never lived where frequent untimely deaths take place may find it difficult to understand their emotional and economic effect on the stability of everyday life. For India even in this century, brief life expectancies indicate that untimely deaths were common. From 1921 to 1930, the average life expectancy for males was 26.91 years; for females, 26.57 years. By 1961–70 the expectancies had risen to 47.1 years for males and 45.6 years for females (Res. and Ref. Div., Ministry of Inform. and Broadcasting, Gov. of India, 1978: 8, tables 1.4, 1.5). It is noteworthy that, as calculated for periods around 1960, India and Sri Lanka (Ceylon) are among the few exceptions to the general rule that females have longer life expectancies than males (Wyon and Gordon, 1971: 263). The frequency of untimely death is related to ghost beliefs and ghost illness, for persons dying before their allotted time are believed to become wandering ghosts until the allotted time has elapsed.

Demographic statistics in India and the Delhi region must be considered with caution, for the problems of gathering accurate data were, and still are, many. Chandrasekhar (1959: 32–37) stated that from 1901 to 1955 births were less often registered than deaths, that causes of mortality and ages of the deceased were difficult to obtain, and that the legal restrictions on marriageable age resulted in inaccurate recording of age. The system of gathering and reporting data from village India has long been inefficient. In the Delhi region before 1969, the head of a household was supposed to report deaths and births to district officials. With the passage of the 1969 Registration of Births and Deaths Act, effective January 1, 1971, it became the duty of the head of a household to register live and stillbirths within seven days of occurrence at the nearest registration center. Registration of deaths within three days is also part of the law. Upon the registration of a birth or death, a certificate stating the facts of each is given free of charge to the informant. Violation of the act is theoretically punishable by a fine of 50 rupees, but during our fieldwork some deaths and births went unreported and remained unknown to the Government so no fines were levied (Gazetteer Unit, Delhi Adm., 1976: 855–856).

There were reasons both for reporting and not reporting births and deaths. Landowners might not report the birth of a daughter because of the Hindu Succession Act of 1956 by which women may inherit equally with men (S. Freed and R. Freed, 1976: 197). On the other hand, landowners reported the births

24

and deaths of males to keep the record straight for the patrilineal inheritance of land. After the passage of the 1969 Registration of Births and Deaths Law, the landless were careful about reporting births because when they presented their birth certificate, they received a ration card for the new family member. Many landowners also carefully registered births. A ration card allowed the purchase of grains and other commodities at a government fair price shop at controlled prices. Some villagers did not report deaths as long as possible because they wanted to continue to use the ration card of the deceased.

WAR AND OTHER TURBULENCE

Figures for the number of deaths from war, raids, riots, and confrontations are difficult to evaluate or may be missing entirely. High and low estimates may vary by an order of magnitude. If figures for medieval combat are taken at face value, the slaughter in those times was impressive. Some of the 17 (or 12) annual raids into the heartland of northern India by Sultan Mahmud, who came to power in the Sultanate of Ghazni in A.D. 997, resulted in tens of thousands of deaths and the enslavement of hoards of prisoners. The most celebrated of his expeditions in A.D. 1024 was undertaken to sack the temple of Somnath. The fierce battle is said to have left more than 50,000 dead (Smith, 1958: 205–208). Balfour (1885, 2: 782) said that only 5000 Hindus fell in the battle at Somnath. When Shahab-ud-Din defeated Prithvi Raj in A.D. 1193, "Then followed scenes of devastation, plunder, and massacre that have too often been enacted in Delhi" (Balfour, 1885, 3: 296).

In 1398, Timur invaded India. He ravaged the country, slaughtering the inhabitants of every place he passed. He defeated Mahmud Tughlak at Panipat. Upon reaching Delhi, he was enraged by a surprise attack and massacred an alleged 100,000 Hindu prisoners whom he had taken along the way. Delhi surrendered, but plunder and violence aroused resistance which in turn provoked a general massacre. Delhi was almost depopulated for two months. Timur reduced the city to a mass of ruins from which it took more than a century to emerge. Timur quit India leaving be-

hind anarchy, famine, and pestilence (Balfour, 1885, 3: 888; Smith, 1958: 260–261; Encyclopaedia Britannica, 1966, 7: 199, 22: 233). Medieval historians call attention to the ferocity of the Muslim invaders from central Asia who slaughtered "hundreds of thousands" (Smith, 1958: 237).

In modern times, casualty statistics for both sides in otherwise well-documented wars are sometimes difficult to obtain. For example, we have found no figures for total casualties on the British side during the Mutiny of 1857 although precise numbers are available for specific battles. Figures for casualties among the mutineers are very sparse. However, figures for major engagements suggest that the toll both for the Government and the mutineers was not light. Balfour (1885, 2: 1025) reported that some 2000 mutineers died in Lucknow in the fight at the walled garden called Sekundar Bagh. The battle for Delhi cost the British 3817 (or 3835 or 3837) casualties (Leasor, 1957: 362; Collier, 1964: 264; Gazetteer Unit, Delhi Adm., 1976: 89). According to Leasor, of a total of 3817 casualties (992 killed, 2795 wounded, and 30 missing), 2140 were Europeans. The number of mutineers who died is unknown, but it almost certainly exceeds the British figure. Moreover, after Delhi fell to the British, in reprisal, ". . . the whole population of Delhi was driven out into the open, and thousands were killed after perfunctory trials or no trials at all" (Encyclopaedia Britannica, 1992, 21: 97). One estimate places the number of people killed in the eight months after the reconquest of Delhi at 26,000. It is likely that many more people died in the aftermath of the fighting than in military actions. So many people either died or fled Delhi that its population is estimated to have fallen to one fourth its former number (Gazetteer Unit, Delhi Adm., 1976: 91–92).

India enthusiastically supported the British at the beginning of World War I in August 1914. Smith (1958: 779) noted that ultimately India recruited 1.2 million men for the war of whom 800,000 were combatants. O'Dwyer (1925: 215) specified that the Punjab contributed about 100,000 men. Lucas (1926: 342 and fn.) reports that India put some one million soldiers into the field, an effort which he calls magnificent; the Indian

Army suffered according to official figures 64,449 killed or died and 69,214 wounded.

There are figures of casualties for some of the conflict attending the campaign for Independence; for example, a prohibited meeting held in Amritsar at an enclosed space known as Jallianwallah Bagh was broken up by troops under General Dyer. Casualties were an estimated 379 killed and 1200 wounded (Smith 1958: 785). An Indian estimate for this engagement is 1000 dead (Gazetteer Unit, Delhi Adm., 1976: 100). Such figures, while quite impressive in the context of a political meeting, pale into insignificance when compared to the massacres that attended partition. Published figures of people killed in 1947 as a result of Independence and the partition of India and Pakistan are only guesses. Collins and Lapierre quoted estimates that range from one to two million, the most extravagant guess, to 500,000 by the foremost Indian student of the massacres, to 200,000 to 250,000 by Britain's two leading historians of the period. In any case, reports of violence are graphic (K. Singh, 1956; Tandon, 1968: Chap. 17; Collins and Lapierre, 1976: 396).

FAMINE

Until rather recent times in India, greater and lesser famines due to drought have taken place with a rough periodicity. The lesser droughts occurred at intervals of about six or eight years. At intervals ranging from 13 to 24 years, substantial failures of rainfall led to bad famines. This latter generalization cannot be accorded too much weight, however, as shown by the two bad famines within a few years of one another in the 1890s. The periodicity of all droughts taken together has resulted in a ratio of about two bad to seven good seasons. Famines were sometimes accompanied by warfare which interrupted agriculture and aggravated food shortages. Moreover, the same atmospheric conditions that produce famine contribute to epidemic diseases, which kill more people than a fatal deficiency of food, although starvation reduces the ability of victims to withstand illness. The combination of famine, pestilence, and succeeding swarms of insects and rats

results in the staggering mortality rates that follow major droughts (Balfour, 1885, 1: 1072–1076; Moreland and Chatterjee, 1957: 300, 409–410).

The part of India that has an average annual rainfall from about 20 to 35 inches is susceptible to drought when the southwest monsoon fails, a region that includes Delhi, Punjab, and Haryana (Balfour, 1885, 1: 341). Now protected by a network of irrigation canals, agriculture in this region was at one time much more dependent on rainfall. A severe famine in the Punjab which formerly included the Delhi region was recorded in A.D. 1345. War was a factor in this famine. Wood and Maconachie (1882: 19) stated, "Muhammad Tughlak's savage extravagance in his war schemes brought on . . . the famine of 1345, wherein men ate each other." Wood and Maconachie (1882: 18–20) reported that famines in the Punjab have occurred twice in the 17th century, three times in the 18th century, and eight times in the 19th century up to 1868. An unusual famine which took place in 1816 was a result of the eruption of the Tamboro volcano on the island of Sumbawa in the East Indies in 1815, which caused considerable climatic changes and damage to crops in India and as far away as England, Scotland, and New England in America (Sigurdsson and Carey, 1988: 71–72). Balfour (1885, 1: 1072) listed five great droughts in the Northwest Provinces in the 19th century and four less serious ones up to 1877. A series of famine years in the first three decades of the 19th century led to the bread riots of 1837–38. Riots also occurred due to the famine of 1860–61.

The last quarter of the 19th century saw terrible famines. The Great Famine of 1876–78 may have been the worst. This famine started in the south and covered all peninsular India; the next year, the Punjab and the Northwest Provinces were hit. In 1877, 36 million people were short of food in South India; the following year, 22 million in the Northwest Provinces and the Punjab were affected. The famine was accompanied by cholera and smallpox in Bombay Presidency. The misery of the affected population was enhanced by a great rise in the price of food grains because of hoarding by private traders in the expectation of still higher prices. Although the Government of India took relief measures, it did not interfere with the normal course of private trade. Beyond an expected 6.5 million deaths in India at the time, an estimated additional 5.25 million deaths took place due to famine (Tinker, 1966: 128; Wyon and Gordon, 1971: 176; Kulkarni, 1990: 13–14).

The famines of 1896–1897 and 1899–1900 produced suffering and mortality comparable to the Great Famine. Each one at the time was officially described as the most disastrous of the 19th century (Guz, 1989: 197; Kulkarni, 1990: 15–18). Although famine may appear suddenly, both these famines were preceded by a year of bad harvests and developed slowly. In each case the immediate precipitating factors were a failure of rainfall and drought. The first famine was widespread over much of India; the second was more limited in area. The Punjab was affected by both famines with Hissar district suffering the most. Hissar, one of seven districts of the former Delhi Division of southern Punjab, is now part of Haryana, the state that borders Delhi Union Territory on the north, west, and south. Although Delhi was somewhat outside the area of maximum distress, it suffered considerably as indicated by the grain riots and looting of grain shops in Delhi during the 1896–97 famine. The Government of India again, as during the Great Famine, refused to interfere with private trade in food grains. The price of wheat, whose supply was roughly normal, rose along with the price of scarce grains, but there were no price differences between famine and nonfamine areas. Mortality during the famine years of 1896–97 exceeded the normal level by 5.65 million. Although the mortality during the second famine was officially 1.25 million, it was probably three or four times that figure. In Hissar, the 1899–1900 famine had noticeable mortality consequences in 1901 and 1902. Most excess postfamine deaths were attributed to "Fever," which for villagers was the sign of ghost illness. Malaria was in all probability prominent among the victims of Fever, although at the time the cause of the disease and its method of transmission had just been discovered and were unknown in the general population. During famine, malaria is absent due to lack of water, but when the rains return, so does malaria, which is particularly lethal because of the lingering debilitating effects of famine (Guz, 1989: 197–207, 214–216, 218–219; Kulkarni, 1990: 15–18, 23, 24).

As Guz (1989: 214–219) noted, famine is a complex phenomenon. Although food may generally be in short supply in a region as vast as the Punjab, there may nonetheless be areas where supplies are more or less normal. The Punjab as a whole was a net exporter of food grains in every year of the famines of 1896–97 and 1899–1900. The transportation system was adequate for moving food into needy areas. The problem was not so much the availability of food. People starved or were hungry because they did not have the money to buy food. Crop failures eliminated the purchasing power of farm laborers, artisans, and small landholders because there was no alternative employment outside agriculture. Moreover, a needy person had to meet rather severe qualifications to be eligible for the governmental relief program. Famine caused by drought involves not only a shortage of food but also a failure of the water supply. Village tanks dry up. Villages are deserted as their inhabitants take to the roads. People die of thirst on the roadside. Milch and draught cattle are killed because there is no fodder and they can be eaten, at least by non-Hindus, which means that farmers have to obtain loans to purchase bullocks when plowing is again possible. Not only does mortality increase during a famine but the birth rate declines. The Government cannot end its emergency programs with the first normal harvest.

Beginning with the 20th century, rail transportation, canal irrigation, and governmental and private relief measures put an end to famine until 1943 when famine struck in Bengal. Food shortages due to World War II contributed to the recurrence of famine, especially in 1943 (Moreland and Chatterjee, 1957: 520–521, 544). Bengal might have escaped the tragedy, but the fall of Burma in 1942 ended imports of Burmese rice. This famine was "'more man-made than an act of God'" (Kulkarni, 1990: 19). After the Independence of

India in 1947, regional food shortages resulted in faminelike conditions and food was obtained from the United States, Canada, and Australia to avert catastrophe (Tinker, 1966: 129–130).

The dread of famine is well expressed in the following verses extracted from a popular folk ballad of the Punjab collected by Usborne (1905: 17):

A Ballad of Famine

Loaf on loaf there it stood;
I had baked all I could
All the jewels — they were sold
All the silver and gold,
To buy flour to make bread for the children;
No more could I beg, buy or borrow.

Up came an old man and he emptied the pan.
Fie, Fie.
Grey-beards should die,
And that soon, and not let children starve.
From where will come bread for tomorrow?

DISEASE

Wood and Maconachie (1882: 18), reporting on health in the Delhi District in 1868, noticed that many men had bodily defects and seemed to be suffering from spleen, malnutrition, lameness, were semiparalytic, or one-eyed. A high degree of drunkenness was common. Records from the then Delhi District provide a general description of disease of the spleen, from which 75 percent of the population suffered. This disease was probably due to excessive drinking and to malaria that existed in the canal-irrigated portions of the Delhi District (Wood and Maconachie, 1882: 16–18). Standing water provided a favorable breeding environment for the anopheles mosquito, the vector of malaria. Malaria at that time had not yet been identified. The diagnosis as disease of the spleen was based on Ayurvedic humoral theories of disease. The theory is that disease caused by imbalance of bile, *pitta*, one of the three humors of Ayurvedic medical theory, affects the organ then known in Ayurveda as the spleen, which today is recognized as two organs, the liver and spleen (Kutumbiah, 1969: 43). At that time the population tended to report all

illness as due to "Fever," the messenger of Hara (Death the Remover, Shiva) in Hindu belief (Daniélou, 1964: 196–197).

Flora Annie Steel (1929: 33), reporting on her early introduction to India and the Punjab in 1867, described dining with Sir Henry Cunningham, when suddenly he asked her not to pay attention to him or look at him because he was shaking with Fever. This was her first encounter with a person suffering from malaria, which then was identified as "Fever." From her many years in India, she tells about other diseases such as typhoid and cholera, and problems of diagnosing diseases by British physicians in India. About to leave India after her last visit in 1898, she came down with an acute attack of malaria. She later wrote, "The malarial mosquito had not been invented in those days, but in my delirium, I drew a picture of the beast which I averred was coursing through my veins" (Steel, 1929: 241). (For the discovery of the malarial parasite and mosquitoes as vectors, see Append. I: 1877–1901: Malaria.)

Despite epidemic diseases, such as cholera, in the Delhi District in the 19th century, the most often named cause of death was still "Fever." In traditional village belief, Fever is due to ghost illness. Complaints of Fever were frequently heard in the autumn months. Since this period marked the end of the monsoon and its often extensive flooding, many deaths may well have been due to cholera, malaria, and typhoid. In the late 1950s and 1970s, villagers still identified illnesses and causes of death with the term Fever. For example, in the fall of the year after the destructive monsoon of 1977, villagers complained of being ill with Fever (Wood and Maconachie, 1882: 16–18; Steel, 1929: 33, 130–131, 178–179, 240–241; Kutumbiah, 1969: 43; Wyon and Gordon, 1971: 173; Gazetteer Unit, Delhi Adm., 1976: 853–859; R. Freed and S. Freed, 1979: 327; 1985: 134).

Devastating epidemics, prominent in the history of India, were cholera, smallpox, plague, and influenza. Although villagers most often attributed deaths from these diseases to Fever, their true identities were known to government officials. Prior to 1901, smallpox, cholera, and famine were the main causes of death (Wood and Maconachie, 1882: 16–18; Wyon and Gordon, 1971: 173). A great

Indian epidemic of cholera broke out in 1878, during which time the death rate was very high (Wood and Maconachie, 1882: 18). In 1916, a cholera epidemic erupted in India, which escalated into the greatest cholera pandemic of the century (Sigurdsson and Carey, 1988: 72). Wyon and Gordon (1971: 56, 76, 173) stated that epidemics of cholera contributed to irregular population growth from 1872 until 1921. During the decades from 1910–50, the death rate from cholera was two to three times that of smallpox (O. Lewis, 1958: 278). In 1958, villagers in Shanti Nagar stated that there had been no cases of cholera in the village for the past ten years although a murder was covered up by reporting it as a death from cholera (Append. I: Cholera).

Smallpox has an ancient history in India and has been estimated to have been present there in the Indus River Valley before 1000 B.C. The earliest evidence of smallpox is a description in the Susruta Samhita, which was written in 600 B.C. The Susruta Samhita contains a description of smallpox, known as *masurika* in Sanskrit (Hopkins, 1983: 13, 16) and also in Hindi. Kutumbiah (1969: x–xxxvi) discussed the compilation of the Samhitas at different dates by the physicians, Charaka and Susruta. He stated that the Samhita period from 600 B.C. to A.D. 200 was the creative period in Ayurveda. Before A.D. 1500, the main evidence for smallpox, other than the Susruta text, may be found in references to Sitala Mata, Goddess of Smallpox. Holwell, an English surgeon, who lived in India several years, claimed that the Atharva-Veda describes "temple services and prayers used by Brahman priests for worship of a smallpox deity" and also mentioned the inoculation of people against the disease (Hopkins, 1983: 17).

The process of inoculation was called variolation and consisted of inserting pus or powdered scabs obtained from sufferers of relatively mild cases of smallpox into the skin of a susceptible person, one who never had smallpox, hopefully to cause a relatively mild case of the disease. Anyone who recovered from smallpox whether acquired by variolation or in the natural way had lifetime immunity. The death rate from variolation was less than from naturally acquired smallpox, but the procedure may have spread the disease. Variolation differs from Jenner's later vaccination with cowpox, which provides only short-term immunity against smallpox, thus requiring periodic revaccinations. Variolation was employed in India and other parts of Asia before it was introduced in Europe and England. However, variolation was not used everywhere in India (Hopkins, 1983: 6–7, 16–17; Append. I: 1796, Smallpox Vaccine; *see also* Append. I: Smallpox—Variola).

In India smallpox spread rapidly during the dry season before the monsoon, which begins at the end of June or in early July in Delhi (Hopkins, 1983: 8–9). In Shanti Nagar, the festival of Sili Sat, at which time the Seven Sisters (Mother Goddesses) are worshipped, the main Sister being Sitala, Goddess of Smallpox, takes place on the seventh day of the dark fortnight of Chaitra (toward the end of March). Sitala is also identified as Mata Rani (Mother Goddess Queen) (R. Freed and S. Freed, 1962: 262–271); Append. V: Calendric Events).

Although smallpox vaccinations were introduced in Bombay in 1802, the practice spread slowly. Epidemics of smallpox occurred throughout India in 1868–69, 1872–79, and 1884–85, during which periods at least 2.5 million people out of the 180 million in British India were reported as having died of the disease. Smallpox continued to be epidemic in the 20th century despite the passage of the Vaccination Act of 1880, and its amendment in 1908, because it was not possible to enforce the law (Hopkins, 1983: 152, 153, 155). Although smallpox epidemics were feared at the beginning of the 20th century, by 1943 the registered cases in the Delhi region numbered 1265; the death rate was 0.6 per thousand of population with a total of 624 deaths. By 1968, there were only 70 registered cases with 13 deaths; the death rate was 0.039 (Gazetteer Unit, Delhi Adm., 1976: 867, table 7). During fieldwork in 1977, one woman pointed to facial scars on a four-year-old child, who she said had smallpox two years previously. In 1980, the World Health Organization announced that smallpox had been eliminated throughout the world (Berkow, 1982: 188; Hopkins, 1983: 310).

An epidemic of plague started in Hong Kong in 1895 and spread to Bombay by the beginning of 1896. Fraser (1911: 271) described the city, especially the slums, as a breeding ground for plague during 1896, and "that first mad exodus at the end of 1896, when the railway stations were crammed with people who fought for places in the trains" and fled the city carrying "the plague with them." Thereafter it spread throughout India, persisting until 1921. It has been estimated that one-third of the 6.5 million deaths from plague between 1901 and 1911 were in the Punjab (Wyon and Gordon, 1971: 174). By 1918 (or 1921) the toll had risen to about 10 million. The first cases of plague detected in the Punjab were in October 1897, but the epidemic and mortality rate did not become acute there until 1902. In 1904, plague deaths in all India numbered 1,143,993. There were fluctuations: plague mortality throughout India in 1907 was 1,315,000 dropping to 156,000 the following year. Then in 1911, the number of deaths again rose; for the first six months ending June 1911, the deaths were reported as 650,000 (Fraser, 1911: 272). The Punjab was the most severely hit, having lost over 2,250,000 people by the end of 1910 out of a total population as recorded in 1901 of less than 22 million. Mortality in the Punjab was greatest in the villages (Fraser, 1911: 271–272). The epidemic cut down many young men and women in the early years of maturity. Numerous remedies were sought to control plague, such as quarantines and inspection of travelers on the railroad, but the most important step, the discovery of the causal bacillus, had already been made by Shibasaburo Kitasato and Alexandre Yersinin in 1894–95 (Harris and Levey, eds., 1975: 2161; Append. I: 1894, Bubonic Plague; *see also* Plague—also called Bubonic Plague, Pestis, and Black Death).

When the plague epidemic became acute in the Punjab, a Mr. Haffkine, who had carried out research on plague, came up with "a prophylactic fluid," which Fraser (1911: 274) mistakenly called a sterilized virus of the disease. It was to be used to inoculate and provide a limited amount of protection. Unfortunately, the first inoculations, which were given to 19 people in the Punjabi village of Malkowal in 1902, came from a single bottle of the fluid, and all who were inoculated died of tetanus. No one knew how the tetanus organism got into the vaccine, but preventive

inoculations for plague stopped because thereafter the population feared the inoculations (Fraser, 1911: 274–276).

Later as a result of the plague epidemic, Lord Curzon and others established a British Plague Research Commission, and the primary step they took was a crusade against rats in India inasmuch as bubonic plague is transmitted from them by fleas to human beings. They also continued research for the prevention of plague through inoculations.

The following excerpts from a very long song collected by Usborne (1905: 38–41) reflect the extent of the Punjabis' fear of plague and inoculations. The people in Malkowal, who escaped death because they were not inoculated, did not understand what caused plague and tetanus. They simply knew that 19 people were inoculated and all 19 died; thereafter they had great fear and distrust of inoculations forced on them by the Government. Like the people of Malkowal, villagers in Shanti Nagar still feared inoculations in the 1950s and 1970s, but much less in the 1970s.

Song of Plague

Oh, Lalaji, you ought to have died as soon as you were born.
Take out all the beds. The plague has entered the house.
Before this only a yard of cloth was wanted to bury a corpse, now you want a whole piece.
The dead used to be carried by their brethren and friends,
Now low-caste leather sellers carry them to burial.
They used to weep in the streets, but now they are crying in every house.
There is a city called Rahun where the lacemakers live; that is where the plague first came.
Then the plague took up its abode at Shankar and the English erected a standing camp.
They found a device. There will never be such a remedy again.
Then the Sahib gave orders: 'If a man be inoculated, perhaps he will escape from the disease.
This is my remedy.'

Then the people collected and combined against it and were quarrelsome.

In Ludhiana the plague created such havoc that a quarter of the people died at once.

In the lane, called the Mud Alley, a shopkeeper died every day;

No one went near them;

Sons and mothers wept from a distance.

There was the wailing of death in every house.

The undertakers made much profit.

There was no end to the firewood burnt in the funeral pyres.

Each corpse required 200 lbs. of wood.

40 lbs. cost a rupee.

The dead consumed large quantities of wood.

Plague spreads to humans in two ways. Bubonic plague spreads from the bite of fleas who obtain the bacillus from infected rodents; pneumonic plague spreads from the inhalation of droplet nuclei spread by coughing patients with bubonic or epidemic plague, who have developed pulmonary lesions (Berkow, 1982: 110). Today plague can be successfully treated with streptomycin, and immunization can be obtained with the standard-kill plague vaccine. It can also be controlled by the use of repellents to minimize the bites of fleas, as well as by rodent control (Berkow, 1982: 110–111). In the Delhi region in recent decades three cases of plague with two deaths were reported in 1944 and one case with one death in 1946. This reduction in reported deaths from plague has been brought about by systematic trapping, baiting, and cynogassing rat burrows, in addition to anti-plague inoculations in the Union Territory of Delhi (Gazetteer Unit, Delhi Adm., 1976: 868).

The worldwide pandemic of influenza, killing tens of millions of people in less than a year in 1918–19, had a serious effect on the population of India, where 12 to 13 million people died in three to four months (Wyon and Gordon, 1971: 175; Crosby, 1977: 5). It first entered India in Bombay and Calcutta in June 1918 and peaked in Bombay in October, when the mortality rate for influenza in India was reported as "without parallel in the history of disease" (Crosby, 1977: 8). Crosby (1977: 5–6) reported that the incidence of influenza was high "for the very young, higher yet for persons between twenty and forty, and lower than normal for the elderly." Wyon and Gordon (1971: 175) on the other hand refuted the statement that influenza was particularly fatal to young adults based on "the subsequent distribution of populations of India and the Punjab." (Append. I: 1933–1940s, Influenza; *see also* Influenza—also grippe, grip, or flu).

Although the great epidemics of the past gradually came under control, many contagious diseases persist in the Delhi region. Important among them are diphtheria, malaria, pneumonia, influenza, poliomyelitis, tuberculosis, puerperal fever, tetanus, and rabies. High death rates of women from puerperal fever and infants from tetanus neonatorum are due to unsanitary delivery practices, but are usually blamed by village women on a ghost taking the mother and the infant (Gazetteer Unit, Delhi Adm., 1976: 859–872).

CHAPTER 6: DEATHS OF FEMALES AND THE FAVORED STATUS OF MALES

The preference for sons in most of India except Kerala has resulted in a population with more males than females, as consistently reported in the Census of India beginning with the first one in 1868. The census in 1981 reported 22.9 million more males than females. This demographic characteristic of the Indian population has been most pronounced in the northern states of Punjab, Haryana, and Uttar Pradesh (Visaria and Visaria, 1981: 1729, 1731, 1733, tables 2, 3). A preliminary report based on data from India's 1991 census indicates a ratio of 920 females to 1000 males (Crossette, 1991: A6 L). The preference for sons and the low status of females are intertwined with the customs of patrilineal descent, fraternal polyandry, dowries, crude and unhygienic midwifery, better care for sons than daughters, Sati (widow burning), female infanticide, female feticide, dowry and other murders, and suicides of wives and daughters.

The total population of the Delhi District of the Punjab in 1868 was 608,850. There were 866 females per 1000 males (Wood and Maconachie, 1882: 91, 93, table 1). For the decades from 1901 through 1961, the proportions of females per 1000 males were 916, 869, 845, 860, 846, 837, 847 (Gazetteer Unit, Delhi Adm., 1976: 129–130, tables 1, 2). In 1958 in Shanti Nagar, there were 392 females and 407 males, a ratio of 963 females to 1000 males (S. Freed and R. Freed, 1976: 37, 38, tables 1, 2). In 1977, there were 629 females and 695 males, a ratio of 905 females to 1000 males (S. Freed and R. Freed, 1985a: 239, table 2).

In Shanti Nagar and usually in North India, descent is traced patrilineally. Daughters marry out of their own clans and most castes also avoid the clans of the mother and father's mother. Children belong to the husband's family. The village is also an exogamous unit. Because daughters leave their natal villages at marriage and sons stay at home, sons are preferred to daughters for economic reasons: they carry out the work on the land and/or otherwise contribute to their family's economy. In recent times, employment in modern salaried occupations, principally in metropolitan Delhi, has become a mainstay. Daughters and wives also work in the fields, but the management of the land usually devolves on sons. Thus, parents count on their sons to remain in the village and take care of them in their old age.

An important consideration in the desire for more sons than daughters is the dowry and cost of a daughter's wedding. In addition, a father must provide gifts at yearly festivals and at life-cycle events for his married daughters and their children, and his sons assume this responsibility after their father's death. Gifts and dowries given and received more or less balance out if a man has an equal number of sons and daughters. More sons than daughters means more dowries received than given and a positive balance of gifts at festivals and life-cycle rites. The whole matter is summed up in the saying, "A girl is the dacoit of India." Another important factor in the preference for sons is that in Hinduism sons are necessary to carry out the proper ceremonial functions for the funerals of their parents. If they are not carried out properly, then it is believed that the parents will become lingering ghosts.

An important aspect of the preference for males is that few couples are satisfied with just one son, for the mortality rates in India are still high enough to make parents with only one son very anxious. Parents generally want two or three sons, hoping that one will survive to take care of them in their old age. Because sons are so highly valued, the deaths of infant sons have a greater impact on the women than the deaths of daughters. They believe that a lurking, malevolent ghost of a wife who died without issue or in childbirth has a penchant for taking the souls of infant sons.

The belief that more male than female children die leads some villagers to think that there are more females than males in India. In 1978 two elderly Jat brothers were discussing the matter, and one of them, whose daughters-in-law had born only daughters, commented that there were more females than males in India. We argued that there have been more males than females in the Indian population for over 100 years. Both men insisted that we were wrong and asked the source of our information. We pointed out that the censuses of India for over 100 years have shown a higher proportion of males than females. One of the men responded that the facts were wrong and that they "were all lies." Not at all impressed by the work of the Government, both men said that "One can't believe such reports."

BIOMEDICAL DIFFERENCES

India and Sri Lanka are among the few countries in today's world where men live longer than women. Both biomedical factors and cultural practices have effects on longevity. That women outlive men almost everywhere suggests that genetics and current medical practices are, on balance, more favorable to them than to males. Thus, an exception to this worldwide trend, like the one that currently occurs in India, is best explained by reference to cultural practices. However, before turning to the cultural practices that favor males, we briefly summarize some recent discussion concerning the genetic and medical bases for gender differences in longevity (Goble and Konopka, 1973; Verbrugge, 1982; Waldron, 1983; Wingard, 1984; Otten, 1985; Roth, 1985). The three articles most applicable to India are by Otten and by Roth, who consider cultural and biological differences, and by Goble and Konopka, who emphasize the effects of various diseases on the sexes.

Male mortality exceeds female mortality in almost all stages of life, especially during the interuterine and neonatal periods (Goble and Konopka, 1973: 325; Roth, 1985: 238). Although some diseases are more serious for males, and others, for females, males on balance suffer a disadvantage with regard to infectious diseases, such as tetanus, typhoid, typhus, and dysentery, which are major causes of death in India, especially the death of infants. The incidence of malaria, a serious disease in India, is about the same for both sexes, but females are more seriously affected by it during gestation, parturition, and lactation (Goble and Konopka, 1973: 329). Although immunity develops from previous malarial attacks, the balance between the parasites in the blood and immunity is such that pregnant women experience a decline in immunity (Davey and Wilson, 1971: 156).

Despite the difficulty of extracting an average susceptibility to disease from a complex situation involving many different diseases, the male disadvantage appears to be pronounced and has the effect, providing that cultural factors do not intervene, of evening the sex ratio (males/females $\times$ 100) at the age of reproduction (Otten, 1985: 185). The sex ratio at birth is about 105 males per 100 females. A commonly cited explanation for the "male disadvantage" is based on the difference in sex chromosomes between males and females. Females have two X chromosomes; males have an X and a Y chromosome. For males, sex-linked genetic material is transmitted almost exclusively on the X chromosome, which means that harmful or lethal alleles, whether dominant or recessive, will be expressed phenotypically. The XX configuration of females offers protection against genetic disadvantages that males, hemizygous for the X chromosome, lack. Moreover, X-linked immunoregulatory genes seem to be involved in the clear advantage shown by females in resisting infectious diseases, for women carry higher concentrations of immunoglobulins than men. Although women benefit from their vigorous antibody response to infection, they are more vulnerable than men to autoimmune disorders (Goble and Konopka, 1973: 339–340; Otten, 1985: 204–205; Roth, 1985: 238).

The male disadvantage based on genetics may have been enhanced in the modern era because of gender differences in reaction to widely used chemotherapeutic agents. The effectiveness or toxicity of particular agents is a matter of concern in India where many largely untrained curers distribute modern drugs with insufficient knowledge of the appropriate indications and dosage. It is not clear whether males or females benefit more from the panoply of modern drugs, but antibiotics appear to be more effective for females than males. Before antibiotics, more boys died than girls; after their advent, the gender disparity in mortality became greater (Goble and Konopka, 1973: 334).

That resistance to disease would, on balance, favor females and lead to their longer life expectancy would be difficult to show just on the basis of data from India, but in most countries, females outlive males, which suggests that this tendency reflects basic biological differences and should also characterize India. Why therefore do Indian males live longer than females? For the answer, we turn to cultural practices that reduce the life expectancy of females.

SATI

As indicated in Chapter 2, Sati (Faithfulness) is the name for the consort of the god Shiva (Daniélou, 1964: 122). She destroyed herself in the fire of her anger when Daksha, her father, would not allow Shiva to partake in the ritual sacrifices of the other gods. The custom of high-caste widows burning themselves on their husbands' funeral pyres derives from this story. The basis for the story of Sati and the conflict between her father and husband resulting in her demise can be traced to ancient texts of the Vedic Age: the Rig-Veda, Atharva-Veda, Upanishads, and Brahmanas; the Mahabharata, and last, the Puranas (Dowson, 1950: 117, 296–300; Daniélou, 1964: 188–198, 321–322; Doniger O'Flaherty, 1980: 132, 154, 162, 272–275; Append. II: Sacred Hindu Texts). British officials and missionaries in India generally used the variant spelling "suttee" for the custom of a woman immolating herself on her husband's funeral pyre, but Sati is preferable (Basham, 1954: 187).

The custom of Sati has persisted in North India and the Deccan as reported in historical accounts and recently in newspapers. Widows were known to burn themselves immediately after the deaths of their husbands, even up to 35 years thereafter. The castes that practiced this custom generally, but not always, prohibited widow remarriage (Stutchberry, 1982: 27, 65, note 9). Since the lot of a widow was difficult and sad, Sati may have been preferred by some widows, but pressure on a widow to join her husband's soul, whether at the time of his death or thereafter, was often exerted by members of her husband's family, "and some cases were shockingly cruel" (Balfour, 1885, 3: 781). The custom persisted because it was deemed to be the proper

action for a faithful wife, thus following in Sati's footsteps.

It is rather odd that this custom arose from these tales about Shiva, Sati, and Daksha, inasmuch as Shiva did not die and Sati was not a widow. However, in the context of the Cosmic Sacrifices of the Vedic Gods, it makes sense. Daniélou (1964: Pt. 2, Chap. 4: 63–69) described these sacrifices and their components. He stated (p. 63): "All this universe, conscious and unconscious is made of fire (agni) and offering (soma)." The ritual sacrifices are based on Agni, God of Fire, fed by Soma, the food of the ritual fire. Soma is also the ritual offering, the elixir of life, and the ambrosia which is given to the partakers in the rituals. Most importantly, "Soma is identified with the beverage-of-immortality (amrta), the beverage of the gods" (Daniélou, 1964: 66). Soma is also semen, the essence of life, and is one of the most important gods of the Vedas. The ninth book of the Rig-Veda has 114 hymns praising Soma, and the whole Sama-Veda is addressed to Soma. When Soma is drunk by those partaking in the rituals, "procreative energy is produced in the lower region" (Daniélou, 1964: 76–77, 121–122). Thus, the gods are created and fed through the ritual sacrifice.

Daksha had incestuous tendencies toward Sati and did not want Shiva as his daughter's husband. If Shiva was barred from these cosmic sacrifices, he would no longer be able to partake of Soma, would then be unable to procreate, would lose his immortality, and like an ordinary human being would die, which explains Sati's consummation and death in the fire of her anger. This story emphasizes the importance of Soma (semen), reproduction, immortality, proper behavior in the ritual sacrifices, and it invokes the tabu against incest. From it came the custom of high-caste widows burning themselves on their husbands' funeral pyres.

The first recorded Sati in the Mahabharata is that of Madri, the second wife of Pandu; other Satis are also described in this epic (Balfour, 1885, 3: 781). Additional evidence for the practice of Sati in India has been found in Greek accounts of Alexander's invasion of India. Sati stones with memorial inscriptions, an imprint of the widow's hand, or a single, upraised stone arm, may still be seen in parts of India, commemorating the many wives who followed their husbands in death. The earliest stone was found near Saugor (Sagor) in Madhya Pradesh with an inscription recording the cremation of man and wife in A.D. 510 (Basham, 1954: 187–188; Moreland and Chatterjee, 1957: 29, 46; Hutton, 1963: 35, 246; Stutchberry, 1982: 34–35, 66, note ll). One stone was found which depicted a woman about "to tub a kicking child." Inquiries revealed that the stone was a memorial to a mother's love, for she was cremated alive along with her beloved son on his funeral pyre and thus became a *Ma-Sati*, or Mother-Sati. "Mother-Satis were of all classes from the potter woman to the princess" (Temple, ed., 1883–87, IV(39): 44).

Two Muslim Emperors were against Sati. Akbar, in the 16th century, allowed the practice only if immolation was voluntary. In the 17th century, Aurangzeb passed a law forbidding Sati. Despite these actions, the custom was still strong in the early 19th century (Moreland and Chatterjee, 1957: 218, 250).

When the British first came to India, they were said to tolerate Sati and female infanticide (Rawlinson, 1965: 407–408). James Tod, for years a British official in Rajasthan, described the custom of Sati among the Rajputs and indicated that the wife's burning herself on her husband's funeral pyre was an act of faith whereby she atoned for her husband's and her own sins (Tod, 1920, 2: 737–738). Balfour (1885, 3: 781–786) discusses several examples of Sati, some involving the immolation of several score wives. For example, he mentioned Tod's recollection that when a ruler of Marwar (Mewar), Raja Ajit Singh, died in 1780, his queen whom he had married in his old age, along with other queens married earlier, and 58 "curtain" (harem) wives burned themselves on his pyre. Balfour also noted other than religious motives for encouraging Sati. ". . . satis were often urged for political reasons, and to get rid of the encumbrance of lone widows. When the Rajput Jawan Singh of Edur died in 1833, there was a forcible sati of his widow" (Balfour, 1885, 3: 782).

Some Hindus favored the abolition of Sati. One early reformer for the rights of women and abolishment of Sati was Ram Mohan Roy (ca. 1772–1833). He was a Bengali Brahman who was born and passed his childhood in a village near Calcutta. He later lived in Calcutta and London. From 1800 to 1833, he played an important role in movements for social reform. He learned English, was influenced by British social concepts as well as by Islam and Christianity, and was prominent in the Brahmo Samaj, a reform sect of Hinduism, which believed in one God. He was horrified at witnessing the burning of his sister-in-law on her husband's funeral pyre and attempted reforms, such as the abolishment of Sati and the passing of a law permitting high-caste Hindu widows to remarry. He wrote a series of pamphlets regarding women and associated reforms, which he published from 1815 to 1830. During the time when he was active, Calcutta was the capital of India, and he came in contact with many members of the British Raj, including their wives, whom he admired (Mayo, 1932: 83; Rawlinson, 1965: 410; Borthwick, 1982: 110–111; Mukherjee, 1982: 155–156, 158, 161, 167–168).

Toward the end of the 18th century and into the early 19th century, records from Bengal indicate that there was an increase in the number of Satis. The recorded yearly total never exceeded 900 from 1815–1829, at which time the estimated population of Bengal was around 60 million. By 1829 the climate of opinion had changed and the British Government passed a law making Sati an act of murder in British India (Stutchberry, 1982: 28–29), but the custom did not end.

Sleeman, another British official, expecting the passage of the law of 1829, issued a proclamation in his district of Jubbulpore (Jabalpur) in March 1828 banning Sati. Later, the relatives of a Brahman widow asked that she be allowed to burn herself on her husband's pyre. When Sleeman investigated the matter, he found the widow sitting near the Narbada River, where her husband's pyre had been placed, as was customary. She remained there without eating or drinking even after her husband's corpse had been burned. When Sleeman returned again after a few days, he found her still there. She told him, "I go to attend my husband, Umaid Singh Upadia, with whose ashes on this funeral pyre mine have already been mixed three times [i.e., in former lives]. My pulse has long since ceased to beat, and I shall suffer nothing in the burning." That she spoke her husband's name for the first time was a sign she considered herself already dead. Sleeman then consented to her immolation. The fire was prepared and the widow walked around it once, muttering a prayer and throwing flowers into the flames. Before entering the heat of the flames, she wrapped herself in a wet cloth, saying that it would counteract anything impure falling on her in the fire because it had been moistened in the holy Narbada River (Sleeman, 1915: 18–23).

Another Sati reported by Sleeman took place in 1809, when a Brahman banker died. The wife of a low-caste Lodhi cultivator claimed that she had been a Sati with the banker in six previous lives and that she would now join him on his pyre for the seventh time. Many people tried to dissuade her and convince her that she had never been the Brahman's wife in former lives, but she claimed that in her last birth she had been living with her husband, the Brahman, in Benares and by mistake had given a holy man salt instead of sugar with his food. He then told her that in her next birth she would, therefore, be separated from her husband and be born in a low caste. Since she was already 60 years old and no one could stop her, she was burned by her Lodhi husband and his brother (Sleeman, 1915: 30–31).

Derrett (1978: 81, 212), commenting on the Hindu Widows' Remarriage Act passed in 1856 and the further amendment to the act in 1976, claimed that the 1856 Act marked the death of the Hindu Marriage law and linked his statement with Sati and the remarriage of widows. He claimed ". . . no respectable Indian consistently or powerfully championed the abolition of suttee; it was the work of squeamish Europeans. The question of the remarriage of widows was a more genuine concern for learned and pious Hindus." Commenting on the passage of the Hindu Widow's Remarriage Act in 1856, Derrett (1978: 81) stated: "It is notorious that it had very little effect since very few widows took advantage of it." As Lamb (1975: 161) pointed out, ". . . to pass a law is not necessarily to effect reform."

This statement applied in Shanti Nagar where, in the late 1950s, the remarriage of Brahman widows, the only sizeable twice-born group, was still frowned upon. By 1977, this attitude had changed to some extent, for two Brahman widows did remarry. Both of them had never born children and one had not mated with her first husband who died when she was 12 years old. Childlessness and an unconsummated marriage were apparently accepted as mitigating factors. A childless Brahman woman after her father had her first marriage annulled also remarried (Chap. 19: Forthright's Remarriage; College Man, City Girl, and Tricky; Chap. 21: Beauty).

Widowhood is believed to be due to the actions of the widows' souls in past and present lives, i.e., they become widows because of those actions. Widows in 1958–59 were looked upon as inauspicious, especially if they became widows while relatively young. Early in the day, villagers avoided crossing the path of one elderly widow for fear she might cast the evil eye and they would have bad luck all day. Although no Satis took place in Shanti Nagar during our fieldwork, a possible souvenir of the custom remains, for men say that women are not allowed to go to the cremation grounds when a corpse is burned. Instead of mentioning the possibility that a grieving wife might immolate herself, villagers simply say that women cannot bear the sorrow and sight of a cremation.

The occasional observance of Sati even in recent years and the intense emotion that the custom stimulates reflect the position of females in Hindu society. Despite legislation permitting the remarriage of Hindu widows, the remarriage of high-caste widows has generally been frowned upon. The Delhi Gazetteer (Gazetteer Unit, Delhi Adm., 1976: 169) noted that "Although the Hindu Widow Remarriage Act of 1856 had legalised such marriage for all castes of Hindus such marriages hardly ever took place. Even today, in urban Delhi, the percentage of widows who marry is extremely small."

Just as widows still rarely remarry, Satis still take place. Recently a number of Satis have been reported. Baxi (1982: 356) wrote:

. . . on November 28 [probably in 1979] a group favouring revival of sati decided to celebrate a 'Sati Day' by taking out a massive procession in the streets of Delhi and announcing plans to build a temple dedicated to the memory of a Rajasthani princess who became a sati in the fourteenth century. News concerning revival of sati is trickling in in [sic] the national media. On August 20, a sixteen year old girl became (or rather was forced to do so) sati in Rajasthan, drenched in 'pure ghee and incense' with crowds chanting "Sati Mata ki jai" [Hail Sati Mata]. Twelve days after the immolation, a shrine was built at the site and a crowd of about one hundred thousand people assembled, which included local politicians and notables. This is only one of the many reported incidents; the number of unreported incidents is anybody's guess.

In Rajasthan on September 4, 1987, Roop Kunwar, whose husband had just died, ascended his funeral pyre and was burned with his body. A crowd of 100,000, among them politicians from the Janata Party and young men from the youth branch of this party, attended the cremation and offered prayers. The incident and its aftermath have been reported in a series of articles in *India Abroad*, 1987, 17(52): 4; 18(2): 6; 18(5): 35. At first it was contended that Roop Kunwar voluntarily immolated herself. Investigations by representatives of women's organizations and the media cell of the Bombay Union of Journalists stated that this 18-year-old widow was forced to commit Sati, and that she tried to hide in a barn when she learned about the preparations for her immolation but was found and dragged back home for the cremation. One news report stated that people in the district collected about 5 million rupees to construct a temple in memory of Roop Kunwar but that they profited from the collection. In Madhya Pradesh, the police prevented the Sati of a 60-year-old woman (*India Abroad*, 1987, 18(4): 40; cf. Datta, 1988, for a historical study of Sati).

FEMALE INFANTICIDE

Female infanticide, the intentional killing of a female infant, has long been practiced in India. In past and present times, it may have been accomplished by direct means, such as suffocation, or indirectly by neglect, exposure, or abandonment. Female infanticide is a counterpart of the general preference for sons in North India. Whether the deaths were or are due to intentional killing, exposure, or neglect, female infanticide in the 19th and 20th centuries has been difficult to prove. The principal evidence for it rests on the longtime preponderance of males over females. In addition, a substantial amount of anecdotal evidence attests to the practice.

Female infanticide reflects the general preference for sons, which in turn is related to patrilineality, patrilocality, the dowry system, and required yearly and life-cycle gifts to married daughters, as described earlier. The problem is that more than one daughter may be regarded as an unacceptable drain on family resources. This conjunction of social structure and family economics is the major stimulus leading to female infanticide. There is also a concern that uncontrolled female pubescent sexuality has the potential for compromising family honor. This problem has traditionally been handled by sending a daughter to her husband for Gauna very shortly after menarche, but nonetheless, premarital pregnancies (or pregnancies between marriage and Gauna) may still happen.

Infanticide has been, and to some extent remains, a worldwide practice. Among its functions are population control, the spacing of births, and the concealment of illicit sexual activity. Considerations of land inheritance in patrilineal societies are likewise associated with female infanticide. In ancient China, Greece, Rome, and India the authority to kill an infant vested in the family head, but cases from India suggest that other members of a family killed infant girls or arranged for their deaths (Maine, 1963: 119, 147–149; Slater, 1971: 29, 222–223; Harris and Levey, eds., 1975: 1337; Simon, 1980: 246). Among hunters and gatherers, a woman often could manage only one baby at a time and had to abandon a newborn while the older sibling was still an infant. Female infants have been more readily abandoned than male. A similar motive is present in rural India. Raising children in rural areas is hard work and a mother has limited energy. A mother with many children can regard the raising of another daughter as more than she can bear (Chapple, 1970: 178; Langer, 1974; Chagnon, 1977: 15, 74–75; R. Freed, 1977: 594–595, Williamson,

1978; Simon, 1980: 246; Lindholm, 1982: 163; Hrdy, 1984: 49).

For the subcontinent of India, Tod (1920, 2: 740, fn. 2) referred to an early report on the Ghakkars, a Scythic tribe living on the banks of the Indus River, who practiced female infanticide. When a female infant was born, someone took her to the marketplace, held her in one arm, displayed a knife, and announced that whoever wanted the infant as a wife could take her. Otherwise she would be killed. This example of potential infanticide or the sale of an infant was later denied during Tod's time despite the fact that the Ghakkars had a preponderance of males over females.

L. Dube (1983: 279–280) noted that "preference for boys depends very much on the social structure features of the society." She linked female infanticide and the scarcity of females in India with fraternal polyandry and wife sharing in particular castes in Haryana, Punjab, and parts of Rajasthan. In the Himalayan region, fraternal polyandry is still openly practiced. This custom of a number of brothers sharing one wife prevents fragmentation of land, pools family resources, and controls population. Recently Goldstein (1987) has delineated the practice and its role in the control of population in Nepal.

In North India the Jats practiced polyandry and female infanticide in the 19th century. Crooke (1896, 3: 310) stated that "an extraordinarily large number of Jats remain bachelors" and "in every pedigree table where the elder of the number of brothers only is married or perhaps one or two . . . it is most probable . . . that a modified system of polyandry does prevail." Female infanticide led to a shortage of marriageable women, so Jats sometimes purchased low-caste girls as wives (Crooke, 1896, 3: 1, 10, 29).

The tradition of fraternal polyandry persisted in the form of limited plural matings within a joint Jat family in recent decades. If a husband was in the army or otherwise absent, songs were sung about a younger brother who remained at home and mated with his sister-in-law. Family and caste members looked on these matings as insurance against the patrilineage dying out for lack of male issue (O. Lewis, 1958: 189, 192–193). Mandelbaum (1974: 34, fn. 6) also referred to the

practice of polyandry as still existing in North India.

Vishwanath (1983: 407) claimed that female infanticide characterized dominant castes in villages and was caste specific. It is not surprising, therefore, that through the 19th century the Rajputs, Jats, and possibly the Ahir, Gujar, and Ror castes, often the dominant castes in their villages, practiced female infanticide which resulted in a shortage of wives. Fraternal polyandry is logically connected to female infanticide. However, no one in Shanti Nagar admitted to the practices of fraternal polyandry or female infanticide although a Jat volunteered the information that Jats formerly purchased low-caste women as wives, a custom which was linked with female infanticide (Crooke, 1896, 3: 28–29).

Since the 16th century in North India, bards have sung a ballad about star-crossed lovers, somewhat like Romeo and Juliet, who mated outside the rules of their caste. The romantic legend partly serves as an excuse for female infanticide. The hero and heroine were Ranjha, a cowherd, and Hir. Ranjha's praenomen was Dido, but he is known by his patrilineal clan name, Ranjha. He belonged to the Jat caste; Hir was a member of the Siyal clan, which claimed descent from Rajputs, a higher ranking caste than Jats. Because of the caste difference and Hir's childhood marriage, which however had not been consummated, Ranjha and Hir were not allowed to marry. They then eloped, thus flaunting the rules of marriage. Pursued by the Siyals, members of Hir's clan, the couple somehow became separated. The Siyals overtook Hir, killed her, and buried her in a tomb, for they were Muslims as were the Ranjha Jats. Before the tomb was sealed, Ranjha arrived on the scene, entered the tomb, and buried himself alive with Hir. So like Romeo and Juliet, they both died. The mausoleum for these lovers may still be found in the Jhang District of the Punjab where the Siyals lived. After the death of Ranjha and Hir, a blood feud arose between the Siyals and the Ranjhas. Public opinion blamed Hir for the tragedy and resulting feud. Thus, daughters came to pose a potential danger to family honor and customary marriage practices, a belief that has been used to justify female infanticide. The names of Ranjha and Hir were shouted in Shanti Nagar during Akhta in 1958, a ceremony exorcising cattle disease (Temple, ed., 1883–1887, 3(15): 29; Temple, 1885, 2: x–xi, xvi, fn., xvii, 177–178, 499–580; Temple, 1900, 3: xii; R. Freed and S. Freed, 1966: 684–685).

Female infanticide was relatively common in 19th-century North India and parts of the Deccan. The Rajputs were notorious in this regard. W. H. Sleeman, an official of the British Raj, described examples of infanticide that he encountered while journeying through Oudh (an area east of Delhi, part of the present-day state of Uttar Pradesh, in which both Jats and Rajputs were settled). The procedure among the Rajputs was to kill an infant girl (allegedly by poisoning her with the milk of the *mudar* shrub and suffocating her with her own feces), to bury her in the room in which she was born, and to plaster the floor with cowdung for purification. His informant explained the practice on the grounds of economics and prestige. The great cost of a daughter's marriage could reduce a family to poverty, and to accept Kanyadan (in this context, gifts, or payment, for a virgin) was a stain on family honor. ". . . it was the dread of sinking, in substance from the loss of property, and in grade from the loss of caste, that alone led to the murder of female infants . . ." (Sleeman, 1858, 2: 38). The experience could be traumatic for a young wife. ". . . mothers wept and screamed a good deal when their first female infants were torn from them, but after two or three times . . . they become . . . reconciled . . . and said, 'do as you like. . . .'" (Sleeman, 1858, 2: 37).

Common as it was, infanticide was still considered bad karma, and among the Rajputs there was a ritual for expiating guilt and restoring a family to its normal ritual status and prestige. On the 13th day after the death, a village priest, a Brahman, cooked and ate his food in the room where the infant was buried. By eating food cooked in ghee (clarified butter), it was believed that the priest took the sin of killing the baby upon himself (Sleeman, 1858, 2: 38). Later in his journey, Sleeman quoted a Brahman farmer: ". . . 'much sin, sir, is no doubt brought upon the land by the murder of so many female infants. I believe, sir, that all the tribes of Rajpoots murder them; and I do not think

that one in ten is suffered to live. If the family or village priest did not consent to eat with the parents after the murder, no such murders could take place, sir; for none, even of their nearest relatives, will ever eat with them till the Brahman has done so'" (Sleeman, 1858, 2: 55).

Pakrasi (1972) has delineated the attempt to eradicate female infanticide, beginning with the measures taken by the East India Company in 1789 in Benares and culminating with the All-India Act of 1870 banning female infanticide that was passed by the British Government. The Proclamation of 1834 in Western India was particularly applicable to the Jhareja Rajputs in Kathiawar, for it was based on the great preponderance of males over females there as evidence of female infanticide. Despite the Proclamation, the census of 1849 for the Jharejas of Kathiawar enumerated 7535 males to 3239 females (Pakrasi, 1972: 29). Before 1840, their sex ratio had been four males to one female. Although after 1840 the sex ratio for the Jharejas began to decline, still in 1854 it was 204 males to 100 females (Pakrasi and Sasmal, 1971: 218).

Tod commented on the practice of female infanticide among the Rajputs of Rajasthan. He quoted a Rajput as saying, "Accursed the day when a woman child is born to me." Tod explained the reasons for female infanticide among Rajputs as based upon complex rules regulating marriage, namely, tabued clans (*gotra*s) and tribes, all of whose members were considered to be the equivalent of consanguines and therefore barred as spouses. He said that a ruler who wished to arrange a marriage for his daughter or daughters paid excessive sums for the weddings and dowries. The ruler felt that this show of prestige was necessary because of bards singing the praises of former rulers who emptied their coffers for their daughters' marriages. Thus, female infanticide was blamed on the problem of finding a possible match for a daughter and the great expense of a marriage (Tod, 1920, 2: 740–743; quotation: 740). As early as 1829, Tod (1920, 2: 743–744) provided another explanation for the almost universal practice of female infanticide among Jhareja Rajputs. He said that originally they were Hindus but then converted to Islam, thereby losing their high-caste Rajput standing as Kshatriyas. After a while, they separated from Muslims to regain their previous high-caste standing as Hindus, but once having lost it they found that it was difficult to find other Rajputs to intermarry with them.

The Jat rulers of Bharatpur followed the custom of killing their daughters. Sir Michael O'Dwyer (1925: 102), acting as Political Agent to the Maharaja of Bharatpur, where female infanticide was practiced in the 19th century, mentioned the costly arrangements for the marriage of the Maharaja's sister. To determine how much should be spent on the wedding, O'Dwyer asked what precedent existed for the amount of money requested and was told no precedent existed because no daughters in the family line had previously been allowed to survive.

It was not until the second half of the 19th century that several anti-infanticide acts were passed for different parts of India, which at first were unsuccessful. Legally required measures included the registration of births, marriages, and deaths, with which the rural population even today does not completely comply. A significant event was a great durbar, a reception for rulers from princely states as well as other high ranking persons, merchants, and landlords from the Punjab, which was held in 1853 in Amritsar, Punjab, to suppress and ultimately to abolish female infanticide (K. W. Jones, 1976: 24–25, fn. 45). The Infanticide Act of 1870 was the first infanticide act to cover all India. British administrators concluded from the problems of enforcing these early acts that it was necessary to educate people that killing infant girls was a crime (Pakrasi, 1972). Despite educational efforts and the passing of laws, female infanticide still proved difficult to exterminate.

Flora Annie Steel, a contemporary of Sir Richard Temple, linked female infanticide, the importance of sons, and the low position of women in India. Referring to Kautilya's Arthashastra on statecraft and aspects of ancient Indian life (Basham, 1954: 50–51, 79–80), she stated that ". . . a man may marry any number of women since women are created for the sake of sons," indicating the slight importance of females and the nil importance of a woman without sons (Steel, 1929: 243). Steel was a forthright, outspoken woman during her long stay in the Punjab in the last half

of the 19th century but generally regretted not having "put her oar in" against some practices, especially when she had specific knowledge. However, she did state, ". . . it was I who told the Western police officials in the Panjab that it was the woman's habit when she had no sons, to expose her new born female infant outside the village for the jackals to carry off; since, if they dragged it from the village, her next conception would be a male one" (Steel, 1929: 183).

Steel's comment about the importance of a woman bearing a son is as true today as in the 19th century. In Shanti Nagar in the 1950s and 1970s, a female learned at an early age that her function in life was to marry and to bear children, preferably sons. Although we never heard of any specific instance of female infanticide, a few cases might have occurred, for in Shanti Nagar, as is generally true in North India, males outnumber females. Female infanticide would be difficult to establish either by impartial visual confirmation or an autopsy. Births until the late 1950s took place in the home attended by a midwife and a mother-in-law or other related senior females. A female infant might easily be suffocated at birth or a few days later either by the mother, the mother-in-law, or a midwife who was paid by the father or senior male in the household to do so. Although formerly babies were buried immediately, in recent decades they have been cremated. Autopsies were never performed on the dead unless the death was reported to the police before cremation or burial. It goes without saying, that cases of female infanticide were not reported to the police. Asphyxia was reported as a major cause of infant death in a dominantly Sikh community in Punjab where Sikhs formerly were known for the practice of female infanticide (Wyon and Gordon, 1971: 192, table 20). Suffocation was in all probability a technique of infanticide.

Minturn and Hitchcock (1966: 96–97) suspected that female infanticide survived into the mid 20th century. Reporting on their fieldwork among the Rajputs of Khalapur, Uttar Pradesh, a village 90 miles north of Delhi, they wrote: "Until the turn of the century, the prejudice against girls was experienced in the custom of female infanticide. Today . . . differential medical treatment still causes twice as many girls as boys to die before reaching maturity." They also noted (fn. p. 96): "The British outlawed infanticide in the region in 1848. A government officer was sent to the village about 1900 to enforce this law. Because of his necessary violation of purdah restrictions, he was murdered by some outraged men. However, government pressure and Arya-Samaj influence may have brought an end to infanticide as a widespread custom, although isolated instances still occur." Minturn and Hitchcock are here making a distinction between infanticide by abrupt action and infanticide through neglect, in this case the withholding of medical care.

FEMALE FETICIDE

A recent development beginning in the last half of the 1970s is the abortion of female fetuses. This development came about as a result of the amniocentesis test, which makes it possible to determine whether a fetus possesses undesirable genes. If so, the fetus may then be aborted. As people in India soon found out, an amniocentesis test also reveals the sex of a fetus. The knowledge makes it possible selectively to abort female fetuses.

The only time that we heard a villager allude to the role of modern science in controlling the sex of a newborn was in a conversation between a Jat Farmer, whom we call Actor, and Manipulator, his Brahman friend. Manipulator, a high school graduate and urbanized man, brought up the subject although he did not mention amniocentesis and abortion. However, he indicated to Actor that science somehow could determine that a son rather than a daughter might be born. This conversation foreshadowed the concern of the Government and others about the manipulation of the sex ratio in favor of sons.

Actor had been expressing his worries about changes in the law regarding the inheritance of land. Although he had four sons who would inherit his land, so far his daughters-in-law had born only daughters. Manipulator, to allay the Jat's worries, stated, "Customary law allows the sons and grandsons to inherit." He did not mention that under statutory law daughters and granddaughters might claim a share of their father's or grandfather's land, for he knew that daughters seldom did so

because their fathers arranged and paid the costs of their marriages including their dowries and also continued to send them gifts at festivals and at life-cycle rites for their children. Actor, still thinking of his lack of grandsons, claimed that their births depended on Bhagwan (God). He said, "It is up to Bhagwan to give you a son." Manipulator replied, "If you pray honestly and devotedly, you can mold Bhagwan to make the decision to give you a son." Actor retorted, "There is no need to pray because it is up to Bhagwan to make the decision." Manipulator added that he had read in the paper that "now there is a medicine that can be given up to three months of a pregnancy, then after giving it, a boy will be born." Actor was disturbed by this statement and said, "I do not believe scientists can do this. Scientists cannot change the world, only Bhagwan can determine such things. If scientists can or have determined the sex of a child before birth, then I will kill the scientists." In Uttar Pradesh, one informant replied when asked about some people believing that folk medicine could change the sex of a fetus: "If it worked there would be no girls born in India" (Jeffery and Jeffery, 1983: 655).

The early amniocentesis test was developed in the late 1960s. A prenatal diagnostic test, a chromosomal-genetic analysis of the fetus, is made to determine whether the fetus possesses any chromosomal abnormalities that would affect the fetus and the child after birth. Clinicians withdraw fluid from the womb of a pregnant woman, cultivate cells from it, and examine their nuclei. While checking for abnormalities, the clinicians can determine the sex of the fetus. This procedure cannot begin until the second trimester of pregnancy, and the analysis of the cells cannot be finished until the fetus is five months old, at which time the parents-to-be can elect to have the fetus aborted. A more recent technique called chorionic-villus sampling allows the clinician to snip off a piece of tissue from the placenta in the eighth week of gestation. With this technique there is no need to incubate the cells. The analysis can be obtained in the first trimester of pregnancy (Berkow, 1982: 1931; Konner, 1987b: 2–3).

The technique of amniocentesis-cum-abortion was introduced in India in 1974 and rapidly became popular. Between 1978 and 1983, 78,000 female fetuses were reported to have been aborted in India. In 1982, a male fetus was aborted accidentally in a sex determination clinic in Amritsar, Punjab, "and all hell broke loose" (*India Abroad*, 1987, 17(28): 1). A study in Bombay revealed that 8000 abortions took place following amniocentesis sex testing, of which 7999 were female fetuses. In 1985, 40,000 female fetuses were aborted in the Greater Bombay area (*India Abroad*, 1987, 17(28): 8). Obviously the technique had captured the public's fancy, but it resulted in a spate of polemical articles on the subject (Ramanamma and Bambawale, 1980; Balasubrahmanyan, 1982; Bardhan, 1982; Mutiah, 1982; D. Kumar, 1983a, 1983b; L. Dube, 1983; Vishwanath, 1983; Jeffery and Jeffery, 1983; Jeffery et al., 1984). Although female feticide has the same result as female infanticide, i.e., discrimination against the female sex and a preponderance of males, according to L. Dube (1983: 279) "infanticide is clearly seen by the people as destruction of a full-fledged human life, not so feticide." Further, because amniocentesis-cum-abortion is scientific and modern, it may have given feticide prestige.

Recent field research in the Bijnor District of Uttar Pradesh, a region where female infanticide was formerly practiced by the Jat caste and where female infanticide by neglect may still take place, provides further information about the ramifications of the new practice of female feticide (Jeffery and Jeffery, 1983; Jeffery, et al., 1984). Amniocentesis-cum-abortion was available only in a few health centers at the price of Rs. 500, which meant that the people who obtained it were primarily urbanites or well-off landowners. Vishwanath (1983: 406) argued that female feticide is urban and class centered. He claimed that mainly the educated, who are aware of scientific advances, will favor it. However, the practice may become more democratic if the number of centers for testing expands and the cost is reduced due to competition and future medical advances (Jeffery and Jeffery, 1983: 656). Whether or not a relative scarcity of women will enhance their value, Jeffery et al. (1984: 1211) commented:

... in our view, any further reduction in the sex ratio in Northern India would signify a continuing decline in the relative status of women there, and would be highly unlikely to offer any benefits to the women who survive. That is, there is no evidence that women are an economic commodity for which scarcity will raise their value . . . rather, their scarcity is symptomatic of their low value. In the states where sex ratios are the lowest [i.e., where there is a preponderance of males, Punjab and Uttar Pradesh], there are no signs that social mechanisms are developing to raise the value of women.

The time when the soul vests in the fetus may be important in predicting the continuation of the practice of female feticide. In the Bijnor District of Uttar Pradesh, the belief is that the fetus has no soul or determined sex until the third month of pregnancy (Jeffery and Jeffery, 1983: 655). In Shanti Nagar, some women had no idea when the soul vested in the fetus, but the general belief was that it did not take place until the sixth month of pregnancy. Formerly Brahmans performed a ceremony at the beginning of the seventh month of pregnancy to mark the vesting of the soul. Because of the belief that it vested in the sixth month, women in Shanti Nagar, under the Government of India's sterilization program, did not hesitate to be aborted and then sterilized in the third month of pregnancy, for only after six months with the vesting of the soul was the fetus the equivalent of a human being. Thus, the chorionic-villus test, which permits early identification of the sex of a fetus, would be attractive to women in Shanti Nagar who might be considering the abortion of a female fetus. However, feticide after the vesting of the soul would be tantamount to murder. In such a case, the soul of the fetus could become a ghost and haunt the mother.

Instead of raising the value of women, the scarcity of women which is the aim of those who practice female infanticide and female feticide, may well result in fraternal polyandry, which was practiced among the Jats along with wife purchase when necessary. Among the Rajputs, who formerly practiced polygyny and kept harems, they obtained their women through their political power and wealth, but since those times have passed, they too may resort to fraternal polyandry. Leela Dube (1983: 279–280) is inclined toward the theory that continued female feticide along with the preponderance of males will result in wife-sharing by a set of brothers or a set of brothers and patrilineal cousins, which comes under the rubric of fraternal polyandry, for patrilineal cousins often live in a joint family with their cousins and are considered as similar to brothers and are so addressed.

Recently the Government of India has issued circulars directing that action be taken under the penal code against anyone using a prenatal sex determination test and then obtaining an abortion. No government hospital now is permitted to conduct sex determination tests (*India Abroad*, 1987, 17(28): 8). Further, a bill aimed at preventing doctors from violating the ban on sex determination tests leading to feticide was introduced in the state legislature of Maharashtra (*India Abroad*, 1988, 18(23): 19). Despite government efforts, the banning of this practice may prove difficult to enforce.

DOWRY AND OTHER MURDERS, AND SUICIDES

During our fieldwork in Shanti Nagar, we learned of several teen-age girls or young brides who were either murdered or were forced to commit suicide. A few brides were killed by their husbands in order to obtain another dowry in a subsequent marriage or because the husbands did not care for the wives chosen for them by their fathers. A number of older wives also committed suicide for various reasons. These girls and women were believed to have become ghosts (R. Freed, 1971; R. Freed and S. Freed, 1985: 143–146; Chap. 15).

A dowry murder is the killing of a bride or a young wife by her husband, mother-in-law, and/or other in-laws because the husband's family is dissatisfied with her dowry and had unsuccessfully demanded more. The economic advantage of dowry murder is that the young widower can then remarry and obtain another dowry. Dowry deaths have apparently increased in recent years, or at least more of them have been identified as such. The sheer number of dowry murders is a matter of governmental concern; in 1985, 999 dowry deaths were reported; 1319 in 1986; and 1786 in 1987 (*India Abroad*, 1988, 19(10): 39).

In a review of urban dowry murders, Bordewich (1986) pointed out that demands for additional dowry have led to murders and suicides of brides. A husband and his family encouraged bridal suicide by beatings and other harassment. Bordewich correctly linked the low status of women to dowry murder and suicide. Bordewich, however, failed to recognize completely the interworkings of the social network between affines and consanguines at the village level, the importance of patrilineal descent, the inferior status of the bride vis-a-vis the husband, and the fact that a new bride leaves her natal village to live in her husband's natal village. Thereafter, she is under the jurisdiction of the head of her husband's family and subordinate to the senior woman in the family. An interesting factor in dowry murders and suicides is that they are primarily reported in the urban areas. They may still be found in rural areas but go unreported to the police or when known to them are classified as accidents (Gazetteer Unit, Delhi Adm., 1976: 650).

Dowry murder persists despite the Dowry Prohibition Act of 1961 (Derrett, 1978: 72, 96, 211) and additional acts against the practice that were passed in 1983 and 1985. In April 1987, the Indian Supreme Court took further action against people who committed or abetted dowry murder. The court ruled that the maximum penalty under the law should be imposed on anyone found guilty of murdering a bride for having brought an "insufficient dowry" (*India Abroad*, 1987, 17(32): 4). Anti-dowry laws have generally proved to be ineffective because dowries have long been entrenched in the marriage system of North India. It remains to be seen if the latest rulings will put teeth into the laws prohibiting dowry and thus prevent dowry murder.

INFANT AND MATERNAL MORTALITY

Many Indian women and their infants die in childbirth or shortly thereafter. One main cause for mothers is puerperal fever; for infants, tetanus neonatorum (Gordon et al., 1965a, 1965b). Almost all cases are the result of unhygienic conditions during lying-in, relatively untrained midwives, or inadequate treatment of postpartum disorders. Primiparous mothers are more vulnerable than women bearing their second, third, or even fourth infants; after the fourth birth, the mortality rate increases (Chandrasekhar, 1959: 115–118, 136; cf. Jeffery et al., 1989, for birth practices in Bijnor, Uttar Pradesh.) Until the Indian Government's Family Planning Programme was introduced, which has been accepted only gradually and partially, women bore many children and most still do, thus contributing to maternal mortality. Conditions are especially bad in the rural areas, where maternal mortality is high and the neonatal mortality rate is almost double that of the urban areas. However, infant mortality in India has been declining gradually since the 1920s from 45 deaths per 1000 infants to 15 per 1000 in the mid-1970s.

In the rural areas, the female death rate in the age group five to nine years is about 20 percent higher than the male death rate. The higher death rate for females persists until termination of the reproductive years (Padmanabha, 1982: 1285–1290). The higher death rate of newborn females is particularly noteworthy because three times as many newborn males as females die from tetanus neonatorum, the principal killer of newborns in rural India. Therefore, the mortality rates favoring males are generally seen as due to the fact that boys receive better medical care than do girls (Wyon and Gordon, 1971: 195), and also to the possibility of hidden female infanticide. Thus, females die in infancy and early childhood more often than males, contrary to the generally greater number of biologically based deaths of male infants at the beginning of the life cycle, as indicated by Goble and Konopka (1973), Otten (1985), and Roth (1985).

Contrary to the facts, women believe that male infants die more often than female infants. Their belief in the vulnerability of males is reflected in the saying "One Son is No Sons." They want sons and believe that it is necessary to have at least two sons to ensure the survival of one, which results in an average family of four or more children (S. Freed and R. Freed, 1985a: 248–250, 1985b: 2172–2173). They are not particularly interested, or even aware, that more infant boys are born than infant girls. They are almost entirely concerned with the infant boys who die, which concern reflects their desire for sons and their greater sorrow when a male infant dies than when a female infant dies.

CHAPTER 7: HEALTH CULTURE

The present health culture of Shanti Nagar is an amalgam of concepts and practices from five discernible cultural traditions, which form a time series, with significant overlap between some of the stages and persistence of some traditions into the present. There is also some sharing of concepts among the traditions. Nonetheless, a cultural and historical analysis in terms of disparate traditions is essential for understanding the current complex situation where the variety of traditions, concepts, and practices means that the villagers' cognitive structure of health, illness, and curing varies by individual, family, lineage, and caste (Angel and Thoits, 1987).

The earliest concepts are from Prevedic times. Next in time are important concepts and practices from the Vedic Age, followed by the periods when the Epics and the Ayurvedic Samhitas (texts) evolved. Ayurveda, a system of medicine based on the Ayurvedic Samhitas, arose after the main events described in the Mahabharata, but the Ayurvedic Samhitas probably paralleled the period during which the Mahabharata was assembled as a written composition. The beginning of Ayurveda dates to about the 6th century B.C. Islamic influences, the fourth cultural tradition, entered village medicine with the spread of Islam, first from Arab traders in the 10th century, then with the Moghul invasion and conquest of Northern India late in the 12th century. The British conquest of North India in the 19th century brought western medical traditions: homeopathy, Western medicine (allopathy), and, after World War II, popular pharmaceutical medicine. Since the Independence of India, the latter has been further promoted by commercial agents from Great Britain and the USA (Moreland and Chatterjee, 1957: 152, 159, 210 ff., 265; Bürgel, 1976; Porkert, 1976; Taylor, 1976; Jeffery, 1988: 45–46). Elements of contemporary medical theory and practice in the health culture of the village have a historical depth of at least three millennia and a geographical scope reaching from China to England and the USA. Only a cursory history of the elements contributing to the health culture of Shanti Nagar can be depicted here, but enough information is given to furnish an adequate understanding of the historical dimension of the current village health culture.

PREVEDIC AGE

Prevedic culture was an amalgamation of the Harappan Culture, indigenous tribal cultures, and the impact of the Indo-Aryan invasion, all with their various languages. The elements of health culture of the Prevedic Age are difficult to reconstruct because of lack of written records. The seals of the Harappan Culture, depicting concepts of the Prevedic Age, have yet to be translated or clarified. However, archeologists have found statues and depictions from the Harappan Culture suggesting the existence of mother-goddess cults. They also uncovered a figure in the Yogic position, which may have been the prototype of Rudra-Shiva. The statues, seals, and other representations from the Harappan Culture show individuals, animals, snakes, and the lingam, and suggest tree spirits, the ritual value of trees, and souls of the dead, all of which, together with The Grand Bath at Mohenjo-daro and ritual centers, are indications or forerunners of aspects of Hinduism, which through time have been related

to life, death, and therefore health. That exorcism existed in the Prevedic Age is evidenced by words related to "shaman" in both Sanskrit and Pali. Although the Harappan Culture may have been overcome by the Indo-Aryan invasion, the invaders in all probability adopted aspects of the culture of the vanquished, as usually happens in such cases. The Indo-European invaders were an agricultural, pastoral, nomadic people, who spread their beliefs widely in North India (Eliade, 1964: 4, 237, Chap. 14; 1978: 127, 190–192; Embree, 1972: 3–4; Thapar, 1976: 24–25, 29; Gove, 1986: 1824).

What remains from the Prevedic period are ubiquitous animistic beliefs which apply to sickness and death. When people fell ill and died, it was recognized that something, the soul, escaped from the body. In turn, the belief that soul loss causes death may have led to the fear of supernatural beings that could take the soul and had to be countered by supernatural techniques, such as exorcism. Although the origin of the complex of ideas about the soul, death, and the cycle of rebirths that is associated with health would be hard to pin down in ancient Hinduism, it is generally believed that animistic concepts, namely, the belief in souls and supernatural beings, may be very ancient because of their pan-human distribution, including tribal groups that in all likelihood were living in India before the Aryan invasion. The belief in spirits or souls of plants and animals apparently also derives from Prevedic times. From the viewpoint of village health culture, one of the most important beliefs stems from the mother-goddess cults of the Prevedic age, for the belief in the Mother Goddess persisted and was again evidenced early in the Rig-Veda (Banerjea, 1953: 66).

One basis for the persistence of the belief in a mother goddess, a deity that has developed into a number of specific mother goddesses, many of which serve as the names of diseases, especially those of childhood, is related to the fact that primarily women have charge of children in sickness and health. Thus, in Shanti Nagar, women more than men worship and make offerings at the village shrines for the mother goddesses to propitiate them when their children and other members of their families fall ill. Protective amulets, the idea of which is no doubt ancient, are part of the complex relating to the care of children. They are made of iron, gold, silver, beads, cloths, and/or strings and are placed on childrens' wrists, ankles, and around their necks to guard against ghosts and the evil eye. The mother goddesses are: (1) Sitala, also known as Chechak (smallpox, still worshipped as one of the Seven Sisters); (2) Khamera (measles); (3) Khasra (itches and miscellaneous skin diseases); (4) Marsal (mumps); (5) Phul ki Mata (boils); (6) Kanti (typhoid during which a rash appears); (7) Masan also known as Kalkaji (Goddess of the Cremation Grounds); (8) Kali (Goddess of Death and Destruction); (9) Chaurahewali (Crossroads Goddess, generally propitiated for the welfare of children). The first seven are known as the Seven Sisters. A Brahman Priest from a neighboring village gave us a somewhat different roster of names, one of which was Khelnimelni Mata (the sickness does not bother the child who can go on playing).

These goddesses are best known for the poxes they are believed to bring, especially as they affect children. Mother goddesses not only bring poxes, they also take them away when properly propitiated (R. Freed and S. Freed, 1962: 262–271; 1979: 306–309, 329). Propitiation of the mother goddesses is an important part of village Hinduism. Because of the connection of childhood illnesses and the mother goddesses, their propitiation still rests largely in the hands of women, for the care of infants generally is in their domain. Women make offerings, usually food, at the shrines of the mother goddesses when any family member, but especially a child, falls ill. At the yearly festival of Sili Sat, women honor the mother goddesses with offerings (R. Freed and S. Freed, 1979: 306–309).

VEDIC AGE

Concepts prominent in village health culture can be traced to the Vedic Age and are based on the four Vedas, the Brahmanas, and the Upanishads. Dates from various authorities vary but the most generally accepted are 1200 or 1000 B.C. to 900 B.C. (Append. II). The Rig-Veda, earliest of the Vedas, refers occasionally to diseases and their cures. Ve-

dic medical theory affirms that illness is caused by supernatural beings, such as deities and ghosts, due to the bad actions (karma) of the soul. The Atharva-Veda consists of rituals and mantras to be used by Brahman priests to exorcise the supernatural beings causing illness (Müller, 1898, AV: 36–37; Dowson, 1950: 350–351). Specific diseases are mentioned in it and linked with different supernaturals. For example, "Varuna sends dropsy to punish crime and especially falsehood." (Kutumbiah, 1969: xi). In addition to what Kutumbiah (1969: xi–xiii) described as Magico-Religious Medicine, the Atharva-Veda contains information on anatomy, the medicinal properties of herbs, and the use of the products of the cow for health purposes.

Vedic beliefs are perpetuated and elaborated by tales from the Mahabharata, the events of which took place about the 9th to 8th centuries B.C. and, therefore, are related to the Vedic Age, and by the tales in the Puranas of much later date (300 B.C. to A.D. 1500) but which are intended to reinforce the teachings of the Vedas (Append. II). These tales strongly influence village beliefs about ghost illness and exorcism. In particular, tales from the Mahabharata and Puranas developed the earlier concept of Fever found in the Vedas as an index of illness, which became associated with a ghost that brings the illness and tries to take the afflicted individual's soul. Thus, it is not unusual for women today to call exorcists to cure their children when they have Fever with delirium and a ghostly voice speaks from the child. Even when an infant cannot yet speak, Fever, convulsive movements, and incessant crying are considered sufficient symptoms of ghost illness for a mother to call an exorcist. Although the Atharva-Veda specifies that Brahman Priests should exorcise the illness and use specific rituals and mantras, exorcists come from a number of castes. In Shanti Nagar they are Brahmans, Chamars, and Chuhras. Exorcists called from beyond the village also come from a number of castes, and a few are Muslims.

AYURVEDA

Ayurveda is a major component of the Hindu health culture of today. It is based on the Samhitas of Charaka and Susruta. Both these texts distinguish between supernatural treatments and natural remedies, such as herbs and minerals. The Charaka Samhita is the work of three authors: Agnivesa, Charaka, and Drdhabala, in that order. The dating of the Samhitas is difficult, but Agnivesa's work is about the 6th century B.C. Charaka's work could be 58 B.C., A.D. 78, or A.D. 123. The last date has the most support, and Charaka is credited with most of the Samhita named after him. Drdhabala is much later, the 9th century A.D. The Susruta Samhita is primarily on surgery, which at first in 600 B.C. was associated with warfare. The name Susruta stands for two Susrutas: the elder and the younger. Susruta, the younger, broke the elder Susruta's association of surgery with warfare and merged surgery with the science of Ayurveda, probably by the second century A.D. (Kutumbiah, 1969: xv–xxi, xxv, xxix, xxx). Thus, the Susruta Samhita began in the 6th century B.C. and was completed in the 2nd century A.D. The period for both Samhitas and the development of Ayurveda is generally given as 600 B.C. to 200 A.D. Although this school of medicine is called Ayurveda, it is not part of the Vedas or the Vedic age even though the word Samhita has been used for the Vedas and the Ayurvedic Samhitas (Gove, 1986: 2007).

Ayurveda has long been a part of village health culture, but the villagers knew more about it in the 1970s than in the 1950s. Over two decades, more villagers had become literate. Moreover, they were influenced by a government program which promulgated the knowledge of Ayurveda and provided local dispensaries for the medicine and *vaids* (Ayurvedic physicians) in the clinics.

Ayurveda is based on the relationship of foods, climates, and seasons to human health. Foods have characteristics: hot or cold; and tastes: sour, bitter, sweet, and acid. The characteristics of a food make it appropriate for human consumption in a specific season, for example, hot foods in winter, cold foods in summer. Foods and when they are consumed have effects on the balance of the *tridosa*s (the three humors: bile, phlegm, and wind) and hence on human health (Kutumbiah, 1969: xv–xxi). In the 1950s, villagers knew the Ayurvedic categories of hot and cold foods,

but not everyone correlated them with the sweet, sour, acid, and bitter categories, the seasons of the year, and the three humors. An example of a hot and cold food classification made by a Chamar in 1958 follows:

> Rice is colder than ice. If you eat it in the winter, you will get pain and wind in the joints. Cooking makes no difference. It stays cold. But if rice is cooked or eaten with meat, it becomes hot; and if you eat meat with something whose essence is cold, the heat of the meat makes the other hot. Carrot is cold, also buttermilk, millet, and butter. Bajra [bulrush or pearl millet] is hot. Wheat has a uniform essence throughout the year, neither hot nor cold. [See also Chap. 13: Troubled.]

For North India, Planalp (1971: 145–193) has made a comprehensive study of Ayurvedic food classification correlated with the seasons. One of his findings is that differences of opinion regarding what foods are hot or cold vary from region to region in India and that a staple food, such as bread made from wheat eaten throughout the year in North India, would be classified as just right or neutral. In Shanti Nagar too there are differences of opinion concerning hot and cold foods and bread is also regarded as "neutral" (cf. Planalp, 1971: 150; Taylor, 1976: 293; R. Freed and S. Freed, 1979: 299, 312; Foster, 1984).

The gunas (qualities) and their associated personality types are sometimes related to food. They are mentioned in the Bhagavad Gita, a late addition to the Mahabharata around A.D. 300, but not in connection with food. They are also a part of Ayurveda. Primarily we will deal with the gunas from the point of view of Ayurvedic medical theories. They are referred to as qualities and are made up of threads and strands, which when mingled in various proportions make up all matter. A preponderance of different threads and strands determines the character or personality types of living human beings. Three basic types are recognized. When sattva (goodness, purity) dominates, a person is a *sattoguna*, a truthful person; rajas (passion, activity) is the main quality of a *rajoguna*, kings and men with physical power; tamas (darkness, dullness, inactivity) is the dominant quality of *tamoguna*, people who are predominantly devils (Daniélou, 1964: 23, 24, 26 ff.; Edgerton, 1965: 141, fn. 9; van Buitenen, 1980: xiii–xxv).

The gunas were mentioned by a few men of the Brahman and Jat castes in the 1950s, one of whom, Manipulator, was taking a mail order course in Ayurveda. They talked about the connection of food to the gunas and the personality types based on the gunas, pointing out that food contributes to the personality types. A similar expression in the West is: "You are what you eat." They said that milk, raw fruits, and vegetables without spices are associated with the *sattoguna* personality; strong food is associated with the *rajoguna* personality; and for the *tamoguna* type, onions and chili peppers are indicated.

Kutumbiah (1969: xxii) stated that gunas are defined and enumerated in the Charaka Samhita as various qualities. The sensible qualities are sound, touch, color, taste, and smell. Then there are 20 physical qualities: a few examples are heavy, light, cold, hot, viscous, and dry. Foods are compounds of the five *bhuta*s (elements: earth, water, fire, air, and ether), possessing various qualities (gunas), which are important in digestion and metabolism. One of the most important qualities is taste, *rasa*, involving the categories of sweet, acid, bitter, and sour (Kutumbiah, 1969: 36–37). Other qualities pertaining to food are: heavy and light, cold and hot, oily and dry, mild and keen, etc. For example, "Foods called 'light' contain largely properties of wind and heat" (Kutumbiah, 1969: 38). This Ayurvedic description of the gunas deals with the senses, matter or the elements, and physical and psychological attributes and is related to different types of foods. (For complete lists of these gunas, see Kutumbiah, 1969: xii, 35–40.)

Kutumbiah (1969: 177), commenting on the early Ayurvedic physicians, stated: "Charaka and Susruta try their best to liberate medicine from the stranglehold of animism. . . . They leave animism severely alone with regard to diseases which can be explained by the *tridosa* theory. It is only in the treatment of mental diseases, which are beyond the pale of rational medicine, that animistic explanations are invoked and magical therapeutics applied."

Jolly (1951: 175–183) described the Ayurvedic classification of nervous and mental diseases in relation to the way the humors affect the body. Under the heading of Madness and Possession, he listed six kinds of mental diseases; *unmada*, translated as madness, is due to disturbance of the humors: (1) imbalance of air causes laughing without reason; (2) imbalance of bile causes violence or violent ghost possession; (3) imbalance of phlegm causes loss of intelligence, memory, and appetite, and results in silence, loneliness, sleepiness, and general lack of grooming; (4) imbalance of all three humors results in an incurable condition; (5) painful excitation due to too much joy or sadness results in madness; and (6) poison causes madness. The cures for madness and possession are different medicines, and, for some patients, shock treatment. For example, they can be thrown into a well and kept there without water or food; chastised by lashing; left in a dark, empty place; or may be frightened with serpents, lions, or elephants. "Along with these violent remedies, it is also recommended to cheer the lunatic with friendly talk" (Jolly, 1951: 179). Although no villager described all six types of madness, some mentioned individuals whom they considered mad, *pagalpan*, the village term, or somewhat disturbed, who fit these categories. The fifth category of too much joy or sorrow was heard most often.

Wig (1983: 80) commented on DSM-III (1980) that rather than two emotions, such as anxiety and depression, which in the West "have been raised to the status of discrete disorders," an excess of emotions, such as too much joy or sadness may also be psychologically unhealthy. He adds that the European or Western tendency to think in terms of duality, for example, good or bad, body or mind, does not work in countries such as India and China where thought moves in terms of a continuum rather than as opposites. His comment applies to Ayurveda regarding mental disorders and also to the villagers' expressions regarding them.

In Ayurvedic theory, the worst form of madness is not due to disturbance of the *tridosa*s or the emotions but is possession by a ghost or demon. The recommended cure is appeasement of the ghost or supernatural being with gifts of food, drink, clothes, and jewelry (Jolly 1951: 179–180). This mental illness is called *bhutonmada* (madness due to a ghost or spirit). The remedy is exorcism. *Mada* in *bhutonmada* could also be translated as intoxication or excitation, similar to alternate, altered, or dissociative mental states (Jolly, 1951: 178–180; R. Freed and S. Freed, 1985: 109–113, 121, 125).

The nine *graha*s (sun, moon, the five planets visible to the unaided eye, and the ascending and descending nodes of the moon, known as Rahu and Ketu) and the astrological, zodiac-sign, *rashi*, under which one is born are thought to affect the health and fortune of children and adults. Ayurvedic theory claims that diseases peculiar to children may be due to the stars and that specific *graha*s cause specific diseases. An example is the planet Skanda (Mars), which is believed to cause convulsions, cerebrospinal meningitis, and encephalitis (Kutumbiah, 1969: 199–200) (cf. R. Freed and S. Freed, 1964: 73, table 2; 1980: 385–387, Fig. 6; Harris and Levey, 1975: 171–172, 638, 3047).

In the 1950s, Ayurvedic practitioners, *vaid*s, were not rated as highly by urbanized villagers as physicians trained in Western medicine. However, by the 1970s attitudes changed somewhat, and the following statement was heard a number of times in the village: "Allopathy puts down the disease, but Ayurveda roots it out." The increased prestige of Ayurveda was due to the government program upgrading Ayurvedic professional training and government funding of local Ayurvedic clinics with dispensaries for villagers. Kutumbiah (1969, Preface to the 2nd ed.: xvi) commented on the new look in Ayurveda: "Ayurveda looks very venerable and dignified in her own ancient lineaments but with this 'new-look' given to her she looks a flirt coquetting with modern medicine for petty favours and recognition."

LAWS OF MANU AND HEREDITARY DISEASES

Although the Laws of Manu are not part of the Ayurvedic Samhitas, villagers tend to regard as part of Ayurveda the laws and concepts from Manu relevant to health that Saraswati passed down to modern times. During the period when Ayurveda was introduced,

the Laws of Manu covered hereditary diseases in the context of contracting good marriages. The Laws of Manu are classified as part of the Dharmashastras (ethical law books) and were compiled between 200 B.C. and A.D. 100 (Sternbach, 1951: 117–120). The name Manu, however, first appears in the Mahabharata and belongs to at least 14 progenitors (Dowson, 1950: 199–202; Daniélou, 1964: 166, 515). Among the many Laws of Manu are those prohibiting marriage with persons having supposedly hereditary diseases or undesirable hereditary traits, a number of which are listed (Bühler, 1969: 76). The best known example found in Shanti Nagar is phthisis (pulmonary tuberculosis). The hereditary diseases are not based on the principles of modern genetics but on observations that specific diseases or traits recur frequently among members of the same family and their close relatives.

THE ARYA SAMAJ

The founder of the Arya Samaj, Swami Dayananda Saraswati, perpetuated the list of so-called hereditary diseases from The Laws of Manu in *The Light of Truth* (1956: 117). The traits he listed when he wrote the book in the 19th century are similar to those in the Laws of Manu: a hairy body, piles, epilepsy, white leprosy, albinism, phthisis, asthma, and bronchitis. The list in the Laws of Manu was compiled when the scientific bases for contagious and hereditary diseases were unknown. Saraswati also was unaware of the basic genetic principles regarding inherited traits. In the 1950s and 1970s, the belief in inheritance within families persisted in Shanti Nagar for tuberculosis, epilepsy, and other traits noted in the Laws of Manu. The basis of the concept of inherited traits may also be linked to the beliefs that due to past actions and family resemblances the same souls may be reborn in the same family lines and will be afflicted with the same diseases or traits.

ISLAMIC PERIOD

From Hindu medical theories we proceed to Islamic medicine and the practices derived from Unani and Unani Prophetic medicine. Islamic traditions were introduced into India by Arab traders in the 10th century and subsequently in North India by waves of Islamic invaders from the end of the 12th century. Unani medical theory incorporates Greek humoral theory and the theory of the wandering uterus (*hustera*), from which the theory of hysteria originated. This theory was preceded by the belief that possessions are caused by supernatural beings. In Unani Prophetic medicine, the Prophet Muhammad introduced the concept of disease inflicted by supernatural beings on humans as retribution for sin. This doctrine is compatible to some extent with karma in Hinduism. The Prophetic doctrines of ghost possession and curing by exorcism are similar to the corresponding concepts of Hinduism (Bürgel, 1976; R. Freed and S. Freed, 1979: 314–315; Simon, 1980: 65–72, 220–225; R. Freed and S. Freed, 1985: 113–114; 116–119).

Pulsing, also known in the village, which came from China via Arab traders in the 10th century, was incorporated in Unani medicine. "Wang Shu-ho (ca. 265–316) . . . became famous for his lucid and detailed book on pulse diagnosis, the *Mo-ching (Classic of the Pulse)*" (Porkert 1976: 72–73). This monograph became the point of reference for all later investigations of pulsing in the 10th century and influenced Islamic medicine and ultimately curing practices in Shanti Nagar.

Villagers believe that pulsing is essential to diagnosis and cure. They expect a curer to feel the pulse and at the same time look closely at the patient to discern the cause of illness. Patients have little faith in curers who do not follow this technique (R. Freed and S. Freed, 1979: 310). According to Opler (1963: 33), the pulse is taken with the width of two fingers away from the root of the thumb. The forefinger indicates whether wind is causing the disorder; the middle finger detects bile; and the ring finger, phlegm. The curer pulses the right wrist of a male and the left wrist of a female because it is assumed that the circulatory systems of males and females differ. Also, the left hand, used for ritually polluting activities, is inferior to the right hand, the latter used when it is important to maintain ritual purity, as in eating. Hippocrates and Galen in their medical theories contributed to the inferior position of women: Hippocrates with the theory of the wandering uterus as the basis of hysteria, and both Galen and

Hippocrates with concepts regarding anatomical differences in the right and left sides of males and females (R. Freed and S. Freed, 1985: 117–118). As practiced in Shanti Nagar, pulsing is compatible with village beliefs about male and female differences (cf. Lloyd, 1962, on the right and left sides of the body).

Daniel's (1984: 115) description of pulsing in Siddha medicine, found in South India, is somewhat similar to Opler's description. Six pulses are taken: three from the right wrist and three from the left. Both males and females are treated the same, in that pulses are taken from both wrists.

In a seminar given by psychiatrists at the National Institute of Mental Health & Neuro Sciences in Bangalore, Neki (1979: 113, 119), commenting on Unani Tradition, "discussed the introduction of the Unani system in India and provided this popular anecdote about pulsing by Avicenna, an Arab doctor who was called to examine a young royal patient in Damascus, whose symptoms had baffled other doctors. His diagnosis and prognosis was based on keeping his fingers on the pulse of the patient. While doing so, he first had the names of all the towns in the province repeated. At the mention of a specific town, he felt a flutter in the pulse. Then Avicenna called for someone to recite the names of the houses, streets, and quarters in the town. When a specific street was mentioned, again there was a flutter in the pulse. Then the name of a particular inhabitant in that location was mentioned, and he again felt the flutter and provided this diagnosis: "It is finished. This lad is in love with such-and-such a girl, who lives in such-and-such a house in such-and-such quarter of such-and-such town; and the girl's face is the patient's cure" (Neki, 1979: 118–119). This example is somewhat similar to techniques employed by exorcists for cases of ghost possession in Shanti Nagar. They often spend time talking with members of the family of a patient to build rapport and find out about problems within the family. Then they use the information in the course of treatment (Chaps. 17, 18).

Unani Prophetic medicine has points of compatibility with Prevedic, Vedic, and Ayurvedic health practices and reinforces the animistic concept of intrusive ghosts, called jinns by Muslims. The Chuhra Sweepers in particular were influenced by Islam from the beginning of the British Raj. The British built railroads and raised an army. Sweeper men were peripatetic and traveled to find work on the railroads and in the army in what is today Pakistan where a dominant Muslim population lived. Consequently, they came in contact with many Muslims and learned to be curers and exorcists from fakirs and hakims, the Islamic terms for these curers. Thus, Unani Prophetic medicine reintroduced the belief in intrusive ghosts, jinns (Chap. 16: The Headless Sweeper). As part of Unani Prophetic medicine, the Prophet Muhammad taught that to suffer pain expiated sin, that disease was a sign of holiness, and that suffering was a religious virtue. It is of major significance that Unani Prophetic medicine reinforced the concept of curing by exorcism and employed amulets as protection against the evil eye and ghosts; both techniques are found in Shanti Nagar (Bürgel, 1976: 54–61).

WESTERN INFLUENCES

The last of the major medical influences are Western and include Western medicine, also known as *Angrezi* (English) medicine and allopathy; popular pharmaceutical medicine; and homeopathy. Homeopathy was introduced by the English and other European doctors in the 19th century. It appealed to an urban elite as a modern type of medicine, which did not require a great break from traditional ideas. There is some question as to what extent Indian doctors of homeopathy practiced a standard version of this medical theory. Homeopathic training and registration as a homeopathic physician were primarily through correspondence courses. Homeopathic doctors could then use a variety of practices (Jeffery, 1988: 45–46). In 1977–78, we knew a journalist in the City of Delhi, who also practiced homeopathy; in the village, Manipulator took his daughter to a homeopathic physician who practiced in a temple in Delhi.

An early event in the introduction of Western medicine in the 19th century was the use of vaccinations for smallpox in 1802 in Bombay. In Delhi, the British built hospitals, and Western medicines were dispensed in pharmaceutical shops. Although the acceptance

of Western medical theory and treatment by physicians has been slow, the adoption of the actual medicines, such as aspirin and later antibiotics, has been rapid. The concepts of germs, contagious disease, and other sources of infection are still not well understood by many villagers. They have interpreted germs as worms, and in terms of their earlier knowledge of illness caused by an intrusive ghost, which could be coped with to some extent by injections of antibiotics to reduce Fever and to combat the ghost. (For worms, germs, and tuberculosis as a contagious disease, see Chap. 13: A Group Discussion). In any case, the Government sponsors Western medicine in hospitals and other public health facilities in the Delhi region, especially the city, and in recent decades has extended these facilities, including primary health centers, dispensaries, clinics, and hospitals into the rural region and often directly to villages (Gazetteer Unit, Delhi Adm., 1976: Chap. 16).

Western medicine has brought gradual changes in birth practices. Until the end of the 1950s, pregnancies and childbirth were primarily in the hands of a family's women and the village midwife. Toward the end of the decade, the Government sent trained midwives, called Auxiliary Nurse Midwives, into the rural area. Their charge was to improve delivery practices, especially hygiene, whose neglect was a major factor in the high rate of infant mortality. Simple but important steps were taken, for example, the use of sterilized instruments, knives or scissors, to cut the umbilical cord. For difficult cases, they arranged for hospitalization of the expectant mother. The Government recognized that in order to reduce the birth rate, a goal of the Family Planning Programme, the infant mortality rate would have to be lowered to convince parents that many children were not necessary in order to have enough survivors, especially sons. Trained midwives, maternity and child welfare services, and inoculations of infants and children against disease have helped to reduce the infant mortality rate substantially. To control the rate of population increase, due in some measure to the decline in infant mortality, the Government promulgated abortion and sterilization. Western medicine has played the leading role in these developments (Gazetteer Unit, Delhi

Adm., 1976: 857–858; Jeffery, 1988: 49–50, 128, table 34 on 227, 238–241).

In the 1950s, a few of the wealthier and more urbanized villagers consulted Western medical physicians. A larger number of villagers patronized various pandits, swamis, sadhus, and *vaid*s who practiced popular pharmaceutical medicine, mainly the injection of penicillin. The villagers went most often to Sanskritist, a Brahman teacher of Sanskrit, who lived in a nearby village, and to sadhus, holy men, at an ashram located near the same village. These men were untrained in Western medicine but injected their patients with penicillin (Chap. 18: The Health Network).

With the advent of Ayurvedic and Western medical clinics and dispensaries near the village by the 1970s, a large number of absentee men working in cities, and a loosening of purdah restrictions, many women made use of the services of this miscellany of curers without obtaining authority from the male head of the family. The health care of children recently and presumably from earliest times rested with their mothers. A mother first treated her child herself. If unsuccessful, she next consulted a village curer, then perhaps a physician or *vaid* in a nearby town, or she might take the child to a nearby clinic or dispensary. The choices varied depending on whether the illness was considered serious, whether the mother believed in ghosts and ghost illness, or was a follower of the Arya Samaj. Of equal importance was the amount of time, energy, and money the mother had, and whether she was willing or able to seek help outside the village. From a historical and analytical point of view, women often combined the Prevedic and Vedic traditions with other forms of health care. For example, some mothers took a sick child to a Western medical physician or to a curer who used popular pharmaceutical medicine for injections to help drive out Fever, thus reducing the symptom in the child. Then they called an exorcist to get rid of the ghost causing the illness, or they exorcised it themselves, as will be described later.

By the late 1970s, the practice of popular pharmaceutical medicine in Shanti Nagar and throughout India was extensive. Taylor found in Punjab that indigenous practitioners used Western medicines, which they obtained from pharmaceutical shops. Pharmacists instructed them in the techniques for injections and kept them up-to-date on new techniques and remedies. Taylor reported one indigenous practitioner who established a very good reputation and became wealthy. His practice was based on the use of penicillin. The only gesture he made toward sterilizing his needle was to pass it through a pan of dirty antiseptic. Other practitioners used the most powerful drugs to obtain quick results. Many used chloramphenicol, unaware of its toxicity (Taylor, 1976: 288–289).

A study of "Traditional Healers and Modern Medicine" in three states of India—Madhya Pradesh, Uttar Pradesh, and Haryana (the last two adjoining the Delhi region)—found that villagers preferred Western medicine but not the physicians practicing it. Their attitude gave indigenous curers the opportunity of adding the use of Western medicine to their practices. *Vaid*s used Ayurvedic and Western medicine; homeopaths used homeopathic and Western medicine. Among the indigenous practitioners, those who used Western medicine the most had a larger clientele, charged more, and were younger than other practitioners. Curers who used only indigenous medicine were losing patients. They were older and less well educated than the others. Traditional healers, who had been trained in Ayurveda or homeopathy, mainly practiced Western medicine. They obtained their knowledge of Western medicine from druggists and representatives of medical companies. Some relied upon what they already knew about Western medicine and did not risk the use of recently introduced medicine (Bhatia et al., 1975). This analysis is generally valid for curers in Shanti Nagar and for treatment given by *vaid*s and compounders (pharmacists), who used antibiotics (Chap. 18: The Health Network; Chap. 21: Gabbler and Student Doctor).

To what degree the use of antibiotics will affect the immune systems of patients and lead to new diseases is anyone's guess. The indiscriminate use of popular pharmaceutical medicine brings to mind the Greek myth of Pandora's Box. The story goes that Pandora's curiosity led to her opening the box and releasing all the ills afflicting human beings

(Nilsson, 1964: 184). Slater (1971: 77) claimed that instead of a box Pandora opened one of the great jars used for burying the dead and in so doing released many evils in the world, which is somewhat akin but not the same as the belief in ghost illness in Shanti Nagar. In the present era some blame for deaths may lie with the indiscriminate use of antibiotics, often injected with contaminated needles, by indigenous practitioners with little knowledge of Western medicine, rather than the spread of diseases caused by Pandora's curiosity.

The following quotation from an M.D. practicing Western medicine for tuberculosis control in Kerala, South India accurately describes the practice of popular pharmaceutical medicine:

> Looking at the medical situation in the villages beyond the walls of the government hospital is even more alarming. Homeopaths, ayurvedic doctors, druggists, and people with even lesser claims as medical investigators are the first to administer new drugs in rural areas, using indications and dosages that are original and startling, injecting streptomycin, penicillin, vitamins and calcium and administering *per os* huge amounts of purgatives, dyspeptic mixtures, digestive enzymes and unhappily isoniazid, para-aminosalicylic acid and acetylamino-benzaldehyde thiosemicarbazone (Thiacetazone). The situation is chaotic. [McCreary, 1968: 706]

Despite the criticism of popular pharmaceutical medicine, the villagers in Shanti Nagar have continued its use, adapting it to the eclectic village health culture. Along with this adaptation, the majority of villagers cling to the traditional animistic beliefs about ghost illness, including ghost possessions, but are willing to use Western medicine to help drive out Fever in conjunction with exorcism. The villagers' unfamiliarity with Western medical practitioners is largely due to the circumstance that most physicians practice in an office or hospital without any rituals, mantras, or other techniques used by village curers and exorcists. Western medical practitioners are further hampered by the villagers' lack of the fundamental concepts pertaining to infectious diseases, which could be remedied to some extent in the village schools. As of 1978, primarily cleanliness and hygiene were taught, not science. Even at the higher secondary level, properly equipped laboratories for teaching science were lacking. Two young village men commented on the lack of science education in school. One was a Chamar, age 17, who said he had been rejected by the Navy because he had no science courses in school. The other, a Brahman, age 25, was studying to be a physician. He claimed there was no proper guidance in the schools for his chosen profession.

CHAPTER 8: IDEOLOGY: SANATAN DHARMA, ARYA SAMAJ, ECLECTICISM

> Superstition, in common parlance, designates the sum of beliefs and practices shared by other people in so far as they differ from our own. What we believe and practise ourselves is, of course, Religion. It is in this loose sense that Tacitus uses the word *superstitio* when speaking of Christians, about whose beliefs and practices he knew nothing and cared less. It is in the same loose sense that the word is used to-day by professional writers and laymen alike [Krappe, 1964: 203].

In other words, the village beliefs about ghosts should not be treated as superstition. They should be understood as part of the villagers' ideology. To understand ghost beliefs, it is essential to probe the ideology behind them. The term ideology has been used "to refer . . . to the several component aspects of all peoples' systems of belief about themselves and the reasons for their being: about their relations to others, to the world, and to the universe as they perceive it. Such explanations both provide a means of comprehending peoples' relation to their environment and serve as guides to the actions necessary to maintain or secure their place within it." As part of his definition of ideology, Hammond stated that ideology is a universal aspect of culture, which focuses on supernaturally based systems of belief and observance and includes secular beliefs, values, and ethical and moral systems (Hammond, 1978: 318). Therefore, we use ideology instead of religion.

In addition to the encompassing concept of ideology, the word dharma is used here as part of ideology when referring to Hindu beliefs and rules governing ethical and righteous behavior. Dharma is the linchpin for Hinduism, providing rules for the behavior of families, castes, sexes, and people of different ages and stages of life (R. Freed and S. Freed, 1966: 674; Mathur, 1964: 78, 83).

The ideology of the village refers to the eclectic system of beliefs about life, death, the soul, what happens after death, supernatural beings including ghosts, and the relation of the world of the villagers to the world of supernatural beings. Thus, it has elements of animism, namely, the concepts of the soul and supernatural beings (Tylor, 1958: 10).

This eclectic system derives primarily from Hinduism, which in turn seems to have evolved from a combination of cultural influences from the Indus civilization, the ancient Indo-Aryan invasion from Europe, and from trade with the Sumerian and Mesopotamian regions. Numerous similarities and evidence of trade have been found at Harappa and Lothal in India, at Susa in the Sumerian region of Western Iran, and at Samarra in Mesopotamia. The material products from this trade provided cultural symbols which indicate that concepts from Susa and Samarra spread to India, such as the swastika and planetary system reflected to this day in Hindu rituals. Hinduism has been further subjected to changes and consists of many sects and cults. It shows similarities to concepts found in Greece, Rome, Islam, and the British Raj, which resulted in ideological changes in the Punjab and Delhi regions in the 19th and 20th centuries (Eliade, 1978: 81–82, 128–129, 187; Redman, 1978: 246, 247, 252–253; Gadd, 1979: 115; Gadd and Smith, 1979; Mackay, 1979: 123, 125; Rao, S. R., 1979; Sayce, 1979; S. Freed and R. Freed, 1980: 87, 89, 90, 101, 102).

We follow Lowie (1948: 151) in his statement that, "The sociological distinction between magic and religion is untenable." In separating magic from religion, Durkheim stated, ". . . religion in its historical forms is invariably linked with a church" (Lowie, 1948: 150). We go a step farther and suggest that the separation of magic from systems of supernatural beliefs, such as Hinduism, presented by Western scholars was ethnocentrically influenced by concepts present in the church religions of Western culture. By using and defining the terms, ideology and dharma, we avoid the word religion and again follow Lowie (1948: 339), who recognized that not everyone classifies in the same way. However, he wrote that "it is highly desirable that we should understand the basis of one another's classifications."

With regard to ideology, villagers generally refer to themselves as Hindus and as followers of Sanatan Dharma or the Arya Samaj. We distinguish a third eclectic group, whose ideology comes in varying degrees from Hinduism, Buddhism, Jainism, Islam, and atheism. The dominant groups are Sanatan Dharma and the Arya Samaj. The latter, a reform sect of Hinduism, originated in the last half of the 19th century. Sanatan Dharma is the more traditional form of Hinduism. It existed before the Arya Samaj and has persisted because of its Brahman adherents, who act as family priests, *purohits*, for other castes who follow Sanatan Dharma. These two sects of Hinduism stand out because Brahmans are most often followers of Sanatan Dharma, and Jats, of the Arya Samaj. Both castes are large and their members own most of the village land. Hereafter followers of Sanatan Dharma are sometimes referred to as Sanatanis; and those of the Arya Samaj, as Samajis. Most but not all Sanatanis believe in many deities and other supernatural beings, such as ghosts; they also believe in the cycle of rebirths as well as release from the round of rebirths and union of the soul with the Ultimate Reality, also known as the Universal Absolute. Samajis believe in Bhagwan (God) but do not believe in multiple deities or other supernatural beings, thus barring ghosts (Saraswati, 1956: Chap. I). Although they believe in the round of rebirths, they either do not believe in release from the cycle of rebirths or at best are skeptical about it. Samajis tend to follow some but not all of the teachings of Swami Dayananda Saraswati, the founder of the Arya Samaj. For example, they maintain that anyone can wear the sacred thread, not only the twice-born castes of Brahmans, Kshatriyas, and Vaishyas, and they also claim that they can and should perform their own fire ceremonies instead of having Brahman priests do so; but they do not wear the thread nor do they consistently perform fire ceremonies. They do not follow a number of Arya-Samaj precepts set down by Saraswati (1956: 43–

44, 118–119); for example an infant after the first six days from birth should be nursed by an ayah rather than the mother, and marriages should take place at later ages than was customary in the village.

Saraswati (1824–1883) was influenced by experiences in his early life, the tumultuous times of the Mutiny in 1857, and the conquest of India by the British (Rai, 1967: 8, 44–45). Jordens (1978: Chap. l) described the Sanatan Dharma Brahman family background, in which Saraswati, then known as Mulshankar, grew up and from which he fled when he was 21 years old to escape an early marriage and pursue his search for truth, i.e., what he later claimed to be the basic teachings of Hinduism. In his childhood, he underwent strenuous training as a Brahman, beginning at age five with the reading of the alphabet. He was invested with the sacred thread at age eight, marking him as the son of twice-born Brahman parents. The investiture imposed vows of chastity, purity, and poverty to age 25, daily worship, and recitation of the Vedas among other austerities. His father was a stern teacher and devout follower of Shiva, whose worship included 36-hour fasts. When Mulshankar was 14, his father insisted that he keep one such fast for Shiva worship in a temple. His father fell asleep during the fast and worship. Mulshankar forced himself to stay awake and saw a mouse creep onto the image of Shiva and nibble at the offerings to the god. This raised questions regarding the power of the deity and the idol, for obviously the mouse was not afraid and the deity did nothing. Thereafter he no longer paid homage to the image so he awoke his father and plied him with questions which the incident of the mouse had raised. His father was angry, berated his son, and insisted on unquestioning obedience. The incident marked the beginning of a major rift between father and son (Rai, 1967: 8–11, 44–45).

Numerous authors have written about experiences which possibly affected Swami Dayananda's teachings. It is possible that his brand of monotheism was to some extent influenced by the British community and their missionaries near his home and also by his wanderings as a sadhu in search of truth, especially in North India where he encountered

Muslims who believe in one god, and his further encounters with the Brahmo Samaj, which also fostered the belief in one god. Various scholars have discussed this question (Rai, 1967: Chap. VI; Jordens, 1978: Chap. V). His brand of monotheism, namely, that all the names of deities in Hinduism and ancient Sanskritic texts are but the characteristics of a single deity, and his strong criticisms of beliefs outside the fold of Hinduism and of various Hindu cults and customs may be found in *The Light of Truth* (Saraswati, 1956; R. Freed and S. Freed, 1980: 331–333).

One reason why members of the Jat caste may have become followers of the Arya Samaj is the competition between Jats and Brahmans based on the fact that Brahmans were at the top of the caste hierarchy and Jats were ranked as clean Shudras. The Jats were not members of the three twice-born varnas (classes of castes) although at least by 1958 the Jats had some Kshatriya pretensions. A second reason is that previously the Jats were not well informed about many orthodox Hindu practices. Because the Jats were the dominant caste and major landowners in the village, they resented the power that Brahmans had with respect to the many rituals of Hinduism, were not inclined to practice all of them, and did not favor enriching Brahmans with fees and gifts for providing ritual services for the rites of passage and festivals.

In the 1950s when Jats were the only Samajis in the village except for one Baniya family, none of them performed the fire ceremony for weddings. Mainly they used Brahman priests, but one Jat family employed a swami from a nearby ashram to act as priest. Some Samajis conducted minor fire ceremonies, and on one occasion the Arya-Samaj Jats joined the Brahmans in a fire ceremony on Akhta, a time when cattle disease was exorcised, which the Jats called fumigation. By the 1970s, although competition between Jats and Brahmans remained, Jats no longer performed any fire ceremonies and again employed *purohits* (family priests) for life cycle rites of passage, thus, disregarding a major tenet of the Arya Samaj (Saraswati, 1956: Chap. I, 46, 66–67, 91, 125, 245–246, 325, 348–349, 854–855, 874; R. Freed and S. Freed, 1966; 1980: 331–334; Juergensmeyer, 1982: 5).

Not everyone professed to be followers of Sanatan Dharma or the Arya Samaj, and even Samajis and Sanatanis were eclectic as were other villagers. Although Brahmans were said to be Sanatanis, some of them blended beliefs from Sanatan Dharma, the Arya Samaj, and the Brahmo Samaj, a reform sect believing in rational theism, which started in Bengal and was influenced by Christianity. Those who followed such a mixture of beliefs were not always aware of their origin. Strict Samajis tended to follow the austere teachings of Saraswati, namely, that there is but one god and no other supernatural beings, thus excluding ghosts. In the 1950s, other castes, Shudras and Harijans, followed Hinduism as they knew it and also adhered to various animistic and Islamic beliefs. For example, they worshipped at the shrine for the Panch Pir, five Muslim saints, and members of all castes celebrated Guga Naumi, a festival for Guga Pir, who had been born a Hindu prince but died a Muslim (Append. V: Month of Bhadrapad). By the 1970s, a few younger members of a number of castes, including former Harijans, had learned more about Hinduism from attending school. Some younger men from different castes, who claimed to be followers of the Arya Samaj, were primarily interested for political reasons, seeing in the teachings of Saraswati a justification for blurring caste lines. Saraswati taught that in the beginning there was only one class of human beings. Later, according to the Rig-Veda, there were two classes of humans: Aryas, who were learned and virtuous, and Dasyus, evil doers and ignorant. Then the Atharva-Veda divided people into four classes: Brahman, Kshatriya, Vaishya, and Shudra. To supersede these divisions, Saraswati advocated education and learning for all children regardless of class or caste (Saraswati, 1956: 51–52, 315; R. Freed and S. Freed, 1966: 675–677; 1980: 331–333; 1985: 150, fn. 19; K. W. Jones, 1976: 43).

Islamic beliefs affect village ideology indirectly through the monotheism of the Arya Samaj and directly by the belief in ghosts and exorcism, which serve to support comparable Hindu beliefs, by the observance of a few festivals and rituals for Islamic saints (pirs), and by the concept of fate (kismet). To attribute a belief in fate only to Islam is misleading since *bhagya*, a Hindi word for luck, fortune, and fate, is linked with Lakshmi, Goddess of Fortune, and beliefs about luck were found among villagers. Saraswati's teachings attempted to free Hindus from beliefs in luck, fate, ghosts, other spirits, and multiple deities, including the mother goddesses of illness, along with what he called superstitions, such as the predictions of astrologers and the wearing of amulets as protective devices against malevolent deities and ghosts (Saraswati, 1956: Chaps. XI–XIV).

Buddhist influence is connected to politics and involves chiefly two related families of Chamar Leatherworkers. The Chamar whose pseudonym is Buddhist I illustrates the political motives of Chamars who take up Buddhism. He practiced the same ceremonies, festivals, and rituals as did other members of his caste, but he was attracted to Buddhism due to the attempts of Gautama Buddha in ancient times and of Dr. B. R. Ambedkar in modern times to abolish caste. In 1956 in Agra, about 120 miles from Delhi, 2000 Jatavs, members of a subcaste of Chamars, converted to Buddhism under the auspices of Dr. Ambedkar. Born a Chamar and educated for a time in the USA, Ambedkar was a political figure of consequence during the struggle for Independence and afterwards. He played a leading role in writing the Constitution of India. Ambedkar's mass movement was what prompted Buddhist I to convert. Despite his conversion, he believed in multiple, supernatural beings, including Hindu and Islamic ghosts. Although Buddhism foregoes all supernatural beings, many Buddhists believe in them, as Spiro (1967) has shown in his study of *Burmese Supernaturalism* (Saraswati, 1956: 45–50; Lynch, 1972; Mandelbaum, 1972, 2: 463; Juergensmeyer, 1982: Chap. 16).

The British introduced schools, Christian missions, and standing armies consisting partly of Indian sepoys. These changes led to the turmoil of the Mutiny in 1857, followed by viceregal rule, and contributed to the founding of the Brahmo Samaj in Bengal and its spread to the Punjab and elsewhere, along with the parallel spread of the Arya Samaj, both monotheistic movements, which were against idol worship. In the Punjab these movements, the large Muslim population, and Christian missions advocated the belief in one god (Farquhar, 1915: 101 ff.; Tandon, 1968: 12–15, 25; K. W. Jones, 1976: Chaps. 1–3; Ghosh, 1986: 118).

Prior to the 19th century, Hindus had been in the minority in the Punjab except for the more southerly portions, which included the Delhi region. Far more people were nonliterate than literate. Only learned Brahmans, few in number, had any knowledge of Sanskrit, the language of the sacred texts of Hinduism. A revival of Sanskrit resulted from a reaction to Christianity and the British Raj. With it came renewed interest in the Vedas, the most ancient and holy of Sanskritic texts, and debates between Samajis and Sanatanis. This revival was important in the modernization of Sanatan Dharma, for Samajis soon learned that few people knew any Sanskrit so they used Swami Dayanand's interpretation of the Vedas to propagate his teachings in public debates. Therefore, Brahman Sanatanis found it necessary to learn Sanskrit, especially since Saraswati's main tenet (1956: Chap. I) was that the multiple deities of the Vedas were merely characteristics of one deity, thus buttressing his position that there was but one god, Bhagwan (Basham, 1954: 3l6, 386–391, 398; Gumperz et al., 1967: ix–xi; K. W. Jones, 1976: 21–25, 27–29, 70).

The innovations that took place in the Punjab began to affect Shanti Nagar in the late 19th and early 20th centuries. A few men from the village traveled as merchants and civil servants in the Punjab and were influenced by the Brahmo Samaj, the Arya Samaj, and the modernization of Sanatan Dharma. Dr. Ramji Lal, a Jat from Hissar, educated in England, helped to popularize the Arya Samaj among Jats in Delhi, Hissar, and Rohtak Districts ca. 1886–1892 (K. W. Jones, 1976: 158). Proselytizers for the Arya Samaj introduced its teachings in the village in 1923. These influences are evident in the following comments of villagers on life, death, the soul, action, dharma, the round of rebirths, release from the round, and supernatural beings, including ghosts. Sanatanis and Samajis generally express somewhat different perspectives.

CHAPTER 9: IDEOLOGICAL INTERVIEWS

The aim of this presentation of quotations from ideological interviews is to let the villagers speak for themselves. In 1958, Brahmans and Jats, both men and women, often volunteered information about the differences between Sanatan Dharma, the Arya Samaj, and other beliefs. Many of the quotations were gathered randomly in the course of open-ended eliciting interviews. A limited number were collected in an exploratory survey about the deities of Hinduism; related comments were encouraged. The survey was based on an opportunistic sample, which covered all castes. All interviews on ideology, including the survey, employed the open-ended eliciting technique. One unsurprising finding was that Brahmans, including women, knew more about Hinduism than did members of other castes. The Jats ranked second owing to their knowledge of the Arya Samaj and some aspects of traditional Hinduism. They, however, were not well informed about the ceremonies for Hindu rites of passage, for such ceremonies had long been conducted by Brahmans. Among the Shudra castes of Bairagis, Jhinvars, Lohars, Malis, and Nais, the women were oriented primarily toward the mother goddesses; however, women of all castes worshipped these goddesses, including Brahman and Jat women. Nai Barbers knew more about the order of ceremonies, especially births and weddings, than did other castes with the exception of the Brahmans. The Nai Barbers attained their knowledge because they served at births and weddings and carried gifts to married daughters at festivals. The Mahar and Gola Potters, Chamar Leatherworkers, and Chuhra Sweepers had the most limited knowledge of Hinduism except for some literate men. Due to their eclectic, historical background, many villagers had a composite of ideological beliefs deriving from tribal and caste origins as described by O'Malley (1935: Chap. 1) and Crooke (1896: 1–4; 1968: 1, 2). These general categorizations of village Hinduism had changed to some degree by the 1970s due to education and access to the mass media.

To reflect differences and changes in village ideology, comments of villagers are identified in the following pages by sex, dominant ideology, and the last two digits of the first year of each field trip in which the information was obtained. Pseudonyms for people, who have been given them, are a fourth element in the identification. Caste is also given but is not used in the code. These identifications are in parentheses at the beginning of each interview. The coding is as follows: M for male, F for female, (if two participants of the same sex were in the interview, the number 2 appears before M or F), SD for Sanatan Dharma, AS for Arya Samaj, B for Buddhism, A for Atheism, E for Eclecticism, 58 for the field trip in 1958–59, and 77 for the field trip in 1977–78. Examples: a female follower of Sanatan Dharma in the 1958 trip is identified by this code: (F, SD, 58); two males who jointly participated in a discussion in the 1977 trip, both followers of Arya Samaj, are identified thus: (2M, AS, 77). A person with a pseudonym who follows Sanatan Dharma and was interviewed in the 1958 trip has this identification: (M, SD, 58, Raconteur).

Although Sanatanis might worship more than one deity on different occasions, they were devotees either of Shiva or of Vishnu or one of Vishnu's avatars, more often Rama Chandra than Krishna. When they referred to the main god they worshipped, they sometimes spoke of the god as Bhagwan-Vishnu or Bhagwan-Shiva; sometimes they simply said Bhagwan, which was the only term used by followers of Arya Samaj. To avoid ambiguity regarding the deity worshipped, we follow the system of identifying the deity as Bhagwan for the Samajis, and as Bhagwan-Vishnu or Bhagwan-Shiva for Sanatanis. Other villagers used Bhagwan without further identification. The women generally identified the mother goddesses. Many Sanatanis stated that they believed in release from the round of rebirths and implicitly in union of their souls with the Universal Absolute, the neuter, formless deity that souls are believed to join upon release from the cycle of rebirths, also known as the Universal Spirit or Ultimate Reality. However, they rarely used the name of this neuter deity (Dowson, 1950: 56;

Basak, 1953: 83; Sarma, 1953: 11, 29; Morgan, 1953: 407). The joining of souls, which have been released from the cycle of rebirths, with the Universal Absolute is called monism and was found most often among Brahmans. Jats knew about it but because of the Arya-Samaj dogma did not expect to be released from the round of rebirths.

The first excerpt is from an interview with a Brahman, who said he did not find much difference between Sanatan Dharma and the Arya Samaj (M, E, 58). Therefore, he is classified under Eclecticism. "Followers of Sanatan Dharma believe that if the soul is not disposed of with proper rituals, it might trouble people as a ghost. Sanatanis also believe in idol worship. Arya Samajis do not believe in idol worship, ghosts, or magic. They just believe in fire worship." This informant claimed he was a follower of Sanatan Dharma but he did not worship a deity in the form of an idol, possibly because of Arya-Samaj influence, but also because the village had no temple with idols to be worshipped. He added, "I believe in the Universal Absolute, a deity with no form. The Jats are Arya Samajis although some believe in Sanatan Dharma. Arya Samajis don't follow Arya Samaj strictly. If someone is ill and going to die and you tell him that if he worships a god or idol he'll then get well, he'll do it. Dharma is molded according to needs. Mostly one realizes or looks to the Universal Absolute when one is in trouble."

The foregoing excerpt provides one man's view of differences between Samajis and Sanatanis despite his opening disclaimer. Except that he did not worship idols, that is, pray to statues of deities, his statement reflects traditional Sanatan Dharma ideology about souls, ghosts, the Universal Absolute, and rituals. He referred to the need to follow proper funeral rituals for the deceased to prevent, as Sanatanis believe, the soul of a dead person from becoming a ghost and haunting family members. Samajis do not share these beliefs in ghosts and the funeral rite of passage.

The following comments are from two Brahman men, members of the same household (2M, SD, 58, Old Priest and Raconteur) (Chap. 12). Old Priest was a professional priest, 92 years old at the time of the interview; Raconteur was 60 years old. The interview is noteworthy for its historical information and comments about followers of the Arya Samaj. Raconteur said, "There are two major sects of Hinduism, Arya Samaj and Sanatan Dharma. Sanatan Dharma is the traditional dharma. A Hindu abides by one or the other, irrespective of caste. I remember when Arya Samaj came here in 1923. There was a lecturer from Punjab, who talked and preached. People in the village then joined the Arya Samaj. Maybe 50 of them said they would follow it, but very few keep to it. Everybody who follows Sanatan Dharma keeps to it, but maybe only ten of the Samajis follow their rules." Old Priest added, "I was the president of the village meeting although I don't remember the year exactly. I do remember the man came and talked for five to seven days; then they started singing. I'm a follower of Sanatan Dharma, but if there's some work to be done for the Samajis, I'll do it. If anyone wants something done for another sect of Hinduism, I'm willing to do it."

Old Bachelor, another Brahman, headed a family whose members appeared to have selected their own rules of dharma (M, E, 58) (Chap. 21: Breakup of Old Brahman Lane; Append. III: Chart 10.1). His brother had been in government service in the Punjab in the 1930s but died young. Then Old Bachelor, a lifelong celibate, took care of his brother's family. He said that the members of the family did not celebrate a number of festivals usually observed by most villagers. However, he went to the Ganges on pilgrimage every year in the month of Karttik (the traditional time) and observed solar eclipses. He did not accept Yama, God of Death, saying, "Why should I ask about Bowana [a large town] if I only want to go to the next village." His explanation of this statement was, "Why should I want to know about Yama when I don't accept him and have no interest in him." Although he did not worship his ancestors, he remembered their names. In conjunction with his statement about ancestors, he said, "I don't accept Kanagat," the fortnight in the fall of the year reserved for their worship and remembrance. It is also known as Shraddha and was observed by most Brahmans who followed Sanatan Dharma but seldom by Jats (Daniélou, 1964: 307; R. Freed and S. Freed, 1964: 87; Append. V: Pilgrimage to the Ganges for Ganga Nahan in the month of Karttik; Shraddha in Ashvin).

Old Bachelor further commented that strict Arya Samajis should not follow mourning rituals after cremation, nor should they observe Kanagat, for Swami Dayanand Saraswati (1956: 854) stated, ". . . nothing should be done for the dead after cremation." However, the reason Old Bachelor gave for not observing Kanagat was because of what he had learned about Karna. According to him, "Karna was a character in the Mahabharata, who in his after-life went to the land of the dead where Yama ruled, and there he found only gold waiting for him. Therefore, Karna returned to earth for two weeks and gave away food so that he would have food waiting for him in the land of the dead" (for Karna, see Dowson, 1950: 150–151).

Old Bachelor did not approve of worshipping and leaving offerings at the Bhumiya shrine for the village founding ancestor, a shrine tended by Brahmans (Wood and Maconachie, 1882: 115; Crooke, 1968: 95), because "When people leave food at the Bhumiya shrine, dogs and cattle eat it." He closed the interview with the statement that he did not accept the ghosts of Sanatan Dharma. In a number of respects he seemed to have been influenced by the Arya Samaj, Brahmo Samaj, and his own proclivities. His statements about Yama, Karna, the land of the dead, offerings, and charity may have derived from Saraswati's statements on the same subjects (Saraswati, 1956: 37, 499–500; R. Freed and S. Freed, 1980: 518–519). An important factor in Old Bachelor's attitude regarding food is related to his position as the head of the family when his brother died. Although the family owned some land, they were not particularly well off. He and his brother's widow, Pure Goddess, strove very hard to educate her three sons and did so successfully, but the effort meant that they went without many amenities and did not waste food.

In a discussion with two Brahman women (2F, SD, 77), the younger woman told us, "The Arya Samaj is not strong now. None of the Samajis perform the Arya-Samaj rituals." Her mother-in-law said, "Only one Jat in the village is a Samaji now." The daughter-in-law added, "The prime reason is that Samajis are supposed to perform their own fire worship instead of having it performed by a Brahman priest. The Jats no longer do so." She also referred to two dead Jats, who were brothers, Womanizer and Schemer, who, although supposedly Samajis, worshipped all the deities. Schemer in 1958 told us he was fond of the old gods (M, AS, 58).

The son of Womanizer, Dissembler (M, AS, 77), a Jat who had been an ardent Samaji in the 1950s, informed us at the beginning of the 1977–78 field trip that the Arya Samaj was not as strong as it had been. Although he called on the services of Raconteur, a Brahman priest, to perform the ceremonies for birth and marriage in his family, in other ways he was a strong Samaji, for he absolutely and vehemently denied the existence of ghosts. A ten-year-old girl in his joint family attended an Arya-Samaj boarding school with a strict regime, which required that she sleep on the floor at night and learn archery and other skills so that she would become a courageous woman, part of the Arya-Samaj effort to impart nationalistic pride among Indo-Aryans.

Two unrelated women from different castes were atheists. Atheist I (F, A, 58) was a member of the Bairagi caste, whose members generally followed Sanatan Dharma. This woman's mother-in-law, Fearful, worshipped mother goddesses and believed in multiple deities and ghosts. Mother-in-law and daughter-in-law, needless to say, were not congenial, and the nuclear families which had been joint separated in 1958. However, both families continued to use the services of the Brahman, Manipulator, as the family *purohit* for the weddings of their daughters. (Chap. 20: The Bairagis: Fearful, Handsome, and Delicate Flower).

Atheist I was an atheist due to her natal family background, her problems with her mother-in-law, Fearful, and the relative poverty of her husband's family. Concerning ideology, Atheist I said:

I have never been on a pilgrimage and have never gone to the Ganges for a pilgrimage or to the Yamuna River on Amavas [the dark night of the moon when people bathed in the river, especially widowed persons, to fulfill a vow as a form of dharma]. I have never gone to the Bhumiya shrine. I don't pray during the day, and I don't believe in anything. My own mother did not do any praying. In my parents' village, my mother never went to the mother-goddess shrines, but if anyone would take me with her to these places, I would go. I don't believe in any goddesses and don't know anything about them [Append. V: Calendric Events— Amavas; Append. IV: Map 4, Crossroads, Pond, Cremation Grounds, Buildings and Other Places Associated with Ghosts].

Although Atheist I said she never did anything for festivals, she qualified her statement by stating that she sometimes drew pictures on the walls of her house for her children at the time of a few festivals, which was customary among mothers of children. She ended by stating, "Doing so, depends on my own sweet will."

Atheist II, also known as Mrs. Illusionist, (F, A, 58, 77), a Chamar, when a young woman, had followed all the beliefs in ghosts, mother goddesses, and Muslim saints. She consulted exorcists when her infants fell ill. Since a number of them died at birth or shortly thereafter, she supplicated the mother goddesses at the village shrines, made vows to Jahar (a Muslim-Hindu saint, also known as Sayyid and Guga Pir), and through the exorcists made offerings to Kalkaji, Goddess of the Cremation Grounds, whose shrine was near Chiragh Delhi. Her babies, however, continued to die. In time, her husband, Illusionist, became an exorcist (Chap. 17). Because of the deaths of her infants and multiple family problems, she eventually did not believe in anything.

In a discussion of ideology in 1978, Atheist II said "I don't worship any goddess or god. My husband does; he worships Shiva, Hanuman, and Kalkaji." Then she talked about the film of Santoshi Mata. "The film ran a lot of times. Many people saw it, even twice. There was difficulty getting tickets. Santoshi Mata is a goddess, but I don't know anything about her. However, my son [age 12], sitting here, has a picture of her. He fasted three months for Santoshi." The boy, whose pseudonym is Bright Light, then fetched the picture and explained his fast, which he maintained in order to pass examinations (M, E, 77). His mother added, "All the daughters-

in-law in the family keep the fast for Santoshi; now the boys have started keeping it so this son does too."

The foregoing interview with Atheist II and one of her sons shows the eclectic ideological concepts in a single family: Atheist II, her son with a combination of beliefs from his mother and father plus the incorporation of a modern mother goddess, Santoshi Mata, from the cinema; and Illusionist, who became an exorcist and worshipped Shiva, Hanuman, and Kalkaji. Other members of the family worshipped Santoshi Mata, and all observed Guga Naumi, the festival for Guga Pir (Append. V).

The recent worship of Santoshi Mata has incorporated ancient Hindu traditions, such as the belief in action (karma) in the form of devotional (bhakti) worship. In effect the piling up of good deeds is expected to counteract bad deeds from past and present lives. Worshipping a deity and fasting are viewed as good actions. By the end of the 1970s, Santoshi Mata had become an object of worship by adult women, including Jats, schoolchildren, and members of all castes. This worship of a new goddess in a traditional way was due to the cinema. It also perpetuated the belief in numerous supernatural beings (E. Smith, 1977, personal commun.; Das, 1980; Wadley, 1983: 151; Kurtz, 1984).

Atheist III, also known as Student Doctor (M, A, 77), a Brahman and the 25-year-old brother of Dr. John, a compounder, in a discussion about ghosts during the 1978 malaria epidemic, gave examples of why he did not believe in ghosts and also claimed not to believe in Bhagwan, saying that his medical training had done away with these beliefs. However, his family background and general conversation indicated that regarding ghosts he might be ambivalent about his beliefs, as were Fence Sitter and other men in the village (Chap. 21: Gabbler and Student Doctor).

LIFE, DEATH, SOUL

These bodies come to an end
It is declared of the eternal embodied [soul]
Which is indestructible and unfathomable.
(Edgerton, 1965: 11)

This verse from the Bhagavad Gita, part of the Mahabharata and familiar to the villagers from story-telling sessions, *katha*s, held throughout the year, indicates that the body is no more at death, but the soul endures. It provides the background for the following interviews. According to traditional Hinduism, after cremation the soul is released from the body, which returns to the earth. For 13 days after death, the soul remains in the cremation grounds. The soul then journeys for a year to the land of the dead, the kingdom of Yama, a deity and Lord of the Dead. As the ruler of the southern direction, Yama is called Lord of the South. He is king of ancestors and ghosts (Daniélou, 1964: 132). Yama with the assistance of Citra-Gupta, his scribe and recorder of the actions of souls, balances the good and bad actions of each soul. Yama then judges the record to determine whether the soul should be reborn and in what form, should be released from the cycle of rebirths and joined with the Universal Absolute, or should become a wandering ghost (Daniélou, 1964: 134).

Some people express variations on this basic theme. Samajis believe the soul is judged by Bhagwan rather than by Yama. Sanatanis believe that if the soul is released from the cycle of rebirths, it is joined with the Universal Absolute, the moral governor of the universe and judge of the fruit of a soul's actions, which includes dharma according to villagers. Alternatively when a person dies before the allotted time, the person's soul may become a wandering ghost after lingering 13 days in the cremation grounds, or the soul may journey to Yama and after one year, having been judged there by Yama, may become a wandering ghost (Dowson, 1950: 56; Basak, 1953: 83, 84; Chatterjee, 1953: 252–256; Dandekar, 1953: 117–122; Sarma, 1953: 30–31; Daniélou, 1964: 23, fn. 5; 132–134; Mathur, 1964: 82–83, 86; R. Freed and S. Freed, 1980: 526–527).

Although the Upanishads, ancient philosophical and mystical texts of Hinduism (Append. II), state that after death the soul may go to one of three or four worlds, these worlds symbolize many possible worlds. There are various lists of these worlds. For example, the following list of five worlds: (1) the world of the ancestors, (2) the world of the demigods, (3) the world of the deities, (4) the world of Brahma (masculine), the Creator, a male

deity, and (5) the world of the Universal Absolute, a neuter deity, (rarely referred to as Brahma or Brahman, neuter). Another list of 14 worlds is described as seven stages ascending from the earth and as seven descending. The Puranas, ancient legends and tales, also depict various heavens and hells (Dowson, 1950: 56–57, 325–326; Basak, 1953: 90–91; Morgan, 1953: 407; Append. II: Puranas).

Swami Dayanand Saraswati (1956: 856) denounced the common usage of heaven, svarga, and hell, *naraka*, maintaining these terms referred to conditions of the soul. He also claimed, contrary to Sanatan Dharma, that the soul was separate from the Universal Absolute and could not become one with it, nor could a soul be released from the round of rebirths. A soul, however, might temporarily be deferred from rebirth, but "enjoyment of the release from the round of rebirths would be for a limited time, after which the soul would be reborn" (Saraswati, 1956: 851).

Villagers customarily did not express complex beliefs about heavens and hells. They occasionally spoke the words, heaven or hell, when referring to suffering from difficulties, but their beliefs about life after death were in terms of the soul's rebirth, release from the cycle, or becoming a ghost, depending on whether they were Sanatanis, Samajis, or eclectic in their choice of beliefs (R. Freed and S. Freed, 1980: 525–527, 535–542). As will be noted in the following interviews, for most villagers what happened to a person after death depended on Yama's or Bhagwan's judgment of the sum of the soul's actions. They believed that judgment depended on a person living out the time allotted by Yama or Bhagwan before death and rebirth. As for the joining of a soul with the Universal Absolute, villagers, who were not Sanatanis, were often neutral. A fair number of villagers did not know about the Universal Absolute.

Thoughts about life, death, and the soul are contained in the following quotations, which refer to one's allotted time on earth, the soul, action, dharma, rebirth, and release from the cycle. The first quotation is from a Brahman (M, SD, 58), who indicates why the soul becomes a wandering ghost:

Bhagwan-Vishnu will give birth to the soul of a dead man whose time on earth has been completed. When a person dies at the ages of 60 to 65, or beyond to 80 or 85, then the soul is reborn. But if a person dies at the ages of 12, 18, or 30, then the soul becomes a ghost and is reborn only after the allotted time has been completed. If a man dies accidentally before a natural death or the allotted age of death, then 'til the allotted time, he'll wander as a ghost. Then the spirit roams here and there until the time of natural death comes.

The next quotation comes from a Brahman grandmother (F, SD, 58, Honesty): "When a woman has had all her desires fulfilled, has married, had children and grandchildren, and then reaches old age and dies, death is celebrated by relatives because she leaves her body in happiness. The celebration is like a second marriage. The death of an old woman like myself is like a marriage." Honesty's viewpoint was partially based on the belief that after death her soul would again be reborn and join the rebirth of her dead husband's soul. In her soul's next life she would have the same husband.

Snakebite Curer (M, SD, 58), a Brahman whose pseudonym describes his curing ability, provides the next statement about the soul, death, and becoming a ghost:

There are two theories about the soul after death. One is that the soul gets another life immediately after death. The second is that the soul waits twelve months after death before it gets another life. No one knows which is right. Everyone has a definite number of breaths allotted to him. A sudden death means that those breaths do not run the allotted course. The soul goes around unsatisfied at that time. These two theories allow for the soul to become doomed to wander as a ghost shortly after death or after one year.

During the 1977–78 field trip when we asked a group of women (Jats and one Mahar Potter) about ghosts, Mrs. Authority (F, AS, 77), a Jat, age 75, whose family members had always been considered the strictest Samajis, said, "If everyone became a wandering ghost, then there would be no one left in the world. If a person dies in his time, he won't become a ghost. No one knows when his time comes,

but when the time for death comes and he dies, then he won't be a ghost. If he dies before his time, he becomes a ghost."

Several Chamars recounted a case of mistaken identity, which emphasizes beliefs about dying at or before the allotted time. Two village men, a Jat and a Chamar, had the same name. Both men fell ill and were dying. The Chamar "died" first. In his death, he saw four men taking him to distant mountains (the Himalayas) where a very strong man (himself) was about to be cremated. Then someone said that the Chamar was the wrong person because his allotted time had not come, that instead the Jat with the same name should have been sent. Fortunately, the Chamar's body had not yet been cremated so his soul was returned to the village, i.e., he did not die. Another Chamar added that someone saw the dying Chamar's big toe wiggling as he was about to be cremated, so the cremation was stopped. At the same time, the Jat with the identical name died; his allotted time had elapsed. Because this story was told by more than one Chamar who had witnessed the so-called death and return to life, it illustrates Chamar beliefs about life and death, and the far-off mountains, the Himalayas, as the place where the soul goes at death (Thompson, 1946: 254; Sabom, 1982: 10–11).

ACTION, REBIRTH, RELEASE

The following quotations touch on action, rebirth, and release from the round of rebirths. A Jat, the son of Mrs. Authority (M, AS, 58, Nutmeg), said:

When a person dies, it's just like changing clothes. The soul takes another form. If by accident I died at the wrong time, my soul would wander until it reached the age of 100 years. Whether a person is progressing or retrograding in life depends on past deeds. Good and bad deeds are weighed against each other for determining rebirth in the next life. What we have cooked yesterday, we'll eat today. If wheat is sown in this season, we'll eat it next year.

Although he did not mention ghosts, Nutmeg said that if he died by accident, his soul would wander until it was 100 years old. The omission of the word ghosts is due to his being a Samaji, but even so the statement was unusual for a strict Samaji, which is what he claimed to be. He asserted a viewpoint characteristic of other members of his family. As successful agriculturists, they believed that hard work was necessary for good deeds, karma. The metaphors he used indicate this work ethic.

In the following long quotation, a middle-aged man (M, SD, 58, Brahman, Plowman), presents Sanatan Dharma beliefs about death, rebirth, action, and caste.

> Nothing will happen when I die. A dead man is gone. How can I come back? There is rebirth. If this is my second birth, then there will be a third, fourth, and so on. The soul moves in a cycle and always goes on taking birth. If you die, you may not be born in America; you may be born in India; or you may even be born as an animal. There's no escape from the cycle of rebirths. It is Bhagwan-Vishnu's will that souls move like this; they don't stay. No person can tell whether the soul goes to a better or worse place. If a person does good deeds, then the soul is born in a better place. If the person is cruel and does bad deeds, he will get a worse birth. If there's a person who gives sweetmeats and nice food to a Brahman on a festival, he gets a better birth. If a person is a Brahman and always does good deeds, or is a person of any caste who did good deeds, then he will be born again as a human being. If the person does not do good deeds, he'll be born as a dog, insect, or any animal. When a person is reborn, there's no way of knowing what he was in his last life. Although caste is only man-made, not god-made, still Yama provides the caste into which a person is born. We should keep caste, for when the caste system started it was for the welfare of human beings and still is. Kshatriyas protect the country from enemies. Chuhra Sweepers do menial work; Chamar Leatherworkers work with leather. Jats do agricultural work. Vaishyas or Baniyas do mostly business. The Shudras are mostly Chamars and Chuhras; there are no clean Shudras.

Plowman, considered by some villagers to be the most skilled village plowman in 1958,

had gone to fourth grade. He presented the traditional Sanatan Dharma position on rebirth, action, and the place of caste in the cycle of rebirths. He stated that a person dies, but a soul is reborn and goes on in the cycle of rebirths, depending on past actions of the soul; there is no way of knowing what the sum of one's past actions are and, therefore, of knowing what kind of rebirth one may have. Plowman mentioned good actions, such as giving traditional gifts to Brahmans, as contributing to a good or better rebirth. Failing to perform good actions, a soul may be reborn in a lower status than a human being, i.e., as a dog, insect, or any animal. He believed that his own rebirth would depend on the sum of his soul's past actions and Yama's decision about them. Then Plowman diverged from the concepts of death, action, and rebirth, and expanded on the subject of caste and its divisions in order to indicate that caste is for the welfare of human beings. He said that there are no clean Shudras, that mostly Harijans, the lowest castes into which one may be reborn, are Shudras, and that membership in a specific caste is determined by dharma (Mathur, 1964: 86–87). Saini (1975: 48) said that the ancient level of Shudra, the fourth varna, has been out of favor in modern times, which explains Plowman's placing Harijans, the panchamas or fifth level, as Shudras. Although Plowman's discussion of caste seemed to be a change of subject or divergence from rebirth, he was thinking of caste in terms of rebirth based on the sum of past actions of a soul.

The following excerpts from the interviews of eight villagers, both men and women of several castes, about death, action, rebirth, and release from the cycle of rebirths represent Samajis, Sanatanis, and Eclectics. The first quotation is from a woman (F, E, 58, 77) of the Chhipi Dyer caste, who had small children and was pregnant at the time of the 1958 interview. Only one Chhipi Dyer family, who migrated from a large, nearby village shortly after we started fieldwork in 1958, lived in Shanti Nagar. The Chhipi immigrants were sponsored by a Jat family, who let them live in one of their houses rent-free in exchange for tailoring. The house was near the Gola Potters. Although the Chhipi caste is identified with the traditional occupation of dying and printing cotton cloth, this family derived its living exclusively from tailoring. We rank them approximately above the Nai Barbers and close to the Jhinvars, Lohars, and Malis (S. Freed and R. Freed, 1976: 95–96, 101). To some degree, they were a bit unsure of their status in the village, and the Chhipi woman seemed hesitant to commit herself during the first interview.

The Chhipi woman was asked, "What happens to a person after death?" She answered, "I do not know. After a person dies, he is gone." In response to a question on rebirth, she said she had not heard of rebirth. When asked whether a dead person becomes a ghost, she replied, "I do not know whether a person becomes a ghost because he dies an unhappy or accidental death. I have heard of ghost possession, but I have never seen a person possessed. But some people say that if one dies, one becomes a ghost."

Her responses were not unusual for people who tended to say that they had never seen a ghost or ghost possession, or who said that they had not heard of a specific deity or of release from the cycle of rebirths, and could not tell if a soul was reborn because they had never seen it. Other people said that they could not prove that a person could be reborn so they did not know if rebirth existed. Although the Chhipi woman had heard of ghosts and ghost possessions but had never seen them, she mentioned that a person might die an unhappy or accidental death and become a ghost. She placed iron amulets on the wrists and ankles of her children to protect them from ghosts. When she was asked what happens to a person who has done good deeds all his life, she replied, "I do not know, but I think that if a person does good deeds all his life, he will be rewarded; if he does bad deeds, he will be punished."

By 1977, the Chhipi woman was more at ease in the village, and she and her husband had friendly relations with us so that she told about the death of her daughter and her own possessions and fits. She suffered first from ghost possessions and then from fits, *daura*, brought by the ghost of her daughter, who died at age 23 in 1972. Between 1958 and 1972, the Chhipi woman and her husband had raised and educated this daughter and were very proud of her. Although relatively poor,

they were educating all their children and were ambitious for them. The death of the daughter at childbirth was a severe blow to her mother. She added, after mentioning her possessions and fits, that whenever she heard a sad story or received bad news, her stomach pained her so much that she had to sit down to avoid having fits. Having experienced ghost possessions and fits, she told about them, but not in great detail, for she was a reticent woman.

In 1958, A Jhinvar Watercarrier man (M, E, Jhinvar, 58) disclaimed both the Arya Samaj and Sanatan Dharma. Although living fairly near Jat Samajis, he was a neighbor of Brahman Sanatanis and had close friendly relations with them. On special festivals, the Jhinvars gave uncooked food to be cooked by a neighboring Brahman woman so that the Jhinvars could attain good karma by feeding Brahmans. Despite these good relations, the Jhinvar said, "I do not not follow Arya Samaj or Sanatan Dharma. One just has to do what one has to do to eat and that is all. Bhagwan is always there if you do your own work. He is also there for the welfare of the village and the village cattle." This man outlined his Hindu practices: worship at shrines and temples for deities, including the mother-goddess shrines and the Bhumiya shrine in the village; pilgrimages to the Ganges when he could afford it; and trips to fairs for the worship of saints (Islamic pirs). Not all males said that they worshipped and made offerings at the shrines of mother goddesses, but some did. On the subject of the avatars of Vishnu, the Jhinvar said that he did not recognize Vishnu and had never seen a deity born on earth. Regarding the rebirth of human beings, he said that he had heard that they were reborn but had never seen it so he could not say if it took place. He thought that the soul was immortal so it might take rebirth in the form of a plant, animal, or human; but he repeated that he had never seen any of these events so he did not know. His main statement, which was consistent with his background and agricultural way of life, was that he worshipped Dharti Mata (Mother Earth).

In the 1950s the adult members of the Jhinvar Watercarrier families were nonliterate, but they had started educating their children. In the 1970s, the son (M, AS, Jhinvar, 77) of the Jhinvar interviewed in 1958 became a teacher of Sanskrit and art in a school in the City of Delhi, and his wife taught school before her children were born. The young couple were strong adherents of the Arya Samaj, which may have been due to the changing times, their education, and their caste ranking close to the Jat caste (S. A. Freed, 1970: 12, tables 4, 5).

A very old Chamar woman (F, E, 58) said that she worshipped Bhagwan, but whenever ghost illness took place in her household, she and other women worshipped and left offerings at the various mother-goddess shrines to help fight off the ghost. She called a bhagat (exorcist) to drive out ghost illness and ghost possession. The old woman had never heard of an avatar of a deity being born on earth but thought that people became ghosts when they died, and she did not know whether a person would be reborn as a human being or as an animal. How the soul would be reborn, according to her, depended on Bhagwan's will. She did not know what would happen to the soul of a person who committed suicide in a well, i.e., whether the person would be reborn or become a wandering ghost.

The 72-year-old head (M, E, 58) of the only Mali Gardener family in the village provided these views about death and rebirth. "There are two kinds of life. One is the life that breathes; and the second is the life that speaks. The life that breathes lives once and then leaves the house. The life that speaks must not die. It can always go to a place where the life that breathes cannot go. Jiva, life, continues and is born into some other body." He then told a story about a number of rebirths of a woman to illustrate the life that speaks but not the life that breathes. He ended with these statements: "Life is like a Persian wheel. It goes up and down. These boys here are my sons. I might die and be reborn to them as a son." His life that breathes is analogous to the living body; his life that speaks is analogous to the soul, which at death may become a ghost for a while and then may be reborn. The Mali's statements to some extent represent Sanatan Dharma, but the forms of worship followed by him and his family placed him in the eclectic category. The Malis had relatively recently migrated from Rajasthan and had their garden and

dwelling near the village cremation grounds, which lay outside the boundaries of the village habitation site (Append. IV: Map 4, B, CG). They did not participate in all village festivals but did employ a village Brahman as priest for their weddings.

A 25-year-old schoolteacher (M, E, 58), a member of the only Mahar Potter family in the village, did not want to be interviewed but cooperated grudgingly. The members of this family were no longer potters and had not been for a number of generations. Although the Mahar Potter caste ranked relatively low in the village caste hierarchy, this family was wealthy. Most of its members lived in the city. The brevity of the teacher's response reflected his resentment of his caste status, which was in conflict with his education and the wealth of his family. He stated that he was neither Arya Samaj nor Sanatan Dharma, and said, "I believe in Bhagwan straight out and that is it. I do not worship idols or go to temples." When he was asked where he learned his beliefs, he replied, "My parents never taught me anything. I just learned by myself." He did not know what happened when one died, nor did he know whether souls were reborn. His final statement: "I do no pujas (worships) and leave no offerings. I just believe in Bhagwan and that is definitely all."

Buddhist I (M, B & E, 58, 77), a Chamar, held views about life, death, rebirth, release from the cycle, and ghosts similar to those of other interviewees. He was bright, self-taught, and considered himself a self-made man; he read pamphlets about Hinduism, which he bought in the city markets. Although he claimed to be a Buddhist, his beliefs primarily stemmed from Hinduism. In 1958, he said:

A man is born after he has been an insect, animal, and all the beings of the world. Only after these stages is the soul born as a human being. A person, who worships Bhagwan intensely, goes into the jungles to meditate, and is a celibate, might obtain human birth again. If he worships very intensely, he might even see Bhagwan. As a result of intense worship, he might become a king or a saint in this world. When a man goes into the jungle to worship, he stays there without regard to hunger or thirst.

Bhagwan tries to scare him in many ways to see if he will run away and not worship. When Bhagwan sees that he cannot be scared, then Bhagwan visits him. When he has proven himself, Bhagwan sees that he is freed from rebirths in this world. Intelligence is given by Bhagwan; but effort is needed. Whatsoever Bhagwan has written in his luck, so it will be. Luck is determined by Bhagwan. When a child is in the mother's womb, then Bhagwan writes on his skull what he will be; whether happy or not. After a man dies and is cremated, on the second or third day his bones are picked up and one can see the writing of Bhagwan on the skull. Then the bones and skull are taken to the Ganges. Mukti means freedom from bondage and if no freedom, the soul goes on wandering as a ghost in this world. I worship Bhagwan-Shiva and believe in ghosts and ghost possessions.

Buddhist I then spoke about the ghost possession of a woman in the City of Delhi and about Lord of Ghosts, a village exorcist, whose wife and daughter-in-law were possessed by ghosts. He distinguished between ghosts and the evil eye. He said that a ghost was the wandering soul of a dead person, and that the evil eye was cast by a living person, who was not conscious of so doing. Although he stated that Bhagwan wrote an infant's fortune on its skull, village women attributed it to Bemata, a goddess who visited mother and child after midnight on the sixth day after the infant's birth. Despite his claim to be a follower of Buddha, Buddhist I believed in multiple supernatural beings and his statements reflect an eclectic selection of beliefs.

Two widows provided additional insight regarding death, the soul's actions, the possibility of being reborn in the same family, and the desire for release from the round of rebirths. The first widow, a Jat (F, AS, 77), with the pseudonym of Widow-in-Between, described the recent death of a five-year-old Brahman boy and then added, "Previously they buried children, but there were cases where the dogs dug up the children and even ate one. A Chamar child was dug up and dragged by dogs into a tomato field. For children, they do not do death ceremonies. They just give bread to a cow for 10 to 13 days."

When she was asked what happens to the soul of a child, she replied:

I don't know what happens to the soul of a child when it dies. Bhagwan may be knowing. Children have a soul. Everybody has a soul. Even trees have a soul because when you cut them down, they are no longer green. The soul does not die; it goes some place else. It never dies. No soul ever dies. In my case, when I die, Bhagwan will dispose of me wherever I should go. I might like to go into a house where there are no problems, but Bhagwan will dispose. I have been so unhappy in this life that if I were born to the same parents and in the same house in the next life, I would pray to Bhagwan to release me from these hardships. I would like to have the same sons, but I would pray to Bhagwan that if I cannot have peace in this life, please destroy my soul. I do not know what to do about all of this. I have had many hardships and now see my daughter-in-law having the same hardships.

Widow-in-Between's unhappiness was due to the death of her husband, Short Life, when she was still a young woman; the ghost possessions of her daughter, Resourceful, when she was eight years old and later at the time of her marriage; and the death of her grown son, Only Heir, who was killed in an accident a year previously. She has been given her pseudonym because her mother-in-law, Matriarch, became a widow at a relatively young age and then her daughter-in-law, Widow III, was widowed when Only Heir died. To die before the allotted time and to become a widow were believed to be due to the soul's past actions. Therefore, the deaths of the three husbands leaving three widows were brought about by the sum of the past actions of each of the six people. It is not surprising that Widow-in-Between hoped that she would not be reborn into the same family to lead a similar troubled life (Chap. 22: Widows, Patriarchs, Twins).

Death, burial, and cremation of children were linked to changing funeral customs in the 1950s and thereafter and to beliefs about what happened to children who die young. When infants died in the 1950s and 1970s, it was assumed by all but Samajis that their actions in past lives were so bad that their allotted time to live was very short. Their souls were not expected to linger long as ghosts. Therefore, in the 1950s burials of infants were accepted. However, at one time, all Harijans (adults and children) had been buried, but in the 1950s adult Harijans were cremated. By the 1970s, all children were cremated. The reason Widow-in-Between gave for switching from burial to cremation for children was that animals sometimes dug up the corpses, based on actual occurrences. Other reasons for the change to cremation may have been due to the decline in mortality rates for children and the increasing number of families who could afford the fuel necessary for cremation. The practice of cremation was consistent with Hindu beliefs about carrying out the proper funeral rituals in order that the soul of the deceased be quickly released from the body so it would not linger as a ghost.

The second widow was Mrs. Householder (F, SD, Brahman, 58, 77), 70 years old in 1978, who was interviewed during both field trips (Chap. 21: New Brahman Lane). In 1958, she described the shrines and places at which she worshipped: Bhumiya, at weddings and when a child or calf was born; mother goddesses for diseases, such as smallpox; pilgrimages to the Ganges in the month of Karttik or to the Yamuna River on Amavas; and the worship of Hanuman, the monkey god and lieutenant of Rama Chandra on Tuesdays. The latter worship was characteristic of Brahmans who were devotees of Rama Chandra. Despite worshipping at shrines for Bhumiya, a male godling, and the mother goddesses, she stated, "Although I do these worships, there is only one god, Bhagwan-Vishnu, but it is said that there are millions of names for him. Then she discussed life after death:

A person dies and is burnt; then the ashes are put in the Ganges River. When the body is burnt, the soul is burnt too, but for the sake of the soul for one month the pipal tree has water placed around it, a cow is fed, and alms are given. The soul, made of all the elements, probably may go to Parameshwara [the Supreme Ruler, Vishnu], but the body which is made of earth stays

as dust in the earth. While alive the body is beautiful. A person who has done good deeds will be reborn; a person who has done bad deeds will be reborn as a dog or a cat. If one does good deeds, he or she will always be reborn as a good person. The soul of a person wanders around until the prescribed period for it to live expires. Parameshwara prescribes the time. If a person dies an accidental death, Parameshwara won't have him. He should not come to Bhagwan-Vishnu before his allotted time is up. Suppose I had done some good work and am about to die, I might be reborn as the child of this woman sitting here beside me because of my good deeds. In case of an accidental death, a person becomes a ghost. He will be a ghost until the end of his allotted time. When a person commits suicide, his soul wanders as a ghost. A person obtains rebirth when he dies at his allotted time.

Some of the foregoing statements were similar to those of other Brahman women. All women commonly referred to the worship of mother goddesses, especially if their children fell ill, but Brahman women were better informed about other deities and aspects of Hinduism.

Mrs. Householder's 1958 statements were similar to those she made in 1978, which follow. However, her 1978 statements were tempered by a number of sad and troublesome events during the preceding 20 years, including the recent death of her husband, for whom she was still mourning. When she was asked whether she had changed any of her beliefs during her lifetime, she responded: "Everything has changed. I still believe in Bhagwan-Vishnu, but there's nothing now which was previously. Before one could buy two seers of wheat for a rupee. I used to be much heavier; now I am thinner and weak." Asked which deities she now worshipped, she replied: "Hanuman, Devi, and Ganga [the Goddess of the River Ganges, worshipped by widows and widowers on Amavas, the day following the dark night of the moon] [Append. V]. Also in the morning and the evening I light a lamp and take Ram's name [Rama Chandra]. The whole family worships Ram. The real worship is when a mother and father are treated like deities and served properly."

Her statements indicate why a soul becomes a ghost and is reborn; her comments about the worship of deities are representative of Sanatanis. The last sentence about parents was characteristic of dharma among Brahmans. Questioned as to what this widow thought made a soul come to life in a body, she responded, "A pig is happy in its skin; and in whatever type of body a soul takes birth, it is happy. Happiness and sadness cannot be divided because of someone else's luck."

Answering a question as to what makes a person die, she said: "Some sickness inside causes the machine to stop functioning and man cannot breathe. When breathing is cornered, life goes away. Breathing and the soul are the same in the way that if one breathes happily, the soul will be happy, and it will be the opposite if one breathes sadly. If someone does good, he will be happy."

When asked what she meant by luck, she replied, "This life of mine was affected by the fruit of actions in past lives so it was my luck that actions in past lives have caused me troubles in this life."

Queried as to what happens to the soul upon death, she answered:

Hollowness becomes hollowness; the body becomes part of the earth. The soul goes into the air. Those persons who die unnaturally become ghosts. Dying unnaturally means being beaten to death, being cut up under a train, killing oneself. But if an old man or old woman dies, they do not become ghosts. They go straight to the Universal Absolute, or they may be reborn. My old man died eight months ago and no one has seen him since [i.e., as a ghost], but he will be born again some place. I do not know where or when. I want to be released from rebirth when I die because rebirth means hell. Anyone may say anything they want, but I have never committed a bad deed. I have never stolen or cheated. If I found something, I always returned it to the person who lost it. Bhagwan-Vishnu may do anything with me.

This widow emphasized her good deeds in her present life, but she believed that the sum of her actions in past lives had affected her present life. She hoped to be released from the round of rebirths when she died because of her many troubles, including her recent widowhood. Because she believed she had performed only good actions in this life, she thought she might find release. Thus, she as well as Widow-in-Between expressed the wish to be released from another life full of trouble.

Mrs. Householder's two interviews, the first in 1958 and the second in 1978, were characteristic of Sanatan Dharma. Her interviews covered the worship of multiple deities, rebirth, action, release from rebirths, and types of rebirth. She indicated that becoming a ghost was related to dying before the allotted time, accidental deaths, suicides, or murders. Her statement about breath stopping when a person dies was based on the identity of the soul with breath and the belief that the soul escapes from the body at death.

CHAPTER 10: FRUIT OF ACTION, FATE, DISCIPLINE

What is action, What inaction?
About this even sages are bewildered.
So I shall explain action to thee.
Knowing which, thou shalt be freed from evil.

(From the Bhagavad Gita, Edgerton, 1965: 24)

The widowed Mrs. Householder linked the sum of her actions from the past lives of her soul with the luck of her present life, but she distinguished between the two concepts, action and luck. In his review of a book on karma, Spiro criticizes the way in which karma has been interpreted to mean fate or the control of one's fate. According to Spiro:

Karma as a term denotes any volitional act, and doctrinally it refers to a theory of retributive justice (over eons of time) in which karma is cause and moral retribution (good and bad fortune) is effect. Hence, . . . karma does not connote, let alone denote . . . fate or destiny . . . for according to the doctrine of karma, one's present fortune is a consequence of one's own actions (karma) performed in previous lives (and to some extent in one's present life) [Spiro, 1984: 1003–1004].

Spiro's reference to "one's own actions" should be one's soul's actions. Spiro's interpretation of the word karma is in accord with the village ideology and the Bhagavad Gita.

Western fascination with the word karma may have contributed to different interpretations of the word among English speakers. For example, some English language dictionaries provide a number of definitions for karma, such as fate, destiny, and the sum of a person's actions during successive rebirths which determines the destiny of a person (Morris, 1969: 715; Gove, 1986: 1223).

Manipulator, a Brahman, used the following example to illustrate the concept of the fruit of one's actions. He recounted how a holy man, whose actions in this life were all good, took ill in midlife, was hospitalized for a long time, and then died at a relatively early age. His early death was due to the fruit of his soul's actions from his past lives. According to this Brahman, the holy man would be born again and again until his bad actions

were completely eradicated by his good actions. The concept of the fruit of actions presents an answer for many villagers when people whose lives are exemplary die at a relatively early age and become ghosts.

Two anthropologists who contributed to the volume criticized by Spiro are Wadley and Pugh. Based on fieldwork in the well-known village of Karimpur located in Uttar Pradesh that was studied by C. V. and W. R. Wiser (1930) and her own research on popular literature in North India, Wadley (1983) pointed out that *vrats* (vows) and the performance thereof can change one's destiny. In Shanti Nagar vows may be a form of bhakti worship, linked with love and devotion to a chosen deity, for example, Santoshi Mata. Thus, vows and their performance constitute good actions. Although individuals may hope that the fulfillment of vows will contribute to a preponderance of good actions over bad actions, no one knows the sum of a soul's actions or whether good or bad actions predominate. Although Wadley stated that vows and their performance transform one's destiny, a more accurate statement is that good actions, such as vows and their fulfillment, would to some extent change the balance of good actions against bad actions. Pugh (1983: 23, fn. 2) linked astrology with karma and traced astrology back to the Vedas. She found in Varanasi that Hindus consult astrologers to dispel anxiety about the effect of their actions in past lives and to seek predictions and advice about good actions that they might perform in their present lives to circumvent trouble.

In Shanti Nagar, despite Swami Dayanand's aspersions about astrology (Saraswati, 1956: 47–49), Brahman Priests cast horoscopes for the sons of many castes, including Jats, shortly after their birth. Horoscopes were seldom, if ever, cast for daughters because as more than one man said, "A daughter is a burden." Setting the time of a wedding was based on the horoscope of the groom, but not of the bride because of this general belief that a girl is a misfortune.

The belief in astrological predictions is grounded in the further belief that the time of one's birth and type of rebirth are decided by Yama or Bhagwan and are based on the fruit of action, i.e., the sum of the soul's actions. Thus, fate and astrology are linked with one's birth date and karma. Moreover, villagers believe that, short of past actions so bad as to cause death, there is a certain amount of leeway between an absolute and invincible fate and a relative fate. Thus interpretation of one's actions in the process of life, death, and rebirth may result in a fate other than expected. One can never know what one's past actions in previous lives may contribute to one's future lives or to release from the round of rebirths, anymore than one can be sure that some small action in this life may not result in a lower or higher form of rebirth or release from the cycle. The odds are unknown so life and death are a gamble. Although a soul may be reborn or released from the cycle of rebirths, villagers generally believe that they will be reborn. Rebirth to them is a kind of immortality and is more understandable than release from the cycle of rebirths and union with the Universal Absolute.

Ingalls (1957) has pointed out that the popularizers of Hinduism, the Mahabharata and the Ramayana, have contributed considerably to the great mass of Hindu believers, ordinary everyday people, rather than the professional specialists and innovators, such as Dayanand Saraswati, who studied and interpreted Sanskritic texts. For example, what appeals most to ordinary people in the Mahabharata and the Ramayana, in addition to the battles and other dramatic events, are answers to moral problems governed by dharma, the rules by which they should live, which are provided by the protagonists in these two epics. Ingalls then gives examples of moral decisions based on the concept of the gunas from the Bhagavad Gita.

The value of the *Mahabharata* to the Indian readers, the joy they have taken in it, derives . . . from a series of moral problems to which there are usually three answers given: the answer of Bhima, which is the answer of materialism, egoism, brute force; the answer of Yudhisthira, which is the answer of piety, of social virtue, and tradition; and the answer of Arjuna, which falls between the two, and so reveals the finest moral qualities of man: courage, energy, pity, self-discipline.

He further noted that Bhima may be characterized as *tamasa*; Arjuna as *rajasa*; and Yudhisthira as *sattvika*. Yet the hero is Arjuna (Ingalls, 1957: 43–44, fn. 43–44).

These answers were familiar to villagers from attending *katha*s, story-telling sessions, from the Mahabharata, especially the Bhagavad Gita, and from the Ramayana, recited by Story Teller, a Brahman teacher of Sanskrit in a higher secondary school, who explained the text while the audience commented on the explanations, asked questions, and agreed or disagreed with him (R. Freed and S. Freed, 1981: 145–146). An important point that the Mahabharata emphasizes is the virtue of self-discipline. The Sanskrit word for discipline is yoga, translated as yoke. Such self-discipline, according to Ingalls (1957: 44), becomes second nature, and only when intensely frustrated and overcome with unbearable grief does an individual believe that what has happened is a matter of predestination. Moksha (release from the cycle of rebirths) as a goal then becomes freedom from suffering.

To attain release from rebirth requires discipline. The paths or ways of discipline, which lead to release are: (1) action or karma-yoga; (2) love and devotion to a deity, bhakti-yoga; and (3) spiritual knowledge, jnana-yoga. Jnana-yoga may include meditation and abandonment of action, both of which involve choice and thus along with bhakti-yoga are forms of action. Most villagers rely on karma-yoga reinforced by dharma, but followers of Sanatan Dharma and eclecticism additionally may have a chosen deity whom they worship with loving devotion. A few old Brahman men sought self-disciplined, spiritual knowledge in the form of meditation as a means of release from the round of rebirths. When parables from the epics and Puranas seem contradictory and villagers are unsure of their meaning, they tend to follow the rules of dharma regarding family and caste customs and to worship a deity or deities (Avalon, 1913: cxliv; Sarma, 1953: 3–5, 26; R. Freed and S. Freed, 1962: 251–252; Edgerton, 1965: 24–25, 63).

The combined ways of action and devotion suit most villagers, especially since they are more interested in rebirth than in release from the cycle. Strict Samajis, according to Saraswati's dicta, do not believe in moksha, permanent release from the round of rebirths, and, except in cases of extreme frustration and grief, as in the case of Widow-in-Between, are not interested in it. According to Ingalls (1957: 45, 46, 48, fn. 20), the concepts of moksha and dharma in Hinduism arose in different milieus, later than the Vedic Age. Moksha was then added to the three Vedic stages of life: student, householder, and retirement. Evidence exists that the concept of release (moksha) first appeared among practitioners of trance and ecstasy. Swami Dayanand Saraswati claimed that his teachings came from the Vedas, the earliest written source of Hinduism, which claim may account for his exclusion of the belief in release from the round of rebirths and union with the Universal Absolute.

BELIEVERS AND NONBELIEVERS

Since two opposing doctrines stand out in village ideology, belief in multiple supernatural beings as against belief in only one supernatural being, Bhagwan, people who adhere to the first position generally believe in ghosts; people who hold the second, usually do not believe in ghosts. These two positions divide the villagers into two groups: believers and nonbelievers in ghosts. Although a number of people profess adherence to one or the other point of view, as will be shown, men, who follow Sanatan Dharma or eclectic beliefs sometimes hedge their position or say they do not believe in ghosts, but later contradict themselves. This ambivalence is due to the influence of male followers of the Arya Samaj in the Jat caste, who claim that fear is the ghost and only women fear ghosts. The interviews in this section illustrate the views of believers and nonbelievers of several castes, beginning with the account of one Sanatani.

FENCE SITTER'S AMBIVALENCE

An interview in 1958 with Fence Sitter, a 25-year-old Brahman Sanatani, shows how an ambivalent man may accept the idea that the belief in ghosts is based on one's fear of them and yet may continue to believe in them, as indicated by his extensive information about ghosts. Fence Sitter had attended higher secondary school but failed his matriculation examination, so he worked in a factory in Old Delhi, often coming home late at night. The members of his lineage, followers of Sanatan Dharma, were known for a family legend about Merchant, their ancestor, and Muslim Ghost (Chap. 12).

When Fence Sitter was asked to tell what he knew about ghosts, he began by saying:

Akhta, basa, and *kins* are three trees. You can become afraid of these trees if you see them. The *kins* is what is used to thresh wheat. The *basa* wood is what you put beneath houses. You have a bunch of sticks and use them as flooring in the house. Then water cannot seep through the floor of the house. *Akhta* is what goats eat because a kind of milk comes out of it. If you see one of these three trees, you might be afraid, for they can become ghosts. When I come from the factory at night and pass these trees, I recite the Gayatri Mantra over and over again. It has been proven that when you recite this mantra you can overcome any obstacle [Append. II: Mantras]. So when I come home, I never have to fear any obstacle.

When Fence Sitter came home at night, he said he was occasionally frightened by animals which followed him and may have been ghosts. He added, "When a ghost takes the form of an animal, it terrifies the person and makes a noise like an animal. If it is a cat, it mews. Then when the person looks behind him and sees nothing there, he is terrified." The animals he named as possible ghosts were camels, cats, dogs, water buffaloes, cows, jackals—chiefly animals sometimes encountered in the fields at night. Fence Sitter continued:

Late one night when I was coming home from the mill, just beyond the next large village a mile from here, I met a jackal. Jackals are of two kinds: a normal one and a mad jackal. I faced a mad jackal, a very frightening animal because it will attack a man. In a ditch nearby, I found some stones and started throwing them at the jackal, but the jackal kept dodging the stones. Then a gardener came along with a dog and the jackal ran away. If a mad jackal howls on the low side of the village, cattle will die. If he howls in the cremation grounds, a man will die. If he howls on the high side of the village, a son will be born. If he howls on the north side of the village, there will be a theft.

When Fence Sitter was asked whether he thought that the mad jackal he had encountered was a ghost, he answered, "There is no relation between the jackal and a ghost. All this about ghosts is a way of saying the actual ghost lies within you. If you are fearful of some place that you are going, then you will be afraid there. If you are dishonest, you will have fear. There are some undue deaths. The souls of such dead people cannot find rebirth so they stalk around unhappily. The ghost is within you; otherwise there are no ghosts."

In this interview with Fence Sitter, particularly his statements about reciting the Gayatri Mantra for protection and about undue deaths ("the souls of such dead stalk around unhappily") Fence Sitter contradicted himself and showed his ambivalence about admitting a belief in and fear of ghosts, and instead projected the masculine adage that it is fear that is the ghost. Fence Sitter recounted another incident:

One day a wolf would have finished me off. It was night and I was riding home along the canal. At the village nearest to home, I saw a wolf drinking water. I cycled on, but the wolf followed me. I then saw the nearby village, but the wolf was still there. When I came to the bridge over a ditch, I braked my cycle and turned to the left. The wolf continued on and then wheeled around and faced me. I lighted a cigarette and the wolf edged away. Then I lit a firecracker, which frightened the wolf off. Although I was afraid of the wolf, I continued homeward. Finally, I crossed the railroad tracks

and saw an animal who lives near the tracks and whose eyes were shining brightly. Some people believe this animal is a ghost, but I say it is an animal. I continued on until I came to the cremation grounds of this village. A Chuhra Sweeper had been cremated there the day before and near his smoldering ashes lay a stick with a kite [a scavenger bird] sitting near it. I thought that the kite was the ghost of the Sweeper and was afraid, lost control of the cycle, and fell. [Note: the equation of a Sweeper, a scavenger, with a kite, also a scavenger]. Then the kite flew away. As a result I decided that the kite was not a ghost. Probably because I was afraid of the wolf, I thought the kite was a ghost. Then I concluded that there are no ghosts and that it was just the fear inside of me.

Fence Sitter reasoned that if one is already afraid, then when one encounters what seems to be a ghost, one will believe that it is a ghost. If one realizes that fear causes the belief that one has seen a ghost, then one can rationalize the fear and the ghost. However, would Fence Sitter have carried firecrackers with him or recited the Gayatri Mantra if he did not believe in ghosts and was not afraid? Did he carry the firecrackers only to frighten animals or to frighten them and ghosts who appeared in the forms of animals? Fence Sitter's interview is noteworthy for the contradictory statements he made about both believing in ghosts and denying their existence, hence his pseudonym, Fence Sitter.

Carstairs (1958: 52–53) commented on behavior similar to Fence Sitter's in Deoli, Rajasthan, and provides a somewhat similar example of a man claiming that he never saw a ghost and "in the same breath" telling about a ghost he had recently seen in the jungle. Carstairs found this contradiction among a number of informants, all of whom used two categories derived from the gunas. They claimed to be *dev-gun* (godlike) by birth rather than *rakshas-gun* (demonlike), and therefore unable to see ghosts. They stated that they were nonbelievers in ghosts and then later related an experience with a ghost. Carstairs (1958: 52–54, quotation p. 54) decided that such behavior was due to "an inner sense of instability and insecurity—nothing and nobody can be relied upon, not even one's own self." To some extent this characterizes Fence Sitter because of his family background, for in his childhood his mother died and his father neglected him. Further in Shanti Nagar males may deny a belief in ghosts to demonstrate their masculinity and courage.

JAT VIEWPOINTS

The following two interviews of Jat men, which took place in 1977–78, are somewhat different because the older man illustrates the firm position of Samajis, unchanged since 1958, whereas the younger man, also a professed Samaji, reflects recent change in some aspects of Samaji belief and practice. Dissembler, a 64-year-old man, when asked about ghosts, answered, "There are no ghosts so how can I believe in them." He was then asked how he knew that there were no ghosts. He replied, "If you have a doubt about anything, then that becomes a fear and that is a ghost from fear. But there are no ghosts. The next question was, "Why do people believe in ghosts and believe that a ghost can possess them? He answered, "People are stupid. They know nothing. If a person is ill, they won't give him proper treatment. They'll think a ghost is causing the illness. If their feet are cold and their head hot, they believe a ghost has possessed them. People can't think. It's some illness in the body. People just make excuses. They have no thinking power. I have been everywhere, and I have never seen a ghost."

When asked in the course of a survey on change about the Arya Samaj, ghosts, and other beliefs, the younger Jat, age 20, whose family in the late 1950s were staunch followers of the Arya Samaj, said, "Nobody is Arya Samaj now. Since I was born, I have seen people worshipping idols. Some people may be saying no idols are worshipped, but they believe in these deities and worship them. In my family, we don't believe in Santoshi Mata or ghosts. The belief in ghosts is due to imagination." Although he accused other Samajis of departing from important beliefs of the Arya Samaj, he declared his own family's steadfast opposition to the belief in ghosts and multiple deities.

DISCUSSION IN
A CHAMAR BAITHAK

This discussion took place in 1978 among the members of a Chamar lineage, in which a wedding party, consisting solely of men of the lineage, had returned the previous day from the bride's village. We had been following the chain of events leading to the wedding, namely, a feast in Shanti Nagar for the 20-year-old son of Kin, who was to be married, and all the accompanying rituals before the groom went to the bride's village. The feast had been held in the large house of Host so we went there to see him. Possibly to avoid comments about the drunken brawl which took place in the bride's village but also to limit the number of people crowding around us, Host took us to his men's house. It was relatively new, well built, and dimly lit by electricity with an altar above which were pictures of deities. More than 20 men, all of this Chamar lineage, were crammed into the room so it was difficult to identify everyone, especially since many Chamars worked in the city during the day and were rarely seen in the village.

The conversation started with a discussion about the education of Host's children and the difficulties of finding jobs for them after they left school. He mentioned that when a family had no "access" to a person with a job opening it was difficult to find jobs. He also described the procedures for looking for jobs. The subject of drunks and drinking was brought up, but Host avoided it by stating that only one or two men in his lineage drank. However, he said, "No five fingers are alike," a metaphor used to express the range of individual differences. This expression was used in the village and has also been found in Pakistan (Berland, 1982).

We then introduced the subject of ghosts, which provoked a debate between partisans of two basic positions: belief or disbelief in ghosts. The discussion took on a personal dimension between Buddhist II, a nonbeliever in ghosts, and the others, all believers, with Host diplomatically acting to maintain peace.

When asked about ghosts, Host replied, "I can't see them." Another man commented, "If you meet a ghost, just look on the ground and pass by. You can see ghosts have different qualities. A ghost can grow small or large. In ghost possession, the ghost speaks inside the person and identifies himself." Host mentioned that one can obtain information about ghosts and ghost possessions from Illusionist, an exorcist. Buddhist II interrupted, "Illusionist is just a propagandist." To prevent Buddhist II from continuing, Host said, "Ghosts and ghost possessions are out of our hands. If someone tells us what to do, we do it, and where to go for curing ghost possessions, we go there. Women are possessed more than men." Another man added, "Women are possessed more than men because they are afraid of ghosts."

Buddhist II forcefully asserted his disbelief. "Only blind-fold people believe in ghosts. For people who don't believe in ghosts, there are no ghosts. I don't believe in any ghosts; the belief is complete nonsense. Just as a person drinks and acts funny so when a ghost is said to possess a person, the person acts funny. I am only saying what other people say about ghosts." A man asked Buddhist II, "If there are no ghosts, why does the person act funny?" His reply, "When people drink liquor, they show off to impress others, so too some people act abnormally just to impress others."

A young man who believed in ghosts but had not spoken previously agreed tactfully that there was some truth in what had just been said. He was asked, "Is there something wrong that is not understood about the person who is said to be possessed and who acts funny?" He replied, "In a person into whom the ghost will enter, the person dimly sees the ghost; then the ghost starts bothering the person, enters, and speaks as a voice. A ghost can be seen only by the person in whom the ghost will enter." He reaffirmed Host's position that some people see ghosts and others do not, but that those who do not see ghosts are not necessarily nonbelievers. They are just not subject to ghost possessions. Another man spoke up to suggest that we make a study of what a ghost is and where the ghost starts. In effect, he was calling for their scientific study. His question was perceptive, for that was what we were doing and said so.

We asked, "If many ghosts exist, how can souls be reborn?" Buddhist II, instead of answering the question, discoursed as follows: "I don't believe in Hinduism. It is all lies. We should follow Buddhism. It propagates the ideas that man is born to man, that the chain goes on, and what is born will die, just like a tree. There is no basis to this belief in ghosts." Another man dissented from Buddhist II's viewpoint by asking, "What if you die accidentally before a natural death or your allotted time to die, will you wander as a ghost? Does not the soul of the deceased roam here and there until the allotted time has passed?" Buddhist II replied, "Only Hinduism has this theory of ghosts. Non-Hindus do not believe in them."

Still another man queried, "Suppose all this about ghosts is trash, then what is an apparition? Why does a ghost regularly enter Kin's wife and now his daughter?" Pointing to the son of Buddhist II, who lived separately from his father, he asked, "Why does a ghost enter the wife of this man standing here?" Buddhist II's son, a believer in ghosts, replied, "There must be a ghost. He speaks and says, 'my name is so-and-so.' I come from here and I want this. Then the ghost wants to take my wife with him."

Buddhist II retaliated: "I don't know why people blindly follow these ideas. I don't believe in ghosts and am not affected by them." Buddhist II's strong opposition to belief in ghosts persisted despite the repeated ghost possessions of his wife, daughter, and daughter-in-law. Ignoring all comments, questions, and suggestion, he kept on his own track, stating, "Here there are Brahman dharma, Radhaswamis, and many other forms of sects and cults. People run these sects to benefit themselves. They dupe other people into giving them money. I know the case of a holy man who swindled money acquired from devotees. He escaped to America and married there. To this day his disciples are propagating his message blindly." He named the so-called holy man and his elder brother, saying that they were from the Himalayas.

Buddhist II's stance on Hinduism and ghosts was based on the possessions of family members and the expenses entailed for curing them. He had been a Hindu but then took up Buddhism because of his caste's recent orientation toward Buddhism, his elder brother's influence (Buddhist I), and disillusionment with ghost beliefs and the cures of exorcists. In 1958 before Illusionist became an exorcist, Buddhist II and Illusionist were close friends. Once they described for us the techniques of exorcism used by Lord of Ghosts (Chap. 16).

The men who attacked Buddhist II's position did quite well in this discussion, for Buddhist II never directly answered their questions. Instead he simply stated his nonbeliefs. The believers' attacks, including Buddhist II's son, were subtle, for indirectly the points made about the possessions of Kin's wife and daughter and the treatment by Illusionist were analogous to Buddhist II's problems with his own wife, daughter, and daughter-in-law.

In response to Buddhist II's last remark, Host responded politely but firmly, "They took a man who was ill to the All India Medical Institute and tried all sorts of medicine on him and kept him in chains, but all to no effect. So the doctors decided some female ghost was affecting the man." Thus, Host added the crowning argument of the believers, namely that even India's most prestigious doctors diagnosed ghost possession in a specific case.

The group at large was then questioned as to whether they believed that people possessed by a ghost suffered, to which Host responded, "There have been cases here where men affected by ghosts were taken to doctors. The medicine had no effect and the patients eventually died. If one cannot help, then go to another. Some things are unexplained. I might sit here and a man a hundred miles away may know what I am doing. Thus, you can't tell what truth is. Even though people say, 'ghost, ghost,' still take the person to a doctor or curer for treatment. If one isn't good, go to another."

Buddhist II again began to complain, this time about the cost of Hindu festivals and having to spend his money on candy for his children. The other men, long accustomed to his behavior, silenced him, for by this time Host had skillfully closed the discussion by referring first to the case at the prestigious All India Medical Institute and then stating that people who continued to suffer should be taken to doctors or curers to see if they can be cured.

Although the debate was over, we asked what ghost possessions had taken place recently. A number of possessions were named along with some identifications of the exorcists. Buddhist II, aroused again by these cases, asked why it was that no ghosts entered dogs and horses. Our answer was, "How would you know whether a ghost entered them?" No one replied; the session ended as the men filed out of the *baithak*. Then Host told us Buddhist II is a greedy man who doesn't believe all that he says but stops others from getting anything done.

During the session in the *baithak*, the following ghost possessions were mentioned: Kin's wife and daughter (Chap. 17); Buddhist II's wife, daughter, and daughter-in-law; an anonymous patient at the All India Medical Institute; and one man said that Eluded, the youngest brother of Lord of Ghosts, formerly was possessed but now suffered from fits (Chap. 16).

JAT CHILDREN

A group interview held in 1978 with five Jat children from Arya-Samaj families, four girls and a boy, revealed how the children came to believe or disbelieve in ghosts. These children belonged to the same patrilineage and represented different degrees of patrilineal cousins, except for two girls who were sisters. The four girls were Pragmatic, age 13; Faithful, age 10; Little Goddess age 10; and Shy, age 6, the sister of Faithful. The boy was Little Charmer, age 8. The children became accustomed to hearing us question adults and wanted to be asked questions too. Before this group session, they were sometimes present when we were asking adults the questions on the Health Opinion Survey (HOS), which tests stress, anxiety, and depression (Crane and Angrosino, 1974: 135–142; Append. VI). All but the youngest child and Little Goddess expressed interest in answering the questions. Before giving them the HOS, we introduced the subject of ghosts.

The children were first asked the meaning of the following terms for different types of ghosts: "What is a bhut?" "What is an *oopra*?" "What is a preta?" To each question they replied, "We do not know." Then Pragmatic, the leader of the group, volunteered, "None of them have come into us so we cannot tell about them. When a person dies, the soul of that person possesses another person, and they call the soul a preta, *oopra*, or bhut." Pragmatic then modified her previous statement, saying that Little Goddess had experienced ghost possession, which made Little Goddess uneasy so that she turned her face away from Pragmatic. With Pragmatic prompting the group, they all agreed, "We can't see a ghost so how can we say what it is?" Pragmatic said that she had heard from another person that ghosts were just air. All the children then expressed their fear of ghosts. Faithful added, "If the air comes from the east and the person is sleeping, the air gets in the person's mouth. It may be bad air which is mixed with ghosts." This statement was based on a belief that if one slept with one's mouth open, sneezed, or yawned a ghost could enter one's mouth and cause death (cf. Saini, 1975: 84, for similar beliefs in Punjab). The belief about sneezing derives from the danger of pollution from mucus expelled from the nose or mouth with a sneeze, but when Indra (Might), one of three main aspects of Shiva, sneezed and other deities said, "Live," it was then possible, by repeating the blessing "Live" after a sneeze, for people to survive (Daniélou, 1964: 199; Doniger O'Flaherty, 1980: 153–154).

The next question was, "Will you go with us to the cremation grounds tonight to see a ghost?" Pragmatic replied, "You can't see a ghost. I won't go." Faithful also would not go because she said that she was afraid. Pragmatic, displaying her practical reasoning, said, "If you go, nothing will happen because when people go there to cremate the dead, nothing happens to them."

We asked, "If you have never seen a ghost, how can there be any ghosts?" The three older girls and the boy declared that their mothers told them about ghosts, and added, "Mothers always tell the truth." Pragmatic recalled that once her mother told her that the Mali Gardeners, whose house and garden were next to the cremation grounds, said that they hear ghosts beating drums and fear them.

Although the children belonged to Jat families whose members claimed to be followers of the Arya Samaj, they believed in ghosts and to some degree were afraid of them. Mothers were the first and most important mentors of these children until about age six. Thereafter boys were separated from the women, girls, and younger boys. The boys then slept in the *baithak* with the men and older boys and began to emulate them. Thus, the expression, "Mothers always tell the truth," affirmed their early belief in ghosts. Women in Arya-Samaj families were less apt to follow Arya-Samaj teachings than men. At the end of the 1970s, for example, Jat women talked openly about worshipping Santoshi Mata and believing in ghosts.

Common village beliefs about the haunting of the village cremation grounds, pond, and crossroads were reflected in the comments of the children (Append. IV: Map 4, CG, P, CR). First, one might see or be possessed by a ghost and suffer from ghost illness after passing these places. Night was the most dangerous time. During a cremation, which always took place in daytime, a number of people were present. Therefore, no ghost would harm anyone because ghosts avoided crowds. Someone who was eating or had just eaten sweet food and passed by or near the foregoing places was a potential victim of ghosts. If children had just eaten something sweet and were planning to go out, their mothers had them wash out their mouths with a salt solution so as not to attract ghosts. Mothers admonished their children about going near haunted places while or after eating, especially after eating sweets. Children were instructed not to eat outside. Some people who owned and farmed land near these haunted places were susceptible to ghosts while working there.

During the group session with the children, the electric lights, which could never be depended on, flashed off and on. The children, who were used to the lights failing, were asked whether they thought the flashing lights were caused by ghosts or rats. Pragmatic in her customary way said, "Probably the wires are disconnected. It is not due to a ghost or to rats biting the wires."

We asked the children what they would think if we told them that we saw a ghost walking outside in the lane and then mounting the stairs to our quarters. Pragmatic said, "You might have dreamed it. My mother

Fig. 3. Cremation of a Bairagi man, 1978. The pyre of dung cakes is ignited with burning straw. The crude ladder used as a bier to carry the corpse to the cremation ground is shown leaning against the pyre.

says that once I dreamed I saw a rat and was sick for two days." Despite Pragmatic's outlook, she volunteered that a ghost came into her mother periodically and that Little Goddess, too, regularly suffered from possessions. This discussion reminded Pragmatic and Little Goddess that they had heard that Resourceful, the daughter of Widow-in-Between, was possessed by a ghost twice, once when she was eight years old and again at the time of first mating with her husband. However, Resourceful no longer suffered from ghost possessions, was happily married, and had children. The happy ending pleased the children.

When the children were told about the case of a young married girl who was possessed and then given vitamins to dispel the ghost, Pragmatic emphatically responded, "Ghosts do not go away that easily. You have to call a bhagat. Illusionist was not a bhagat previously, but now he is and he cured Little God-

dess. She had typhoid and her hair was cut off because of Fever. Four to five days after recovering from Fever, the ghost came into her. The ghost was a girl friend [Whose Daughter], who drowned in the pond while she and Little Goddess were washing a water buffalo."

When Little Goddess was asked about Illusionist, she answered, "He does *jhara* [to drive the ghost away], but I do not know what happened because I was unconscious." Pragmatic, ever helpful, added, "Her mother was crying." By this time, the children had grown restless so we closed the interview. As they left, they said that they would think about ghosts and let us know if they knew any more about them. Because the children liked visiting us and being asked questions, within the next two days Pragmatic, Faithful, and Little Charmer took the HOS. Faithful and Little Charmer, who were close friends and in the same grade in school, took the HOS together, each responding to the questions in their own way. Some questions provided information about ghosts, and successive sessions with the children indicated how children became conditioned to ghost beliefs and disbeliefs through their mothers, other family members, friends, and from possessions that they saw. We present the comments and visits of the children along with some facts about them.

Little Goddess did not visit often and suffered more than one ghost possession during 1977–78. A stress factor troubling Little Goddess was that her father, a policeman, often was drunk. Drinking in the late 1950s was relatively rare in the village and was generally carried on in the city. By the late 1970s men of many castes, including Brahmans, drank openly at weddings and other times, and teen-age boys would sneak off into the fields and drink during festivals (Chap. 14: The Ghost of Whose Daughter; Chap. 22: Little Goddess).

Little Charmer visited every day before and after school, and in the evening after eating his meal so we knew him quite well. By age eight, he had spent a goodly portion of his time with the male members of his family of many brothers, all but one older than he. In school, the children were segregated by sex. Boys were taught by men; girls, by women. As role models, the men professed not to believe in ghosts so Little Charmer followed suit. However, in later discussions, he contradicted himself by first describing ghost possessions and then stating that he did not believe in ghosts or ghost possessions because he was afraid of ghosts (Chap. 17).

Little Charmer also commented on drunks in the context of a question in the HOS about dizziness (Append. VI). He was disturbed because drunks acted as though they were possessed by a ghost. He compared drunken behavior to feeling dizzy when he twirled around, but he could not understand why grown men would act thus. What most disturbed him was the unpredictability of drunken behavior, which did not fit into his idea of how men should act. To him, such behavior was the same as a person's behavior when possessed by a ghost. Romanucci-Ross (1983: 273–274) described drunken behavior in a New Guinea village as equivalent to ghost possession. Drinking liquor, considered a form of European behavior, was looked upon as "taking the spirit," which is compatible with the belief that spirits could enter one's body and possess one's thoughts and acts. Little Charmer, in comparing drunkenness with ghost possession, presented a similar equation.

Pragmatic, who also visited us daily, was a bright young girl who excelled in school. She was fond of her mother and grandparents but disturbed because her mother suffered periodically from ghost possessions. Living in her grandparents' home in Shanti Nagar kept her from the emotional impact of the family situation in her natal village, which fostered her mother's possessions (Chap. 22: Widows, Patriarchs, Twins). Pragmatic approached the subject of ghosts as practically and logically as possible but was emotionally involved where her mother was concerned. Faithful, too, visited daily, gave us small tomatoes during the harvest, and was very loyal to Little Charmer and Little Goddess.

CHAPTER 11: GHOSTHOOD

This chapter continues the discussion of ideology which started in Chapter 8. It summarizes ghost beliefs as covered to this point, adds information from ancient traditions and pan-Indic beliefs, and includes a brief discussion of village terms for ghosts.

Two basic questions are posed: What is a ghost? How does one become a ghost? A number of meanings and terms are attributed to the word ghost, deriving from classical texts of Hinduism, pan-Indic sources from the 20th century, and village usage. The term ghost may refer to the disembodied spirit or shade of a dead person, who may haunt living persons and locations where the deceased lived or died. It may refer to the soul rather than the body of a deceased, to an apparition, specter, phantom, or wraith seen by a living person, or may be a haunting dream, memory, or image of the dead.

In village belief, 13 days after death the soul becomes a wandering ghost who may haunt the living. Ghosts haunt specific places, such as cremation grounds, crossroads, ponds, wells, and locales where the deceased lived, worked, played, and died. A person may be haunted by a ghost because the deceased is unforgettable, or because of a former relationship between the ghost and the living person, or because a vulnerable individual imprudently ventures into the locale frequented by the ghost. A ghost may appear in a multitude of forms, may be silent, speak to a living person, or, upon possessing someone, speak from within that individual, or may attack a person and knock, rap, upset furniture or various utensils, the latter traits characterizing a poltergeist, a specific type of ghost. A ghost may be malevolent and/or benevolent. In Shanti Nagar, seeing or dreaming about a ghost may cause ghost illness. An attack by a ghost may result in ghost possession or harassment by a poltergeist.

ANCIENT TRADITIONS

Well-known terms for ghosts that come from ancient Sanskritic texts are bhut and preta. In ancient texts, the spirits of darkness ruled by Shiva include antigods, demons, male and female genii (yakshas and yakshin-

is), evil spirits (bhuts), ghosts (pretas), elves, magicians, mermaids, witches, scorpions, serpents, and tigers (Dowson, 1950: 55, 242; Daniélou, 1964: 137, 213). Shiva is known as Lord of the Spirits of Light and Darkness, as Hara, and as Bhutesvara, Lord of Ghosts. Bhuts are described as souls who died violent deaths, but they are not always distinct from pretas, souls formerly of the living who have not yet been released from the round of rebirths or been reborn. Both bhuts and pretas haunt cremation and burial grounds. The pretas have as their subsidiary leader, Yama, the King of the Dead. Cruelty, a love for unclean polluting places, and being in constant pain are traits of pretas. Human beings are said to come under their influence when they are afraid (Daniélou, 1964: 196, 311). Rudra, The Destroyer, is a Vedic god, who brought disease. He later developed into Shiva, who is said to haunt cremation grounds attended by bhuts and pretas (Dowson, 1950: 269–270; 296–300; Daniélou, 1964: 12, 192; cf. Morris, 1969: 1521, kei-1, II(3), III, on etymology of cremation or burial grounds and Shiva, Lord of the Dead). Since cremation and burial grounds in Hinduism are by definition polluting, because death is polluting, ghosts are expected to tarry there. After leaving the cremation grounds in Shanti Nagar, mourners bathe, or at least wash their hands and face, and thereafter go through a mourning period to attain purity, thus ridding themselves of death's pollution (S. Bhattacharyya, 1953: 173; Sarma, 1953: 12).

The soul of an ancestor, pitri, in ancient Hinduism had a higher status after death than the soul of a bhut or preta. The souls of ancestors were believed to consist of the first progenitors of the human race and of all the dead who thereafter were given the proper funeral ceremonies. These ancestral souls were believed to be immortal, similar to deities, and to dwell in a space of their own or in the sphere of the moon (Daniélou, 1964: 307).

Daniélou (1964: 371) confirmed the early belief in multiple supernatural beings and the gunas (qualities), which result in different temperaments, by quoting Krishna's statement in the Bhagavad Gita: "Man becomes what he worships . . . Those who worship the gods become gods; those who worship ancestors become ancestors; those who worship the elements master the elements, and those who worship me gain me." Thus, in the context of qualities, human beings are inclined to worship different aspects of the universe. Those in whom consciousness is dominant worship the deities; persons in whom action or existence is important worship genii and antigods; those in whom sensation or enjoyment are significant worship ghosts and spirits (Daniélou, 1964: 22, 26–27). Ingalls (1957: 43–44, fn. 10), as indicated earlier in commenting on the influence of the Bhagavad Gita regarding the gunas, stated that three answers are usually given to moral problems and gives the examples of Bhima as tamas; Arjuna as rajas, and Yudhisthira as sattva, but adds, "It is true that Bhima has a considerable infusion of *rajas* and Arjuna of sattvam, but the Gita calls a man rajasa if only rajas predominate among his strands." (Ingalls, 1957: 43, fn. 10).

PAN-INDIC BELIEFS

Although the following short selection of studies reveals regional differences about ghosts for this century, mainly it shows the overall belief in ghosts and the reasons for becoming ghosts. From information collected during a 1957–58 field trip in and around Sirkanda, a village of the lower Himalayas in western Uttar Pradesh, Berreman (1963) listed the following characteristics and types of ghosts: all or nearly all ghosts have backward turned feet; some take the form of snakes; women who die in childbirth become ghosts, and new mothers and infants are vulnerable to them. These female ghosts described by Berreman, similar to the yakshinis of yore and the *oopra*s of the Punjab and Delhi regions, are called *churail*. The ghosts of women who became Satis on their husbands' funeral pyres torment their neglectful descendants. A *shaiad* is the ghost of a Muslim. Not all the ghosts in Sirkanda could be identified. For the first 13 days after cremation, all souls become ghosts and are feared. Ancestral ghosts as well as other ghosts can return to torment the living because they die prematurely, are improperly mourned, or

their sons do not give proper charity for the deceased father, but they are worshipped as household godlings (Berreman, 1963: 110–113). Citing Morris Opler (1958: 566), Berreman (1963: 89) noted that prevalent anxiety about health may be related to beliefs about ghosts and ghost possessions. Berreman (1963: 111) further stated, "Ghost possession is qualitatively different from possession by a god. Once a ghost has 'caught hold' it will usually not leave unless forced out by exorcism. During the time it is in possession, it causes illness, unusual behavior, and even death."

Based on his fieldwork in Deoli, Rajasthan, 1951–1952, Carstairs (1958) stated that ghosts haunted houses, the countryside, and numerous specific places. He reported *bhopa*s, exorcists, going into possession-trance and ghosts possessing various members of a family. In one case the ghost spoke through his widow, who was in possession-trance, because the ghost was said to be worried about family affairs and the handling of money. Ancestors became godlings and returned to their families because they worried about family members (Carstairs, 1958: 53, 89, 92–93). In connection with ghost beliefs and the gunas, Carstairs stated that twice-born informants claimed people had one of two personality types or qualities, gunas, from birth. These types were *dev-gun* (godlike) and *rakshas-gun* (demonlike) (Carstairs, 1958: 53, 328, 332).

Saini (1975: 83, 84), relying on sources from the 19th and early 20th centuries about the Punjab, gave the following causes for ghosthood: (1) improperly performed funeral ceremonies, (2) death during or after childbirth, the woman's soul becoming a charel, (3) painful or violent death, (4) an untouchable sweeper buried with his mouth upwards is sure to become a bhut, (5) sneezing and yawning may allow a ghost to enter the nose or mouth, thus causing untimely death and ghosthood. Saini's sources reflect a time when a strong Muslim influence existed in many parts of the Punjab, and jinns (Muslim ghosts) were believed to possess women.

For the period around 1911 in Kathiawar, Gujarat, Stevenson (1971: 200) described three classes of ghosts: ". . . the Mama are very tall, so tall that their heads reach the sky; they live in *khadira* (acacia) trees. . . .

the kharisa . . . is headless. . . . the Jinn . . . like most aliens, is the worst of all." All three types frighten people and possess them.

Majumdar (1958: 234–238) noted many haunted spots, particularly ponds and cremation grounds, in Mohana, a village about eight miles from Lucknow, Uttar Pradesh, which he studied from 1946 to 1955. He related the cases of three low-caste women, probably suicides, who thus became ghosts. His term for them is *churail*, which he defines as the spirit of a low-caste woman who dies an untimely death. He also pointed out that men who became ghosts only attacked men, and females who became ghosts attacked females. To some extent this last finding is similar to a statement made in Shanti Nagar in 1958–59, which did not consistently hold, namely, that female ghosts attack females, and male ghosts, males.

Hockings (1980: 162 ff., 176) from his 1963 and 1972 fieldwork among the Badaga, who live in Tamil Nadu on the Nilgiri Massif, reported that their ghosts have feet pointing backward and make a frightening sound. If a person dies before his time, he becomes a ghost. Apparently women who commit suicide become ghosts, but unlike women from the Delhi region, they cannot drown themselves in a well because the terrain provides virtually no wells. Instead they take opium.

S. C. Dube (1955: 129) in his 1951–52 study of Shamirpet, Hyderabad, provided a relatively full list of reasons for people becoming ghosts: (1) too much attachment to sex, wealth, and children, (2) dying without satisfying sexual cravings, (3) death during pregnancy, (4) accidental deaths by falling from a tree, drowning, or being struck by lightning, (5) suicide, (6) dying with an intense hatred of someone, (7) victims of murder. Dube (1955: 127) also listed diseases and calamities caused by supernatural forces which result in people dying before their time and becoming ghosts. Diseases imputed to supernatural causes are: "persistent headaches, intermittent fevers, continued stomach disorders, rickets and other wasting diseases among children, menstrual troubles, repeated abortions." The calamities are "failures of crops, total blindness, repeated failures in undertakings, deaths of children in quick succession and too many deaths in a family within a short time. Smallpox, cholera, and plague are always attributed to the wrath of various goddesses" (S. C. Dube, 1955: 127–129).

Minturn and Hitchcock (1966: 75–76, 80–81) in a study carried out in 1954 among the Rajputs of Khalapur, located 90 miles northeast of Delhi in Uttar Pradesh, found that people become ghosts: (1) immediately after death until the death ceremonies are performed, (2) if the ceremonies are not properly performed, (3) if the death is unnatural or takes place in the prime of life with worldly desires unsatisfied. Unnatural and untimely deaths include: suicides, persons killed intentionally or accidentally, deaths of unmarried individuals, persons dying without issue, women dying in childbirth, and death after a long, lingering, undiagnosed illness. An infant whose mother dies in childbirth is in danger from the mother's ghost who will try to take her infant with her. If the mother succeeds, the infant becomes a ghost. They also reported briefly on ghost illness in infants and other children (Minturn and Hitchcock, 1966: 106). Carstairs (1983: 54–56) also noted that ghosts and ghost illness were found especially among children but also in the whole population of Rajasthan.

VILLAGE TERMS FOR GHOSTS

Although village terms for ghosts have been used previously in this study, they are given here for comparison with ancient and pan-Indic usage, to indicate variations and differences from other usage, and to recapitulate the roles ascribed to the ghosts. The general village term for a ghost is bhut. *Oopra* is used for daughters-in-law (wives) who become ghosts. Luthra (1961: 58) reported that *opra* (sic) is used as a general term for "evil spirit" in Jhatikra, Delhi. *Oopra*s seize or possess the souls of children, especially their own infants or the newborn infants of second wives, and haunt or seize the souls of successive wives of their husbands. Villagers more readily suspect a daughter-in-law's ghost of ill will than a daughter's ghost. This suspicion is expressed when a daughter-in-law dies for reasons believed to have caused her to become a ghost. The fear of in-marrying women, who become ghosts, may have an ancient origin based on wide distribution, for the

Chetri of Nepal believe that wives may be sorceresses, who send ghosts to cause sickness (Dowson, 1950: 55, 242; Daniélou, 1964: 137, 313; Gray, 1982: 220–221, 234–235; R. Freed and S. Freed, 1985: 134).

Preta was used on a few occasions when referring to a ghost haunting the cremation grounds. Although some Pan-Indic sources use the word churel with variant spellings for a ghost with feet in the reverse position or for women who become ghosts, this term was not customary in the village. A young teenage boy from Nepal, who worked for us, used churel and told us that in his village of birth the feet were not in the opposite position of the face; instead it was the face which was opposite to the feet!

We first heard the phrase *upri hawa* in 1978 from a young village woman who had attended school, went to cinemas, and watched television. *Upri hawa* referred to a married woman who had died, become a ghost, and was seen by living persons; although an apparition, she was described as "just air." An *upri hawa* was believed to be amiable and benevolent, as seen in the television film. According to the young woman's description from the film, the *upri hawa* had nothing to do with ghost possession.

When the *hawa* (air) comes, the *hawa* sits and talks to a person calmly. Only those persons can see the *hawa* and no one else. I saw a film on television. In it, the woman had died at a very young age after giving birth to a son. The boy cried a lot without her, and her husband missed her. They had a big house and were very rich. Her husband's father was a very strict person. He kept a watchman for the house and gave him full instructions not to let anyone in the house. The child did not eat or drink anything without his mother and kept on crying. The husband remembered her a lot because they loved each other very much. She [the *upri hawa*] was haunting here and there because she wanted to visit her son and husband. The watchman saw her and asked her to go away because no one was supposed to enter the house. She replied that she was *hawa* [air], and no one could stop any *hawa*. She said, "You can't even see *hawa*," and so saying disappeared from

before his eyes. She went straight to the room where her son and husband were waiting for her. Both of them saw her and were very pleased. The child embraced her. She fed both her husband and child and then disappeared. Afterward she visited them regularly.

Then the woman relating this story said, "One can have *hawa*, and no one can stop *hawa* because no one can stop air."

This film effectively impressed on the viewer the belief in *upri hawa* as a benevolent loving ghost of a wife and mother. Traditional beliefs about ghosts still lingered in the film. The woman died before her allotted time; the *upri hawa* was just air, a substitution for the word ghost, and was benevolent; she returned to her loved ones and the place in which she had lived with them. The ghosts of wives are generally feared only if their husbands remarry. Then the ghost becomes malevolent, a danger to the second wife and her infants. The screen husband did not remarry and his dead wife remained a loving ghost.

Hoch (1974: 675) wondered whether in Kashmir the authority of the deities would be lost with secularization and westernization. Since the cinema and television, according to her are "neither 'here' nor 'there,' neither 'I' nor 'you'" but insubstantial and unreal, she suggested that these media may replace the realm of deities and ghosts. Her point is somewhat limited when applied to Shanti Nagar, for the Santoshi Mata film, mentioned earlier, and this television film of a benevolent ghost, the *upri hawa*, have perpetuated supernatural beliefs. Both films recast a number of old beliefs in new forms, a process by which change with persistence of old beliefs takes place because the new beliefs are to some degree compatible with the old.

Ancient beliefs about ancestors influenced the villagers. A male, who was a husband and a father and then died, usually but not always having lived his allotted time, was referred to as a pitri (ancestor). Occasionally a male ancestor was referred to as a *devata* (godling). *Devata* was used for both males and females who died and were believed to be benevolent ghosts who hovered around the living members of their family to help them, similar to the *upri hawa* in the television film.

Although the general belief was that the proper and full funeral ceremonies and mourning periods should be carried out for both sexes, the observation of these procedures was more scrupulously followed for males than for females. If the rituals were not followed according to the standards for each sex, the deceased was expected to become a bhut or an *oopra*, who would then haunt the family. When proper funeral ceremonies were not carried out, it was usually because the deceased had violated sexual and other tabus, committed suicide, or was murdered. When mortality rates ran high in past times during epidemics, it was not always possible to observe all funeral rituals, thus providing an additional reason why numerous ghosts were associated with the souls of people who died in epidemics. They died tortured from disease, attributed to Fever, often before their time without issue. Therefore, many reasons existed for their ghosthood.

When the soul of a dead woman was believed to become a *devata*, she usually died in her family of marriage after she had born children, had grandchildren, and lived her allotted time. As the patrilineal system extolled only male ancestors, these women were not called pitris. If they were loved or remembered for their good deeds, they became *devata*s. For example, Forthright, the urbanized, married daughter of Manipulator, a village Brahman, claimed she saw the ghost of her second mother-in-law in dreams for one year after her death; then she said that her mother-in-law became a *devata*, after which she still visited Forthright. If Forthright had any problems, this mother-in-law would appear in a dream and tell her what to do (Chap. 19). This example illustrates the belief that the soul of the deceased was an *oopra* for one year after death. When deeds from her soul's past lives had been judged, she became a *devata*. It also confirms the belief that when a person who has died appears in a dream, it is the equivalent of seeing the ghost of that person, even when the ghost has the higher status of a *devata*. The same belief applies to a pitri, an ancestral male ghost.

Village beliefs regarding how long pitris or *devata*s might visit the living were vague, but it depended on the memories of relatives, friends, and neighbors and on how long they told stories about them. Theoretically, after one year, providing the soul was not doomed to become a lingering ghost, it was eligible for rebirth or release from the round of rebirths. Some Brahmans believed that a pitri or *devata* was released from the round of rebirths but could return to visit the living. Members of other castes held similar beliefs. For example, some Jat and Bairagi families erected shrines, *than*s, to their male ancestors, worshipped them there, and expected them to protect and help them.

Although jinn is the Muslim term for ghost, it was used in the village for the ghost of a male Muslim, who therefore was a stranger. A headless jinn was considered the most malevolent and dangerous ghost. A jinn, like other ghosts, could just let itself be seen or could possess an individual. Although the jinns in Aladdin's tales are often benevolent, the villagers expect Muslim ghosts to be only malevolent or both malevolent and benevolent.

BECOMING A GHOST

When a person dies, three main reasons are given for the soul of the dead becoming a ghost: (1) dying before the allotted time, (2) dying tortured, and (3) behavior contrary to village customs. The allotted time is set by Yama (for believers in ghosts) or Bhagwan (for disbelievers) based on their judgment of the sum of the soul's actions in past lives. Since no one knows the sum of a soul's actions, villagers interpret the allotted time in terms of the average natural length of a life, that is the average time villagers expect to live. When people die before the end of the average life span, they are expected to become ghosts and haunt their families and village until their allotted time expires. Uncertainty about the allotted time leads in some cases to doubt as to whether those who die become ghosts.

Dying tortured encompasses most deaths before the allotted time. Tortured deaths include dying from dread diseases, famine, murder, accident, or suicide. Additional reasons for becoming a ghost, which are subordinate to dying tortured, are dying without issue, especially a son, and never attaining the pleasures of adult life, which include sexual pleasures, diverse experiences, and other satisfactions. For a male (adult or child) to die without issue is generally but not always related to dying before achieving sexual satisfaction. Great emphasis is placed on the misfortune of a man becoming a ghost because he died without a surviving son, a death reported as dying without issue because of the emphasis on continuing the patrilineal line of descent. Dying without a son or daughter applies to young females who have not yet conceived or born a child, who die during their first pregnancy, who die during childbirth, the newborn also dying, or who commit suicide or are killed because of a pregnancy out of wedlock, all deaths believed to be before the allotted time. Married women, who die young without a surviving child or die during a pregnancy or immediately after the birth of a child, are regularly believed to become *oopra*s. They are expected to haunt a second wife when the husband remarries, as he usually does. If the dead woman's infant survives, the mother's ghost is expected to take her infant's soul. This expectation is usually fulfilled if the infant is a daughter, for she is more likely than a son to die shortly after the mother. If the second wife bears children, it is believed that the ghost of the first wife will attempt to seize the souls of the second wife's infants.

Behavior that violates village custom is contrary to dharma, and nonconformity to dharma constitutes bad karma. Strangers in the village, such as Muslims and wives who die before their allotted time for whatever reason, are believed to have died because they violate village customs. Forbidden actions for all villagers are mating with or marrying a consanguine, a person of one's own *gotra*, within one's village of birth, or out of caste. Fornication is generally forbidden, although as a rule only females suffer from violating this prohibition. They are believed to become ghosts only if they are found out and are killed by their fathers or husbands, or commit suicide (R. Freed, 1971; R. Freed and S. Freed, 1985: 143–146).

An exception to the rule applying to an early death is that of a child younger than six years. If children die before reaching the age of reason, six years, after which they are held responsible for their actions, their deaths fall within the allotted time because they are not expected to accrue bad actions until some time after six years of age. Death before this age is believed to be due to the great preponderance of the soul's bad actions from previous lives, which means that Yama gave it a short time to live after rebirth. The allotted time is even shorter for a fetus that miscarries after the soul is believed to enter the fetus in the sixth month of pregnancy. The souls of dead children might tarry as ghosts anywhere from 13 days to one year from death as do all souls (Chap. 14: Pregnancy, Deaths of Infants and Children, and Ghosts). Thereafter the children's souls are expected to move on to another rebirth. (For an exception to this belief, see Chap. 21: Mrs. Earnest.)

Beliefs about becoming a ghost reinforce desirable customs. For example, the proper funeral ceremonies must be performed; otherwise the soul of the dead is believed to haunt kin who neglect the ceremonies. The bad karma that accrues to those who neglect the ceremonies and the haunting by the ghost act as deterrents to people who may want to neglect proper funeral rituals. Moreover, it is believed by all but the strict Samajis that unless the proper ceremonies are carried out the soul of the dead person cannot be released from the cremation grounds for judgment and will not achieve rebirth or release from the cycle. Instead the soul becomes a ghost and haunts those who neglect the ceremonies.

Another belief reflects a conflict between ancient traditional curing practices and Western medicine. If an infant or small child falls ill and the parents take the child to an indigenous curer, then they lose faith in the curer and take the child to a Western medical practitioner after which the child dies, the death may be blamed on the Western practitioner for lack of supernatural power to cure. This conclusion is tied to the belief that a ghost causes illness and is trying to take the child's soul and therefore only the indigenous curer has the power to ward off the ghost. It is also thought that when the child is taken to a Western practitioner, the indigenous curer originally consulted becomes angry and uses his supernatural powers to cause the child's death (Chap. 13: Deaths of Little Boy and Scapegoat).

Chapters 8 through 11 on ideology have

provided the village views on life, death, the soul, action, rebirth, release from the cycle of rebirths, the fruit of action, fate, discipline, differences between believers in ghosts and nonbelievers, ancient, Pan-Indic, and village beliefs, terms for types of ghosts, reasons for becoming a ghost, ghost illness, and ghost possession.

CHAPTER 12: MERCHANT, MUSLIM, PRIEST

Chapters 12 and 13 present two lineage histories, which reach back to the beginning of the 19th century, covering seven generations by the end of the 1970s. The first lineage history, "Merchant, Muslim, Priest," concerns a Brahman lineage, whose members follow Sanatan Dharma; the second, "Old Fever," covers a Jat lineage, whose members by the fifth generation became followers of the Arya Samaj and thereafter claimed not to believe in ghosts. Significantly, both lineage histories reflect the impact of numerous deaths and their relation to ghost beliefs. Most members of the two lineages were neighbors, living on the same lane (Append. IV: Maps 1, 2).

Our knowledge of the 19th- and 20th-century history and times of the Brahman lineage is based chiefly on the oral autobiography of Old Priest, who was an affine of the lineage, and on a legend about a Muslim Ghost and a ghee (clarified butter) merchant who was a lineage ancestor. Their pseudonyms are Merchant and Muslim Ghost. In 1958 Old Priest resided in a large joint-family household headed by Raconteur, a grandson of Old Priest's sister. Lineage members lived in three separate dwellings in the village, and some lived in an apartment building which they owned in the City of Delhi. In 1977–78 other members were located in various parts of India, and one man worked in a foreign country.

Old Priest was 92 years old in 1958 (1866–1962) when he told us the story of his life and provided historical information about Shanti Nagar and the lineage into which his sister had married sometime around the mid-19th century. As a child, Old Priest was adopted into the lineage of his sister's husband after having been orphaned due to famines and diseases that led to the deaths of his other relatives.

Raconteur in 1958 was 60 years old when he provided genealogical information about the patrilineage and recited "The Legend of the Merchant and the Muslim Ghost." Only 13 individuals were identified in the first four generations of the lineage: A founding male ancestor in Generation I; Merchant and his younger brother in Generation II; Merchant's son, the son's wife, her brother (Old Priest), and two sons of Merchant's younger brother in Generation III. The eldest of these two sons died without issue. The younger had a son who survived to adulthood, married, and was a member of Generation IV. He in turn had two successive wives. Despite a number of live births, his line of descent eventually dwindled to a married daughter in another village. Merchant's son and his wife had two sons, Generation IV (Append. III: Introduction and Chart 1.1).

OLD PRIEST'S AUTOBIOGRAPHY

Old Priest helped shape and inform the children of the lineage about their ancestors and traditions and told them "The Legend of the Merchant and the Muslim Ghost." The lineage followed Sanatan Dharma, and the legend helped to perpetuate the animistic, traditional Hindu beliefs in ghosts and the curing powers of exorcists. When Old Priest was interviewed in 1958, he was blind and very old. He did not relate the legend because he had grown tired telling about his life history. He and Raconteur said that when he was tired he went through periods of dissociation and could not speak clearly. However, his long, well-expressed oral autobiography provided information about the last half of the 19th century along with details of his early life, training for the Brahman priesthood, and changes and persistences within the village.

When Old Priest first came to live with his sister, Merchant had been dead for some years. He learned about Merchant from Merchant's younger brother and Merchant's son, to whom Old Priest's sister was married, all of whom lived jointly. His account follows:

I am 92 years old and can read and write. I learned when I studied to be a priest. I went to Kashi [Varanasi] and studied Sanskrit. At one time I gave sick people medicine and was a hakim. Because I cannot see now, I no longer treat people who are ill. When I was a little boy, my parents died and I came to this village to live with my sister who was married here. I have never married. My sister had two sons but no daughters. I have been looking after the children in this family for four generations. My sister's and my *gotra* [clan] is Vaishist; it was one of the first *gotra*s of the Gaur Brahmans who came to this region from Bengal. Four Gaur Brahmans came, who were so gifted that it was said they could walk on air. When they came here, people offered them milk and other food and they accepted. When they wanted to return to Bengal, the air did not work so they said one person had become impure because he accepted food from another caste and left him here. He is the ancestor of all these Gaur Brahmans. People who take donations are called *danishwari* [wise, learned] so these Gaur Brahmans are called *danishwari*. All the Gaur Brahmans have descended from this one man.

I came to the village at the age of 10 to 11 years to live with my sister. She was 16 or older. My mother died and I do not remember her. I was brought up by my sister. My father was also dead. My sister's husband was about 18 years old when I came here. During the lives of my sister and her husband, they had two sons. Then, in their time, the eldest son had three sons; and the youngest, two sons. [The eldest son's three sons are Raconteur, Lieutenant, and Security Officer; the youngest son's two sons

are Progenitor and Gentle Soul in Generation V (Append. III: Charts 1.1, 1.2, 1.3).]

I started going to the priest's school in a nearby ashram. This was a school for Brahman priests. Since I did not have the sacred thread, the pandits [Brahmans learned in Sanskrit and Hinduism] at the school said I would have to have one so I was invested with it at age 11 [cf. R. Freed and S. Freed, 1980: 443–451 on the sacred thread rite]. I was the only boy from this village who studied the Shastras [Append. II: Sacred Hindu Texts]. I went there for nine years. I would go around the village where the pandits' school was located and beg for flour. The people used to let us cut wood from the forest. Just as in Kashi, the students lived near wealthy people so that we could go to them and eat their food and beg. I would take clothing from my sister's family and visit back and forth constantly. Once I had started working as a priest, I obtained clothing from the people I served on the occasion of a wedding or when a son was born. For the birth of a son, they would call me on the tenth day to perform the fire ceremony. Then they would give me money and raw materials for food and lots of clothing.

When I was first brought here as an orphan, my sister's family of marriage began to talk about what I should do as I had nothing. As a result, I went to the head pandit at the school and told him I was living with my sister. The pandit asked me what I could do about expenses. I answered that I did not know. The pandit then said, "It is all right. You live here and go around the villages asking for food and then you can study here." I started school at age 11. I could not even enter the kitchen of the school without the sacred thread so I was invested with it. I studied there for eight to nine years. Then when I had become clever there, a man passed through who said to me, "Come to Kashi and I will pay your fare." In Kashi, there were areas belonging to various people and one belonged to Bowani Wallah [a man from Bowana who took him to Kashi]. He lived there.

When Old Priest was asked whether his mother and father died at the same time, he replied:

I do not remember. I do not know exactly how old I was when I came here. It may have been six months to a year before I began to study with the pandits. I lived in this village in the same location as I am now living, but the house then was kachcha [a mud hut] [Append. IV, Map 1]. The front part of the house was pukka [made of bricks] in 1930. The back part of the house was not pukka until the end of 1957. When I first came here, there were no pukka buildings; they were all kachcha. The wells were pukka. The village has grown a great deal since that time. Then the people were paupers and short of grain due to famine. The railroad came here in my lifetime. It used to be all jungle and wild around here. Since I came, they have broken new ground and individual farmers have started harvesting hundreds of maunds [a unit equal to 37.3 kg] of grain. Previously when it rained, the place was waterlogged; then there was less rain and the water was drained off and people were better able to work the land. The rain used to accumulate and form lakes; then the government had the ditches and the canal dug. Wherever a big lake had formed, the government dug the canal which led into the River Yamuna. The canals for draining flooded lands were dug during the time I was studying [ca. 1877 to 1887]. The irrigation canals were dug first; then the rain increased; too much water accumulated; and more canals were dug. When I was a boy, they already grew sugarcane here. When I first came here, no schools existed in this village, but two schools where Urdu was taught were located in nearby villages. Maybe one or two children from this village attended the schools.

I remember when Dry Stick [the pseudonym for a Brahman, not a member of the "Merchant, Muslim, Priest" lineage], who was younger than I, was one of the first people for whom I performed the wedding ceremony. He was 10 to 15 years old at that time. I gave him the sacred thread too. The sacred thread was given just before the wedding as it is now. When the sacred thread ceremony is performed, any number of men can come to take the thread. The ceremony is for those who do not have the thread. Other men can put on a new thread at the time if their thread has become broken or dirty. When the thread is put on for the first time, it constitutes a ceremony, which is a matter of dharma. Any time a thread is broken, it is like the death of a person, and the whole thread has to be changed. With a break, it becomes impure.

I studied for one year at Kashi and there learned to be a pandit. The Baniya, Bowani Wallah, who took me there, had an inn in an area. An area is a place where food is cooked and maybe 10 to 15 people are fed there. The Baniya paid for all of this; he used to give the students food, clothing, and books free. Anybody with money can have an area there. When I finished at Kashi, I returned home to the village and did not leave. That is when I became a pandit here. I worked for whomever called me from this village and surrounding villages. I was paid Rs. 5 for the fire ceremony in weddings; Re. 1 for Teva [writing the letter for the Lagan ceremony before a wedding] [R. Freed and S. Freed, 1980: 423–426].

A letter goes from the bride's family to the groom's family a month or so ahead of the wedding so that Lagan can be performed; then another letter goes two weeks later. I was paid Re. 1 for each. The first letter contains the names of the bride and groom, names of people of the village to which the letter goes, and the date of the wedding. It also gives details about the stars relating to the bride and bridegroom and the suitable date for the wedding. If they do not find such a date, then the letter does not go. The two letters are called the letter of marriage and the letter of reminder [R. Freed and S. Freed, 1980: 423–424].

Old Priest's recollection of his training to be a professional priest is somewhat similar to what was and may still be in some parts of India the training of a Brahman boy. It began in the boy's family. Primarily it consisted of memorizing verses from the Vedas, starting when the boy was eight years old and continuing for eight years. Old Priest's training began when he was 10 to 11 years old and lasted for eight to nine years (Ingalls, 1958: 209–212). He emphasized his memorization of the Bhagavad Gita. His final training as a professional priest was in Kashi. The information that he gave us about vesting the sacred thread, marriage customs, and auspicious astrological times for fixing a wedding showed the continuity of these ceremonies to the time of this interview in 1958.

By the time Old Priest had gone through this long session, he was exhausted and had to stop. His account was lucid and forthright. Although he was 92 years old, he remembered events going back to about 1876 when he first came to Shanti Nagar, which at that time was a poor hamlet with a small population. Of particular importance were the ravages caused in the population and in Old Priest's life by famine and disease. Malinowski's comment (1984: 202) on the ability of old men to remember past events and experiences characterizes Old Priest's autobiography, which touched on schools, canals, irrigation, famines, the coming of the railroad, introduction of sugarcane as a crop, and the gradual replacement of mud houses by brick houses, events which were verified by other villagers. (Wood and Maconachie, 1882: 17, 19–20; Moreland and Chatterjee, 1957: 355–357, 409–410; Wyon and Gordon, 1971: 174–178; Gazetteer Unit, Delhi Adm. 1976: 853).

THE LEGEND OF MERCHANT AND MUSLIM GHOST

The legend of two men, Merchant, who became a pitri, and Muslim Ghost, a jinn, provides a glimpse of the traditional background which conditions children in successive generations to believe in ghosts. Lineage members readily accept the two ghosts because they are both spectacular and benevolent. An interesting facet of the legend is the coupling of the ancestor worship of Merchant, a Hindu, with Muslim Ghost. The tale, told by Raconteur in 1958, does not describe the ghosts of other family members within the lineage, who are part of the lineage history. They are described in the context of their families.

The events behind the legend took place sometime between 1840 and 1850 when Merchant was in his thirties. With the advanced age of Old Priest, Raconteur took over telling the legend while Old Priest listened. He said:

My great grandfather was a ghee merchant. Once when he was going some place near Hissar [now in Haryana] to buy ghee, he passed through a Muslim graveyard where some sweets and other offerings were lying. These offerings were for the ghost of the grave. He was in the company of a number of people, who were frightened by the graveyard and the offerings. My great grandfather said, "There is nothing to be frightened of. I can eat everything offered here and then urinate on the spot." The other people were not convinced so Merchant ate some of the food, urinated, then became sick, and had to return home without buying ghee. He was ill for six months. First he had ghost illness and thereafter ghost possessions. Various inquiries were made as to how he could recover, and a *siyana* [an exorcist, wise man, sorcerer] was found in another village. He told my great grandfather to offer at the grave five times the amount that he had eaten. He did so for the ghost, and a lot more in addition, so much that Merchant was then able to provide cures for the troubles of other people.

The son of an Englishman fell ill and was cured by my great grandfather, Merchant. Sometime later, one of the ancestors of the Jat who lives across the way [a member of the Old Fever lineage] wanted a son to be born in his family [Append. IV: Map 1, Dwellings in the 1950s for both lineages]. This Jat went to my great grandfather, who by this time had the reputation of being an accomplished *siyana*, and he told him that if he would see that a son was born, he would give him nine bighas of land [.76 ha]. When the son was born, he did so. The Muslim Ghost now stays in our fields and makes everybody leave the fields except members of the family. There is a stone [in a *than*—shrine for an ancestor], which came from Hardwar, and Old Priest worships at it every morning as if it were the god Shiva.

Additional tales about Merchant and Muslim Ghost were related by other lineage members in 1958–59. A motif in their stories, as well as in Raconteur's account, was that the

Fig. 4.   Ancestor shrine of the family of Merchant, Muslim, Priest, 1977. The shrine contains a stone Siva linga from Hardwar, a place of pilgrimage on the Ganges River.

ghost of Merchant and Muslim Ghost protected their fields. This motif is similar to Sleeman's (1915: 221–222) account that the ghost of the ancient owner of the soil, properly propitiated, protects the land and its crops, except that in the present case, only Merchant, not Muslim Ghost, was the owner of the fields.

Merchant was the great, great grandfather of Fence Sitter, the nephew of Raconteur. Here is Fence Sitter's description of the regular worship at Merchant's shrine:

> On Dusehra, Diwali, Holi, and other festivals, we present the first food at the shrine, light a lamp, throw water around, fold our hands in prayer, and come home. At the shrine, we meet neither Muslim Ghost nor Merchant, our ancestor. This worship satisfies both Muslim Ghost, Merchant, and all the deities. We never again see in the same forms the men of the family who died. We have a black snake in the fields, which never goes into any other fields; some people say the snake may be Merchant.

Of the snakes found in this region, a black snake was considered to be the most poisonous and fatal. An old saying in the Delhi region was, "In the presence of the black snake, the lamp won't burn." As a proverb, the saying means "Nothing can be done against a powerful person or a ghost of a powerful person, the owner of the fields" (Wood and Maconachie, 1882: 29).

Fear of an ancestral ghost appearing in the shape of a black snake to protect the fields was not unusual in the 19th century and persisted into the 20th century. Sleeman (1915: 224) wrote about a man who did not believe that an ancestral ghost haunted land which he had leased. When he went there to supervise the plowing, he sat under a banyan tree and railed against the superstitious men who were afraid to plow the field. He then looked up, saw an enormous black snake coiled in the branch above him, stood up, mounted his horse, and never again returned to the field he had leased.

The dual roles of Merchant and Muslim Ghost are explained by Merchant having urinated on the Muslim's grave, the equivalent of blasphemy (bad karma). Then Muslim Ghost caused Merchant to have ghost illness. A *siyana* told Merchant to make offerings at the Muslim's grave. When he did so, Muslim Ghost became his familiar and returned with him to his home. The events after the initial desecration were a logical result according to Hindu beliefs about ghost illness and the attainment of curing powers. The elements of desecration and retaliation have been found in Deoli, Rajasthan, by Carstairs (1958: 89), who was told by his patients that their illnesses were caused by a ghost who was angry because they had urinated on his territory.

By 1958 more than a hundred years had passed since the events upon which this legend was based. When Merchant died and became an ancestral ghost, he and Muslim Ghost continued to care for the property and affairs of the lineage. Although guarding the fields by Muslim Ghost is a prominent motif in the legend, Merchant's ghost in the form of a black snake also guarded his land. The link between Merchant and Muslim Ghost is based on Muslim Ghost acting as his familiar and helping him with his supernatural curing powers. Although this legend reflects the pervasive animistic beliefs in ghosts, ghost illness, ghost possession, and the power of exorcism, it is based on events in the past century, regarded as true by Raconteur, and as a legend is "the counterpart in verbal tradition of written history" (Bascom, 1984: 9–10).

MERCHANT'S DESCENDANTS

Information about the lineage history was first obtained at the end of the 1950s and added to at the end of the 1970s. Events which fell in this 20-year period are recounted in the context of the family line in which they took place. Families beginning with Generation V are identified by the name of the head of the family and include his descendants in Generations VI and VII. Six family lines begin with the men of Generation V: Raconteur, Lieutenant, Security Officer, Progenitor, Gentle Soul, and Dead Issue (Append. III: Charts 1.2, 1.3, 1.4).

By the end of the 1950s, Merchant's kachcha dwelling had become a large brick house in which Old Priest lived with Raconteur, the family head, his wife, and their two youngest sons, 21 and 18 years old. The house was also shared by Mrs. Lieutenant, the wife of one of Raconteur's brothers, and their youngest son and three daughters. Raconteur had a third grade education and had learned to read and write Urdu. After the Independence of India when Devanagari became the official script, he as well as other men and some women attended adult education classes in the village for one year to learn to read and write Devanagari. Raconteur had a reputation as a curer of sorts, but not as an exorcist. He had lived in the City of Delhi for 17 years while working as a compounder in a pharmacy. Then he became a vaccinator in Bowana. In 1958 he was 60 years old and, as the head of his joint family, directed the family's affairs from the village.

Raconteur's eldest son, Guard, lived in the apartment building in Delhi, which was owned by Raconteur and his two younger brothers, Lieutenant and Security Officer. In 1958, Guard was 30 years old, married, and had three young daughters living at home. At that time Lieutenant and Security Officer lived together in quarters provided by the younger brother's employer. The eldest son of Lieutenant, years later known as New Priest, lived with them (Append. III: Charts 1.2, 1.3, 1.4).

Many children in this family line visited or stayed with Raconteur in the village. All of them were fond of Old Priest. On the occasion of festivals and marriages, the older children saw that Old Priest was carefully shaved, had his hair cut by the Nai Barber serving the family, and was properly dressed in a clean white dhoti, shirt, and turban.

In 1959, the wedding of Conductor, the 21-year-old son of Raconteur, took place in the natal village of the bride. Conductor had recently obtained a job as a bus conductor. Shortly after the wedding, he was in a traffic accident and was hospitalized with an eye injury. The parents of the bride were afraid that their daughter might have a one-eyed husband so they visited the hospital to see whether he would recover the vision in his eye, which he did. Had he been blinded in one eye, they might have had the as yet unconsummated marriage annulled due to the inauspiciousness of a one-eyed man. Consummation takes place at the time of Gauna, generally the second visit of the bride to her husband's village when the bride has attained menarche and is ready for first mating. She then brings the balance of her dowry (R. Freed and S. Freed, 1980: 497–498).

Progenitor, the patrilineal cousin of Raconteur, lived with his family in Old Brahman Lane, the area first settled by the Brahmans. When his third infant son died shortly after Well Worship, a ceremony held on the fortieth day after birth, his first wife, the mother of the dead son, committed suicide in the well where the ceremony took place. Since her soul became a ghost, the family stopped Well Worship and did not mention the suicide. Cowherd and Fence Sitter, her first and second sons, were then left without a mother. Progenitor married his second wife, Fertility, and they had a number of sons and daughters. In 1958, Cowherd was absent from the village. When Fence Sitter, his younger brother, separated from his father in 1959, Cowherd returned to the village, lived with Fence Sitter's family, and herded cattle for villagers. Progenitor neglected Fence Sitter and Cowherd because their mother committed suicide and was believed to be the ghost who haunted Fertility, his second wife. Because of his mother's death and his father's nature, Fence Sitter was closer to Old Priest and Raconteur in his childhood than to his father.

Progenitor had a younger brother, Gentle Soul. When the parents of Progenitor and Gentle Soul died during the plague and influenza epidemics, their souls became ghosts. Progenitor neglected to arrange a marriage for Gentle Soul, who married late. He separated from Progenitor and moved next door to Raconteur. In the late 1950s, he had two sons and one daughter. His second son, age seven, had been ill with *piliya*, a term translated as yellow, indicating jaundice, possibly due to hepatitis or malaria. He recovered, but thereafter was afflicted with intermittent illnesses.

DEAD ISSUE

The line of descent from Merchant's younger brother ended with Dead Issue and his infant son (Append. III: Charts 1.1, 1.4). Merchant's younger brother had two sons; the eldest died without issue, thus becoming a ghost. The youngest had one son, who had two wives in succession. The first wife had 15 or 16 children, whose sex was not remembered by informants, for they died as infants. When she died, her husband remarried. The second wife had two sons and one daughter. The first son was one-eyed, never married, died in early adulthood without issue, and became a ghost. The second son, Dead Issue, married Strong Minded. Dead Issue's sister married and went to live with her husband and eventually was the sole survivor of this line of descent.

Dead Issue had married early in the 1940s, and in 1947 Strong Minded bore him a son, who died immediately after birth. Shortly thereafter Dead Issue died. According to informants, the two brothers, the one-eyed man and Dead Issue, died of tuberculosis. Thus, beginning with the son of Merchant's younger brother, there was a line of ghosts ending with Dead Issue and his infant son. Lineage members never mentioned the ghosts' names for fear that the ghosts would attack them. The fear was reinforced by the belief that tuberculosis was inherited. Only through a fluke in the process of gathering information about Strong Minded in 1958, did a Brahman daughter-in-law of the village, married to a man in another lineage, provide the details about the demise of this whole line of descent. Although Merchant's younger brother had lived jointly with Merchant, the members of this line of descent ending with Dead Issue and his infant son lived in the small dwelling next to Raconteur and Old Priest, which Gentle Soul took over in 1947 after Dead Issue's death.

When Dead Issue died, his widow, Strong Minded, could have continued living in her husband's house but under the control of Raconteur. At that time, Brahman widows followed the long honored custom of not remarrying, but their lot was difficult unless they had grown sons to protect them, who would inherit their father's property and take care of their mother's interests. When the childless Strong Minded was widowed at an early age, no Brahman widow in Shanti Nagar had ever remarried.

Although a law had been passed in 1856 sanctioning the remarriage of widows of all castes, the first public remarriage of a Brahman widow did not take place in Western India until 1869 (R. Freed and S. Freed, 1980:

503–504; Mukherjee, 1982; Pearson, 1982: 137). Derrett (1978: 81) noted that the law "had very little effect, since very few widows took advantage of it. . . ." In 1937 the Hindu Women's Rights to Property Act was passed (Derrett, 1978: 82, 89), which halted the passing of property to male heirs during the lifetime of a widow. If a widow remarried, she lost her rights in her dead husband's property. In any case, the pressure of custom and subordination of women to men were such that widows usually lived under the authority of a male family head. This would ordinarily have been the fate of Strong Minded after her husband's death.

Strong Minded had no surviving children, so her status was lower than that of widows with children. It was low to begin with because widows were held to be inauspicious, for widowhood was due to bad actions in past and present lives. Since Strong Minded was a young woman, she chose to deviate from Brahmanical custom by marrying another Brahman, who lived near Progenitor's house (Append. IV: Map 4). To complicate the situation further from the viewpoint of village Brahmans, the man she married was one-eyed. As one-eyed men were considered inauspicious, his parents had not arranged a marriage for him. As the saying goes, "A one-eyed man is unlucky. If he comes to a party, the merriment stops at once" (Temple, 1883–87, 1(4): 41, Item 359). Although one Brahman woman said that Strong Minded's parents would have arranged another marriage for her, Strong Minded and One Eyed arranged their own marriage shortly after the death of Dead Issue instead of waiting one year for the elapse of the period of mourning, thus further deviating from custom. Since the couple had flaunted custom, and One Eyed worked as a clerk some distance from the village, the newly married couple lived there.

With the demise of Dead Issue and the remarriage of Strong Minded, the land and buildings of Dead Issue reverted to the males who were next of kin in the patrilineage: Raconteur and his two brothers; and Progenitor and Gentle Soul. Raconteur and his brothers received half the land; Progenitor and Gentle Soul received the other half. On the separation of any of these brothers, each would be entitled to his share. Thus, although many

family ghosts resulted from the line of descent ending in the death of Dead Issue and son, more distant relatives benefited from the deaths and the widow's remarriage. Strong Minded and One Eyed at first felt the ostracizing brunt of Brahmanical opinion. By the 1970s when the attitude toward the remarriage of Brahman widows had been modified, this couple returned to live in the village (Chap. 21).

DEATH OF OLD PRIEST

During fieldwork in 1977, Raconteur described the memorial service for Old Priest and recounted lineage events. Old Priest died in 1962 at the age of 96. Raconteur combined an account of his death and subsequent mourning ceremonies with the retelling of "The Legend of Merchant and Muslim Ghost" in the context of the ceremony held 13 days after death, the time at which the ghost of the deceased is believed to leave the cremation grounds and journey to Yama, the Lord of the Dead. Raconteur said:

On the thirteenth day after Old Priest's death, we sent food to the Merchant's ancestral shrine. We do this for any ceremony. That day, my brother, Lieutenant, had a big headache at 3:00 p.m., a sign that the ghost was troubling him, and he asked whether the food had been taken to the shrine. We answered, "Not yet," so he said to send it. We did so, and then we burned a *jot* [wick of ghee and cotton] for the offering and worship. Present were two of my brother's sons. The eldest son looked fixedly at the burning *jot*, staying there a long time, then he saw a ghost and fell asleep. He was supposed to awaken at 4:00 a.m. to ready himself for work, but when we went to wake him, we found he was unconscious. I was greatly troubled by this so I took a 5:00 a.m. train to Palam [where Muslim exorcists were known to live] because a mullah [a Muslim prayer leader] is a fakir and priest at the mosque there.

I returned with the mullah to the village. He asked questions about my brother's son's condition and said that at 8:00 p.m. he would be all right and he was. For the next 12 days my brother's son fell unconscious one to four times daily. The name of Old Priest would come to him regularly, and Old Priest's ghost said that he had chosen him to be his priest. He then told my brother's son many things. While he was doing so, we wrote them down. He also said that my brother's son would be a good son and would become famous for the whole family. The ghost of Old Priest said he would continue to reside here until the festival of Holi [Append. V: Calendric Events—Phalgun, Purinmashi] and asked us to make a shrine [*than*] for him. The family did so. Everything Old Priest told us has turned out to be true. This new shrine is at the same place as the shrine for my great grandfather, Merchant. The old shrine was originally a few feet from the well. Now we have shifted it to a new location for safety and the two shrines are together. The shrine was originally placed there for Merchant so Old Priest could act as priest. Now Old Priest is a ghost and my brother's eldest son is the new priest for Old Priest and his shrine. Muslim Ghost never possessed Old Priest.

Since the mullah said New Priest would regain consciousness at 8:00 p.m., I brought the mullah here simply to confirm his prediction. Muslim Ghost instructed New Priest and the ghosts of Merchant and Old Priest to go to Hansi in Hissar [where the Muslim cemetery is located] to make offerings. Muslim Ghost spoke to all of them—Merchant and Old Priest through New Priest. Offerings of blue cloth were brought there. New Priest, at the time the *jot* was burned, saw the sayyid, Muslim Ghost. He was a strong man clothed in blue cloth. For all three men, Merchant, Old Priest, and New Priest, Muslim Ghost was the sayyid.

According to Raconteur's account, the tradition about Merchant and Muslim Ghost was perpetuated when New Priest was possessed by the ghosts of Old Priest, Merchant, and Muslim Ghost. In the 1977 version of the legend, Raconteur elevated Muslim Ghost to a sayyid, a Muslim saint claiming descent from Muhammad, the Prophet, and added other minor elaborations (Temple, 1884, 1: 121–209; R. Freed and S. Freed, 1985: 150, fn. 19).

Hoch (1974: 670) described the power obtained through heredity by pirs in Kashmir. Fakirs, according to her, may be Muslims or Hindus whose powers are not hereditary but who are self-styled healers using intoxicants, fumigation, singing, drumming, and dancing. Although Hoch did not say so, these activities may act upon endorphins and the central nervous system and contribute to alternate mental states, such as dissociation and ghost possessions (Ludwig, 1966; R. Prince, 1982a, b). Kakar (1983: 63), describing a Brahman possessed by a Muslim ghost, indicated that Hindus fear Muslim ghosts more than Hindu ghosts because less is known about Muslim ghosts. To some degree these statements account for attitudes about and persistence of Muslim Ghost in this lineage legend, but they do not explain Muslim Ghost's benevolence inasmuch as antipathy often existed between Hindus and Muslims. The rationale implicit in the legend is that the offerings to Muslim Ghost and supplications for his forgiveness tamed him and tied him to Merchant, to whom he transferred supernatural power as his familiar. Thereafter, Muslim Ghost protected the interests of Merchant and his descendants.

The legend was perpetuated and augmented by events at the 13th-day ceremony, namely, erecting a shrine for Old Priest, and then the journey of New Priest accompanied by the ghosts of Old Priest, Merchant, and Muslim Ghost to Hissar to visit Muslim Ghost's grave. New Priest's series of possessions after the death of Old Priest and his trip with the ghosts to the grave of Muslim Ghost theoretically imbued New Priest with supernatural power. Furthermore, Raconteur elevated Muslim Ghost to the rank of sayyid, when he was described as wearing blue clothing after New Priest offered blue cloth at his grave.

In retelling the legend of Merchant and Muslim Ghost, Raconteur added that after eating the sweets and urinating on the grave of the Muslim, Merchant fell ill from the effects of mosquito bites, a new element in the legend. Raconteur thought that the mosquito bites resulting in ghost illness were directed by Muslim Ghost, who also possessed Merchant. After Merchant recovered he derived his supernatural powers from his familiar,

Muslim Ghost. However, in the first version of the legend after Merchant ate the food offerings on the grave and then urinated on it, he had Fever, the index of ghost illness. At that time malaria had not been identified though it existed in the region. British government reports in 1847 indicated that 50 percent of the total rural population had disease of the spleen, a symptom later associated with malaria. Again in 1867 an unusually high incidence of disease of the spleen was reported and correlated with swampiness and lack of drainage of the region. The landowners complained that the canal water brought Fever and impotence to the men, and villagers refused to drink canal water although chemical analysis showed no noxious substances in it (Wood and Maconachie, 1882: 11–12, 16–18).

It was not until 1898 that Ronald Ross proved that malaria in birds was transmitted by the anopheles mosquito and that Grassi showed that human malaria was transferred in the same way (Append. I: Discoveries—1877–1901, malaria; see also Descriptions—Malaria). Despite these findings, it took a long time for the knowledge of the cause of malaria, its effect on human beings, and the means of controlling and treating it to spread. By the time bits and pieces of this knowledge had percolated into Shanti Nagar, Merchant had long been dead. Thus, there is no way of proving that Merchant fell ill from malaria, but it was known that he experienced Fever, a long period of ghost illness with delirium, and then ghost possessions over a six-month period. The presence of Fever marked the condition as ghost illness and the possessions led to his becoming an exorcist.

What stands out in the legend is the description of Merchant's long illness with forms of dissociation, his achievement of supernatural curing power, and a bit about his personality, namely, that he scoffed at his comrades' fears about desecrating the Muslim's grave. Because of his blasphemous acts, Muslim Ghost caused his long illness. In order to recover from ghost illness and his repeated possessions, he made reparations to Muslim Ghost, who became his familiar. This description of the transformation of Merchant into an exorcist includes three characteristics of exorcists: (1) a profound emotional experience; (2) a miraculous recovery from ghost illness and possessions which could kill; and (3) unusual personality traits (Landy, 1977: 416–417). A fourth characteristic was the attachment of Muslim Ghost to Merchant as his familiar, the conduit for his supernatural power.

RACONTEUR, HIS BROTHERS, AND THEIR FAMILIES

By 1977 Raconteur and his brothers, Lieutenant and Security Officer, had separated their families, divided their possessions, and the large family dwelling had been split into four apartments. Raconteur's wife died in 1964, and in 1977 the only son living with him in one of the four apartments was Conductor. Conductor's wife had borne him six daughters and two sons, but three of the children died. The second child, a daughter, died when she was six months old; another daughter died at age eight; and an eight-year-old son died early in 1978. The last death was particularly worrisome because Conductor's wife had been sterilized in 1977 during the height of the governmental sterilization campaign. The death reduced the number of family sons to one, a perilous situation, succinctly expressed in the adage, "One eye is no eyes and one son is no sons."

The two children who died at age eight reportedly died of the same illness. Manipulator, the Brahman, who had been an urban worker until retirement, said that the deaths were due to dropsy, a popular term for edema. Edema, an excess of fluid in the body tissues, has a number of causes (Lyght, 1956: 164–167; Wingate, 1972: 135, 302–303). Another informant claimed that the disease from which the children died could not be diagnosed at the hospital to which they were taken. A cousin of Conductor and nephew of Raconteur, Young Lawyer, said that the boy had an enlarged spleen and the disease from which he and his sister died was inherited. These informants were adult men who spent most of their time in the city. Mrs. Fence Sitter, a daughter-in-law of Progenitor, pinpointed the boy's symptoms as a swollen stomach, similar to a pregnant woman's, and a pale, thin body. She added that he had been taken to an urban hospital for treatment a year before his death and then had been withdrawn from school. She attributed the illness and death of both eight-year-old children to their habit of eating mud but also believed that their deaths were caused by a ghost or ghosts.

The description and symptoms given by Mrs. Fence Sitter are similar to those for edema, which may be caused by helminths, such as *Wuchereria bancrofti* or *Brugia malayi* (the latter found in the dry Western Gangetic Plain). These are parasitic, filarial worms, whose vectors to human beings are mosquitoes (Davey and Wilson, 1971: 57, 70, 194–200). Other insect-born infections which could have caused the deaths of these two children are leishmanial, in particular kala azar (visceral leishmaniasis). The leishmanial infections have sandflies as their vectors and have been found in the plains and delta of the Ganges River (Append. I: Disease—Kala azar).

Eating mud or clay, sometimes called pica, "the perverted craving for substances unfit for food" (Hochstein, 1968: 88–89) was noted in 1958–59 in Shanti Nagar among pregnant women who ate clay. Like children, women who eat clay can become infected by helminths, hookworms among them. Moreover, pica is a symptom of hookworm (Append. I: Disease—Helminths). Men said that women followed this practice so that the infant would be born with a fair skin (R. Freed and S. Freed, 1979: 339). Hochstein (1968: 88–89) stated that pica may be due to a complex of factors: psychological, anthropological, sensory, nutritional, microbiological, and physiological. A study of hookworm in Bengal postulated that infection by helminths may have ecological, genetic, social, and behavioral causes (Anderson, 1985: 1537—38). Recently I. Prince (1989: 177, 193–194), calling the practice of eating earth "geophagia," has traced its distribution in culture context, including India.

Villagers regularly use the fields for defecating. Since Raconteur's dwelling was near the edge of the village, the children could have eaten earth where people defecated (Append. IV: Maps 1, 2). Deposits of human feces support a dense population of infective larvae. Taylor (1976: 291, 296, table 8) reported informants saying that the main cause of infection by roundworms (nematodes,

somewhat like hookworms and other helminths) in Ludhiana (Punjab) and Lucknow (Uttar Pradesh) was due to children eating mud. Thus, the habit of eating mud may well have been implicated in the deaths of these two siblings.

The two children were remembered by their parents and siblings, and, according to Hindu belief, their souls were eligible for ghosthood inasmuch as they died tortured, before their allotted time, and without issue. In this family whose members believed in ghosts and perpetuated the legend of the ghosts of Merchant and Muslim Ghost, the ghosts of the two children because of their youth were expected to tarry for a short time around the house, fields, and cremation grounds.

Quite a few members of this lineage had become urbanized and visited Shanti Nagar only occasionally. Therefore, information about some family ghosts may be lacking. Raconteur's eldest son, Guard, continued living in the family apartment in the city. After 1958, two sons were born to Guard's wife; by 1977 they were 11 and 15 years old. One boy had a twisted leg from polio. Two of Guard's daughters were married and lived with their husbands; a third daughter worked as a telephone operator, an index of modernization and urbanization. For all his working years, Guard was employed in the same mill; by 1977 he had been promoted to an administrative position in the mill's security department. His apartment was regularly used by all members of the family when they visited the city or wanted to get together with other lineage members who lived in or visited the city.

Lieutenant, Raconteur's brother, served a long time in the army but had retired by 1958. Thereafter he was somewhat peripatetic, working in various parts of the country. He was born in 1912, fourteen years later than Raconteur, and in 1958 was 46 years old (Append. III: Chart 1.3). At that time he was working in the security system of a large mill in the City of Delhi. Lieutenant's eldest son then lived with his father and uncle, Security Officer, while he was apprenticed to an iron worker. Later he lived in Shanti Nagar and became New Priest when Old Priest died. Lieutenant's six children were born before his retirement from the army; all but the eldest son stayed with their mother, Mrs. Lieutenant.

During the fieldwork, we never saw Lieutenant in Shanti Nagar, but once or twice saw him in the city apartment. From 1959 onward Lieutenant joined the Hyderabad police and later a reserve branch of the same police. He then moved to a position as company commander of police on the India-Pakistan border. He injured his leg in a border dispute, recovered, and moved to Madhya Pradesh as a security officer in a factory. By 1977 his daughters had married and gone permanently to live with their husbands. Both sons lived in separate apartments in the ancestral village dwelling. New Priest had become an Assistant Traffic Manager in the city, commuting daily to work. He and his wife had four children, three sons and one daughter. Mrs. Lieutenant, his mother, lived with him, his wife, and children. Raconteur stated that New Priest and his father, Lieutenant, were still joint with regard to their major properties, especially their land. However, neither man farmed the land; instead Lieutenant leased it to Gentle Soul, who lived next door (Append. III: Charts 1.2, 1.3; Append. IV: Map 2).

Lieutenant's youngest son always lived in the village. When he married, he and his wife had two children, a son born in 1976, a daughter born in 1974. He had separated from his father and occupied the third apartment in the ancestral dwelling. When he first started to work, he became a policeman but did not care for the occupation. He learned to drive and then obtained experience working in an auto repair shop, became an auto mechanic, and a dealer in automobile parts. He, too, commuted daily to work.

Lieutenant's wife lived in the village. Men serving in the military or working away from home often do not have their wives living with them. Mrs. Lieutenant, a pleasant, affable woman, never appeared unhappy with her lot. She filled a need both for her own children and as a surrogate mother for the other children who visited back and forth. When Raconteur's wife died in 1964, it was fortunate that Mrs. Lieutenant could carry on the household chores until Raconteur's sons and nephews married.

The youngest of Raconteur's brothers, Security Officer, left Shanti Nagar early in life to join the army. On his retirement from the army, he lived in Delhi and worked in a mill (Append. III: Chart 1.2). He was still employed by the mill in 1978. He rented one room, in which he lived by himself, and from time-to-time visited his relatives. As usual the gathering point was the city apartment, in which Guard and his family lived. Guard and Security Officer were close together in age, for Security Officer was 57 in 1978 and Guard was 50. Thus, though Security Officer was Guard's uncle, in age he was more like a brother or cousin.

Security Officer had been married early. When he first joined the army, his wife lived in the ancestral dwelling. She died in childbirth along with her infant shortly after he enlisted, and she was believed to have become a ghost. When Security Officer remarried, his second wife bore him two sons: the first was born in 1945, the second in 1948. The second wife died at the birth of the second son. Her death was attributed to the ghost of the first wife. However, both her sons survived. They were raised by Raconteur's wife and Mrs. Lieutenant. Security Officer did not remarry and never again lived in the village. He did, however, see that his two sons were well educated. By 1977, the eldest son, Physician, had received his MBBS degree (medical degree) from an army medical school and was a practicing physician and major in the army. He practiced in an army hospital in the greater Bombay region. He met a nurse there and arranged his own marriage to her; it was rumored that he married out of caste. The couple had three daughters by 1977; the first born were twin girls. Early in 1978, Physician was transferred to a hospital in the City of Delhi.

The second son of Security Officer, Young Lawyer, practiced law in the city but lived with his wife and three-year-old daughter in the fourth apartment of the ancestral village dwelling. Mrs. Young Lawyer had received an M.A. in Sanskrit studies at Delhi University. Her father was a high-school teacher of Sanskrit, whose example probably influenced her to study the language. Although Young Lawyer and his wife were well educated and quite urbanized, they preferred living in the village. Mrs. Young Lawyer, who

Fig. 5. Guga Pir on horseback surrounded by snakes, drawing by Fertility, a Brahman woman, 1958.

had been raised in the country, took over some of the agricultural chores.

THE FAMILIES OF PROGENITOR AND GENTLE SOUL

Progenitor (born 1906) married his second wife, Fertility (born 1917) shortly after the death of his first wife (born 1909). His first wife, who committed suicide in the main village well (ca. 1934) after the death of her third son, left two small surviving sons, Cowherd and Fence Sitter (born 1927 and 1932). Since there was a five-year gap between the two boys, probably one or more infants died at birth in that interval or some miscarriages (spontaneous abortions) took place. The long-remembered ghost of the first wife was greatly feared, and relatives were reluctant to speak of her and her dead child. A few married women, neighbors in the Lohar and Bairagi castes and unrelated Brahmans who lived near Progenitor, provided information about these two deaths and claimed that he contributed to the suicide. They offered no facts but said that he was a bad character and an immoral man. When wives commit suicide, their husbands do not mention them. Progenitor was one such husband; his feelings were reflected in his poor relations with Cowherd and Fence Sitter, his first wife's sons.

The death of Progenitor's first wife reinforced the well-known stepmother belief, namely, that children of a dead first wife do not receive good treatment from a second wife. If the first wife commits suicide, she becomes a ghost and the attitude toward the suicidal wife has further ill-effects on her surviving children. Cowherd and Fence Sitter,

the two surviving sons of Progenitor's first wife, suffered from the suicide of their mother and the second marriage of their father. In such cases usually the stepmother is blamed for whatever goes wrong between a father and his offspring by a first marriage; women, who rank low, become convenient scapegoats.

Fertility, the second wife of Progenitor, bore her first surviving son, Luck, in 1937. She was pregnant 15 times; four of the pregnancies, probably including the first, resulted in miscarriages. One infant died shortly after birth, and a son died at two years of age. The deaths and miscarriages were attributed to the ghost of Progenitor's first wife. Fertility's five surviving sons were born in 1937 (Luck), 1940 (Policeman), 1951, 1952, and 1955. She had four surviving daughters, who were born in 1939, 1941, 1944, and 1948. When Fertility's last child, a son was born, she was approximately 38 or 39 years old. She nursed him until he was four years old.

In 1958–59, Fertility was a pleasant woman, who told us about festivals, rites of passage, and her children. On the occasion of Guga Naumi, a festival celebrating the birth of Guga Pir, women usually draw pictures in charcoal above their cookstoves of Guga Pir seated on a horse. When we were surveying the villagers' observance of Guga Naumi, Fertility explained her drawing, which depicted Guga Pir on horseback surrounded by many snakes (Append. V: Calendric Events— Guga Naumi on Bhadrapad *badi* 9). Fertility said:

> I usually put snakes in the picture because they often come to me in my dreams. When I am asleep at night, I feel snakes all around me. Probably the souls of ancestors take the form of snakes. I am afraid of snakes. If I did not draw the snakes, I would probably see them in the daytime also. The snakes move around in my dreams, but when I distribute sweets, they stop coming in my dreams. Two to three days ago my husband saw a black snake in our fields so I thought I had better do a worship for snakes. I usually perform the worship only on Guga Naumi. It keeps the snakes away. If it does not, then I distribute the sweets and perform the worship again.

Although no women in this lineage told us

the tale of Merchant and Muslim Ghost, they knew the legend and that the black snake seen in their fields was believed to be the ghost of Merchant.

The Freudian concepts of a snake symbolizing the male organ or of the snake as vermin representing children are so well known that they scarcely require comment. The snake as a phobic element and thus an anxiety symbol, which Fertility expressed in her fear of snakes, is also well known. In a region with many poisonous snakes, including the black snake, it is not unusual for people to fear them, especially when they are believed to be ghosts. Hinduism is replete with stories and symbols of snakes. For example, Shiva, a fertility deity, is described as carrying a snake around his neck; snakes surround his image in temples; and a snake is usually coiled around his phallus (lingam). Among celibates attempting to conquer their sexual desires and attain liberation in order to journey to other worlds (jivanmukti, release while living), *kundalini*, the latent energy which must be awakened or controlled for spiritual power, translates as "the coiled" or serpent power (Freud, 1962: 161–162, 417–418; 1967: 392; Daniélou, 1964: 151, 162–163, 178–180, 217; R. Freed and S. Freed, 1980: 401–403).

Cowherd and Fence Sitter, the two sons of Progenitor and his first wife, had little education and help from their father. The poor relations between Progenitor and these two sons were due to Progenitor's dominating, nonaffectionate, and somewhat cruel nature, which no doubt had contributed to the suicide of his first wife and in time affected his other sons and Fertility, his second wife. Cowherd and Fence Sitter suffered all the more from Progenitor's personality because they had no mother to act as a buffer between them and their father. Cowherd was so neglected that he ran away from home when he was 17 years old and joined the army (ca. 1944). While in the army, Cowherd acquired the habit of smoking ganja (cannabis) (cf. Gove, 1986: 210, 934, 1381, for bhang, ganja, marijuana). Later Cowherd became a policeman, was caught smoking the drug, and dismissed from the force. He then returned to the village where in 1959 he was living with his brother, Fence Sitter. Thereafter he earned his living herding cows for villagers. He died in the early 1960s. The cause of death was reported as Fever, the indication of ghost illness. His father had never arranged a marriage for him so he died before his allotted time without issue, tortured from Fever, and was believed to be a ghost. As late as 1978, his ghost and his mother's ghost were still haunting Progenitor's second wife, her sons, their wives, and children.

When Mr. and Mrs. Fence Sitter separated from Progenitor in 1959, they took over the family cattle shed for their dwelling. At the time, Fence Sitter was working in a flour mill in the city. Mrs. Fence Sitter represented the trend of increasing female education of her generation, for she had attended school through the fifth grade. The couple already had two daughters, ages 3 and 5, and in January 1959 another daughter was born, who fell ill with Fever about six months after birth. In 1978 Mrs. Fence Sitter recalled that the ghost illness was due to something in the child's throat, but she did not know exactly what was wrong and the child died. Shortly after this daughter's death, the same illness beset another daughter so Mrs. Fence Sitter immediately took the child to a hospital in a suburb of Delhi, where the illness was diagnosed as diphtheria, treated, and the child recovered. However, Mrs. Fence Sitter herself also exorcised the ghost troubling the child.

By the late 1970s, Fence Sitter and two of his half brothers, Luck and Policeman, with their families lived separately from Progenitor, who refused to divide the land while he lived. The sons of Progenitor and Fertility, who lived in the village, helped Progenitor farm his land and took a share of the produce. The cattle shed, in which Fence Sitter lived in 1959, had been rebuilt into three separate apartments for Fence Sitter, Luck, and Policeman (Append. IV: Map 4). Another son of Fertility and Progenitor moved out of the village. The youngest son had not yet married and in 1977 took a job in one of the Persian Gulf countries.

Fence Sitter seldom talked to any of his half brothers and had not done so for many years. He had not spoken to his father or Fertility for five years. He avoided his half brothers, who lived in apartments adjoining his, because their children wandered in and out of his apartment and stole things, which led to quarrels. He was tired of the problems which arose from association with his brothers, father, and stepmother, none of whom had ever contributed to his welfare, and he wanted to lead his own life. Therefore, he did not talk to them, they did not speak to him, and he had peace.

By 1977, Fence Sitter was employed as a watchman and general superintendent of agricultural work for a large landowner in a nearby village. Mrs. Fence Sitter, who had never been able to adapt to her father-in-law and Fertility, seemed content with her husband's way of life. She was an excellent housekeeper and added to the family income by sewing clothes for women and children.

Mrs. Fence Sitter's ability to adapt to modern ways and still adhere to her early beliefs about ghosts and ghost illness is shown in the way she cared for her children when they fell ill. For example, her 18-year-old son had ghost illness in 1978. He had failed his matriculation examination and was studying to retake it. The pressure on him was heavy because obtaining a good job and then having a marriage arranged for him by his father depended on passing the exam. That both his father and his uncle, Cowherd, had failed the same examination and thereafter never earned a very good living added to his stress.

When he fell ill with Fever, he became delirious and the voice of a man (the ghost) spoke through him. Although Mrs. Fence Sitter took her son to a doctor in a nearby town, she believed that a ghost caused the illness because of Fever, delirium, and the strange man's voice speaking from him. Moreover, just before falling ill, he had been eating sweets when he passed the village cremation grounds, making him vulnerable to ghost illness.

For her son's ghost illness, Mrs. Fence Sitter followed a dual procedure, which she used for all her children beginning with her daughter who had diphtheria. First, she took them to a doctor; then she carried out a simple rite of exorcism to drive off the ghost causing the illness. To exorcise ghosts, she used *Loban*, a commercial canned product, which she bought in the City of Delhi and kept in the house to use in cases of ghost illness.

Loban is translated as benzoin and is sometimes identified as gum benzoin. The commercial product consists of several substances: resins used in ointments, perfumes, medicines, and extracts from shrubs and trees. These substances form crystals. Benzoin has also been called benjamin, and the term and substances derive from the Arabs (Pathak, 1976: 969; Morris, 1969: 123, 124).

For her curing, Mrs. Fence Sitter started a small fire and had her son sit close to the fire looking into it; then she threw the crystals on the fire and had her son smell and inhale the fumes. For good measure, she had him smell chili peppers, a time-honored remedy used by villagers and exorcists when a person was believed to have ghost illness. Sometimes she put black pepper in her children's eyes or mouth and/or placed ashes on their foreheads, also ancient practices, if the other procedures did not work. In using *Loban*, Mrs. Fence Sitter was following the Hindu tradition of exorcism, where fumes produced from substances such as those contained in *Loban* have been used for centuries.

Mrs. Fence Sitter knew about the ghosts in Progenitor's family line and about many other ghosts who, in the late 1970s, were said to be haunting the village. She claimed never to have seen the ghost of her husband's mother but knew that Fertility had seen her. Because of Cowherd's closeness to his brother, Fence Sitter, and her fear of calling his ghost, she did not mention his name, but the ghost whom she believed caused the ghost illness of her 18-year-old son was Cowherd.

Mrs. Fence Sitter's account of the visit of Bemata (the goddess who visits women after midnight on the sixth day from the birth of a child) indicates her early exposure to the belief in visitations by deities and, by extension, other supernaturals:

It is said that Bemata comes and writes the fate of the child. She comes on Mother Sixth [Chhathi] and keeps her hand on the forehead of the child. She is just like Bhagwan-Vishnu, who sends Bemata to the earth to bless children. We are not supposed to sleep throughout the night of Mother Sixth. My mother once held the hand of Bemata. It was on the sixth night after the birth of my younger brother. When Bemata came, she was tall and wore a long skirt. My mother caught hold of her hand, and then she blessed my brother. Bemata then ran away without identifying herself. I also woke up throughout the night of the sixth when my first son was born, but I did not see anything.

Asked whether she was afraid of danger befalling her or the child on Mother Sixth, Mrs. Fence Sitter replied, "There is danger to both." We asked this question since Mother Sixth is celebrated because the first six days from birth are the days during which infants, especially sons, and mothers are apt to die. As indicated earlier, their deaths are associated with a ghost taking the souls of mother and infant, although many infant deaths are due to tetanus neonatorum, and maternal deaths, to puerperal fever (Nautiyal, 1961: 54; Wyon and Gordon, 1971: 176, 184; Sehgal et al., 1980; R. Freed and S. Freed, 1980: 372–374; 1985: 135).

Mrs. Fence Sitter continued: "We in this family are afraid that we might have an *oopra* attack us because my father-in-law had two wives. The first one died so there was danger of her ghost causing ghost illness." Asked who in her husband's family line was troubled by this ghost, her answer was: "My father-in-law's second wife was troubled by this ghost."

At the end of the interview, Mrs. Fence Sitter emphasized, "I believe in Bhagwan-Vishnu because he always helps us. For example, whenever I travel in a bus, I definitely get a seat. It is because I believe in Bhagwan so much that whenever I start any work, I take Vishnu's name."

Other ghosts arose in Progenitor's family line. Fertility's first surviving son, Luck, was married twice. His first wife suffered an extremely difficult first pregnancy. Her whole body became swollen, and she was in such pain that she committed suicide in the main village well before the infant was born, contributing another *oopra* to haunt the family, particularly Luck's second wife. This suicide happened shortly before 1958 so many neighboring women feared her ghost and referred to the death. By 1960, Luck and Policeman had married two sisters. Both men with their wives and children sometime later moved into the apartment complex where the Fence Sitter's lived. As usual, they never mentioned

the name of Luck's first wife. Luck worked as a farmer, and Policeman was a constable who farmed on weekends.

Another death in this family line was due to the chronic illness of the youngest daughter of Fertility and Progenitor, who was born in 1948 and died in 1973, by which time she was married and left two children. She was quite ill in 1958 when she was ten years old. She had aching and brittle bones and emitted pus in her urine. The disease, from which she suffered all through her childhood, was described by her mother, who said she had it from birth. It was ascribed to her soul's actions in past lives, and therefore was a form of ghost illness.

It is possible that she suffered from a form of tuberculosis, what was formerly called infantile scrofula and has been described as a chronic illness found in children between the ages of two to fifteen. It is characterized by enlargement of the cervical lymph glands, abscess formation, and discharge of curdy yellowish pus through one or more bodily apertures (Lomax, 1977: 356). Until the discovery that tuberculosis is a contagious disease caused by a bacillus, tuberculosis in its various forms was believed to be hereditary. In 1978, many villagers still believed that tuberculosis was an inherited illness, which a mother passed on to her children. The villagers' position is by no means irrational; there is plenty of empirical evidence supporting it. While TB is not an inherited genetic defect, it nonetheless can be acquired from an infected mother by transplacental spread, by aspiration of infected amniotic fluid, or simply by close contact. About 50 percent of the children of mothers with active pulmonary TB will contract the disease in the first year of life unless treated (Lomax, 1977; Myers, 1977: 75, 77, 79, 142, 145; Append. I: Discoveries—1882–1908, Tuberculosis; 1913–21, Tuberculosis; Descriptions—Tuberculosis).

Although Fertility's youngest daughter was ill all her early life, a marriage was arranged, and she was wedded when she was 15 years old. When she died, no information was given as to the cause of her death. If it was diagnosed as tuberculosis, no one in the family line would have mentioned it, for it would then have been difficult to arrange further marriages in this branch of the lineage. Since the belief was that her soul became a ghost, she was expected to haunt her husband's village where she died. Although she was consistently ill throughout her early life, her parents had to arrange her marriage. The reason rests on dharma. It is dharma for parents to see that their children, especially daughters, are married. Not to do so results in bad karma (Bühler, 1969: 328). Progenitor never arranged a marriage for his son, Cowherd, nor did he arrange a marriage for Gentle Soul after his parents died. Perhaps his lack of respect for dharma was one reason why he was said to have a bad moral character. As he grew older, he may have realized he had already accumulated more than enough bad karma and therefore arranged his daughter's marriage.

In 1978 Progenitor and Fertility still lived in Old Brahman Lane, where Progenitor had lived from the time of his birth. Except for occasional visits of sons and grandsons, they were often alone. Only two other families of Brahmans remained as neighbors (Append. IV: Map 4, no. 17, 18, 20). Fertility occasionally lapsed into states where she forgot events, mumbled, was anxious and afraid, and especially feared visiting the nearby clinic when she was ill because she feared injections. Possibly she was becoming senile.

The family and descendants of Progenitor's younger brother, Gentle Soul, were far fewer than those of Progenitor (Append. III: Chart 1.3). Gentle Soul, born in 1913, was seven years younger than Progenitor. He married late, not surprising since his mother died during the plague and influenza epidemics, and his father died shortly thereafter, leaving no concerned person other than Progenitor to arrange his marriage. It was difficult to determine the year of his marriage, but his wife, born in 1923, was ten years younger than he so the first mating would have been when the bride was about 15 years old, approximately 1938 or later.

About the time of the birth of his first child, Gentle Soul separated from Progenitor and moved into the building left by Dead Issue. This building was part of the original plot of land owned by Merchant and his younger brother. Gentle Soul worked in a mill in Delhi in the 1950s; he was retired by 1978 and farmed a small amount of land.

By 1977, this couple had four surviving children. The eldest son was born in 1947, another son in 1951. The second son was ill most of his life, starting with the bout of *piliya*, described earlier, which was probably hepatitis. He was then seven years old. A third son was born in 1958, and a daughter, Love Song, was born in 1954. These four children were born before Old Priest died. They lived next door to Old Priest and Raconteur and were much influenced by them (Append. IV: Maps 1, 2). As was the custom with patrilineal cousins, Gentle Soul's children and the children of this lineage who lived next door treated each other as brothers and sisters, using the appropriate kinship terms.

Love Song was particularly close to Young Lawyer, the youngest son of Security Officer. When Young Lawyer was wedded, Love Song suffered a series of ghost possessions. In 1978, Goody, a Brahman girl from another lineage, described the possessions as follows: "Gentle Soul's daughter had ghost possessions. She is now about 24 years old. She suffered from the ghost shortly before her marriage and was treated in New Delhi by a bhagat. He tied a *tawiz* [an amulet in the form of a locket] around her neck. I saw her being possessed the first time on the day that her brother [Young Lawyer] was married. The two were close like real brothers and sisters." No one identified the ghost possessing Love Song.

Goody was then asked why she believed in ghosts, but she avoided a direct answer by saying, "We do not have them in our house." This interview was conducted in the apartment of Mrs. Young Lawyer, whom Goody was visiting. Mrs. Young Lawyer had just claimed that "only uneducated people believe in ghosts and suffer from ghost possessions," and her statement affected Goody's reply. Despite her claim that they had no ghosts in her house, Goody knew that recently her brother, Welder, had suffered a series of ghost possessions by Whose Daughter, his recently drowned patrilineal cousin (Chap. 14).

Despite Mrs. Young Lawyer's comment about ghost beliefs, she said that she and her husband as well as other lineage members worshipped at the shrine of Merchant, her husband's ancestor, but did not mention Muslim Ghost or the new shrine for Old Priest. Obviously, pitris (ancestral ghosts) had a higher status than bhuts, and worship at ancestral shrines was an acceptable form of behavior for Mrs. Young Lawyer. Still her attitude was somewhat surprising coming from a village-born Brahman woman. Possibly her advanced education was in conflict with the ghost beliefs to which she was exposed as a child.

Gentle Soul's eldest son passed tenth grade, joined the army, and was posted to Jammu and Kashmir. His wife and son lived there with him. His wife had also been educated through the tenth grade. Gentle Soul's second son finished seventh grade and was employed as a laborer in the city. His daughter, Love Song, finished eighth grade, married, and lived with her husband. In 1978, Gentle Soul's youngest son was completing studies for the B.A. at Delhi University. These changes in the education of males and females reflect the changing times. For a small landowning farmer with little help from his lineage mates, Gentle Soul had done well with his children.

CHAPTER 13: OLD FEVER

The second lineage history, "Old Fever," depicts a group of Jats in the 19th and 20th centuries, roughly contemporaneous with "Merchant, Muslim, Priest." Through at least the first quarter of the 20th century, these Jats followed "Popular Hinduism" (O'Malley, 1935: vii–viii) and relied on Brahman priests for Hindu rituals, especially ceremonies of the life cycle. Then they became followers of the Arya Samaj although the Senior Branch of this lineage was not as strict about Arya-Samaj principles as was the Junior Branch. As befits followers of Arya-Samaj principles, members of Old Fever, except those in the older generations, did not believe in ghosts. In this regard, they contrasted with the members of the Merchant-Muslim-Priest lineage, many of whom were their neighbors (Append. IV: Maps 1, 2). Two senior and important men, one in each lineage, Raconteur of Merchant-Muslim-Priest and Old Codger of Old Fever, were approximate age mates and neighbors. Comparison of the ghost beliefs and practices of these two men helps to highlight the differences between their lineages and between the Arya Samaj and Sanatan Dharma. The comparison also shows the tenacity of ghost beliefs among Samajis, especially older individuals, as indicated by Old Codger's recourse to a Muslim exorcist.

FEVER, OLD FEVER, TUBERCULOSIS

Both in 1958–59 and 1977–78, villagers tended to avoid using the terms, tuberculosis or TB, especially in front of anyone who had the disease or was related to a family in which tuberculosis was known to exist, because of the belief that the disease is inherited. From the point of view of karma, such inheritance is due to a soul's bad actions in past lives. Ayurvedic medical theory has held that hereditary diseases are passed on through diseased semen or menstrual fluid and are subdivided into diseases inherited from the father's or the mother's side (Kutumbiah, 1969: 80). These hereditary alternatives likewise have been attributed to past actions of the soul.

In ancient times, pulmonary tuberculosis existed among Egyptians, Persians, Hindus, and Greeks along with different beliefs as to the cause of the disease, from affliction by supernatural beings to contagion or inheritance, and with various cures. Hippocrates named the disease phthisis, meaning "melting or fading away," and considered it to be an inherited disease. He also described phthisis in animals and pointed out that scrofula (a form of tuberculosis) could be found in animals and humans. Galen, on the other hand, considered phthisis to be contagious and observed that many persons in the same family died of the disease. Despite Galen's observation, Celsius and other physicians discounted Galen and considered tuberculosis to be inherited within a family line (Myers, 1977: 6–15). In Ayurvedic and Greek humoral medicine, the most persistent theory was that phthisis was inherited. This theory was passed on through Hindu and Muslim traditions in Shanti Nagar, where many villagers thought that the disease was inherited from the mother (Append. I: Descriptions—Tuberculosis).

In 1977–78, although a few urbanized villagers used the initials TB to identify the disease, other villagers used "Old Fever." The first time that we recorded the euphemism, "Old Fever," was in 1978 when we interviewed an elderly Brahman couple, who were reluctant to name persons who were believed to have died and then became ghosts. They finally said that Ill Fated, a member of this Jat lineage, died of Old Fever and was believed to have become a ghost.

TWO BRANCHES OF OLD FEVER

The Senior and Junior Branches of this lineage are descended from three of four brothers in Generation II as shown in the kinship diagrams (Append. III: Charts 2.1, 2.2, 2.3). The Senior Branch descended from the two eldest brothers; the Junior Branch, from the next to youngest brother, the youngest brother having died without issue. In the late 1950s, the members of Old Fever lived in a group of houses at the side of the village farthest from the main roads leading into it (Append. IV: Map 1). A cluster of large brick dwellings, erected between 1925 and the 1940s, was inhabited by two families headed by two brothers, Forceful and Taciturn, representing the Senior Branch. Two smaller buildings belonged to the Junior Branch.

SENIOR BRANCH

Forceful and Taciturn had two younger brothers, one of whom died in childhood. The other younger brother, Ill Fated, died in 1925, age 18, before his allotted time and without issue. These four brothers constitut-ed Generation IV of the Senior Branch. Within the households of Forceful and Taciturn lived two widows, Dancer and Long Lived, who had been married to Old Groom and Fateful, Generation III. Dancer was wedded at age five to Old Groom, a man considerably older than she. He died in 1924 when she was 21 years old and he was 40. They had no children. In 1958, the widowed Dancer, then 55–56 years old, lived in Forceful's household. Long Lived, Fateful's widow, age 70, resided with Taciturn. Like Old Groom and Dancer, Fateful and Long Lived had no children (Append. III: Charts 2.1, 2.2). Dancer, who was known for her sprightly dancing at celebrations for the birth of a son, died in the 1960s. Long Lived died at age 90 in January 1978.

Forceful, Taciturn, Dancer, and Long Lived provided details about the history of the first four generations of the Senior Branch. The two old widows, reared in the tradition of ghost beliefs, remembered details about deaths and related ghosts from past times. Dancer recalled information about all the male members of Generation III and their wives, who lived in one joint-family household. The senior men were Dancer's husband, Old Groom, who was the only surviving son of the eldest brother in Generation II, and Old Groom's patrilineal first cousins, Capable, and his brother Fateful. Capable, the oldest male (born 1877), headed the joint family. He and his wife, Sparrow, had four sons: Forceful, Taciturn, Ill Fated, and one son born before Ill Fated who died in childhood (Append. III: Charts 2.1, 2.2).

Capable and Fateful died during the first two decades of the 20th century when the region was first devastated by plague and then ravaged in 1918–19 by influenza. When Capable died, Old Groom became head of the family. The other family members were Dancer; the widows of Capable and Fateful, namely, Sparrow and Long Lived; and three sons of Capable: Forceful, Taciturn, and Ill Fated. Forceful and Taciturn were absent from the household at the beginning of the third decade; Ill Fated and Old Groom were the resident males. The three women were sisters as it was the custom to arrange marriages of sisters with brothers and cousins so that young girls would have at least one consanguine in their marital village (Append. III: Chart 2.2).

In 1916 when Forceful, the eldest son of Capable and Sparrow, was 19 years old, he ran away from home and enlisted in the army. The family did not learn where he was or what he was doing until notified by the military a year later. Forceful served nine years in the army. From 1916 until the end of World War I, he traveled to Sikanderbad, Hyderabad, the Suez Canal, Baghdad, Basra, and then France. After the war, he returned to India where he was stationed in many cantonments. He was with the cavalry as a stableman. He enjoyed army life but left it when he was notified of the death of Ill Fated. By the time he returned home in 1925, much had happened in his family.

After the death of Old Groom, the three widowed sisters, Dancer, Sparrow, and Long Lived, were left in the care of Ill Fated. He was responsible for farming the family's 500 bighas of land (42 hectares), caring for the cattle, and in general seeing that the family's affairs went smoothly and effectively. Although he was about 18 years old, his wife, Felicity, had not yet come for first mating because of her youth and the absence of a senior, adult man in the household.

From 1924 to 1925, Ill Fated was bedeviled by the ghosts of the recent past and the troubles of the present. He was young, under considerable stress, and, in addition to taking care of the family estate, was responsible for three women. The strain was such that he suffered ghost possessions and villagers began to talk about the ghosts possessing him, who were identified as his two uncles, Old Groom and Fateful, and his father, Capable. In 1958 Dancer named Old Groom and Capable as the ghosts haunting Ill Fated; other villagers named combinations of the three men. They said that once when Ill Fated was possessed, the ghost of Fateful spoke from him in a strange voice and talked about events which had happened in village families. A number of the villagers decided that a curer should be called to exorcise the ghost. Ill Fated claimed he heard the villagers discussing his possessions and the suggestion that a curer be called although he was not present when they did so. He then told the members of his family and other villagers that they should

not call a curer because no one could cure him.

One day Dancer found Ill Fated unconscious and gradually brought him back to consciousness. He said to her, "The house is full of food, but there is nothing to eat. I am always hungry; yet I have drunk so much milk. Now see in the evening, there will be no milk." According to Dancer's account, that evening the cow gave no milk. Dancer folded her hands and asked that whatever she may have done be forgiven; then the cow gave milk. Dancer claimed that her husband's ghost, Old Groom, troubled Ill Fated. Thereafter, whenever Ill Fated fell unconscious, ghosts spoke from him, relating some events that took place between the widows and their husbands before Ill Fated was born. According to the three widowed sisters, these events were secrets known only to them and their spouses so Ill Fated could not possibly have found out about them, thus reinforcing the belief that the ghosts of their dead husbands spoke from him. Ill Fated then fell ill with Fever, and Old Priest, who lived across the lane, was called to cure him of ghost illness. Old Priest recited mantras and asked the ghosts why they came. The ghosts replied, "We want to take the boy away with us." A few days later in 1925 Ill Fated died, and he too was believed to have become a ghost.

It seems reasonable to suppose that with the successive deaths of Capable, Fateful, and Old Groom, the three widowed sisters, who were often left to themselves, talked about their husbands and past events. Regardless of what they thought, Ill Fated must have heard some of their conversations and those of other villagers, especially about the many dead who became ghosts during the first two decades of the 20th century. Kakar (1983: 69–70) described a similar possession possibly related to gossip. When Ill Fated died, he was 18 years old, an age at which he normally would have been mated with his wife. Instead he was alone in a house with three widowed sisters: his mother, Sparrow, age 45; Long Lived, age 38; and Dancer, age 22. The fact that Dancer, the youngest of the trio and the closest to his age, joined her hands to pray that she be forgiven for whatever she might have done could be interpreted that she flirted with or teased Ill Fated and that she believed her husband's ghost became jealous and possessed Ill Fated. At that time the Arya Samaj had only recently been introduced and ghost beliefs were still strong among Jats. Both Dancer and Long Lived believed in ghosts until they died.

After Ill Fated's death, the family sent word to Forceful to return home to head the family and manage the land and household. During Forceful's military service, the young girl to whom he had been engaged died. Sometime after his return, he, therefore, took as his levirate spouse, Felicity, the widow of Ill Fated, whose marriage to Ill Fated had never been consummated (Append. III: Chart 2.2).

The younger brother of Forceful, Taciturn, was married twice. His first wife died without any surviving children. Either she never bore any, or if she did, they died as infants. In any case, she, too, was believed to have become a ghost. Taciturn then married the younger sister of Felicity, here called Timely. She was born in 1927, and the consummation of the marriage occurred around 1942 when she was 15. The wedding had taken place when she was 12 years old. Before the death of his first wife, Taciturn separated from Forceful, and each brother built brick dwellings between 1925 and 1940. Forceful retained the original mud hut of the joint family as a storage place, which still stood in 1978. Despite the separation into two families, the brothers remained loyal to each other as did all the Senior Branch members in Generation IV and succeeding generations.

Forceful and Taciturn had surviving children at a relatively late age. Forceful's first surviving child, a son, Politico, was born in 1938 when Forceful was 41 years old. Four sons, born earlier, died as infants. Taciturn's first surviving child, a daughter, was born in 1947 when Taciturn was 44 years old and Timely, his wife, was 20 years old. The second wives of Forceful and Taciturn were much younger than their husbands. The second marriage of Taciturn to Timely when his first wife died, Forceful's taking of Felicity, the widow of Ill Fated, as his spouse when the girl to whom he had been engaged died, the large differences in age of husbands and wives, and the relatively advanced ages of the husbands at the births of their first surviving

children reflect the high death rates through the first two to three decades of the 20th century (Append. III: Chart 2.2).

Although Forceful was in service when his father, Capable, died, he later erected a *than* to him. The family had gathered Capable's bones from the cremation grounds on the third day after death as was customary. They were placed in a container to be carried to the Ganges River when Forceful returned from service. He chose instead to erect a *than* and place the bones in the ground under it, following the ancient tradition of ancestor worship observed by landowners. Thereafter members of the family regularly worshipped at Capable's shrine. The *than* for Capable elevated his ghost from a bhut to an ancestral ghost. Members of the Senior Branch expected the ancestral ghost of Capable to act in a benevolent way and protect them. For weddings and births of children and calves, the family lit a lamp and brought fruits and sweets there. Forceful said, "We do so even when the child is a girl." On the dark night of the moon, Amavas, and the full moon, Purinmashi, they worshipped at the shrine for 10 to 15 minutes (O. Lewis, 1958: 233; R. Freed and S. Freed, 1964: 82, 85; Append. V: Calendric Events). These customs are contrary to Arya-Samaj beliefs regarding worshipping or commemorating the dead (Saraswati, 1956: 145).

In 1977, Forceful and Felicity had six surviving children: four sons and two daughters. Their last surviving child, a son, was born in 1954. Taciturn and Timely had 10 surviving children: six sons and four daughters. The last child, a son, was born in 1969, when Timely was 42 years old (Append. III: Chart 2.2).

POLITICO

The education of Forceful's sons, especially, Politico, illustrates the emphasis that Forceful and Taciturn placed on the education of boys. When Politico was 20 years old, he took the matriculation examination for the fourth time, having failed it three times. When he attempted it the fourth time, his father said he would take it again if he failed. He passed and later studied three years to be a physical training instructor. Politico's next oldest brother also had trouble in school so his family sent him to a special school. By 1977 he was in the army.

Neither Forceful nor Taciturn had gone to school. It is rather common for youngsters with nonliterate parents to have trouble in school. They tend to fail the matriculation examination more often than children whose parents have some schooling. Because non-literate parents do not appreciate the need for their children to attend school regularly and to be on time daily and because they have little idea of the difference between learning household and agricultural tasks on the one hand and, on the other hand, the abstract cognitive problems of learning reading, writing, and arithmetic and how in general to learn by reading, many of their children fail in school or drop out early even though their parents pressure them to do well and continue their educations (R. Freed and S. Freed, 1981: 123–129).

Politico's personality developed in the context of violence, both at home and in school. It was accepted that a schoolmaster could and should beat children when they were naughty, late for school, or did not apply themselves. The practice was also part of family life. Moreover, beatings were not confined to children but were extended to wives, for it was the duty of husbands to discipline them (R. Freed and S. Freed, 1981: 75, 125). Considerable violence might be generated within a family by such treatment though many families were peaceful and not inclined to beat anyone. In any case, beatings in Politico's family and in school may have contributed to his hair-trigger temper and tendency toward violence. In the mid-1960s he was involved in a fight with two Brahman brothers, who had attacked his uncle, Taciturn. In anger, he killed one and wounded the other. After serving ten years in prison, he was released in 1977. When he returned home, he ran for election to the office of pradhan, head of the village panchayat, and won. His success was partially due to his having learned to work with many castes while in jail and the power which his father and uncle, wealthy farmers, had over a number of castes (S. Freed and R. Freed, 1987: 25–27, 61).

THE TUBERCULOSIS SCOURGE

With the denial by the Arya Samaj of ghost beliefs, tuberculosis as an inherited disease replaced ghost illness as a source of anxiety in the Old Fever lineage. During 1977–78, a number of people in the village said that Timely, the wife of Taciturn, had suffered from tuberculosis for many years and that some of her offspring had the disease. In a discussion of health attitudes with a group of Jats from another lineage, one man mentioned that both Taciturn's wife and son had TB and had been hospitalized with the disease. Others in the group said that the son and mother were all right after the hospitalization, but they could not work hard. These men voiced the opinion that tuberculosis was a disease inherited from the mother. They said that in Taciturn's family, the disease came from Timely. Others claimed that it started with Sparrow, the wife of Capable, thus indicating the possibility of earlier cases of tuberculosis. Although the elderly Brahman couple claimed that Ill Fated had died of Old Fever, no one else said so.

Two lengthy group interviews with members of Taciturn's family elicited information on the family history of TB. The first interview took place in Taciturn's house in the fall of 1977. The 26-year-old wife of Friendly, Taciturn's next to eldest son (age 27), was in a tuberculosis hospital, but family members said she was there because she suffered from malaria. The subject came up while we were censusing the family because one of Taciturn's married daughters had been called from her marital home to help during her sister-in-law's stay in the hospital. Timely, her mother-in-law, daily took food to Mrs. Friendly in the hospital. This practice was customary when a family member was hospitalized.

The census interview revealed that the eldest son of Taciturn, Troubled, had separated from his father and lived in a small hut built nearby for him, his wife, and small son. His wife was a sister of Friendly's wife, then in the hospital. Later we learned that Troubled's separation from his father was partly due to his fear of tuberculosis. Friendly, the second eldest son, operated his father's tractor. He had dropped out of school in the ninth grade because he was not good in his studies. He then took a test to be a bus driver but failed, so he drove the family tractor. Troubled used bullocks to plow his land. Like his brother, Friendly, and patrilineal cousin, Politico, Troubled had been a slow learner in school, spending three years in first grade.

The third son of Taciturn, Athlete, was the first son to contract tuberculosis and to be hospitalized. He had a government job in a city. Part of the job entailed playing volley ball and kabaddi, a strenuous game involving bodily contact (R. Freed and S. Freed, 1981: 83). In 1975 he had gone to Chandigarh to play in a tournament when he fell ill. He attributed his illness to becoming very hot when he played and then drinking a glass of cold water. He stayed one-and-a-half months in two hospitals specializing in tuberculosis, and his father, Taciturn, took him to many curers: *vaid*s, physicians, and compounders, claiming to have spent Rs. 10,000 on him to no avail. Athlete lived at home but could not work in the fields. However, when there was no one to look after the fields, he spent an hour or two acting as a watchman. Despite his illness, he continued to smoke cigarettes. His father had recently built small, sunlit, one-room apartments on the roof for each of his sons. When Athlete fell ill, the family of the girl to whom he was engaged broke the engagement. Later Taciturn tried to arrange another marriage for him, but Athlete would not consent to an engagement.

In the early spring of 1978 as we were passing Taciturn's dwelling, Friendly called out inviting us into the courtyard. It was very sunny, immaculately clean, and Friendly was reclining on a cot. Mrs. Friendly greeted us and said, "When you first came here, I was in the hospital because blood was coming out of my mouth." Thus she tended to confirm that her illness was tuberculosis.

Friendly's mother, Timely, came into the courtyard, sat insouciantly smoking her hookah, and asked that we take her photograph. We were startled to see her smoking after she had been cured of tuberculosis, but Friendly also smoked a cigarette during this session. With three people smoking the hookah or cigarettes who had suffered or were suffering from TB, Timely, Friendly, and Ath-

lete, it is dubious that they understood the damage that smoking does to the lungs. Since village men and women claimed that hookah smoking helped their digestion, it might be difficult to convince them to give up the habit.

As for the transmission of tuberculosis in the tropics, Davey and Wilson (1971: 103–104) listed the following factors: spitting (sputum) of an infected person, consumption of raw milk infected by *Mycobacterium bovis*, the eating utensils of infected persons, communal eating from a single dish, early marriage, frequent child bearing, hard farm work of women and young children, and heavy household duties of women (Myers, 1977: 116–117; Berkow, 1982: 127; Append. I: Discoveries—1882–1908, Tuberculosis; 1913–21, Tuberculosis; 1944–51, Antituberculosis drugs; Descriptions—Tuberculosis). The factors of early marriage, frequent childbearing, and hard work were especially prominent in Shanti Nagar.

Friendly invited us to take tea. When it was served, Timely's brother came in and launched into a series of stories about the members of this family with whom he had lived in the 1950s. He was currently visiting because of the death of Long Lived for whom a memorial feast had recently been held.

Friendly then told us about his current illness. He had been ill for one month with recurrent attacks of malaria. He took medicine from Home Trained, a village curer of the Nai Barber caste, but found no relief, so he went to a particular clinic, which was a tuberculosis clinic although he did not specifically identify it as such. There they checked his blood and sputum and x-rayed him. A doctor said there was something wrong with his blood and gave him medicine and directions for taking it daily for 30 days: one injection of streptomycin, one tablet of isoniazid, and a vitamin-mineral tablet, all three daily for 30 days. Although Friendly did not say who injected the streptomycin, he or other members of his family may have been taught how to give the injections, or they might have had Home Trained, one of the village curers, do it. The first two drugs are generally prescribed for tuberculosis (Davey and Wilson, 1971: 108–109; Berkow, 1982: 130–131; R. Freed and S. Freed, 1985: 187;

cf. Weiss, 1992, for more recent information). Friendly said that he had been feeling better the last five to seven days. He showed us the containers for the medicine, and we read the labels and instructions to him.

During this interview and discussion, a daughter-in-law from Forceful's household came into the courtyard and placed her two-year-old child on Friendly's cot. Friendly immediately told her to remove the child who should not be on the same cot with him due to his illness. She then picked up her child and sat down at a distance from Friendly. This description of Friendly's illness and treatment is characteristic of home treatment for tuberculosis. It shows that Friendly was following some of the instructions given him regarding contagion from TB. A few months later, Friendly, apparently recovered, was happily driving his tractor.

TROUBLED

In 1977–78 villagers said that Taciturn's eldest son, Troubled, had attacks of madness, during which he beat his wife and threw tools and utensils around. Villagers believed that Troubled's separation from his father and his attacks of madness were due to his fear of tuberculosis.

Troubled provided the following details and descriptions of his attacks. He had intermittent attacks of malaria, which he called Fever (Append. I: Descriptions—Malaria). In 1975 when he first suffered from malaria, he went to a swami in a nearby ashram. The swami told him to eat only watermelon and sweetened, fruit-flavored water for one week. He did so but grew worse. Some people in the village were passing out chloroquine tablets and gave Troubled four of them. He took them all at once with milk, a staple food which, like wheat, is believed to be appropriate at all seasons. One informant said that milk serves as an antidote to the "hot" pills and therefore prevents "heat in the brain." In any case, by evening Troubled was unconscious. His father then took him in a borrowed Jeep to a hospital in Delhi. In the hospital he was delirious and unconscious for two to three days. He said, "I was in a state of madness, during which time I grabbed hold

of the doctor and nurses, shouted, and tore my clothes. A patient's wife was visiting in the same ward, and I either bit her hand or tried to bite it. At 8 p.m. on the third night I was given an injection; then I hit the doctor." The police were called and Troubled was removed from the hospital, after which he and his father returned to the village.

The next morning Taciturn put Troubled on a cot and the cot on a trolley, which he attached to his tractor, and drove to a mental hospital in Punjab, which had been recommended by a relative. Troubled was there 15 days. Every day he was given injections, pills, and electroshock treatments, i.e., electroconvulsive therapy (Andreasen, 1985: 200–203). During shock treatments, he was unconscious. The doctor prescribed a diet of cow's milk and porridge. He also massaged him with clarified butter (ghee). In the afternoons Troubled was given orange juice. He went home for ten days. When he returned for a checkup, the physician said he was all right.

This illness struck in June, 1975, and lasted for a month. In 1976, he had a recurrence. The doctors in the hospital had given him a list of medicines to take for a recurrence so he went to Dr. John, a Brahman villager and compounder. Dr. John gave him injections and other prescribed medicine. Then he was again all right.

Dr. John had studied to be a compounder and passed his examination in 1959. By the late 1970s he had been practicing for some time in a government clinic some miles from Shanti Nagar. In addition, he and a woman physician jointly owned a pharmaceutical shop in a large village of over 8000 people. Compounders were called doctors by the villagers; the word compounder is equivalent to pharmacist. Villagers equated the giving of medicine with being a doctor, and the status of a doctor was associated with men, not women. Once when we accompanied a WHO (World Health Organization) group of women physicians to a village on the western edge of New Delhi, the physicians gave written prescriptions to individuals, who then had them filled by a compounder at the WHO van. The patients addressed the compounder as doctor, but did not show the same deference to the women physicians. Due to this cultural orientation, Dr. John's partner was usually referred to as nurse, rarely as doctor, while he was always given the title of doctor.

When asked for a description of his symptoms, Troubled said that he had a great deal of heat in his brain. Heat in the brain is an expression used to describe what appears to be heat syncope as recognized in Western medicine. It is also known as heat stroke and *loo lagna* (affected by the *loo*—a hot wind). In the Delhi region the *loo* occurs in the hot season, which begins in April and reaches its peak in May and June. The hottest temperatures are in May when the average high temperature is about 105°F (40.6°C) and days with temperatures of 110°F (43.3°C) or more are not uncommon. Heat stroke takes place during the hot season before the monsoon which begins in early July; heat exhaustion occurs during the monsoon. A study of Indian troops in Iraq during World War II, who were struck by "subacute heat effect," found that they were first admitted to hospitals as mental patients because their behavior was maniacal, which is comparable to Troubled's state when he had "heat in the brain" (Planalp, 1971: 230, 234, 285, 388–389, 398–399; Append. VII: Daily Temperatures).

When he first fell ill, Troubled said he was totally unconscious and did not know what he was saying so he said, "the wrong things to people." He claimed that he had eaten a lot of bajra *kicheri*, food consisting of cooked lentils and bulrush (pearl) millet. Bajra *kicheri*, according to humoral theory, is classified as very "hot" (Planalp, 1971: 149, 150). It is usually eaten in winter, when it is considered healthy, but he had been eating it well into the spring. The villagers, following Ayurvedic thinking, believe that very hot foods generate heat in the brain and body. Troubled said that bajra *kicheri* along with the four chloroquine tablets caused too much "heat in the brain" and resulted in his attacks of madness.

Other villagers believe that chloroquine tablets generate much heat in the body and brain. For example, Unfortunate, a young Brahman, said that the Government passed out tablets for malaria and that four should be taken when one had an attack of malaria, "but if a person is weak, he cannot stand them because they are very hot. For such a person the number of tablets should be reduced."

Unfortunate described these tablets as being very hot, but if one did not eat rich food, the heat broke out in a rash. He said that new blood is not manufactured when one has malaria because the red blood corpuscles fight the malaria; then the quantity of blood is reduced and the person develops jaundice, *piliya*. His statements were based on his own experience with malaria followed by jaundice. When chronic malaria persists and is not treated, mild jaundice usually develops because the spleen and occasionally the liver become enlarged (Lyght, 1956: 938).

During the malaria epidemics in the last half of the 1970s, the village pradhan distributed chloroquine tablets from the beginning of the hot season in April until November 1, and maintained a record of the people to whom he gave them. Villagers went to him, to two clinics in a nearby village, to pharmacists and doctors (*vaid*s and Western medical physicians) for chloroquine or purchased chloroquine tablets themselves. However, some villagers were wary of taking pills, tablets as they called them. The well-known case of Troubled may have contributed to more people avoiding chloroquine. The recurrence and rise in the incidence of malaria from 1965 to epidemic proportions beginning in 1974 through 1978 hit the population hard as many of the villagers had never experienced malaria and had no immunity to it. Troubled was one example. (W. Peters, 1975; Sarkad, 1975; Pattanayak and Roy, 1980).

To advocate the prevention of malaria by taking chloroquine once a week was relatively ineffective because most villagers did not recognize the concept of preventive medicine, i.e., taking medicine in order to avoid being ill. A number of elderly villagers did not take any pills unless they were suffering badly. Some villagers were willing to have injections to rid themselves of Fever, which included malaria, because they believed that injections drove out Fever, somewhat akin to exorcism by a curer. For this last reason if an inoculation against malaria is ever perfected and described as preventing Fever, it may be readily acceptable (O. Lewis, 1958: 169; Silverman, 1977; R. Freed and S. Freed, 1979: 317, 319, 327; Kolata, 1984; Trager, 1984; Vohra, 1985). A vaccine against malaria does not seem likely in the near future. Two recent articles report that the promise of a vaccine has failed and that the most lethal strain of malaria, *Plasmodium falciparum*, is now resistant to chloroquine. Moreover, there are already signs of resistance to the new drug, mefloquine (Marshall, 1990: 399–400; Cherfas, 1990).

Davey and Wilson (1971: 188–189) wrote that chloroquine is one of the recommended drugs for the control of malaria, which was epidemic in the Delhi region when Troubled took the four tablets, and that the drug should be directly administered to each person. At the village level such control is not practical. For example, during the epidemics in the malaria seasons of the 1970s, an assortment of government and volunteer workers passed out the tablets without supervising how they were taken. An immediate adult dosage is 600 mg of chloroquine, followed by doses of 300 mg once a week. When Troubled took four tablets all at once in 1975, the hot season and the epidemic of malaria had peaked.

The malaria epidemic was so severe that radical treatment for malaria was undertaken; the former five-day treatment was reduced to a one-day dosage of chloroquine of 600 mg plus either pyrimethamine 50 mg or primaquine 45 mg. The villagers did not mention the latter two drugs; generally they referred to the pills as quinine tablets. Quinine was an old, established term for the medical treatment of malarial fever, which had not been replaced by the name of the new drug any more than "Fever" had been replaced by "malaria." (W. Peters, 1975: 167; Sarkad, 1975; Pattanayak and Roy, 1980: 1–4 (table 1), 5, 6).

Since Troubled lived across the lane from Raconteur and New Priest, we asked him whether his illness was similar to the ghost possessions and ghost illness of Ill Fated, who was treated by Old Priest, or the possessions of New Priest when Old Priest died. He replied that he knew about their possessions and the death of Ill Fated, but that he himself was not possessed by a ghost. He added that Long Lived thought that a ghost had entered him. He recalled that the doctors had named his illness, but he could not remember the term. Whether the doctors used the term manic-depressive or the more recent bipolar terminology, which includes mania and de-

pression, both terms would have been new to him, and it would not have been easy for him to remember either one. Moreover, he had electroshock treatments which affect the patient's memory. (For ECT, electroconvulsive therapy, for forms of mental illness, see Abrams, 1989: 28–30). The first time he fell ill, he had no warning; the second time he felt heat in his brain, knew he would be ill, and went to Dr. John for the injections and other medicines he had been instructed to take.

Treatment at the Punjab hospital was free, but his father had to pay for the medicine and hospital stay of 15 days. The total expense was Rs. 1000–1100. The expense for the earlier three days in the City of Delhi hospital was Rs. 500–600. Troubled's father remained with him and bought the medicine. The physicians at the Punjab mental hospital told Taciturn that Troubled needed more work to do. This statement tends to fit the depression aspect of the bipolar syndrome.

One morning in May or June 1977, Troubled was passing through the village on his way to catch the bus to go to the city and was bitten by a dog. The dog's owner, Tippler, was drunk, talkative, and pulled Troubled around in order to make him pay attention. Because the dog thought the two men were fighting, it bit Troubled a number of times. Tippler, an alcoholic, was often belligerent when drunk so people tended to avoid him as much as possible. Troubled, however, had to pass Tippler's house to reach the bus stop. Troubled did not see a physician about his bites. The village remedy for dog bites is to soak the seeds of chili peppers in mustard oil and then apply the mixture to the bites and bandage them.

The number of village dogs had increased from the 1950s. Many of them had no owners and had to beg for food and forage in the village lanes and fields, sometimes killing and eating rats and wild animals, a source of rabies (Berkow, 1982: 177, table 12.2). The problem of rabid animals, especially dogs, exists throughout the Union Territory of Delhi. In 1985, about 60,000 dogs were in the region. Unless a dog is foaming at the mouth, most rural victims of dog bites do not have injections against rabies because it is too far for them to travel to a medical center for

regarding supernatural beings, especially ghosts, ghost illness, ghost possession, and exorcism. He attempted to ban Akhta, a cattle-curing festival for exorcising cattle disease, which falls in autumn in the Delhi region (R. Freed and S. Freed, 1966), and in later years he favored Western medicine. In many ways Reformer's adherence to Arya-Samaj beliefs might be compared to followers of the Protestant Ethic (Tawney, 1947; Weber, 1958). He led a temperate life, was one of the first in the village to practice birth control, was careful of his own and his family's health, worked hard, and instituted new business undertakings. He believed in only one deity.

Barker, who had a governmental clerical position in Delhi, also did not believe in numerous supernatural beings. He took advantage of working in the city to enjoy its pleasures, particularly liquor despite the prohibition laws in effect in the 1950s when he already was well on the way to being an alcoholic. In 1958, despite his Arya-Samaj beliefs, he regaled a group of Jats with a story about a man in his office whose house was regularly visited by an unseen ghost, causing furniture and other objects to move about (a poltergeist). No doubt, he also told the tale to members of his family.

In the late 1950s, Curmudgeon and his wife, the younger sister of Scapegoat, had four surviving children; two sons (born 1933, 1942) and two daughters (born 1923, 1929). His eldest son, Soldier, was in the army and seldom in the village. His two daughters had married and lived in their husbands' villages. His teen-age son, Cattleman, wrote lyrics for songs on the festival of Holi, was a good student, and planned to become a veterinarian. He was the favored child of his father, who gave him more freedom than was customary, providing him with spending money to attend the cinema and visit the city when he so desired. Although Curmudgeon gave Scapegoat the *orhna*, she did not mate with him. She was six to seven years older than her sister, and two to three years older than Curmudgeon (Append. III: Chart 2.3).

Because Curmudgeon was deaf, it was difficult to elicit information from him. His hearing defect not only made him irritable but to some degree paranoid. He was suspicious of what went on around him. If he came home while we were interviewing the women, he stopped the sessions. He had arranged the levirate espousal of his eldest son, Soldier, to Misfortune, the widow of Unknown's son. Misfortune was five years older than Soldier, who was posted to the Punjab during his military service. Misfortune and her children lived with Curmudgeon. She and Soldier had four children (Generation VI): three daughters (born 1953, 1957, and 1963) and one son (born 1955), Little Boy, who in 1958 at age 3 died of typhoid complicated by diarrhea (Append. III: Chart 2.3).

DEATHS OF LITTLE BOY
AND SCAPEGOAT

Curmudgeon, who like all men in the village was much concerned about the perpetuation of the male line of descent, blamed the death of Little Boy on his levirate spouse, Scapegoat. Claiming that she had not taken proper care of the child, he abused her when the boy died. As a result, she committed suicide by drowning herself on a hot summer day at high noon in the main village well, a time when most people were off the lanes resting in the shade or indoors. Her body was left lying at the well so that the police could investigate the death before cremation. No one went near the corpse, nor could anyone draw water from the well. During the long hot week after the suicide, temperatures hovered between 110°F (43°C) and 115°F (46°C) while the police investigated and villagers drew their water from small wells in the fields and a few private hand pumps. The police had the body autopsied and then cremated. Because Scapegoat committed suicide and died tortured, no funeral rituals were performed in the village and it was said that Scapegoat became a ghost.

Honesty, a Brahman grandmother and friend of Scapegoat and Amiable, said that when Little Boy fell ill, the women in the household called a *siyana*, a Brahman who was a professional priest and curer, to treat the boy. He gave them a *ganda* (piece of paper with mantras written on it) and a *tawiz* (locket in which to put the *ganda*). The *ganda* in this case read: "This boy should not catch the evil eye [*nazar*], should be well, live long, and should have no Fever" (the index of ghost illness). The locket was tied around the child's neck with a blue, untwisted thread which had a series of knots in it, a protection against the evil eye, ghosts, and bad dreams of ghosts. Honesty claimed that whoever took the *tawiz* and *ganda* from the priest should have taken pills from him for the child but did not. Had Little Boy been given pills from the priest, he would have lived.

When the child became quite ill, Curmudgeon took him to a *vaid* (an Ayurvedic doctor), which action according to Honesty caused the child to die. Honesty's point of view is typical of the belief that only supernatural cures can fight off a ghost trying to seize a child. One must follow the curer's instructions completely, whether priest, bhagat, or *siyana*, or the patient will die. Instead, Curmudgeon, a strong follower of the Arya Samaj, took the child out of the priest's care. Curmudgeon blamed Scapegoat for Little Boy's death because she sought the aid of an exorcist to drive out the ghost causing Little Boy's Fever, which was contrary to his beliefs as a follower of the Arya Samaj. Blaming Scapegoat, the usual target of his rage, provided an outlet for his grief and anger.

For two months after Scapegoat died, it was rumored that a number of women had seen her ghost. A neighboring Nai Barber woman, who served Curmudgeon's family, said that she saw Scapegoat's ghost twice. Her ghost appeared to Honesty when she was in the fields. She was afraid of the ghost and ran away. The woman most troubled by her ghost had been her closest friend and next door neighbor, Amiable (age 60), the wife of Old Codger. After seeing Scapegoat's ghost, Amiable suffered from ghost illness.

Honesty, an excellent source of information about ghosts, gave Scapegoat as an example of a woman who died tortured and became a ghost because she jumped in a well and drowned. She claimed that so many males in Curmudgeon's family had died that Scapegoat committed suicide because she was tortured by grief. She added that Amiable quite often saw the ghost of Scapegoat in her dreams and that the ghost spoke to her. Amiable was frightened and fell ill. Old Codger, her husband, called a *vaid* who gave her medicine.

According to Honesty, Amiable had it in her to live and so she did.

More than two months after Scapegoat's death, Amiable was interviewed. She was first asked whether she had fallen ill because of the evil eye. She said not the evil eye, but that she saw the ghost of Scapegoat and it affected her heart. She went on to say that it was like a bad dream, a terrible nightmare. She first saw Scapegoat's ghost in a nightmare; the ghost talked to her and she replied. In describing her experience, Amiable avoided using Scapegoat's name and never said that she had deliberately committed suicide. Instead Amiable said, "She fell in the well. If a person falls in a well, then the soul is distracted and wanders. This is so for anyone who intentionally or otherwise falls in a well." Amiable added that her dead friend was grief-stricken because of many deaths in the family: first her husband when she was very young, then her son, and last of all the grandson of her sister and Curmudgeon.

Amiable described seeing Scapegoat's ghost again when she was sitting on her cot. "When The Lady [a euphemism for a female ghost] appeared, I said, 'You must go away from here. The children will be terrified; you must go away.' The ghost said, 'I have been here 27 years '" and then repeated the statement, after which Amiable fell unconscious. Although Amiable may have fainted from fear of the ghost, her unconscious state was interpreted as due to the ghost appearing before her and trying to take her soul, which resulted in the ensuing ghost illness. The 27 years referred to the time since Scapegoat's husband died (1931). Scapegoat then became a widow and a levirate spouse. Amiable noted, "Many people have seen the ghost: the barber's wife saw her twice, and other women, but most of them will not admit to having seen her. Only a person who has experienced ghost illness from seeing or being possessed by a ghost can see a ghost. If a number of people come together, the ghost vanishes. A ghost only comes to people who are alone."

OLD CODGER, BARKER, AND MRS. BARKER

In the fall of 1977, Old Codger was still alive, but his wife, Amiable, died earlier that year. Old Codger was the only man in the Junior Branch who identified ghosts and people possessed by ghosts. He mentioned the ghost possessions of his daughter-in-law, Mrs. Barker, although his son, Barker, and nephew, Reformer, were adamant that there were no ghosts. Old Codger was helpful when other people in the village suffered from possessions. According to Old Codger, two old men, Farmer, a Jat, and Withdrawn, a Brahman, had recently been possessed by the ghost of the Headless Sweeper. Old Codger brought a mullah, a Muslim exorcist, from Palam, the site of the International Airport, to exorcise the ghost. He claimed that both men had been cured by the exorcist and that the ghost of the Headless Sweeper no longer bothered anyone (Chap. 16: The Headless Sweeper; Chap. 21: Withdrawn; Chap. 22: Farmer).

Within his joint family, Old Codger had his own troubles. His son, Barker, was hit by a truck outside a police station in 1971. At the time of the accident, Barker had long been a heavy drinker and was in all likelihood an alcoholic. Villagers commented that Barker was drunk when the accident took place. A bone in his lower left leg was broken, and he had other injuries. He was said to have been in a coma for two months and in the hospital, seven months. The accident left scars on his face. Later he went to a Catholic hospital for surgery. He said that he was there for four months and spent Rs. 42,000. An orthopedic surgeon diagnosed deterioration of a bone in his left hip so that he needed an operation. The operation and hospitalization took place in 1974. A steel rod was inserted in his leg, which did not work because of bone deterioration. In 1975, the surgeon took out the rod and grafted bone in its place. Barker believed that he had been cured, as the leg was functional. He walked with a limp, used a cane, and continued to commute by bus to work.

Given the high incidence of tuberculosis in this lineage, the fact that all the houses of its members were clumped together, and that in earlier decades, members of the third, fourth, and fifth generations of the Junior Branch lived in either one or two houses together, Barker's bone deterioration may have been caused by tuberculosis (Append. IV: Maps 1 and 2). Tuberculosis may cause chronic, destructive lesions of bones and joints. Although any bones or joints may be attacked, more often the hips, spine, knees, or hands suffer (Lyght, 1956: 1137–1138; Berkow, 1982: 138).

In comparing Barker with the most notorious village alcoholic, Tippler, Helpful opined that Tippler was dangerous and hurt people while Barker's "bark was worse than his bite." He was irascible and short tempered. Two elderly Jat women, Mrs. Patriarch and her best friend, disapprovingly discussed the behavior of Barker and Tippler. Mrs. Patriarch declared, "Tippler is mean and breaks things. He used to beat his wife, but now she beats him. Barker's wife also beats him when he is drunk." Both women agreed that Barker was drunk at the time of his accident. They added, "Wives are not supposed to beat husbands. It formerly was the custom for a husband to beat his wife and then kick her out of the house. Her parents would then take her in. In time she went back to her husband. But now, sooner or later, the wife grows tired of being beaten and then beats the husband."

During the latter part of Barker's hospitalizations, which began in 1971 and stretched through 1975, his wife felt that something was pressing her chest and parts of her body at night and believed it was a ghost. In those years Mrs. Barker was 40 to 44 years old and went through her menopause, a time of stress for women, which along with the family problems may have contributed to the ghost attacks. Old Codger fetched a Muslim exorcist from Palam to exorcise the ghost and later declared that the ghost of the Headless Sweeper had troubled her. The following description fits the belief regarding a ghost trying to take Mrs. Barker's soul but is somewhat akin to sleep paralysis found among Eskimos and the Old Hag folk symptoms in Northeastern North America (Hufford, 1982; Hughes, 1985a: 3–4; 1985d: 480, 488, 495; Ness, 1985). Mrs. Barker's ghost attacks were characterized by disturbed sleep and nightmares and occurred at a time when she was much troubled by her husband's traumatic accident, its high costs, family problems, and her menopause, all of which caused intense anxiety. The nightmare element is significant, for nightmares may take place at any age.

Studies show that some take place in midlife. A large number of people with nightmares talk in their sleep. In Mrs. Barker's case, if she talked in her sleep, it may have been interpreted as a ghost speaking from her. Mental stress usually increases the frequency of nightmares. The word "nightmares" includes frightening or bad dreams and an incubus (ghost or evil spirit) attacking an adult (Kales et al., 1980: 1197, 1199). The evil spirit is believed to descend upon and have sexual intercourse with a sleeping woman (Morris, 1969: 667). Moreover, Barker when drunk may have disturbed Mrs. Barker at night, or she feared and dreamed that he would. She also may have had a guilty conscience about some of her actions as will be pointed out below. The classic example of such disturbed sleep is Shakespeare's Lady Macbeth who, suffering a mental collapse brought on by strain and the crushing disappointment of her hopes, walked and talked in her sleep (Parrott, 1938: 826; Krueger, 1989: 36; Westermeyer, 1989: 17–19). A doctor called to witness Lady Macbeth's sleepwalking offered a diagnosis that would have touched a chord in Shanti Nagar 350 years later: "[Her] heart is sorely charged. . . . Foul whisp'rings are abroad; unnatural deeds/Do breed unnatural troubles. . . . More needs she the divine than the physician" (Macbeth, Act V, Scene I).

Mrs. Barker's sleep disturbances resemble mainly a poltergeist, a ghost which infests a house or workplace, especially in the form of someone or something pressing her at night. Recently it has been found that poltergeists may be related to intrapsychic and interpersonal family or community conflicts, which sometimes are resolved as a result of the poltergeist (Hess, 1989). This type of ghost will be described in more detail in the case of Farmer, also a Jat (Chap. 22).

Barker's eldest son had married and remained living jointly with his father and grandfather, Old Codger. He worked in the same government department as his father. This son's wife had borne five children (Generation VII) but three of them, an only daughter and two of four sons, died shortly after birth during Barker's hospitalizations. The surviving children were two sons, one born in 1971 before Barker's accident, and the other, the couple's fifth child, born in 1977 two years after Barker's last operation. The mother, age 24 to 25 at the time of the interview, stated that all her children were born about a year apart and that the three dead infants were premature births not fully formed. It seems odd that the second child was born about a year after the first if the mother nursed the first surviving child, because nursing contributes to amenorrhea and associated anovulation so that a nursing mother usually does not conceive. The fact that this woman's first child was normal at birth and survived raises the question of why the following children were premature. One possibility is that her mother-in-law, Mrs. Barker, may have beaten her during her pregnancies (Chap. 14: Daughter-in-law vs. Mother-in-law). It was not unusual for a first infant to be premature and die but less common for successive births to a young woman (R. Freed and S. Freed, 1985: 131, 135). For three children out of five to die shortly after birth was no longer as customary as it had been in earlier times, especially in a family whose head consulted modern Western medical physicians and was treated by them. In the case of Barker's eldest son's wife, the first surviving child was delivered by the government midwife, the next two children by the village midwife. The information about the birth of the fourth child was vague and may have been by another village midwife or the government midwife. When Barker recovered, his son's last child was delivered in a hospital and survived.

Obtaining exact information about these deaths was difficult. Old Codger, 79 years old and the great grandfather of the children, answered the questions for the household census. His information regarding the sex and birth order of the infants was incorrect. The children's mother gave the correct information in our Medical Childbirth Survey (1978). When the session began, she was alone with the interviewer. By the fourth question her mother-in-law, Mrs. Barker, entered the house and stopped the interview by telling her daughter-in-law to take her bath and then wash clothes. When the interviewer returned about an hour later, Mrs. Barker told the interviewer that her daughter-in-law was still bathing, and it was obvious that Mrs. Barker would not allow the session to continue.

From 1971 through 1975 was a chaotic time in the household due to Barker's drinking, accident, and hospitalizations. As a result, the daughter-in-law did not have adequate medical care although Barker did. In addition to worries about her husband and a chaotic household, Mrs. Barker's poltergeist attacks may have been partially due to a guilty conscience about the three infant deaths of her son's wife and that of her own infant daughter in 1961. Two of Mrs. Barker's three infant grandchildren who died were males and all three died immediately after birth. Infanticide of male babies is extremely rare, but Mrs. Barker may have beaten her daughter-in-law during her pregnancies and called the village midwife because it was more convenient than sending for the government midwife, despite the latter's superior training. Thereafter she may subconsciously have rationalized the deaths of her grandchildren as somewhat fortuitous, relieving her of the burden of three newborn infants during Barker's hospitalizations.

REFORMER AND FAMILY

Old Codger's nephew, Reformer, contracted pulmonary tuberculosis five years before Timely, the wife of Taciturn. He was cured circa 1969 to 1970. In 1971 or 1972, he was voluntarily sterilized. He had begun practicing birth control in the 1950s but said that his wife was not enthusiastic about a limited number of children. Therefore, to avoid further conceptions he had a vasectomy after the birth of his fourth child and second son. In a number of ways, Reformer's life was quite successful. He earned a Junior Basic Training degree and began to teach the lower grades when he was 22. By 1973 at the age of 41, he was headmaster of his school. In 1974, his mother, the sister of Amiable, died. After recovering from tuberculosis, Reformer was careful about his health and that of his family. He, his wife, and four children were consistently clean and neat (Append. III: Chart 2.3).

Reformer discussed his own and village health practices. He said that the Government had promised to send medical personnel to visit the villages, but by 1977–78 none had yet come to Shanti Nagar. The plan was to provide medicine for villagers. Mainly the medical visitors were to distribute medicine (chloroquine) for malaria, tell people about the medicine, and keep them posted about medical developments. However, there was another channel for sending malaria medicine to villages. The pradhan, head of the village council, gave out medicine for malaria free of charge. In 1977, the distribution ended on November 1. However, one could have malaria throughout the year.

Reformer and the members of his family each took two tablets of chloroquine once a week to prevent malaria. Reformer also kept medicine and equipment for giving injections in his house, and he, his wife, and eldest son gave injections of streptomycin and penicillin. His wife, who had pains in her joints, took daily doses of both *Tandran* (a commercial medicine) and penicillin. Family members purchased both medicines in the market place. For eye infections, they kept a tube of terramycin ointment. For eczema, they used an ointment called *Betnovate*. Reformer called these products *Angrezi* (English) medicine, a synonym for Western medicine. Reformer thought that *Angrezi* medicine was better than desi (indigenous) medicine which he equated with Ayurvedic medicine. He did not trust it although he once used it. He claimed *Angrezi* medicine worked faster and commented that there was no point in staying in bed for ten days and wasting money. Thus, Reformer was an advocate of Western medicine and more informed about it than most villagers.

As a Jat and Arya Samaji, he did not believe in ghosts, ghost illness, and ghost possession. He said that what Illusionist, one of the village exorcists, did was false and that he did not trust him because one day he almost killed a boy. In June–July 1977, one of the Nai Barber boys was ill from typhoid and ran a very high temperature. The boy's father called Illusionist to exorcise the illness. Reformer went there to see what was going on and told the boy's father and other members of the family to ignore Illusionist and take the boy to a hospital. They would not listen to him, but when another man also told them to take the boy to the hospital, they did. He was in the hospital a month and almost went mad. The physicians said that had the boy stayed in the village another night he would have died. Reformer added that nonliterate people do not want to spend money on medicine. He said, "They call a bhagat. The people who call a bhagat believe that a ghost gets into the person."

When Reformer was asked about the ghost possession of a young bride in 1958, he replied, "About fifty years ago, the women did a lot of work in the house, much more than now. In order to have an excuse from all the work, they acted as though they were possessed and arranged with a bhagat to tell their in-laws not to make them work so hard. Now they do not have as much work, but young girls have problems because of their menses and leukorrhea so they call a bhagat instead of going to a physician."

On the subject of women's problems, Reformer discussed the midwives who delivered infants. His wife had the government midwife deliver her infants from the time this midwife was first introduced in the 1950s. Reformer said they were trained for the work and, therefore, should be used. Because she used the government midwife, his wife had no problems when she was delivered of her four children. However, as a nonsequitur, he mentioned that one of his sons was ill about one-and-one-half years after birth. He had diarrhea, which infants may have if given food other than mother's milk at that age (Wyon and Gordon, 1971: 187–188), and eczema so Reformer took the boy to a hospital. He was then all right.

Reformer had picked up some knowledge of Western medicine because he went to a Western medical doctor whenever anyone in the family was ill. He read the prescriptions and asked the physician about the illness. The doctor whom he consulted was in private practice in a nearby town. Another physician in the nearby Catholic dispensary taught Reformer how to give injections. Reformer knew the nuns at the Catholic clinic quite well and invited them to hold Catholic song sessions in his house. He showed interest in Catholicism, seeking information about the differences between Catholicism and Protestantism. He may have influenced Barker's decision to go to a Catholic hospital.

Reformer ran his farm systematically, regularly having his soil and seeds tested at the Pusa Agricultural Institute. He used the most advanced agricultural implements then available in the region. He owned not only his own tractor, trolley, and thresher, but also a mill for grinding grain for villagers, a service for which he charged. While he taught school, his wife and eldest son ran the mill and tractor. In 1978 his wife was the first and sole woman in the village not only to run a tractor but also to be elected to the village council.

Without mentioning the incidence of tuberculosis in Reformer's lineage, which could have put him on the defensive, but because of it and the possibility that an infection of tuberculosis, and perhaps other diseases, could spread from cattle, we interviewed Reformer about cattle disease, the treatment of milk, and contagion in general. Concerning cattle disease, he said:

It is up to the farmer to see that cattle are inoculated by the government veterinarians. Usually the farmer calls them and has his cattle inoculated. Sometimes the veterinarians come about every one to two years. For inoculations, however, the Government does not have a good arrangement; they don't come regularly. They should come at least every six months. When they come, it is proclaimed by the village watchman beating drums. When the cattle make a gargling sound in their throats, it is a sign of an infectious disease so they then inoculate the cattle. This disease is neither a cough nor pneumonia, but the windpipe constricts so it is difficult for the animal to breathe.

Reformer named two remedies for this disease. A veterinarian may be called to inoculate, but some people heat an iron instrument and mark the neck of the animal. Reformer did not recommend the latter remedy.

Reformer said that cattle might suffer from fever if they have pneumonia or *afara* (indigestion or wind in the stomach). He claimed never to have heard of an epidemic among cattle, but in fact he had. He opposed the holding of Akhta, a rite to exorcise epidemics of cattle disease. In 1958 when an epidemic of cattle disease took place, the villagers held Akhta to drive out the disease, but they did so then and thereafter when Reformer was absent from the village (R. Freed and S. Freed, 1966).

The question of the transmission to humans of disease from cattle was raised especially because bovine tuberculosis can be transmitted through drinking infected raw milk. It spreads from the milk of cattle to the intestines of humans and thence to any part of the body but most often to lymph nodes or bones (Myers, 1977: Chap. VII). Reformer did not mention this possibility and seemed to see few potential health risks from cattle. He mentioned only the possibility that cattle might cause eczema (*khaj*), but he was not sure. However, he was emphatic about the need to boil milk before drinking it. He said, "You will find many who drink milk without boiling it, but I do not because I have read that it should be boiled, and doctors say milk should be boiled before drinking it. Most people do not know much about boiling milk." However, many women left a pot of milk heating over smoldering dung cakes for hours, a treatment which might have pasteurized the milk, but due to exposure in the air and no control over the actual temperature, might not have. Any milk not drunk the day it was drawn was converted to butter and then to ghee because of lack of refrigeration. According to the United States Public Health Service, *Mycobacterium tuberculosis* can be destroyed by heating milk to a temperature of 143°F (61.7°C) maintained continuously for at least 30 minutes. Milk can be pasteurized in 15 seconds at a temperature of 161°F (71.7°C) (Lyght, 1956: 1516; Wingate, 1972: 434–436; R. Freed and S. Freed, 1979: 331; 1985: 137, fn.13). Davey and Wilson (1971: 265) stated that in the tropics, "Milk should be pasteurized at a temperature high enough to kill all organisms (80°C (176°F) for one minute is recommended). . . ."

On the subject of contagious disease in general, Reformer said "Educated people understand [contagion]. I have the members of my family inoculated regularly against diseases. When my 12-year-old son was born, I called the government midwife, who reports the birth and sees that a man in the health department of the Government inoculates new born children with BCG [against TB] and with other vaccines" (Append. I: Discoveries: 1913–21, Tuberculosis [for BCG];

and Descriptions: Diphtheria; Tetanus; Pertussis [for DTP]).

CURMUDGEON, CATTLEMAN, SOLDIER, AND FAMILIES

In 1977–78, Curmudgeon, an elderly widower, lived with his youngest son, Cattleman, Cattleman's wife, and their five children: two sons and three daughters (Generation VI) (Append. III: Chart 2.3). Cattleman had become a veterinarian and was employed in a government program for milk production. He commuted daily to Delhi for work. None of his children had died, but his oldest child, a daughter, aged 15, dropped out of school after finishing sixth grade because of pulmonary tuberculosis. Cattleman regularly took her to a city hospital for treatment.

Cattleman's elder brother, Soldier, had retired from the army and returned to the village with a second mate, Concubine, and their children. His levirate spouse, Misfortune, was still alive with three surviving daughters but no sons after Little Boy died in 1958. Soldier spoke of Concubine as his wife. Although she may have gone through a wedding ceremony with him, no one mentioned having attended such a ceremony. He and Misfortune had not gone through the standard Hindu wedding ceremony because she was a levirate spouse. Concubine was 15 years younger than Soldier and gave him two sons and one daughter. She was a resolute, physically powerful woman willing to challenge men to a fight and quite capable of beating them. Her combative nature may have derived partly from her somewhat ambiguous status as wife. The two women, their children, and Soldier lived separately from Curmudgeon and Cattleman (Append. III: Chart 2.3). Soldier worked in the city as a bus conductor after leaving the army, but while boarding a moving bus he broke his kneecap. He had a long horizontal scar on his leg and could not bend his knee easily. After this injury, he worked in the bus company's office.

One day Concubine went to her natal village to obtain a powder for Soldier's indigestion. After some questioning about his ailment, Soldier stated that eight years previously when he lived in Delhi with friends, he ate out a great deal, attended many marriages and parties, drank a lot of liquor, and started smoking marijuana (cannabis). He claimed that this behavior spoiled his digestion and so he began taking a powder with opium in it for his digestion, which Concubine obtained for him. It was not unusual to find opium in some patent medicines. For example, in one Jat family, a patent medicine containing opium was given to a small infant so that he would stop crying and go to sleep.

According to Soldier, some years earlier his first spouse, Misfortune, had Fever and walked to a nearby clinic for injections. She walked back to the village in a high wind and driving rain. After that, one of her legs was partially paralyzed. She was no longer able to walk normally, had a swelling in her shoulder, and suffered acute pain. Soldier spent Rs. 400 to 500 on her treatment, claiming her illness was due to something wrong with her veins from taking too much medicine. Since there was no relief and Soldier was reluctant to spend more, she went to Illusionist, the exorcist, for relief. He prescribed ground pigeon excreta as an internal medicine. Ground birds' excreta was one remedy among his roster of medications. Sometimes when her pain was extreme, Misfortune had Home Trained, the Nai Barber, give her an injection.

Concubine also had an ailment. She had a boil or chancre which had grown inward. For a month, Soldier spent Rs. 1200 to Rs. 1300 for a series of treatments by different curers, more than he spent on Misfortune. Finally he located a surgeon in private practice, who formerly practiced in a tuberculosis hospital. This doctor gave Concubine some injections and capsules. He charged Rs. 52. When it was suggested that Concubine should go to a hospital, Soldier said, "There would be too many difficulties. A woman would have to stay with her and someone would have to bring her food daily," thus reducing the number of women for work in the house and fields.

Concubine described her illness as a swelling on her right shoulder which caused acute pain. She attributed it to something having gone wrong with her veins and blood. Although first she went to the doctor, she claimed he was no use. She then consulted a *vaid*, who gave her some medicine to mix with ground pigeon excreta. She made a paste of the mixture and applied it to the swelling.

She planned to have an operation if the paste provided no relief from the pain.

During the wheat harvest in the spring of 1978, we noticed Soldier watching Misfortune, Concubine, and his daughter while they were cutting wheat. Misfortune was obviously crippled in one leg. Later as the sun was setting, the poor woman limped home alone. Her teen-age daughter was as yet unmarried. She was mildly retarded and attended the first grade for seven years before dropping out of school. She was a pleasant teenager, willing and able to work under directions, but was seldom, if ever, left alone.

In 1979, Soldier, age 46, died. We were informed of his death by mail with no details other than that the cause of death was paralysis, which covers a number of possible diseases (Berkow, 1982: 207, table 12–5, 209, 1616, 1617, 1359). The afflictions of Soldier, Misfortune, and Concubine may have been due to tuberculosis, venereal syphilis, or both. Although venereal diseases are frequently found in men who serve in the army, the possibility of tuberculosis exists for these three people because of the history of tuberculosis in the lineage, which like syphilis has skin and bone lesions as symptoms. However, the symptoms of Soldier, Misfortune, and Concubine tend toward syphilis. Soldier's knee injury may have contributed to deterioration of the bone as in Barker's case, but since the cause of his death was described by the vague term paralysis, venereal syphilis may have invaded his central nervous system while he was in military service. Syphilis goes through three stages, is not always discovered in the first stage, and may be relatively quiescent in the first and second stages (Wingate, 1972: 407–408; Berkow, 1982: 1616–1619; Append. I: Descriptions—Syphilis). If syphilis is discovered and properly treated with penicillin in the first stage, it can be cured. The description of Misfortune's limp and paralysis of one leg could have been an indication of tabes dorsalis (locomotor ataxia), which begins with pain, affects the legs, results in an unsteady gait, and indicates a late stage of syphilis, which has affected the central nervous system (Wingate, 1972: 408; Berkow, 1982: 1619). Thus, it would seem that in 1978, Misfortune may have been in a later stage of syphilis than Concubine. Concubine's chancre would have been the first sign of having been infected by syphilis. We do not know when it first took place. This primary lesion, called a chancre, generally appears in the first stage of syphilis within four to eight weeks of the infection and may be found on a number of parts of the body (Berkow, 1982: 1617). The original source of syphilitic infection for these two women would appear to have been from Soldier. In 1978, Soldier too had a limp, which he attributed to breaking a kneecap when he boarded a moving bus. If he was syphilitic, the disease was most probably acquired when he was in the army and by 1978 he was in the third and last stage of the disease. It is possible that he knew he had syphilis and would never acknowledge it, or it may never have been discovered by the usual test for syphilis. Soldier's life history and personality fit the type of soldier most apt to contract a venereal disease: drinking a lot, smoking marijuana, coming from a large family, having a limited education, and intercourse at an young age due to early marriage in India (Hart, 1973: 542, 546). Army service when young and long absences from his older, levirate spouse freed him from family responsibilities and the usual authority of Curmudgeon, the head of the joint family.

No villagers noted cases of venereal disease in the village, even when questioned during the Health Opinion Survey, and it is doubtful that they would have mentioned any. A visit to another village in this region with a team of medical workers for the World Health Organization revealed that venereal diseases were a problem in the Delhi villages, possibly because of their nearness to the city, but the health workers mentioned that it was difficult to get the men to say so (Lyght, 1956: 652, 653, 1137, 1536, 1606, 1607–1608, 1695–1697; Davey and Wilson, 1971: 127, Chap. XI; Wingate, 1972: 407–408; 433–436; 446; Berkow, 1982: 127–128, 135, 138, 1616–1619).

A GROUP DISCUSSION

Toward the end of our fieldwork when malaria and ghost epidemics struck Shanti Nagar in March–April 1978 along with the rise in daily temperatures, we interviewed a number of Jats from both branches of Old Fever and Helpful, a Jat from another lineage, about ghosts and illness (Append. VII: Daily Temperatures, March–April 1978). We began with Old Codger, a lively, chatty elder, who was sitting in the sun outside his *baithak* with little to do at his age other than talk with neighbors and visitors. In 1958–59, he had told us about the ghost of the Headless Sweeper and in 1977–78 again told about this ghost. The Headless Sweeper, who had become a bogeyman to scare children and susceptible adults, was the only ghost named by Old Codger, which suggested that he liked to tell the tale but may not have been too interested in ghosts (for the two versions, see Chap. 16). Old Codger may have retained some of his early ghost beliefs but was also influenced by the Arya Samaj.

After three Jat men, Barker, Politico, and Helpful joined us, Old Codger said, "I have never seen a ghost myself. Ghosts are just air which can be seen by some people but not by everyone." Although Old Codger may have wanted to entertain us with the tale of the Headless Sweeper, when the other men joined the group, all ardent followers of the Arya Samaj, he took a different stance. We then asked whether it might not be better to talk with women about ghosts because they know more about them than do the men. Old Codger replied, "Yes, you're telling the truth. Women have smaller hearts so they are afraid of ghosts." The implication of fear owing to smaller hearts followed the stereotypes regarding women, men, fear, and ghosts.

Helpful then added, "There is no such thing as a ghost, but the women here believe in them. Do you have ghosts in America? If you do, how do the ghosts come and overpower other people?" (i.e., possess them). We answered, "Some people believe in ghosts and others do not in America, just as in this village."

Barker launched into a semantic explanation pertaining to ghosts. He said, "*Bhut* means past. There is *bhut kal*, past time, and *vart* (*vartman*) *kal*, present time. Then there is *bhawishya kal*, future time. We have the past, present, and future so this is how I have interpreted the word *bhut*, or the belief in ghosts. Only foolish people will think about the past. One should make efforts for the present and future and not the past." Since

Pathak (1976: 827) stated that in addition to its meanings of ghost, demon, and evil spirit, *bhut* also means past or past time, Barker had grounds for his interpretation.

Barker's viewpoint derives from the teachings of Swami Dayanand Saraswati (1956: 45–47) showing that the Sanskrit words *bhuta* and *preta* are not synonymous with ghosts, spirits, genii, goblins, etc. Saraswati defines *preta* as the body of a dead person and *bhuta*, a body which has been cremated. He wrote that these words are used to indicate that the dead persons lived in past times.

Politico then explained the connection of supernatural beings and disease in terms of a lack of medical knowledge in former times. "In olden times when there were no hospitals or clinics, people called diseases bhut. Take tuberculosis for example, they called it bhut or *ghal*, [which he said meant killer or destroyer]. When a patient lay unconscious, they thought it was due to some supernatural being." Thus, he was referring to one of the alternate states in ghost illness or possession.

The group was then asked for the differences between the following words: bhut, *ghal*, *oopra*, *hawa*, preta, and jinn. Helpful responded, "All of these words are one and the same. In a way, they are similar to the many words for Bhagwan [God]. They derive from prevalent beliefs in early times, which were due to lack of education and medical knowledge."

Old Codger commented on *ghal*, "Previously when someone was suffering from TB, people did not understand this disease. There was no sure cure for TB so they would say that a ghost put this killer [*ghal*] in a man. The man then died in one to three years if he had TB." Helpful chimed in, "Now they have a hospital in Kingsway Camp which specializes in this disease." Others present added, "There are a number of places where TB is treated. They admit the patient, give him x-rays, check his blood, urine, and other things. They test the blood to see if there is any deficiency in it."

When asked what causes TB, Helpful replied, "It is due to hard work." Barker answered, "Something affects the lungs. There are three stages. In the first stage, it can be cured." Old Codger added, "Some worms inside the lungs cause TB. The doctors can see

and kill the worms." Helpful stated, "They can see them in the x-ray and then provide medicine and injections so the worms are killed." The Atharva-Veda lists worms as one of five causes of disease. Ancient Egyptians also had the idea that disease could be due to worms (Kutumbiah, 1969: 78–79; Myers, 1977: 10).

Helpful then asked us, "Do germs cause contagious disease?" We answered, "Yes." He dissented, "It is not so. TB is not a contagious disease. These germs are present in everybody." Both Helpful and Old Codger had seen x-rays of lungs and saw what they thought were worms, which they equated with germs. The concept of germs held by most villagers was little more than semantic, for few villagers had studied enough science in school to understand the concept. Furthermore, villagers thought that tuberculosis was inherited, which accords with the ancient belief that phthisis, pulmonary tuberculosis, is inherited and therefore cannot be contagious (Bühler, 1969: 76; Myers, 1977: 13). In a survey about the causes of tuberculosis taken in Ludhiana, Punjab, and Lucknow, Uttar Pradesh, Taylor (1976: 295, table 7) found that one of the causes given was "germs in the lung," a response similar to Old Codger's statement of worms in the lungs and Helpful's remark that these germs are present in everyone.

Then Barker interjected, "After 40 years of age, no one can have TB." When asked about BCG, Barker said that BCG is not an inoculation for a disease; it is the name of a person who invented the inoculation for TB. He then distinguished between inoculations to prevent disease and injections once one has a disease. He was half right and half wrong about BCG (Bacillus Calmette-Guérin), for it is a vaccine named after the people who developed it, Albert Calmette and Camille Guérin. In 1978, the Government used it as an inoculation against tuberculosis, but it does not provide permanent immunity (Append. I: Discoveries—1913–21, Tuberculosis; Descriptions—Tuberculosis).

Barker's statement, "After 40 years of age no one can have TB," is false but has long been accepted, possibly due to the short life span in past times. For India in the 1960s, the average age at which TB infection took place was 15; the average active case might not be identified until age 39. Thus an early infection might not become active until later in life (McCreary, 1968: 699). In recent years up to 1978 in the United States, most active cases occurred in older individuals (Berkow, 1982: 127). TB has been on the rise in the United States during the past decade or so; for example, in New York City the number of cases almost tripled from 1978 to 1990. Usually tuberculosis is contracted early although it may not result in the disease, or may be activated or reactivated later in life. On the other hand it is possible to contract tuberculosis at a later age (Myers, 1977: xvii, 159–160). In the City of Delhi the prevalence of tuberculosis for males shows a steady increase with age. For females, prevalence reaches its peak about 25 to 35 years of age (Goyal et al., 1978: 77). Gothi (1982: 135) reported that infection rates increase with age for both sexes up to 45 to 54 years of age. The rate of increase slows for females after age 15. Infection rates were about the same for the rural and urban areas of Delhi.

Politico, an impatient man who did not want to waste time, rose to leave. Before his departure, we inquired about the number of people in the village currently suffering from malaria and tuberculosis. All answered, "Many." Politico said "Ten to 16 have malaria. I can't tell for sure how many have TB." Barker rejoined, "If people will not tell when they have TB, they will die. They cannot hide the sickness and need to be treated. They should not feel bad about it because there is no connection between disease and moral character. A disease can visit anyone, but due to deficiency in intelligence, people tell no one and do nothing. If you don't know something, there is no harm or sin in asking and finding out." Barker's statement about there being no connection between disease and moral character is interesting, for in effect he was saying that actions (karma) in the past and present do not cause misfortune or retribution in the form of illness. But he expressed the same opinion earlier when he said, "Only foolish people will think about the past. One should make efforts for the present and future and not the past."

The men were then asked why science, which would be helpful in understanding disease, had not been introduced in the schools earlier than was the case. Barker answered, "I do not think you can start science education very early because young children do not have enough brain. Here they start teaching science in the sixth class. The first subject taught is hygiene, for which they have an expert teacher. Once or twice I have talked with teachers, and they agree with me about the subject and the books used. If the child has good marks in hygiene, it means that the child is doing well."

We asked, "Do young children ever say anything about hygiene or cleanliness?" Barker replied, "My children don't have a chance to comment because my wife keeps a very clean house. She is very particular about cleanliness. She cleans the nooks and corners of all the utensils. Using cups is unhygienic because there may be cracks in them so we drink from glasses, and from cups only without cracks. When I am not at home, I don't take tea from any shop and I use my own glass." The practice of drinking from glasses instead of cups which might have cracks in them was known, but not always observed, throughout the village. However, it was not linked with the fear of contagious diseases but with avoidance of dirt and Hindu pollution concepts. Although contagion was not well understood by many villagers, some village sufferers from tuberculosis followed medical instructions from TB clinics to keep their own dishes and utensils separate from those of other family members and to clean them themselves (R. Freed and S. Freed, 1985: 189).

In spite of Barker's emphasis on cleanliness, one of his current practices led to adverse village comment, although it probably was the result of circumstances. After having recovered from his accident and hospitalizations but still suffering from lameness, he did not follow the village custom of going to the fields to defecate and urinate. Instead he performed these functions on his roof-top reportedly without benefit of a chamber pot or a sweeper to clean up after him. The use of a chamber pot and/or sweeper would have made the situation acceptable to village opinion. Comparable adjustments were made by other villagers who were incapacitated or too ill to use the fields.

COMPARISON OF THE MERCHANT-MUSLIM-PRIEST AND OLD-FEVER LINEAGES

Although the lineages represent two castes, Brahman and Jat, each with its own subculture, in earlier times members of both castes believed in ghosts, ghost illness, and ghost possession. In 1923, the Jats adopted the Arya Samaj, which recognizes but one God, Bhagwan, and renounces multiple deities and ghosts. The Brahmans continue to follow the more traditional beliefs of Sanatan Dharma. Ghost illness, possession, and protective ancestral spirits fit easily into the beliefs and daily lives of the Brahman lineage (Merchant, Muslim, Priest), especially the pitris, whose memory is passed on from generation to generation. The Jat lineage (Old Fever) shows greater diversity of belief as befits the relatively recent change in ideology brought about by the Arya Samaj. The Junior Branch of Old Fever represents a more complete switch from beliefs in multiple supernatural beings to one deity and a disavowal of ghosts than does the Senior Branch. This viewpoint was best expressed by Barker in the preceding group discussion. However, older members of the Junior Branch still retained noteworthy beliefs in ghosts and supernatural curing, as was indicated by Old Codger's securing a Muslim exorcist from Palam to treat Mrs. Barker's poltergeist attacks and Scapegoat's earlier recourse to a *siyana* for Little Boy.

Members of both lineages hold some of the same theories about various illnesses, for example, the belief that tuberculosis and edema are inherited. The belief about tuberculosis is stated in the Laws of Manu and reiterated by Saraswati. This theory was reinforced by the number of people in the Old Fever lineage who contracted TB and the two children in Conductor's family believed to have died of dropsy interpreted as an inherited disease although they probably died because they ate mud, thus ingesting helminths which could have blocked the lymphatic system. The belief that past actions determine illness and other unhappy events during one's lifetime was generally accepted in the village despite the statements of Barker.

In both lineages, the ghosts most remembered from early times were males, many of whom died without issue in Generations I and II. In the Merchant-Muslim-Priest lineage, the best remembered ghosts are Merchant and Muslim Ghost because of the well-known legend about them and the retention of Brahmanical beliefs in ghosts. In this lineage, female ghosts in later generations are remembered because of the belief that first wives who die and become ghosts will haunt the second wives of their husbands. Examples are the first wives of Progenitor, Luck, and Security Officer. In the Old Fever lineage, the ghosts recalled by Dancer and Long Lived, who knew them during their lifetimes, were males in the Senior Branch who died during the plague and influenza epidemics. They were Capable; his brother, Fateful; their cousin, Old Groom; and Ill Fated, the brother of Taciturn and Forceful. With the introduction of the Arya Samaj in 1923, the men in the Junior Branch of Old Fever no longer referred to ghosts who in life had been members of their lineage. However, Amiable, the wife of Old Codger, described how the ghost of Scapegoat possessed her and caused her to fall ill. Old Codger, who like his neighbor and age-mate, Raconteur, liked to spin a good yarn, recounted the legend of the Headless Sweeper and described how Mrs. Barker, his daughter-in-law, had been attacked by the Headless Sweeper. The Sweeper, however, was not a member of his lineage, but a Chuhra Sweeper. Despite the Arya-Samaj beliefs among the Jats, some Jat women believed in ghosts.

In both lineages, some ghosts (Merchant, Old Priest, and Capable) evolved from bhuts to pitris, and Muslim Ghost, Merchant's familiar, became benevolent after supplication by Merchant and later was promoted by Raconteur to a sayyid, indicating he had more power than a pir (Kakar, 1983: 63). Although the Senior Branch of Old Fever worshiped at the ancestral shrine of Capable, the father of Taciturn and Forceful, the Junior Branch practiced no comparable ancestor veneration. The Brahmans not only worshiped at the ancestral shrine of Merchant, but set up a new shrine for Old Priest, who was a member of the lineage through adoption.

Brahmans have a tradition of acting as exorcists and Jats do not. In the Brahman lineage, Merchant was an exorcist; Old Priest was also a hakim and practiced exorcism, serving among others the Gola Potters; New Priest occasionally practiced as an exorcist for the Gola Potters, thus following in the footsteps of Old Priest. As far as is known, Merchant was the first to establish the tradition of curing in his lineage; Raconteur worked in a pharmacy, and later as a government vaccinator. The culmination of this line of curing in the 1970s was the son of Security Officer, Physician, who in military service obtained the MBBS in Western medicine. He and his brother, Young Lawyer, exemplified the advantage the Brahman lineage had over the Jat lineage regarding education, although one village Jat had become a lawyer. The greater degree of education in the Brahman lineage did not seriously affect the belief in ghosts. From the time that Old Priest was adopted into the lineage until his death, he strongly influenced the children of the lineage. After his death, Raconteur elaborated the legend of Merchant and Muslim Ghost. Although the Jat lineage had no exorcists among its members, in 1977–78 a bhagat regularly visited Forceful and Politico, but the nature of his visits was not revealed. The Senior Branch continued the custom of having a Brahman Priest act as their family priest; in 1978 Raconteur fulfilled this function.

CHAPTER 14: DEATH OF CHILDREN

Women who were born in the last decade of the 19th century or the first two decades of the 20th century often said that formerly all their infants and small children died. They blamed their deaths on ghosts. A few children died in accidents, and an unknown number were victims of infanticide, many probably from deliberate neglect. But the prevalence of infectious disease marked by Fever led villagers, especially mothers, to attribute the great majority of infant deaths to ghosts.

PREGNANCY, DEATHS OF INFANTS AND CHILDREN, AND GHOSTS

Whether fetuses, infants, and children become ghosts and for how long depends on their age at death in terms of three basic principles: (1) the soul vests in a fetus in the sixth month of pregnancy, (2) until six years of age, a child does not know the difference between good and bad actions, and (3) the time allotted by Yama or Bhagwan for a soul to live. Therefore, in the case of a fetus, death before the sixth month cannot result in a ghost, for the fetus has not yet acquired a soul. From the point of view of the villagers, an induced abortion in the first trimester is uncompli-cated by concern about taking the life of a human being endowed with a soul. Theoretically, villagers would regard an induced abortion in the fourth and fifth months in the same light; however, the sterilization program of the Government of India avoids induced abortions after the first trimester because of the risk of complications (Berkow, 1982: 1706–1707, 1723–1724).

When spontaneous abortions, popularly called miscarriages, take place, the soul has not yet vested unless the fetus is six months old or older. If a fetus or premature infant dies any time after the soul has vested, it is considered the equivalent of a live infant dying, and believers in ghosts blame a ghost for taking the infant's soul. If a premature infant or a mature infant dies shortly after birth, their souls become ghosts, but only for a short time, namely, the 13 days after cremation. When a child survives childbirth but dies before the age of six years, it is assumed that the soul had not yet accumulated bad actions in its recent life, and the death is attributed to bad actions in past lives. The soul of such a child suffers the same fate as that of an aborted fetus after the vesting of the soul or a stillbirth (technically, death of a fetus after the 28th week of pregnancy or at delivery); it may become a ghost but only for 13 days.

Villagers believe that a soul may be reborn in the same family. This possibility depends on the timing of a death and a subsequent conception in the family. According to one belief, the soul of a dead ancestor cannot enter into a fetus until a year from the ancestor's death when the mourning period ends. For example, if a person dies at the same time that an infant is conceived, the soul of the dead person cannot vest in that fetus. If a person dies at least one year before a woman's sixth month of pregnancy, the soul may vest in her fetus except when it is believed to have become a wandering ghost. An alternative theory, which is not well known, is that the soul is eligible for rebirth after the thirteenth day from death. The soul then may enter the fetus of a woman who is in her sixth month of pregnancy.

Some villagers believe that a soul may be reborn at any time. This belief may have derived from early Ayurvedic medical theory, for Susruta, the early Ayurvedic physician, taught that the fertilized ovum is endowed with a soul (K. B. Rao, 1952: 210). Kutumbiah (1969: 2–4) expanded this theory, claiming that two Ayurvedic physicians, Charaka and Susruta, believed that when the semen of the male joined with the secretions of the female, the soul came in touch with these substances and the embryo was formed. Parkin (1988: 3–9) presented variant beliefs from Middle India regarding an ancestral soul vesting intergenerationally.

DEATH: TERMS, TIMES, CAUSES, AND CASES

The following biomedical terms and related time periods pertinent to infant mortality are used here. (1) If a pregnancy ends with the delivery of a dead fetus less than 28 weeks from conception, it is classified as an abortion, whether spontaneous or induced. (2) If the fetus dies any time after the 28th week of pregnancy up to the time of delivery or is dead at delivery, it is classified as a stillbirth. This statement is qualified by the medical terminology for a *premature birth*, which applies to delivery between the 20th week and the 38th week of pregnancy. "Pregnancy is

considered to last 266 days from the time of conception or 280 days from the first day of the last menstrual period if menses are regular at 28 days" (Berkow, 1982: 1710). "Delivery between 20 and 38 wk is considered *premature birth*" (Berkow, 1982: 1723). (Note: 38 weeks = 266 days.) (3) If an infant dies in the period from birth to the seventh day after birth, the death is termed perinatal. Villagers mark this last period by the ceremony of Mother Sixth (Chhathi), celebrated on the sixth day from birth; they recognize the first six days as the most dangerous time for the survival of mother and child. (4) Deaths of children after the perinatal period but within the first 28 days after birth are classified as neonatal deaths. (5) Deaths of children who die in the remainder of the first year from birth are designated as postneonatal deaths (Davey and Wilson, 1971: 376–377; Wyon and Gordon, 1971: 152).

Many of our findings in the late 1950s in Shanti Nagar are similar to those of the Khanna study carried out in 11 villages in the Ludhiana District of Punjab from 1953 to 1960. A prominent similarity is the noteworthy number of stillbirths and spontaneous abortions, especially for primiparous mothers and for older women (ca. 35 years old or older), who already had born four or more children. First pregnancies had the greatest possibility for spontaneous abortions, stillbirths, perinatal, and neonatal deaths. Tetanus neonatorum appeared to be the greatest cause of perinatal deaths although government trained midwives had been instructed to tell the village midwives to request a new, clean, unused knife when cutting the umbilical cord rather than a sickle or any implement used for agricultural or household tasks (Chandrasekhar, 1959: 115–118, 136, Chap. IV; Gordon et al., 1965a; Wyon and Gordon, 1971: 160–161, 184; Padmanabha, 1982: 1288–1289; Levine, 1987: 293–297; Append. I: Descriptions—Tetanus).

In 1977–78, we asked a group of men whether they bought clean, unused knives or scissors for the midwife to use when she delivered an infant. They asked why such implements should be used. When we explained the risk of tetanus neonatorum, they claimed never to have heard that this disease was the cause of many infant deaths. Village men regarded childbirth as women's business and showed little interest in it. They were barred by custom from attending a delivery. Moreover, childbirth was considered to be ritually polluting. Depending on the caste, in prior times the husbands generally did not see their wives and infants until seven to ten days after delivery. However, this practice began to change at the end of the 1950s and had changed by the 1970s. Fathers saw their infants a day or two after delivery except in very strict orthodox Brahman families (R. Freed and S. Freed, 1980: 383).

Tetanus neonatorum has been a major persistent health problem in India. The incidence and mortality rate of the disease for the years 1965 and 1975 in the Union Territory of Delhi, despite many health programs instituted there including inoculations of tetanus toxoid during the third month of pregnancy and advanced treatment, did not "show even the slightest downward trend in Delhi" (Sehgal et al., 1980: 88, 90). Sehgal et al. (1980: 81) believed that an expanded immunization program, health education, and door-to-door immunization are the only way to eradicate tetanus.

People may learn from programs of health education, but they do not necessarily change their behavior. Gulani et al. (1977 unpublished article) conducted a study of fathers in the rural region of Delhi in three villages surrounding the Chhawla Subcentre of the Najafgarh Primary Health Centre. The study aimed at teaching fathers the benefits and necessity of having their children inoculated for diphtheria, pertussis, and tetanus (DPT). After the teaching sessions, fathers returned for post-testing. It was found that they retained information but had not changed their behavior, for they failed to complete the schedule of inoculations. The men gave a number of reasons for this oversight, such as the busy harvest period and flooding during the monsoon. We suspect that a subconscious reason was that rural males do not pay much attention to female teachers, in this case nurses who taught them and asked the questions. Villagers are not oriented to preventive inoculations for diseases with which they are only vaguely familiar and which they do not, as a rule, recognize as causes of childhood

mortality (Append. I: Descriptions—Diphtheria, *see also* Pertussis).

The Khanna study lists causes of infant deaths comparable to those found in Shanti Nagar in 1958–59 and in 1977–78. The causes and unknown causes of infant mortality from 0 to 11 months from birth are given in rank order from highest to lowest:

1. Peculiar to infancy, immaturity
2. Diarrheal disease
3. Tetanus
4. Birth injuries, postneonatal asphyxia, atelectasis
5. Pneumonia
6. Unknown causes
7. Other residuals and measles
8. Infections of newborn and accidents
9. Typhoid fever
10. Tuberculosis
11. Other known causes (Gordon et al., 1965: 906–908, table 1).

Matching the reports of villagers about the causes of infant death to the foregoing list would involve considerable uncertainty. The all-purpose term, Fever, which is compatible with ghost illness, was often reported in Shanti Nagar and was also recorded in the Khanna study (Wyon and Gordon, 1971: 173). It could be classified in several categories. Categories 6 and 11, which are in effect residual categories, might be overly used for want of greater precision by the recorder. It should also be noted that there is considerable overlap among the categories. Although such a list gives a general idea of the relative importance of various causes of infant death, there is clearly large scope for greater precision. Moreover, we found other causes of death for infants and children, such as neglect, sibling rivalry, and dangerous disciplinary measures. While they do not appear in the above list and except for neglect may be relatively rare, they are nonetheless of considerable ethnographic and psychological interest.

Compiling a complete list of diseases in the Delhi region is not possible, but in addition to the foregoing illnesses, chicken pox, enteric fever, cerebrospinal meningitis, diphtheria, and poliomyelitis may be mentioned. Smallpox had been completely eliminated by the end of the 1970s. Diphtheria had increased in reported incidence from 1945 through

1968, but the bulk of the cases were from 1961 through 1966, as were the deaths from diphtheria. In the lineage of "Merchant, Muslim, Priest," Mrs. Fence Sitter reported cases of diphtheria for two of her children, one of whom died, but she also exorcised the ghost or ghosts causing her children's illness. She was the only village woman who mentioned diphtheria to us, which does not necessarily mean that no other village children had diphtheria or died from it. According to government records, by the first half of the 1970s, decreases in many contagious diseases had taken place in the Delhi region. The infant mortality rate had decreased from 217.2 per thousand in 1921 to 55.5 (a provisional figure) in 1971. Fever, however, was still reported as a major cause of death. Although tuberculosis remained a problem, many cases were treated and cured (Gazetteer Unit, Delhi Adm., 1976: 857–870, tables 2, 4).

Part of the decline in infant and childhood mortality can be attributed to inoculations provided by the Government for newborn children: BCG for tuberculosis; DPT for diphtheria, pertussis, and tetanus; typhoid; and the oral vaccine for poliomyelitis. Plague inoculations were given in parts of the Union Territory of Delhi although the last reported deaths from plague were two in 1944 and one in 1946 (Gazetteer Unit, Delhi Adm., 1976: 863–869).

From January 1, 1958, to June 1, 1959, we recorded the births of 33 infants: 13 males and 20 females. During the same period, five boys and five girls died (table 2). Five of the ten deaths had a supernatural cause, either ghost illness or Kanti Mata (typhoid). Three deaths were due to passive infanticide, one was an accidental drowning, and one was a stillbirth. Three of these five children became ghosts. Thus, eight of the ten infant deaths had a supernatural component, either as cause, outcome, or both.

Infants who fell ill could not indicate that they had been attacked by a ghost, but the usual symptoms of Fever, struggling for breath, body convulsions, and incessant crying were believed to be due to a ghost trying to take the soul of an infant. Although these symptoms could be caused by various illnesses, village women most often attributed infant deaths to ghosts both in the 1950s and

the 1970s, but by the late 1970s, they sometimes linked an infant's death with tetanus, and some at the same time attributed the cause of tetanus to a ghost.

Multiple births usually resulted in stillborn infants or death in the perinatal period. If twins survived infancy, one of them commonly died by early adulthood, but since death struck very often, such deaths were not necessarily due to the person having been a twin. However, the belief that multiple births are inauspicious perpetuates the belief that such infants will die and may in fact contribute to their deaths. All but one of the multiple births that we recorded were twins, but there was one case of triplets, all of whom died at birth or shortly thereafter. Saini (1975: 81–82) indicated that the birth of twins was believed to be inauspicious in the 19th century in the southern Punjab, which then included the Delhi region, and that parents might give away, sell, or kill one twin because of this belief. In 1958, twin daughters were born to the Outsiders, Potters, who already had many children. They were quite poor and, anticipating problems in caring adequately for so many children, offered us one twin for adoption. In any case, one twin died in early childhood, but the other was still alive in 1977–78 (Chap. 20: The Potters and The Lady). Children born under an inauspicious sign might also be given away or killed. Twin births have been regarded with awe by various societies, and such infants have been done away with in some places (Krappe, 1964: 207).

When a twin sister and brother are born, they may be considered even more inauspicious than other twins due to the mythology of Yama and Yami. Yama, who later became the God of Death, and Yami, his twin sister, are considered to have been the first human pair. Before they became deities, Yami urged Yama to mate with her (incest) in order to perpetuate the species. Yami loved Yama passionately. When he died, she mourned him and later became the river Yamuna. The river flows by the City of Delhi, and on the new moon, widows and widowers go to the river to bathe (R. Freed and S. Freed, 1964: 82, 85). Thus, the River Yamuna is associated with death and widowhood. Details about Yama and Yami may be found in the Rig-Veda, the Mahabharata, and the Markandeya

TABLE 2

Deaths of Children Younger than Three Years in Shanti Nagar, January 1958–June 1959

Caste	Age	Sex	Circumstances
1. Bairagi	6 days	M	Died of ghost illness according to the child's grandmother. A neighboring Brahman man blamed tetanus neonatorum. Child became a ghost (Chap. 14: Death on Mother Sixth).
2. Chamar	3 yr	F	Drowned in pond and became a ghost.
3. Chamar	9 mo	F	Typhoid, attributed to Kanti Mata, a supernatural being. Death was also regarded as ghost illness. Infant became a ghost.
4. Chuhra	3 yr	M	The boy went blind in the summer of 1958, probably from measles. Then he was kept in a kind of cage until he died in 1959, at age 3. The family was extremely poor and no one seemed very bright. This same family lost another child, case 5 below.
5. Chuhra	1.5–2 yr	M	Similar circumstances and outcome as case 3 above.
6. Chuhra	2 yr	F	Fever, the index of ghost illness. Child became a ghost.
7. Jat	ca. 3 yr	M	Typhoid and dysentery, similar to case 3, except that the child was not reported to have become a ghost. After the boy died, his grandfather's levirate spouse committed suicide and was said to have become a ghost.

TABLE 2—(*Continued*)

Caste	Age	Sex	Circumstances
8. Jat	2–3 mo	F	Daughter of Dissembler and Worn Down. Had she been a boy, she might have lived. Brahman and Bairagi women said that the mother and baby died of ghost illness and became ghosts (Chap. 15: A Maternity Death).
9. Jat	Stillborn	M	Difficult primiparous delivery.
10. Jhinvar	1 wk	F	Born with clubfoot and massive growth in lumbar region after 10–11 months pregnancy. Passive infanticide because the parents and grandparents were terrified by the deformity and did nothing to save the infant. Became a ghost (Chap. 14).

Purana (Dowson, 1950: 373–375; Daniélou, 1964: 133; Doniger O'Flaherty, 1980: 27; Append. II: Sacred Hindu Texts; Append. V: Calendric Events—Amavas).

In 1958, Pure Goddess, a Brahman, related how she had borne twins, a boy and a girl, when she was 36 years old. At that time her husband had a government job and the couple lived with their other children, two sons and a daughter, in government quarters in northern Punjab. When her husband told her that he was going to sell the girl twin, Pure Goddess packed her belongings and took all her children back to Shanti Nagar to live with her husband's relatives. The girl lived only a few years; the boy, Story Teller, was alive in 1978.

Many of the cases of infant and childhood death presented below involve ghost illness and are described in family context. The causes of death are based on village beliefs regarding ghosts and ghost illness. Possible biomedical causes are mentioned when they can be plausibly ascertained. Some identifications are reasonably strong but others are tenuous.

The births and deaths of children have both short range and long range economic consequences. In the short term, a baby is another mouth to feed and a drain on its mother's time and energy. In the long term, a boy will become an economic asset and a girl, a liability. Although her labor balances her cost to her natal family from a relatively early age, her marriage is costly and the expenses do not end when she moves to her husband's family. If births and infant deaths result in a family having significantly more girls than boys, the family can be in trouble economically. The economic consequences for a family where infant deaths resulted in a single male ultimately having the responsibility for several females are illustrated below in the three-generation case of Sad Memories.

SAD MEMORIES

These deaths were reported in 1958 by Sad Memories, a Bairagi grandmother, who was 60 years old or older. Their economic consequences had become apparent in 1977–78. Sad Memories said that her husband's father and his wife had five sons and seven daughters, but that four sons and five daughters died as infants. Sad Memories was married to the surviving son, constituting the second generation, and she and her husband had four sons and three daughters. Two sons died as infants and another son died without issue. The fourth son survived and he and his wife had four sons, three of whom died as infants; their fourth son and three daughters survived. These children were Sad Memories' grandchildren. By 1958, her husband, son, and daughter-in-law had died, and the only surviving male in this direct line of descent was her grandson who was about 22 years old. He and his wife, about 19 to 20 years old, as yet had no children. He worked as a clerk with a low salary and farmed his small plot of land. He was responsible for arranging the dowries and marriages of two of his sisters, as yet unmarried, and for sending gifts to his married sister in the regular cycle of gift-giving as well as doing so for his other two sisters when they married. He also sup-

ported his mother, wife, and the two unmarried sisters. The heavy costs of a woman's wedding, chiefly for the dowry and hospitality for guests, are born by her male relatives, especially the head of her family. The burden does not end with the wedding. A woman's natal family must send gifts to her marital family at various festivals, when she bears children, and when her children are wedded. Therefore, this grandson was saddled with expenses for his sisters that drove him into debt.

By 1977, Sad Memories' son, then age 42, had suffered the predictable slide into debt. Although he had a better job and greater income than 20 years earlier, he owed Rs. 10,000. He and his wife, who had scrofula in the neck (TB), had four children: two sons, aged 8 and 14 years; and two daughters, 1½ and 11 years old. If the sons survived and were wedded, the family would receive dowries from their brides; on the other hand the two daughters would need weddings, dowries, and gifts yearly. The family's tenuous economic position was due largely to the deaths of so many male members. Had they lived, they would have helped pay the wedding and ceremonial costs of the family's women. This case is an example of the many deaths of children in earlier times and their connection to ghost beliefs, for Sad Memories, who was a follower of Sanatan Dharma, said that a ghost or ghosts had caused her sons and her husband's brothers to die of ghost illness and they, too, became ghosts. Moreover, the case well illustrates the economic importance of at least a sexual balance among progeny. A single male in modest circumstances can be driven into debt by his obligations to sisters and daughters.

THE GHOST OF CAT WOMAN

Cat Woman, a Chuhra Sweeper, was so named because her ghost was believed to take the form of a cat. Ghosts are thought to appear sometimes in the form of an animal, plant, or tree. In 1958, two Chuhra Sweeper women, who were next-door neighbors, described seeing a flickering light at night in the empty hut opposite theirs where the ghosts of the former inhabitants were believed to linger. The ghosts were Cat Woman and her

Fig. 6.   Hoi Mata, drawn by Mrs. Fence Sitter, a Brahman woman, 1977. Sun (Surya), moon (Chand), and Hoi Mata are written across the top of the drawing. The Goddess is worshipped by women who want to become pregnant and to protect their children from illness and death.

husband who had died there. The women reported that the ghost of Cat Woman died without children, was malevolent, and was taking the souls of their infant sons. One of the women reported that Cat Woman's ghost had taken her two infant sons a few days after birth. The other woman claimed that her infant son had also been taken by the same ghost. The most probable cause of the deaths was tetanus neonatorum because the babies died in the perinatal period before Mother Sixth.

DEATH ON MOTHER SIXTH

In 1959, a young Bairagi bore her first child, a son. On Mother Sixth, the sixth day of life, he died with symptoms that resembled tetanus neonatorum. The couple believed that a ghost had taken the boy's soul. This belief was reinforced by a relative, Fearful, a firm believer in ghosts, who said that they had forgotten to make an offering to ward off disaster when the boy was born and therefore a ghost had taken the infant (Chap. 20: The Bairagis).

THE MEDICAL CHILDBIRTH SURVEY

In 1978, information about 11 infant deaths was obtained in a Medical Childbirth Survey of 13 women who had given birth to at least one son and one daughter. The survey shows changes that were gradually taking place in birth practices. Ten of the women were in their twenties and three, in their thirties. They represent nine castes (one informant each from the Bairagi, Baniya, Jhinvar, Lohar, and Nai castes; two informants from the Brahman, Chamar, Jat, and Gola Kumhar castes, the castes with the greatest number of people). These infant deaths took place during approximately two decades.

The majority of children in this survey were delivered by the village midwife, a few by other midwives, and some by the government midwife. Many of the women did not know whether the implement used to cut the cord had been bought for the delivery or had been sterilized. The few who did know said that the implement was most often a scissors. Sterilization was described as (1) immersing the implement in boiling water; or (2) pouring *Detol* (the trade name for a disinfectant) in warm or hot water and then placing the implement in the liquid. To avoid infection from puerperal fever, the government midwife placed a plastic or rubber sheet on the bed where the mother would give birth (cf. Gordon et al., 1965b; Append. I: Discoveries 1847, Puerperal fever, *also* 1864, Antiseptic surgery; Descriptions—Puerperal fever, *also* Tetanus). The village midwife used rags and pieces of jute for this purpose, which she threw away after delivery. The 13 women bore a total of 55 children, an average of four plus children per woman. Only one spontaneous abortion was recorded, which ended a four-month pregnancy. Of the 55 children born by the 13 women over a period somewhat longer than two decades, 11 died; 44 were still alive.

TWO TRAGIC DEATHS

During her interview for the Medical Childbirth Survey, a Potter woman told how two of her seven children died. Her first child, a son, died when he was five years old. He had been playing with some boys but came home because he was not feeling well. He lay down on his cot. His father called a bhagat who was visiting Forceful and Politico, the Jats of Old Fever. As the bhagat was trying to exorcise the ghost causing the illness, the boy suddenly died. Just before his death, according to his mother, black clouds formed over the house and it started to rain. The mother considered the clouds an omen that a ghost was about to take her son.

The second child to die, a daughter, was this woman's fourth child, born after two surviving sons. The youngest of these sons was three years old at the time of his sister's birth. One day the mother went to the fields to work, leaving her one-month-old daughter in the care of her mother-in-law with whom she, her husband, and children lived jointly. According to the mother-in-law, the three-year-old boy wanted to play with the baby, took her in his arms, went outside, and threw her down on the paved lane, killing her immediately.

Soon after their daughter's death, the mother, father, and their two sons separated from the joint family of her husband's mother and father. The mother related the death of her infant daughter so as to imply that her mother-in-law was to blame. The three-year-old boy may have been jealous of the infant and wanted to get rid of her, but at his age he may not have had sufficient strength to throw the infant down forcefully enough on the paved lane to kill her. If he did throw her down or drop her, he was too young to realize what killing an infant meant, and his act would not have been regarded as bad karma because of his age. Although there is no evidence to prove it, the grandmother may have prompted the boy's actions, or herself killed the child because she was a girl.

DAUGHTER-IN-LAW VS. MOTHER-IN-LAW

During the Medical Childbirth Survey, a 22-year-old Nai Barber mother told about the births of her four children and the death of one of her twin daughters. After the birth of two sons, her third pregnancy resulted in the premature births of identical twin daughters. Her interview reflects changing birth practices, emphasizes her relationships with her husband and her mother-in-law, and indicates the mediating role that the hospital employment of her husband and elder brother-in-law played between a modern urban institution and traditional village people.

The government midwife delivered her first two children, both sons, in her husband's village house. The use of the government midwife was an advance over the villagers' sole reliance on the traditional village midwife, a step in the direction of modern medical treatment. The mother's third lying-in represents the final step toward the use of modern Western medicine. The twins were delivered in a hospital in the city because the lying-in was expected to be more dangerous than usual; twins were expected but the births were premature. Not only was modern medical treatment available to villagers but also it was being used more and more. Recourse to hospitals was not yet routine, however. In this case, the fact that two family members, the father of the twins and his elder brother, worked in hospitals made it easier for the mother to deal with an unfamiliar institution.

The young mother was first taken to one hospital for delivery, but then she and the twins were immediately transferred to another hospital where the twins were put into incubators. The mother referred to the incubators as "some machine" and said the babies were placed there because they were very weak. Fourteen days later, one of the twins died; after the other twin spent 21 days in the incubator, the mother took her out of the hospital because she was afraid that she, too, might die. Mother and child stayed in the city in the home of a friend of her husband who worked in the hospital. It was a large government apartment with inside toilets, bathrooms, and a television set. The baby flourished in this environment as did the young mother, who was reluctant to return to the village when her husband brought her home.

This young mother endured brutal beatings from her husband and mother-in-law until just before the twins were delivered, in all likelihood a cause of their premature birth. Almost from the time of first mating of the young couple, the mother-in-law accused her son's wife of illicit relations with men and incited her son to beat her. The young woman said that she still had pains in her back from these many beatings.

In 1977 the mother-in-law had been attacked and badly bitten by a pack of dogs, was treated for rabies, and needed some time to recover. She took her misery out on her daughter-in-law. Moreover, she was jealous of her daughter-in-law, fearing that she would cause her younger son to establish his own family separate from his parents, as had her eldest son. Her younger son finally realized that his mother had created trouble between him and his wife so he separated from his parents shortly after the premature birth of the twins.

Although the case of the Gola Potter woman and her two children illustrates a ghost belief based on the omen of the black cloud and calling a bhagat to exorcise the ghost, in this Nai Barber case, ghosts were not mentioned. Nai Barbers in 1958 believed in ghosts, but later this young husband and his elder brother became followers of the Arya Samaj. Urban employment, like Arya-Samaj beliefs, may also have led to an apparent disinterest or disbelief in ghosts.

The cases of the Potters and Nais conform to the theme that mothers-in-law may treat their daughters-in-law badly. The myth that grandmothers, who are likewise mothers-in-law, always love their grandchildren is weakened by some cases in this study, for sometimes the grandmothers are so worn out from childbearing, hard work, and worry about dowries and other ceremonial costs for daughters that they no longer love children. Another theme in the relationship of mother-in-law and daughter-in-law is the older woman's fear that her daughter-in-law will steal the affection of her son, as illustrated by this Nai mother-in-law (Mandelbaum, 1970, 1: 84–86; S. Freed and R. Freed, 1976: 71).

A GHOST TOOK MY SON

In 1978, Truthful, a nonliterate Brahman 29 years old, told us about the death of her infant son in 1967. A ghost was believed to

have taken his soul. She told the story in the course of a long interview which illustrates the ghost beliefs then current. Although Truthful was the main informant, the session was a group interview which took place in the house of Truthful and her husband, Teacher, located on a lane where Brahmans of Teacher's patrilineage lived. We visited Truthful to learn about her ghost beliefs because villagers mentioned that one of her children had been seized by a ghost and died. In addition, an elderly man, Affine, who was living with her and Teacher and was married to Teacher's mother's sister, had recently been possessed by a ghost (Append. III: Chart 3).

This session was somewhat hampered because three Brahmans, two elderly men and one young girl, had died during the past two years in the lane where Teacher and Truthful lived and the inhabitants of the lane feared their ghosts. During the first part of the interview three teen-age Brahman girls were present, one of whom was the granddaughter of Wealthy Landowner. Also present were Teacher's sister's 12-year-old daughter, who was staying in his household, and a neighboring woman, the daughter of a man in Teacher's patrilineage. Wealthy Landowner had died tortured from an eye operation, age 72, five months earlier. His ghost was believed to be wandering in the lane because the year of mourning had not yet passed. Whose Daughter, another granddaughter of Wealthy Landowner and the younger sister of the granddaughter present at this session, drowned in 1976. Her ghost was believed to haunt this Brahman lane as well as the village pond and other parts of the village (described in this chapter and in Chap. 22).

Another Brahman family who lived near Teacher's house suffered two tragedies in 1977. Two senior men, devoted brothers married to two sisters, democratically ran the household. The younger of the two brothers accidentally cut off one of his hands while operating a mechanical fodder cutter. The shock of the accident reportedly caused his older brother, age 70, to die of a heart attack, thus dying tortured. However, it was thought that his ghost would not tarry long because he was believed to have died at the allotted time. The surviving brother and two wives were shattered by the misfortune. The widow never recovered from her husband's sudden death; she could not reconcile her widow-hood to her past actions, for she believed that she had led an exemplary life. She died in 1981.

To be maimed, crippled, or one-eyed were considered inauspicious and due to one's past actions. Since these Brahmans were quite good people, the injury of one brother, the death of the other, and widowhood, all believed to be due to past actions, were difficult to reconcile with their own view of themselves. Due to the several deaths in this Brahman lane and the year of mourning for each, the three teen-age girls and the neighboring Brahman woman present during the interview were extremely reluctant to speak of ghosts.

We entered Teacher's house by passing through a hallway on one side of which was the men's sitting room and on the other side, a courtyard (Append. IV: Map 3, Dwelling of Truthful and Teacher). Entering the hallway, we met Teacher and Affine emerging from the sitting room to greet us. They directed us to the courtyard where Truthful, her mother-in-law, the neighboring woman, and the three teen-age girls were chatting.

Truthful's mother-in-law, with whom we had been quite friendly in 1958—59, started the conversation by remarking that her married daughter's 17-year-old son, who was living with them, was not feeling well but did not seem very ill although he had taken leave from work (Append. III: Chart 3). He was lying down in the men's sitting room. The young man was currently being treated by Home Trained, the Nai Barber dispenser of popular pharmaceutical medicine. When Truthful's mother-in-law was asked why they chose Home Trained instead of going to the government dispensary for treatment, she answered, "The village man provides proper medicine, the medicine gives relief, and he charges less. It takes time to go there, and this man is right here. He comes at night when anyone calls him." Shortly thereafter she went to see how her grandson was faring. Her statement is in accord with Taylor's (1976: 287) finding for Punjabi villagers, namely that they preferred curers who were near them and came as soon as they were called.

To bring the conversation around to ghost illness and ghost possession, we asked wheth-er anyone had heard about the recent ghosts and ghost possessions in the Chamar section of the village. At first no one said anything, then reluctantly one of the girls said that they had not heard about the ghosts. Truthful told the girls that if any of them knew about any ghosts, they should speak up. No one said anything, so she prodded them:

Why be shy? My mother-in-law's sister's husband [Affine] saw a ghost recently. The ghost took hold of him, threw him on the ground so he was hurt. He saw the ghost, who told him "I'm going to kill you," and then the ghost picked him up again and threw him down three times. The ghost was a Muslim. Because he is a practicing priest, he can recognize a ghost easily. He knows everything about such things, but women and girls do not. Then the ghost left him but he was ill a few days and was treated by a *vaid*. Haven't you seen the bandages on his face?

One of the girls then said, "Ghosts don't come here. They go to the Chamar section. If you go to a fair in Meerut, you will see some great things there." Truthful added, "People who die under a train, drown, or die in a fire, cannot find release so their souls wander around in air and they are ghosts."

We asked whether a certain man, who had been murdered in 1974, haunted their lane or the next lane where he had died. Truthful replied, "It is not essential that ghosts stay here and attack people. They can wander anywhere. When a person becomes a ghost, he wanders around worrying about his wife and children. I heard something like this on the radio."

Replying to the question, "What happens if the person who dies is a woman and then becomes a ghost"? Truthful said, "If a woman becomes a ghost, she enters another woman and makes her jump around and play. The ghost plays in this way, but the victim becomes unconscious and knows nothing of what happens."

Next we asked the girls whether they would want to become *siyana*s. One girl answered, "I would not. These *siyana*s are empowered by Bhagwan and only Bhagwan knows what education and training they receive. There are no *siyana*s in this village, but there are some in Palam, some in the City [of Delhi], and some in the Gurgaon District."

A question that offered the girls a hypothetical choice, "Which would you prefer, to see the ghost of a man or the ghost of a woman," produced an immediate and forceful reply from all three. "We don't want to see any ghosts," they said. "When you see a ghost, you become afraid. Who wants to be afraid?" The neighboring woman said, "Go to the cremation grounds at midnight and you will see a ghost, but I won't go with you because you will die." At this point Truthful interjected, "Not if you are unafraid." Our reply was that we would take Hanuman to protect us, for Hanuman, the monkey god and lieutenant of Rama Chandra in the Ramayana, is often the familiar of bhagats and other exorcists. Truthful agreed, "Yes, then you will be all right."

Truthful then recounted how her husband, Teacher, one day at high noon brought a dead man's bone from the cremation grounds because a buffalo had given birth to a calf but had not given milk for 10 days. Plowman, a son of Teacher's grandfather's younger brother, advised Teacher to fetch a bone from the cremation grounds, bury it, drive a peg into the ground on the spot, and tie the buffalo to it (Append. III: Chart 3). Then the buffalo would give milk. Teacher followed the instructions, and the buffalo gave milk.

We asked the girls if they had heard about the ghost of the Brahman girl who died about 20 years earlier. Although her death and the belief that she had become a ghost were well known among the village Brahmans, the girls answered that they had not heard of her and that one should not say who had become a ghost (Chap. 15: Illusion's Death). Thus, they linked the naming and appearance or haunting of a ghost with ghost possessions.

The girls were next asked, "Are you afraid to talk about ghosts and identify them?" They replied, "Yes. One should not take the name of a ghost." Truthful then said:

I have seen a ghost. When I gave birth to my first child, a son, my husband was in training to be a teacher and lived away from here. One night when the infant was 14 to 15 days old, I was sleeping with the baby on my bed in the room off this courtyard

[Append. IV: Map 3, Room 1]. One of my sisters-in-law slept in the next room [Room 2], and another sister-in-law slept in the courtyard in front of the same room. [Teacher's two married sisters had come to his house for the delivery of his son to perform the nipple-washing ceremony (Chuchi Dhona) before the baby was first nursed by the mother. For the ceremony, sisters were customarily given gifts of money or jewelry (R. Freed and S. Freed, 1980: 369 ff.). They stayed a while and were present during the ghost episode.] My mother-in-law slept outside my room. An oil lamp was burning in the courtyard. The ghost came from the inner room [Room 5], the men's sitting room, blew out the lamp by waving his hand, came into my room, and snatched my child from me. I awoke and found my breasts had dried up, no milk was flowing, and the baby's mouth was open gasping for air. He made sounds as though he was having difficulty breathing [which indicated that a ghost was trying to take the soul of her son].

The girls and the neighboring woman had grown uneasy from this account and departed, but Truthful was unperturbed and went on with her narrative.

After awakening, Truthful called her mother-in-law, who in turn woke her two daughters (Truthful's sisters-in-law) and Affine, who was sleeping in the men's sitting room. Affine was staying there so that an adult man would be present in case of emergency. At the time, Teacher was living in Delhi. Affine immediately dressed and took the child to a *siyana* in a nearby village. The *siyana* gave him a *tawiz*, a protective amulet in the form of a locket, into which the *siyana* put a piece of paper on which he had written a mantra. He told Affine that if the child lived through the night, they should bring the infant back to him in the morning before nine o'clock, at which time he would leave for work. Like many curers, he practiced curing as a part-time occupation while holding a job in the city.

Truthful continued:

The next morning instead of going to the *siyana*, we took the baby to my relatives who live in the city. They said, "This going to a *siyana* is all nonsense. If the boy has life in him, he will live. Don't bother with the *siyana*." My husband wasn't there, but my brother was so I asked him to fetch my husband from the training center. When he came, we took the child to a hospital. [The group consisted of Truthful, her brother, Teacher, Affine and his wife, and the infant.] No doctor asked what had gone wrong with the child, but they said, "You have brought the child when he is in a serious condition." They then gave the infant oxygen. At first he revived and looked beautiful again. My husband started playing with him, and Affine said, "Now the child will be saved. Let's have tea." While we were drinking tea, my son died.

We asked Truthful what Teacher and Affine said when the boy died. She answered:

They did not say anything except that the child had been all right when they left. I think that a ghost took the child. After this baby died, all of my children have been born alive and survived due to the help of the *siyana*. When my first child died, we continued going to the *siyana* to rid ourselves of the ghost. The *siyana* took us to the Ganges because we believed that if we made offerings of *pindas* [balls of cooked flour used as offerings] to the Ganges on behalf of the ghost, the soul of the ghost would find release. I don't remember all the details of what we did there because the work was carried out by the *siyana*. My husband and I only took a dip in the river. Now we go there after every Holi and Diwali [Spring and Fall festivals in Chaitra and Karttik, Append. V] and obtain a *tawiz* from him. When I wear the *tawiz*, none of us eats any food brought from outside the house. If someone dies whom we know, I am not supposed to go there. If I must go, then I have to take off the *tawiz* and leave it here. When I return, I take a bath, light incense, and touch the *tawiz* with smoke from the incense before putting it on again. When my next child was born after the first died, I went to the Ganges and offered the new baby there.

Asked how this was done, she replied:

As you have seen, women go to worship the well after the birth of a son, so we go to a place near the River Ganges and buy *karvas* [pitchers] and offer them to the Ganges. My sister-in-law, mother-in-law, and sometimes other relatives accompany me. We worship near the Ganges, and a priest and my sister-in-law hold a piece of cloth in the water. I drop the infant into the water above the cloth. Immediately my sister-in-law and the priest bring the child up by pulling on the cloth. Then I take the child from them and give them money, as if I am buying the child from them.

These rituals were necessary to protect Truthful and her offspring from a ghost or ghosts, for Truthful believed that her son would have lived had they taken him to the *siyana* rather than to the hospital.

Truthful said that when she awoke and found her baby gasping for breath, the sounds indicated a ghost was trying to take his soul. The sounds were similar to a death rattle, which villagers interpret as the soul leaving the body. Villagers believe that dreaming of a ghost is the equivalent of seeing it and forewarns an attack. They expect that they or someone close to them, in this case Truthful's infant, will have ghost illness. The dream, the infant's symptoms, and his death a day later convinced Truthful that a ghost took the soul of her baby.

Truthful had fallen asleep while nursing the child, but the infant continued to suck. The fact that her breast had run dry bothered Truthful because of the fear that one's breast can be sucked dry by a malevolent ghost or supernatural being. Thus, a ghost might have already possessed her baby. Moreover, since the nursing ability of women was highly valued, women became anxious at signs of lactational failure. The story in the Bhagavata Purana (the Krishna myth) of Putana, the witch, trying to poison Krishna with her milk, which had no effect on him because he sucked her breasts dry until she died, had a negative emotional affect on women who nursed infants (Kakar, 1982: 147–148; R. Freed and S. Freed, 1985: 136–137).

At the end of the interview, we asked Truthful if the Sat Narayan feast that she and her husband had given a few months previously was for one of her children. She said,

"At that time some of my children were sick and I wanted to spend money in a good way so my husband and I decided to invite neighbors and relatives to a feast and take the name of Bhagwan. We did this because Bhagwan gives us happiness so we should remember him and do something for him" (Narayan or Naryana is commonly used for Bhagwan-Vishnu [Dowson, 1950: 221]).

From a Western medical viewpoint, Truthful's infant probably suffered from atelectasis, a respiratory distress syndrome due to incomplete expansion of the lungs. The syndrome arises from lack of an agent that reduces surface tension in the lungs so that they can be filled with air. Until birth, a fetus has no air in the lungs; after birth, the newborn's lungs should contain air for the first time. Atelectasis may occur after birth if the lungs shrink and lose their air. This shrinkage and loss of air, known as hyaline-membrane disease, is a common cause of death among newborn babies. Unless breathing can be maintained by artificial respiration with oxygen, the baby will probably die of asphyxiation. The disease is found a number of days after birth, often in premature babies. We do not know whether Truthful's first child was premature, but premature births among primiparas are not unusual. The symptoms exhibited by Truthful's baby arose 14 to 15 days after birth. This period, Truthful's description, and the administration of oxygen in the hospital accords with atelectasis and hyaline-membrane disease. Even with artificial inflation of the lungs with oxygen, many infants so afflicted do not live. As the physicians in the hospital said, the child was brought to them in a serious condition. Had he been brought sooner, his life might have been saved (Gordon et al., 1965c: table 1, 907; 906–908; Wingate, 1972: 48–49; 213–214). Atelectasis, which occurs a number of days after birth in the neonatal period, is not included in SIDS (Sudden Infant Death Syndrome), which is recognized as a leading cause of death in the postneonatal period (Bochner et al., 1988: 469; Hasselmeyer and Hunter, 1988: 3).

The history of the joint family into which Teacher was born illustrates the sexual tension and strain that a number of untimely deaths resulting in two widows and a widower imposed on the joint family, and which affected land inheritance, as well as the economic and psychological well-being of family members (R. Freed and S. Freed, 1979: 302). The family situation in 1958–59 was augmented by the belief in ghosts, the fear of them, and of ghost illness and ghost possessions.

Teacher was born posthumously seven months after his father's death in 1945, by which time Snakebite Curer, the younger brother of Teacher's grandfather, had not only become head of the family but also assumed that the land of his dead elder brother's son was his to handle as he pleased. He did not know that Teacher's father had left a pregnant widow, only that the widow had two surviving daughters and no son. Because of his early demise and lack of a male heir, Teacher's father's soul was believed to have become a ghost. Snakebite Curer had survived his eldest brother (Teacher's grandfather); his youngest brother, the father of Plowman; and Teacher's father. Thus, he became the head of the family and acted as though all the land belonged to him. His main occupation was farmer, but his pseudonym indicates he also cured snakebites (Chap. 18: Brahmans as Exorcists and Curers). Teacher's widowed grandmother was the senior woman and virtual tyrant supervising the other women in the joint family. She died sometime after 1959. Snakebite Curer was a widower, for his wife died in 1939 shortly after giving birth to her third son. She too was believed to have become a ghost. In addition, Snakebite Curer's eldest son worked and lived far from the village, coming home only on vacations, but his wife and children lived with Snakebite Curer, which added to the sexual tension in the household. All the members of the family were ruled by him and his tyrannical, widowed sister-in-law (Append. III: Chart 3).

The youngest brother of Snakebite Curer left one son, Plowman, who had little or no recollection of his parents. Plowman looked on Snakebite Curer as his father. Plowman was married twice. When his first wife and two children died, he married again. Not much was said about these dead, for they were believed to have become ghosts. Plowman believed that his first wife and their two children died because he and his wife belonged to the same *gotra*, which constitutes a forbidden marriage in Hinduism. Although a son of Snakebite Curer as well as Plowman had married within their *gotra*, these marriages and some others within the same Brahman *gotra* were justified by the *gotra* having split into two *shasan*s, groups which are geographically separate. By the late 1950s, a Brahman stated that marriages between these two *shasan*s were no longer acceptable because descendants of such marriages were believed to be weak and die early. Marriages between the two *shasan*s had originally taken place due to the decimation of the population from plague and influenza (cf. R. Freed and S. Freed, 1980: 411–414).

Plowman continued to be disturbed by his first marriage to a woman from the same *gotra*. When children of his second marriage died, he believed that the violation of clan exogamy was still working against him and his offspring, another way of saying that due to his past actions a ghost was taking his children. He did not name the ghost, but the likely candidate was the ghost of his first wife. The first three of his five sons died at birth; then one survived, but the next son died. However, two daughters survived (Append III: Chart 3).

Teacher not only grew up in a joint household haunted by ghosts but also his posthumous birth was a problem. In the case of a son who would inherit land and who is born long after his father's death, such a birth may raise the question of illegitimacy. A posthumous only son, such as Teacher, or in fact any only son, who if he lived would inherit land from his father's estate, was in danger of being surreptitiously killed as a child by males to whom the land would revert if the son died. Suspicion of illegitimacy might make such a step easier for the eventual beneficiaries. In Teacher's joint family, Snakebite Curer at that time managed a total of 6 acres (2.43 ha) of land, two of which Teacher was entitled to inherit as his father's share. His widowed mother had the right to maintenance from the land during her lifetime unless she remarried. Unaware at first that the widow of Teacher's father was pregnant, Snakebite Curer believed that the land would be his to handle as long as he lived and would eventually go to his three sons and his younger brother's only surviving son, Plowman.

This premise was dispelled when Teacher was born and survived.

The generations of Teacher's father and his grandfather were afflicted by famine, plague, influenza, and other contagious diseases. Conditions were such that a lineage could harbor many ghosts. Any of the male adults who died during the period from the first decade of the century through the 1950s could have been the ghost that Truthful believed took her son. In any event in 1967, the ghost was a man who in her dream came from the men's sitting room.

In 1960, Teacher, then 15 years old, and his mother separated from the joint family, dividing the land and part of the joint family dwelling and later enlarging their part. By that time, Teacher's sisters had married and were living with their husbands. Because there were only two of them, Teacher and his mother, his mother asked her eldest daughter if a one-year-old son might come to live with them. He was still there in 1977–78. Later Teacher's eldest sister's daughter also came to live with them. From time-to-time Affine, his wife, and some of his children visited Teacher and his family, and in turn Teacher and Truthful visited them when they went to the city. The somewhat anomalous position of Affine in Teacher's house in 1967 when the infant son died and thereafter when he, his wife, and later his two youngest children came to live with Teacher appears to be related to his later ghost possessions. Although elderly childless widowers might end their days living with a sister's family, a man with a wife and sons would not ordinarily do so. However, there were practical reasons for Affine's presence in Teacher's household. He was an affinal relative due to his marriage with Teacher's mother's sister, and his presence served to protect Teacher from possible assault by land-hungry consanguines. Moreover, several of his children were living in nearby Delhi.

Teacher and his mother were afraid of what might happen to them because of the land hunger of their patrilineal kin. This was one reason that Affine and members of his family frequently visited. Teacher's mother and her sister were very close so Teacher's mother had learned that she could trust Affine. The distrust that Teacher and his mother had of

Snakebite Curer was reinforced by his failure to arrange the marriages of Teacher's sisters. His mother had to resort to her brothers and received some help from Affine to make the arrangements.

Around 1963 to 1964, Teacher and Truthful married and their first son, the infant who died, was born in 1967. Because of their close tie, when Affine retired in 1974 he came to live with Teacher. Affine's land in Uttar Pradesh at that time was flooded so he did not return to his natal village. He had never farmed, and his land was worked for him on half shares while he worked in the city. He continued the same arrangement after retirement. Four of his married children, three sons and a daughter, lived, and worked or attended school in the City of Delhi. His two youngest children, a 10-year-old son and a 12-year-old daughter lived with him and his wife in Shanti Nagar and attended school there. After living in Delhi for 40 years, he was more a native of the city and surrounding region than of his place of birth (Append. III: Chart 3).

In general, villagers followed these rules regarding affines: a son-in-law should not live with his wife's natal family; a brother might visit or stay in his sister's marital village if a need to safeguard her arose, but not as a general rule; and a father should rarely go to the village in which his daughter was married. Exceptions to the rules took place, but Brahmans tended to follow the rule that an adult male should not live with in-laws. In 1978 one Brahman woman, Pure Goddess, 79 years of age, recited the following verse:

Those who keep a dog as a pet are dogs;
And those who beat a dog are dogs;
And if a son-in-law lives at an in-law's
     place, he's a dog.
The chief of such dogs is the man who goes
     to live in his daughter's house.

Affine had lived in the city from 1934 to 1974 and ignored or opposed some aspects of village life, especially since his natal village was in Uttar Pradesh. In any case, he seemed to have trouble building relationships in Shanti Nagar. Affine had been active in promoting the remarriage of Brahman and other widows, partly because he knew how much

his wife's sister, the widowed mother of Teacher, suffered. Even though widow remarriage was gradually accepted in the village, many village Brahmans were still uneasy in open discussions of widow remarriage. Affine ignored these nuances of opinion and talked openly about his early advocacy of widow remarriage.

After retirement, Affine began attending classes in a Durga mandir (temple to the goddess Durga) where he was learning to be a professional priest. He learned that Hindus in early times had treated women much better than they had been treated during his lifetime, so he began to preach on this subject, too. Since he was an affine and a relative stranger, his activities were unwelcome. He had already begun acting as a priest for birth and marriage ceremonies, but before his ghost possessions he had ineptly performed a Brahman birth ceremony. In addition, Manipulator, an elder, retired Brahman was also building up a clientele as a professional priest. Although he appeared to welcome Affine, in fact he was his competitor.

During Affine's 40-year residence in the city, four of his ten children (three sons and a daughter) died as infants (Append. III: Chart 3). Affine died in the early 1980s, reportedly from an asthma attack, an unverified village diagnosis. His ghost possessions, in which he fell and had hallucinations, were at least partially due to psychological stress from retirement and a difficult adjustment to village life.

Because of the death of her first son, Truthful went to a hospital for the delivery of her second child but feared the strange hospital environment. For delivery of her third child she went to her elder married sister's home. For subsequent deliveries, this same sister came to stay with her and supervised the births, seeing that a sterilized scissors was used to cut the umbilical cord. Truthful continued to follow the *siyana*'s instructions and made semiannual pilgrimages to the Ganges. Although she believed that a ghost had taken her firstborn son, she differed from women in earlier times who claimed an *oopra* caused such deaths. Instead she blamed an unidentified male ghost.

The group session with Truthful showed the fears of the neighboring woman and the three teen-age girls, all of the Brahman caste, who refused to identify or discuss ghosts for fear the ghosts would attack them. Moreover, the ghosts of two old Brahman men and of Whose Daughter were believed to be haunting their families and people living in the lane. Further, the ghosts of Teacher's father and grandfather, of Plowman's parents, and of Snakebite Curer's wife were believed to haunt the former members of the joint family ruled by Snakebite Curer. Still Affine's presence in Teacher's household may have subconsciously disturbed Truthful and been reflected in her dream of a male ghost coming from the men's sitting room and taking her son. By 1977–78, Snakebite Curer was 79 or 80 years old, senile, and lived with his next to oldest son. His other two sons and Plowman had separated from him.

THE GHOST OF WHOSE DAUGHTER

The ultimately fatal physical maladies of Wealthy Landowner and of one of his sons, Wrestler, were never mentioned in connection with ghost illness. Fever and the other signs of ghost illness were not indicated. Wealthy Landowner's problem was the aftermath of an operation on his eyes. Wrestler had a persistent skin condition that was unique as far as the village population was concerned. Wrestler sought relief from physicians at first and then began to consult *vaids*. Neither the bungled operation of Wealthy Landowner nor the unsuccessful efforts to cure Wrestler were likely to bolster the confidence of villagers in operations and physicians. On the other hand, Mrs. Wrestler had one mastectomy and in 1978 was to have another. She did not hesitate to display the surgeon's work to people, whether or not they wanted to see it. We do not know whether the operation was performed by an Ayurvedic or a Western medical surgeon. Although Mrs. Wrestler seemed to flaunt her mastectomy, some people were disturbed by her behavior. She herself at times seemed highly emotional in 1978, not surprising considering the death of Wealthy Landowner, Wrestler's physical condition, and the drowning of her daughter [Whose Daughter] in 1976.

The one prominent ghost in this Brahman family was Whose Daughter. Other Brahman ghosts lurked about, including Wealthy

Landowner's, but the ghost of Whose Daughter was the only one to possess people. One of her victims was a family member, the other, a school friend. The ghost of Whose Daughter entered the scene when a family member was under considerable psychological stress.

Although Wealthy Landowner's lineage had a distant lineage connection with the other village Brahmans, it had been continued through an adoption. Wealthy Landowner's great grandfather had adopted the son of a daughter from his own line of descent, who became Wealthy Landowner's father, thus continuing the lineage and providing an heir for his land. Adopted men were treated with some caution because the adoptee was from another village and was more or less a stranger. Although the descendants of such an outsider were gradually accepted, the family's outside origin was not forgotten. In this case the large amount of land inherited by the descendants of the adoptee helped family members to establish themselves firmly.

Wealthy Landowner's unsuccessful eye operation was in 1975. Where the operation took place and who performed it were never mentioned. It could have been performed by an Ayurvedic or a Western medical surgeon (cf. Jeffery, 1988: 185–186). According to village reports, the operation damaged his brain so that he was never the same thereafter. Although he continually complained that he was ill and that something was very much wrong with him, he refused to see another doctor or go to a hospital. When he died in the fall of 1977, his funeral ceremonies were carefully carried out. Then the family began the customary year of mourning. Because he lived until he was 72 years old and the proper funeral ceremonies had been observed, he was expected to become a pitri after the year of mourning, despite having died tortured. However, during the year of mourning, his ghost was believed to hover around family members, their buildings, and the lanes where he formerly had walked.

Wealthy Landowner left two widows, 60 and 70 years old. When his first wife had borne no children after several years of marriage, he took a second wife. Cowife I then bore a son. Although both wives thereafter had children, a number of them died. Cowife

I had six children, three of whom died; one daughter and two sons survived. Cowife II bore seven children, five of whom died; the two surviving children were daughters. The cowives said that all the children who died, except one, died of typhoid. The other child died from smallpox. By 1977, the daughters of both cowives had married and gone to live in their husbands' villages. The two surviving sons of Cowife I, the elder dubbed Steady and the younger, Wrestler, married and their wives had borne children by 1958. Steady failed in the ninth grade and left school; Wrestler had no education. The cowives and their daughters-in-law had no education.

The cowives had a traditional Brahman background, which included ghost beliefs. When grandchildren were born, the cowives, who lived quite amiably together, supervised the delivery, lying-in, and 40-day seclusion of their daughters-in-law. They set up a bulwark in the lying-in chamber against ghosts, other supernatural beings, and sources of pollution, which might harm the mother and child. Supernaturally effective substances placed in the delivery room included fire, water, and iron which were believed to purify the room and protect mother and child from ghosts and other supernatural beings. A small glowing fire of cowdung was maintained throughout the 40 days of seclusion and a heavy iron chain, as a magical device against malevolent ghosts, circled the bed upon which mother and child rested. Grain was scattered on the floor for the same reason, and a pitcher of water was placed near the mother's bed. For nine nights after delivery a lamp burned in the room, not only to provide the mother with light in case she needed it but also as a protection against ghosts. In addition, neem leaves were hung from the doorway indicating that the mother was in seclusion and that no woman who was mourning or menstruating (states regarded as polluting and therefore dangerous for the new mother and child) could visit the house (R. Freed and S. Freed, 1980: 381–383).

Wrestler had an unnamed disfiguring skin disease, which was said to cover his entire body. A number of people both in 1958–59 and 1977–78 told how he caught the disease. Steady, his older brother, said that his brother was impotent when he married so he went to a hakim who gave him some medicine. The impotence was cured (he had an eight-month-old baby daughter in 1958), but the general belief was that the medicine had not been properly purified so that it caused Wrestler's skin disease. In 1978, Wrestler himself said that the disease first occurred in 1958 when he was 26 years old. Actually he had it before 1958, for we saw clear evidence of it in January 1958 at the beginning of our fieldwork. As described to us, he first had a boil on his nose, but then the disease spread throughout his body. As of 1977, his skin was peeling away and he wore bandages on many parts of his body. Family members once took him to Irwin Hospital where doctors prescribed some medicine which gave him temporary relief, but he stopped taking the medicine and then sought relief from *vaid*s and a variety of curers and compounders. By 1977, he could no longer bathe himself and his wife bathed him. He was then 45 years old; he died late in 1978 or shortly thereafter.

In 1958, a neighboring Brahman offered another version of Wrestler's disease. He said that Wrestler had been a famous wrestler in his youth and traveled around for wrestling matches. He defeated the disciples of another famous wrestler, named Hanuman. At that time, Wrestler's status was a matter of izzat (honor or prestige) in Shanti Nagar. According to this informant, whose account was supported by another informant also in 1958, a contending wrestler put mercury in Wrestler's food which caused the disease. Another version from 1958 was that mercury was given to Wrestler when the first signs of his disease appeared.

In a trial reported in 1875 at Lahore, Punjab, the question raised in the case was whether mercury was a poison. A Dr. Brown stated that metallic mercury was often used by Indians in order to injure people who had offended or hurt them. He said that such people believed that when mercury entered the body it would erupt in sores and leprous spots on the skin. The victim in this legal case was a woman. After changing the description of mercury to "an unwholesome drug," a conviction was obtained (Goldwater, 1972: 28). Thus, the contention that an opponent of Wrestler put mercury in his food is not far-fetched.

In 1958, we wondered whether the skin disease might be yaws or syphilis, the visible symptoms being due to the use of mercury to cure the disease, for before the introduction of penicillin, mercury was used to treat syphilis. Goldwater (1972: Chap. 15) traced the use of mercury in treating syphilis from the last decade of the fifteenth century until the use of penicillin. Although he considered the use of mercury in treating syphilis to be the most colossal hoax perpetrated in the history of the medical profession, he also pointed out that it was the first drug used for killing pathogenic microorganisms. However, mercury is a cumulative poison, not easily discharged from the body (Harris and Levey, 1975: 1751; Berkow, 1982: 2444, table 290–294).

The last stage of Wrestler's disease showed similarities to the late stage of syphilis, that is, tissue hypersensitivity with ulcerations, necrosis, and degenerative processes in the central nervous system (Berkow, 1982: 1616). Because village families would rarely if ever have acknowledged that a member of their household had syphilis, confirmation of the speculation that Wrestler had it would have to come from neighbors, and no one whom we questioned regarded it as a possibility (Append. I: Discoveries—1905–1912, Syphilis; Descriptions—Syphilis).

A Jat in 1977–78 told us that skin diseases were inherited, an assertion which offered the opportunity to ask about Wrestler. We asked him whether the family of Wealthy Landowner suffered an inherited skin disease, specifically if Wrestler had one. He said, "No skin disease exists in the family," attributing Wrestler's disease to poisonous medicine. He said that mercury could cause the disease. When we told him that formerly mercury was the treatment for syphilis, his son who was standing by said, "Syphilis is not common here." We asked them what they thought caused syphilis, and the young man said that it was heat coming out of urine. We pointed out that venereal diseases were transmitted by sexual contact, and they replied that villagers were not apt to have such diseases, that venereal diseases were more characteristic of cities than villages.

These questions were partly stimulated by what we had learned when we accompanied a group of physicians and nurses working with the World Health Organization in a tour of some villages in the Delhi region where, in addition to other diseases, venereal diseases were found. The group said that it was not easy to collect information about venereal diseases or to obtain the cooperation of males, especially husbands, with regard to such diseases, inasmuch as the physicians and nurses were women and they interviewed only women.

No statistics were available regarding the incidence of venereal diseases in the Delhi region, but two venereal disease clinics reported 3361 cases in one clinic, and 2050 in the other. However, the figures include the city. Our informants' claim that venereal disease is less likely in the villages than in the city is probably valid. In any case, the identity of Wrestler's ailment cannot be answered by informant testimony, and the doctors at Irwin Hospital apparently offered no specific diagnosis, although their failure to do so probably eliminated leprosy from consideration. Doctors would have recognized the disease, and in the Delhi region it is primarily confined to beggars and leper colonies (Gazetteer Unit, Delhi Adm., 1976: 871–872). (For information on leprosy and the treponematoses, cf. Davey and Wilson, 1971: Chaps. III, XII; Wingate, 1972: 407–408, 464; Wood, 1979: Chap. 6; Berkow, 1982: 140–143, 1616–1623, Kumar et al., 1982.)

The information about Wrestler is pertinent to the drowning of Whose Daughter, the alleged daughter of Wrestler. According to reports, Whose Daughter and Little Goddess (the Jat girl in the group interview of children) were school chums (Chaps. 10, 22). After school one day they took a water buffalo belonging to Wealthy Landowner to the pond to be bathed. The pond lay on the north side of Lane III, running from the highway into the village, forming part of the crossroads (Append. IV: Map 4, Lanes I, II, III). There were no dwellings on this lane except at the intersection of the lanes in the village proper. It was common for children to take care of cows and water buffaloes. While washing the animal, they talked and played. Something happened to stampede the buffalo. Little Goddess said that she was leading the buffalo by a rope but dropped it when the buffalo stampeded. Whose Daughter stepped backward into deeper water, and the buffalo pushed her down into the water where she drowned. The tragedy happened at a time when few people passed by the pond. The Brahman servant in the household of Wealthy Landowner retrieved her body for cremation. Although the drowning was accidental, Little Goddess felt guilty and feared Whose Daughter's ghost. The ghost possessed her several times in 1977–78.

It was rumored that Whose Daughter was not the daughter of Wrestler, but of Wrestler's wife and their Brahman servant. The girl was said to resemble the servant. She was dark-skinned as was he, while Wrestler and his wife were relatively fair. The servant was very fond of Whose Daughter and bought her presents regularly. When she died, he was said "almost to have gone mad." His profound grief at her death suggests more than just affection. This rumor about Whose Daughter ties into Steady's statement that his brother, Wrestler, was treated for impotence. If Wrestler was indeed impotent for any significant period, his wife's alleged liaison with the servant may have been condoned by Wealthy Landowner to perpetuate the family line.

After Wealthy Landowner died in 1977, his joint family separated into three households. The cowives lived in one apartment in the old family house; Wrestler and his family occupied another apartment. Steady, the eldest son, moved his nuclear family to the cattle shed which he converted to a dwelling. At the time, Steady and his wife had three unmarried sons, ages 22, 18, and 13, and an unmarried daughter, Goody, age 16. The 18-year-old son was studying to be an electrician. Steady's eldest son, Welder, had finished higher secondary school and then trained as a welder, but was unable to find a job. He was under considerable pressure to find a job, which was almost a requirement before his marriage could be arranged. As happened among some other young men in the village in such circumstances, he suffered a series of ghost possessions. The ghost was identified as his cousin, Whose Daughter. His mother said that he was possessed the first time because he passed the cremation grounds while eating sweets. She explained that after eating sweets or any sweet foods, including milk, one should rinse one's mouth with salt water before going outside. Otherwise a ghost might be attracted and seize a person. Mothers commonly taught their children that they should not eat outside, especially sweet foods, or a ghost would get them. When Welder's possessions continued and became quite severe, a Brahman, here called Respected Leader, who was an Air Force officer, was fetched from a nearby large village to drive off the ghost.

THE BOY HAD TO DIE

A five-year-old Brahman boy died suddenly in the fall of 1977, despite treatment by a practitioner of Western medicine. His mother and grandmother, who were most involved in the case, were sure that a ghost had taken the boy and that his death was inevitable. The sudden death stunned not only the boy's family and close kin but also other villagers. Widow-in-Between said, "He died suddenly. In the morning he went to the Baniyas' shop and bought sweet potatoes and *khil* [popped rice], ate them, then came home, went upstairs, slept, and there they found him dead. On that day the whole village was shocked by his death because he was an active small boy, who ran around and was very playful. They cremated him. For children they don't do death ceremonies. For children's deaths, they give *roti*s [unleavened bread] to a cow for 10 to 13 days." The shortness and simplicity of funeral rituals for children can be interpreted as representing their brief life, the hope that their souls will soon be released from the round of rebirths, the cost of funeral rituals, and the high mortality rates of infants and children.

The following complex and often interrupted interview took place some months later in the home of Grief Stricken, the mother of the boy who died. She, her husband, and children lived with her husband's mother, father, and their four unmarried children, ranging in age from 10 to 16. When their five-year-old son died, they then had two surviving children. Their first child, a daughter, was born dead. The next child was the five-year-old boy who later died; then another son and daughter, aged three and two, were born. Less than a month after the five-year-old boy died in 1977, another daughter was born. A total of 11 people then lived in the house.

We visited this household because Bruised Flower, the dead boy's grandmother, a woman 45 to 50 years old, was on our list of respondents to be interviewed for the Health Opinion Survey (Append. VI). Family members kept entering and leaving the room during the interview and an 18-year-old man, the son of the grandfather's elder brother, was present the entire time. In 1974 he failed his 10th grade examinations and ran away from home. After wandering for three years, he returned home in 1977. Since his return, he had been underfoot, in and out of his father's and uncle's houses. His pseudonym is Hippie because of his former unconventional, peripatetic existence. A neighbor, Sudden Grief, whose husband, Victim, was killed in the 1960s, also drifted in and out during the interview.

The questions and answers had barely begun when Bruised Flower and Grief Stricken, the mother of the dead boy, began telling about the child's death with interjections from Hippie. Grief Stricken was pregnant and soon to give birth when her son died. Bruised Flower said that the boy came home, said he wasn't feeling well, and went upstairs; then he vomited, excreted, had Fever, lay down, and never spoke again. Hippie then went to fetch Doctor John from his shop in the nearby town. He was not in his shop so his partner, Lady Doctor, a physician with an MBBS degree, came in his place.

She examined the child and found that he had a temperature of 107°F and was delirious. She gave him two injections: one for pneumonia and one to reduce Fever, the sign of ghost illness in the view of his grandmother and mother. The child then stopped vomiting and excreting, the Fever went down, and the child slept. Lady Doctor instructed Bruised Flower to see that a pot with a smoldering dung fire was placed under the bed, a step customarily taken when a person was quite ill. The doctor had given the injections and instructions about noon and said that the child would be all right. She further told them not to talk to the boy. Then she left.

Shortly thereafter Bruised Flower, Grief Stricken, and Hippie looked at the boy and decided he was either dying or dead. Although Hippie was fairly certain he was dead, he carried the boy to the bus stop to take him to the government medical center in the nearby town. He found that the bus would not come until 2 p.m. There he waited at the bus stop about an hour. When he reached the medical center, as he expected, the child was pronounced dead. Grief Stricken did not accompany her son because of her advanced pregnancy.

Hippie brought the boy's corpse home so that he and Bruised Flower could prepare the body for cremation, which they delayed until the boy's father returned from work. Because the child was under six years of age, the two women said that no special service was held for him. Grief Stricken added that the villagers did not know any ceremonies for children so whatever was done for a child was incomplete. She also commented that when her son came home on the day of his death, she gave him some bread and an unidentified tablet.

Although Lady Doctor had been called, Bruised Flower said, "It [the treatment] was all foolishness. This death had to happen. The boy had to die. The child went upstairs at about 10 to 11 a.m., vomited, excreted, and stopped talking."

After Bruised Flower and Grief Stricken finished their account of the boy's death, we continued with the Health Opinion Survey. The eighth question was whether Bruised Flower had frightening dreams. Instead of answering for herself, she said that her daughter-in-law had a number of bad dreams. Grief Stricken then told about her dreams:

I had four bad dreams before my son died. In one I saw the house had fallen down. In another dream someone stole something from the house. In the third dream there was a loss of money. In the fourth dream Hippie struck me on the head and I lost a lot of blood. These four dreams foretold that someone in the family would die. Three days before my son's death, I dreamed that two men entered the house and called out, "Are you sleeping?" I replied, "I'm awake." Then I woke my husband and said, "Some thieves are in the house." We looked around, saw nobody, and went back to sleep. The night before my son died, I had the same dream but the men entered this room. When you see the ghost of a person who has died come into a house in a dream, it is a bad omen. One of the two men was my father's dead younger brother. I asked him, "Why, if you are dead, do you come here?" Then I awoke.

I believe that when I dreamed the first time the boy was already sick. I had the first dream at 1:00 a.m. and was afraid one of the children would fall ill so I felt the foreheads of my two sons and daughter, but they seemed normal. At 2:30 a.m. I did so again and found my five-year-old son had Fever. He asked for water, and then I knew he had Fever.

Grief Stricken was asked whether she worried about her children's health, food, and clothing. She replied briefly that such concerns are usual and cannot be avoided but also spoke about her own health. "Since the death of my son, I often feel dizzy, and yesterday from the dizziness I had a headache. The dizziness started from the day my son died. Almost a month later my infant daughter was born. The government nurse delivered the child and inoculated her against diseases."

It was clear from Bruised Flower's responses to the Health Opinion Survey that she suffered from a number of physical ailments, claiming to have many aches and pains, leukorrhea, and thin blood. The last two diseases were often diagnosed and treated by Home Trained, who combined Ayurveda with the practice of popular pharmaceutical medicine learned from his brother-in-law, a compounder. (On leukorrhea in Ayurveda, see Kutumbiah, 1969: 180–181; and for Western medicine, see Berkow, 1982: 1674.) Bruised Flower had one of the highest stress scores on the Health Opinion Survey. Her total was 51, anxiety 16, depression 13, indicating too much stress (Append. VI). The conditions under which the questions were administered may have added to the total score, but the main elements were the recent death of her grandson, listening to Grief Stricken's dreams whose meaning was now clear after the boy's death, the crowded living conditions, and other family problems.

Bruised Flower, her husband, and children lived jointly with her husband's elder brother and his wife. The older couple often fought with each other. When they were not fighting, the wife would fight with her brother-in-law. After fighting with her husband and brother-in-law she would beat her younger sister-in-law, Bruised Flower, who was the scapegoat after the scraps between husband and wife. For 14 to 15 years of her married life until the two families separated, Bruised Flower's sister-in-law, the senior female authority figure in the household, beat her. The sister-in-law was also her patrilineal cousin, following the age-honored pattern of marrying sisters or patrilineal cousins to brothers or patrilineal cousins with the hope that they would live together more peaceably than unrelated women.

The two families separated at the end of the 1950s, but they continued their bickering because the land was still held jointly by the two brothers. The younger was not very industrious, which was the elder brother's wife's main complaint against him. Thus, his pseudonym is Loafer. His wife, Bruised Flower, said that all he ever did was run the tractor and play cards. During the interview, both women commented that women really do the work of weeding and harvesting the tomato crop, while all the men do is run tractors, play cards, and smoke the hookah. Bruised Flower claimed that when she was unable to work and direct the other members of the family, they all sat around doing nothing.

The two brothers had built a *baithak* across the front of their houses, which, with the introduction of electricity in the 1960s, became one of the places where village men played cards late into the night. Construction of the *baithak* reduced the size of the women's quarters. One of the families had 11 members and the other, 13. The houses were small for the number of people. Villagers tolerate rather dense concentrations of people, but even by village standards, we thought that the two families were crowded.

In both these families through the years a number of children died. The elder brother's wife had born 13 children: the first child, a daughter, died at three to four months of age; the sixth child, a son, died at age 12; for her eighth pregnancy this woman bore triplets, two girls and a boy, all of whom died 10 days after birth. Out of 13 live births, five died: three girls and two boys.

In Loafer's family, he and his wife, Bruised Flower, had nine children, three boys and six girls. Of these nine, the third child born, a girl, died when six days old; the fourth child, a boy, died when he was one month old; and the fifth child a girl, died when she was four to five months old. The last two deaths happened between the end of the 1950s and the beginning of the 1960s, when adult members of the joint household were embroiled in bitter fights and finally separated. The two families were still joint when Bruised Flower suffered severe beatings at the hands of her sister-in-law. Once she attempted suicide in the main village well. She was rescued and an effort was made to cover up the attempted suicide by saying that she had accidently slipped and fallen into the well. After the separation, the younger brother's family was quite poor.

Neither Loafer nor his brother had gone to school. The elder brother, however, joined an adult education class in the 1950s so he could read a little and sign his name. Loafer learned to read a bit when he was in the army, having run away to enlist when he was 18, and he traveled to Java, Sumatra, Singapore, Malaya, and Assam while in service. He returned home six years later and married Bruised Flower who was ten years younger than he. The children of these relatively nonliterate brothers went to school and did fairly well except for Hippie who failed in the tenth grade. The husband of Grief Stricken and father of the five-year-old boy who died was well educated, having finished higher secondary school with additional training for composition and proofreading so that he had obtained a job with a large printing press. His wife, Grief Stricken, was nonliterate.

At first, Grief Stricken and Bruised Flower blamed Lady Doctor for the death of the boy.

One reason she was criticized is that village women had no previous experience of women as curers. As a result, they were reluctant to accept a woman in the role of a curer or doctor although some women were midwives and nurses. Hippie attempted to correct the women when they called Lady Doctor a nurse, saying she was a compounder, but many villagers called a compounder a doctor because their experience with compounders was that they were men and curers.

Grief Stricken and Bruised Flower said that Lady Doctor had mishandled the case. They did not understand why two injections were given or why they should not talk to the boy and should leave him alone. When someone falls ill in the village, it is customary for a number of people to rally around and not leave the person alone. This custom is related to the general belief of villagers and other Indians that one should not be alone. "To be left alone for any length of time becomes stressful" to Indians (Surya, 1969: 389). All told, Lady Doctor and her treatment did not fit into the composite village picture of a doctor or how to take care of a person who was ill. Although the grief experienced at the sudden death of the child turned into anger and criticism of Lady Doctor, still the mother and grandmother believed the real cause of death was due to the omens in the dreams of Grief Stricken, particularly the presence in one dream of the ghost of Grief Stricken's father's younger brother. Her son also had Fever and therefore died of ghost illness.

During the discussion of the five-year-old boy's death, not once did his mother or grandmother mention his name because they believed the boy had become a ghost. Grief Stricken did not use the name of her dead uncle for the same reason. The strong belief in ghosts as a cause of illness and death underlies the grandmother's statement, "It [Lady Doctor's treatment] was all foolishness. This death had to happen. The boy had to die."

CHAPTER 15: DEATH OF ADULTS

Most of the adults (people 15 years of age and older) who die tortured and/or before their allotted time and are believed to become ghosts die from a dread disease. Homicide, which includes murder and manslaughter, provides an additional reason for souls to become wandering ghosts, as does suicide. Fatal accidents, chiefly falls and drownings, are rare among adults. Children are more likely to drown than adults. The only adult death that we recorded where a fall was a factor also involved drunkenness linked with robbery; it was therefore described as murder in the course of robbery. Although tales of homicide and suicide circulate endlessly in the village, only 20 well-documented adult cases came to our attention: 8 murders; 11 suicides; and 1, either a suicide or a murder. In addition, other deaths of adults are reported here; it is debatable whether some of them are homicides, suicides, or deaths from other causes. However, the individuals may have died without issue or before their allotted time, thus their souls became ghosts. The ghosts of individuals who are murdered or commit suicide haunt Shanti Nagar longer than other ghosts.

HOMICIDES

The chief types of homicide (the killing of one person by another) are manslaughter (without premeditation or intent to harm) and murder (with malice aforethought). In terms of village custom, killing a person, whether manslaughter or murder, is called murder and is so categorized here. Villagers recognize self defense as grounds for justifiable homicide, as in the West, as well as the protection of "family honor." At this point, however, Western and Indian customs diverge. For example, the so-called "unwritten law" of adultery in parts of the United States would some decades ago have excused in the eyes of a jury an outraged husband who caught his wife *flagrante delicto* and killed her lover in hot anger (cf. Hoebel, 1968: 286). We never heard of such a homicide in Shanti Nagar. However, comparable acts would be a father's execution of his daughter for fornication, especially if an illicit pregnancy results, or a brother's slaying of his sister's lover. Sisters and daughters in this patrilineal society are important to family honor because they are blood relations rather than in-laws, but within a caste, village men might try to kill a married woman who was an adulteress. In former times, it is said that an adulteress was marked by having her nose cut off (Mandelbaum, 1988: 10–11, 20–21).

Implicit in the foregoing comments is the principle that crime, law, social control, and the resolution of disputes should be analyzed in relation to social structure and custom. In any complex society or nation, several legal systems, each one particular to a subunit of the social structure, may be operating, sometimes in conflict concerning the propriety of specific behavior. Legal systems often form a hierarchy that reflects the increasing inclusiveness of subunits. In the case of rural North India, family, caste, village, and state form such a hierarchy. An individual is a member of several subunits simultaneously and therefore may be under the control of somewhat different legal systems. Thus, individual behavior that is proper at one level may be illegal at another (cf. Pospisil, 1971: 97–126). People generally resolve conflicts between long-established customary law and more recent laws enacted at high governmental levels by ignoring or evading the latter for as long as and to the extent possible. For example, the custom of the levirate may result in a man having two spouses at the same time. This form of polygyny was permissible formerly but became illegal in 1954 under national law. Prior to 1954 widows were taken as levirate spouses under certain conditions by a brother or patrilineal cousin of the late husband, the man then managing the land and other property. This village custom was continued after the passage of the law, widows being given the option of accepting or rejecting a levirate marriage as either a first or second wife. Moreover, even village men with modern views in 1977 would suggest that a childless man marry a second wife. The need for children, especially a son, took precedence over conflicting law. Both national laws and laws of the Delhi region have allowed daughters as well as sons to inherit property, widows to hold and manage the property of their husbands for life, and have forbidden the payment of dowries under the following acts: Hindu Women's Rights to Property Act 4 of 1937; Delhi Land Reforms Act, 1954; Hindu Succession Act, 1956; Dowry Prohibition Act, 1961 (S. and R. Freed, 1976: 90; Gazetteer Unit, Delhi Adm., 1976: 597, 601; Derrett, 1978: 72, 82, 89, 96, 121). However, dowries are still routinely paid and daughters usually do not claim a share in their father's land if they have brothers.

To handle this complex legal situation, villagers adhere to the important maxim that the village should manage its own affairs, with the corollary that castes and families also have their proper quasi-autonomous domains in which they enforce codes of conduct recognized as proper in those domains. The state is to be kept at arm's length. "The highly developed state with its powerful law looms so large," writes Redfield (1967: 6), "that perhaps we do not always see that within it are many little societies . . . enforcing [their] own special regulations." When the enforcement of village customary codes came into conflict with state and national law, villagers, especially the Jats, the dominant caste, tried to circumvent outside intervention. Circumvention was also the order of the day even in the case of disapproved behavior that was considered to be "family business." When disputes could not be managed by the traditional means—which ranged from informal counseling by respected elders, to ad hoc panchayats, caste panchayats, and the village panchayat—and the matter came to the attention of higher authority, the disputants sometimes successfully manipulated the police and courts to their own advantage (Cohn, 1965: 104–106; Pospisil, 1971: Chap. 4; R. Freed, 1971; S. Freed and R. Freed, 1976: 169; Baxi, 1982: 329–331, 339–345).

Baxi, formerly Dean of the University of Delhi Law School (recently Provost of the University), described this state of affairs as "cross-sterilization." Baxi divided Indian legal systems into the State Legal System of the Government of India and the Non-State Legal Systems, which include the kind of customary law encountered in Shanti Nagar. An important aspect of the village type of legal system, which he pointed out, is that villagers have two sets of dominant social relations: one is to the village community; the other, to the *biradari* (the brotherhood of locally resident caste-mates) and *jati* (subcaste). He further stated that in village nonstate legal systems, due to patterns of caste dominance, the village panchayat (governing council) becomes the extension of the dominant group in the village. Conflicts which arise between the village legal system and the state system raise questions not only of differences in values but also of the interests of the dominant group. The dominant group in Shanti Nagar has long been and still is the Jat caste (Baxi, 1982: 329–334; S. Freed and R. Freed, 1987: 22–24).

Because two major legal traditions operate simultaneously in Shanti Nagar, official governmental law and informal village law, information about murder and suicide can be difficult to uncover. The principal reason is that people can use the formal legal system to harass enemies or competitors, who are usually members of other lineages or parties (*dhars*) (S. Freed and R. Freed, 1987: 23). Therefore, villagers are not much given to discussing murders if the information can be used against them. However, members of castes, lineages, or parties hostile to the group in which a murder took place are often happy to offer information and more or less informed speculation. Women are sometimes easier to approach about suspected murders and suicides because they do not generally participate in village politics, the domain of men. Several police officers live in Shanti Nagar. Concerning crimes committed in the village by fellow villagers, they follow village custom rather than codified law. Since they work in jurisdictions other than the one that includes Shanti Nagar, they have no jurisdiction in their village of residence and feel no need to intervene in village matters. Moreover, they understand village power and politics and want to avoid unnecessary personal trouble due to ties of family, lineage, and caste.

CASE HISTORIES: MURDERS AND MANSLAUGHTER

In our selection of case histories, we concentrate on murder and suicide because these deaths result in the soul becoming a wandering ghost. In addition, they reveal social, political, legal, family, and individual aspects of village life. We also describe some questionable deaths that possibly involve homicide. Homicides are interesting in their own right both as drama and in terms of karma and dharma. An element of mystery is sometimes involved in murders or in determining whether a death is murder or suicide, which brings out the latent detective in anthropologists. On this point, Sir Cecil Walsh, an ex-Sessions judge who served during the British Raj, wrote, "Mysterious murders, arising out of cold blooded conspiracies and ambushes, in which well-to-do people are often involved for various reasons . . . are extremely difficult to unravel" (Walsh, 1977: 22).

The cases of homicide and suicide feature more women (14) than men (6). Five men were murdered and one committed suicide. By caste, the murder victims were one Brahman (killed by a Jat man), one Chamar (killed by a Chamar man), and three Jats (two killed by Jat men and one by an unknown robber). In addition, one Jat man was either poisoned by his wife or died of a dread disease. One Mahar Potter man committed suicide.

Three females were murdered, 10 committed suicide, and one case was either murder or suicide. By caste, the murder victims were two Jats killed by their husbands, and one Brahman murdered by her father. The 10 female suicides list six Jats, two Brahmans, one Lohar Blacksmith, and one Mahar Potter. Of the 14 female homicides and suicides, all were wives, i.e., daughters-in-law of the village, except the murdered Brahman daughter.

We also describe one case of a man who clearly died of a dread disease, and one case of a maternity death, both representing common deaths. Villagers frequently discussed in detail the cases presented here, which can be taken as substantial documentation. Regarding the three chief motives for murder, namely, land, women, and money, it is important to note that most village land was owned by Jats and Brahmans, the most numerous castes in the village.

TIPPLER'S FIRST WIFE

Tippler, so-called because of his drunkenness, was the son of a lambardar, a government official formerly appointed by the British to collect land revenue, which posi-

tion was abolished by law in 1954. However, the former lambardar still had considerable prestige in the village. He was born around 1900–1901; his wife, a few years later. The couple had two sons, Rival and Tippler, born in 1926 and 1929 respectively, and one daughter, who at the time of our fieldwork was living in the village of her husband. Rival never attended school. Tippler went as far as higher secondary school but failed his final examinations. His mother had no education. Although we have no information about the lambardar's education, he may have learned to read and write Urdu (the written language used by lambardars). Rival attended an adult education class held in the village in the 1950s, so he could read and write.

Although the lambardar was a member of the most powerful Jat lineage in the village, his family was nuclear, rather unusual for Jats in the 1950s. In the lambardar's nuclear family of birth, an elder brother died young without issue, and since the lambardar had no other brothers, he succeeded to his father's position. Thus, when Rival and Tippler were youngsters, they too lived in a nuclear family consisting of their mother, father, and sister. A Chuhra Sweeper was their regular servant. For a short time a young girl lived with them to attend school in Shanti Nagar because her mother, a schoolteacher and friend of the family, lived and worked some distance from Shanti Nagar. The lambardar owned 21.1 hectares (250 bighas) of land and was wealthy. His property occupied a large corner plot located at the junction of the two principal village lanes (Append. IV: Map 4, Lanes II, IV, no. 9, 10, 11). The buildings included a place for the servant, and the land surrounding the buildings was well tended. Tippler's father wielded considerable political power in the village and region, and was highly respected.

The history of Jats in this region of North India has some bearing on the behavior of Tippler and his brother, Rival. In the 19th century Jats practiced female infanticide and fraternal polyandry. As late as 1938, Prince Petros of Greece reported that some Jats (Hindus and Muslims), albeit somewhat reluctantly, admitted that some families still practiced fraternal polyandry (Prince Petros, 1963: 122–123) although the custom was sporadic and kept secret. Again in 1950, he learned from a Sikh student at the University of Delhi that a younger brother mated with the wife of an elder brother during the latter's prolonged absence from home. Petros correlated the custom with the close relationship and solidarity existing between males of the joint families and patrilineage. He further stated, "Polyandry is a latent male homosexual and near incestuous form of the marital institution correlated with excessive economic and social pressure on the nuclear family" (Petros, 1963: 568–569). Polyandry is an adjustment to the scarcity of women in former times due to female infanticide. Survivals of polyandry in India have lingered well into the 20th century. For example, songs were sung in the 1950s and thereafter about a Jat who mated with his brother's wife when the brother was away in the army. Thus, the belief persisted that a wife was the property of a family, and that men in the family might mate with her in the absence or death of a husband (Crooke, 1896, 3: i, 10, 29, 310; Mandelbaum, 1974: 34, fn. 6; R. Freed and S. Freed, 1989: 144–145, 148–151; Chap. 6: Female Infanticide).

Due to the paucity of sons in the former lambardar's line of descent for a number of generations, Rival and Tippler did not enjoy as much male companionship within the family as was characteristic of many village families, particularly the Jats. From age six, Jat boys usually lived in the *baithak*, the men's house, and spent their time mainly with male relatives and friends. In fact, the separation of the sexes took place early in most village families. In school, boys and girls were generally kept separate with teachers of their own sex. Thus, boys from an early age had as their main companions males of their family, lineage, and caste. In any case, Tippler's companions were primarily men, which was not unusual in the village where men and women tended to be segregated from each other due to purdah. Rival and Tippler were not friendly, especially since the lambardar favored his younger son.

In 1958, Tippler led up to the death of his first wife by dwelling on his early childhood, blaming his mother for his poor performance in school, and indicating he much preferred his father to his mother. He said that he had not done too well in school because his mother

never had his food ready for him on time so that he was often late and sometimes missed school entirely. As a result, his male schoolteacher beat him. His statements about his mother and teacher were echoed by other boys whose schooling was interrupted by mothers who took them out of school to run errands and did not understand the importance of being on time. The practice of teachers' beating students was traditional in the schools, a custom associated with British schoolmasters in India. Further, there was very little formal schooling in villages before the 20th century, and what did exist in the early 20th century was primarily for boys. By the time Tippler was 17 years old in 1946, educated boys were beginning to ask that their wives be able at least to read and write. Although Tippler would have liked an educated wife, such was not the case with his first wife nor was it to be for his second (R. Freed and S. Freed, 1981: 119–125, tables 3, 4).

Tippler mentioned that he was first introduced to liquor in a hospital after recovering from 63 hours of unconsciousness, the result of an automobile accident. His father brought him liquor to ease his pain. The accident took place in the City of Delhi after he ran away from home in order to avoid his first wife when she came for first mating at Gauna. He said:

I was first married when I was five to six years old; the girl was three to four years old. The wedding seemed just like play. She did not come for first mating until I was 17 to 18 years old when I was taking my higher-secondary examinations. The whole village knows when she came here because I left the village. I did not understand what marriage should be. I did not know why I was married and I hated her. The girl came here three to four times, but I did not go to fetch her from her home and later she died. Then I was married again. When my father selected her, the only thing he wanted was to see that the girl came from a good family, was fair, and strong.

Later in the interview Tippler recounted, "One day my first wife went to the well to wash clothes. I do not know whether her foot slipped and she accidentally fell into it or whether she jumped." When asked which of the two it was, he answered:

> I don't know because I had no hate for her, but I never thought of her as my wife because I did not know what marriage was at the time. [Note: the contradiction regarding hating her.] Even when she had been here a number of times, I frankly told her that I had no love for her because we had been tied together forcibly with no choice. All this happened to me because of my own luck due to past actions and was no concern of the girl.

According to various village versions, Tippler murdered his first wife by drowning her in a well. A village Chamar who saw Tippler kill his first wife said:

> When Tippler was a child, he and his elder brother, Rival, were married in a double wedding to two sisters. When Tippler's wife came for first mating, he did not like her so he snuck up behind her when she was on the way to wash clothes at the well. He then tried to push her in; she was strong and struggled, but finally he choked her and threw her into the well. He spread the clothes around to make it appear as though she had been washing them, broke off two bricks near the edge of the well, and threw her bucket into the water so it looked as though she had slipped when the bricks broke, and thus he made the death appear accidental.

The Chamar, standing nearby, witnessed the murder unbeknownst to Tippler. The case never went to court because Tippler's father at that time was the most influential man in the village. The Chamar's version spread through the village, and the consensus of villagers was that Tippler murdered his wife and that her soul then became a malevolent ghost who haunted Tippler and the village thereafter.

Before Tippler became an alcoholic, his main interests were attending cinemas, eating in elegant restaurants in Delhi, and drinking. He claimed that he had learned more about life and how to live from the cinema than if he had attended college where all one did was read, thus further excusing his failure to pass

his higher-secondary examinations. Sometimes he saw as many as four films in one day, mostly by himself.

His father took him to his first cinema when he was nine years old. What he most enjoyed in his early years were films with beatings and fights. At that time, this vicarious violence was an outlet for his aggressions and tension. Later in life, he became openly violent, beating his third wife and becoming pugnacious when drunk. He tried to follow a life style which fit the romantic, sometimes violent, films that he enjoyed. During his early attempt to escape village life and his first wife, he ran away from home, was in the automobile accident and hospitalized, was said to have killed his first wife, joined the police, and after having been dismissed for some wrongdoing, he went to Bombay in an unsuccessful attempt to make films.

Around 1956 or 1957, Tippler married his second wife, about whom in 1958 he said, "She only visited me two or three times and spent most of the time in her parents' village. The second marriage was against my wishes, and I was not happy with it. I would be willing to allow her to divorce me and remarry except that it would cast a blot on my family." Asked whether he had ever been in love with a woman, Tippler replied, "Although I like women and am friends with a number of them, I have only seen what love is in the cinema and have never experienced it myself."

During 1958–59 when Tippler was living in Shanti Nagar, he had a realistic attitude regarding the property he owned and the income obtained from it, but his notions of romantic love and marriage were formed from films and did not fit village customs. In his autobiographical discussion, he showed a clear preference for his father. A number of times, he described his mother in the same derogatory terms he used for his first and second wives. Later in the 1960s after his second wife left him, he took a third wife.

The effect of the cinema on Tippler and his remarks about it reflect to some extent the influence of modern media on youngsters. In Tippler's case, he was the only nine-year-old village boy exposed to the cinema in the late 1930s as far as we could ascertain. The psychiatrist, Erna Hoch (1974: 675), with many years of fieldwork in Kashmir and associated with the Hospital for Psychiatric Diseases, Srinagar, Kashmir, India, commented on this influence: "It seems to me that, in present India, the world of the cinema and, most recently, also of television, is to a great extent replacing the former realm of the gods and ghosts, as a means for 'realizing the undeveloped possibilities.'"

Hoch's statement is most apt when applied to Tippler. For both him and his father, films provided a fantasy life much more than did the supernatural realm. This substitution partly reflects Arya-Samaj beliefs, largely hostile to the populous spirit world of the traditional village. As a Jat, Tippler was a follower of the Arya Samaj and was taught that there are no ghosts, other spirits, and no deities other than Bhagwan (God). However, the position of Tippler and his parents regarding Arya-Samaj teachings was ambivalent, for the family did not follow all of its practices. When the lambardar died, the two brothers conducted traditional funeral ceremonies, observed a year of mourning, and erected a *samadhi* (a special memorial building) to him. One of Rival's daughters mentioned seeing the ghost of her grandfather after his death. Tippler said that his father helped him after death, thus placing him with the *devata*s and pitris. Tippler frequently consulted astrologers and had his fortune told, all contrary to the Arya Samaj. Within a year after the death of their father, the two brothers separated, their mother going with Rival, leaving Tippler alone except for his second wife, who soon left him.

We first became acquainted with the lambardar, Rival, and Tippler at the beginning of our fieldwork in 1958. At that time, the lambardar was not well and soon died from cardiac arrest. He had been a heavy drinker and introduced his sons to drinking, both of whom drank heavily. This family drinking should be viewed in terms of Jat custom as compared to Brahman custom. Traditionally, Jats, like Rajputs, drank alcoholic beverages. The Rajputs in Deoli, Rajasthan, drank *daru*, a spirit distilled from the flowers of the mahua tree. They considered it their right and a means of relieving tension (Carstairs, 1958: 97, 118–119). The Jats in Shanti Nagar followed the same tradition but drank

distilled commercial or country-made liquor in the late 1950s, despite a prohibition law then in effect. At that time, Tippler sometimes drank with a group of friends, one a Brahman and the rest Jats, usually in Delhi but sometimes surreptitiously in the village. Alcoholic beverages are tabu to Brahmans; instead their traditional and accepted form of intoxication and release of tension is bhang, an infusion from hemp (*Cannabis sativa*). Carstairs (1958: 118) said that his Brahman informants told him that bhang was a sacred drink used by the great god Shiva.

In 1958–59, Tippler was not yet a confirmed alcoholic. He was often likable, entertaining, a shrewd analyst of village politics, and at first a successful politician. He gladly shared his knowledge of village politics with us, and his aid was invaluable. He pushed very hard to step into his father's shoes after his death and thereby managed to tread on the toes of much older, skilled village politicians. In the 1960s, the Government of India was encouraging the settlement, development, and irrigation of arid lands for agricultural purposes, known as colonization projects. Tippler took over one such project at a distance from Shanti Nagar and was absent from the village for long periods. His colonization project was financially successful, but he soon tired of it. His driving ambition for political power was often defeated by his impatience, drinking, and aggressiveness, all of which, but especially alcohol, contributed to his downfall. However, in the late 1950s and early 1960s, he was active in village politics and President of the nearby Jat higher secondary school.

After marriage to his third wife, who was 16 years younger than he and could read and write, Tippler immediately left the village without consummating the marriage and spent his time on the colonization project, leaving his bride with her parents. During Tippler's absence from Shanti Nagar, Rival sent word to Tippler's bride to come to the village. He mated with her; she became pregnant and in 1963 bore the first and only son of Rival who had five daughters. Three days later Rival legally adopted the boy, dubbed Whose Son, thus laying claim to a son, who otherwise legally would have been recognized as Tippler's son. Rival thus followed the traditional practice of fraternal polyandry in his brother's absence, but also resorted to codified law by adopting the child.

The birth of Whose Son brought about legal complications which increased when in 1972 Rival was found by the police unconscious in a ditch far from Shanti Nagar. The supposition of the police was that Rival was quite intoxicated when a dacoit knocked him out, broke his neck, and robbed him. The police brought him to the village; he was hospitalized, never regained consciousness, and died. When Rival died, no hint of foul play on the part of Tippler in arranging or being responsible for his brother's death was mentioned, but the possibility exists because of the sibling rivalry between the brothers and the birth of Rival's son to Tippler's third wife. When Rival died tortured, he qualified for ghosthood, but his ghost was not mentioned in the village, only the complications arising from the birth of Whose Son. After Rival's death, his widow, the sister of Tippler's first wife, an implacable enemy of Tippler, managed her husband's affairs.

By 1977, Tippler was no longer respected in the village but retained a few loyal friends. He had been defeated for the office of pradhan (head of the village council) twice because of his drinking and aggressive, violent behavior. His neighbors regularly complained about his fights with people, beating his wife, and his wife beating him in retaliation, which was a change in wifely behavior from earlier times. (Chap. 22: Mrs. Patriarch on wife beating). Some time after returning from his colonization project, Tippler finally mated with his third wife, so that by 1977 he was living with his wife, Whose Son, and his own children—two sons and a daughter. From Tippler's own statements he never mated with his first two wives, neither of whom bore children.

From Tippler's marital history and autobiographical description of his relations with his mother and father, it seems that Tippler feared mating with a woman and may have been impotent for long periods. His drinking started when he failed his higher-secondary examinations, ran away from mating with his first wife, and was injured in an accident, thus establishing a pattern of release when he could not cope with life crises. Said to have killed his first wife, he never suffered from ghost possessions, but he did undergo a life crisis situation at the time he was expected to mate with his first wife. His drinking became an escape from his guilt and his failures. Outwardly, he was a strong, dark-skinned, good-looking man so villagers compared him to Krishna, the avatar of Vishnu, but by the 1970s, his persistent daily drinking made it difficult to talk with him or even to pass his house.

Tippler and Rival's widow fought bitterly over Rival's land. The dispute took the form of conflict over whether Whose Son had been adopted by Rival. Sons, a widow, and unmarried daughters are potential heirs. After the death of Rival, the Government sent a summons to Rival's widow to come to the government office for the mutation, that is, the recording in governmental records of the transfer of land. As a rule, land mutations are done publicly; the government official should come to the village and declare the mutation openly. In this case, Rival's widow went to the government office with the village pradhan and her lawyer, both of whom testified that Tippler had refused to accept the summons and therefore there was no objection to the mutation.

Tippler learned of the mutation only after the period of appeal had expired. He then filed a case on behalf of Whose Son. The case dragged on for two or three years and was eventually decided against the boy; all the land went to the widow. The court allegedly decided against Whose Son when Tippler failed to appear for a hearing. The widow's lawyer is said to have bribed a court clerk to call the case on a day when Tippler could not be present. Tippler appealed to the judge, who reopened the case. It would be treated as a new case and the whole long expensive procedure would have to be gone through again.

At this point, Manipulator advised Tippler that a compromise was in order. He summoned Tippler's lineage to hear the matter. Tippler argued that the land should go to the boy as the adopted son. The widow's position was that the boy was not hers and she should get the land. The compromise was that she would have the land in her name during her lifetime but that she would make a will in favor of the boy so that when she died the land would pass to him. She admitted that Rival, her husband, had adopted the boy, and he was made to live with her. Tippler's overriding consideration was to neutralize the fact that the land was registered in the widow's name in the land records. This could be done only if the boy was Rival's and her adopted son and she made a will in his favor. Thus both adoption and a last will and testament would favor the boy. Rival's widow could not will the land to anyone other than her adopted son, and the daughters would be out of the picture because of the will. Without the will in favor of the boy and with all the land in her name, the widow could will it to anyone she wished. Tippler would lose all control. The will in favor of the boy protected Tippler's interest to some extent. After Tippler's death, his land would be divided between his two sons with Whose Son inheriting Rival's widow's land. If the adoption were not recognized, Tippler's land would be divided among the three boys, making a lesser share for Tippler's two sons. Manipulator remarked, "Now they all live happily."

Aside from a possible genetic predisposition, which would be speculative, the reasons for Tippler's descent into alcoholism began with his running away from rather than mating with his first wife and his father providing him with liquor after his accident. Family circumstances and relationships, especially with his mother, father, and wives, and his own specific personality, contributed to his downfall. However, his first wife's death was the main reason for his becoming an alcoholic. Individuals can adjust to painful circumstances without recourse to alcohol. The rejection of alcohol is easier in societies where drinking is scorned, as it generally was in Shanti Nagar in 1958–59, a disdain reinforced by the legal prohibition then in effect. However, Tippler was a Jat and there is no tabu on drinking among Jats; it is considered a relatively acceptable form of masculine behavior. Thus, the lambardar introduced his sons to drinking at an early age with no hint of it being disapproved behavior. In 1977–78, drinking was seen at the Holi festival, at some weddings, on Sundays, and during election campaigns, but drunken behavior, especially constant drunken behavior as in Tippler's case, was frowned upon.

As for personality traits, a key determinant in predicting or analyzing a person's relations to others is the individual's ability to integrate the good and bad in his or her self (Foulks and Schwartz, 1982). Tippler's main problem was that his mother was to him a bad object and his father generally a good object, and based on his opinion of his mother and thus women generally, he criticized the wives that his father chose for him. Thus, Tippler blamed his mother for his poor performance in school. In later years, he cast his wives in a similar role as the cause of his problems, for they did not fulfill his cinema-based fantasies about what women should be. Additionally since his mother was barred to him sexually, he transferred the same tabu subconsciously to his wives. His inability to form a warm mature relationship with women was reinforced by the customs of companionship confined chiefly to males, purdah, and the low status of females compared to males.

Another of Tippler's problems was that he had very few people upon whom he could depend, and as he grew older, almost none. The death of his father, who until that time had been the only person he loved and the main support in his life, was an irreparable loss. Although he must have had some dependency needs, he could not acknowledge them and would not have sought out women because of his conflicted view of them based on his concept of the bad mother. At times Tippler seemed to be in a state without object relationships because of his narcissism, but there is no information regarding his possible regression to infantile sexuality in the form of masturbation. Because Hindus fear semen loss, masturbation may lead to anxiety rather than release from tension. Thus, drinking was the main outlet for Tippler. Since liquor was not frowned upon but instead was offered as a panacea by his father, it is not surprising that Tippler became a drunkard (Fenichel, 1945: 63, 83–89, 379 ff.; Freud, 1965: Pt. II; Foulks and Schwartz, 1982: 256–258; Angrosino, 1989: 206–207; Konner, 1989: 5).

Tippler in 1978 was between the second and the last stage of alcoholism. He was physically dependent on alcohol, had lost control over his drinking, and would have denied that he had a drinking problem. He showed no signs of malnutrition, but he drank at any time of the day, was definitely estranged from his brother's family, and was at odds with his wife (Angrosino, 1989: 208). Except for fondness for Whose Son and his own children, Tippler had only two or three male friends in the village. The Western concept of ending up on Skid Row did not apply because he owned substantial property, but if he continued drinking, he might in time dissipate all of it.

The ghost of Tippler's murdered first wife continued to haunt the village through the years. For example, the ghost possessions of two neighboring girls were attributed to her (Chap. 20: Bairagis; Chap. 22: Resourceful). She probably haunted Tippler, too, whether as a ghost or through his conscience. In 1977–78, her ghost was still said to be one of a gang of female ghosts haunting the village. Because the villagers believed that she was murdered, she became a long remembered, malevolent ghost. She was seen by her victims in the neighborhood of Tippler's house. However, no one would have told him that she was still haunting the village because villagers were wary of his violent nature and would not mention her to him to avoid provoking him or for fear that her ghost might attack them.

LITTLE BRIDE

Another well-known case of murder in the 1950s is named for the victim, a Jat bride who was said to have been unusually small or short, the reason her husband gave for not liking her. We first learned of Little Bride's death in 1958 from Schemer, an economically and politically powerful elder Jat. He visited us fairly regularly, so that when he came to see us after not having visited for two weeks, we asked him where he had been. He answered, "I've been to Delhi. I was invited to a birthday party for the son of a friend of mine who is a refugee from Pakistan."

When Schemer was asked what else he had been doing in the city, he replied, "I was there about Young Groom's wife, the little bride who fell into a well." We wanted to know how the accident occurred. He said, "I don't know; it happened at night." We pressed further, asking whether many people fell into

wells and drowned. He answered, "Young women in this country may be unhappy with their husbands but they do not get divorces. They jump into wells instead." When he was asked whether this was what Little Bride did, he replied that he did not know because he had not seen her drown. During the conversation, he avoided direct answers to some questions, but implied that Little Bride committed suicide. With continued questioning, he became more evasive and then changed the subject. He did, however, say that part of the reason he had gone to the city was to testify in court on behalf of Young Groom to the effect that he had a good character and was innocent of killing his wife. As Schemer was a prominent Jat, his testimony was weighty enough to contribute to Young Groom's acquittal.

Because of Schemer's visit, we later asked Nutmeg, a Jat who lived near Young Groom, about the death of Little Bride. Nutmeg said, "Young Groom was married and when the girl came to this village, she committed suicide. She had a lover in her village, considered herself to be his wife, and told Young Groom not to touch her. He did anyhow so she committed suicide by jumping into a well." This suicide version of the story turned out to be a cover-up to protect the principals, all Jats, involved in the case. On another occasion, however, Nutmeg said that Young Groom killed his wife in order to remarry and have another dowry. We interpreted this version in terms of two dominant Jat factions at that time. Young Groom's family belonged to one faction and Nutmeg, to the other. We were new to the village and discounted Nutmeg's pejorative comment as factionalism, not yet realizing that husbands sometimes did murder wives for reasons that to an outsider might appear strange.

In June, 1958, Scapegoat drowned herself in the main village well (Chap. 13: Deaths of Little Boy and Scapegoat). The event stimulated renewed discussion of Little Bride's death. Consensus among villagers was that Little Bride was murdered. She was strangled on her cot. Late at night, her body was lowered from the roof, dragged to a Bairagi well located in the fields, and dumped into it (Append. IV, Map 4, BW). The general opinion was that Young Groom killed her but that someone helped him. Little Bride was described as short but heavy, so the villagers claimed that he could not have carried out the job by himself. Although many people in the village knew of the murder and discussed it among themselves and with us, they did not pass on their remarks to the police, despite pressure.

Because the renewed discussion of the case brought many facts and much informed speculation to our attention, Nutmeg decided to tell us in some detail the relevant background of Young Groom and his family, although he stuck to his opinion that Little Bride had committed suicide. Young Groom was a member of a joint family organized around three brothers. It was headed by Devious, the eldest brother. The next oldest was Army Officer, who was stationed in South India but came home for weddings. When the father of Devious and Army Officer was alive, one of the father's brothers died leaving a widow and her two sons. Their father took the widow as a levirate spouse. She bore him two daughters. After he died, her sons separated from Devious, and she with her two daughters came to live with them. Devious, as the eldest son of his father, was responsible for arranging the marriage of his two half sisters, but had not done so until after the wedding of Young Groom, his youngest brother. Once Young Groom had been wedded, Devious was able to use Little Bride's dowry for the double wedding and dowries of the two half sisters.

Nutmeg confirmed the wealth of Little Bride's family and said, "When she came to her husband for first mating, she brought her full dowry and was wearing beautiful, golden jewelry and brought silver ornaments for the cattle." All was proceeding as planned by Devious until Little Bride's death on the night of the double wedding of Devious's half sisters, at which Army Officer (a brother of Devious), and his wife, Passion Flower, were present. Passion Flower was about four years older than Young Groom and had lived in Devious's household before moving with her husband to South India. The relationship between a younger brother and an elder brother's wife, especially if their ages are not too far apart, could become intimate. This sister-in-law–brother-in-law relationship has been alluded to in songs and stories as the means of readying a young man for marriage (O. Lewis, 1958: 189, 191, 192, 193).

Nutmeg hinted that the intimacy between Young Groom and Passion Flower may have contributed to the death of Little Bride. He blamed Devious for not paying attention to what was happening in his own household. Nutmeg said Devious did not keep a close watch on the people in his family and as a result Little Bride committed suicide. According to him, Devious was so busy with political factions that he made enemies. One enemy reported to the police that Little Bride had been murdered. The police, in turn, went to Devious and informed him that a boy from the Chamar caste told them that Young Groom's wife was murdered.

Tippler presented this version of the demise of Little Bride. "Young Groom wanted to enter military service since a tradition of military service exists in the family. However, he believed he would not be accepted if he was married so he murdered his wife. He did so by fastening her on a cot which had stakes on each side. He strangled her with a rope and the ends of the rope ran across her throat to the stakes. Then he threw her body into a well." According to Tippler, whose informant was a Chamar boy, the marks on her throat proved that she had been strangled. He said that Devious paid Rs. 400 to the police who investigated the case, so it was hushed up for a while. However, members of Little Bride's family were certain that she had been killed and made a statement of accusation to the police. When a new police officer became suspicious and started asking questions, the case was reopened.

In December of the same year, after Tippler had become successful in village politics, he regaled us with panchayat and court cases which had taken place in the village, and talked about his experiences as a police officer. In the case of Little Bride, he stated:

At first the police accepted the testimony of Devious and Young Groom, but due to the report of the Chamar boy and the pressure put on the police by Little Bride's parents, they reopened the case. Devious in his first statement to the police said Little Bride had fallen into the well. The police at that time were unable to obtain evidence to the contrary. When the parents of the girl brought police pressure, the head of the police station told Devious that he should testify that Little Bride and Young Groom had quarreled so she jumped into the well. However, Schemer advised Devious to stick to his original statement that Little Bride accidentally fell and drowned, and so he did. As a result, the police took Young Groom to the station, slugged him, and he confessed. He spent six months in jail and the family spent thousands of rupees to have him acquitted.

What Tippler did not say was that he was responsible for the Chamar boy going to the police, for Tippler's party was in opposition to Devious and Schemer, and the Chamar boy and his father were in debt to Tippler and worked for him.

College Man, a university student, the son of Manipulator, home during the month of June, provided brief but pertinent information. He said that Little Bride's parents believed she was murdered because Young Groom had made two previous attempts on her life. After each attempt the girl visited her natal home and told her parents. College Man reported, "When Little Bride first came, Young Groom tried to overturn the tonga in which she was riding. Another time he attempted to throw her off the roof of their house. The girl was the only child of her parents and brought a great deal of jewelry and wealth with her—even silver ornaments for the cattle."

A young Brahman, Policeman, the son of Progenitor, provided an eyewitness report of Little Bride's murder (Chap. 12. The Families of Progenitor and Gentle Soul). He began by speaking of a grandmother within his own lineage, who had either been murdered or committed suicide. He did not know which because he was a young child when she died. He then continued:

I, however, do know that Young Groom murdered his wife. He was my classmate, and we were friends in school. He did not like his wife because she was short. At first he would not bring her from her parents when he should have, but pressure was brought on him by Devious and the girl's parents, so he brought her to the village. The day before he killed her, he told me that he was going to kill her. I did not believe him because he was my classmate and I did not think he would do such a thing. The next day during the big wedding in Devious's house, while everyone was making a lot of noise, Young Groom strangled his wife with her headcloth. The wife of his brother, Army Officer, helped him. I saw him do it because I was in my cattle shed which is located right next door. Young Groom knew I saw him do it, and now he does not talk to me because he feels ashamed. I did not say or do anything about the death of his wife because he was my classmate and because my parents told me not to do so. That night two Sweepers from a nearby village came and carried the body to the Bairagi well and dropped it into the well. They work for Young Groom's family. Thus, there was complicity within the family.

Policeman's family had a tradition of civil and police service. Another Brahman from Old Brahman Lane had carved out an excellent career with the police (Chap. 21: New Brahman Lane). He and Policeman received their appointments for training through the connections of their mothers' brothers. Such connections were known as access, i.e., the intervention of someone in a position to obtain an appointment or employment. The decision of Policeman and his parents about what to do in the case of Little Bride reflects the attitude and custom that village affairs should be settled within the family and village.

Although Manipulator was a Brahman like Policeman, he was politically involved with the Jat factions through his friendship with the lambardar and then with his son, Tippler. Manipulator's version of the case was that Little Bride was pregnant but not by Young Groom. He therefore killed her. Manipulator added, "I do not have a very high opinion of Young Groom, but he is merely a child." Elders commonly invoked youth to excuse the bad actions of males and females under 20 years of age. Manipulator continued, "The village has stuck together regarding the court case against Young Groom and nothing further will come of it. If the girl's family had not become suspicious, it would never have gone to court. Devious has two daughters, and he will see to their wedding this coming marriage season; they are about 15 and 17 years old. Then he'll arrange another marriage for Young Groom if someone comes looking for a boy." Manipulator took the safe, political position with regard to Little Bride but knew more about the case than he revealed, for his son was College Man. Furthermore, Honesty, Manipulator's mother, subscribed to the village position that Little Bride was murdered by Young Groom and she became a ghost.

Manipulator correctly predicted the marriage of Devious's two daughters and the remarriage of Young Groom a few years later. After acquittal, Young Groom continued his education and then began working for a bank. Twenty years later he was still working there and doing well. Late each evening he came home from work and quietly walked down the lane to his home. He and his second wife had separated from the joint family of Devious and lived across the lane from them. It is likely that Young Groom's second wife knew that her husband murdered his first wife, for in the spring of 1978 when the village was rife with the ghost epidemic, the soul of Little Bride was one of the malevolent ghosts. Young Groom's second wife daily talked with the Jat and Brahman women who lived around her. These women were familiar with the village ghosts and passed on the village lore about them. Passion Flower, Little Groom's accomplice in the demise of Little Bride, by this time had returned to the village to live, and village women would have long ago told Little Groom's second wife about Passion Flower's role in the murder of Little Bride. (See Append. VI. The HOS score of Young Groom's second wife shows borderline stress.)

This case might be classified as a dowry murder except that the stated motives for the death of Little Bride were that Young Groom did not want to be married to a woman so short and, in any event, was not yet ready for marriage, as was also the case with Tippler. Generally, most of the village was united in concealing this murder, although Tippler used the occasion to make trouble for a prominent

member of a hostile party through the use of a Chamar boy to inform the police. Both the cover-up and the effort to use the police and courts to harass an enemy are typical village strategies. The case also illustrates the economic importance of dowries and the potentially intimate relationship of an older brother's wife and a husband's younger brother. The main points are that murder is very bad karma, and the soul of a murdered person becomes a lingering, malevolent ghost.

ILLUSION'S DEATH

Illusion, a teen-age Brahman girl, was killed by her father in 1958. The circumstances were such that she was expected to become a ghost. This prophecy was fulfilled, as we learned in our 1977–78 fieldwork when her ghost was said to be haunting the village and causing the possessions of young girls and women. She had been wedded but the marriage had not yet been consummated. Justice, her father, never went to school, tried working in the city, did not like it, and for the balance of his life, he farmed. He needed Illusion's help in the fields, and moreover did not have sufficient dowry to send her to her husband for first mating just after menarche as was customary (R. Freed and S. Freed, 1980: 407–408, 497–498; 1985: 159–160).

Justice, his wife, and children lived and worked closely with the family of a patrilineal second cousin, Indecisive. Their wives were sisters. When Indecisive's father died before he was born, he and his mother continued to live in the same joint household with Old Grandfather, the father of Justice and Householder, and the granduncle of Indecisive. When Indecisive became an adult, he and his mother separated from Old Grandfather. Justice also later separated from his father, and the families of Justice and Indecisive lived together (Chap. 21: Breakup of Old Brahman Lane; Append. III: Chart 10.2).

Because Indecisive's mother became a widow at an early age and her son was born after his father's death, she was regarded as inauspicious and was not welcome at happy events such as weddings and visits to a new mother and infant. Her pseudonym is Inauspicious, for she was believed to cast the evil eye; men avoided crossing her path at the beginning of a day for fear misfortune would befall them. Despite her troubles, Inauspicious persevered, raised her son, and obtained a good education for him with the help of her brothers. In time he found an office position working for the railroad. To achieve her ends, Inauspicious habitually dressed in the drabbest, most bedraggled widow's weeds, was obsequious, joined her palms beseechingly when asking for help, and generally acted out the ancient traditional role of a Brahman widow, which by the 1950s other Brahman widows in the village no longer did. Although she obtained what she needed and wanted, her behavior contributed to the molding of Indecisive's hesitance in taking action.

In addition to being born posthumously, Indecisive started life with another drawback. He had strabismus in one eye, and was called one-eyed by villagers although he had vision in both eyes. He reminded one in some ways of Dickens's Uriah Heep and of Harischandra, two anxiety ridden characters, who in trying to please everyone pleased no one, not even themselves. The tribulations of Harischandra, the slave of the god of Justice (also known as Dharma) disguised as a hideous Chandala (low-caste man), are depicted in the Markandeya Purana (Balfour, 1885: 1: 649; Dowson, 1950: 118, 364, 367; Append. II: Puranas).

Because Indecisive was a railroad employee, he was absent from home for long periods so Justice farmed his land for him on shares. Indecisive owned more land than Justice, for he was the only son of his father whereas Justice had a brother, Householder, and Old Grandfather was still alive in 1959. This farming arrangement stopped when the Delhi Land Reforms Act of 1954 was put in effect. The law allowed people who had cultivated a plot of land for a number of years for an owner to lay claim to the owner's land (Aggarwala, 1956: 3–4, 20). Indecisive, not so indecisive with regard to his land, thereafter either farmed it himself with the help of his eldest son and wife, or more often had one of a number of people in the village farm it for him for one year at a time, under which terms it could not be alienated. Justice, who

had regarded the land as almost his own, no longer had any say about it, obtained no share in Indecisive's crops, and was in reduced economic circumstances.

What contributed to the ultimate antagonism between Justice and Indecisive was the sexual promiscuity of Indecisive's wife, Adulteress, and her influence on her son and Illusion, the daughter of Justice. The two families separated partly due to Adulteress's behavior. The combined impact of land reform, adultery, and separation ultimately resulted in Illusion's death and her soul becoming a ghost.

Because Justice did not have the funds for the balance of his daughter's dowry, he could not send Illusion to her husband for first mating although she was wedded and had attained menarche. Illusion and the son of Adulteress were thrown together by Adulteress to the extent that she arranged to have her son look at Illusion while she was bathing. Sexual relations between the cousins developed and Illusion became pregnant. When Illusion's parents discovered that she was pregnant, they hurriedly gathered the rest of her dowry and sent her to her husband for first mating. Her in-laws recognized that she was pregnant and immediately returned her to her father. Her father then killed her for the sake of family honor, for she had committed adultery since she was already wedded, incest (a patrilineal cousin is similar to a brother and tabu as a mate), and violated both village and clan exogamy. If Illusion had lived and born her child, the prestige of both her natal and marital families would have been ruined. One recourse would have been to send her from the village and sever all ties forever. Since she was nonliterate and knew only village life, she would have then been an unprotected young girl, and her only recourse to stay alive would have been prostitution or begging. An alternative was suicide (Williams and Jelliffe, 1972: 118; R. Freed and S. Freed, 1985: 143). Indecisive had an urbanized and more modern approach to the problem, for he suggested an abortion, but Justice would not countenance it and late at night hanged Illusion and cremated her before daybreak. Illusion's death was reported as due to cholera. No one questioned the report although two men in her lineage were policemen and knew all the facts (R. Freed, 1971: 423).

This case illustrates a father's rage toward a daughter who has shattered his image of her and damaged her family's prestige by having illicit sex. This element is present in other cases which have come to our attention of daughters who were raped and/or had illicit pregnancies (R. and S. Freed, 1985: 143–146). By no means do all fathers react in such circumstances as did Justice, especially when the abortion option is available. However, there was no public disapproval of Justice at the time. Because Illusion was a daughter of the village and her death had a strong emotional impact on her mother and patrilineal cousin, villagers were very disturbed by her death, but no one reported it to the police as murder.

Illusion had a number of counts against her, which for two or more decades led to her persistence as a wandering ghost who might possess teen-age girls about to be wedded or mated. She had violated serious tabus and died tortured before her allotted time. For a year after her death, Brahmans discussed it and the acts that led to it over and over again. Illusion was an illusory person; not too much was known about her. In discussing her death, Old Soldier, a Brahman seeking moksha, said, "What was, was not, and what is, is not." He was invoking the concept of maya (illusion), a basic Hindu concept. (On maya, illusion, cf. Daniélou, 1964: 28–31.)

Illusion's death and subsequent ghosthood were attributed to her past actions, which were deemed very bad, not only for the life which her father took but for her earlier lives. Therefore, death as a solution meant that her soul would be able to start another life, hopefully with good actions, after her time as a wandering ghost elapsed.

From the village viewpoint, the law in this case was that a family head decided what should be done with a family member. Informal family law was consistent with Maine's theory of *patria potestas*: namely, the power of ruling and taking care of family affairs vested in the head of the family. He enforced family law or breaches of it within the family, negotiated with other family heads for his

members, and had the power of life and death over family members (Maine, 1963: 147–149). Thus, Justice had the right to execute Illusion. Although the execution of his daughter represented ancient customary law, still the village was part of a state and nation. A few villagers acknowledged that under state law Justice's deed constituted murder. What Justice did was accepted by members of the Brahman caste with the exceptions of Indecisive, Adulteress, and their son. Still, the act of killing his daughter tormented Justice. It is not surprising, therefore, that in 1977–78 Illusion's ghost was reported as still haunting her father and members of his lineage. Justice, an insatiable smoker, was dying of lung cancer (Chap 21: Beauty; cf. R. Freed, 1971, and Baxi, 1982: 334–340 regarding this case).

After Illusion's death, her father and other members of his lineage blamed Adulteress for leading Illusion astray. Because Indecisive was rarely in the village and possibly because of his ineffectiveness, Adulteress had a reputation for liaisons with other men. A year previous to Illusion's death she had been beaten by the adult men of her husband's lineage for adulterous activities. Later, some months before Illusion's death, Adulteress was caught *flagrante delicto* with a Jat. Adulteress encouraged Illusion to mate with her son by leaving them alone together and by calling her son's attention to Illusion while she was bathing. Perhaps her actions constituted her revenge on Justice and other members of the lineage who beat and threatened her.

Because of Adulteress's behavior, the men in the lineage tried to kill her. Indecisive, his usual anxiety-ridden self, did nothing except injure himself by accidentally or intentionally falling off a train. A few villagers hinted that he had attempted suicide. Meanwhile Adulteress reported the men of her husband's lineage to the police. A panchayat of three well-known men from outside the village convened in the village meeting house. Adulteress was allowed to speak but could not mount the steps of the meeting house, for women were not permitted to enter while men sat there in a panchayat. The panchayat recommended that no action be taken by the police against the men who had threatened Adulteress but warned both sides to desist in their behavior. By filing her complaint with the police, Adulteress put the threats on record and so protected herself. One Brahman said, "Indecisive's wife could have been killed by this time. If a man can kill his own daughter, killing a woman in the village is an easy thing. The whole village will cover it up" (R. Freed, 1971: 434). Although it was against state law, the Brahmans outcaste Indecisive's family by refusing to attend or participate in a premarital banquet for his son, the young man who had impregnated Illusion. After his wedding, he never returned to the village.

We startled Indecisive and Adulteress when we asked them in 1978 about Illusion's becoming a ghost because they were frightened by hearing her name and afraid that the ghost would attack them if they talked about her. Adulteress, who formerly took great care of her personal appearance, had become a slattern. She and her husband, who had retired, could best be described as being on the fringe of their caste community though he was more acceptable than she. At times she acted as midwife in emergency deliveries for women of the Brahman and Jhinvar castes. Other times she was seen talking with teen-age Brahman girls, rarely with adult men and women of her caste.

BROTHER VS. BROTHER

One night in 1974, Woodsman, a Jat, was allegedly murdered by his elder brother, Favorite. The murder had been planned by Favorite and his father, Schemer, who always favored his eldest son and did not care for Woodsman. The motive was the inheritance of land by sons. At dispute was the paternity of two young men, the sons of a widow, Bangle Wearer. It was alleged in the court case over the inheritance rights that she was the levirate spouse of Woodsman and her sons were fathered by him. However, villagers who knew the family well said privately that the sons of Bangle Wearer had not been fathered by Woodsman.

Jat history and the structure of Schemer's family provide clues as to why Woodsman was murdered. Schemer was born in 1898 when polyandry and female infanticide still persisted among the Jats. He and his elder brother both inherited a large amount of land,

which made them well-off landowners. Schemer and his wife had four sons and three daughters. By 1958, his daughters had married and gone to live with their husbands. The four sons were Favorite, born 1920; Postman, born 1924; Woodsman, born 1940; and Marketeer, born 1941. Favorite as the eldest son was indeed his father's favorite; the two worked hand-in-hand.

The trouble in the family started in 1948 when Postman, then 24 years old, and his mother died of typhoid fever. Woodsman was then eight years old. Postman's widow, Bangle Wearer, was between 23 and 25 years old. She had born one child, a daughter who died at birth before Postman's death. After Postman and his mother died, neighboring villagers reported that Schemer's behavior changed without his wife's steadying influence. Stories circulated in the village about the carryings-on of Schemer, Favorite, and Bangle Wearer. One of the stories was that Schemer took a necklace belonging to Favorite's wife and gave it to Bangle Wearer. When Favorite's wife discovered it was missing, Schemer told her that a Jat neighbor had stolen it. However, Favorite's wife must have learned about her husband's relationship with Bangle Wearer and that Bangle Wearer had the necklace because she took her only child, a son, and left Favorite, thereafter living with her father. Since her son would inherit from his mother's father (according to a later report from Favorite's second wife) and probably because Favorite and Schemer wanted no revelation of their activities, they let her go. When Favorite's first wife left, Schemer arranged a second marriage for him with another wealthy and powerful Jat family, which took place in 1949. Favorite and his second wife had ten sons and one daughter.

When Schemer provided the information about his family for our census in 1958, he stated that Postman and Bangle Wearer had two sons. The two sons were born in 1955 and 1957, but we did not find out until our second field trip that Postman had died in 1948. An elderly Brahman who knew the history of the members of Schemer's family quite well provided this information. In the same 1958 census, Schemer also said that Woodsman had given the widow, Bangle Wearer, the bangles, i.e., a ceremony indicating that she was his levirate spouse. This statement, too, was false, for the bangles are given one year after the death of a husband, at which time Woodsman was eight to nine years old so the ceremony would have been unlikely. Either the bangles were never given to Bangle Wearer, or more probably, they were given to her by Favorite, which may have contributed to his first wife leaving him. The marriage to his second wife and the dowry she brought with her probably hinged on there being no levirate spouse or earlier children who would inherit.

In the opinion of knowledgeable villagers, the two sons of Bangle Wearer were Favorite's sons. One year after her wedding the second wife of Favorite bore her first son in 1950; a daughter in 1954, and another son in 1956. The last two pregnancies coincide with the time when Favorite would have mated with Bangle Wearer resulting in the birth of her two sons in 1955 and 1957. It is customary for a wedded couple to refrain from sexual intercourse beginning with the second to third months of pregnancy. Thus it is highly likely that Favorite temporarily shifted his attentions from his second wife to Bangle Wearer, with the result that she bore two sons.

Sometime after 1958, Woodsman arranged his own marriage, for his father had never arranged one for him. He and his wife then had one son and two daughters. Woodsman himself knew that he was not the father of Bangle Wearer's sons and he adamantly rejected them in order to conserve the eventual inheritance of his own son. His son would lose too much land if he had to share it with Bangle Wearer's sons. Favorite and his acknowledged sons would have a lesser inheritance if Bangle Wearer's sons were taken care of in any way other than as the sons of Woodsman because Favorite and his second wife had 10 acknowledged sons. With so many sons to inherit his land in equal shares, every bigha was important to Favorite. Faced with a stubborn antagonist who was no fool, Schemer and Favorite realized that they would have to do whatever was necessary to settle the affair in their favor. They were not the kind of men to shy away from drastic measures and plotted to murder Woodsman.

Their strategy was to provoke a confrontation. They had selected a favorable time, for a member of their lineage, Actor, held the highest political office in the village. He would do what he could to shield the conspirators from justice.

Ostensibly to settle their differences with Woodsman, Schemer and his allies proposed a meeting at 9:00 p.m. one evening in June, 1974. Woodsman was willing to talk, and proudly drove to the meeting in a tractor that he had just bought. As allies he brought along his wife, Outspoken, and her two brothers. Expecting a peaceful discussion, they were unarmed. As they turned into the lane toward Schemer's house, they saw Favorite and six other men with clubs advancing toward them ready for a fight. Favorite's allies were his two older sons, two brothers of his wife, and the two sons of Bangle Wearer.

When Outspoken's two brothers saw that they were outnumbered, they ran away, leaving Woodsman and Outspoken to fight alone against seven armed men. It was no contest. Woodsman was stabbed a number of times and fell in the lane in front of Manipulator's house. Manipulator and Helpful, a neighboring Jat, had come outside to see what was going on and witnessed the fight.

Favorite and his cohorts dragged the mortally wounded Woodsman to his tractor, tied him and Outspoken on it, and drove it into Schemer's courtyard, shouting that Woodsman was a thief. Woodsman's intestines were falling out and he was on the point of death. With his dying breath, Woodsman called to his father for a drink of water, but Schemer ignored him. Moments later, Woodsman died. It all happened in no more than five to ten minutes.

When the fight began, Favorite and Schemer shouted, "Villagers, come to our help. Dacoits have come to rob us." This was the prearranged signal for Politician, a powerful Jat supporter of Schemer, and a small group of his close kinsmen armed with clubs to arrive on the scene after the fight was already over and Woodsman was dead, as had been planned. The idea was to make it appear that the attack on Woodsman was not premeditated but was due to dacoits and to enable Politician and his group to appear as impartial witnesses in any court case concerning the death of Woodsman. No other villagers responded to Schemer's call, for the spectators did not want to get involved in the family business of a powerful Jat lineage, and no one wanted to make an enemy of the formidable team of Schemer and Favorite.

Favorite and Politician then took Favorite's eldest son, Vector, who had been wounded in the fight by his own father to prove that dacoits had attacked Favorite's group, to a hospital where they phoned the police anonymously. When the police came to the village, Actor showed them around and manipulated them in favor of Favorite and against Woodsman's wife, whom he labeled a bad woman. When she and her brothers complained to the police, Favorite and his cohorts were jailed for six months but were acquitted because no villager would testify against them. However, Helpful and Manipulator saw Favorite kill Woodsman, and Helpful said that he saw Favorite wound Vector to make it look as though dacoits had done so. The explanation offered by Favorite and his cohorts in their defense was that they had been assaulted by dacoits; Woodsman was killed in the fight and Vector was wounded.

Actor was one of the principal witnesses in the criminal court case. In telling us about his courtroom testimony, he admitted committing perjury to protect the defendants out of loyalty to the brotherhood and to Schemer's family. To justify himself, he claimed that the bad characters on Outspoken's side bribed the police to bring the case against Favorite and his party. He explained that it was better for him to testify as he did than to bring further misfortune on the defendants by having them convicted of murder. The case cost Favorite and Schemer Rs. 40,000. Manipulator said that Politician lent money to Favorite for legal expenses and also supplied witnesses in order to get into Favorite's good graces. Schemer died toward the end of the trial at the age of 76.

After her husband's murder, Outspoken immediately took her three children to her natal village and stayed there a while. When she returned to the village, she left her son with her father and brothers, fearing that as heir to his father's land he might be murdered by her husband's kinsmen. During Outspoken's absence, Schemer recalled Bangle Wearer from her natal village and had her

and her two sons installed in Woodsman's house to further their claim that Woodsman was the father of the two boys. To maintain her own claim, Outspoken and her two daughters then had to return to Shanti Nagar and live side-by-side with Bangle Wearer and her sons. Whenever Outspoken was interviewed, they sat nearby, listened, and the eldest son occasionally commented. Bangle Wearer said nary a word.

A subsequent case in Civil Court concerning the disputed paternity and the inheritance of Woodsman's land also ended in victory for Favorite, the court deciding that the two sons belonged to Woodsman, based on Schemer's and later Actor's testimony that Bangle Wearer was the levirate spouse of Woodsman. Woodsman's widow lost both her husband and a substantial part of her son's inheritance. Moreover, her husband's murderer escaped punishment.

According to Outspoken, her husband's soul became a ghost. Sometime after his death and the verdict of the courts, Outspoken dreamed that a black snake appeared to her in a dream. At first she was frightened, but the snake said he was her husband and told her not to be afraid. In the traditional form of a black snake, he told her that he had come to protect his land. But despite the protection of her husband's ghost, she feared to live in the village. Further weakened by tuberculosis and malaria, she lost the will to live and died. Her brothers came to the village to oversee the cremation and then took her two daughters to live with them and their little brother in their village.

JATS VS. BRAHMANS

One day in the spring of 1967, a serious dispute erupted over a rather common occurrence, trespass by water buffalo into cultivated fields. These large powerful animals can do a fair amount of damage in only a few minutes. Depredations by cattle frequently lead to disputes, which are usually not too serious. However, one such fight caused the death of a Brahman man. In the course of a dispute over trespassing water buffalo between some Brahman brothers and Taciturn, an elderly Jat, one of the Brahmans, known for his impulsive nature, struck the Jat with his club, knocking him to the ground where he pretended to be dead. Word reached his nephew, Politico, who snatched his rifle and rushed to the scene to defend his uncle. In the melee which followed, with the Brahmans carrying pitchforks and clubs, Politico shot one of the Brahman brothers, whose pseudonym is Victim. Shortly thereafter he died. He also wounded Victim's brother, who recovered. Villagers called the death of Victim murder. To judge from the general facts of the case, the accused murderer did not have malice aforethought but killed Victim in a state of anger; therefore, legally it was manslaughter. In any case, Politico was convicted of murder and sentenced to be hanged. The penalty was later commuted to life imprisonment, and eventually he was released from prison on probation (S. Freed and R. Freed, 1987: 25–26).

Although the soul of Victim was a prime candidate for ghosthood since he died tortured while still in the prime of life, his ghost was never specifically identified in any cases of possession except that of his widow, Sudden Grief. In 1977–78, she was seen wailing and crying while sitting near a hand pump and was reported by neighbors and relatives as suffering from ghost possessions. No further information about her attacks was available except that High Strung, a village exorcist and eldest brother of Victim, exorcised his brother's ghost. Sudden Grief lived with her eldest son in 1977. He was a policeman, married, with two small daughters, and was head of the family. Other family members were Sudden Grief's other son, unmarried, and her daughter who was born one year before her husband died in 1967.

Sudden Grief's persistent mourning and her possessions ten years after Victim's murder are best understood by taking into account her hearing deficiency, her family circumstances, and village social organization and politics. As a child, Sudden Grief had measles and was left somewhat deaf, which can lead to relative social isolation and a sense of insecurity. Her parents recognized that this handicap would cause her problems. They therefore arranged her marriage to a man of Shanti Nagar so that her two older sisters, already married to men of the village, could help her if necessary. However, her chief

source of aid was one of her sisters-in-law. At the time of the murder, Victim and one of his brothers, the one who was shot but recovered, had a joint household. It was this brother's wife who was a good friend of Sudden Grief and helped her to communicate, as she did when we interviewed Sudden Grief. The close friendship of the two women is shown by the fact that this sister-in-law helped to nurse Sudden Grief's children, her own children, born about the same time as Sudden Grief's, having died.

Her sister-in-law was a nearby source of strength, but her husband was away from the village most of the time. He and his brother owned land in another village, and Victim spent most of his time there. A largely absentee husband heightened Sudden Grief's insecurity from deafness. However, she was fond of her husband and was shattered by his sudden death when he was 33 to 34 years old and she was 32–33, as well she might have been in view of her loss of status and, as a Brahman woman, almost no possibility of remarriage.

The noteworthy feature of this case is that Sudden Grief's mourning was still intense 10 years after Victim's death. The 10-year lapse between the trauma of sudden widowhood at a young age and her possessions serves to highlight chronic grief as the principal element in her possessions. Prince and Paris (1991) emphasized that grief, as a causal element in ghost possession, deserves more attention than it would receive as only one of several stress factors. Pathological grieving reactions may derive from an intense love-hate relationship with the deceased. One possible outcome is: "To prevent being overwhelmed by grief and guilt the bereaved denies the loss; the loved one is incorporated or brought inside the bereaved (sometimes to be re-projected as the feared ghost)" (Prince and Paris, 1991: 304).

While such an analysis makes sense in the case of Sudden Grief, it must be qualified by the village context. Sudden Grief's sense of loss, anger, and insecurity was in all likelihood given fresh impetus by the pardon of Politico, his return to the village in 1977, and his election to the office of pradhan in December of that year to the dismay of the Brahmans, in particular the close relatives of Sudden Grief. On the surface, animosity had to be repressed. In fact, one of Victim's sons declared that (under the circumstances obtaining at the time of the election in 1977) he held "no enmity" for Politico (S. Freed and R. Freed, 1987: 27). Since Sudden Grief suffered more than anyone from the murder of Victim, her husband, she then repressed her anger and the revival of her sorrow at the triumphant reappearance and election of Politico. The repression, however, was short-lived and resulted in her weeping and wailing at the hand pump and a series of ghost possessions. Her behavior was understandable in view of the cultural conditioning to the belief that the soul of a murdered person will long tarry as a ghost.

Psychiatric disorders are multidetermined so that when analysis takes into account social structure, especially the joint family, educational and employment pressures, finances, and governmental programs perceived as threatening, one soon has a menu of plausible explanatory factors at the social or cultural level. They are transformed at the psychological level into grief, fear, anxiety, guilt, pressure, or stress, or a combination of any or all of these mental states which in turn may be manifest as ghost possession (R. Freed and S. Freed, 1991: 75).

Several reasons why grief is not more prominent in analyses of Indian ghost possession are suggested. First, suicide may be a reaction to grief, which is even more dramatic than ghost possession. For example, one of the causes of Scapegoat's suicide (Chap. 13: Deaths of Little Boy and Scapegoat) was grief. Another reaction to grief is death simply from pining away (the "giving-up-given-up complex") (Chap. 19: College Man, City Girl, and Tricky). Moreover, the concept of karma focuses attention on the personality of the deceased which may add or detract from the feelings of the mourner about the ghost. Finally, lingering ghosts in Shanti Nagar due to accidents, suicides, and murder are believed to be malevolent whereas the ghosts of other dead persons, who are mourned for one year, are viewed as benevolent. The television program about the benevolent wifely ghost who comforted her grieving husband and young son illustrates this aspect of ghosthood (Chap. 11: Village Terms for Ghosts).

CHAMARS VS. CHAMARS

A murdered Chamar man, whose soul might have become a ghost, was not so reported, probably because he was in his 50s, an age at death interpreted as his allotted time to live, and he died defending family prestige, an honorable death. He was killed in a dispute over his daughter's love affair with a young Chamar of the village, a transgression against the principles of female premarital chastity and caste and village exogamy. When the girl's father found out about the liaison, he had to take action, for his daughter's behavior was an affront to family honor. He gathered some men from his lineage and protested to the young man and his father. The boy's side and the girl's side fell into a heated argument, augmented by the fact that the two sides were members of unfriendly lineages. The father of the young man, known for his plotting and skillful political moves, told the father of the girl and his companions to meet with him and his son on their roof later that night. They did, a fight ensued, and the girl's father was knocked off the roof. Badly injured, he was taken to a hospital where he died.

Although the death was reported to the police, the young man had political influence beyond the village, and his father was feared by the opposing Chamar lineage as well as by other villagers. Thus, when no one from the village would testify in court, the young man and his father were acquitted for lack of witnesses and also on the grounds that the girl's father and his allies were judged the aggressors because they came to their opponents' house where the fight ensued. The young man, with whom we had always had friendly relations, told us with no hesitation that he murdered the girl's father. The daughter, who was about 14 to 15 years old, may have been sent to her husband shortly thereafter, but her natal family did not discuss her. Her brother, Host, an active participant in the group session of Chamars on believers and nonbelievers in ghosts, became the head of the family when his father died. Although he said that he himself did not see ghosts, he believed in them. However, he never said that his father became a ghost (Chap. 10. Discussion in a Chamar *Baithak*).

Fig. 7.   Village well, 1958, where most suicides occurred. Water is drawn in buckets and poured into earthern or brass vessels that women carry home on their heads. Three basic styles of women's clothing are shown: (1) sari with blouse, (2) a silwar suit of a long shirt and pajamalike pants, and (3) long shirt and skirt.

CASE HISTORIES: SUICIDES AND QUESTIONABLE DEATHS

With two exceptions, all the persons reported as having committed suicide ended their lives in the main village well. One exception was an old man of the Mahar Kumhar caste, who lived in Old Delhi for many years and committed suicide in the well of a dharmsala, a place of refuge. Many years earlier he had beaten his wife and she committed suicide in the main village well. The other exception was the murder or suicide of Housewife, a Jat, to be discussed under "Murder or Suicide."

The main village well, situated in a neighborhood mainly of high-caste families, Jat and Brahman, had a long history of suicides by women (Append. IV: Map 4, MW). In 1978, Pure Goddess, a Brahman woman born in 1899, who had worshipped at this well after the birth of each of her sons, said she had never seen a ghost there or anywhere else

but admitted that other women had seen the ghosts of women who committed suicide in this well. She then related her own recollection of how the well was built, claiming that the circumstances surrounding the construction of the well accounted for women committing suicide in it.

The reason women have died when jumping or falling into this well is due to what happened when it was made. There was a Brahman, who was the ancestor of the man who recently died of shock when his brother's hand was cut off in the fodder cutter. This ancestor constructed the well but died before its completion. His sister hit her head against it and cried, "Who will complete the well?" Next morning the people saw that the wall which had been constructed around the well had sunk by itself. Then some people constructed a similar wall, and the two walls sank in the well. The well is very deep and the two walls needed to be sunk. Nobody can come out alive. The way in which the well was constructed was miraculous and accounted for women committing suicide in it. The belief is that a woman who goes to a well, which has a ghost reputation, can be attacked by the ghosts of the well.

Actor, the pradhan, who had considerable experience having wells dug in his fields, described how this kind of well is built and added that there was nothing miraculous about the construction or sinking of the second wall of the well.

When a well is built, they dig down to the layer where they find the clearest water, and then they build a circular wall around the digging. The water remains standing in the well from 10 to 15 feet; the sand and mud settle down. If water is drawn out, the well water remains clear and clean. In putting in the wall around a well, first a round wall is set up on the surface of the land. Then they go on digging to the level of the water. The round wall slips down to the level of the water. Previously they used mortar and lime for a wall; now they use cement. First, they dig down to 20 feet where they reach water. Then they start building the second round wall, all of it above the land surface. Then they start digging out water and mud below the round wall. The next step is to put weights on top of the round wall so the wall sinks. They keep on digging until the wall slips into place and the water rises to the right level.

The myth about this well, its location, and its familiarity, for neighborhood women had to go there twice a day for water before the introduction of hand pumps, made it a prime means of suicide, especially for high-caste women. The size and depth of the well were also important. Once a woman jumped or fell into it, she could not escape from drowning without assistance. Ten women, all daughters-in-law, were named as having committed suicide in it. Two were Brahmans, the first wives of Progenitor and Luck, father and son (Chap. 12). One was the first wife of the Lohar Blacksmith (Chap. 20: The Lohar Blacksmiths). The fourth suicide was the first wife of a Mahar Potter, mentioned above, who long ago lived near the well. Her husband had beaten her badly so she committed suicide. All the foregoing were believed to have become ghosts. The other six women were Jats. The first Jat case has already been described in Chapter 13, the case of Scapegoat, the levirate spouse of Curmudgeon, who was a member of a lineage different from that of the women in the three following cases of Jat suicide. Their lineage was under the rule of a well-to-do, highly respected Jat man with the pseudonym of Mr. Authority.

RULE OF AUTHORITY

A series of homicides (murder, suicide) and questionable deaths took place over a number of decades among members of a group of related Jats, who in the 1950s and thereafter were more or less under the rule of Mr. Authority. Three of the Jat women who committed suicide were the wives of men descended from a common grandfather. In 1958, his descendants, who formed three families, lived in separate apartments in a large house next to the main well. The apartments were arranged around an inner courtyard. The largest apartment was inhabited by Mr. and Mrs. Authority, their son Nutmeg and his wife and son, and the wives and children of some of their other sons. These men lived and farmed land at some distance from Shanti Nagar but left their wives and children with their parents. Mr. Authority wielded considerable influence among the Jats and in the whole village (Append IV: Map 4, no. 30).

Deaf Woman, the levirate spouse of Military Man, lived alone in the second apartment. Many years prior to the 1950s when she was young, she was married to a first cousin of her levirate spouse, but he died without issue. A younger brother of Military Man then took her as his wife. He was the secretary of a private school; his pseudonym is Secretary. He, too, died without issue. His elder brother, Military Man, then took Deaf Woman as a levirate spouse although Military Man's wife, Suspicious, opposed it because of Deaf Woman's inauspiciousness and peculiar disposition. She was doubly inauspicious because her first and second husbands died young without issue, and these deaths plus her deafness were attributed to bad actions of her soul. Suspicious said that Deaf

Woman had poisoned her second husband, Secretary, an accusation that Suspicious spread around the village because she did not want to live in the same household with the woman and was afraid that she or her husband, Military Man, might be poisoned. Part of Deaf Woman's troubles was due to her deafness, for she walked around the village interrupting conversations and ignoring what was said to her because she could not hear the replies. Because of her deafness and the gossip about her, she was generally ignored, had been living alone in her apartment for some time, and was socially isolated. Thus, she became more and more difficult through the years.

Military Man, his wife and children lived in a suburb of Delhi. Before he moved there, his mother committed suicide in the main village well soon after Secretary died because she believed that someone in the immediate family had killed him. Although there were two versions of the cause of Secretary's death—that he died from poisoning by Deaf Woman, or that he suffered from a disease that caused great pain—his mother believed that he had been poisoned. Thereafter no one lived with Deaf Woman. Military Man and Mr. and Mrs. Authority saw to it that she did not cause any trouble.

Head Clerk and his two half brothers, Advocate and Business Man, lived in the third apartment in the 1950s. Head Clerk's mother had committed suicide in the main well decades earlier; his father married again and his second wife bore two sons, the half brothers of Head Clerk. They later moved to a house outside the village habitation site. Married when a young man, Head Clerk enlisted in the army and served ten years. During his enlistment, his wife also committed suicide in the main village well. Family members did not discuss the reason for her suicide.

Young wives were often lonesome when they came to live in their husbands' villages. Sympathetic in-laws allowed new brides periodically to make long visits to their parents during the early years of marriage while they were adjusting to their husbands and in-laws. They generally permitted a young wife to visit her parents after her first child was born. Sometimes economic necessity militated against these visits, or a senior woman or

male head of a joint family would not allow the young bride to visit her natal home. Then the girl might commit suicide or attempt it, especially if her in-laws or husband mistreated her or if her husband was in the army and she was lonely. In a song cast as a dream by a husband serving in the army, his wife sings:

Either you come home and leave the army,
Or I will die by jumping into the well.

(O. Lewis, 1958: 193).

This refrain suggests a possible reason for the suicide of Head Clerk's wife.

A murder took place among the descendants of Mr. and Mrs. Authority in the 1970s, but it transpired far from the village so the dead man, who lived in the village only as a child, was not expected to haunt it. By the time it happened, Mr. Authority had died, but his widow and her eldest son, Retired Inspector, with his wife continued living in the village apartment. Retired Inspector's life was blighted by the murder because the victim was his eldest son, Libidinous, who had been carrying on an affair with the daughter of Nutmeg. The girl and Libidinous were patrilineal first cousins, for Nutmeg was a brother of Retired Inspector. Nutmeg's son, who operated a gas station in Uttar Pradesh, learned about the affair. One night when Libidinous came to the gas station, Nutmeg's son allegedly shot and killed him when his back was turned. When we asked Libidinous's mother years after the murder whether suicide or murder constituted bad actions which would determine whether the suicide or murderer became a ghost, she said, "Death by murder is due to the actions of the person murdered and Bhagwan determines who kills the murdered man, and not the murderer." Part of her statement accords with beliefs about karma, for death by murder is death before the allotted time due to bad karma. However, to murder a person is also bad karma. The death crushed Retired Inspector and yet he could not complain publicly, passing the murder off as a "tragic accident." "What could he say?" explained Manipulator. "It was a family matter."

The Brahman and Jat women living around the main well recalled the suicides of the mother and first wife of Head Clerk and of Military Man's mother and said that their ghosts still haunted the well. Rarely someone remembered the death of Secretary and said that he became a ghost because he was poisoned or died of a disease many decades ago. The first husband of Deaf Woman had receded into the past by 1978, and only two old women mentioned his dying without issue and becoming a ghost. In general, women more often spoke of female than male ghosts. Most ghosts, other than ancestors, are eventually forgotten, but there are always new ghosts and some remembrance of old ghosts that foster basic village ghost ideology.

BREAKDOWN AND HIS THREE WIVES

The case of Breakdown and his three wives, from another Jat lineage, shows the common sequence of the ghost of a previous wife haunting her successor. It also underlines one of the common motives of female suicide, namely, the failure to bear children. When the first wife of Breakdown bore no children, he told her that she might as well commit suicide and so she did in the main well. He remarried and predictably her ghost haunted the second wife, who, in turn, drowned herself in the main well because a physician told her that her mind was being destroyed by a dread disease. She too bore no children. Breakdown married again but died a few years later without issue of a dread disease at age 30 to 31. It is possible that the barrenness of his three wives and his second wife's medical diagnosis were related to his physical condition and in some way related to the profligate life of his grandfather. Since none of his wives bore children, Breakdown died tortured without issue. Whether he became a ghost was never mentioned.

Wastrel, the grandfather of Breakdown, once owned considerable land and wielded political power in the village, but his wealth, power, and health declined due to his dissipation and dissolute character. He reduced his family's wealth by selling a large amount of land to pay for his dissolute habits. He died at age 90 or 91, shortly before his grandson's death, having been feeble and almost blind for a number of years. In his declining years, he lived by himself in a shed at one end of the village. The death of Breakdown took place during our 1958–59 study and was the subject of much comment among Brahmans, Jats, and other villagers. They implied that Breakdown's death was due to the dissolute life led by Wastrel, even though they described his death in terms of Ayurveda as a total breakdown of his system.

When Breakdown died, his third wife was about 24 years old. The ghosts of his first two wives were said to haunt her, just as his first wife had haunted his second wife. In the late 1970s, the third wife was no longer in the village. If she came from a well-off Jat family, she probably returned to her natal family, for she was relatively young, childless, and could remarry. In past times customarily a Jat widow became a levirate spouse of one of her deceased husband's brothers or patrilineal cousins, but not this third wife, even though her dead husband had a younger brother, for the levirate was fast disappearing. It was not unusual for a daughter-in-law to drop out of village life without a trace.

MURDER OR SUICIDE

In the spring of 1977 near the end of the Emergency Period (1975–77) when government employees or their spouses were under intense pressure to be sterilized if they had three or more surviving children, Housewife, a Jat woman, was sterilized. She had gone to her parental home to have the operation. When she returned to her husband's home in Shanti Nagar, her brother accompanied her. Later that evening her family noticed that she was missing and in retrospect claimed that they believed she had gone to a hospital because she was in pain from the sterilization operation. When she did not return after a day or two, a visiting married daughter of the head of the family started looking for her and went out into the fields to a small well on family land. There she found Housewife's body floating in the well (Append. IV: Map 4, DW). The police were called and told that Housewife committed suicide because of the painful aftereffects of the operation. They accepted this statement because numerous women complained of pain after sterilization.

Uninvolved villagers, however, said that

Housewife had been murdered. Several features of the case support this point of view. It is odd that Housewife's unexplained absence in the evening seemed to have caused her family little concern, for it had the potential for harming the family's reputation. Other villagers would be quick to suspect misbehavior on Housewife's part. Moreover, her choice of the particular well in which to kill herself suggested murder rather than suicide. The well of choice for suicides of high-caste women, such as Jats, was the large main village well. This well was close to Housewife's house, and not far out in the fields as was the small well in which her body was found. The murders of women that were made to appear as drownings or suicides usually took place in out-of-the-way, small wells. It is therefore surprising that the visiting daughter of Dissembler, the family head, happened to go out into the fields and find her body in the small well unless she suspected or knew something.

Finally, the liaison of Housewife and her father-in-law, Dissembler, offered a motive for murder. Dissembler's wife, Worn Down, died in 1958 when his son, Pawn, was 13 years old. Dissembler at that time planned to marry the boy to an older woman in order to have an adult woman to keep house and to work in the fields. Pawn and Housewife were married ca. 1960. Shortly afterwards, Pawn caught pneumonia, was hospitalized, delirious, arose from his bed, ran out of the room and jumped down an air shaft. Hospital attendants pulled him up with long hooks. After recovering from pneumonia, he began having epileptic fits. Hospital physicians prescribed medicine to be taken regularly to control his fits, but like many villagers Pawn did not see any point in taking his medicine regularly when he thought he was well. The fits recurred and a number of villagers in 1977–78 commented that he was an epileptic. Dissembler never acknowledged his epilepsy, but Pawn's eldest sister told us about his epileptic fits and that he started taking his medicine again regularly after the death of Housewife (cf. Trostle et al., 1983, on epileptics not taking their medicine). Pawn's fits and his dislike of Housewife affected their marriage, and, according to village gossip, they never mated. Although this was gossip, the intimate knowledge villagers have of one another's lives is often extraordinary. Housewife bore three sons and one daughter, who in birth records were attributed to Pawn but, according to villagers and the government midwives who delivered the children, were fathered by Dissembler.

In 1978 the Government Midwife, who served the village and was generally well informed about matters concerning women, said:

All the children of Pawn's dead wife are Dissembler's children. The woman who was formerly the Government Midwife and held my job told me this. Another Lady Health Visitor who knew everyone in the village and everything about them also told me that the children were Dissembler's. These matings happen in all castes. Only a few bad families do such things, but they do not speak about them. The women in such families like it when their father-in-law cohabits with them because they think he will give them good things. Those who do not like it, when the father-in-law acts in this way, tell. Now women are worse than ever. Whenever I ask about a child, some woman may state who the father actually is. When women sit together at a wedding or at a death, then they talk over these affairs.

If Housewife was indeed murdered, sexual jealousy and Pawn's hatred of Housewife for giving him the name of a cuckolded husband, which was common knowledge, would constitute sufficient motive for her murder. When his father was in the prime of life and Pawn was an adolescent, Pawn at first may not have realized what was going on, but as he grew older, the situation was an affront to his manhood and prestige (izzat). Then Housewife was sterilized and he was left with a wife whom he hated and with no children of his own. By this time he was frustrated, very angry about his position, and under great stress. Manipulator, who knew the family well, was emphatic that Housewife's death was murder, not suicide. He said, "Pawn killed her because he hated her. Only one reason exists for such hate. She was carrying on illicit relations with his father, Dissembler."

However, from the viewpoint of Dissembler, his behavior was an extension of the principle of polyandry formerly practiced by Jats to assure that sufficient male heirs continue the line of descent. Prince Petros (1963: 568) in his study of polyandry in India commented: "Fraternal polyandry becomes the rule with these peoples. On the very good excuse that close association between males is essential and jealousy must therefore not be given free rein, incestuous desires find considerable satisfaction in the fact that access to a sister-in-law is possible, as it is too, in certain circumstances, even to a step-mother or a daughter-in-law." Bock (1980: 158–159) pointed out that Freud insists that family members may be the object of erotic desires, which the custom of polyandry fostered.

Whether she was murdered or committed suicide, Housewife was eligible for ghosthood. By the fall of 1977, her ghost was said to have been seen a number of times as one of a gang of ghosts of murdered women, Tippler's first wife and Little Bride, all of whom were labeled malevolent because they were murdered. The malevolence of Housewife's ghost and the spectral group with which her ghost consorted indicate that her death was more likely murder than suicide.

AN ATTEMPTED MURDER OR SUICIDE

In order to avoid trouble with the law and to protect family prestige, villagers preferred not to report deaths of women in wells as either murder or suicide, instead passing them off as accidents. A noncommittal "She fell into a well" reflected the common cover-up. For women, this deception was credible because most female suicides and murders involved drowning in wells, which could be accepted as accidental. Unless the police received a complaint regarding a woman who was said to have drowned in a well, they did not inquire further into the case to ascertain whether it was an accident, suicide, or murder (Gazetteer Unit, Delhi Adm., 1976: 649, 650, table 3). Douglas (1961: 159–160, 227–231) and Bock (1980: 201) have pointed out that the classification of a death as suicide is influenced by community attitudes.

Villagers usually treat attempted murders or suicides in the same way as fatalities, that is, to dismiss them as accidents. Such evasion may be possible for attempted suicides but difficult for murders, for the intended victim would have to complain, if only as a defense against future attempts. Murder or attempted murder has much more serious consequences than suicide, so involved villagers usually try to transform an attempted murder into an attempted suicide. Even so, the soul of a murder victim or a suicide becomes a ghost, according to village belief, thus indicating how the person died. The case of Mr. and Mrs. Newcomer here outlined is not one of accomplished murder or suicide; rather it illustrates both the reaction of a woman who believed herself targeted for murder and of village leaders who wanted to treat the case as suicide and keep it out of the hands of the police.

Mr. and Mrs. Newcomer settled in the village in 1965 because Mr. Newcomer could obtain work at a nearby brick kiln and was related through his mother's brother to one of the local patrilineages of Gola Potters. His mother's brother had died but left a son. A number of Gola Potter families lived in the village; generally they were not well-off (Append. III: Chart 4: The Newcomers).

The Newcomers rented a hut near the other Gola Potters from a Jat who was living in Delhi. Some time between 1966 and 1969, Mr. Newcomer's younger brother and wife and his elder brother visited him. During this visit, the youngest brother's wife jumped, fell, or was pushed into a well. She was rescued. She accused her husband and his two brothers of trying to murder her. Mrs. Newcomer, our only source of information about the case, claimed that some of the Gola Potters were their enemies and that they had talked the young wife into accusing her husband and his two brothers of attempting to kill her by pushing her into the well. The case was settled by Benevolent, the Jat pradhan. He decided that the young woman had herself jumped in the well to make it look like her life was threatened. He also kept the case from going to the police. The pradhan died before we learned of the case so we could not ask him about it.

A MATERNITY DEATH

Deaths of women in childbirth were not unusual; mainly they took place with primiparous young mothers or when a woman had born four or more children, as in this case. In August 1958, Worn Down, a 40-year-old Jat woman, the wife of Dissembler and the mother of Pawn, bore her seventh surviving child, a daughter. Although Jat women customarily had a lying-in of 40 days after delivery, Worn Down started to work in the house and fields on the seventh day after delivery because there was a shortage of workers in the nuclear family, which had recently separated from a joint family. By September, Worn Down was seriously ill. One of her legs and an ankle were swollen; her knee was badly discolored; and one breast was swollen, infected, and painful. Her infant daughter had become emaciated because Worn Down could not nurse her very well. Toward the end of the month, Worn Down asked to be taken to a doctor in the city, but not until a fortnight later was she finally taken to a city hospital.

When we asked her brother-in-law, Actor, about the delay in taking her there, he said:

Every disease comes from stomach trouble. My brother's wife is so sick that they have taken her to a doctor in Delhi. Depending on the doctor's recommendation, they will take her to the Lady Irwin Hospital. Her liver is bad and is not making blood. It is turning out water. Anyone can tell by looking at her that this is so. When she clenches her hands and then opens them, her palms are white. Her trouble is such that only the doctors in the Irwin Hospital can handle it. What she has is very common, and usually the patient is taken to a local *vaid* [Ayurvedic doctor]. We did not know she would not get better.

Matriarch, an elderly Jat woman, who had delivered Worn Down's seventh child, accompanied the dying woman and her husband, Dissembler, to the hospital. When the physician examined her, he said, "She is almost dead. What can I do for her now?" He then told them to take her back to the village to die.

She was unconscious by the time she was brought home. The word had spread that she was dying, and six Jat women sat around her bed, including her eldest married daughter. Also there were her husband and a 17-year-old nephew of her husband, Marketeer, the

son of Schemer. Mrs. Authority, a next-door neighbor, was the only optimist in the group and kept saying "Nothing has yet happened and while she is still breathing, there is hope." The other women kept repeating that they did not think she would live through the night. Her husband was not disturbed and said, "When she dies, I will think about her for a few days and then forget." One woman then said, "If she dies, her husband will arrange a marriage for his 13-year-old son to an older woman so that there will be someone to take care of the house." This prophecy proved to be correct.

Worn Down died during the night and was cremated early next morning. Her infant daughter died 12 days later. The souls of Worn Down and the infant qualified for becoming ghosts. None of the Jats mentioned that they became ghosts, but neighboring women of the Brahman, Bairagi, and Lohar castes said that Worn Down died of ghost illness, became a ghost, and then took the soul of her infant daughter because she loved her.

DISCUSSION

Eight well-substantiated cases of murder, which by village definition includes manslaughter, are presented above. Six took place in Shanti Nagar; two others happened at a distance from the village, namely, the robbery and murder of Rival and the murder of Libidinous, shot by his patrilineal cousin, the son of Nutmeg. The case of Housewife was ambiguous. The police recorded her death as a suicide, but more probably she was murdered by Pawn. Secretary was either murdered by poison or died from disease. The motives for killing women were sexual transgressions that reflected badly on family prestige, as in the case of Illusion, and a husband's dislike or hatred of his wife, for example, Little Bride, Tippler's first wife, and probably Housewife. All four females were believed to have become malevolent ghosts. Men were murdered in disputes over the ownership of land or damage from trespass (e.g., Woodsman killed by Favorite; Victim killed by Politico), or because of tabued male-female relations (the Chamar killed by his daughter's lover, and the killing of Libidinous by his male cousin because he was having an affair with the murderer's sister).

With one exception, all suicides were women. Where motives are known, kin-based unhappiness was almost always involved: intolerable marital family relationships, often with a husband; despair over a death; abuse by a spouse; excessive pain during pregnancy, as in the case of Luck's first wife; and the loneliness of a young wife unable to visit her natal family. Painful relationships, in turn, might involve sterility, which a husband would blame on his wife. The single case of male suicide mentioned here took place in Delhi and we do not know the motive. In Chapter 16 on the Headless Sweeper, we describe the perpetuation and elaboration of the legend of a man cutting off his own head and the actual facts of the case. Suicide as an alternative to suffering a painful disease was mentioned in the case of Breakdown's second wife, who was said to have committed suicide because a physician told her that her mind was being destroyed by a dread disease. A number of motives for suicide were suggested in the case of Little Bride in order to cover up her murder and have Young Groom acquitted.

We compare our findings with a few studies of murder and suicide that use data from governmental records. Our principal impression is that not much confidence can be placed in official records when they concern the villages. Villagers, who are the source of all such data, make sure that little that will cause trouble comes to the attention of the police. Infanticide is never reported, murders of women become suicides or accidents, and suicides become accidents or "unnatural deaths," as they are termed in the statistics. The police, many of whom are themselves villagers, have few compunctions about accepting what they are told. More attention may be paid to the murders of men than to those of women because this is a patrilineal society which values males more than females. Moreover, the murders of men may be more spectacular than those of women, involving public fights with guns, clubs, and knives which cannot be ignored, especially if the victims and/or perpetrators are socially prominent.

Both murder and suicide in the rural areas are probably underreported. Two studies in India (Singh et al., 1971; A. V. Rao, 1983) and one in Sri Lanka (Dissanayake and Silva, 1983: 171) based chiefly on governmental statistics run into this problem of underreporting. The same, however, holds for our data, both for suicide and murder, since we were not present in the village for many of the years covered in the testimony of our informants. Memories may be short; informants, recalcitrant or silent because of, among other reasons, the custom of not naming the dead believed to have become ghosts. Relatively complete and valid information on the causes of death and the identity of ghosts cannot be obtained by surveys although if the person being questioned is allowed to elaborate and go beyond the survey questions, important information sometimes is revealed. The best information derives from holistic fieldwork through established rapport with individuals in lengthy, in-depth interviews.

Singh et al. (1971) conducted a study of suicide in the Union Territory of Delhi for a period of one year from April 1, 1967, to March 31, 1968, based on police reports of suicides. The number of reports was small and the sample was reduced further because some people could not be located for the interviews which were an important aspect of the study. Major findings were that the rate of suicide (per 100,000) was higher for females, 3.15, than for males, 2.76, and higher in the rural areas, 8.92, than in the urban, 1.53 (Singh et al., 1971: 413, 414 and table 3). The authors attributed the higher rural rate to the proximity of Delhi; villages located near the city are said to have few advantages of village life but nearly all the disadvantages of being close to the city (Singh et al., 1971: 417). However, another interpretation is equally likely: i.e., villagers in the Union Territory of Delhi have the advantages and disadvantages of both country and city life.

Another dubious interpretation in the study of Singh et al. (1971) is the authors' claim that the joint family provides stability for individuals while at the same time suggesting that one of the causes of female suicide is problems with kin, especially with husbands and children but also with in-laws in the joint family. At the heart of the matter, especially for young brides and to some extent for older wives, are their loneliness and isolation away from their natal families and the fact that they are subject to the authority of fathers-in-law, mothers-in-law, husbands, and the male heads and senior women of their joint families. The loneliness of young brides falls within Durkheim's concept of anomie. The subordination to a number of people telling a young bride what to do and what not to do is hard to bear and often creates confusion and conflict.

A. V. Rao (1983: 213–214) listed further reasons for suicide in current times in various parts of India, including the Delhi region: stressful marriage negotiations; conflict within the family; mother-in-law–daughter-in-law confrontations; barrenness, which in a woman is considered inauspicious; cultural pressure to bear a son; and accusations that a wife is unfaithful. Rao commented that accusations of infidelity may or may not have a basis but still may cause a woman to commit suicide. One cause of male suicide, according to Rao, is the belief that impotence and other disorders are due to masturbation. This concept is connected with the ancient admonition not to waste semen (Carstairs, 1958: 72, 87–88). The belief may be stressful to young males, widowers, and celibates who then suffer from ghost possessions.

Far more females than males were reported to have committed suicide in Shanti Nagar. It is possible that male suicides may have been underreported more than female suicides, just as male cases of ghost possession are reported less often than female cases. In fact, one of our Chamar informants suggested as much when he said that men tended to commit suicide in front of trains and away from the village. However, he mentioned only the one elderly Mahar Potter man who had committed suicide away from the village. Village males and females have different attitudes in some areas. Men do not want to admit their fear of ghosts or that they have been possessed; women speak more readily about ghosts, ghost illness, and ghost possession.

In addition to drowning in wells, the female choice, and throwing oneself in front of a train, allegedly preferred by males, other ways to commit suicide are used. A common method for both sexes may be poisoning with insecticides, although only one unsuccessful attempt was reported in Shanti Nagar. Other methods are hanging (males) and burning oneself alive (A. V. Rao, 1983: 220, 226–227). Dowry murders may have been reported as suicides by burning, but Rao does not mention them. Suicides by poisoning could well pass unremarked in Shanti Nagar, where many causes of death are unknown and cremation takes place immediately after death.

The belief that good and bad actions determine what happens to the soul at death, i.e., that the soul may become a wandering ghost, be reborn, or be released from the round of rebirths, should be a deterrent to murder and suicide. Although there are circumstances in which villagers accept homicide as justified, village opinion mostly views the killing of a human being as extremely bad action. Except for strong followers of the Arya Samaj, villagers generally believe that the soul of both victim and killer become ghosts. The soul of the person who is killed is believed to suffer this fate due to bad actions in past and present lives; the soul of the killer may suffer the same fate because the killing adds a weighty bad act to the sum of past and present actions.

CHAPTER 16: THE HEADLESS SWEEPER IN A LINE OF HEREDITARY EXORCISTS

The case of the Headless Sweeper and his descendants is analyzed in family context. It is based on partly legendary information about the man whose ghost is called the Headless Sweeper, a member of the Chuhra Sweeper caste, and his ancestors but also on detailed interviews with some of his descendants: a son (Old Survivor), a grandson (Lord of Ghosts), and several members of Lord of Ghost's family. The relations among the members of Lord of Ghost's family and between them and a related affinal family suggest one kind of familial milieu in which ghost beliefs thrive, namely one marked by jealousy and paranoia.

We first learned about the ghost of the Headless Sweeper in 1958 when Withdrawn, a Brahman, was said to have suffered a series of possessions by this ghost. Although the Headless Sweeper was a real person who was born in the 19th century, he became a malevolent ghost when he died and something of a legend with the passing of the years. We heard two versions of the legend of the Headless Sweeper, one in 1958 and the second in 1978. These versions perpetuated the fear of his malevolent ghost. Old Codger of the "Old Fever" lineage related both versions to us, apparently unaware that our fieldnotes showed that his 1958 version differed from the later one. The 1958 version follows:

During the plague and influenza epidemics, a member of the Chuhra Sweeper caste wandered from place to place. By the time he arrived in Shanti Nagar, he was quite ill with a painful inflammation in his neck. The villagers, including members of his own caste, shunned him and would not let him stay in the community. Since he could go no further, he stopped at the periphery of the village. In his illness he called for his son [whose pseudonym is Absent Son]. His wife told him that his son had left the village. The man then became very angry and started shouting. When his wife asked him not to make a row, he grew even angrier. He demanded that his hookah be filled, had a cloth spread on the ground [so he could sit there], smoked his hookah, took a long

knife, and cut off his own head. This was deliberate death [suicide]. The man died tortured, before his time, and his soul became the ghost of the Headless Sweeper. Some members of the Sweeper caste dug a pit outside the village and buried the body.

Two Brahmans, Raconteur and Plowman, when questioned about the Headless Sweeper, said, "To die in an epidemic and to take one's own life are unnatural causes of death so the soul of the Headless Sweeper was doomed to go 'round and round.' Any person into whose body this headless ghost enters may or will be killed. The soul of such a person cannot find a home in the next life." Raconteur noted that the Headless Sweeper was a villager and member of the Chuhra Sweeper caste. Politician, a Jat, added that the Headless Sweeper was one of the three most powerful ghosts in the village. All three were men. The Headless Sweeper could wander anywhere, attack anyone, and he drove two other powerful ghosts into distant fields. All the foregoing comments were recorded in 1958.

In a long interview in 1978 on the subject of ghosts with Buddhist I (a Chamar), he defined a jinn as the ghost of a man whose head was cut off. It could be cut off when the man placed himself deliberately on the railroad tracks to be killed, or by someone intentionally cutting off his own head (both are suicides), or by another person cutting off a man's head (murder). Buddhist I recalled the ghost of the Headless Sweeper and linked him with Muslims when he used the term jinn for his ghost. He recalled that the ghost of the Headless Sweeper formerly entered everyone and did not spare a soul. The people who were possessed eventually died. According to him, the Headless Sweeper was finished. He no longer haunted the village.

When the malaria and ghost epidemics swept the village in the spring of 1978, we asked Old Codger about the Headless Sweeper without referring to his 1958 recitation. Old Codger launched into this account:

I was a young man then and there was the

first World War with Germany. Germany attacked with gases that caused great harm in India. There was an epidemic and many people died. I remember that for 15 days no one walked through the village lanes. Everyone was ill. The Sweeper came from outside the village and was roaming around. He was sick. One night he needed water and entered the Sweeper compound. The Sweeper men beat him soundly and threw him across the road. One to two days later he died. I have some fields across from where he died. Then the Sweepers dug a pit there and buried him. The pit was shallow so animals dug out the body of the Sweeper and ate his flesh.

The ghost of the Headless Sweeper attacked Ill Fated, [the younger brother of Forceful and Taciturn. Chap. 13, Senior Branch]. Ill Fated was then 17 to 18 years old and died within a year of the time when the ghost attacked him. The ghost attacked after sunset when the clock struck midnight. The ghost then declared, 'It's midnight and I'll come back and take you away with me.' The family did not know a *siyana* or bhagat so the young man died. Whenever the Headless Sweeper attacked, the person died. He did not spare anyone. A bhagat came here and overpowered the ghost when he attacked Withdrawn [Chap. 21, Withdrawn's Possessions]. The bhagat then took the ghost away.

As a rule of thumb, an early version of a legend is more apt to be accurate regarding facts than a later version. In the second version not only had Old Codger elaborated and dramatized the tale of the Headless Sweeper, he changed some facts. For example, Ill Fated was not attacked by the Headless Sweeper. The ghosts his family members reported as having possessed him were his father (Capable) and his two uncles (Old Groom and Fateful), members of Generation III in his own patrilineage (Chap. 13). Old Priest tried to cure him to no avail. Further Old Codger said the Headless Sweeper came from outside the village, inferring that he was not a villager but a stranger. Although Old Codger in the second version construed the Headless Sweeper's death as having been due to the influenza epidemic of 1918-19, adding a bit

of whimsy about the poisonous gases from Germany, the death was most likely due to the disastrous epidemic of bubonic plague, which persisted in India from 1896 until 1921 (Wyon and Gordon, 1971: 174). The evidence for plague from the 1958 version of the legend is the inflammation in the Sweeper's neck. Early writers about the influenza epidemics from 1793 through 1847 claimed that influenza was not contagious but was caused by poisonous gases or miasmas spreading over the land (Beveridge, 1978: 1–2), obviously a fallacy which lingered on and was added by Old Codger to his second version of the legend. The inflammation in the Sweeper's neck is linked to bubonic plague, which begins with fever and chills, followed by prostration and then swelling of the lymph nodes, which form buboes in various parts of the body, such as the neck. Instead of suicide the Headless Sweeper probably in a fit of madness called for his hookah to summon his supernatural power to cure his illness and used a knife to pierce the painful bubo in his neck. Instead he killed himself since mania sometimes develops in bubonic plague (Lyght, 1956: 958–959; Davey and Wilson, 1971, Chap. XXII; Berkow, 1982: 110; Append. I: Disease: Descriptions—Plague).

Since Old Codger was born in 1898, he was 20 to 21 years old at the time of the influenza epidemic and 27 years old in 1925 when Ill Fated died. Ill Fated was a member of the Senior Branch of the Old Fever lineage and lived near Old Codger. Thus, he knew the facts of Ill Fated's death but enjoyed telling the legend of the Headless Sweeper, which he changed by 1978. His age-mate, Raconteur, also enjoyed reciting a specific legend, namely, that of Merchant and the Muslim Ghost.

The Headless Sweeper manifests the traditional attributes of ghosts. He was fond of sweets and attacked anyone who had been eating them outdoors, especially near the village cremation-burial grounds. The known location of his grave outside the village between the shrines of Kanti Mata and Kali Mata on the lane that passed by the Sweeper compound added to the perpetuation of the legend (Append. IV, Map 4, XX on Lane II). Due to Old Codger's elaboration and perpetuation of the legend, the Headless Sweeper was believed to be a stranger and a Muslim, so he was feared. This fear accords with van Gennep's (1961: 26–27) theory that a stranger may be viewed as having supernatural powers and may be malevolent or benevolent. Mainly he was feared because he brought the plague to the village. The story of cutting off his head made him an even more dangerous ghost, for the act was unnatural.

We attribute the strength and longevity of the legend of the Headless Sweeper partly to the influence of Islam in the Punjab, for it added an alien element to his persona. By the middle of the 19th century, Muslims accounted for half the population of the Punjab. Chuhra Sweepers worked there for the British army and the railways. By 1891, Hindus made up no more than 40 percent of the population and the proportion continued to decline as indicated in subsequent census reports (K.W. Jones, 1976: 1, 2, 5, 12). Because Sweepers had no land to farm, many of the males were peripatetic and traveled, worked, and lived in what is now Pakistan, which was dominated by Muslims. Some converted to Islam; many were influenced by Muslim customs. When plague and the influenza pandemic struck the Punjab, some men returned to Shanti Nagar but had been gone so long that they were not known or remembered by other castes. Such was the case of the Headless Sweeper. Headless and a stranger, he became the most feared ghost of all the people who died during the dread bubonic plague and influenza epidemics, which wiped out whole families and decimated generations. Thus, his ghost symbolized those who died during the epidemics; they, like the Headless Sweeper, died tortured, before their allotted time, and became ghosts.

THE BEHEADED

The horror stemming from the Headless Sweeper's ghost is reinforced by stories from the Vedas and the Ramayana. For example, Kabandha, the Beheaded, ruled over all five forms of Vedic ritual sacrifices and was the earliest teacher of the Atharva-Veda. Kabandha is described as "covered with hair, vast as a mountain, without head or neck, having a mouth armed with immense teeth in the middle of his belly. . . ." In the Ramayana he advises Rama Chandra how to fight Ravana,

the demon king of Sri Lanka (Dowson, 1950: 137–138). Daksha, Ritual-Skill, another such example, was beheaded by Shiva (Dowson, 1950: 77–78).

Still another example of beheading is Rahu, the ascending node of the moon and one of the nine *graha*s (astronomical bodies with the attributes of deities). Once Rahu was an antigod (*danava*). While the gods were drinking soma, he disguised himself and imbibed some of the ambrosia. The deities discovered him and severed his head from his body. He should have died but since he had drunk soma he had become immortal, and thus a god. His head became the ascending node of the moon, known as Rahu, and his tail, the monster, Ketu, the descending node of the moon (Daniélou, 1964: 98–99, 315–316).

Another legend about a Hindu-Muslim saint, Guga Pir, is associated with beheading. Different versions of the legend date it differently, but the events took place among the Rajputs of Bikaner. The bards who told and retold this legend, which may originally have been partially based on fact, no doubt changed and elaborated it. Temple (1884, 1(6): 121) wrote: "The whole story of Gugga [sic] is involved in the greatest obscurity." Nonetheless, Temple (1900, vol. 3(52): 261) specifically stated, with some reservations about historical validity, that Guga died defending his country against the expedition of Mahmud of Ghazni into India in A.D. 1024.

The story told in Shanti Nagar in 1958 by senior women, who first drew a picture on the wall above their cookstoves of Guga on horseback surrounded by snakes (fig. 5), is that Guga kills his two brothers by cutting off their heads. He then presents them to his mother, who thereupon declares that he is no longer a Hindu. Thereafter he becomes a Muslim and dies by burying himself alive. This story is told on Guga Naumi (Guga's Ninth), his birthday in the dark fortnight of the month of Bhadrapad (R. Freed and S. Freed, 1985: 150, fn. 19; Append. V: Calendric Events).

Temple (1884: 1(6): 121–209) provided a full Punjabi version of this legend with an English-Punjabi text in poetic form as performed annually in Ambala District. In this version, replete with miraculous feats attributed to Guga, Raja Jewar and Queen Bachchal anxiously want a son, so Queen Bachchal beseeches Guru Gorakhnath, with his miraculous powers, to help her bear one. Bachchal's sister, Kachchal, also a mate of Raja Jewar, disguises herself as Bachchal and visits Guru Gorakhnath, too, in order to obtain sons. He does not realize she is not Queen Bachchal and promises her that she will bear two sons. Then she and a sister of Raja Jewar spread gossip about Queen Bachchal being in the royal garden at midnight with a yogi, implying that she has ruined her reputation and become pregnant. They repeat this gossip to the Raja who then banishes Queen Bachchal from the palace.

Although Bachchal is 12 (sic) months pregnant, she begins her travels to her natal family in transport pulled by bullocks. When the coachman stops to water the bullocks, a snake bites them and they die. While Queen Bachchal bewails the bullocks, Guga miraculously speaks from his mother's womb and tells her how to bring the bullocks back to life by using a branch from a neem tree, calling on Guru Gorakhnath, making an offering for the Guru, repeating eight charms for snakes, and then praising the Guru. This is the first step in establishing Guga's miraculous power with snakes. Bachchal follows Guga's directions, and the bullocks stand up immediately. A snake and a partridge are favorable omens taken by a Brahman priest when determining the time of Guga's birth in the month of Bhadon, an alternate term for Bhadrapad (August–September). With these omens, Raja Jewar and Bachchal are reconciled and happy with the birth of their son.

Guga's betrothal and marriage also illustrate Guga's power over snakes. This power accounts for the worship of the drawing of Guga Pir on horseback surrounded by snakes. Shortly after Guga's betrothal, his father dies so the engagement is broken. Guga then goes into the forest and calls on Guru Gorakhnath to put him in touch with the Chief of Snakes, Basak Nag, who in turn sends his servant, Tatig Nag (a snake), to Guga. The Chief of Snakes tells Tatig Nag to do whatever Guga orders because Guru Goraknath is known to have special power over snakes. Then according to Guga's instructions, Tatig Nag disguises himself as a Brahman and visits the garden of Guga's former fiancée's father where

she is sitting. When she sees Tatig Nag after he resumes his snake form, she faints. He then has another plan. When she goes to the lake to bathe, he enters the lake in his snake form, bites her toe, and she dies. Guga, known for his power with snakes and snake bites, is then called. By using the same procedure that he told his mother to use for the dead bullocks, he revives the girl. They are again engaged and soon wedded.

After the wedding, the twin sons of Kachchal, Surjan and Urjan, ask for a share of Guga's property. He refuses, so they plot to kill him while hunting together. When they try, Guga draws his sword to defend himself, kills each of them with one stroke apiece, and cuts off their heads with a second stroke. He next places the heads on the pommel of his saddle and takes them to his mother. She curses him, saying that he is no longer a Hindu, and tells him to go down into the earth to die. He then asks Mother Earth to take him, but this goddess tells him that to be buried he will have to become a Muslim. He seeks a Muslim teacher, learns the creed, and goes down into the earth to die, for Muslims are buried. This legend reflects the influence of Islam in North India.

A later version of the legend incorporates some of the above features and adds that Queen Bachchal nurses the twin boys because their own mother is unable to do so, thus accounting for Bachchal's feelings about their death. This version is based on a collection of relatively recent oral presentations about Guga throughout North India with a map showing the distribution of the legend (Blackburn et al., 1989: 19, Map 1, Chap. 16). The atavistic interest in the well-known horror tales of beheading may further account for the perpetuation of the belief in the ghost of the Headless Sweeper.

Doniger O'Flaherty (1980: 149, 275) has called cases of beheading in Hindu mythology heresies of Hinduism. However, village Hinduism has no central temple or institution that hands down dogmas or rules specifying that actions are heretical or unorthodox; therefore, no heresies may be said to exist. From the villagers' point of view, the stories about beheaded supernatural beings and people who commit suicide by cutting off their heads or who are murdered by decapitation would not contravene Hindu beliefs. Karma, rebirth, release from the round of rebirths, and becoming a ghost cover a multitude of beliefs regarding the results of one's actions. Further, the villagers' attitudes toward the supernatural beings in Hindu myths tend to coincide with beliefs about themselves. Just as their view of deities, spirits, and ghosts is often anthropomorphic, so too the view of their behavior is anthropopathic. They believe that supernatural beings, like human beings, vary in their behavior and may be malevolent, benevolent, or both, depending on the situation. This attribution stems from villagers' identification with the supernatural beings in the epics and the Puranas, and the parables raised by them, in which the moral or ethical behavior to be learned from the stories is not always clear any more than are their own decisions in everyday life. Even though the villagers debate the meanings of these parables, they accept the actions of supernatural beings as illustrative of their own dharma and of good and bad karma. Thus, they would not say that the beheaded in Hindu stories contradict Hindu beliefs but rather that they reinforce their ideology regarding karma, dharma, rebirth, and release. Their acceptance of the stories is incorporated into their everyday view of life.

With all these stories about beheading and the headless, it is not surprising to find that Kakar (1983: 28), a psychoanalyst practicing in New Delhi, considers a *sirkata*, a headless ghost, to be one of the core Muslim and Hindu fantasies in India. By way of illustration, he described the encounter of a policeman with a headless ghost. The *sirkata* wanted to drink water from a well near the Jama Masjid, a famous mosque in Old Delhi. In order to do so, he asked the policeman to pour the water from a bucket down his headless neck. The policeman soon tired of the endless task of pouring the water and threw away the bucket in disgust. The *sirkata* asked, "Aren't you afraid of my anger?" The policeman retorted, "Why should I be afraid of someone who doesn't even have a head." Then the *sirkata* ran away; but the policeman fell ill the same night. He was cured by a Muslim pir known to Kakar (Kakar, 1983: 15, 28).

The case of the Headless Sweeper is by no means a heresy of Hinduism. In fact, it fits well into Hindu myths, legends, and other tales, as well as into village beliefs and the historical developments that took place in the Punjab in the 19th and 20th centuries as they affected, especially, the peripatetic Chuhra Sweeper caste. Just as the Headless Sweeper was influenced by a complex sociohistorical environment, his death from the dreaded plague and subsequent ghosthood had an effect on those who followed in his footsteps.

OLD SURVIVOR

In 1958, Old Survivor, the second son of the Headless Sweeper and his oldest living descendant, was blind but mentally quite alert. He was then 80 years old, which places his approximate birth date around 1878. The following interview with him clearly illustrates an important aspect of the lives of Sweeper men of Shanti Nagar from the last quarter of the 19th century until 1958, namely, long employment away from home chiefly in what is now Pakistan. Old Survivor led such a life.

The interview started with Old Survivor telling about his family, his ancestors, and the founding of the Chuhra Sweeper caste in the village. The earliest identified ancestor from whom all the Chuhra Sweepers claimed descent was a man from Narela, who was not a Sweeper, but a Banjara. The Banjaras were one of the classes of Indian society, a group of wandering grain merchants, some of whom settled at least for a while in the tract under the northern hills lying between Gorakhpur and Hardwar. They had a number of *gotras* (clans) and were either Muslims or Hindus. However, Banjaras moved around, were scattered all over India, and were known under a variety of names. From the description of the wandering life of Banjara men, it is possible that they often took wives temporarily from different castes and then wandered off in the course of their travels. With the coming of the railroads, it was expected that in time they would disappear or be absorbed into other castes and enterprises (Balfour, 1885 (1): 270–272).

The Banjara from Narela took a Sweeper woman as a wife, and their son settled in Shanti Nagar where he founded the Chuhra Sweeper caste. Founder (his pseudonym) apparently considered himself a Sweeper and had two wives, both of whom were Sweeper women. These two wives each had four sons; thus the eight sons were brothers. All the village Sweepers trace descent from Founder. Only the descendants of Founder and his second wife were curers or exorcists. The eldest son of the second wife was the man whose ghost, through the elaboration of the legend, became the Headless Sweeper, but Sweepers did not refer to him that way. Instead in reciting the Chuhra Sweeper genealogy, they used his name but never said he was a ghost. His name was the same as the word for an amulet used as protection against ghosts.

In reciting the Chuhra Sweeper genealogy, Old Survivor said that at first he never knew about the Banjara and the descent of the Sweepers from him until some old men told him. We estimate that Founder was born about 1825 or earlier, and the Banjara at the end of the 18th or beginning of the 19th century. The so-called Headless Sweeper was Founder's son, and his birth date is estimated at about 1850, inasmuch as Old Survivor was the Headless Sweeper's second son. His eldest son, Absent Son, was born ca. 1868 to 1875. This patrilineal descent is from the Banjara to his son, the founder of the Sweeper caste in the village, then to the Headless Sweeper, and from him to his sons, the eldest of whom, Absent Son, was the father of Lord of Ghosts, who was also an eldest son. Lord of Ghosts was the grandson of the Headless Sweeper. Although Lord of Ghosts had three sons, as far as is known, none of them became exorcists (Append. III: Chart 5).

Old Survivor had only one surviving son; three others died. When he was asked whether he had more than one wife, he replied, "I have had only one marriage, and one is hard enough. What would I do with three or four wives. More than one cause trouble."

In the context of his, his wife's, and his children's past illnesses, he spoke about curing and his curing techniques:

One can treat the evil eye and cure it completely but one cannot do much with a ghost. Only a ghost can catch a ghost. There's a mantra which I read and then wave a broomstick. If a person has a headache, pain in the back, or breasts, or if a scorpion bites the patient, then you do this treat-ment. I learned how to do it from an old babaji [respected elderly man], a fakir, when I was in Sukkur. To learn one can give four to five rupees, a turban, *kamiz* [shirt], or *silwar* [baggy trousers, formerly worn by Muslim men; still worn by women in North India]. I learned in two to three months. If one is bright, one learns quickly; otherwise it takes longer. For example, if I bought a book for four to five rupees, I read it during the day and sold it by night time. I read Hindi.

I used to go to the job at 8 a.m. and was home by 4 p.m. Then I cooked my meal and studied two hours. I learned Hindi in this way. I worked with railway engines in Sukkur. I moved from one job to another. First I worked cleaning pipes, pushing long steel rods in and out; then ashes fell out. I also stoked fires; but I never worked with the broom; I was not a sweeper. When I joined the railway, I started with a pay of eight rupees per month. When I left I was earning two rupees a day. Salaries were low then; an engineer received about 20 rupees a month. I had Government quarters to live in, but they did not furnish food. I bought my own. There were heaps of coal around the railway yards and I used the coal for my fuel. When you work at a place, you use what is there. The coal was for the Government, but since I worked there, I took it and did not pay for it. I would look around and then stick some coals under my shirt. I do the same here in the village for gur [brown sugar]. You are not supposed to do this, but I do and I eat a little here and there.

I went to Sukkur when I was 15 years old [1893]. My bones were not yet visible then. People used to come home on leave and others would go back with them. I went with my elder brother [Absent Son]; I was already married but I do not remember my age then because the wedding took place in my childhood. My wife came to Sukkur about two years later. I joined the railway at age 25 [1903] and retired at age 55 [1933]. I worked there until I retired and received a lump sum on retirement of Rs. 608.50. I owed some money so I paid it out of this lump sum. Then I bought some grain, came home, arranged the marriage of my only son and a daughter, and built this house. After Independence I fell ill and did not work any more. I was ill three years and could not move off the bed; I still cannot move my fingers in this hand. My wife and children were also ill.

After Old Survivor's retirement in 1933, he returned home, worked at odd jobs and as a curer, and raised goats, chickens, and pigs, the latter two animals traditionally kept by the Sweepers of Shanti Nagar. His training by a fakir continued the tradition of curing within this Chuhra Sweeper lineage. Yet he did not have the power to drive out ghosts.

LORD OF GHOSTS

Several examples of the eternal triangles of jealousy which sometimes occur between members of families cropped up in the 1950s in the case history of Lord of Ghosts. In this instance, the triangles of jealousy were linked with ghost possession and the fear of sorcery. Lord of Ghosts was an exorcist although not particularly powerful. His efforts to counter the actions of a more powerful *siyana* illustrate the hierarchy of power among exorcists. Lord of Ghosts used more than one technique of exorcism. Villagers sometimes distinguish among exorcists on the basis of their most characteristic technique.

LIFE AND FAMILY HISTORY

Lord of Ghosts, the eldest son of Absent Son, grandson of the Headless Sweeper, and nephew of Old Survivor, like many other Sweepers spent most of his life employed away from the village. His pseudonym derives from one of a number of names by which the god Shiva is identified. Born in 1898 and 60 years old in 1958, he was recruited in the army at Jhelum, Punjab when he was 25 years old. He retired from the army in 1947 at age 49, after serving throughout India, in Australia, and having once visited London. He said that he could read and write a little although he had never gone to school. After his retirement he continued with his curing practice which he began to learn from Old Survivor and his father, Absent Son, but he added to his knowledge while in the Punjab. Because of his curing practice and visits to his two broth-

ers living in Delhi, he was often absent from the village.

Lord of Ghosts had two successive wives. The first wife became a ghost along with her first infant when she and the baby died shortly after the baby was born. The second wife, Lady of Ghosts, was somewhat younger than her husband, 50 to 55 years old in 1958. Husband and wife were the parents of six surviving children: three sons and three daughters, all of whom were married by 1958. The two older sons worked: the eldest for the railway as a sweeper in the city, and the next eldest, Good Natured, for his father as a field watchman. The third son was in ninth grade. Lady of Ghosts had long been the village midwife, but three to four years prior to 1958 she began to suffer from possessions by the ghost of the first wife which then turned into what the villagers called madness, *pagalpan*. The widow of a son of a brother of the Headless Sweeper took over the midwife practice temporarily until she went to live with her sons in the city.

TECHNIQUES FOR CURING THE EVIL EYE AND GHOST POSSESSION

Lord of Ghosts was the first male sweeper whom we came to know fairly well. At the behest of Honesty, Manipulator's mother, he performed a curing ceremony for Ruth Freed, a description of which follows, when Honesty believed she had been attacked by someone casting the evil eye. She was in fact suffering from a streptococcal throat infection and was cured with Western medicine. However, Lord of Ghosts' ritual curing opened the way for further interviews with him and other Sweepers.

Lord of Ghosts was referred to as an *ojha*, bhagat, or fakir. For relatively simple cures but not ghost possession, his curing technique was similar to Old Survivor's. Called *jhara*, meaning to take off or exorcise the ghost or evil eye, the technique was relatively simple. Lord of Ghosts and his patient faced each other over a pan of water on the ground. Holding a broom in his right hand throughout the curing session, he waved it in front of his patient and recited verses to coax the effects of the evil eye out of the patient and into the water. He gave patients pieces of rock salt to hold and directed them to squeeze the rock salt very hard and then drop some into the water, after which he recited a mantra or verse. After reciting a number of verses, if any rock salt remained, he directed patients to throw the balance into the basin of water. Thereafter the basin was emptied where no one could step over its contents to avoid additional influence from the evil eye. The foregoing curing techniques are somewhat similar to those reported from Nepal (L. G. Peters, 1981: 117), which consist of reciting a spell or magical formula and brushing away bodily pain with a broom.

Lord of Ghosts claimed that the basin of water, rock salt, waving of the broom, and recitation of verses drew off the evil eye. He recited a collection of verses learned from a fakir in northern Punjab, now part of Pakistan. He claimed some were Hindu mantras, others were from the Islamic Koran, and one was a religious hymn from the Granth, the book of the Sikhs. Another cure for ailments, such as toothache and backache, was to circle the head of the sufferer with grain and to throw it into a fire.

During the 1958 fieldwork, two Chamars, Buddhist II and Illusionist, described a more intense form of curing by exorcism that Lord of Ghosts practiced for cases of ghost possession. The cure involved singing and smoking a special hookah which only he used while a companion beat a drum. They said: "Bhagats are of two types: those who through words try to overpower the ghost possessing a patient, and those who sing in order to control the ghost." Lord of Ghosts was said to be the second type. The Chamars compared the process of smoking, singing, and drumming to a snake charmer charming a snake with his bin (flute). While the drum was beaten, Lord of Ghosts sang a song to call his familiar, a ghost. The ghost then came and entered Lord of Ghosts. Lord of Ghosts was thus able to communicate through his own ghost with the ghost possessing the patient. In this way Lord of Ghosts overpowered the ghost in the patient, and the patient was released from the possession. This type of cure was what was meant when Old Survivor claimed that only a bhut can catch a bhut.

The description of a special hookah which only Lord of Ghosts smoked suggests that it provides the exorcist with special powers. General social intercourse requires that a hookah be passed from man to man when smoking in a group. In this curing ceremony it is not. *Nicotiana persica* (a slow burning tobacco suitable for the hookah, grown in Asia) when smoked in excess or taken in liquid form has intoxicating and/or hallucinogenic properties. Thus, Lord of Ghosts' intensive hookah smoking along with the semihypnotic effect of singing and drumming was believed to enable him to call his own ghost and catch a ghost (Dobkin de Rios, 1973: 81; Harris and Levey, 1975: 2759; R. Prince, 1982b: 410). The rhythmical, sensory stimulus to the neurotransmitters in the central nervous system along with the intoxicant could result in an alternate mental state, in which the smoker believed he was in contact with his familiar, a ghost (Ludwig, 1966; Tart 1979; Jilek, 1982: 326–328, 337–340; R. Prince, 1982a: 303–316; 1982b; Saffran, 1982: 322–324). Weiss (1973: 43) stated "Tobacco is not an hallucinogen, but in massive doses it is a powerful intoxicant . . . it is credited as the source of a Campa shaman's powers to see and communicate with the spirits and to cure. . . ." *Nicotiana persica* belongs to the family *Solanaceae* (Nightshade); its most characteristic constituent is the alkaloid nicotine, which is responsible for its narcotic, soothing qualities (Harris and Levey, 1975: 1939, 1943).

Lord of Ghosts began learning his curing techniques from Absent Son, his father, who, in turn, learned from his father, the man whose ghost came to be known as the Headless Sweeper. If this curing technique with the hookah was passed down from the Headless Sweeper, it would account for the Headless Sweeper calling for his hookah, smoking it, and supposedly cutting off his own head, but more probably puncturing the lymphatic inflammation (bubo) in his neck, which resulted in his death. Further evidence for passing down the occupation of curing in this family line is that Old Survivor was taken to Sukkur by his brother, Absent Son, who was the eldest son of the Headless Sweeper, who had also been taken to Sukkur by his father, another eldest son of the second wife of Founder.

Jhelum, a predominantly Muslim area

where Lord of Ghosts was recruited into the army, is far enough north to share curing practices current in Kashmir. Hoch (1974: 669–670) described the curing practices of Muslim pirs and Hindu and Muslim fakirs in Kashmir. The pirs have an inherited position; their disciples or apprentices have no hereditary claim, but in time may become pirs and thereafter pass along their status to their descendants. The more powerful pirs by long practice of meditation are able to go into possession-trance which is helped along by drumming, singing, and fumigation. In this state, they call one of their ghost familiars to talk with the ghost possessing a patient. The Muslim and Hindu fakirs do not have an hereditary role, but they may proclaim themselves as healers by various characteristics, such as eccentric or unusual costume, the use of various intoxicants or drugs, for example, Indian hemp (hashish), fumigations with incense and smoke, drumming, singing, and dancing. Lord of Ghosts' curing practices show a combination of the pir and fakir traditions. While in Shanti Nagar, however, he never dressed differently from the usual villagers or members of his caste.

FAMILY JEALOUSIES AND SORCERY

Honesty, a Brahman grandmother, told us about trouble in Lord of Ghosts' family caused by a ghost controlled by a *siyana*, the father of Lord of Ghosts' daughter-in-law. She said:

Lord of Ghosts' son's [Good Natured] wife had a ghost seize her mother-in-law. Because of this action, Lady of Ghosts is crazy. The daughter-in-law's father was a *siyana*, and he released a ghost to seize Lady of Ghosts. Lord of Ghosts has spent two to three thousand rupees on his wife's illness.

A *siyana* grabs hold of people who have died and orders them around. He keeps all these dead people strung up and asks them to go wherever he goes. Then he writes out statements, which have the power to hold these dead people. When the dead bodies are cremated, the *siyana* takes away the bones and orders the bones about. He has to have the bones for his work. When he has them, the ghost is under his control. If

the *siyana* knows he has an enemy, he can control the enemy through the ghost.

This particular case illustrates the role of a *siyana* as a sorcerer. In this region of India, it is believed that people who control supernatural power can both cure and cause illness and death. Most of the activities of bhagats, *siyana*s, and other curers that came to our attention were aimed at curing ghost illness and possession, except when a curer possessed of supernatural means became angry because his patient had sought treatment by another curer.

The problems that afflicted the family of Lord of Ghosts point to a possible case of sorcery in the context of domestic tension as the result of the triangles of jealousy between Lady of Ghosts, her son, and her daughter-in-law; and between the mother-in-law, daughter-in-law, and Lord of Ghosts. In addition, Lord of Ghosts was disturbed by the superior power of his daughter-in-law's father, a *siyana*, and his disciple, also a *siyana*. These triangles will be described below.

Before the foregoing conversation, Honesty had been talking with Nutmeg, one of the Jats who professed not to believe in ghosts. The conversation reflects the sensitivity exorcists feel toward those who doubt their powers, including a *siyana*'s power to kill. When Honesty began to talk about Lord of Ghosts curing *masan* pain (death pain), she said:

Lord of Ghosts would not go to Nutmeg's house when Nutmeg asked him to cure his wife of *masan* pain. Nutmeg's wife often miscarries so Nutmeg wanted Lord of Ghosts to cure her of *masan*. There are two kinds of *masan*: one when a child is born healthy and dies suddenly; and the other when women miscarry. [In both cases a ghost takes the soul. A similar description of *masan* is "the ghost killer of unborn babies" (Kakar, 1983: 74)]. These pains can only be cured by a *siyana* or bhagat. One son of Nutmeg had *masan* and died suddenly.

Honesty added that a *siyana* had provided a charm to tie around the neck of Nutmeg's son, but when the boy became ill, they went to a doctor. The *siyana* then became furious and caused the boy to die. This *siyana* came from another village. Later when Nutmeg wanted Lord of Ghosts to come to his house to treat another of his sons, Lord of Ghosts refused because he said Nutmeg did not believe that these pains were caused by Masani, an alternative name for Kalkaji, Mother Goddess of the Cremation Grounds.

Mrs. Authority, Nutmeg's mother, then made an offering at Hardwar, a famous pilgrimage spot on the Ganges River, saying that she would perform the same offering for the health of the child in five years. The ceremony is one where a mother goes to the Ganges with her infant, and says, "Here is the child whom I offered to you five years ago." Then she gives something like Rs. 5000 to the priest and takes back the child. Honesty said that it is a way of providing money for good works (i.e., good karma) and that some women even donate ornaments. This account of the ceremony, recorded in 1958, is similar to the one described by Truthful in "A Ghost Took My Son" (Chap. 14).

Having learned something about Lord of Ghosts' family from Honesty, we visited the Chuhra Sweeper compound and found Good Natured, the second son of Lord of Ghosts, but not his father. Good Natured had just brought his wife, Timid, from Karnal, and he wanted us to meet her. She was a pleasant woman with two children, who jokingly asked for a rupee for unveiling her face in front of us, a traditional custom for a new bride, but not for a mother of two children.

Good Natured also jokingly began, "My wife is a very timid woman, and if I slice her ears, she will become even more timid and obey me very well." He then mentioned that he had wanted us to go with him when he fetched his wife from her parents because they had been saying "No, no" to him. Finally he told them he would report them to the police so they sent her to him. At this point, his wife smiled and indicated by a gesture that he was just joking. Good Natured then said, "My wife has been at her home for two-and-one-half years because my mother has been ill. The illness may have been due to evil spirits, some said; others said other things. I think her illness is a physical thing, but my mother thinks she is possessed by a ghost. I think that when her blood gets too hot she gets

attacks. She has been ill for the last three years."

Then Good Natured talked about his late father-in-law, whom he called a babaji, which literally means respected elder male (i.e., a *siyana* or exorcist, another term for a wise man or sorcerer). Good Natured's father-in-law had a disciple, and everybody in Lord of Ghosts' family thought that the disciple, also a *siyana*, acting as a surrogate for his late mentor, had done something to Good Natured's mother, Lady of Ghosts. She was convinced that somebody put something in her food which brought on her illness. Good Natured said:

My mother becomes violent, starts abusing even her husband and destroys things. Her attacks continue for 24 hours. For three years she has been suffering. She is never all right. She behaves this way all of the time. She never rests even for an hour. If you go over there where she is sitting, she'll talk to you nicely. She is nice to outsiders, but she abuses her own family except the children. She is more violent with me, my wife, and my father because of my wife's relationship to her father, the *siyana*, and also to his disciple, who my mother believes has done this to her. My wife formerly was possessed for one to two hours and my father treated her. My mother did not like it when he treated her [i.e., she was jealous]. It is believed that when my father treated my wife, he may have abused her [in this context, abuse means cursing her, using insulting or threatening terms], and she reported this to her own father, who brought this sickness to my mother. [It is noteworthy that the victim of the sorcery was not the target, that is, Lord of Ghosts was regarded as culpable but the ghost was sent to attack his wife, possibly because the wife did not have the powers of an exorcist but the jealousy of Lady of Ghosts is also involved. In a sense, Lord of Ghosts was punished indirectly through his wife in an effort to make him amend his behavior.] My father abused my wife because she spoke to him while he was treating her for one of her attacks. A daughter-in-law should not speak to a father-in-law. He called her some foul words. Probably he only incidentally did so, that is, he lost his temper and swore, but she should not have reported the incident to her parents. My wife used to start trembling all of a sudden due to an evil ghost.

Lord of Ghosts suddenly appeared on the scene and said, "Probably the disciple affected her. He lives in my son's wife's natal village and stays in a gurdwara." Lord of Ghosts then left as precipitately as he came. Good Natured continued:

This disciple has been in this village many times but has not been here for the last year. He was here before my wife had her attack of ghost possession. I have been married to my wife 14 years; I was 9 to 10 years old when we were wedded; she was 8 to 9 years old. She came to live here permanently when she was physically mature [ca. 14 to 15 years old, the average age at menarche for village girls in 1958–59]. She bore her first child [a daughter] the third year after she came here [ca. age 17 in 1952]. She had her attacks after the first child was born and then again after the second child [a daughter] was born when she was 19. My mother [Lady of Ghosts] was the midwife. Because we believed that the disciple caused her attacks, we made a *tawiz* for her. When we did this, for a while she was cured.

Then in 1955 my wife's attacks would come from two to five times a day for about one month. My father again tried to cure her to no avail so we took her to her father's disciple and left her there until she was cured. She stayed there two-and-one-half years. Now she has returned. My wife and mother do not get along now. Formerly they were very affectionate to each other. One would not take her meals without the other. My mother does not get along well with me either, but she gets along well with my brothers and their families, but not with me or with my father. I think some fakir might cure her. My father can only temporarily cure her attacks. Probably the ghosts who attack my mother are too powerful for him. Only Bhagwan can give a person the power to cure such attacks or to have intelligence.

Then Good Natured said that we should talk with his mother as she was sitting nearby. We approached Lady of Ghosts, sat down, and she began telling about her illness:

I have been sick for three years and do not think I can be cured. When I lie down, I see animals and insects before my eyes. I want to lie under a train and let it cut me and kill me or put a rope around my neck and die. Everybody watches me so I cannot kill myself. My husband has spent much money on me for cures, but nothing has done any good. This illness began all of a sudden at midnight when I started talking violently. I think somebody put something in my food and my husband agrees. I would kill anyone who did this to me if I could find him. I was the midwife of the village and now I do not do anything. I think this illness is in my luck. You are welcome to sit with me, but I am unlucky, just cry and feel bad. I have been to far off places and seen many curers, spending Rs. 100 a day, but I won't be cured by anyone. I've been taken to Karnal, Gurgaon, and other holy places but nothing helps. I was never afraid of anyone, but now when I see many animals and insects moving in front of my eyes I am terrified. Two to three animals come in a group and then go away and others come in a group. This goes on before my eyes all of the time and I cannot close them and go to sleep.

Lady of Ghosts yawned throughout the interview, but kept on talking. "I used to be a very affectionate, nice woman, but this illness has changed me. If one feels an illness can be cured, one does not feel as annoyed as when one knows it will go on forever." Lady of Ghosts interspersed her remarks during the interview by crooning and muttering. Sometimes she seemed to be falling asleep although still sitting up talking; then she became a bit more alert. She occasionally uttered, "Lar, lar," a kind of moaning sound. Intermittently she would tell her husband to take the hookah and smoke. At the end of the interview, Lady of Ghosts was asked whether she presently saw any animals or insects in front of her eyes. She answered, "No." Lord of Ghosts interjected, "She sees them only when she is alone. Her mind is affected by evil spirits."

Lady of Ghosts then asked that we leave her because she could not talk any more.

JEALOUSY, PARANOIA, AND FOLIE À DEUX

Lord of Ghosts' being a bhagat and the family tradition of exorcism going back to the Headless Sweeper and beyond him to Founder and his second wife were important factors in this family situation. Timid's possessions may have been related both to growing up in the family of a *siyana*, where involvement with supernatural events would have been commonplace, and also to the stress of living in the household of Lord of Ghosts and her mother-in-law, a milieu with similar traditions and experiences. Villagers sometimes believe that ghosts afflicting them can spread by contagion from one person to another. To complicate the situation, Timid's father, a *siyana*, had greater power and prestige than Lord of Ghosts, a bhagat. The *siyana*'s disciple, who had the same powers, visited Shanti Nagar after his mentor's death possibly to carry out his wishes, or so it seemed to Lord and Lady of Ghosts. Lord of Ghosts could not cure his wife and had to take her to exorcists with more power than he had.

The triangles of jealousy started when the amicable relationships between Lady of Ghosts and her daughter-in-law, Timid, deteriorated around 1952 and 1953, beginning with the ghost possessions and then the madness of Lady of Ghost. Their relationship ultimately became quite stressful. Timid's first and second pregnancies at ages 17 and 19 contributed to the stress she was undergoing in her marital family. Lady of Ghosts by that time had been suffering from ghost possessions and jealousy and had become very difficult to live with. She may have leveled much of her animosity at her daughter-in-law, who was more vulnerable than her husband or children. Already verging on paranoia, she delivered Timid's first two children. The birth of the children increased Lady of Ghost's jealousy of Timid concerning her son's affections and thereby helped to trigger Timid's possessions.

When Lord of Ghosts attempted to exorcise the ghost possessing Timid, she spoke to him and he cursed her. Ideal behavior requires that a father-in-law and daughter-in-law are not left alone together and do not touch one another or converse together. Because of these rules of avoidance, Lord of Ghosts should not have treated his daughter-in-law. Whatever happened, he lost control and cursed her. Since a bhagat, *siyana*, or fakir can practice sorcery, his cursing someone is believed to be especially harmful. Thus, Timid may have feared for her life when Lord of Ghosts cursed her. His actions were disturbing enough for Timid to report the incident to her father. Thus, Lord of Ghosts expected retaliation by the *siyana* and his disciple. Thereafter, Timid did not return to her husband for two-and-one-half years.

After this incident, Lady of Ghosts was even more jealous of Timid because she believed that her husband should not have been alone with her. In effect, Lady of Ghosts was entangled in yet another triangle of jealousy involving the relationship between Timid and her husband. To find paranoia in a jealous person is not surprising, especially if it is believed that a bhagat or a *siyana* can aim his supernatural powers against the jealous person.

Lady of Ghosts' illness fits the symptoms of a paranoid disorder, which may have its onset in middle age or later. The identifying symptom is delusions of persecution; in her case, the belief that someone tried to poison her. Before he died, Timid's father had been accused; but when the illness persisted, Lord of Ghosts and Good Natured blamed the disciple of Timid's father. However, Lady of Ghosts may also have believed that her daughter-in-law tried to poison her since her madness began in 1953, or even that her husband gave her something to cause her to see animals and insects because he was attracted to Timid. Jealousy once started spreads like sickness. However, because Lord of Ghosts had cursed Timid, the *siyana* and his disciple were the main suspects.

Lord of Ghosts may have tried to cure his daughter-in-law because he wanted to demonstrate his own power. His failure to do so created self-doubt about his curing powers and prestige, especially since he also could not cure his wife. That Timid's father was a *siyana* was an additional threat to his confidence. On the other hand, Lord of Ghosts spent quite a sum of money for cures for his wife and may not have had the money to spend on his daughter-in-law, for he was heavily in debt.

Carstairs and Kapur (1976: 117) found in Kota, South India, that women are reluctant to go to *Mantarwadis* and *Patris*, curers who follow the principle that all trouble originates from past actions, usually the violation of village customs and tabus. Their reluctance is not due to their fear that a past indiscretion will be exposed but rather to their belief that these curers are endowed with excessive "sexual heat," which attracts women. Although no such statement was heard about Lord of Ghosts or other curers in this village, they were believed to have special powers for good or evil.

Erna Hoch (1974: 672–673) listed two points regarding pirs, fakirs, and psychiatrists. Her first point is that the alien and alienated somehow belong together. Psychiatrists are also called alienists, a word referring to those treating the mentally ill, and derived from the Latin *alienatus*, meaning estranged (Morris, 1969: 33). The two terms should be regarded as linked, indicating that whether they refer to pirs, fakirs, exorcists, or psychiatrists, these individuals are different from most people. These terms also fit village ideas regarding strangers, Muslims, and those foreign to village customs, as well as curers. Alienation also applies to the caste of Chuhra Sweepers who are peripatetic and before the Independence of India were called outcastes.

Curers may be feared by people who believe that they are different and have special powers, such as a psychiatrist's ability to probe the mind. The supernatural powers of exorcists in Shanti Nagar are feared, for they are the source of an exorcist's ability to delve into a patient's mind and cure it, as does a psychiatrist. The curer with supernatural power is thought to be able to deal with the intrusive ghost, the proximate cause of the trouble, with which ordinary people cannot always cope.

Hoch's second point is that pirs, fakirs, and psychiatrists have charisma or exude power which cannot be taught. The sexual heat, of which the women of Kota are afraid, may be similar. The Russian monk, Rasputin, a hypnotist and faith healer, is a classic example

(Massie, 1985: 191–214; DeVinne, 1987: 1395).

Good Natured's account and the villagers' statements that Lord of Ghosts would no longer allow Timid and Good Natured to live with him and Lady of Ghosts, is further evidence that a shared paranoid disorder existed between mother-in-law and daughter-in-law, and also between Lord of Ghosts and his daughter-in-law. Since Lady of Ghosts evinced jealousy of her husband and Timid and was hostile to Good Natured, she probably was suspicious of their intentions toward her. That Timid stayed in her natal village two-and-a-half years shows similar suspicion and fear regarding her mother-in-law and father-in-law.

This case may be one where more than two persons were involved in a folie à deux, a shared paranoid disorder. "Paranoid Disorders are thought to be rare. However, Paranoia involving delusional jealousy may be more common." (Am. Psych. Assn., DSM-III, 1980: 196). In a shared Paranoid Disorder, "The essential feature is a persecutory delusional system that develops as a result of a close relationship with another person who already has a disorder with persecutory delusions. The delusions are at least partly shared. Usually if the relationship with the other person is interrupted, the delusional beliefs will diminish or disappear. In the past this disorder has been termed *Folie à deux*, although in rare cases, more than two persons may be involved," which is what seems to have happened in this case (Am. Psych. Assn., DSM-III, 1980: 197; cf. Berkow, 1982: 1463, 1470; Andreasen, 1985: 149).

One symptom which raises a question about this diagnosis of a paranoid disorder is Lady of Ghosts' hallucinations of seeing insects and animals. Andreasen (1985: 61) stated that "When a person reports visual hallucination, the cause is more likely to be some form of intoxication with drugs or alcohol. . . ." Berkow, (1982: 1469) indicated that typically a paranoid disorder develops without hallucinations. A medical examination of Lady of Ghosts would be necessary to determine if there was a physical basis for her hallucinations. Although alcohol was readily available in the Sweeper community, we saw no indication that she drank, but then we were with her only a short time. The suggestion that Lord of Ghosts may have been surreptitiously giving her a drug which caused her visual hallucinations is based on the general absence of hallucinations in association with paranoia (Am. Psych. Assn., DSM-III, 1980: 1160).

Despite the contraindication of hallucinations, Lady of Ghosts had some common signs of a paranoid disorder, namely, age at onset (middle age), jealousy, and delusions of persecution. She was 50 to 55 years old in 1958. She had delusions that someone was trying to poison her and that the poison caused her illness. The prognosis of her probable disorder, from which she never recovered, is described as follows: "The course of Paranoia and Shared Paranoid Disorder is chronic with few, if any, exacerbations or periods of remission" (Am. Psych. Assn., DSM-III, 1980: 195). Lady of Ghosts died some years before Lord of Ghosts, who died in 1974 at age 76.

FINALE

When Lady of Ghosts died, her midwifery did not pass to Timid. Instead, after the widow who had been acting as midwife for a year or two left the village, the wife of one of Lord of Ghosts' brothers took over the practice and was still carrying on in 1978. During the 1977–78 fieldwork, various Chuhra Sweepers mentioned that Timid and Lord of Ghosts' youngest brother, Eluded, at one time suffered from ghost possessions, and both of them later had fits (*daura*). Their ghost possessions are best categorized as Dissociative Disorders; the later fits, as Somatoform Disorders, but neither individual was called mad, *pagalpan* (Am. Psych. Assn., DSM-III, 1980: 253). Timid worked as part of a team of village Sweeper women that covered about five villages. In 1958–59, Eluded lived in the City of Delhi. Although he lived in the village in 1977–78, he worked in the city and eluded interviews. No further information could be

obtained about him other than that he had always worked as a sweeper in the municipal system and that at one time he had considered becoming a Christian.

Good Natured, Lord of Ghosts' son, ran into us one day in 1978 while we were waiting for a bus. He spoke at great length about past events in the village and described his present job as a sweeper for a group of nearby villages. Formerly he had worked as a sweeper in the city, but did not enjoy commuting. He was very happy when he obtained his present job because he could save the carfare and could return home from work earlier. He mentioned the deaths of his parents, that his wife worked part-time as a village sweeper, and that her ghost possessions had become fits. We later learned that she was blind in one eye.

Lord of Ghosts' itinerant life gave him the opportunity of meeting and adding to his knowledge from diverse curers: Hindus, Muslims, and Sikhs. His status as an exorcist afforded him prestige in comparison to his lowly status as a Chuhra Sweeper. Since he was born into a cultural milieu which primarily attributes illness to ghosts, he himself believed in ghosts and ghost illness, witnessed ghost possessions, and believed in the ability of exorcists to cure or kill. The case of Lord of Ghosts' family shows that people within an exorcist's family may themselves suffer from ghost illness and ghost possession. Both Lord of Ghosts' wife and daughter-in-law were victims of ghosts. When Lord of Ghosts was unable to cure his wife, he sought help outside the village from a variety of exorcists whom he believed to have more supernatural power than he had. Resorting to a hierarchical network of exorcists is a noteworthy feature of persistent cases of ghost possession (cf. Clark, 1970: 183–214; Romanucci-Ross, 1977; R. Freed and S. Freed, 1985: 204–205).

CHAPTER 17: ILLUSIONIST,
A SELF-SELECTED EXORCIST

The life history of Illusionist, a member of the Chamar Leatherworker caste, is a study of how exorcists are recruited, or self-recruited as in Illusionist's case, and trained to cure ghost illness and possession. The vicissitudes in the lives of Illusionist and his wife contributed to his becoming an exorcist.

Illusionist was a member of the caste that ranked second-lowest in the village. Not yet an exorcist in 1958–59, he was 31 years old, economically insecure, and had a wife and two children. In contrast to Lord of Ghosts, he became an exorcist later in life through somewhat different pathways than Lord of Ghosts, who as an eldest son inherited the role of exorcist and was introduced to it by his father, Absent Son. In his wandering life among Sikhs, Muslims, and Hindus, he learned additional skills. However, Lord of Ghosts and Illusionist shared a trait; they were both low-caste men: one a Chuhra Sweeper; the other a Chamar Leatherworker. These castes ranked lowest in Shanti Nagar, the Chuhras at the bottom.

EARLY HISTORY

Early in our fieldwork in the spring of 1958 on the eve of the Holi festival, we were invited to an entertainment in the Chamar compound. A large crowd of villagers attended. The entertainment was provided by Chamar men who danced and played musical instruments. The dancing and the miming which accompanied it called for male and female roles, but both were played by men. The men who dressed as women mimed women's movements and used suggestive gestures. Although all the dancers were good, one performer stood out from the rest. He acted and danced the stereotyped role of a British memsahib. His performance was so good that it raised howls of laughter. This star performer was Illusionist. He and other Chamar men performed at festivals and weddings, sometimes earning as much as 100 rupees for a performance. When these men danced, high-caste men in the audience gave them money. The man who danced the role of the memsahib so amusingly and suggestively received the most money. As a result of his performance, we came to know him early in our fieldwork and became quite friendly. Through this friendship and the fact that we lived on the second storey of a building that looked directly down on his house and courtyard, we soon acquired considerable knowledge about him and his family.

Illusionist was born in 1927. His father, a poor provider, sent him to live with relatives in Old Delhi in 1932 when his younger half brother was born to his stepmother. His own mother had died. We had to delve deeply into his history before we found out that the woman who for many years was designated as his mother was in fact a stepmother. No one mentioned his real mother who was believed to have become a ghost. As a boy, Illusionist was shunted back and forth in Old Delhi between his father's sister and his mother's sister. These two women were the only family security he had in his early years after his mother died. When Illusionist was 12 years old in 1939, he held his first job, working in a factory for two rupees per month. He left that job and worked for two years in another factory where rings and buttons were manufactured. When he was 15 years old, he obtained a job as a laborer in a third factory and after some time became a mason.

In 1947 at age 20, Illusionist returned to Shanti Nagar for his wedding, a double wedding, for his half brother, Dutiful, and he were married on the same day. Afterward, his father's elder brother employed him to cycle to the city to sell milk. By 1958, Illusionist had separated from his father and worked in a textile mill where Kin, the son of his father's elder brother, was employed. In the same year both men were laid off. Kin took up agricultural work, which he had learned while growing up in the village. Illusionist, however, had never done agricultural work so he decided that the mill in time would reemploy him and did not accept a separation settlement from the factory as Kin had done. During about two years of unemployment, Illusionist danced whenever possible at festivals and weddings and cycled to the city where he bought vegetables which he resold in the village. He and his family were quite poor.

Although Illusionist and his wife had no education, Illusionist claimed that he could read and write a little Hindi. His ideological beliefs were eclectic, drawn from Hinduism and Islam. By 1958, Mrs. Illusionist had born four sons and three daughters. The first child, a son born in 1948, was the only child to survive. The other six died in infancy. Because of these deaths and the difficulty she had nursing her babies, Mrs. Illusionist went to a hospital in Delhi in the summer of 1958 for delivery of her eighth child, a daughter. The hospitalization was arranged through her parents, who lived in the city and had access to a Chamar who worked in the hospital.

Illusionist brought his wife and infant daughter back from the city on his cycle after a seven-day stay in the hospital and a week with her natal family in Old Delhi. Mrs. Illusionist enjoyed the hospital where she was given daily plenty of milk to drink, shared a room with another woman, slept on a bed with a mattress, and had clean bed linen instead of the rags she slept on in the village. She and her baby were bathed daily and their clothing was washed and changed. Before leaving the hospital, she was given a prescription for her baby's milk formula, which she lost. She was also instructed to come back whenever she and the child had any trouble. She never did because she depended on her husband, who was often absent from the village, to take her.

The hospital physician assured Mrs. Illusionist that she was perfectly capable of nursing her daughter even though she had experienced difficulty nursing her earlier infants, who she believed died of ghost illness. Their deaths made her fearful for the survival of her new infant, despite the physician's reassurance. It is possible that she could not nurse successfully because of anxiety or because her children had infant hypolactasia, a genetic trait whereby an infant cannot secrete sufficient lactase to digest the lactose in milk. In those days this trait had not yet been recognized, but the gene has a wide distribution in North India (McCracken, 1971; Sahi, 1978; R. Freed and S. Freed, 1985: 136–142, 196–197, 207).

Illusionist's father, Bad Seed, during the early summer of 1958, tried to seduce a young bride by enticing her into his house with sweets. Mrs. Bad Seed found them there and exposed them, trumpeting the liaison to the Chamar community. Bad Seed was an irascible, asthmatic man in his fifties, who had given up regular work, but occasionally carried out odd jobs in the village. Mainly, he depended on his younger son, Dutiful, who worked in a factory in the city. When Dutiful, Illusionist's half brother, was six years old, he started school, but the teacher said he stuttered so he stopped. He was wedded at age 15 along with Illusionist, but his wife was younger than Illusionist's and did not come for first mating until some years later. By 1958, Dutiful and his wife had a daughter age 7, and two sons, 2 and 4 years old. The four-year-old boy had a nervous affliction.

Because of his father's difficult personality and the trauma of being sent from his home at an early age to live in Delhi, Illusionist did not care for his father, complaining that he had not been much of a provider or parent. Illusionist also did not have a close relationship with Mrs. Bad Seed, his stepmother. Illusionist's warm relationship was with his cousin, Kin. They had a number of things in common besides the kinship tie. They had both been employed in the same factory in Delhi, and Illusionist had worked for Kin's father in the milk business. Kin's mother had been the first wife of the eldest of three brothers. When her first husband and infant son died during the influenza-plague epidemics, Kin's father took her as a levirate spouse in addition to his wife. When Kin was born, she named him after her first son who died, dedicating him as a son to her first husband who died tortured without surviving issue. Because of this levirate relationship of his mother, by 1958, Kin separated from his father and his father's first spouse and brought his mother to live with him.

Illusionist was different from the average village Chamar. He had never learned agricultural work, was more of an urbanite than a villager, had a flair for putting on a show, was handsomer than average, and liked to be the center of attention. For special occasions, he wore immaculately clean, white, tailored clothing and a white turban. Moreover, he had been much on his own in finding work from the time he was 12 years old and had not been a permanent resident member of any family until he married. Until then, he had to change domiciles periodically.

We first noticed Illusionist's considerable interest in ghost possession and exorcism in the fall of 1958, when a new bride was afflicted by a series of ghost possessions. We saw one of the possessions when Illusionist was present, and afterward he talked about the possession and subsequent curing session with us. He was clearly interested in everything, and his account was detailed and helpful. He said that the bride was possessed by a girl friend who died, became a ghost, and then entered the young bride in order to take her soul to accompany her as a wandering ghost. He pointed out that only an exorcist could take off or drive away a ghost. To become an exorcist one had to undergo hardships, visit cremation grounds, pick up the bones of the dead so that their ghosts would work for the exorcist, and obtain the power to drive out the ghost.

One of the characteristics of some exorcists was that they were men of low status and sought to change their condition by becoming exorcists. Such was the case with Illusionist. Anything that offered power, prestige, and a steady if small income interested Illusionist, for he was frustrated by his unemployment, poverty, and low status in the village. When he lived and worked in the city, he did not generally suffer from low-caste status. When he danced for weddings and festivals, he was admired and paid, but in the village there was essentially no escape from his position as a Harijan, his unemployment, or from the bad reputation of his father. Becoming an exorcist was one of the pathways by which Illusionist might escape an unsuccessful life to attain relative prestige and power.

Illusionist described worship with a hookah among the Chamars:

Hookah worship among Chamars is guru worship. If the Chamars want something, we take the hookah, pass it around the fire, offer food to the fire, and turn toward the guru, wherever he may be. Usually we do this worship regularly after the festivals of Holi and Diwali. For these festivals, it is compulsory. But if my son were to fall ill, I might promise to do this hookah worship when he got well. It is always done on Sunday. First we fast and then do the worship.

The guru in question was a Chamar and a spiritual teacher, who also functioned as a wedding priest for the Chamar community.

Illusionist and Buddhist II described how Lord of Ghosts used a special hookah to cure ghost possession and the difference between two kinds of bhagats: those who cured by talking and those who cured by singing, drumming, and use of the special hookah. In later years when Illusionist became a bhagat and Buddhist II stopped believing in ghosts, the two men were no longer friends. Despite Buddhist II's disbelief, his own wife, a daughter, and a daughter-in-law were persistently afflicted with ghost possessions and never cured. His son, whose wife was repeatedly possessed, had separated from his father. At first, Buddhist II resorted to curers but later decided that they were fakes. His contentious disposition could have been a stressful factor contributing to the ghost possessions of the women. Unfortunately, we were unable to interview them because Buddhist II prevented it (Chap. 10: Discussion in a Chamar *Baithak*).

In the spring of 1959, conditions in Illusionist's household worsened. His recently born infant daughter became ill and died early one morning. Mrs. Illusionist cried bitterly and various women, including her mother-in-law (Mrs. Bad Seed), tried to calm her. Between sobs as she gradually quieted, she mentioned the deaths of her other children, claiming that mother goddesses and ghosts had taken them, just as they had taken the soul of her most recent infant. She described little poxes like millet seeds which appeared on the infant's chest, a symptom of typhoid.

Then Mrs. Illusionist recounted how formerly she consulted doctors for her children, but a Chamar woman told her that doctors were no good and that a bhagat would be better able to drive off ghosts, so she began to consult bhagats. When her infant daughter fell ill, she took her to a bhagat, a Gola Potter, in a nearby village. He told her, "Tie 1½ rupees around the baby's neck in the name of Kanti Mata [Goddess of Typhoid]. Then

Fig. 8.   Brahman woman making offerings at the shrine of Kanti Mata (1977), situated across the lane from the Kali Mata shrine. Both shrines are located near the grave of the Headless Sweeper. See Map 4: KM1, KM2, and XX.

put 5½ seers of wheat, one cake of brown sugar cut into small pieces and fried, and 1½ rupees into a pitcher. Offer the pitcher at the shrines for Kanti Mata and Kali Mata" [Goddess of Death and Destruction].

Mrs. Illusionist (later also known as Atheist II) prepared the offerings for the mother goddesses and took them to the shrines. The same day she placed five pice (1¼ annas, 16 annas equal one rupee) at the shrine for the Crossroads Mother Goddess and vowed that if the baby survived she would go to this Goddess's temple at Gurgaon to offer a baby pig. She told her husband to buy a small package containing a comb, bangles, and a number of small packets, all the cosmetics a woman needs. She planned to leave these gifts, along with some red cloth, rice, dal, and a dry coconut at the shrine for the Crossroads Mother Goddess. The belief was that such gifts pleased a mother goddess, who would then act benevolently on behalf of the child

(R. Freed and S. Freed, 1979: 306–309). Mrs. Illusionist also bought some batashas (white sugar candy) in case the bhagat needed them. If her infant survived, she planned to cook sweet porridge and give it to an old Sweeper woman. When the child died, she gave the batashas to children in the compound and gave the porridge to the old woman. She placed the gifts for the Crossroads Mother Goddess at her shrine for the protection of future children that she might bear. Before the death of her daughter, she had taken tobacco to the bhagat, but he would not accept anything.

In 1960, Illusionist was recalled to the mill where he had formerly worked and underwent a short training period. Then for seven years he worked temporarily as a substitute before finally becoming a permanent employee. During this period, four sons were born to Mrs. Illusionist, all of whom survived. When the last son was born in 1969, the Government Midwife delivered the boy and then took Mrs. Illusionist, who was bleeding internally, to a hospital in Delhi, where she was treated and sterilized. Shortly thereafter she was ill for three months. In 1978 when she described her illness, she said that first she seemed to have malaria; then she had pains in her stomach but no Fever and nothing wrong with her eyes. She was taken to a hospital and remained there ten days; then she was taken to another hospital. After that she was treated privately but still without relief. Finally she consulted a bhagat and recovered. Malaria, which was resurgent beginning in 1965, may have triggered other ailments which were festering in Mrs. Illusionist. Malaria could have been linked with the aftereffects of bearing many children or sterilization. Tuberculosis was a vague possibility because the first hospital to which she went had a well-known tuberculosis clinic. If she had tuberculosis, she would not have admitted it. In any case, she used a bhagat as a last resort. It is possible that she was on the way to recovery but did not know it before the bhagat treated her, or that the physical component of her illness had been cured but psychological effects remained, which could have yielded to the bhagat's ministrations. By 1978, she was quite well and worked in the fields every day.

Mrs. Illusionist attributed the survival of her last four children, in comparison to the earlier children who died, to delivery by the Government Midwife, who used hygienic practices that greatly reduced the possibility of tetanus neonatorum, a leading killer of infants even though she, like other village women, attributed death from tetanus to a ghost taking the infants' souls. The Government Midwife who treated Mrs. Illusionist was the first of a series and, according to village women, the best of the lot. Another change which in all likelihood contributed to the children's survival was the introduction of inoculations against infant and childhood diseases. When the Government Midwife delivered a child or learned that a child had been born, she reported the birth and shortly thereafter the infant received a series of inoculations against contagious diseases. The infant mortality rate in the Delhi region gradually declined with the increase in government midwifery ser-

vices and inoculations for communicable diseases. Infants and adults were inoculated with the BCG (Bacillus Calmette-Guérin), a vaccine against tuberculosis with limited protection of about ten years, and with DTP (diphtheria, tetanus, and pertussis) (Davey and Wilson, 1971: 111; Gazetteer Unit, Delhi Adm., 1976: 857–858, 864–872; Append. I: Discoveries—1913–1921, Tuberculosis).

LEARNING TO BE AN EXORCIST

Mrs. Illusionist's illness marked a turning point in Illusionist's life. In 1978, he said:

When she fell ill, Lord Shiva came to my house, entered, and went to the altar in my sitting room. I did not see him because I was on night duty, but some of my relatives told me that he came. They saw Shivaji sitting near the altar. Because my wife was ill, I had been praying to Shiva. If she died, I would have had no one to cook for me. When Shivaji came, my relatives thought that a mad woman had come to the house, but Shiva identified himself. Afterwards my wife was completely cured. This happened about eight years ago. Then I began curing people.

Illusionist's statement, "If she [my wife] died, I would have had no one to cook for me," has implications beyond the obvious fact that without a woman, the preparation of meals would be a problem. Having been ousted from his father's home at an early age, Illusionist had no permanent home until he married. Therefore, he greatly feared the instability that would follow the loss of his wife. She gave him permanency and was his anchor. Agni, God of Fire, provides heat, purification, and cooked food; he is essential to many Hindu rituals, including curing, and plays a role in rites of passage from birth to death and cremation. Agni is a manifestation of Shiva; fire destroys but has two aspects: fearful and benevolent. Agni is a domestic deity, forming the center of the household with the cooking fire. Agni's wife is Svaha (Offering, one of the 16 daughters of Ritual Skill, Daksha). These terms, Agni and Svaha, are learned early in life, especially at weddings. With his interest in supernatural beings, curing, and his creature comforts, Illusionist identified with Agni, the kingpin of the household, and saw his wife as Svaha, the one who feeds her husband, Agni or Fire. Without her the fire would go out (Daniélou, 1964: 64, 87–89, 195, 321; Doniger O'Flaherty, 1980: 31).

Illusionist's wife's illness and the belief that Shiva visited his home crystallized his considerable interest in curing and finally led him to become an exorcist. Illusionist told us how he learned to be an exorcist:

I learned how to cure from a guru outside of the village. He lives in a section of Old Delhi where my mother was born. I saw the guru curing a person who had suffered a great deal, and I was very impressed. So I bent down, touched the guru's feet, and told him I wanted to learn to cure. The way I happened to see the curing session was due to a friend of mine, who is a cycle repairman; this friend also practiced curing by exorcism. When he had a patient he could not cure, he called this guru to cure the patient. The guru is a fictive mother's brother to me and a Brahman by caste. [We were unable to verify his caste.] When the guru had finished the curing session, the repairman asked me to take the guru home on my cycle. On the way I talked with the guru and again asked him to teach me to cure. The guru said that since he was my fictive mother's brother, he would do so. When he said this, he placed his hand on my head; then he instructed me to come to his place to learn and to bring some prasad [offerings] with me.

When I went there, I took a garland, two betel leaves, and some food. The guru read some mantras over the betel leaves and instructed me to chew one leaf while he chewed the other. Next the guru recited a mantra in my ear and blew some air into it. Then he had me sit down and learn the first stage in curing: to chant the mantras for a long time. He gave me additional mantras to learn for different types of curing. During the process of learning the mantras, the guru told me how to prepare sacred mantras to be placed in a tawiz [locket]. I went through this training period and learned everything that my guru taught me. While I was learning from my guru, he

had me practice reciting mantras for 20 to 40 days to prove that I would be able to cure. The guru said that medical doctors could not cure ghost illness. To cure it one must recite mantras.

Mantras cannot be learned from a book. The main monosyllabic or seed-mantras are called basic-thought-forms. The number of mantras is endless. Mantras which form sentences are ruled by numerical symbolism. For example, the main Shiva mantra has five syllables; that of Vishnu, eight (Daniélou, 1964: 335–337; Append. II: Sacred Hindu Texts—Mantras).

There are a number of noteworthy points in this account. The man who taught Illusionist was said to be a Brahman and a guru (hereditary priest and spiritual teacher). Although a Brahman, he lived near Chamars. As a result of proximity, he was a fictive mother's brother to Illusionist. This fictive kin tie was his reason for accepting Illusionist as a pupil. Illusionist observed the deferential behavior necessary to persuade the guru to teach him, namely, reverentially bending down and touching the guru's feet and politely asking that he teach him to be a curer through exorcism. The guru acceded, placing his hand on Illusionist's head, thus acknowledging their kinship and his discipleship. Placing the hand on the head could also be interpreted as a way of vesting curing powers in the disciple. Offerings were customarily presented to a guru. The guru's placing of his hand on Illusionist's head and their mutual chewing of betel leaves were the prelude to Illusionist's initiation into curing rituals and implied mystical participation between guru and disciple. The guru, a Brahman, reciting a mantra into Illusionist's ear was similar to a ritual in the initiation of twice-born males, called the janeu or Upanayan rite of passage, when the priest whispers a secret mantra into the ear of the initiate and puts the sacred thread (janeu) on him. Whether Illusionist ever witnessed a twice-born initiation rite is difficult to say. However, he could have seen the rite which occurred frequently in the courtyards of village Brahmans when a young Brahman was about to be wed (R. Freed and S. Freed, 1980: 443–450).

Illusionist also had a Muslim preceptor

who, among other instructions, taught him a mantra to cure babies. Illusionist said:

A very old Muslim from Rajasthan taught me too. He spent seven Thursdays in a row showing me how to light a lamp, meditate, and how to use a rosary [*mala*] made of seeds while I counted the verses in the mantras. I followed his instructions and practiced by myself for seven Thursdays. Then I started using the rosary in my curing. This old Muslim worked in the same factory as I did. When I found out he could cure, I invited him to take tea and asked him for a mantra to cure babies. The Muslim gave me the mantra and told me to light a clay lamp on seven Thursdays in a row, meditate, and then I would come to know the mantra and receive the power which went with it. I did so and obtained that power.

Although Hindus, Muslims, and Christians use rosaries, Illusionist learned to use the rosary from a Muslim. The one Hindu deity pictured with a rosary is Agni, who sometimes carries this string of beads on one of his four arms (Daniélou, 1964: 88–89; Harris and Levey, 1975: 2358). Receiving curing instructions and power from the Muslim reinforced Illusionist's picture of himself as a curer and endowed him with the special ability to cure babies. The number seven is auspicious in Islam as well as in Hinduism. In Hindu weddings, the couple being married goes around the fire seven times. Thursday, *Brihaspat* or *Guruvar*, is named after the planet Jupiter and is Guru's day. The auspicious number seven and Thursday as Guru's day account for the ritual of seven Thursdays in a row. Illusionist and Lord of Ghosts used Hindu and Muslim beliefs and techniques, but unlike Lord of Ghosts, Illusionist did not recite verses from the Sikh holy text (the Granth Sahib).

A significant part of Illusionist's practice was treating babies. He used the mantra learned from the Muslim and other remedies, as illustrated in his treatment of the grandchild of Kin's half brother in 1978. The father of the child brought him to Illusionist and said the infant had never ceased crying from morning to late afternoon. Illusionist chanted a mantra seven times, blew incense fumes over the baby, and placed ashes on the in-

fant's hands, navel, and stomach. When the baby still cried, Illusionist told the father to give him powdered sparrow's feces. The father asked what was wrong with the child, and Illusionist said the boy was feverish from constipation. When asked how he could tell, Illusionist replied that the diagnosis was natural for him because he first felt the pulse of the child (R. Freed and S. Freed, 1979: 314; Chap. 7: Islamic Period).

Responding in 1978 to a questionnaire on change, Mrs. Illusionist said that her family was currently better off than in 1958. They ate better food, including fruits and vegetables; bathed every day with soap; and Illusionist took a bath twice a day, once at home in the morning, and again at the mill before leaving work. They had several sources of income: her husband's salary, revenue from a yearly tomato crop on land which they rented from landowners, and fees from Illusionist's curing practice. She added, "Nowadays I work in the fields. Previously I only gathered fodder and stayed in the house, but now I am in the fields all the time. My health is good." The four sons born after the death of her infant daughter attended school, and her eldest son, who had separated from his father, was a constable in the police. Among this son's children was one daughter, whom Mrs. Illusionist regarded as her own since she had no surviving daughters. She noted that Illusionist worshipped Shiva, Hanuman, and Kalkaji, the deities from whom Hindu exorcists derive power. She herself did not worship any deities and did not believe in anything; thus her other pseudonym is Atheist II. As for Illusionist, his curing, and fortune telling, she said, "This is his pastime. What help can it give?"

ILLUSIONIST'S CURING AND INTERVIEWING TECHNIQUES

Illusionist not only exorcised ghosts and cured minor ailments but also used astrology and numerology to find out more about his patients and to predict their future. After asking a patient or anyone who wanted a prediction to select a number, he would then refer to a book and provide a prediction. For example, he asked Stanley Freed to select a number, which he did, and then Illusionist told him that the work he was doing would be completed at the end of April. Since it was general knowledge in the village that our field trip would terminate by the end of April, this prediction was not surprising.

Two Jats commented on Illusionist's ability to predict. Helpful said that Illusionist could not predict but that he could cure cases of ghost illness. Actor told this story about Akbar, a Mogul emperor of India and one of India's most remarkable rulers. "To please Akbar, a priest told him that he would live to age 125. Akbar had the man killed on the grounds that he was lying." The story was typical of the many stories about the cleverness of Akbar. Jat men, in particular, liked to tell stories about him to emphasize points or just for amusement.

Illusionist offered a prediction for one of our research assistants based on numerology. He foretold, "Your work will be done with the help of friends." This prophecy was in all likelihood based on common knowledge about the way in which our research assistants worked, for they became friends and worked as a team. Illusionist also worked out a more elaborate version of our assistant's fortune based on casting his horoscope. He first went into a discussion of how the nine *graha*s affected one's future, and how bad luck from one's sign of the zodiac might be prevented. Then based on a letter from the young man's name, he told him his sign. He pointed to the sign on an astrological chart. In the course of working through a number of signs and their permutations, he managed to identify some of the young man's personality traits and at the same time present a flattering portrait of him.

Illusionist's divination through astrology and numerology was somewhat similar to the system used by astrologers in Varanasi. The Varanasi astrologers counsel their clients in terms of four aspects of an individual—mind, body, family, and community—which are recognized as components of a single system of thought (Pugh, 1983, and 1984). Illusionist used astrology and numerology to tell his patients about themselves and to help them with their problems. His technique was to probe the personality of his patients, find out what troubled them, and use the knowledge for exorcising ghost illness and possessions. In

the course of treatment, he counseled his patients about their problems. Since patients believed that family troubles as well as illness were caused by ghosts, such counseling was especially effective because it was offered in the context of an accepted theory of supernatural causation. Moreover, during counseling Illusionist gave patients his complete attention which was reassuring, put them in a state of mind conducive to exorcism, and made them confident that the ghosts would be exorcised and that his amulets would protect them against returning ghosts.

For people who had not known Illusionist when he was a young man, his professional paraphernalia and procedures could be rather impressive. He carried an attaché case which opened to form a small altar with pictures of well-known Hindu deities pasted inside the cover. The case was filled with books, scraps of paper, bottles of ink, black pepper and *haldi* (turmeric). The latter was used to make a mark on the forehead, a blessing. In his men's sitting room, he had an altar, surrounded by pictures of deities, with a dim red light over it. A curtain hid the altar. It was drawn aside when the altar was to be used. When he visited a patient, he dressed in immaculate white garments, as he had in earlier years before becoming a bhagat.

Illusionist said:

Mainly what I do is cure people of ghost possession, which happens when the ghost of someone who died an unnatural death enters another person. The condition is known as ghost possession or sometimes fits [*daura*].

For ghost possession, I have the patient sit opposite me. I light incense and have a container of water, and recite mantras. Then I throw some water on the patient. The patient speaks and tells me what is wrong; then the ghost starts speaking and tells from whence he comes and what he wants. I then write three mantras on a sheet of paper, hold the paper over the smoking incense, put the paper in the water, and have the patient drink the water. The ink does not wash off the paper. After drinking the water, the patient feels at peace.

When I write mantras on a paper, I do so in the form of sixteen squares, in each

Fig. 9.   Exorcism to cure a sick child, 1978. The technique shown here is to scratch the ground rapidly with a knife. The attaché case contains the exorcist's curing paraphernalia.

of which is a mantra represented by a number. I recite these mantras while I perform the curing ceremony. [In his astrological book, the mantras were listed with the number of times each should be recited. Typical numbers were 11,000, 22,000, and 44,000.] I use black pepper to drive the ghost away and at the same time recite a mantra while holding the pepper in my hand. I also use incense to drive out the ghost. The patient inhales the pepper and incense which get rid of the ghost.

I have special inks, four kinds, which I use for different purposes. These inks are used to write mantras on slips of paper and then are inserted into a *tawiz*. The *tawiz* is worn by my patient to ward off ghosts. The ink is very costly.

Illusionist seemed most effective in treating ghost possessions. If the death was natural, he told us, then the person did not become a ghost unless the funeral ceremony was improperly performed. If the death was unnatural, then Shiva, as Lord of Ghosts, took possession of the soul of the deceased, who became a ghost. Illusionist's statements conformed to some degree with village opinion about becoming a ghost. Daniélou (1964: 90) covered the subject of the funeral ceremony in terms of the last two of five forms of ritual fires: the ancestors' fire and the funeral fire. The ancestors' fire is one in which offerings are made to ancestors, and the rituals of exorcism are performed with this fire. The closest approach to this ritual fire appeared in the ancestor worship for Merchant in the legend of Merchant, Muslim, Priest, and for Capable, the father of Taciturn and Forceful in Old Fever (Chaps. 12, 13). For a natural death, the funeral fire includes cremation and its rituals along with observances for a year of mourning. The domain of Illusionist as a bhagat was to exorcise the ghosts of persons who died unnatural deaths or whose funeral fire and other observances were neglected.

Thus, he propitiated Shiva, calling on Shiva's help through mantras, substances, symbols, and meditation to drive out ghosts, as did Lord of Ghosts, the Chuhra Sweeper. Illusionist said that while he was curing, deities and supernatural beings did not appear to him but he felt their presence.

ILLUSIONIST'S PATIENTS

In Shanti Nagar, Illusionist treated members of his own lineage and members of other castes when they called him. In his own caste, his lineage and another one distrusted each other, so he did not treat its members. However, they had ties through marriage with a *siyana* in another village and sometimes called him, or else consulted a bhagat from a nearby village, as Mrs. Illusionist did when her child fell ill in 1958 before Illusionist became an exorcist. Thus, for Shanti Nagar, Illusionist's patients in his caste were from his lineage. Other castes called him in emergencies and also because of his good reputation as an exorcist and curer. His practice extended beyond the village. He was known outside Shanti Nagar, for he worked full time in Delhi. He was absent from the village not only for his job in the city but also for visits to his patients who lived outside Shanti Nagar. His other village patients are mentioned in Chap. 13 (the cases of Misfortune and of a Nai Barber boy), Chap. 20 ("The Potters and the Lady"), and Chap. 22 ("Little Goddess").

Within his own lineage, Illusionist treated members of Kin's family. Although Kin's wife had a history of ghost possessions, none took place during our field trips. When Illusionist became a bhagat, he treated her. A number of people mentioned that Illusionist had brought Kin's grandson back from the dead, but no further details were furnished. Kin himself said that Illusionist cured him when he was ill and had treated members of his family.

In the spring of 1978 after the wedding of Kin's 20-year-old son, his 14-year-old daughter, Sunny, suffered a series of possessions in late March and early April when the weather was already quite hot and malaria had become epidemic. Her first possession took place in school; the second, in the Cha-

mar compound. There are slight differences in the following reports of Sunny's possessions, which indicate only the normal difficulty of obtaining exact information about what happens at the time of a possession or any other event.

One day, Little Charmer, the eight-year-old Jat boy who visited us regularly in 1977–78, told us about Sunny's ghost possession. He said:

Two or three days ago in school, Sunny, the daughter of Kin, was possessed. Her father came to school but was informed by the teacher that the ghost had left. Sunny's brother [patrilineal cousin] saw her possession and later told me about it. He is seven years old. When Sunny was possessed, everyone in school stopped studying, and the teachers stopped teaching. The male teachers went from their side of the school to the girls' side to find out what was wrong. Her brother told them, "The ghost has possessed my sister." She was unconscious only two to three minutes. The lady teacher of her class declared that a ghost possessed the girl because Sunny had said so. The lady teachers were frightened, but the male teachers were not. Men don't get afraid. They declared that if anyone brought them a seer [.93 kg] of candy, they would eat the candy at the cremation grounds.

Little Charmer added, "I myself do not eat any sweets there. I enter my house first and then eat sweets. It is all right to eat inside one's house but not outside, or near, or in the cremation grounds," thus indicating how his mother had trained him to prevent ghost illness and possession. After hearing Little Charmer's report, we asked whether he still did not believe in ghosts. He answered, "No, I do not. Nothing happens. I am not interested in being possessed by a ghost because I am very afraid of ghosts." This and other conversations with Little Charmer indicated that because of the Jat masculine stereotype about ghost beliefs, he could not admit that he believed in ghosts although he feared them. This ambivalence is not surprising in a young boy whose mother had taught him about ghosts and whose best friend, Faithful, and other Jat girls, also believed in ghosts. Still he wanted to adhere to the masculine viewpoint of his older brothers, father, and other Jat men who said that fear was the ghost but that there were no ghosts as incorporeal beings.

At the height of the ghost epidemic during the first week in April, Bright Light, a son of Illusionist, related the following incidents about Sunny. He said:

There is somebody in the neighborhood whose first wife died and that woman comes into everybody. Sunny ate some sweets and spat at the place where the ghost was cremated. The ghost who entered her said that she had spit there. Her first possession happened on a Saturday. She was then in school; the teachers sent for her brother to take her home. Then they fetched my father, who talked to the ghost. He sat in his appointed place for a *havan* [fire ceremony, around a *havan kund* (fire-pit) in his yard]. He had Sunny sit beside him and talk to the ghost. After a time the ghost went away. Now Sunny is all right. My father, the bhagat, performed this *havan* ceremony both times that she was possessed.

Bright Light did not identify the ghost by name, but the ghost was Hairless (Chap. 23). A woman standing nearby commented that Illusionist was very busy at present because three or four ghosts had formed a gang and talked together a lot. She said that the ghosts were finished off two days earlier when a *siyana*, who was more experienced than Illusionist, came to the village and joined hands with him. This *siyana* was an affine of the members of the other Chamar lineage in Shanti Nagar. Together they rid the village of these ghosts. The ghosts were Housewife, Little Bride, and Hairless (Chaps. 15, 23). When the woman was asked about the ghost of Tippler's first wife, she said that previously her ghost had not visited the Chamar side of the village. She added, "When the ghost of Government Worker's first wife [Hairless] entered a woman, she declared beforehand that she would enter her victim at a specific time, and then she did so."

Bright Light commented:

This ghost [Hairless] possessed Sunny, and then the ghost announced, "Now I have to possess Constable's wife" [i.e., Immature]. Constable was standing next to Sunny and heard the ghost. It was the day on which his bride [Immature] had come from her parents' village, and the ghost [Hairless] then possessed Constable's wife (Chap. 23).

Another time in the morning when Sunny was taking her food, the same ghost stood near her, but Sunny went on eating *rotis* [unleavened bread] until they were all consumed. A family member asked what happened to all the bread. Sunny answered, "They have taken it; they have taken it." The ghost was under a nearby neem tree, and Sunny saw the ghost of Government Worker's first wife [Hairless] there and said that she had taken all the bread. That evening Sunny could eat only two pieces of bread because no ghost was around.

After telling about Sunny, Bright Light was asked whether he wanted to become a bhagat. He replied that he planned to finish school and find a job but did not want to be a bhagat.

In the spring of 1978 when Sunny was possessed, she was 14 years old and in fifth grade. Her brother had just been married and her first possession struck shortly thereafter. Sunny was close to her brother. During the wedding rituals in the bride's village, members of the wedding party drank too much and started a brawl. As the daughter of Kin, Sunny belonged to a family haunted by a number of ghosts with her own mother having an ongoing history of ghost possessions. Sunny's possessions began after the wedding when the weather had become quite hot. Because of her age, it is possible that she had attained menarche and was menstruating. The stress of her favorite brother's marriage, the drunken brawl, the heat, and the onslaught of menarche could well have contributed to her possessions. A description of Sunny's possession in school seems similar to a brief fainting spell, but the episode of eating all the bread was quite unusual and differed from other possessions. In all she suffered three possessions in the spring of 1978.

In a discussion about ghosts and ghost illness with a Chuhra Sweeper woman, Loyal, and her daughter, Loyal said that people attacked by ghosts should call a bhagat. Her daughter commented, "Illusionist is a bhagat, but he is not always good. However, he did bring Kin's grandson back to life when his soul was seized by the ghost of Government Worker's first wife [Hairless]." Loyal said that this ghost had affected everyone among the Chamars. In another interview, Loyal claimed that Illusionist was a good curer because he immediately helped anyone affected by a ghost, took care of a person, and also gave some relief.

College Girl, a Brahman, attending a college for young women, related this experience with Illusionist. She said that when she was in ninth grade she became very ill. Her patrilineal granduncle, Old Bachelor, had died a few months previously so everyone thought that his ghost was causing her ghost illness because he was very fond of her. When her father, Trusted Employee, who worked in the city, thought her illness was caused by the ghost of her granduncle, he called Illusionist to treat her (Append. III: Chart 10.1; Chap. 21: New Brahman Lane). Illusionist put ashes on her forehead and tied a *ganda* on her arm. That night when she was trying to sleep, the *ganda* tied around her arm bothered her. She was so frustrated by it that she arose from her bed and opened the *ganda*. Inside was a piece of paper on which a swastika was drawn. She was furious because Illusionist had taken five rupees for the treatment, including the *ganda*. Shortly thereafter the girl said that she went to a hospital where they cured her of worms.

The swastika is a very ancient symbol in Hinduism. Its use is not confined to curers or priests; anyone in the village can draw one. It was drawn as an auspicious sign by housewives to replace another symbol drawn on an outside house wall for a festival. The replacement was to prevent a ghost or any evil spirit from occupying the empty space. It was also drawn by Brahman priests for ceremonies marking a beginning, such as birth and marriage, and was used to represent the nine *graha*s. Thus, the swastika represented the known planetary universe in early times and the supernatural world governing the affairs of humans (R. Freed and S. Freed, 1980: 336–337; S. Freed and R. Freed, 1980: 87, 95–101). Illusionist drew the swastika to ward off the ghost of his patient's granduncle, who died a celibate without issue.

ILLUSIONIST AS EXORCIST

Landy (1977: 416–417) and Spiro (1977: 419–427) describe personality traits and biographical reasons for becoming a curer or exorcist. The applicable traits for Illusionist from Landy are: (1) self selection to become an exorcist; (2) undergoing a profound emotional experience, namely, the fear of losing his wife; (3) a complex personality; and (4) exceptional personality traits. Points three and four are not identical. Illusionist's complex personality partly reflects his unstable and difficult childhood as well as the problems encountered in the early decades of his marriage. His exceptional personality traits are his standing out from others and his acting ability, both of which are very helpful to an exorcist or curer.

Although Spiro's characteristics of exorcists derive from his fieldwork in Burma, the following traits apply to Illusionist: (1) Before becoming exorcists, recruits have low status and come from a wide range of occupations. These traits characterize Illusionist because of his caste and his unskilled employment early in life in the mill with gradual betterment through experience, but still without prestige. (2) The work of exorcism is usually part-time combined with full-time work in a relatively low occupation. (3) Instead of an hereditary claim to supernatural power, or obtaining it through the technique of ecstasy, the latter a characteristic of shamans, exorcists may acquire power through becoming a disciple of an exorcist. (4) Exorcists may be found throughout the villages of Burma, true also for villages in the Delhi region. (5) A code of ethics is requisite for a respected exorcist. Illusionist fulfilled *aan*, that is, all the obligations and ethics of his profession as taught to him by his guru or gurus, except that he received payment. (6) An exorcist is respected by his fellows, which is linked with Spiro's first point. Prestige was especially important for Illusionist who before he became an exorcist was not respected in the village or elsewhere. (7) A dramatic trait found among exorcists in Burma was that they wore white clothing, thus standing out from others.

Illusionist's white clothing made him stand out. The color is characteristic of exorcists and is linked with his chosen deity Shiva, who is Lord of Death, whose messenger is Fever, and who is also Lord of Ghosts and ruler of spirits of darkness, i.e., many supernatural beings who are feared and might need to be controlled by an exorcist (Daniélou, 1964: 213–214). The link to Shiva is particularly important for all curers because in the Shiva Purana, Shiva says, "I am omnipresent but I am especially in twelve forms and places." The twelve forms and places are the twelve great lingas (phalluses) associated with Shiva. The sixth linga, Vaidya-natha, is Lord of Physicians, another of Shiva's titles. Thus, it is not suprising that Illusionist, the Sweeper exorcist whose pseudonym is Lord of Ghosts, and Dr. John, a compounder, had Shiva as a chosen deity (Dowson, 1950: 177–178, 331; Daniélou, 1964: 14, note 7; 224–227; Chaps. 16, 21).

As for Illusionist's motivation and personality, his decision to become an exorcist was self-motivated; he was not possessed by a supernatural being and endowed with power which he henceforth was obliged to exercise. His early history shows that he was interested in ghost illness and possession and the work of exorcists before he became one. Illusionist's dancing, acting, story-telling, and intelligence were well above average. He also deliberately chose to stand out from others rather than fit into the role of the average villager or mill worker. He continued to display these personality traits as an exorcist. Thus, he fitted the alienated role of "Pir, faqir, and psychotherapist," noted by Hoch (1974: 669, 671). With this background, Illusionist approached two gurus for instruction in exorcism after Shiva visited his house, a Brahman guru whom he had seen curing, and a Muslim who worked where he did.

Several traumatic experiences in Illusionist's life also were involved in his becoming an exorcist: first, the death of his mother whose soul became a ghost; second, having a stepmother; and third, being sent from his parental home to live in the city among relatives. The fourth was beginning to work from age 12 with no schooling or training and thereafter experiencing periods of unemployment and insecurity. These experiences resulted in privation, family instability, and lack of prestige. Also traumatic were the deaths from ghost illness of his children as infants. The ultimate trauma which finally pushed

him into becoming an exorcist was the illness of his wife. He feared that she might die. Her death would have been the equivalent of his abandonment as a young child by his mother's death and by his father and stepmother.

Before becoming a curer, Illusionist had a low status. He was a Harijan, landless, poor, and without steady employment. Although by effort and luck he could escape poverty and unemployment, he could never change his ascribed status of Harijan. However, as a curer, his caste identity was largely irrelevant. He could treat anyone and, for the duration of a curing session at least, think of himself as the equal of anyone. For Illusionist, his role as curer ameliorated his ascribed caste status (Carstairs, 1969: 407, 409).

Spiro (1977) distinguished between shamans and exorcists, stating that exorcists control harmful supernaturals but shamans do not. Exorcists in Shanti Nagar do attempt to control malevolent supernaturals. They try to drive out the ghosts causing ghost illness, sometimes successfully, other times, not. However, they do more. They find out what troubles the victim and other family members and counsel them. This counseling was characteristic of Illusionist who used his personality, numerology, astrology, and various props to win the confidence of his patients. The exorcism of ghosts is the spectacular part of what a village curer does, but his counseling function should not be overlooked.

A final point applicable to Illusionist is that at no time was he possessed by a supernatural being, nor was he known to have entered any unusual, alternate mental states except the self-satisfaction and exhilaration of dancing and acting at festivals and weddings. In other words, he did not have "the technique of ecstasy" of shamans, which Eliade (1964: 493) stated reproduces a situation available to others only through death. Although Illusionist never experienced a state where he believed he was possessed by a supernatural being or where he saw a supernatural being or said that he could see Shiva, Kalkaji, or Hanuman when he was curing, he did say that he felt their presence.

COMMENTS

Hinduism has the belief that a devotee of a deity may be possessed by the deity and still remain alive. Such possession is called jivanmoksha or jivanmukti, living release or living liberation from the world. It is temporary. Seeking jivanmukti through devotion to a deity (bhakti-yoga) or through spiritual knowledge (jnana-yoga) are two paths provided for attaining release and eventually at death may result in release from the round of rebirths (moksha or mukti) and union with the Universal Absolute, the neuter deity which joins all deities and all souls together (Avalon, 1913: cxliv–cxlvi; Dandekar, 1953: 126–127; R. Freed and S. Freed, 1962: 251–252). Illusionist showed no signs of seeking jivanmukti during his life or mukti after his death.

Warner (1980: 50) has pointed to deception and self-deception among shamans and psychiatrists and concluded "that the medicine man is a sincere practitioner who maintains his self-esteem, despite his knowledge that he deceives his patients through a process of self deception." He compared this process with the methods and techniques of psychiatrists, who do so too. However, he indicated that indigenous curers, such as shamans and exorcists, do cure their patients.

CHAPTER 18: THE HEALTH NETWORK

The health network of exorcists and other curers found in the village and elsewhere, some of whom are identified in various parts of this study, is here discussed with regard to individual curers, their castes, the kinds of curing they practiced, and how the villagers obtained their services. Our picture of exorcists, other curers, and the health network deals with the men so identified during both field trips. Relevant points from the lists of the common personality traits and other characteristics of exorcists and curers compiled by Landy (1977) and Spiro (1977) were used in chapters 16 and 17 on Lord of Ghosts and Illusionist. The full lists are outlined here and then applied to the network of men from the village and beyond who treated villagers.

Landy (1977: 415–417) listed eight points, characteristics, and pathways by which men become curers: (1) inheritance of the role; (2) selection by others; (3) self-selection; (4) undergoing a profound emotional experience; (5) self-dedication to a healing cult; (6) miraculous self-recovery from a condition or experience that could kill or disable; (7) genetic, congenital, or acquired physical disability or deformity; and (8) exceptional personal traits.

Spiro (1977: 419–427) described characteristics of Burmese exorcists. (1) They have low status and may come from a wide range of occupations. (2) The curing role is part-time, usually combined with full-time work in a variety of low occupations. (3) The exorcist acquires curing power not through the technique of ecstasy but by becoming a disciple of an exorcist. (4) He controls harmful supernaturals whereas a shaman propitiates them. (5) He must follow an ethical code, as must the patient who may not seek help from another curer without the exorcist's permission. An exorcist may not take on a case which is being treated by another exorcist without that exorcist's permission. (6) Exorcists may be found throughout the villages of Burma, which is similar to the situation in the Delhi region. (7) An exorcist is respected by his fellows, one of the reasons for an unsuccessful man with low prestige to become one. Spiro (1977: 423) stated, ". . . the two dominant motives for recruitment of the exorcist role are status anxiety and power." (8) Exorcists dress in white symbolizing Buddhist beliefs. Burmese Buddhism is a mixture of Buddhism and Hinduism, both derived from India. Thus, the traits listed by Spiro are relevant in the Delhi region. Another trait of exorcists and curers is that they stand out from others. Somewhat along the same line, Hoch (1974: 671) compared them with psychiatrists, alienists, aliens, and the alienated, i.e., people different from others.

Clark (1970: 183–214) and Romanucci-Ross (1977) have reported on the "hierarchy of resort" in seeking a curer. We have expanded this concept to include the network of exorcists, other curers, and institutions—indicating how they are chosen by caste, kinship, relationship by marriage, type or seriousness of illness, personal beliefs, emergencies, and availability. The choices include Western physicians, Ayurvedic physicians (*vaid*s), compounders, practitioners of popular pharmaceutical medicine, bhagats and other supernatural curers, and medical centers, such as ashrams, clinics, dispensaries, and hospitals.

BRAHMANS AS EXORCISTS AND CURERS

Brahman exorcists are part of the network of curers. Their ascribed caste status gives them an hereditary claim to the role. The authority is the Atharva-Veda (Chap. 7: Vedic Age). Old Priest was both a professional Brahman priest and a practicing exorcist before he became blind. Lifelong celibacy and hereditary caste position imbued him with power. As one of the tallest men in the village, he stood out in the population. He was trained as a professional priest in a nearby ashram and had further training at Varanasi in Unani medicine, thus the Muslim title of hakim. Additionally, he was traumatized at an early age because all his relatives except a sister had died. He came to live with her when he was a small boy, young enough to have been influenced to some degree by the legend of Merchant and the Muslim Ghost because his sister was the wife of Merchant's son. As an orphan, his only chance for a reasonably good life was through training to be a professional priest, which led to his also becoming a hakim (Chap. 12: Merchant, Muslim, Priest).

Raconteur's nephew, New Priest, became an exorcist after Old Priest's death. He suffered the traumatic experience of being possessed and instructed by Old Priest's ghost and in the process was selected by Old Priest's ghost to be his successor (Chap. 12). He fulfilled this role in 1977–78 by officiating as a family priest for minor ceremonies and ex-

orcising ghosts for the Gola Potters, who also called Illusionist for ghost possessions and ghost illness. Their choice probably depended on who was available since both men had full-time jobs in the city (Chap. 20: The Potters and The Lady). In 1958–59, these Potters called the brother of Outsider from Rajasthan, who was the disciple of a superior exorcist called Maharajah. He exorcised the ghost troubling Outsider's eldest son. Other curers in the Merchant, Muslim, Priest lineage were: Raconteur who worked for a pharmacist for 17 years and thereafter was a vaccinator for the government until he retired; and Physician, one of Guard's sons and Raconteur's nephew, who while in military service received the MBBS. He remained in the army and practiced Western medicine in 1977–78 in Bangalore and then in the City of Delhi (Chap. 12).

High Strung, a Brahman in another lineage, came to our attention in 1958–59 when he exorcised an epidemic of cattle disease in a ceremony known as Akhta. Accompanied by some Jats, he visited all the village cattle sheds the first evening of Akhta, carrying a pot of *gugal* (incense) and burning dung with which he smoked the animals to take off the disease caused by ghosts. Jat followers of the Arya Samaj denied the ghosts and said the fire and incense fumigated the disease, a belief derived from Swami Dayananda Saraswati (Saraswati, 1956: 64–66). The curing ceremony, always held on a weekend, began Friday night. Twice on Saturday in the morning and evening and once on Sunday morning the village was magically circled by villagers herding all the animals around it. High Strung ran through the village and the herd of cattle and other animals carrying his smoking pot to draw the disease away from the village and across the fields to government land near the canal empty of villages where he deposited the pot, thus ridding the village of cattle disease. In former times this task was considered dangerous because of the risk of working close to many large strong animals who could be startled, and the hazard of depositing the pot on the land of another village. The other villagers might come out and beat the Brahman with sticks for bringing them the disease (R. Freed and S. Freed, 1966). Crooke (1894: 93–

94, 103–110, 191 ff.; 1968, 2: 376–377) described the exorcism of human and cattle epidemics by this method in various parts of India during the 19th century.

High Strung also exorcised the ghost possessing Withdrawn, another Brahman, in 1958–59 (Chap. 21: Withdrawn's Possessions). He obtained *bhabhut* (holy ashes from a ceremonial fire), put them on the afflicted person's forehead, and recited mantras until the ghost departed. Respected Leader, a Brahman in the Air Force who lived in a nearby large village, gave him the ashes. Respected Leader had helped people in Shanti Nagar through the years. For example, in 1978 he exorcised the ghost of Whose Daughter who possessed Welder, her cousin, both Brahmans (Chap. 14: The Ghost of Whose Daughter). High Strung was helped in exorcising Withdrawn's ghost by Sanskritist, a higher secondary schoolteacher of Sanskrit from the large nearby village, who was related affinally to Story Teller, who lived in Shanti Nagar. Sanskritist also gave penicillin injections to villagers in 1958–59. Some years later, he earned a BIMS (Bachelor of Indian Medical Surgery). Thereafter, he practiced a combination of Western medicine and Ayurveda. He was still practicing in 1978. Once a year, he visited the Brahman families that he treated annually in Shanti Nagar and was given grain. He received one rupee for an injection but never charged for medicine. By 1977–78, he no longer practiced exorcism, but High Strung still exorcised ghosts, for example, in the case of City Girl (Chap. 19). High Strung qualified as an exorcist because he was a Brahman and because he was strong and good with cattle. He also acted as a family priest for rites of passage (R. Freed and S. Freed, 1980: 335). His main occupation was farmer.

Another Brahman, Snakebite Curer, born in 1898, specialized in curing snakebites. He said there are many poisonous snakes in the area. He treated a snakebite victim with a decoction made from plants he collected from the wooded area around the village. When the patient drank the potion, it caused the poison to rise up through the patient's body so that he vomited.

In his interview, Snakebite Curer described the ethics of a curer. He would not divulge the names of the plants or how he combined them because he honored his guru, who had admonished him to keep them secret. He added that, when summoned, a curer must drop everything he is doing—eating, working, or sleeping—and immediately set out to cure a patient. He called the curer's prescribed behavior *aan*, the duty or obligation of the curer to his guru who taught him the ethics of curing and how to cure. He was neither to eat at a patient's house nor to take money for curing. He said the disciple of a guru must accept the guru's code of ethics or the guru will not teach him. The man who taught him was a fictive younger brother of his father. The ethics delineated here are somewhat similar to those described by Spiro (1977: 420–421). Similar rules are found among other curers and exorcists in this region but are not always followed. Snakebite Curer was still alive in 1978 but was senile and no longer cured snakebites.

Story Teller, a teacher in a higher secondary school, was another Brahman exorcist in Shanti Nagar in 1977–78. He treated only Brahmans in New Brahman Lane—usually when their possessions were considered to be emergencies. He exorcised ghosts by reciting mantras and placing ashes on the victim's forehead. During the first field trip he was a young man much interested in politics and power. He regularly read the Ramayana and parts of the Mahabharata at night to gatherings of villagers, and produced, directed, and acted in a play about Lord Krishna's birth on Janamashtami, Krishna's birthday. These talents proved useful as a teacher, exorcist, and for his avocation: politics (Chap. 21; Append. III: Chart 10.1).

High Strung exorcised the ghost that possessed the Brahman, Withdrawn, but the elder and younger brothers of Withdrawn, Senior and Junior, also exorcised the ghost possessing him. One of Senior's sons, One Eyed, and his own sons, exorcised ghosts from family members. They also treated Farmer, a Jat. A son of Junior, Doctor John, was a compounder who served people in Shanti Nagar (Chaps. 21, 22). He worked in a nearby clinic and had a pharmaceutical shop in another village with his partner, a woman physician with an MBBS (Chap. 14: The Boy Had To Die).

Still another Brahman, a *siyana* and a specialist in exorcising ghosts, came from the City of Delhi to exorcise the ghost of Illusion who haunted Beauty, a Brahman girl. Her possessions began when she was 12 years old and continued until she was 15. Because the possessions were so persistent, this renown specialist was called (Chap. 21: Beauty; Append. III: Chart 10.2).

A JAT *VAID* AND MISCELLANEOUS CURERS

The only Jat in this network of curers in 1958–59 was a *vaid* who operated an ashram in the town of Narela. It served as a place of refuge and a hospital. His wife was a nurse and Patriarch's sister. Patriarch called the *vaid* when his infant granddaughter, Beloved, had pneumonia. The *vaid* came on his motorcycle, gave her penicillin injections, and she recovered. Patriarch and others in his family reported a series of illnesses, deaths, and the curers or facilities used for treatment from 1959 to 1978: an infant treated by Dr. John; a twin married daughter who went to a city hospital; the other twin who suffered ghost possessions for a number of years in her marital village and then stayed with her parents, the Patriarchs, while she was treated by a Muslim *siyana* in Delhi; a grandson taken to a nearby government clinic for malaria; and Mrs. Patriarch who was treated for heart trouble by Home Trained, who practiced popular pharmaceutical medicine. He also treated the Patriarchs' son for food poisoning but the son died (Chap. 22: Widows, Patriarchs, Twins). This variety of treatments illustrates changes which took place within Patriarch's family regarding the selection of curers, which in turn was related partly to the changing times and the availability of various types of service in the health network.

The joint family of Taciturn, another Jat, also turned to Western medicine for some illnesses. Several of its members went to hospitals for treatment for tuberculosis, and Troubled was treated in a mental hospital in Punjab for the bipolar syndrome due to cerebral malaria. Despite this turn to Western medicine, Forceful (Taciturn's brother) and

his son Politico had a bhagat from out of town visit them.

Sprains and even broken bones were treated by traditional curers. In 1958–59, Fearful said that she went to Delhi to have a bonesetter, who was a wrestler, take care of her broken or sprained wrist. Since it healed very quickly, it most likely was a sprain. Also in 1958–59, Tricky, Manipulator's son, fell while climbing a tree and broke his arm. His grandmother, Honesty, took him to a bonesetter in another village. In 1977–1978, the father-in-law of the girl whose pseudonym is Sita, treated sprains only. If a bone was broken, he referred the patient to a bonesetter in the city, but if the break was bad, he recommended going to a hospital. He did not charge for his services (R. Freed and S. Freed, 1985: 186–187).

In general, however, there has been a shift toward the more professional styles of treatment, except in cases of ghost possession. For example, in 1958–59, villagers often went to an ashram in a large nearby village where swamis and sadhus gave them injections of penicillin and medicine for constipation. By 1977–78, government dispensaries and clinics had replaced the ashram. The Outsiders of the Gola Potters, and Reformer and Barker, both Jats, went to a Catholic clinic in the nearby village. Barker also went to a Catholic hospital for the operation on his leg. Some people treated cases of ghost illness with a combination of both Western medicine and exorcism.

NAI BARBERS: TECHNICIAN, DRESSER, AND PRACTITIONER OF POPULAR PHARMACEUTICAL MEDICINE

The Nai Barbers were one of the smaller village castes, consisting of only three related families in 1958 which grew to six in 1978. The Barbers had a disproportionate number of men enter modern medicine in various capacities. One Nai studied to be a compounder in the late 1950s. In 1977, he told us that his course of study had qualified him for work in the Hindu Rao Hospital in Delhi. He served an apprenticeship of six months for which he was paid, was quite competent, and by 1977 had been promoted to operations theatre technician in charge of several subordinates. Because he had a full-time city job, he did not have an appreciable village medical practice. However, he did play a minor medical role in Shanti Nagar, furnishing modern medicine and injections to his family and other villagers. He once gave an allergy test to Manipulator. He said that he was not authorized to give injections but believed that the medicine that he was dispensing with instructions could not hurt even if it was ineffective. His younger brother studied in Bombay to be a dresser (surgeon's assistant who applies bandages), and he too worked in a city hospital. Mrs. Doctor John took her small son to a Nai Barber a distance from the village for the child's polio treatments (Chap. 21: Mrs. Doctor John, Polio, and Karma).

Home Trained, a Nai Barber in one of the original three families, practiced popular pharmaceutical medicine in the village in 1977–78. He was very popular because he lived in the village, came immediately, had no full-time occupation other than his practice, and had been born and raised in the village. He learned about Western medicine working in the shop of his brother-in-law some distance from the village and claimed to be a Registered Medical Practitioner. The details of his training were vague, but he used Western medicine and Ayurveda.

CHAMARS AS BHAGATS AND USERS OF BHAGATS

Although no village Chamars were exorcists in 1958, Chamars used bhagats; for example, Mrs. Illusionist went to a Gola Potter bhagat when her infant daughter fell ill (Chap. 17: Early History). However, the bhagat's role in Chamar life went considerably beyond exorcism. During a 1958 interview on beliefs in supernatural beings and the ceremonies of the life cycle and calendric round, an 80-year-old Chamar woman discussed the place of the bhagat in Chamar life. She described an aspect of the exorcist's role that neither Landy nor Spiro include among its more prominent features, namely, the curer as advisor. The woman had little contact with Western medicine, depending almost entirely on bhagats and other rural curers. During much of her life, epidemics of contagious disease, such

as smallpox and cholera, identified by the names of the mother goddesses, were exorcised by excluding outsiders from the village and carrying out rituals believed to drive out the disease. In 1958 through 1977, the only remnant of this all-village form of exorcism was Akhta. However, there were other rituals intended to forestall possibly epidemic diseases, such as the annual village-wide worship of the mother goddesses on Sili Sat and personal or familial propitiation of the mother goddesses. A relative of this Chamar woman was a bhagat who lived in another village but at times was available to help with curing. For example, when a family member had smallpox, the elderly Chamar said that she usually gave the bhagat offerings to place at the shrine for Kali, the Mother Goddess of Smallpox, and at the shrine for the Seven Sisters, the mother goddesses of disease (R. Freed and S. Freed, 1962: 265–266; 1979: 306–309; Append. IV: Map 4, CM, KM1, KM2). When her great grandchild had smallpox, the bhagat was too far off, so she and other women in the family took the offerings to the shrines.

When asked about ghosts, she said that a person usually became one at death. She linked this belief with the death of her husband. After he died, there were many family quarrels, so the family consulted their bhagat to find out the cause. The bhagat said that Bhagwan was displeased with the family because our informant's daughters-in-law were not good to her. She added that a bhagat cannot always ask the members of a family about their affairs or tell the head of the household what to do. Instead the bhagat must use his powers to discover what is wrong and then guide or advise the family. The bhagat's effectiveness as family counselor derives from his power to gather information from ghosts, in this case the ghost of the old woman's husband. The old woman finished by saying that when they encountered any sickness or other trouble, they regularly consulted the bhagat mentioned above, who was the son-in-law of a member of her husband's lineage. As a son-in-law, he did not live in Shanti Nagar but some distance away and could not always be reached immediately. When he came, he provided advice and exorcised ghosts causing illness.

In 1958–59, four Chamar exorcists were called to exorcise the ghosts troubling Sita, a newly married Chamar girl. The first exorcist was from a village in the Delhi region; the second was fetched from the City of Delhi by Government Worker who knew of him from working in the city. When the possessions continued, her father was notified and he brought two Chamar exorcists for an all-night session. One came from New Delhi, the other from Mehrauli, a large town south of New Delhi. The assortment of techniques used by these men were hypnosis (the use of a fire at night to focus Sita's attention and the repetitious chanting of mantras), various substances to drive out the ghosts or to cause Sita to be possessed, and shocks, such as pulling her braids and verbal abuse aimed at the ghosts possessing her. These exorcists called on their familiars to aid them. Sita was not cured, and her possessions turned to fits which still persisted in 1978. She used hospitals and Western medicine for complaints that she recognized as somatic but turned to exorcists for her possessions and fits, for she believed that they were caused primarily by the ghost of Taraka (Sita and Taraka: pseudonyms used in R. Freed and S. Freed, 1985). For example, a *siyana* gave her an amulet in 1976 to protect her from Taraka's ghost; she was wearing it in 1978 and believed that it had reduced the number of fits (R. Freed and S. Freed, 1985: 166–171; Chap. 23: Immature and Sita).

MULLAHS FROM PALAM

The last in the series of exorcists who treated the villagers were mullahs (Muslims) who were fetched from Palam, the site of the International Airport near New Delhi. Raconteur called a mullah when his nephew, New Priest, was possessed by the ghost of Old Priest. Old Codger, a Jat, called one for the poltergeists attacking Mrs. Barker and Farmer, both Jats, and the ghost possessions of the Brahman, Withdrawn. Farmer said he went to Palam where a fair was held, and the *siyana* there looked at his palm and said that he would be all right. The same mullah came to the village and pounded nails in his cot to protect him from the poltergeist, but to no avail. As Raconteur and Old Codger were age-mates living across the road from each other, it is possible that Raconteur told Old Codger about the mullah he called in 1962 when Old Priest died.

VILLAGERS AS EXORCISTS AND EXORCISM

Villagers act as exorcists in emergencies or when no exorcist is available. For a sudden or first ghost possession, members of the possessed person's family, neighbors, or whoever happens to be around use well-known techniques to drive off the ghost. When such possessions persist, an exorcist is called, if not from the village or nearby, then from the City of Delhi, Palam, or Mehrauli. If a new bride or an older married woman suffers ghost possessions in her marital village more than once or twice, her father may be notified. He then sees that an exorcist, whom he knows or who is recommended to him, treats his daughter. In what are deemed to be cases more dangerous than average, two or more exorcists may join forces to drive out the ghosts through their combined supernatural powers and practical techniques (R. Freed and S. Freed, 1985: 169–172). In the late 1950s and 1970s skilled exorcists were most often sought through men who worked in the City of Delhi and had heard of such men. Finding an exorcist entails a network of friends, neighbors, relatives, men employed in the city, and references from less skilled exorcists who recommend their gurus. This kind of network is also used by men who are in the process of becoming exorcists or want to become one.

Techniques of exorcism follow a fairly regular pattern although each exorcist to some degree has his own system of exorcising ghosts and establishing a relationship with his patients. What is not fully recognized or emphasized in studies of exorcists and exorcism are the techniques used by relatives, neighbors, and bystanders when a person is afflicted with ghost possession in a public place. The dramatic spectacle of ghost possession is common in the village. Most villagers have seen exorcists in action so that they know what to do when dealing with ghost possession.

Generally, a public possession is preceded by symptoms. The victim starts to shiver, moans, and then falls down unconscious. Spectators fetch quilts and cover the victim. Someone brings burning cow dung or pig excreta and wafts the smoke under the nose of the victim to bring him or her back to consciousness. The victim is then propped in a sitting position. By this time, a number of spectators have gathered who provide suggestions from all sides and endeavor to frighten the ghost or ghosts away. The strange voice that often speaks from the victim is identified as the ghost trying to seize the victim's soul, so the spectators talk to it. First, they try to identify the ghost; then they ask what it wants. Generally, the ghost states that the victim ate something special, usually sweets, and that the ghost wants its share. The idea here is that the ghost has been slighted or is jealous of the person eating the sweets, but in fact the cause of the possession may be that the victim has not been given as favorable treatment as other family members. The deprivation of sweets thus represents a broad range of complaints of ill-treatment endured by the possessed. Identification of ghosts is difficult because they use different personae, usually the names of people who figure in the victim's life history. These conversations with ghosts are not necessarily logical or coherent on the part of the voice of the ghost speaking from the victim, but the remarks and actions of the spectators follow a pattern of behavior similar to that of exorcists.

Part of an exorcist's technique is to frighten or threaten a ghost by calling on his familiars, that is, his supernatural powers. Ordinary villagers do not have such powers but they still can abuse a ghost in two ways: verbally and/or physically. For example, during the possession of a teen-age bride when the female ghost was particularly evasive in stating what she wanted, the ghost, speaking from her victim, finally said that her victim had been fed sweet noodles that morning but that she (the ghost) was not given any. An old woman insultingly shouted at the ghost, "I'll give you cow dung to eat." The ghost replied, "You stop talking rot." Then the old woman retaliated, "You mother-in-law, you bastard, you eat cow dung." Insulting, threatening, and frightening the ghost by such means are part of the techniques of exorcism.

Sometimes a possessed person may try to commit suicide, or more accurately run toward a well, pond, or railroad tracks, which implies suicide. Therefore, villagers watch a person who is apt to be possessed or is possessed to prevent a suicide attempt. They also instruct a person who has been possessed not to be afraid of ghosts and to threaten them, but we never saw any victims of possessions threatening their ghosts.

Villagers prefer the physical techniques of exorcism, believing them to be more effective than verbal abuse. These techniques require the use of specific substances: ashes, chili peppers, black pepper, incense, and the smoke of burning cow dung or pig excreta. Ground up black pepper is put in the eyes of victims or may be eaten by them, as are chili peppers. Ashes (*bhabhut*) from a *havan*, holy fire of a puja, are generally put on the forehead and/or tongue of the victim by Brahman exorcists while reciting mantras. The ashes are believed to have supernatural power because they come from the fuel used in the holy fire. The usual components are sandalwood, clarified butter (ghee), and incense, but cloves, camphor, and other items may be added to the list. However, exorcists who are not Brahmans also use ashes for their patients. Villagers may put the peppers or ashes in the mouths of victims, but more often place the peppers, incense, and other substances in a fire. The victim breathes the fumes whose effect is to smoke out the ghost. Mrs. Fence Sitter used fumes from a commercial product, Loban (benzoin), to drive out ghosts when her children became ill. Although she took them to *vaid*s and other physicians as well as to hospitals, she still believed that their illness was caused by ghosts so she took no chances and exorcised the ghosts, too (Chap. 12: The Families of Progenitor and Gentle Soul).

Some of the physical methods of exorcism are painful. Villagers may slap a person who has fallen unconscious, or who is "talking nonsense," that is, speech interpreted as a ghost's babbling. They also pull victims' hair or pull out some hairs from their heads, which actions supposedly hurt the ghost's head, for it is believed to be inside its victim trying to take the soul. O. Lewis (1958: 296) quoted a village man in the Delhi region, who said that this technique was a way of catching the ghost.

Another technique to drive a ghost away is to make a victim squeeze rock salt. This technique was part of the repertoire of Lord of Ghosts to exorcise the evil eye (Chap. 16: Techniques for Curing the Evil Eye and Ghost Possession). When such painful techniques are applied, ghosts say that they will leave, but after awhile they return. Villagers say, "Ghosts don't keep their promises."

Since anyone may be vulnerable to ghosts, young people, strangers, and even thoughtless adults are told how to avoid them. First, it is dangerous to eat sweets and immediately go outside, for sweets attract ghosts. If it is necessary to leave immediately, then one should cleanse the mouth with salt or ash to camouflage the sweets. By no means should anyone who has eaten sweets go near or through the cremation grounds (Append. IV: Map 4, CG.; cf. O. Lewis, 1958, Chap. 8 for similar beliefs in the Delhi region). If a ghost is encountered, one must not be afraid. Talking to the ghost and threatening it can drive it away.

In addition to the foregoing techniques, exorcists have other resources for dealing with ghosts, namely, their supernatural powers. At the start of a curing session, they enumerate their supernatural powers and call on them to frighten the ghosts. Most often these powers are Hanuman, the monkey god; the ghosts of well-known sorcerers, conjurers, or necromancers; Shiva, the Lord of Death; and sayyids or pirs (Rosin, 1983: 125). Being able to call his familiars is an important part of the exorcist's technique. His familiars represent a hierarchy of powers. For example, he may first call Hanuman's minister, who in turn calls Hanuman. This hierarchy makes sense to villagers who are familiar with hierarchical social orders based on prestige and power.

In order to induce possession in patients, exorcists sometimes use drugs, herbs, and hypnotism. They achieve hypnotic effects by holding a curing session at night and having the patient look at a fire or the moon for protracted periods and/or by talking, rhythmical drumming, singing and chanting mantras. Possession is induced by visiting exorcists in order to confront a ghost and banish it for good. In difficult cases where the patient has suffered numerous possessions, two skilled exorcists may work together, combining their supernatural powers and practical experience. The primary techniques are the use of substances, physical force, conversation, hypnotic effects, and convincing the victim and the victim's family of the power of the exorcist (R. Freed and S. Freed, 1985: 169–173; Freeman, 1979: 188, 190).

Often the session ends with the exorcist's announcement that he will make certain offerings on behalf of the victim to Kalkaji, the Mother Goddess of the Cremation Grounds. The family of the victim provides these offerings. Sometimes, the exorcist manages to bribe the ghost so that it promises to come away with him. Then everyone believes that the ghost will leave with the exorcist and perhaps never trouble them again. However, they also believe that ghosts can escape the exorcist and wander anywhere, for persons may be possessed repeatedly by the same ghost despite the best efforts of exorcists.

Exorcists supply their patients with amulets to protect them from the ghosts that trouble them. The simplest amulet is a *ganda*, a folded piece of cloth containing a piece of paper on which a mantra is written or an auspicious sign drawn. The cloth is tied around the neck or arm of the patient. Usually a blue thread is used, a color associated with Krishna, an avatar of Vishnu. The thread is described as kachcha, i.e., it was spun but not twisted. A *tawiz* is similar to a *ganda* but costs more. It consists of a metal locket with a mantra written on paper, which is put inside the locket. The locket is fastened around the neck of the patient with blue thread. For example, Gentle Soul's daughter was possessed when her cousin, Young Lawyer, was married. Her father took her to an exorcist in New Delhi, who exorcised the ghost and then provided her with a *tawiz* to protect her from its return (Chap. 12: The Families of Progenitor and Gentle Soul).

Villagers themselves provide protective amulets for their children. Shortly after an infant is born, a necklace of protective charms is fastened around its neck. Strung on a blue string or light chain are gold and silver pieces representing the sun and moon, the latter in various phases; an ivory tooth to prevent toothache; and a doll-sized bag containing salt and grain to ward off ghosts. The necklace is believed both to protect an infant while asleep and also to prevent earache. Mothers say that it prevents unfriendly winds from bringing illness caused by ghosts and other supernatural beings (R. Freed and S. Freed, 1980: 377–378). If it is feared that an infant or small child will be attacked by the ghost of its mother or by the ghost of a woman who died in childbirth or without issue, then iron amulets are placed on both ankles and wrists of the child. Families that do not have much

money use amulets for the wrists or necklaces of black and blue beads to ward off ghosts. These amulets along with the admonition of parents about not going out immediately after eating sweets, not eating sweets or other food outside, not going near the cremation grounds at night or high noon, and being careful at crossroads where ghosts are believed to linger are believed to prevent ghost illness and ghost possession (Append. IV: Map 4, CG, CR).

CHAPTER 19: THREE WIVES AND FOUR HUSBANDS

Ghost illness, ghost possession, and poltergeist attack, while affecting individuals, take place in a social context of successively more encompassing units (family, caste, village, region) and great historical depth, points that have been illustrated in cases previously presented in the text. From the point of view of the individual, the natal and marital families stand at the center of this complexity, for the problems of conflict and adjustment in family life may generate the stress that contributes to ghost possessions and poltergeist attacks. Sapolsky (1988: 38) pointed out that "the word stress is fairly new to the medical vocabulary," deriving from the research of the physician, Hans Selye, in the 1920s and 1930s, when he found that organisms, whether rats or hospital patients, subject to stress showed various physiological responses. Sapolsky (1988: 40–41) compared examples of Western executives under stress with baboons in the Serengeti Plains of East Africa. This concept of stress in human beings has been very carefully documented in Selye's (1956) *The Stress of Life*. His concept of stress is directly applicable to villagers in Shanti Nagar, especially during life crises, and also when the ecological setting is disturbed as was the case in 1977–78.

The studies presented in this chapter and the four chapters that follow it are intended to show how stress in family situations is a contributing factor in ghost possession and

poltergeist attack. The basic data are sketches of life histories from as many individuals, members of their families, and their friends, as possible, enhanced by census and general historical information. Analysis of the lives of individuals reveals both cultural norms and the scope of behavioral variation around the norms. From the point of view of the individual, culture may be a cloak worn either to express conformity to the norm or to highlight or conceal differences from it. Study of life histories has become a part of the holistic method of anthropology. (Casagrande, 1964: ix; Langness, 1965; Mandelbaum, 1973; Freeman, 1979; R. Freed and S. Freed, 1985.) Some examples of this approach appear in previous chapters: Old Priest's autobiography (Chap. 12), Troubled (Chap. 13), the Headless Sweeper and descendants (Chap. 16), and Illusionist (Chap. 17).

The case of the three wives and four husbands emphasizes the slow changes in the position of wives in their marital families from the end of the 19th century through 1978. These changes have come about from the influence of the British Raj and later from the general modernization that has taken place since Independence in 1947. The three wives discussed here represent three generations and highlight the normative patterns of wifely behavior with all their difficulties, which were expressed in episodes of ghost possession for all three women. The principal change concerns remarriage for Brahman women whose first marriages ended either because of widowhood, divorce, or annulment. The first two wives had only one husband each, but the third had two successive husbands, for after being widowed, she married her husband's younger brother. Her case brings up the problem of widow remarriage among Brahmans (Append. III: Chart 6, Generations II, III, IV). The earliest information about the case of the three wives and four husbands dates to the end of the 19th century and comes from the first of the three wives, Honesty (1895–1967), one of our oldest and best informants. We knew three of the husbands and the three wives in this case but not Honesty's husband, Moneylender, who died in the 1940s.

HONESTY AND MONEYLENDER

Honesty was born and raised in Rohtak District, Punjab. Her natal family consisted of her mother, father, and five stalwart tall brothers. Her eldest brother, a lambardar, was born sometime before 1880 and died in 1946 or 1947. Old Soldier (1882–1966) was the brother to whom Honesty was most attached. He lived with her and her husband for many years. A third brother, born in 1886, was alive in 1977 at age 91. We have no further information for the other two brothers except that one was alive in 1977. These brothers fulfilled the ideal role of a brother to a sister, coming to the aid of Honesty, her husband, and their children whenever necessary.

Honesty, a widow who had never attended school, said in 1958:

When I was a child my mother loved me very much. When I was about five or six years old, my mother taught me to embroider and to sweep. Then when I was about eleven, I learned to make cow-dung cakes [for fuel] and to spin cotton. Around that time I started working in the fields and also learned to cook chapatis [unleavened bread]. It is just my luck that my daughter-in-law is no good in these ways.

When I was a young girl, people thought that a girl of 12 to 14 was a fully developed woman and should be sent to her husband. Children were wedded when they were quite young, and when the father of a daughter

decided she was ready, he sent her to her husband. Now they do not follow this rule strictly, but even so my granddaughter who is married cannot go to her husband until my son, her father, sends her. He will not send her until her husband comes here. My granddaughter's mother-in-law is not good. She is very quarrelsome and will not allow her son to come here for his wife. I was sent to my husband for Gauna [first mating] when I was fourteen years old.

When Honesty and Moneylender were wedded, the marriage of young children was common. In 1958, we interviewed 64 women with regard to age at marriage and at first mating (S. Freed and R. Freed, 1971: 282–284). The average age at marriage was 11.7 years. The average age was higher among younger women than among older women, which suggests that the age of marriage was rising. For women 35 years of age and older (N = 34), the average age at marriage was 10.2 years; women younger than 35 (N = 30) married at 13.5 years. However, the age at first mating was almost the same for both groups, 15.5 years for the older group and 15.6 for the younger. We took no survey in 1978 but our interviews and observations indicate that the average age of marriage for females at that time was about 15+ years. Men were two or more years older. The Child Marriage Restraint Act, commonly known as the Sarda Act, passed in 1929 and amended in 1949, finally set 15 years as the legal age of marriage for women, 18 for men (Derrett, 1978: 81). In 1978, the Lok Sabha (Parliament) raised the ages to 18 and 21, respectively. In the *Times of India*, 1978, a column on *Getting Married* commented, "But can legislation alone, no matter how progressive, make any real difference on the ground? It is no secret that the Sarda Act has been honoured more in the breach than in the observance. Why should the fate of the present bill, when it becomes law, be any different?"

Honesty described her preparation for first mating as follows:

My mother talked to me about mating with my husband and told me to be nice to my mother-in-law and my husband. She said I should do all the work given me. If my husband started quarreling with me, I should flatter him. My mother said that it is necessary to flatter a husband. My mother told me that whenever my husband asked me to sleep with him, I should not quarrel or say anything. I should just do as he said. My mother-in-law also said the same things and said, "This is your room." My husband was quite well built and strong so I was afraid and rushed out of the room. My mother-in-law took me back into the room and told me not to be afraid. She said, "Men are never afraid. What have they to be afraid of?" When I started screaming, my husband said, "Be quiet so my mother will not hear you." Then I was quiet, and he was quite nice to me and said that I could do whatever I wanted. Afterwards I was not afraid. My heart used to start trembling at the start of it. Now I remember my husband a great deal because he was my own. When my son's wife or anyone starts quarreling, I remember my husband very much.

Honesty stayed in her husband's home for ten to twelve days at Gauna, then she returned to her natal home and experienced ghost possessions followed by ghost illness. She said:

I saw a ghost once and did not recover for six months. I was 14 years old when I fell ill and had pains all over my body and was reduced to a skeleton. A *vaid* gave me some sweet medicine. My father and brother called the *vaid*. There was a woman in the village who had died; I saw her ghost; then the ghost seized me. This woman was a daughter-in-law of the village, but not married to anyone in my natal family. She fell in a well and died [suicide].

One day when I went to the fields to relieve myself, her ghost was standing there. I was so terrified that I fell down and was unconscious. This woman was 30 to 40 years old and had children. She had quarreled with her mother-in-law who said to her, "Why don't you jump in the well?" And so she did. She had wanted her husband to separate from the joint family, but her mother-in-law was against the separation. They, too, were a Brahman family. The quarrel about separating and then the suicide took place two months before I saw the ghost and she possessed me. She was a bad woman; that is why she became a ghost. She was not chaste, was immodest, and did not have the respect of her family. She was shameless because she never respected her elders and was not polite to anybody. She had not been married very long when she bore her first child and then began sexual relations with other men. Her family scolded her but she continued. Whenever any men visited the household, she would come out to see them although she had been told not to do so. This was why her mother-in-law abused her and told her to jump in a well. She lived as close to my family's house as did the family there across this lane.

In the course of telling about her marriage and how she was possessed by the ghost, Honesty incidentally delineated the proper behavior of a married woman, contrasting the ideal pattern of behavior with that of her daughter-in-law and the woman in her natal village who committed suicide. Honesty said that her daughter-in-law, the wife of Manipulator, did not follow proper behavior, but she never accused her daughter-in-law of sexual immorality.

During Honesty's subsequent ghost illness, Bad Temper, her husband's elder half-brother and the head of the joint family, came to see the lambardar, Honesty's elder brother, to ascertain that she was being properly treated and had the right medicine. Such a visit by an in-law was expected when a daughter-in-law fell ill in her natal family's home. Bad Temper observed the proprieties, careful not to reveal his hostile feelings about Honesty and Moneylender.

Honesty's ghost possessions and ghost illness may be attributed to her separation from her natal family where, as the only daughter, she was well treated and loved in comparison with her life in the disturbed and tense environment of her husband's joint family. The fact that she "became as thin as a skeleton" showed the fear and frustration that she experienced after Gauna in her husband's home. A loss of weight, which fits an "idiom of distress" and may be an indication of depression, has been observed among recently married Havik Brahman girls in South India (Nichter, 1981; Ullrich, 1987a: 262–263, 272–273). Although Honesty portrayed her husband and his mother in a favorable light, Bad Temper and other members of his joint family were hostile to her and her husband. Thus, Honesty suffered from a loss of appetite when she most needed additional calories for the stress placed on her metabolism beginning with Gauna (Selye, 1956: 182). As Honesty told of these past events, she was indirectly comparing her granddaughter, her daughter-in-law, and the woman who committed suicide and became a ghost to what gossips in her natal village might have said about her because she remained there for a long time after Gauna.

At the end of a year, Honesty returned to her husband's household prepared to remain there permanently. The joint family then consisted of her husband's mother, Bad Temper's mother, Bad Temper and his first wife, and Moneylender and Honesty. Bad Temper (1887–1945) was described as a man with a foul temper who at times became violent. When his first wife died without issue, he remarried and his second wife bore him two sons and two daughters. A son and daughter died young; the surviving son and daughter were born some years before Honesty's first child, Manipulator. Then the second wife of Bad Temper died, and he later took a third wife who bore a son in 1923. In later years this son was said to have been driven mad by his wife, so he is dubbed Driven Mad. In 1925, another son was born to Bad Temper and his third wife. This son has the pseudonym Close Mouth because as an adult he silently kept his own counsel. The souls of the first and second wives and of the son and daughter who died became ghosts.

Honesty said that she liked her mother-in-law but never knew her father-in-law, who had two wives, because he died shortly before Moneylender was born in 1893. When he died, Bad Temper believed that he would be the sole owner of his father's land. However, with Moneylender's posthumous birth, the land would be divided equally between the two half brothers. Bad Temper, however, as head of the family, continued to think of the land as his.

When Honesty returned to her husband in 1910 to stay permanently, she paid court to her mother-in-law as was the general practice among young brides. She did whatever her mother-in-law asked her to do, pressed her legs as a sign of respect when she returned to or left the village, and in general fulfilled the proper role of a daughter-in-law. The joint family, however, was under the rule of Bad Temper. After Honesty had returned to her husband, Bad Temper took his third wife. By the time the third wife came permanently, Bad Temper had quarreled quite a bit with Honesty. Therefore, from 1910 to 1914 Honesty visited her parents whenever she had the opportunity and during that time either bore no children or may have had a child who died at birth. Because she firmly believed in ghosts and was afraid of wives who became ghosts and caused the deaths of infants, she never mentioned any infants who may have died, especially since the deaths would have been attributed to the ghosts of Bad Temper's two dead wives.

Bad Temper's mother died sometime after 1910; then Moneylender's mother died. Honesty had counted on her for protection from Bad Temper. Bad Temper's attitude toward Moneylender developed not only because Moneylender was born posthumously but also because Bad Temper's father had taken a second wife while his first wife, Bad Temper's mother, was still alive. When the second wife gave birth to Moneylender, Bad Temper then had a rival heir, a situation resulting in more than the usual sibling rivalry. After both mothers-in-law died, Honesty had to submit to the rule of Bad Temper's third wife.

Because Honesty feared Bad Temper, she returned to her parents' and brothers' village seven months before her first child (Manipulator) was born in 1915 and stayed there five to six years. The lambardar, her eldest brother, would not allow her to return to her husband's home because he believed that Bad Temper threatened the lives of Honesty and the infant. During the years that Honesty stayed with her brothers, Moneylender visited her as much as possible—usually once a week. He was developing several business ventures, became a moneylender, and regularly traveled through the Punjab. Honesty bore a daughter in her natal village about 1918–19. If Honesty and Moneylender had any other children, they died as infants and no one mentioned them. In 1958 Honesty was one of many women who stated that formerly many infants died.

By 1922 Honesty returned with her two children to her husband's village because Moneylender had separated from Bad Temper. At first they lived in a small mud hut and built a separate hut for Old Soldier, Honesty's brother. Old Soldier lived near the young couple and their children to protect them from the threat of Bad Temper. Moneylender feared to leave his family without protection when he was absent from the village on business trips. After the family separation, the inherited land was divided equally between Bad Temper and Moneylender; in time Moneylender's half would be inherited by his son, Manipulator.

OLD SOLDIER

Old Soldier's oral autobiography provides a sketch of the history of the region under the British Raj. It is important in understanding his influence on Honesty and her son, Manipulator. Old Soldier was usually called *babaji* as a sign of respect. "Old soldiers who retired . . . with their small pensions were admired and respected" (Farwell, 1989: 28). He related his life history in 1958 at age 76:

My wife died more than 20 years ago before the 1914 war. She was not too tall or too short, maybe about 5'4". I had joined the army before she died. I was married twice and both wives died. I had one son who died when I was 25 to 26 years old. One of my two sons died when he was five years old; and the other died after he finished tenth grade. My eldest brother then asked me to marry again, but I said, "No." I myself was seven years old when first wedded; she was about the same age [wedding date ca. 1889]. She came for mating seven years after the wedding. She bore one son and the second wife bore the other son. The first wife served me better; the second was not as good as the first. The second wife died suddenly. She had a tumor or growth in her side and died in the Hindu year '62 or '63. Both wives died before the 1914 war and I did not marry again. People asked me to do so, but I said, "No." I thought when two

marriages did not work, what can one do with a third wife. My first wife was 24 years old when she died [1906]. I had taken a job as a policeman before she died.

I served in the Rohtak District of the Punjab and was a lance naik [corporal]. I served at various police stations, always in the Rohtak District. Then I became a havildar [sergeant]. If you are a lance naik, you do not keep watch. When you are a havildar, you command a small group. Of course, I was uneducated. At that time during the British Raj, men who were six feet tall or over, as I was, went to Simla to serve the viceroy. If anyone served the viceroy three years, he became a havildar. That is what happened to me. Men from every field served the viceroy: police, Gurkhas, army, everything. Immediately next to the viceroy's house was a British soldier, then a Gurkha, then the cavalry, the army, and five policemen. The organization was great. I had to obey orders; there was no question of liking to do so or not. It was very cold there. It snows a great deal there in December. I used to feel very cold. Whenever we went on a job, every policeman had a small stove with coal, and we had a lot of warm clothing to wear. People who had always lived there probably did not feel as cold as I did.

I joined the cavalry when I was 16 years old [1898]. I worked in Gwalior in the cavalry for eight years. Then when I was 24 [1906], I joined the police. I left the cavalry because there was a great deal of work. I had to clean horses, go on parade, keep watch, and do a hundred things. There was no free time at all. I had to work all the time. We would go on parade in the morning, take the horses to be brushed and cleaned, then we would eat; then we would have classes. It was work all the time. We were taught about war and enemies. If enemies were to attack us, we were taught what to do.

In the police, they only taught us about such things as cheating, or what to do when you have a criminal with you, or when you see a murder committed, and what to do when arresting a murderer. For a murder, what they taught was that you should pat a criminal on his back and say to him, "Co-operate with me so we can catch the murderer." Then we would take the handcuffs off the man and get him to help take the murderer to the jail. We were also taught when we should arrest with or without a warrant. We learned that we could not arrest everyone.

There were two kinds of rules: police rules and rules laid down by the British. There were different rules for arresting people. Criminals could be arrested without a warrant, so could people who broke into houses without authorization; also escaped convicts could be arrested without a warrant. If a person was found in possession of stolen goods, he could be arrested. If someone interfered with a policeman carrying out his duties, he could be arrested. Anyone who ran away from the King's army or navy on land or sea could be arrested. The last group of people, who could be arrested, were those people who had connections with bad characters and who lived with the bad characters and broke into houses at night.

Work in the cavalry was good, clean work and you did not take bribes; but in the police you took bribes and therefore the work was not good. I did not take bribes. When I wanted to be recruited in the cavalry, I accumulated 400 rupees to buy a horse. My father gave me 200 rupees. He did not want me to join the cavalry but to stay home and eat, but I was enthusiastic about joining. My father did not even want me to join the police. I had seen men who went into the cavalry and from them I had the notion to join. I had a good, strong body and was athletic. I played all the games. In the cavalry I helped with training the horses and playing games with horses where a handkerchief was dropped and the horse was trained to jump over it. We used to place a line or string on the ground, mount the horse, and while running the horse across the line, we would cut the line with a sword. Sometimes we would place a hunk of wood on the ground, run toward the wood on the horse, and pick it up with the sword. I have two certificates from participating in the 1911 and 1924 durbars. I saw the coronation of King-Emperor George V when it took place in 1911 [cf. Farwell, 1989: 28–

29 on recruitment of Indians and their ranks in the Indian Army; Cohen, 1971: 35–45 on recruitment of Indians into the British army.]

Old Soldier recounted the changes he had seen in the City of Delhi:

The main change in Delhi from 1902 to today was that formerly it was very small. Now it is big. It also has expanded as far as Mehrauli [a large town to the south]. First it was only in the neighborhood around the Red Fort [in Old Delhi]. New Delhi is now located where formerly they had brick kilns. The neighborhood around the Red Fort was all in ruins. Now one does not know what is happening. I have not been there for some time. In 1902 the Red Fort was in ruins. In the 1902 Durbar they released a big balloon with two white men in it. They also had mock battles. In 1911, there were no such battles. When they had mock battles, they divided into two enemy factions; one won, the other lost. Sometimes they would have one side of Muslims and the other of Hindus, then have them fight. The British kept up mutual hostility between the Hindus and Muslims. Under Jawaharlal Nehru the Chamars and Chuhras are coming up and the upper castes are going down. The British really ruled India, but now that we have Independence, everyone is trying to cheat and fill up his own house.

King George V ruled two years and when he was made the King-Emperor, he ordered 112 villages around Delhi removed. When the 1914 war started, he died in London and probably was buried or burnt someplace. Everybody died in the 1914 war. So many of our men died that they could not be counted [see Chap. 5: War and Other Turbulence].

Old Soldier discussed the rivalry between Jats, Brahmans, and other castes, and the current rule of Prime Minister Nehru. Apparently he believed that the British were better rulers, kept order, and that the times then were better. He ended by saying, "Whenever anybody becomes strong, they get their way. All these one-eyed people who come and sit with us are bad, as were Sukra and Bali."

Sukra and Bali require explanation. During a sacrifice given by King Bali, Vamana, the dwarf avatar of Vishnu, asked that Bali give him some land. When Sukra tried to prevent Bali from giving this land as charity, Vishnu blinded him in one eye. Thus, Sukra's name became synonymous with being one-eyed (Daniélou, 1964: 325). Bali is as interesting as Sukra, for as king of the genii (asuras) he controlled all three worlds. He deprived the deities of their world so they sought the help of Vishnu, who in his dwarf's incarnation begged Bali to give him as much land as he might cover in three steps. Bali agreed and the dwarf covered the earth in one step, the heavens in another, and when no space remained for a third step, he placed his foot on Bali's head and pushed him into the nether world, where he became ruler (Daniélou, 1964: 169–170). By referring to this story, Old Soldier implied that men had become greedy, did not give charity, and were the equivalent of inauspicious one-eyed men. The village belief in the inauspiciousness of one-eyed men may derive from this story.

Old Soldier began his long residence with his sister and Moneylender in 1922, and it lasted into the 1960s. When he came to stay with them in 1922, he was forty years old. He helped Moneylender and later his son, Manipulator, with the agricultural work and protected their wives and interests when they were absent from the village. An elderly man in 1958 and 1959, Old Soldier spent his days taking Manipulator's cattle to graze and watching over them. At the same time, he was seeking moksha, release from the round of rebirths. While watching the cattle he repeated the mystic syllable and mantra, AUM, over and over again. He had arthritis and for relief used the drug bhang (*Cannabis sativa*), which grew wild near the village. Although he never went to school, when he was in the cavalry he learned to read and write from a friend. He served in the army in World War I, going as far as France where he mentioned seeing the mademoiselles of Paris. In the first half of the 1960s he was still living with Manipulator and Honesty. When his brothers' grandchildren invited him to a wedding in his natal village, they liked him so much that he stayed there until he died in 1966 at age 84. Old Soldier's account of his life, the City

of Delhi, and the British Raj reflect his perception of some of the changes that took place in the Delhi region from the 19th century to 1958. His experiences and values influenced Honesty and Manipulator, for he had an important role in their family.

MANIPULATOR AND FAMILY

Manipulator's memories of his childhood provide an insight to the formation of his personality and characteristic means of handling problems. He related an early instance of manipulating his mother, Honesty, when he was six years old because she had beaten him. He ran out of the house and climbed a *jamun* tree, a fruit bearing tree whose berries ripen in June–July (Maheshwari, 1976: 160–161). Manipulator hid in the branches and began to eat the fruit. No one could find him, even when they came into the garden, because he remained silent. Finally he called to his mother that he was in the tree and she asked him to come down, promising never to beat him again.

When Manipulator first came to his father's village at six years of age, he became acquainted with his patrilineal cousins (brother and sister in Hindi), the surviving son and daughter of Bad Temper and his second wife. The boy, Nondescript, was too old for Manipulator to play with; the girl was ten to twelve years old. Manipulator recounted the following incident about her: (Append. III: Chart 6).

One day I went down to the canal to bathe in the water. I had just dipped into the canal when my sister climbed on my back and I began to drown. A carpenter passed along and asked the girl what she was sitting on. She answered, "I am sitting on my brother who is a big horse." The carpenter pushed her off of me, saw that I was unconscious, and brought me home where I was restored to my senses. My sister was scolded.

Manipulator recounted other incidents about his early years in Shanti Nagar. When Manipulator was seven years old (1922), Old Soldier told his parents that he should start school. The closest primary school was a half hour's walk to a nearby village. One day Manipulator refused to go to school because there were no roads and he thought that the walk was too long. Old Soldier slapped him when he would not go, teaching him the limits of disobedience. After that he never was absent from school. Although Manipulator was quite bright, he did not finish tenth grade until 1934. The discrepancy between completed grades (10) and years in school (12) was due not to failing any grades but to attempts by Bad Temper and his sons to kill Manipulator. Manipulator's wife, mother, sister, and his eldest son, College Man, in 1958 remarked more than once that Manipulator had to live for a number of years in the home of his sister's husband while he was a minor to protect him from his patrilineal kinsmen. Although his sister was born in 1918, she was wedded when still a child and had gone early to live with her husband so the tie between her natal and marital families was well established. The main reason for Manipulator staying with his sister and her husband's family was because he had no brothers, was a minor, and his uncle and uncle's sons wanted his land. They would stand outside Manipulator's house at night and call him to come out and fight. If Manipulator had gone out and been killed in a fight with them, they could have made the death appear to be an accident and then would have inherited the land because Manipulator had not yet mated with his wife, and Honesty and Moneylender had no other sons (Append. III: Chart 6).

After Moneylender's wife and children had settled in Shanti Nagar, Moneylender began building a one-story brick house for the family. The foundation had to be dug next to the dwelling of Bad Temper. As the foundation was dug, water accumulated, so Manipulator tied a rope to a little pot, filled the pot with the water seeping from the foundation and carried it off. When Manipulator recalled this incident in 1977, he said that he had just been playing, but when he was a small boy he thought he was being helpful. The house was finished in 1923.

When Moneylender began building his house, Bad Temper again started to fight with him. Old Soldier and other villagers helped him to settle the fight. Manipulator remembered:

> Bad Temper fought because he never wanted to part with any land or buildings when

my father separated from him. Finally the villagers helped settle the dispute about the separation. When my father and my mother's brother began building the house, they dug the place for the foundation, laid it, and then Bad Temper destroyed the foundation and all the other work. The villagers again joined together and admonished Bad Temper for what he had done.

In 1977 Manipulator said, "My father was afraid of his elder brother and shy of him. There was a difference of five to six years between them. His elder brother never wanted my father to have a son and tried to prevent it as much as possible. My parents used to say that when I was born and growing up, he was jealous of me, but I did not know it." The last sentence was characteristic of Manipulator, for whenever any statement was made about Bad Temper and his sons, he would equivocate as though no such bad relationships existed. In fact, however, he shrewdly protected himself, his family, his property, and other interests from them.

The sibling rivalry that had escalated into open hostility between Bad Temper and Moneylender was due to different temperaments, different mothers, and the posthumous birth of Moneylender, in addition to which Bad Temper had early grown accustomed to being the only son and heir, and later the family head. Other bones of contention were Moneylender's growing independence, success in business ventures, and his separation from Bad Temper, which broke Bad Temper's hold on Moneylender and divided the land. Conflict between an elder brother and a younger brother and the resulting murder of the younger brother may be as much a part of a Brahman's life as of a Jat's or Rajput's due to the structure of land inheritance and family relations. Carstairs (1953) described such a case resulting in murder among the Rajputs of Rajasthan, characterizing it as a culture-conditioned crime.

Although Manipulator and his wife were wedded when they were eight years old, she did not come for Gauna (first mating) until after he had matriculated when they both were 19 (1934). In this case, Gauna was some years later than was customary at the time, especially for a bride. After matriculation, Manipulator took a course in shorthand and typing in Delhi, living with a friend of his father and four other men in one room because poor transportation facilities made commuting impossible. Manipulator began commuting to work from the village in 1940 when the railway initiated a stop in a nearby village. He left for work at 5:00 or 6:00 a.m. and returned home at 6:00 p.m. In those days, office hours were from 10:00 a.m. to 4:00 p.m.

Manipulator and his wife had their first child, a daughter, Forthright, in 1936. The next child, College Man, was born in 1939. Thereafter three more sons were born in 1941, 1945, and 1946, followed by four daughters in 1947, 1952, 1954, and 1956. The last daughter and child to be born is here called Baby. Thus, Manipulator and his wife were the parents of nine children, four sons and five daughters (Append. III: Chart 6).

Manipulator recalled that in World War II a few village men were in the army. He remembered the riots of 1942, which were part of the movement for Independence. He took no part but said that everyone wanted Independence from Britain although when the war ended in 1945, it had not yet been achieved. Manipulator was still working in the city and had slowly advanced from a temporary clerk in a government office to a permanent clerk in the courts. By 1958 he was a law clerk in the court for domestic affairs in Old Delhi, and by retirement in 1976 had reached the apex for a court clerk. As a result of his work, he had become knowledgeable about legal questions and was often consulted by villagers about legal problems.

During World War II, famine and epidemics ravaged the Indian population. In Shanti Nagar, a typhoid epidemic killed a number of infants and adults. Manipulator's father, Moneylender, died in January 1945, age 52, and Bad Temper died in the same year before the end of the war. The ages of the two men at death, however, were within the average allotted time for a natural death so they were not believed to have become ghosts (Append. I: Disease). Manipulator inherited his father's land, standing crops, buildings, cattle, 15,000 rupees in cash, and some outstanding loans. He invested some money in a trucking business and lost part of it. He also added a second story on his house.

In 1947 with the division of the subcontinent of India into Pakistan and India, there were many riots between Muslims and Hindus (Thorner and Thorner, 1950: 645–646). Manipulator helped some Muslim friends to leave the country by lending them money, hiding one man in the house of a shopkeeper, and helping him to obtain a ticket to fly to Pakistan. Later the man repaid him, and in return helped a Hindu leave Pakistan by hiding him and his belongings in his own home, then escorting him to the border.

Manipulator, commenting on the troubled times in 1947, said, "Many rumors spread about Hindus being killed in Pakistan so the nearby villagers stopped a northbound train at the station about a mile from this village and murdered some of the Muslims." He named a village Jat as one of the men who did so. In *Train to Pakistan*, Kushwant Singh (1956) provided graphic descriptions of this period (cf. Collins and Lapierre, 1976). At the time of the riots, Manipulator again stayed in his sister's village because all the adult men were away. During the turbulent period from 1940 to 1948, he alternately stayed in his own village and his sister's village whenever the men of his sister's marital home were absent. Since Old Soldier was still living with Honesty, Moneylender, and Manipulator, these absences of Manipulator from his home were possible. However, intermittent absences beginning early in his married life in time affected the relations between Manipulator and his wife, who was a jealous woman.

Based on several events in 1958–59, behavioral evidence points to two tendencies in Mrs. Manipulator: (1) to inflict mental or physical pain on others; and (2) to seek the same treatment for herself. These traits were also present in her sister, Fomenter, who lived next door, and to some extent in her sister's second mate, Close Mouth, the youngest of Bad Temper's sons. The acceptable village customs of husbands beating their wives, and parents beating their children have been taken into consideration in evaluating Mrs. Manipulator, Fomenter, and Close Mouth (Append. III: Chart 6, Generations III, IV). Their traits stand out from the normative pattern and are best described as sado-masochistic. For example, it was not unusual to see Fomenter beat one of her children quite cruelly and an hour or so later kiss and hug the child (Fenichel, 1945: 58, 73–74; R. Freed and S. Freed, 1981: 75).

Additional features of Mrs. Manipulator's personality and character, namely, her frustration and outbursts of anger and violence, reflect the subordination of a wife to her in-laws, especially her mother-in-law, of wives to husbands, and of women to men (Mandelbaum, 1970: 46, 84–90). Mrs. Manipulator did not want to be subordinate to anyone. At the same time she was insecure and jealous. The cultural setting in which Mrs. Manipulator was expected to be subordinate and deferential to her mother-in-law, father-in-law, Old Soldier, and husband frustrated her and made her very angry at times. The anger sometimes flared into bouts of temper and violence. During her early years of marriage, a wife often carried on a semicourtship with her mother-in-law as described by Honesty and referred to earlier regarding Timid and Lady of Ghosts (Chap. 16). As she grew older, a daughter-in-law was more apt to fight with her mother-in-law and other members of her husband's household (S. Freed and R. Freed, 1976: 63–64, 71. Cf. Ullrich, 1987b, for the subordinate role of married Brahman women in South India over a period of 20 years).

Throughout much of 1958, Honesty and Mrs. Manipulator had many arguments and some actual fights. Other family members either entered into the arguments between them or had their own disputes with Mrs. Manipulator. Manipulator twice beat his wife and for two to three months stopped talking to her or having any relations with her whatsoever, including refusing to allow her to serve his food because he was afraid she might poison him. During this time, Manipulator was absent from the village a great deal in addition to the time he spent at work. His wife accused him of seeing other women because he avoided sexual relations with her, but Honesty refuted this accusation by insisting that he was tending to family affairs and business. When Honesty defended him, it only infuriated Mrs. Manipulator the more. Grounds for Mrs. Manipulator's accusations were that Manipulator always had a great deal of freedom with long absences from home, and it was well known that he was friendly with Tippler and two other Jats, one of whom lived away from the village and had a mistress in the city. All three men ate in city restaurants and drank liquor. In later years, Manipulator admitted that he drank with these men for seven or eight years and only stopped when his son, College Man, asked him to do so.

Close Mouth and Fomenter were another source of friction. They lived together in the adjacent building which had been the home of the joint family of Bad Temper and Moneylender before 1922. In 1958 Close Mouth took care of Manipulator's agricultural work on a fifty-fifty sharecropping basis. Mrs. Manipulator helped with communal weeding, seeding, harvesting, and the daily cutting of fodder for cattle belonging to her household. She and her sister, Fomenter, often hurled bitter accusations back and forth about sharing the work and dividing the crops. Part of the tension between the women lay in the relationship between Close Mouth and his mate, Fomenter. After both of them had been widowed, they continued living together but were not married although Fomenter bore Close Mouth's children. Because of their relationship they were social pariahs, the equivalent of outcastes, despite the illegality of outcasting. Their status reflected upon Mrs. Manipulator, Fomenter's sister.

CLOSE MOUTH, FOMENTER, AND DRIVEN MAD

The events which led to Close Mouth and Fomenter mating but never marrying started during World War II. At that time they and Driven Mad, Close Mouth's elder brother, were living in the City of Delhi where their activities had considerable impact on the rest of their lives. Driven Mad and Close Mouth were both married. Close Mouth was in the army. Driven Mad lived with his wife, Fomenter, the sister of Mrs. Manipulator, and Close Mouth's wife in the city where he worked. He and Fomenter had a son, Unfortunate, born in 1942. When on leave Close Mouth joined them. When Close Mouth was discharged at the end of World War II, he stayed in the city with his brother and his brother's wife. Then in the last part of the 1940s Driven Mad was said to have been driven insane by Fomenter and to have become a wandering beggar somewhere in the city. In the meantime the wife of Close Mouth died without issue around 1944–45, thus becoming eligible for ghosthood. Fomenter and Close Mouth continued living together and a daughter was born to them in 1947 (Append. III: Chart 6, Generations III, IV).

When Bad Temper died in 1945, his eldest son, Nondescript, became the head of the joint family and farmed the land held jointly by him, Driven Mad, and Close Mouth. However, Nondescript and his wife, Mrs. Nondescript, died in the late 1940s. With their death, Close Mouth and Fomenter moved back to the village where Close Mouth farmed his own and his brother's land. Nondescript and his wife left one son, No Trouble, and a married daughter, the girl who almost drowned Manipulator. She lived in her husband's village.

Nondescript's son (born 1933) has the pseudonym of No Trouble because he did not want to become involved in troublesome joint-family affairs. His wife came to him for first mating in 1950. In 1958 she said that she and her husband at first lived jointly with Close Mouth and Fomenter. Fomenter and Close Mouth fought with each other, and Fomenter also fought with her sister, Mrs. Manipulator. No Trouble's wife was scrupulously clean and peace-loving; Fomenter was just the opposite. Therefore, when Mrs. No Trouble became pregnant in 1953, she and her husband separated from Close Mouth, partitioning the dwelling and dividing the land. No Trouble was entitled to one-third of the land held jointly by Nondescript, for the land descended from Bad Temper in equal shares to his three sons, Nondescript, Driven Mad, and Close Mouth. In time Driven Mad's land was to be inherited by his son, Unfortunate, who lived with Close Mouth and his mother, Fomenter.

After Close Mouth and Fomenter returned to live in the village, Fomenter was the equivalent of an outcaste because she was living with Close Mouth and had born him a daughter while her husband, Driven Mad, was still alive. By 1958, she had born two daughters (1947 and 1950); they were followed by the births of four sons in 1951, 1953, 1954, and 1956. Driven Mad came to the village a few times, but the villagers knew the children were not his. According to village standards, Fomenter was blamed much more than Close Mouth because she was a woman. Although the villagers blamed Fomenter, Close Mouth was not a weakling who could be led by a woman. The following statement of a Brahman woman best describes the point of view of Brahmans and other villagers:

In the case of Fomenter, who gives birth to her husband's younger brother's children, because we are all Brahmans our respect is involved so we do not talk about them. However, when the time comes for them to marry their children, anyone who is like them may marry the children. Unfortunate is the son of Fomenter's real husband, who wanders no one knows where. But because he is the legal son, he can be married in a good family.

Fomenter is the cause of her real husband's insanity. He had a job in the city; he took her with him, brought his salary home, put it in a box to save it. She stole the money and never told him. This caused him to go crazy. Then she brought him back to the village, but she did not take care of him. He was cold, hungry, and wandered around begging and suffered more shocks, and he went to the City of Delhi to beg. Whenever she became pregnant from Close Mouth, she would find Driven Mad, bring him back, and say the children were his. She did this with the first three children, but then she became pregnant again and nobody could find her husband. The whole village then told her, "This is Close Mouth's child and you should acknowledge it." When a child is born, the village watchman sees that the name of the father is recorded. Now Fomenter acknowledges the children as being Close Mouth's children, and the whole village has come to know that they are useless people.

If someone among the Brahmans does this sort of thing, no one offers them the hookah or food. They are outcastes. But Close Mouth is not outcaste because the world is becoming full of sinners and people do not bother any more. Because Driven Mad was insane and because Close Mouth was a widower, the case is less serious than the case of the remarriage of Strong Minded and One Eyed [Chap. 12: Dead Issue].

Generally the members of Manipulator's family did not discuss or refer to the status of Close Mouth and Fomenter because Mrs. Manipulator was Fomenter's sister. However, Honesty presented her version:

Fomenter's husband was a clerk and a very nice young man. The couple lived in Delhi and had one child, Close Mouth's stepson. Fomenter stole her husband's earnings and went to her parents' house. Then she had an old sorcerer do something to her husband so he first became dizzy and then crazy. Now he begs in Delhi. When this happened, Driven Mad and Close Mouth were joint; they and their wives lived together. Later when Close Mouth's wife died, my son told Fomenter that she should live in his house and that he would take care of her and her son and even give her ten rupees a month. But Fomenter would not come. She continued living with Close Mouth, but they have never been married. She is a very bad woman and incites my son's wife to fight with me. The two sisters come from a bad family.

Further investigation revealed that Close Mouth, greedy for land like his father, was interested in acquiring the property of Driven Mad as well as keeping his own share of the land. Thus, he usually passed off his stepson, Unfortunate, as his own son. While the boy was growing up, the land was farmed and operated by Close Mouth, for after a while Driven Mad was never seen again and was believed to have died.

Although Fomenter's theft of Driven Mad's money may have affected him, World War II and the way in which the two couples lived together in the city started the trouble. Since insanity is complex, one would need to know more about Driven Mad, his father, Bad Temper, and his mother, and whether his brain had been damaged by the drug obtained by Fomenter from the sorcerer (Andreason, 1985: 111–115, 230–231). No cause of death was given for the wife of Close Mouth. As for Driven Mad, no matter when he died, his madness and eventual death, according to the beliefs of these Brahmans, resulted in his becoming a ghost. The events that led to the death and ghosthood of Close Mouth's first wife and Driven Mad deeply affected the lives of Close Mouth and Fomenter.

FORTHRIGHT'S MARRIAGE

Manipulator did not equivocate when events impinged on the welfare of his eldest daughter, Forthright. Although he arranged her marriage after a long careful search, she had not been married long when her husband began to beat her. She did not like being beaten but accepted it as part of woman's lot, for her own father beat her mother. However, she found out that her husband had a vicious, violent temper, had been married previously, and had murdered his wife. Whenever it was hot outside, his temper became dangerous. His first wife was three years older than he, and he had been mated with her when he was 14 years old. One day his mother, who understood how to manipulate him, told his wife to make dung cakes on the roof of the house. When her son asked where his wife was, his mother implied that she was wicked and had gone off somewhere with a man. The boy became very angry and said, "Wait and see." Next day he took his wife with him to Delhi where he stayed while attending school. That evening he burned her to death with kerosene and attributed the death to an accident with a kerosene stove. He was never jailed or tried because his mother's brother, a police official, intervened.

Although Manipulator spent three years searching for a husband for Forthright and investigated the groom's family as carefully as possible, he never learned of the young man's previous marriage and the murder of his first wife until his daughter told him about it. The first wife was believed to have become a malevolent ghost. Thereafter Manipulator would not allow his daughter to return to her husband. Forthright learned the story from village gossip and was thus able to avoid a similar fate. She described her mother-in-law as a disagreeable, greedy woman, who took all the clothing and jewels she had brought as part of her dowry.

Some villagers said that Forthright's husband returned her to her father because she was dark skinned, and various gossips even hinted that she had done something wrong.

The gossip troubled her and, knowing that she would not return to her husband, she went back to school the following year. She had left school after the fifth grade but eventually finished the eighth grade. In due time, Manipulator had her marriage annulled and arranged a happy marriage for her to a widower who lived in a large town.

MRS. MANIPULATOR AND CHILDREN

Although Mrs. Manipulator showed concern for her children, seeing that they attended school and had new clothes for the beginning of the school year, at times she let out her frustrations on them. For example, in May 1958 when the weather was extremely hot and dry and the the *loo* was beginning, her youngest son, Tricky, age 12, was playing hooky with some boys. He climbed a tree, fell, and broke his arm. Honesty and Mrs. Manipulator tried to keep the facts about Tricky's accident from Manipulator, who thought that Tricky was lazy and stupid. Tricky never applied himself to his studies but had learned some of his father's crafty ways.

When Tricky broke his arm, Honesty rose to the crisis and immediately took him to a bone-setter in another village. Until the arm healed, Honesty prepared halva regularly to serve as a plaster on Tricky's arm and for him to eat. Halva is a cooked sweet containing semolina flour, ground nuts, spices, sugar and milk. Villagers believe that if it hardens on a sprain or broken bone, the injury heals; eating it soothes the person and adds to the cure. Thus, the cure could be described as having elements of sympathetic and imitative magic. For example, when a man broke his finger by bending it backward, he used halva as a plaster and ate some because he believed both actions straightened his finger (R. Freed and S. Freed, 1979: 334).

Both Mrs. Manipulator and Honesty were distressed by Tricky's accident because two sons of the Manipulators had died when they were five and 14 years old. The 14-year-old son died in 1955 as an indirect result of losing one of his shoes. When his mother asked him where the shoe was, he said he did not know. She lost her temper, beat him, tied him up

to a cart outside their cattle shed, and then forgot about him. Early the next morning when she arose to grind the wheat for the day's bread, she remembered him, ran to the shed, untied him, brought him home, and covered him with quilts. Because of exposure he had Fever and died of ghost illness within the day. Another son, born in 1945, died in 1950 of an unidentified illness also attributed to a ghost. The 14-year-old son was eligible for ghosthood because of dying from Fever, an index of bad actions, and without issue; the five-year-old son's ghost illness and death were also laid to his soul's actions in past lives, and he too died without issue.

In 1959 Manipulator talked about the death of his 14-year-old son:

One of my sons died in 1955. He was born under an inauspicious sign, the Mul Nakshatra, a bad configuration. To pacify the stars, my father, who was alive when the boy was born in 1941, invited the Harijans and Brahmans to a feast. My father collected water from 27 wells [at first there were 27 Nakshatras, later increased to 28] and bathed my son in the water. I do not believe in horoscopes and inauspicious signs, but it is said that if a person who is born under an inauspicious sign survives his misfortunes he grows up to be very fortunate. My son had severe illnesses at the ages of 9 and 12 as was anticipated, but survived. However, he died when he was 14.

Manipulator never mentioned how or why the 14-year-old son died. Perhaps he did not know because of his absences from home. If he knew, the knowledge may have added to the gap between him and his wife.

The day after Tricky broke his arm, Bright, the next to oldest daughter, had a bad cold, went upstairs after she finished her chores, and fell asleep in the corner of a little used room. About eight o'clock that night, Mrs. Manipulator went upstairs looking for her and found her sound asleep. She shook her daughter awake quite roughly, slapped her a number of times, kept yelling at her, and complained that everyone had been looking for her all over the village. Then she took her downstairs and beat her. Later she explained

Fig. 10.   Altar design for a fire ceremony to protect a boy born under the Mula Nakshatra, an inauspicious astrological sign, 1978.

that she was afraid that Bright had drowned in one of the village ponds because a month previously a small Chamar girl had, in fact, drowned in one of the ponds. No doubt Mrs. Manipulator suffered great anxiety and fear when Bright was missing, especially so because of Tricky's accident and the death of her 14-year-old son in 1955. If Bright had drowned, Manipulator and Honesty would have blamed her. When such problems arose, Mrs. Manipulator let out her anxiety and fear with physical violence, in this case beating her daughter.

The youngest child in the family, Baby, was 21 months old at the time of Tricky's accident, and Mrs. Manipulator nursed her regularly. Whenever the little girl fell asleep during the day, her mother woke her very abruptly. The child would be startled and cry for a long time. Mrs. Manipulator said that if she allowed Baby to sleep during the day, then Baby would not sleep soundly at night and would awaken her from her own sleep.

Although this sounds selfish or heartless, Mrs. Manipulator had to get up at 4:00 a.m. daily to grind the wheat for bread, worked hard in the fields during the day, breast fed the infant throughout the day on demand, and did not go to bed at night until her children were asleep.

Mrs. Manipulator did not have an easy life, for her husband was absent a great deal, was not fond of her, and the couple often fought. After one of their fights, Manipulator claimed that if she kept on aggravating him and fighting, she would be the death of him. Because Manipulator did no agricultural work and was absent more often than he was home, Mrs. Manipulator had to carry a heavy load of fieldwork. Although the girls sometimes helped their mother, two daughters and the two sons, Tricky and College Man, attended school. As a result of long years of hard work in the fields, Mrs. Manipulator begged and nagged her husband to try to arrange marriages for his daughters so that they would not have to work in the fields. The two surviving sons, College Boy and Tricky, were being educated for jobs in the city so they could avoid much of the agricultural labor as had their father and grandfather.

Honesty, 63 years old in 1958, was exempt from hard labor, but during Mrs. Manipulator's illnesses, she cut fodder for the cattle, a daily job. Otherwise, she controlled the food supplies and cooking, assisted by Forthright. Honesty milked the cows, boiled and churned the milk, and prepared curd, butter, and ghee, jobs usually done by a daughter-in-law but in this household there was only one daughter-in-law, Mrs. Manipulator. The precautions taken against Mrs. Manipulator's cooking and handling foodstuffs were due to Honesty and Manipulator being afraid that she might poison them because of her sister's reputation for having given her husband a drug to drive him mad.

MRS. MANIPULATOR'S POSSESSIONS

Mrs. Manipulator was troubled by a ghost or ghosts three times in April, May, and August, 1958. The first time she looked as though she had fainted, was placed on her cot, and remained unconscious for a while. She lay there limply, eyes closed, jaws clamped together, but lips slack. Even when she was shaken by Honesty, she did not revive. Honesty and Tricky did nothing for her, but Forthright was worried and tried to bring her back to consciousness. Later Mrs. Manipulator said that just before she became unconscious, she saw the ghosts of the eldest son of Bad Temper, Nondescript, and his wife, Mrs. Nondescript. She did not mention their names, identifying them by terms of relationship. The two ghosts said to her, "Come with us." Because this couple was believed to have become ghosts, nothing much was said about them in 1958 or 1959.

When Mrs. Manipulator recovered consciousness, she related a dream that she had about her mother-in-law. She dreamed that she told Honesty that she was dying but Honesty paid no attention to her. It appeared that Mrs. Manipulator was upset and created disturbances so often that the members of her household did not take her seriously. Aside from the dream, Mrs. Manipulator said that

Honesty wanted her to die and that her husband had not accepted food or water from her for two months. She complained that her mother-in-law never gave her any ghee to put on her bread and that Honesty locked up all the food in cupboards.

During the possession and recovery, Honesty ignored her daughter-in-law so one can understand the basis for the dream. Later when Mrs. Manipulator asked her son, Tricky, to rub her legs, he did not do so, a sign of disrespect. Because her husband and mother-in-law did not respect her, neither did her children. The children's attitudes may have been fostered by their grandmother, who did not display anger with them, did not beat or hurt them, and was the person who controlled the food supply and fed them. A month later, Mrs. Manipulator was again possessed. This time she was talking nonsense, i.e., a ghost was speaking from within her. The possession was taken more seriously, for a hakim, also called a swami, from the nearby ashram was called to cure her.

In August Mrs. Manipulator may have suffered an attack of ghost illness. We learned about it while visiting Tippler's mother. Honesty came in carrying a sickle and announced that she had to go to the fields to cut fodder because her daughter-in-law was ill. When she was asked what was wrong with her daughter-in-law, she replied, "Nothing, she is pretending to be sick." After Honesty left, Tippler's mother, like other village women, said that Honesty and Mrs. Manipulator constantly fought and that Mrs. Manipulator was not a very clean woman, a trait unbecoming a Brahman. Then Tippler's mother added that if women were educated they would not fight. We disagreed, saying that we knew highly educated people who often fought with each other. She then laughed and said we were right, for her own son, Tippler, was well educated, had a temper, and fought a lot.

About this time, Honesty encountered a ghost. She went to the jungle to relieve herself and saw the ghost of Scapegoat, who had committed suicide in June. She was afraid, ran away, but did not suffer from ghost illness (Chap. 13: Deaths of Little Boy and Scapegoat).

Although Mr. and Mrs. Manipulator were on better terms by the end of 1958, still in 1959 Mrs. Manipulator's temper resulted in fights. One fight was with her eldest daughter, Forthright. No one knew what started the fight, but whatever it was Forthright almost choked her mother to death. After the fight, Forthright had a black eye. Then Mrs. Manipulator moved her cot from the first floor to a small room on the roof and slept there alone. To cover up the fight, Honesty said that her daughter-in-law was sleeping upstairs to guard the place, which was empty.

Part of the trouble between Forthright and her mother was due to Forthright's nebulous status as a married woman. Manipulator convened a village panchayat to deal with the matter and stop gossip. However, whenever Mrs. Manipulator was angry or unhappy, she would pick a subject on which one of her children was most vulnerable and upset the child. She did this more than once with Forthright, who was 22 years old and had better relations with her father and grandmother than with her mother. Mrs. Manipulator was jealous of Forthright, whom Manipulator favored over his wife.

Although Mrs. Manipulator seemed most at fault in family disputes, there were extenuating factors. First, her husband avoided sexual relations with her, partly because he had five daughters and only two surviving sons, College Man and Tricky. Dowries for the five daughters, which included a remarriage of Forthright, meant that he would have an outlay far greater than the dowries he would receive from the marriage of his two sons. A more acute problem was that Mrs. Manipulator was experiencing the onset of menopause. In 1958–59, she was 42–43 years old, the average age of menopause as reported in the Punjab-Khanna study (Wyon and Gordon, 1971: 163). Furthermore, she was still subordinate to her mother-in-law, not trusted by her or by her husband, and her children did not respect her. At that time, she was the only wife in the household other than her mother-in-law and was overworked. Her physical violence and temper to some extent were due to cumulative stresses, including the fact that she had a sister living nearby, who displayed similar sado-masochistic tendencies by inciting Mrs. Manipulator, with whom she often fought.

Mrs. Manipulator's family and kinship relationships constituted a vicious circle that left her relatively isolated, frustrated, anxiety stricken, and angry. This emotional state was expressed in outbursts of violence and fights with her husband and other family members. These eruptions and her ghost possessions and illness were the only times that she received attention and, in the aftermath, a little rest. It is possible, as indicated by Honesty, that the attack of ghost illness was feigned, but with a husband who was quite manipulative as a model, Mrs. Manipulator might try in her own way to influence the members of her family. Mrs. Manipulator, the second of the three wives featured in the title of this chapter (Honesty is the first), suffered from excessive stress, including anxiety, frustration, and depression due to her own temperament, the menopause, an often absent husband, entrapment in the village environment and culture, and the structure of family life.

MANIPULATOR'S DAUGHTERS

Manipulator managed to have Forthright's first marriage annulled and then in 1961 arranged her marriage to a widower who lived and worked in a city and had no children. Thus, Manipulator began to fulfill the promise he had given his wife that he would arrange marriages for his daughters so they would not have to work in the fields. Although Manipulator avoided discussions about Forthright's first husband having killed his first wife, he said that in order to have Forthright's first marriage annulled, he told her husband that he would pay the legal fees and give him a sum of money with a down payment when he signed the papers for the annulment. Although the husband expected him to make further payments, once he had signed the papers Manipulator made no further payments and never heard from him again. By 1977 Forthright had three sons, the eldest of whom was eight years old and earning special honors in school.

All but one of Manipulator's five daughters had married by 1977. Bright, the second eldest daughter, also a favorite daughter along with Forthright, the eldest, took the Teacher's Training Course after finishing higher secondary school. While teaching in the primary grades she studied at Delhi University. In 1969 Bright and her next younger sister, the third daughter, age 17, were married in a double wedding. The fourth daughter was wedded in 1975, age 21, to another widower, thus reducing the amount of the dowry. The third and fourth daughters finished higher secondary school and were teaching school in 1977, as was Bright. Baby was attending the women's college at Delhi University on weekends, helped in the fields at home, and in 1977 became engaged to a compounder living in the city. Thus, Manipulator fulfilled his promise that his daughters would not have to work in the fields.

COLLEGE MAN, CITY GIRL, AND TRICKY

Manipulator's eldest son, College Man, was his pride and joy. At the end of the 1950s when he was 19 years old, he was attending college, returning home on holidays. He was a pleasant, well-informed young man and quite likable. However, he did not study hard and when final examinations came, he was caught cheating and dismissed from the college. Manipulator was very fond of the boy and ambitious for him to finish college and become a teacher. Therefore, he arranged to have his surname changed so that he could be readmitted to college under the new name. In 1962 he obtained his B.A. degree and began teaching and living in a middle-to-upper class suburb of Delhi.

As early as 1958, a number of fathers of young girls visited Manipulator to try to arrange a marriage between College Man and their daughters. Manipulator insisted that he would not allow his son to marry until he had completed college. Most of the fathers were from the city, but they wanted to marry their daughters to a village man because the dowry demands in the villages were lower than in the city. Additionally, they may have thought that a boy brought up in a village would have fewer vices. The best asset that Manipulator's son had as a candidate for marriage was a college degree. By 1962, College Man had gone through the engagement ceremony, in which the terms of the marriage were stipulated. The engagement took place in the village of the boy and was witnessed by a panchayat of respected village elders. In the same year College Man and his bride, City Girl,

were married and shortly thereafter began living in the suburb where he taught.

After the couple settled in the suburb, Tricky daily brought them milk, curd, butter, and ghee from the village. City Girl said that she sometimes made fun of Tricky when he was late or spilled the milk. Tricky was a few months younger than his sister-in-law. He was just finishing eighth grade, whereupon he left school. Manipulator had tried hard to make a scholar of him, even sending him to private school in the City of Delhi, but without success.

Manipulator wrote to us in the last half of the 1960s to announce that College Man had Hodgkin's disease. Having lost one son and aware that College Man was much more capable than his other surviving son, Tricky, he was clearly worried. He wanted to know what could be done about treating the disease. We gathered information about Hodgkin's disease from a physician and wrote to Manipulator, reporting what we had learned and pointing out that treatment for the disease could be obtained in India.

College Man's affliction with Hodgkin's disease may have started some time before his marriage, for in 1959 when he was 19–20 years old, he had not been feeling well and said that he felt some swellings in his armpits. His father then sent him to a Western medical physician, who had been trained in England and who practiced in New Delhi. This physician did not find anything wrong with him, according to College Man's report, and, therefore, the physician did not prescribe anything for the swellings. This report led his father to believe that nothing was wrong. However, we knew the physician and he told us privately that the problem was masturbation and that Manipulator would be well advised to arrange a marriage for his son as soon as possible. In any case, it is possible that College Man was then in an early stage of Hodgkin's disease.

The course and treatment for Hodgkin's disease is long and painful; remissions occur, and cures are uncertain (Berkow, 1982: 1146–1151; C. S. Kleinman, 1987). One of the symptoms is Fever, which for those who believe in ghosts is a sign of ghost illness. A study of Hodgkin's disease over an eight-year period in Ludhiana, Punjab, showed a trimodal age distribution: in children; among young adults; and in males older than 50. For the Punjab study, the majority of patients presented themselves in advanced stages of the disease (Mani et al., 1982). Manipulator had dabbled for a time with a correspondence course on Ayurveda but in 1958 he nonetheless went to a Western physician in the city for malaria. After the death of College Man, however, he no longer had faith in Western medicine. In 1977–78 when his daughter, Bright, suffered from chronic backaches, he took her to a homeopathic practitioner in a temple in the city. For influenza and pneumonia, family members consulted a *vaid* who practiced Ayurveda in a nearby town.

When College Man was dying in 1967, Honesty took to her bed and died shortly after him. The earlier death of her brother, Old Soldier, in 1966, may have contributed to her demise. Although Honesty was 72 years old at the time of her death, she had consistently appeared to be in good health and might have lived longer, but the motivation to live died with Old Soldier and College Man. Engel (1968) has called this lack of motivation to go on living "the giving-up-given-up complex."

In 1978 City Girl described how Manipulator, after College Man's death, spared no effort to persuade her to marry his remaining son, Tricky. Manipulator did so partly because City Girl was an only daughter, and her father and brothers took good care of her by sending her many useful household gifts, such as electric fans, fluorescent lights, and an iron, and also because a daughter-in-law was needed immediately to carry on the work in the house and fields.

After her husband's death, City Girl returned to her father's house to live. Manipulator went to see her and her father to plead with her to marry Tricky. City Girl refused and told her father that she would prefer any man except Tricky. Manipulator continued to plead, and even cried, saying that he wanted to keep her in his family. Finally, her father agreed to the marriage and she unhappily gave in. After she had been widowed a year, a traditional Hindu Brahman wedding ceremony was performed in 1968 with the bride and groom going around the fire. Thus, City

Girl became the wife of Tricky, the fourth husband of this chapter (the first three are Moneylender, Manipulator, and College Man; Append. III: Chart 6). Afterward, according to Manipulator, many Brahmans slapped him on the back and told him that in arranging the wedding of his widowed daughter-in-law, City Girl, he had finally overcome the feeling against Brahman widow remarriage. Though Manipulator brought about reform in the village, the law and times fostered the change. Reforming Brahman customs was probably far from his mind; he was simply seeing to his own welfare and that of his family. (On culture change brought about by an individual, cf. Mandelbaum, 1964.)

Tricky was not well regarded by most villagers, who adopted his father's opinion that he was not very bright. They also thought that he was a coward. Despite his opinion of his son, Manipulator had managed to find employment for him in government service. Tricky enjoyed working in the city, became friendly with his co-workers, and experimented with minor vices, such as eating eggs and meat, which are tabu to Brahmans. He was shifted from job to job and by 1977 was an inspector at Subzi Mandi (Delhi's large wholesale vegetable market). He said that traffic daily was very congested from the many trucks, carts, and bicycles entering the market bearing produce from the countryside so by the end of each day he was exhausted (cf. Gazetteer Unit, Delhi Adm., 1976: 415, 427–428).

Tricky's reputation was due to his often unreliable and ineffective behavior. He borrowed money from men, who loaned it to him because of his father's position; then he did not repay his creditors unless pressure was put on him. He was labeled a coward by village men because of an episode in the fields. He was in the fields one night when robbers arrived. He was so badly frightened that he allegedly lost control of his bowels and hid for many hours, even after the robbers had long gone. When he was asked questions about his work, he did not seem to have a good grasp of it. This evaluation may be unfair since he had not worked very long as an inspector and the job was complex.

City Girl said she did not like Tricky and did not want to marry him, but she loved

When my health is poor, it changes my complexion. I stopped being plump after the death of my first husband ten years ago. My health has declined steadily ever since he died. Sometimes I pass out completely.

When City Girl was asked whether a doctor treated her when she passed out, she replied, "No, I come out of it." When pressed further about dizziness and passing out recently, she answered that she did not remember the last time she passed out. She again said that she had not been taken to any doctor when this happened, but that she would be unconscious for some time and then people in the family threw some water on her. They pinched her nose closed and put some water in her mouth. She could not breathe and came to. After she returned to consciousness, she felt tired and had to rest. She did not say anything about being possessed, but a characteristic of ghost possession is that the victim does not remember it. Her dissociative states were reported as ghost possessions by women in the family and were treated by family members and High Strung.

Asked whether there was anything she would like to do other than what she was doing, City Girl replied:

I have to do the household work. What else do I have to think about. I cannot do something else. I have to do the work. If I had been better educated, I could have had a job outside the home and village. If I had a good job, I would visit places. When I see other people enjoying themselves, I want to enjoy myself too. The atmosphere here in the village is such that I cannot bring up my children the way I want to. The children go to the village school and do not get a good education. They do not learn good manners, and they repeat what other children say. There are two younger sisters in this family whom the children copy. My mother is dead, and my father cannot take care of any of the children. One of my brothers told me I could send my eldest son to live with him, but I did not because he had recently married and his wife likes to go places. My eldest brother lives outside the city and has five or six children. It would not be practical to let my children go to school in the city and then bring them back

and forth from my brother's house. A child needs proper care, clean clothes, must be helped to ready himself for school on time, and needs his meals at the proper time.

When asked whether she ever was depressed, she answered: "Yes. Sometimes I am depressed when I worry about household affairs. When the household is happy and peaceful, I am happy." The last question was whether she ever thought that everything was useless. Her answer was: "No, never. The household work is very necessary, but when there is trouble in the household, I sometimes think that what I am doing is useless."

City Girl's score on the Health Opinion Survey was 30. She scored 7 on anxiety; 11 on depression. Her overall total of 30 indicated borderline stress (Append. VI). Given her marital history, it is surprising that her test score was not higher. She did not love her husband, had little influence about raising her children, and was the family's drudge. From our observations, she was a good mother and housekeeper but was definitely exploited and taken for granted by the members of her family. She was relatively isolated from her natal family. She said that she did not like to spend time sitting and gossiping with the village women, nor did she have time for it. The love of her children and occasional visits with her brothers and father kept her in reasonably good spirits. Otherwise, she was relatively alone and had little emotional or psychological support. The death of her first husband, her unloved second husband, the change from suburban life to village life, and the burdens placed on her by her in-laws made her vulnerable to ghost possession.

In recent years questions have been raised about the terms anxiety and depression as used in Western psychiatry. For example, as indicated earlier, Wig (1983: 80), an Indian psychiatrist stated, "Two emotions, anxiety and depression have been raised to the status of discrete disorders, to the exclusion of numerous other emotions in human experience—e.g, anger, greed, rage, jealousy, hate or eroticism. In other cultures excess of all emotions is considered bad, and one often wonders why an excess of other emotions is not considered 'mental abnormality' in modern psychiatry." This assertion was apropos of the statement: "In many other cultures, such as the Indian or the Chinese, it is much more natural to think in terms of a continuum without clearly defined boundaries" and "the European mind somehow always likes to think in terms of duality—e.g., good or bad, body or mind" (Wig, 1983: 80). However, the information gathered from City Girl reflects more than anxiety and depression so it is possible to discern the kinds of stress she had to bear. Wig's comments bear out the viewpoint of villagers, namely that mental abnormality could result from too much joy or sorrow, in other words an excess of emotions.

GROUP SESSION

One evening the following people visited us, here listed in the order of their arrival: a Chamar named Driver, Tricky, Bright, Mrs. Manipulator, and Baby. Manipulator came last, made a derogatory comment about the Chamar's presence, and sat as far from him as possible. When he came in, there had been a great deal of talking with Mrs. Manipulator about whom she would be willing to pay to work in the fields. The line of questioning was initiated in a joking manner, which all present understood. The question about paying someone to work in the family fields stimulated Mrs. Manipulator's imagination and she went off into rounds of laughter. Then we asked Mrs. Manipulator whether Manipulator worked in the fields. The thought of him working in the fields again sent Mrs. Manipulator off into a fit of laughter. When she was asked what Manipulator did when he went to the fields, she replied, "He just stands." The women and Tricky were asked whether Manipulator told them what to do. Again with gales of laughter, they said "Yes." Mrs. Manipulator, her two daughters, and her son enjoyed the questions but Manipulator was understandably silent. City Girl was not present because she had too much work to do.

Toward the end of the session each person was asked what they wanted to be in their next life. Mrs. Manipulator said, "I would like to be a man and be born in America." Bright said she would like to be a doctor, and Baby wanted to be a magistrate. The men

expressed the correct, traditional, conservative beliefs: "What Bhagwan wills, to live right and be a good man, to follow one's dharma." Although their answers seemed to indicate that they were satisfied with their lives, their replies, generally similar, were traditional and served to conceal any dissatisfaction. The answers of the women indicated cultural change; 20 years previously they would probably not have so answered. Their interests and desires showed that they preferred the way of life of men who worked in the city at an occupation that they believed was more interesting and satisfactory than their own.

During this session, Bright described her husband's grandfather, whom her sons liked. He was 82 years old, funny looking with red puffy cheeks, very fat, and yet walked rapidly. Once a month he and his son fought. When they did, the women in the household went into another room and laughed. Her husband's father was about 60 years old.

Earlier in the day, Bright, who was visiting her parents, said that she only taught school and did not work in the fields because her in-laws no longer had much land and lived in a town. The only time she ever worked in the fields was when she visited her parents. However, Bright had trouble with her mother-in-law, who expected her to do a great deal of work in the house after she returned from teaching.

This group session reflected tradition, but at the same time showed changes which were gradually coming about in the lives of village women. The phrasing of the men's statements was traditional. City Girl, now a village wife and a daughter-in-law, had the traditional low status of a daughter-in-law, and the daughters of Manipulator still had preferential treatment while in their parents' home. The only exception to this rule about wives is a woman, such as Mrs. Manipulator, who is a mother-in-law, elderly, and has grandchildren.

However, changes were evident. This session would not have taken place in the 1950s because men and women did not sit together then. Also in 1958, Chamars did not stay in the room when Manipulator, a Brahman, was present. However, when Driver, the Chamar, was a boy, he visited Tricky during the day when Manipulator was absent; they were joined by schoolmates from the Jat, Nai, and Gola Potter castes. The friendships of these boys often did not persist into adulthood. Nonetheless, there was a more democratic atmosphere among different castes than was true of Manipulator's generation.

The traditional responses of the men to the hypothetical question of what they wanted to be in their next life require further explanation. All three men, Manipulator, Tricky, and Driver, worked in the city. Driver had the most varied experiences because he had been a soldier, worked as a driver for an important government official, and had traveled as a government employee to Moscow. From the time Manipulator finished higher secondary school, he spent most of his days and many of his nights in the City of Delhi and in the courts. His way of life influenced Baby, who wanted to be a magistrate. Tricky had an eighth-grade education, and about ten or more year's experience working as a clerk in Delhi and then as an inspector in the vegetable market. College Man, too, from the time he entered college lived and worked in an urban or suburban milieu. These men not only had different life experiences than did their wives but they had higher status and more freedom.

The women, except for City Girl and Forthright who with her second husband lived in a large town, had spent most of their lives in villages. Bright, the best educated of Manipulator's daughters, was the most modern but still was subject to many persistent customs, such as a form of purdah after marriage, namely the custom of covering her face in public places and before men of her husband's family and lineage older than her husband. Baby attended a women's college on weekends and was soon to be married to a man who lived in the city. Despite their educational and occupational changes, the women still were controlled by Manipulator as the head of the joint family, except his married daughters who were dominated by their husbands and fathers-in-law. With the less stringent purdah restrictions, the village women had somewhat more freedom of movement than in the 1950s, for they could go to the city without their husbands, fathers-in-law, or brothers, providing they had at least one woman as a companion. The main point is that women, partially due to education,

were experiencing more freedom than formerly although they still did not have the freedom of men. Yet women knew more about the outside world than formerly. The choices of occupations made by them in the group sessions indicated that they realized men led a life which was easier physically, more interesting, and freer than theirs. Even Mrs. Manipulator, who had no education, said she would like to be reborn as a man in America. Despite the changes, City Girl, the only wife raised in the city, was trapped in the subordinate, hard-working village role of a daughter-in-law.

It is not surprising that all three wives, Honesty, Mrs. Manipulator, and City Girl, suffered from ghost possession, and Honesty and Mrs. Manipulator from ghost illness. Honesty was possessed after returning to her natal village from a visit to her husband for first mating. The ghost was a married woman who lived across the lane from Honesty's parents and committed suicide while Honesty was in her natal village. Honesty was afraid of her husband's elder brother, Bad Temper, because he did not want her to bear children and wanted the family land for himself and his sons. Due to her experiences with Bad Temper, she had returned to her parents' home and after her possessions became "as thin as a skeleton," an index of loss of appetite, depression, and ghost illness. Years later in 1958 when she was a widow and grandmother, she saw the apparition of Scapegoat, a Jat woman who had recently committed suicide. She was afraid of the ghost and immediately ran from the field; it was probably the security of her status as mother of the head of her family that saved her from further possessions. However, she passed on her beliefs about Fever, ghost illness, and possession to her children and grandchildren. Her daughter-in-law had similar beliefs. In 1958–59, Mrs. Manipulator experienced ghost possession twice and ghost illness once, triggered by her family problems. It is highly probable that she was possessed at other times in her life.

In the early fall of 1977, City Girl experienced possessions by the ghost of her first husband, College Man, although she had never previously experienced possessions. According to her responses to the Health Opinion Survey, she experienced a number of unconscious states, described by Baby as possessions. Her possessions were due to entrapment in her second marriage to Tricky, for whom she had no regard or respect; to her role as a daughter-in-law, in which she was the family drudge; to her lack of freedom, friends, recreation, and control of her childrens' lives; and to her living in the village which made her more aware of ghosts, particularly since her first son was dedicated to College Man's soul to raise it from a bhut to a pitri. Her answers to some of the survey questions indicate that she was angry, frustrated, and depressed by her situation.

In April 1978 when the malaria and ghost epidemics were at their height, Manipulator was asked whether anyone in his family experienced ghost possessions or saw any ghosts. He answered, "Only Chamars and other Harijans believe in ghosts." When he was told about two Jats who recently had been possessed, he said that ghost possession was a disease of women. When he was confronted with the case of Farmer, a Jat, who in 1978 had experienced ghost attacks, he said, "Some men may have it too." Then he said, "I do not believe in ghosts [bhuts]. Ghost illness is a disease of the liver or some gastric trouble which travels upward."

Manipulator, however, instituted the dedication of the first son of City Girl and Tricky to College Man's soul so the soul could be raised from a bhut to a pitri. His action could be regarded as a contradiction of his asserted beliefs, even though he probably regarded an ancestral ghost as a *devata*. In any case, considering himself an educated man, which he was for his generation, and sophisticated by any standard, he denied the existence of ghosts and attributed ghost possession to the low castes and women. In taking this position, he followed the masculine point of view regarding ghosts, which was strongly held by the Jats, the dominant caste of the village.

Manipulator helped Unfortunate, the stepson of Close Mouth, in his attempt to separate his share of the land from Close Mouth. In the fall of 1977, Unfortunate's second wife bore a son whose horoscope indicated he was born under the bad sign of the Mul Nakshatra. As a result Manipulator organized a ceremony and feast for the infant son as a means of staving off the bad effects of the Mul Nakshatra despite his 1959 statement that he did not believe in horoscopes or auspicious signs. After the termination of our fieldwork in the spring of 1978, we learned in a letter from Manipulator that when Plowman's son was married, the Brahmans in Plowman's lineage, including Manipulator, Unfortunate, and Close Mouth, were in the wedding party which went to the bride's village for the three-day wedding rituals. During this time, there was a lot of drinking, and, according to Manipulator, Unfortunate died from drinking poisoned bootleg liquor. No one else died. Unfortunate's death was viewed as the first of the bad effects of the Mul Nakshatra under which Unfortunate's infant son was born. Unfortunate's first wife died of Hodgkin's disease leaving two small daughters, seven and three years old in the fall of 1977. With Unfortunate's death, the second wife had to care for her step-daughters and her own infant son. We did not learn what happened to her and the children thereafter, but she was educated and had an excellent job in the city. In all likelihood, she and her son lived with her parents, but the daughters of the first wife may have gone to live with their maternal grandparents.

Some months before the wedding, Plowman was interviewed for the Health Opinion Survey. When he came to the question about dreams, he said he dreamed of a wedding, which was an omen of a death. Upon recalling his dream, he was so disturbed that he answered no more questions and left. Some months later his son was wedded, and Unfortunate, a member of the wedding party, died and his body was brought back to Shanti Nagar for cremation by the wedding party. Whether he died from bootleg liquor or was poisoned by someone, after cremation his soul became a wandering ghost. Since Close Mouth may have been a member of the wedding party and wanted Unfortunate's land, he may have poisoned him.

Despite the deaths of his three sons, especially College Man, Manipulator was able to rally, carry on, arrange the marriage of Tricky, and fulfill the promise to his wife to arrange marriages for his daughters so that they would not have to work in the fields. He educated his daughters so they could work as teachers, and he arranged the remarriages of his daughter, Forthright, and his daughter-in-law, City Girl, contrary to the traditional customs regarding remarriage among Brahmans. He was resourceful and not easily beaten down by trouble or misfortune, often relying on his manipulative skills. Born in the village and having worked in the city courts for many years, Manipulator was a half-traditional, half-modern man. He was able to draw on both these domains for strategy and tactics to achieve his goals.

This family history has delineated the difficult ideal role behavior of the three wives and the four husbands along with other family relationships, ghost illnesses, and deaths which contributed to ghost beliefs and the possessions suffered by the wives. The village

setting and absentee husbands added to the problems of the women. Even Old Soldier, whose two wives died early in life in their village of marriage, led a cosmopolitan life and was primarily an absentee husband. After marriage, the three wives, Honesty, Mrs. Manipulator, and City Girl were subject almost exclusively to village culture. The stressful conditions, hard work, frustration, and lack of freedom for the women plus the belief in ghosts and fear of them contributed to the possessions of Honesty, Mrs. Manipulator, and City Girl although she had little experience with ghosts and ghost beliefs until she married Tricky, moved to Shanti Nagar, and was trapped in the role of a village daughter-in-law.

CHAPTER 20: FIRST AND SECOND WIVES

The following three cases of the Bairagi Mendicant Priests, the Lohar Blacksmiths, and the Gola Kumhar Potters illustrate, first, the motif of the ghost of a first wife haunting her husband's second wife or levirate spouse and the second wife's offspring. Second, the cases also show how a general belief in ghosts as well as the fear of particular ghosts are passed from person to person. Third, males and females may be possessed by ghosts of either the same or opposite sex. Fourth, ghost illness and possession, which have biological, cultural, and psychological bases, may be treated by a variety of people: exorcists, other curers, family members, and neighbors.

THE BAIRAGIS: FEARFUL, HANDSOME, AND DELICATE FLOWER

The Bairagi Mendicant Priests were originally from the North-West Frontier Province and Rajputana. When they first came to Shanti Nagar, they were known for their begging. They carried a little bag for money and

a basket for whatever else they might be given. In time, the village landowners settled small parcels of land on them so that they would stop begging. Occasionally some of them persisted in the practice but not within the village. The Bairagis follow Sanatan Dharma in many of their beliefs. Brahman priests serve at their rites of passage for birth, marriage, and death. They believe in multiple deities, ghosts, and mother goddesses. They are Vaishnavas, preferring Rama Chandra as their chosen deity, rather than Krishna; both are avatars of Vishnu (Crooke, 1896, 1: 113–114; S. Freed and R. Freed, 1976: 94–95).

The Bairagi case begins with Fearful, a pseudonym indicative of her fears and anxiety. She was a mother and grandmother, 55 years old in 1958. She earned small sums of money in several ways, as described below, and also worked for us, bringing our water from the main village well and doing some housework. When she did not show up for work one day because she was ill, her son brought our water. Late on the second day of her absence, she returned to work, saying she had been possessed by the ghost of her brother, who died two years previously. Although her reports of the event varied and were somewhat inconsistent, the first account of her ghost possession followed by ghost illness was probably the most accurate. It follows:

The day before yesterday after leaving here I was all right, but that evening just before sunset when the cattle came back from the fields, I went to the gardeners for some ber [a fruit]. I jumped over a ditch as a shortcut. My knees were then acting badly so I went home. I think this was when the ghost caught me. I fell unconscious and my youngest son fetched my oldest boy. They took care of me. At 10 p.m. my youngest son, the one who brought your water, caught hold of my hair and asked, "Who are you?" He wanted to find out who the ghost was. The ghost answered, "I'm Handsome, [a nickname for her dead brother] and I'm her brother." The ghost spoke through my mouth. This brother was very good to me and older than I am. Whenever I had any trouble, he would always help me. He had a lot of money when he died, Rs. 10,000 in silver. My brother's son spent most of this money for his father's cremation and other death ceremonies. Now he is the only person working in the family, and he has the whole family to feed. My son then asked the ghost, "Why have you come here?" The ghost replied, "Why does my brother-in-law beat my sister?" My son retorted, "Don't bother my mother. Go away and in the future, your brother-in-law [i.e., the husband of Fearful] will not hurt your sister any more." All this happened that night. The next day a second ghost came and possessed me so my sons took me to Lord of Ghosts, the village exorcist.

Suddenly, Fearful said, "I have to go now and will tell you more later."

That evening and a few other times Fearful identified the second ghost who possessed her as that of her daughter, Delicate Flower, but did not provide the details until six months later when she recalled her two possessions and talked about her brother whom she described as being, "dark as an umbrella, but good-looking." When she saw his ghost before he possessed her, she said that he was riding a bicycle with Cat Woman, the Sweeper woman who died and was believed to have become a ghost. Fearful said that her brother had dreamed of the Cat Woman's ghost so that was why he died. The ghost of Cat Woman was malevolent and was said to have caused the death of a young wife and new mother in the Lohar-Blacksmith caste in addition to infant sons in the Sweeper caste (Chap. 14: The Ghost of Cat Woman). Fearful claimed that the ghost of Cat Woman frightened her youngest son.

Fearful's two possessions were the first of a series, which we learned about during the 1958–59 fieldwork. At first her sons used the matter-of-fact method of treatment by family, friends, and neighbors when a person is first possessed by a ghost; then Fearful went to Lord of Ghosts, who exorcised the ghosts (S. Freed and R. Freed, 1964: 154–155).

Some of Fearful's activities preceding her possessions appear significant in that they disturbed her. The Gardeners' house and gardens were next to the cremation grounds where ghosts are said to linger. By going to their garden to gather fruit toward sundown, Fearful hoped to avoid the Gardeners, for she was pilfering. She chose a roundabout way into the garden so that she would not be seen, but in jumping over the irrigation ditch she hurt her knees. Moreover, she was risking an encounter with a ghost by going near the cremation grounds and so was afraid. Her fear, the pain from her knees, and the element of guilt because she was stealing fruit were stressful and contributed to her subsequent possessions (Append. IV, Map 4: DD, B, CG).

Fearful later told us that she was again possessed by the ghost of her brother and added, "I have had diarrhea for three days so my daughter-in-law cooked rice pudding for me. I am going to go to the swami in the next village, who will give me some powder for diarrhea and then I'll be all right." Fearful considered her diarrhea to be ghost illness brought on after her possession by Handsome's ghost. Rice pudding, which is cooked with milk, is believed to have a binding effect and to stop diarrhea. In 1958–59, going to the nearby swami for powder was customary among villagers who suffered from diarrhea for a number of days, even though the diarrhea was attributed to ghost illness.

We recognized that Fearful's possessions and subsequent ghost illness were partly due to working for us, strangers from a strange country. Her work disturbed her because she could not comprehend the reasons for our instructions. S. K. Jones (1976: 22–28) reported a similar case when she and her husband were carrying out fieldwork in Nepal. She had a Limbu woman as her cook, and the cook ". . . had to cope with our standards of cleanliness, as well as other culturally conditioned wants and desires" (S. K. Jones, 1976: 24). This cook became possessed two months after she started working for the Joneses. According to the analysis, the possessions were the means by which the cook was able to gain rewards, such as being relieved of some of the burdens of the household in which she lived. To some degree Jones's analysis applies to Fearful's possessions and ghost illness.

Although the stress from our work may have triggered Fearful's possessions, we soon found out that it was slight compared to the troubles she was experiencing due to family affairs and her own personality. She was poor, at times asked for her pay in advance, later pretended that she had not been paid when she wanted more money, and periodically did not show up for work but sent her eldest granddaughter, Pink Flower, 13 years old, or her youngest son, 16 years old, in her place. Since she sometimes contradicted herself, we carefully checked whatever she told us. Fearful, an uneducated, elderly woman, had to achieve her ends by mendicity and cunning.

Fearful was part of a joint family headed by Watchman, her husband. Other members in 1958 were their eldest son (Family Man), his wife (Atheist I) and four daughters, and the youngest son of Watchman and Fearful, who was unmarried at the time and just finishing school (Append. III, Chart 7).

The small landholding of the joint family provided only enough grain for their daily bread. However, Watchman, Fearful, and their eldest son, Family Man, had jobs and all the family helped to farm the small landholding. Although Watchman at 65 years of age could not do much work, he was paid Rs. 15 a month as the village watchman. He was supposed to go around the village three times at night but said that he seldom did so. In addition, he walked through the village announcing important coming events. His job was basically a sinecure for an old man. Early in 1958, Family Man held a temporary job in a mill in the City of Delhi, earning Rs. 2 a day, but then was unemployed and found it difficult to find work. Fearful earned Rs. 25 per month from us and Rs. 7 per month for cleaning the village school. Occasionally she received cash or grain for pounding and grinding wheat for weddings, and she sold rather poor vegetables in the village, which she brought from the city. She intermittently worked for the wealthy, widowed Jat landowner, Schemer. He had political clout in the village and in a limited sense was her patron and protector. Much gossip was spread in the village about Schemer. One of the rumors was that he provided Fearful with wheat and money in return for sexual favors.

At the time of Fearful's possessions, Family Man with his wife and daughters was on the verge of separating from Watchman to form an independent household. This separation worked further economic hardship on both families, resulted in a division of the land, and reduced the number of family members on whom Fearful could rely to help with her jobs and to do household and agricultural chores. Therefore, she coaxed Pink Flower, her eldest son's oldest daughter, to stay with her rather than go with her father. Family Man said to his daughter, "If you are a human being, you will come with me or I will not accept you for the rest of your life." Pink Flower replied, "I am a human being, but I will not come with you." Fearful's temporarily successful manipulation of her granddaughter widened the gap between the two families. The fight over Pink Flower lasted two months while she lived with Fearful and helped with her work; then she returned to live with her father and mother.

In 1958 Pink Flower's mother, Atheist I, was the only known atheist in the village (Chap. 9: Ideological Interviews). Her disbeliefs protected her from her mother-in-law's excessive demands that offerings be made to various goddesses as protection against ghosts and malevolent deities. For example, for events such as a birth or a son finishing school, Fearful insisted that offerings be made to a goddess or goddesses and that sweets be distributed to avert misfortune and to continue good fortune. When bad fortune befell members of the lineage, Fearful blamed them for failing to carry out these actions. The difference in the beliefs of the mother-in-law and daughter-in-law may have contributed to the separation into two nuclear families, but Fearful's manipulations and lies created most of the discord. Fearful badgered and tried to influence the Bairagis in the village, taking advantage of the fact that they were all related. When the infant son of a young Bairagi couple died on Mother Sixth (Chap. 14: Death on Mother Sixth), she told the parents that the death was their fault because they did not make the proper offerings to protect the child from the ghost.

During the altercations regarding the family separation and the tug-of-war over Pink Flower, Watchman beat his wife, as indicated by the quotation from her brother's ghost: "Why does my brother-in-law beat my sister?" Beating a wife is considered to be the duty of a husband if a wife disobeys or acts against a husband's wishes, all the more if she creates a disturbance in family affairs. It is noteworthy that the ghost was believed to be Handsome, the dead brother of Fearful, on whom she formerly relied in times of trouble, for a woman's brother is her protector and source of aid. Thus, Fearful was probably thinking of Handsome as she pondered her problems, and in her unconscious, dissociated state after her fall, she saw his ghost and believed he came to help her.

A week or two after Pink Flower returned to her parents, Fearful slipped and fell again, breaking or spraining her wrist when she was trying to bring her water buffalo out of the rain into a shed. We did not see her for a day or two. When she returned to work, she described her injury and treatment. She bound her wrist tightly with her *dupatta* (headcloth) and the next day went to Delhi by bus where she had it treated by a wrestler who was known for bonesetting. She said he massaged the sprain, clicked a bone back in place, and then bandaged her wrist tightly (R. Freed and S. Freed, 1979: 334). Fearful paid the wrestler Rs. 3. Afterward her wrist ached for a while but within a few weeks she was using the arm which was no longer bandaged so it may have been a sprain and not a broken wrist.

Since Fearful worked for us almost daily, we learned a good deal about her, Watchman, and members of the Bairagis' patrilineage. However, she did not name members of her husband's family or other village Bairagis who died and became ghosts. Fearful's daughter, Delicate Flower, died when she was 14 years old in 1951. A number of villagers reported that the girl suffered from epileptic fits (*mirgi*), whose symptoms are generally known in the village. Delicate Flower was described as dark complexioned and very beautiful. She wandered everywhere and was unpredictable in her behavior. People protected her so she would not fall and hurt herself when she had a fit. She spoke in tongues or gibberish, which no one could understand. She was credited with being able to sense an approaching airplane long before anyone else in the village.

Because it is the duty of parents to see that a daughter is married and it was difficult to arrange a suitable marriage for Delicate Flower, Fearful agreed to her daughter's marriage to a 70-year-old widower, who paid her a large sum of money. The villagers said that Fearful was able to marry her to the old man despite her inauspicious physical condition because he wanted a young wife. Fearful justified the marriage of an old man to a young girl on the grounds that the man promised to have Delicate Flower cured. Watchman, who was supposed to arrange the marriage of his daughter, did not do so. After Delicate Flower's marriage, her husband was unable to understand her or have her do as he wished so he returned her to her parents. Shortly thereafter Delicate Flower died of ghost illness. Fearful's daughter-in-law, Atheist I, said that when Delicate Flower died she had "Fever" for two days, during which time she was talking nonsense (delirium, *sarsam*) (R. and S. Freed, 1979: 326–327; 1980: 505).

According to village traditions, probably deriving from the laws of Manu, to sell a daughter (i.e., take money for her marriage) is bad karma. Copulation with an individual of disordered mind or intellect is also bad karma. Marrying an epileptic should be avoided because epilepsy is believed to be inherited (Bühler, 1969: 76, 81, 84) due to the sum of a soul's past actions. It is not surprising, therefore, that Fearful and other villagers believed that Delicate Flower's epileptic fits were brought on by a ghost or ghosts due to her soul's past actions (Kutumbiah, 1969: x–xxxvii, 79–80, 199–201; R. Freed and S. Freed, 1985: 124–125).

Some time after Fearful's possessions, she began calling Ruth Freed "Delicate Flower." She associated her with her daughter because when she spoke English, Fearful could not understand her and thought that she sounded very much like Delicate Flower. She further resembled Delicate Flower in her mother's mind because she did not work as did village women but wandered around the village talking with people and writing in a notebook. It seems logical to deduce that Fearful's dead daughter troubled her conscience because she had arranged her marriage to an old man, was paid for it, and shortly thereafter the girl died of Fever before her allotted time without issue and thus became a ghost.

Months after being possessed by Delicate Flower's ghost, Fearful said that she vowed to make offerings at her daughter's marital village when her daughter died but forgot; therefore, her daughter's ghost possessed her. After her ghost possessions by Handsome and Delicate Flower, Fearful visited a temple in Delhi, which was well known for a holy man who went down into the earth (i.e., he buried himself alive). She first scattered grain around the temple; then she gathered mud from a nearby hill, which was believed to have supernatural, curative powers. When she returned to the village, she distributed *batasha*s (sugar candy) to all the Bairagis and her patrons.

Fearful's husband, Watchman, was the surviving brother of a twin (birth date ca. 1893). Although the birth of twins is considered inauspicious in the Punjab and the Delhi region due to the myth about the fraternal twins, Yama and Yami, neither of the Bairagi twins was killed, sold, or neglected so that one or the other would die, perhaps because they were boys (Dowson, 1950: 373, 375; Daniélou, 1964: 133; Saini, 1975: 81–82; Doniger O'Flaherty, 1980: 27; Chap. 14: Death: Terms, Times, Causes, and Cases). When the Bairagi twins reached age 18 they were wedded in 1911 to two sisters. The elder sister and wife of Watchman's twin came shortly after the wedding for first mating because she had attained menarche. She then stayed permanently with her husband. The younger sister, Watchman's wife, Fearful, was born in 1903 and was eight years old when wedded. She did not go to her husband for mating for many years. Within six months of his marriage, Watchman's twin brother died, leaving his young widow to become the levirate spouse of Watchman. This woman then bore six infants (sex unknown) in rapid succession. All six infants died at birth or shortly thereafter. The mother along with the last infant died immediately after delivery.

The souls of the dead twin brother, the six infants, and the levirate spouse then became eight ghosts, emphasizing the inauspiciousness of twins. The souls of the six infants did not tarry long as ghosts. From 1911 until 1919 is the approximate period from the first mating to the deaths of Watchman's twin brother, the infants, and mother. This calculation places the deaths in the period when plague and influenza were rampant. Although the deaths of the infants and levirate spouse could have been from many other causes, such as unhygienic or inadequate delivery practices, they were attributed to ghost illness. It is not unreasonable for the mother to have born six infants during this span of eight years because lactational contraception due to amenorrhea and anovulation disappears after the death of an infant when the mother can no longer nurse (Harrell, 1981: 797–805; P. Anderson, 1983: 27–30; R. Freed and S. Freed, 1985: 131).

Fearful was 16 years old when she came to her husband for first mating late in 1919 after the death of his levirate spouse, also her sister. Had she not died, Watchman might have put off Fearful's coming because he had grown fond of his levirate spouse and 40 years later was still melancholy about her death. Although Fearful had first claim as a wife because she had gone around the fire in the Hindu wedding ceremony with Watchman, the levirate spouse had been the equivalent of a first mate in terms of emotional attachment.

Fearful and Watchman had two surviving children in 1958: one son born in 1926, the other in 1941. Although Delicate Flower (1937–51) was the couple's only deceased child that we recorded, they may have had other children who died. If so, their deaths as infants would have been attributed to the ghost of the levirate spouse taking their souls.

In the fall of 1958, Atheist I, accompanied by her four daughters, visited her consanguineal relatives in her natal village. At that time, her husband had no job. She stayed only three days because she had no brothers and her father's brothers would not have wanted her to stay longer as they, too, were poor. Her father and mother were dead. On this visit, she and the children walked there and back. Sometimes her husband took her and the children to her natal village on a borrowed bicycle, but at that time he was away looking for a job. The description of this visit indicates the poverty in Family Man's household, the marginal economic state of his wife's relatives, and the effect that numerous deaths in one's natal and marital families have on surviving individuals. Despite her problems, Atheist I talked very pleasantly about her children, stating that they were never ill. The two oldest girls, 13 and 9 years old, were already engaged to two brothers. Both girls, Pink Flower and Jolly, were soon to be married and each would go to her husband for first mating when she was about 15 years old. The engagements had been arranged two years previously by the girls' father.

During the period that Atheist I, Family Man, and their four daughters lived as a joint family with Fearful and Watchman, some influence from Fearful's belief in ghosts rubbed off on her granddaughters. On a visit to the village in 1978, Jolly said that she had seen the well-known ghost of Tippler's first wife, who had lived next door. The ghost possessed her, and she suffered a series of ghost possessions. The first possession happened just before first mating, which took place shortly after menarche, a characteristic time for ghost possession of young brides. Though wedded and about to mate, they had little or no psychological preparation for menarche or coitus. Because first wives often died young from suicide, being drowned by their husbands, or from disease and then became ghosts, it was not unusual for young girls, who were about to mate with their husbands and subsequently would be expected to stay with them permanently, to be afraid that similar fates awaited them. The fear that marriage, mating, and bearing a child could result in death was founded on known instances of deaths of young wives who then became ghosts.

To sum up, beginning with the death of Watchman's twin brother and thereafter with the death of Watchman's first mate and her six infants, a number of ghosts haunted Watchman and then Fearful. Although Fearful bore three children who survived at least into adolescence, two sons and one daughter, the odds are that she bore additional children who died and were believed to have been taken by the ghost of Watchman's levirate spouse and first mate. Delicate Flower, who lived to the age of 14 years, was an epileptic, whose fits and odd behavior Fearful interpreted as ghost possessions. Fearful's pseudonym is apt, for she was anxiety ridden and troubled by many ghosts: Handsome, Cat Woman, Delicate Flower, Watchman's twin brother, the ghost of Watchman's first mate, who had endeared herself to Watchman as Fearful had not, and for a short time the ghosts of the six infants.

Delicate Flower's ghost weighed heavily on Fearful's conscience, for contrary to custom she had arranged her marriage to an old man for money, shortly after which Delicate Flower died of Fever, i.e., ghost illness. Fearful traced her diarrhea and sprained wrist to the same ghost who caused her own possessions. Although her mother was an atheist, Jolly did not escape the ghost beliefs of her grandmother, Fearful. Before departure for Gauna, she was possessed by the ghost of Tippler's first wife. First mating follows just after menarche, which involves a change in one's body. Therefore, it is not surprising that Jolly, disturbed by the biological aspects of menarche and afraid of what was to come, experienced possessions (R. Freed and S. Freed, 1980: 405–406, 408). By 1977, Fearful had become senile; her younger son and his wife took care of her. Both Family Man and Atheist I were permanently employed in nearby schools as custodians and had added three sons and two daughters to their family, a total of nine children, none of whom had died. Pink Flower and Jolly were married and lived in their husbands' villages (Append. III: Chart 7: Bairagis).

THE LOHAR BLACKSMITHS: SORROWFUL AND DIFFICULT

Early information on the Lohar Blacksmiths, who had relatively recently settled in the village, is scanty. Originally, they came to the Punjab, including the Delhi region, from Rajputana and the North-West Frontier Province, as had the Bairagis. Their Hindu beliefs and practices were similar to those of the Bairagis, for both castes observed the Hindu festivals and major life cycle ceremonies, but the Bairagis were better versed in Hindu rituals because of their former occupation as mendicant priests. Both castes were Vaishnavas, worshipping the avatar of Vishnu, Rama Chandra (Crooke, 1896, 3: 372–380).

Sorrowful, the head of the sole Lohar family in the 1950s, settled in Shanti Nagar in the 1920s. One of the Jat landowners, Schemer, invited him from a nearby village because at that time Shanti Nagar was without a blacksmith. As he was nonliterate, Sorrowful did not know his date of birth or exact age or those of his wife. However, he did know the approximate ages at which he and his first and second wives were married, mated, and the approximate ages of his children. In any case, Sorrowful provided enough information to sketch his family's history (Append. III: Chart 8: The Lohars).

Sorrowful was born ca. 1908. His second wife, Difficult, was approximately his age. Her pseudonym stems from her disposition, physical ailments, family troubles, and fear of ghosts and death, especially the ghost of her husband's first wife. These Lohars suffered the fate of many people born in the first two decades of the 20th century, i.e., the loss of relatives due to the plague and influenza epidemics. Sorrowful was wedded when he was 17 years old in 1925. His first wife came to live with him shortly thereafter when she was 12 years old. All Sorrowful's relatives, except his two small sisters, were wiped out during the epidemics so he brought his sisters with him when he moved to Shanti Nagar. Although it was not yet time for his young wife to come for first mating and to join him permanently, he needed someone to care for his sisters so he asked his wife's parents to send her.

Normally a young bride is instructed by her mother-in-law and older sisters-in-law regarding mating, bearing children, and household matters. Unfortunately, this child-bride had no such advice or assistance. In the first year of marriage, Sorrowful was still learning the blacksmith's trade and was very busy because he had to work unaided. His wife was left pretty much on her own. She was very lonely and wanted to visit her parents, but Sorrowful would not or could not let her go because no one would take care of him and his sisters. Due to loneliness and desperation, the young wife committed suicide by jumping in the main village well and became another village ghost (Chap. 15: Suicides and Questionable Deaths). No further information was obtained about Sorrowful's two sisters, an indication that they probably died in childhood. As late as 1958, Sorrowful still mourned his wife's death, despite the fact that he had remarried as soon as possible. He married his second wife, Difficult, in 1926 when she was about 18 years old. There is no information as to why she was married at that late age, but it may have been due to the scarcity of mates because of the epidemics. She too had little or no help in the early years of her marriage.

The Lohars had many troubles. In the early 1950s when they both were 43–44 years old, Sorrowful stopped speaking to and broke off all relations with Difficult. According to diverse informants including a young daughter-in-law, they still were not speaking to each other in 1977, and by then had lived separately for more than 25 years. In 1958, Sorrowful stayed with his sons at his forge on the periphery of the village; the women and small children lived in another house in the middle of the village across the lane from Schemer. Difficult said that until Schemer's wife died in 1948 the two families had been on good terms. In 1958 and 1959, Schemer, his sons, and his elder brother's two sons harassed Sorrowful and his family in an effort to make them move out of their compound across the lane from them so they could occupy the space. By the 1960s they had moved and the dwelling site became Schemer's cattle shed and *baithak*.

An illness which Difficult began to suffer in 1951 to 1952 when she was 43 or 44 years old may have worsened due to Schemer's harassment and may have widened the gap between her and her husband. In the fall of 1958 she had been suffering attacks of this illness for the previous four months. At the time, she spoke a great deal about her illness as well as family troubles and the ghosts which bothered her, her family, and neighbors. Her symptoms were a splitting headache, swollen skin on her body, and pain. She used lime juice in her bath water which she claimed lessened her pain. She also took various medicines. When she first had the illness, she was cured for one year but then suffered a relapse the following year. First she had prickly heat and then her whole body became swollen. She had this illness during the hot weather and the monsoon. The hot weather began in April; the monsoon generally arrived at the end of June and sometimes lasted well into September. During the winter, she was free of these symptoms. During the hot weather and the monsoon she had them regularly; they would come at intervals for two days at a time. Just when she was feeling all right, they suddenly would start again with a fierce headache. If she took a bath in cold water or if it started raining hard, then she had one of these attacks. The *vaid* who treated her said that something was wrong with her blood. Despite her beliefs, she never said she was suffering from ghost illness.

To some degree her symptoms fit the general description of heat exhaustion characteristic of the Delhi region and Uttar Pradesh. The hottest temperatures of the year are usually in May, but thereafter the somewhat reduced but still oppressive heat and increased humidity with the onset of the monsoon may cause what is called heat exhaustion or climate fatigue in susceptible individuals (Planalp, 1971: 284–285, 388–389, 532). A high salt intake predisposes to this illness, especially for people with high blood pressure or undue stress because they suffer from the heat more than others. Difficult was under stress but the presence of hypertension is an open question. There are numerous causes for hypertension, and furthermore its associated symptoms may also be found in normotensives (people without hypertension) (Berkow, 1982: 389 ff., 1297, 2125). However, disturbing symptoms during menopause may be due to organic diseases, such as hypertension (Berkow, 1982: 1680). In Difficult's case, with the onset of the symptoms when she was 43 to 44 years old, the illness may have started with menopause and high blood pressure. The fact that her husband at that time stopped all relations with her may have been due to her difficult disposition brought on by her physical condition. Later harassment by Schemer and his kin added to her physical and emotional stress.

Sorrowful and Difficult had seven surviving children: four sons and three daughters. The sons were 9, 15, 21, and 24 years old (Append. III: Chart 8). The 24-year-old son worked with his father at the forge while the 21-year-old, Urbanite, worked in the city. The Lohars had educated Urbanite and were also sending their two younger boys to school. Their eldest daughter and first child, born in 1931, had already been married and widowed by 1958. Since she had four surviving small daughters but no sons, the men of her dead husband's lineage were reluctant to take her as a levirate spouse. This situation worried Difficult because she and Sorrowful could not take care of their widowed daughter and four granddaughters. Eventually, however, a man in her husband's lineage took the widow as a levirate spouse. The second daughter of the Lohars was already married and had gone permanently to her husband; the youngest, 12 years old, had been wedded but would not go to her husband for about three years.

A sad event took place in this joint family in 1956 when the first wife of Urbanite died. In 1954 she had given birth to her first child, a son, Sprightly, and in 1956, she gave birth to a second son, who died shortly after his mother. Difficult attributed her daughter-in-law's death to her having arisen from seclusion on the sixth or seventh day from childbirth when she went to the fields to defecate; then she fell ill. Difficult said that three ghosts seized her: the ghost of Cat Woman, the ghost of Tippler's first wife, and the ghost of the first wife of Luck, one of Progenitor's sons. Difficult especially feared the ghost of Luck's first wife because she had lived near them.

Late in her pregnancy her body became quite swollen and she committed suicide in the main village well before the child was born (Chap. 12: The Families of Progenitor and Gentle Soul).

When Urbanite's first wife and second son died, his first son, Sprightly, was two years old. Since Difficult attributed Sprightly's mother's death to ghosts, she placed iron amulets on Sprightly's ankles and wrists to protect him from any ghosts, including his mother's ghost, trying to seize his soul. Because he had not been able to imbibe his mother's milk, he was given goat's milk. In 1958, he was a healthy looking four-year-old boy. A small daughter of Difficult's eldest son and his wife also could not drink mother's or buffalo's milk so she too was given goat's milk. Infant hypolactasia was therefore a possible genetic trait in this family line. As indicated earlier, the genes for this trait have been found in the population of northern India (McCracken, 1971; Johnson et al., 1974; Johnson, 1981; R. Freed and S. Freed, 1985: 136–142).

Difficult was responsible for the main care and supervision of her daughters-in-law during and after the birth of their children, including seeing that they remained secluded. Thus, a daughter-in-law was not allowed to go to the fields to defecate shortly after giving birth. Urbanite's wife did so because of lack of care and supervision by Difficult (R. Freed and S. Freed, 1980: 371–372). At that time the wife of the eldest son of the Lohars was about to give birth, and Difficult was expected to supervise the details of her delivery and seclusion too, but Difficult was lax in the supervision and seclusion of both daughters-in-law. Thereafter she claimed that a ghost took the souls of Urbanite's first wife and second son. An index of Difficult's relations with her daughters-in-law was that when Urbanite remarried, he and his second wife did not live with Difficult but instead lived at the forge with Sorrowful.

Difficult and Fearful seemed to fear ghosts more than most villagers who believed in them. They often discussed ghosts, ghost illness, possession, and knew about many ghosts believed to be haunting the village. Difficult described how her twelve-year-old daughter fell sick whenever she was frightened by ghosts. This girl accompanied her brother,

Urbanite, to the mourning rituals for his father-in-law. The child slept in a cattle shed that night, was frightened by a dream, and cried out in her sleep. Afterward for ten or more days she had Fever. Her mother said that her daughter often dreamed but did not always remember her dreams. Once she dreamed that she was drowning in a well; then she dreamed that she jumped out of the well and was all right. Her mother and other neighboring women often spoke of wives who committed suicide in wells or were drowned in them by their husbands. Therefore, the 12-year-old child's dream of drowning in a well was not surprising, for she was already wedded and would mate with her husband in two to three years. Such a dream was interpreted as a ghost dream and a bad omen as indicated in the case of The Boy Had To Die (Chap. 14). Thus, when Difficult learned of her daughter's dream in the cattle shed and then the girl had Fever, she believed the child had ghost illness.

A somewhat similar attack took place when Urbanite was a small child. He visited his mother's parents' home. At night he awoke frightened; his mother's sister-in-law took him in her arms and he started clawing her. His mother's brother took the boy from her and asked him what he saw. Urbanite answered, "Some woman is eating me." Then he fell sick with Fever. The dream was a ghost dream. Difficult said that first her children were frightened by dreaming of a ghost; then they had ghost illness. She also said that if they did not believe in ghosts, then they would not fall sick. They believed in ghosts, were afraid of them, and then fell sick when they saw them. She added, "There is a power which makes them see the ghost and they are afraid."

Thus, Difficult instilled the fear of ghosts and ghost illness in her children through her constant refrain, her own fear of ghosts, and the closely related fear of dying. She did not like to hear about anyone dying; yet every time one of her children or grandchildren was ill, she made a statement such as: "Sprightly has Fever and is vomiting; he will die." For a small granddaughter afflicted with boils, she made a similar declaration. No matter how mild the ailment, Difficult said that the child would die. These statements revealed Difficult's fear that ghosts were causing illness and trying to take the children's souls. Because Difficult believed that five ghosts, all of them first wives, haunted her neighborhood and the village—Sorrowful's and Urbanite's first wives, Cat Woman, and the wives of Tippler and Luck—she took precautions by placing amulets on all her grandchildren under the age of five years.

Although the ghost illnesses described by Difficult which afflicted her children started with dreams of ghosts, they fit Good and Kleinman's (1985: 311–314) analysis of specific syndromes and anxiety disorders in a cultural context. What they term "fright illnesses" are caused by fear reactions or startling, the latter a reaction to fright. The anxiety and fright of Difficult's children were generated by her indoctrinating them with a fear of ghosts, ghost illness, and death. In particular, the categorization of the children's illness as ghost illness was indicated by Fever and linked with the deaths of wives by drowning in wells which caused them to become ghosts and attack children as well as adults.

Difficult's descriptions of the ghost illnesses of her son, Urbanite, and her 12-year-old daughter, which were caused by fright and being startled, should be classified according to Simons (1985c: 329–331), not as a Culture-Bound Syndrome, but as a fright taxon, a Folk Illness of Psychiatric Interest, because it has a wide distribution. In Shanti Nagar, it is considered ghost illness because of Fever. Simons pointed out that Susto, which is widespread in Latin American societies, is similar to conditions found in many areas of the world. Rubel (1977: 121–122), in describing Susto found in Mexico and among Mexican Americans, stated that sometimes it is caused by fright or an accident and the belief is that the soul of the individual takes flight causing the illness. Rubel et al. (1985: 333) also indicated that illness with symptoms similar to Susto may be found in other areas of the world. A. Kleinman (1981: 4, 195, 251) reported a similar illness from fright in Tapei, China, which includes a number of disorders found in children. Family members may take the child to a Western medical physician and then to a shrine where a ritual is performed "to call back the soul." These two remedies are similar to Mrs. Fence Sitter's twofold cure

for her children (Chap. 12: The Families of Progenitor and Gentle Soul). However, in Shanti Nagar, contrary to Susto, the belief is that when the soul leaves the body, the individual dies. The cure takes place while the ghost is trying to take the soul from the body; the exorcist drives out the ghost in order to keep the soul in the patient and prevent death.

The dreams of Difficult's two children also show similarity to the definition of nightmares, "nocturnal episodes of intense anxiety and fear associated with a vivid and emotionally charged dream experience" (Kales et al., 1980: 1197). Given the ghost beliefs with which the children were inculcated by their mother, the fear, which the daughter had when attending a funeral ceremony and sleeping in a strange cattle shed, was transformed into a nightmare. The dream episode may have been augmented by the onset of illness marked by Fever for ten or more days thereafter. Thus, her illness was ghost illness. Urbanite's nightmare while visiting his maternal grandparents fits the same pattern (on nightmares, cf. Chap. 13: Old Codger, Barker, and Mrs. Barker; Chap. 22: Farmer).

The details of Difficult's own illness and family background together with the ghost illnesses of her son, Urbanite, and her 12-year-old daughter confirm the limitations of using the concept of Culture-Bound Syndromes. In pointing out the problems related to this concept, Simons (1985a: 25) stated: "With increasing recognition that culture-specific factors shape all afflictions . . . the distinction between culture-bound syndromes and other forms of alleged psychological deviance has been blurred. . . . Thus, as currently used, the category 'culture-bound syndromes' seems not only ethnocentric but indefinitely expansible. For these and other reasons several recent papers have suggested doing away with the term which has always been at best a residual category. . . ." Hughes (1985a: 3–24) in questioning the use of Culture-Bound Syndromes suggested that they and Folk Illnesses of Psychiatric Interest be tested in comparison with DSM-III (Am. Psych. Assn., 1987) to see whether they stand up when full descriptions of these illnesses have been obtained. Hughes (1985d: 471–472) further noted that possession and trance are so ubiquitous that they by no means fall into the category of a Culture-Bound Syndrome. In India for example, data pertaining to the behavior defined as possession have been reported in the eleven major languages of the country (A. V. Rao, 1978: 7).

A spate of reviews of Simons and Hughes (1985) *The Culture-Bound Syndromes* appeared in *Culture, Medicine and Psychiatry* [Good, 1987: 11(1); 1988: 12(4)]. In reply, Simons [1988: 12(4): 526] questioned whether the sleep paralysis taxon (Simons, 1985b: 115–116) in the cases of Old Hag of Newfoundlanders and Uqumairineq of Eskimos should be called a Culture-Bound Syndrome, pointing out that "it is necessary to describe that which is to be explained in exhaustive and minute details." Questions of this order are applicable to the poltergeist attacks of Mrs. Barker and Farmer (Chaps. 13, 22) of this study, which are intertwined with sleep, fright, nightmares, and stress in family and cultural settings.

Simons [1988: 12(4): 528] in the conclusion of his reply to reviews of *The Culture-Bound Syndromes* stated that the book "proposes that the causal chains which generate the observed and experienced behaviors include biological, psychological, social, and cultural components which are intertwined in situationally specific ways. The explanatory task is not to assign them relative weights, but to trace those causal chains." This position coincides with our ethnographic and analytical approach to fieldwork.

To continue with the Lohars, the startle and fright behavior, plus Fever, shown by Difficult's two children, her 12-year-old daughter and her son, Urbanite, were part of the causal chain contributing to their ghost illness. By 1977–78, Urbanite, who had grown tired of the problems he encountered in his family and the village, had long been living in Delhi with his wife and children, except for his son, Sprightly, who stayed in the village with his grandfather, Sorrowful. Difficult lived separately from Sorrowful with Mrs. Clerk, the wife of her next to youngest son, Clerk, who was in the air force stationed away from home. His small wife was quite bright and competent. At the end of 1977, she bore her second child, a son. Each of her children had been delivered in a hospital by Caesarean section, and she was sterilized after delivery of the second infant. She had only one surviving son, for her first son died in January 1978 (Append. III: Chart 8).

After her sterilization, she returned to the village and was in the care of her mother-in-law. When we visited the new mother, she was lying in bed. From her appearance and the odor in the room she must have been neglected by Difficult. She did not complain and must have had considerable inner strength and a good constitution, for she survived the Caesarean and sterilization with little aftercare, and the child appeared to be flourishing. However, when her daughter-in-law took to bed, Difficult groaned and moaned, claiming that she too was ill, and went to her own bed.

Some months later in the spring of 1978, Mrs. Clerk said that her first son died when he was one year old. He had always been strong and healthy and looked more like a three-year-old than a one-year-old. In the unusually cold winter the child died after he had recovered from pneumonia some days previously. As was customary, Mrs. Clerk went to fetch water from the well in the morning and left the infant boy in the care of Difficult, her mother-in-law. When Mrs. Clerk returned from the well, the child was dead. She never found out why the child died, whether due to the aftereffects of Fever, pneumonia, or Difficult's negligence.

During the 1977–78 fieldwork, Difficult had become increasingly isolated from family members and other villagers. Whenever we visited the Lohars, she demanded attention. Once when her mother-in-law was not present, Mrs. Clerk said that she soon planned to join her husband with the children. Although our evidence is only indirect, Difficult seemed to be one of those mothers-in-law and grandmothers who, if she did not like her daughters-in-law, in time did not care for her grandchildren either. She may have indirectly through negligence contributed to the deaths of Urbanite's first wife, their second infant son, and Mrs. Clerk's first son.

The marriage of Difficult to Sorrowful after the death of his first wife is similar to the case of Watchman and Fearful, for each woman was the second mate and was haunted by the ghost of the first mate, and both men were alienated from their second mates. Difficult's ghost illness took the form of heat exhaustion, possibly exacerbated by hypertension; Fearful suffered ghost possessions. Both women were steeped in beliefs about ghosts and ghost illness and had estranged relations with their daughters-in-law.

This Lohar case again illustrates the pervasive belief that the ghost of a first wife haunts a second spouse and may cause her death, the death of her infant or infants, and the death of infants of other women. It shows that dreams of the dead are the equivalent of seeing a ghost and an omen that the dreamer or someone in the family of the dreamer will be struck with ghost illness marked by Fever. It also points out the factors pertinent to ghost illness and possession.

THE POTTERS AND THE LADY

The Gola Kumhars came to Shanti Nagar from the Punjab. Although they were Hindus, they knew less about Hinduism than the Bairagis and Lohars and rank lower in the caste hierarchy. The traditional occupation of the caste is making pottery, as befits the caste name (Kumhar means potter), but only two of the Kumhars of Shanti Nagar were potters and they easily supplied all the needs of the village in 1958–59. The same two men remained the only practicing potters in 1977–78. That they were still able to supply the needs of the village, whose population had grown by 65 percent in the 19.5-year interval between our censuses, was because brass pots were more widely used, to some extent replacing earthenware pots. Moreover, itinerant potters visited the village where they did a brisk business. The breeding and trading of donkeys, mules, and horses and their use to transport goods could also be considered traditional occupations of the Kumhars. In 1958–59, all but one of the 12 Kumhar families owned at least one of these animals. Transportation was of equal or greater economic importance to the Potters than the making of pots (Crooke, 1896, 3: 338–340; S. Freed, 1963b: 886, 889, table 5; S. Freed and R. Freed, 1976: 97; 1978: 84–85).

The case of "The Potter and the Lady" involves two men, here called Insider and Outsider, and their lineages, known as the Insiders and the Outsiders (Append. III: Chart 9). Insider's mother died when he was an infant. His father married again, but died when Insider was about one year old and before having surviving children with his second wife. Insider's grandfather arranged for the widow of his dead son to marry a Potter from Rajasthan who was his sister's son. Because this immigrant was related to the Potters of Shanti Nagar through a woman rather than patrilineally, he was an outsider. Insider, his grandfather, father, and children were related patrilineally and were therefore insiders. Mrs. Outsider did not care for Insider, her stepson. Her interest was devoted to the many children that she bore her new spouse, Outsider.

Insider's grandfather lived well into old age and had plenty of time to raise Insider. When the grandfather arranged for his sister's son to come to the village and become Insider's stepmother's mate, part of the agreement was that he was to take over the old man's pottery practice and teach Insider to make pots when he was old enough.

Insider was born in 1931 or 1932. His parents died at a time when epidemic and endemic diseases were still rampant. Thus, Insider's parents became ghosts because both died young and from a dread disease attributed to ghost illness. Insider's mother's ghost was feared more than her husband's ghost because she died shortly after childbirth and her place was usurped by a second wife. Her ghost was referred to by the euphemism The Lady (Append. III: Chart 9).

Outsider kept one part of his agreement with Insider's grandfather: he served as the village potter. However, he did not teach Insider the skill, the other part of the bargain. Insider's grandfather then arranged for Insider to live with Insider's father's sister's husband in his village and there learn to make pots. In 1958, Outsider said that Insider had been apprenticed to him to learn how to make pots, but in fact Insider learned the craft elsewhere. When Insider was ready to return to Shanti Nagar and begin practicing on his own, his father's sister's husband made the heavy potter's wheel for him, a necessity for a potter. When he was 20 to 21 years old, Insider returned to his natal village (ca. 1952–53) and set up his potter's wheel and kiln. Thereafter Outsider no longer had the village monopoly for making pots.

By 1958, Insider had married, was about 26 years old, and had one child, a daughter, age two. His grandfather, who was in his eighties, lived with him and grazed donkeys for other Gola Potters. Insider, his wife, and his grandfather, like Mr. and Mrs. Outsider and the great majority of Gola Potters, were nonliterate. Insider's income came from pot-making and transporting mainly bricks with his donkeys. By 1977, Insider and his wife had three sons and four daughters; all but the eldest daughter had attended school. Two daughters were married and had gone to live with their husbands. Insider's eldest son was 13 years old and helped with chores as did his 16-year-old daughter.

Despite the fact that Insider did not rent land in order to participate in the lucrative truck farming that was common in the late 1970s, he appeared to be doing better than the Outsiders. Through the years, the two potters had steadily competed with each other. No love was lost between their families, whose houses were fairly close to one another, and the ghost of The Lady, Insider's mother, lingered on as a potential menace to her husband's second wife and her children.

In 1958, two events fixed the Outsiders in our memories. First Mrs. Outsider bore twin daughters early in January, increasing the family to ten children. The family derived its income from pottery, transporting bricks from a nearby brick kiln, and trading horses, mules, and donkeys. Despite these activities, the family was poor. Mrs. Outsider not only took care of the children and household but also assisted her husband in some of the hard work of making pots. She found it quite difficult to manage it all, especially with the added burden of the twins. The Outsiders thought of having the twins adopted and even approached us about the matter, but eventually decided to keep them.

The second event, which took place in February 1958, was the wedding of the Outsiders' two eldest sons, ages 14 and 12. Their even younger wives were not to come for first mating for a number of years. After the two sons returned from their wedding in the village of the brides, who were sisters, Eldest Son (his pseudonym) was possessed by a ghost. His mother, Mrs. Outsider, described his illness as follows, "Something is inside of him which gives out a sound that shows a ghost is there. He gives up speaking in his own voice and speaks in another voice. His wife will not come permanently for three years. She is not yet 15 years old. My other son who was wedded at the same time is 12 years old and his wife is 10 or 11 years old."

Mrs. Outsider mentioned that whenever anyone fell ill they called a Brahman priest from a nearby village or a swami from the ashram, both of whom gave penicillin injections. For ghost possessions they called the younger brother of Outsider; he and Outsider's father lived in Bikaner, Rajasthan, Outsider's natal town. The younger brother was said to be a specialist in exorcising ghosts. His teacher was a maharajah, a term applied to a great and well-known exorcist.

Mrs. Outsider was not too well informed about ghost beliefs. For example, she said that she did not know what caused a person to be a ghost, but that she was afraid of ghosts. If a person caught sight of a ghost, then that person would be possessed or fall ill. When that happened, the person would start crying and speaking in the ghost's voice.

By 1977, the Outsiders were somewhat better off than in 1958–59, which was true of most villagers. They participated in the currently profitable truck farming, an enterprise open to landless low-caste people because they could rent land. Truck farming was well suited to large families, for much of the work could be done by family labor. The Outsiders rented land from a large landowner and planted tomatoes, an especially profitable crop. In addition, they still made pots, moved bricks at the brick kiln, transported vegetables from Shanti Nagar to the modern Delhi vegetable market, and traded horses, mules, and donkeys.

In 1958, only two sons of the Outsiders had attended school, but by 1977 all the sons and grandchildren who were old enough went to school. A few of the wives had attended school but none of the family's daughters. The educated boys looked for modern forms of employment besides helping with many tasks at home. Eldest Son, who had been possessed in 1958, his wife, and six children, had separated from his parents, but the Outsiders still had a three-generation household of 17 people. One of their twin daughters died within her first year, but another daughter was born to them in 1963. When the twins were born, Mrs. Outsider was between 38 to 41 years of age, so her last child was born when she was between 43 and 46 (Append. III: Chart 9).

In 1978 the Outsiders' next to youngest son, whose pseudonym is Younger Son, was 22 years old. He had been educated through the tenth grade and was looking for a job as a conductor. If that failed, he planned to enter military service. Younger Son was taking a typing course to help him obtain work. On the side, he worked in the fields, at a nearby brick kiln, and made pots. Although he was married, his wife, who was 17 years old, had not yet come for first mating. With the education of girls and boys, parents of daughters tended to keep them at home until such time as they were sure that the young husband was employed. This change contributed to problems among the youths, who wanted their brides to come earlier for first mating. Because his wife's parents would not allow their daughter to come for Gauna until he had a good job, Younger Son was under considerable psychological stress. He had been possessed a number of times for more than a year by The Lady. Because Younger Son was very busy, he was rarely around and we were never able to interview him.

In January 1978, during a conversation with Mrs. Outsider's 14-year-old daughter about various illnesses in the family (malaria and typhoid during the summer and fall of 1977; colds and her infected ear in the winter of 1978), she stated that the family went to the village curer, Home Trained, for medicine generally, but that she had gone to a nearby Catholic clinic and dispensary for her ear infection. She added that for their ghost possessions caused by the ghost of The Lady, everyone in the family went to New Priest in Raconteur's family or to Illusionist. She continued, "My brother [Younger Son] is possessed by her ghost and goes to Illusionist. He has been troubled by her for one year; he is 22 years old. He eats something sweet, goes

out of the house, and the ghost of The Lady disturbs him." Mrs. Outsider asked whether we could do anything for his possessions, lamenting that she had so much grief in her house that she was not able to cope with it. Then she described how her daughter's ear pained her. It was all right while they used the medicine from the Catholic dispensary, but they were unable to pay for any more medicine so the pain returned. She described the ear problem as "a lot of pus coming out of the ear, which has to be cleaned."

Younger Son's mother and sister stated that a number of family members had been occasionally possessed by The Lady. Crowded living conditions, many illnesses, and the family history of ghost possession made for a relatively stressful family life style and set the stage for ghost possession. The competition between Insider and the Outsiders enhanced family stress and reinforced the memory of the ghost of The Lady and her replacement by Mrs. Outsider. The ghost of the vengeful first wife, Insider's mother, menaced the Outsiders. It is perhaps noteworthy that Insider and his family apparently escaped episodes of ghost illness and possession.

The ghost possessions of Eldest Son and Younger Son, which took place after their weddings but before Gauna, are similar to the 1978 possessions of Welder and the ghost illness of the Fence Sitter's son, both Brahmans (Chaps. 12, 14). These possessions reflect changes regarding the age at wedding and the need in some cases for men to be employed before their marriages could be consummated. The lack of a suitable sexual outlet was almost certainly involved in the cases of these young adults. The belief that wasting semen weakens the body may also have been a factor, for the possibility of masturbation cannot be discounted. In both field trips, villagers mentioned that parents did not discuss sex with their children, that wasting semen weakened a man's body, and a few men voiced the belief that women were sexually more demanding than men. To some extent, they were feared because their excessive demands led to wasting semen. The relation of wasting semen to health has been covered by Carstairs (1958: 83–87). His male informants believed that their strength resided in "the making, storing, and expenditure of a man's semen (virija)" (Carstairs, 1958: 83). When men told him that they were weak and he asked why, they replied with an account of *jirjan*, namely, the loss of semen due to eating what is wrong and doing what is wrong, the latter referring to loss of semen through tabued sexual activity or too much sexual activity (Carstairs, 1958: 84–85). *Jirjan* has also been called *dhat* in India. Simon and Hughes (1985) in *The Culture-Bound Syndromes*, described *dhat* and *jirjan* as "severe anxiety and hypochondriasis with discharge of semen; whitish discoloration of urine; feelings of weakness and exhaustion" (Hughes, 1985d: 479).

Since the subjects of masturbation, wasting semen, and possible impotence plus the above symptoms postulated for *dhat* or *jirjan* are difficult to investigate and probably vary regionally, this whole complex of beliefs, practices, and illness, both physical and psychological, cannot be defined as a Culture-Bound Syndrome. Associated with the fear of wasting semen is the problem of sexual release, especially in the form of masturbation, which has been tabu in numerous societies. As Carstairs (1958: 72, 263) pointed out and as we occasionally observed in the village, children learned about sex to some degree from observation and through erotic stimulation early but secretly (R. Freed and S. Freed, 1981: 67–68, 82, 99–100). Masturbation was condemned as wasting semen, especially in adult life. From the point of view of Hinduism it is also bad karma. Thus, although young men, who were not yet mated with their wives, might seek release by masturbation, they suffered guilt and anxiety. Lifelong celibates and widowers would have somewhat similar problems (cf. Freud, 1965: 80–87 on masturbation; Paris, 1992; cf. Chap. 15 of this text for a discussion by A. V. Rao, 1983).

SUMMATION

The case of Insider and the Outsiders provides a further example of the ghost of a deceased first wife haunting the second mate, a wife or levirate spouse, her infants, and other members of her family. Insider's family members suffered no possessions, as the ghost of The Lady was believed to be benevolent toward her surviving son, but not toward her husband's second wife, who, when widowed, married again and left Insider to be raised by his grandfather. The Lady, who haunted the Outsiders, symbolized the relations between Insider and the Outsiders.

The foregoing cases of the Bairagi Mendicant Priests, Lohar Blacksmiths, and Gola Kumhar Potters are examples of the same motif, namely, that the ghost of a first wife may continually haunt the second mate and her children, sometimes causing her and/or one of her infants to die. In the case of the Gola Kumhars, two sons of the Outsiders suffered from ghost possessions by The Lady shortly after they had been wedded but before they could be mated. Mating deferred until a young man was employed constituted a change in custom and contributed to the possession and ghost illness of males, as was pointed out in the case of two Brahman males (Chap. 12: Fence Sitter's son in The Families of Progenitor and Gentle Soul; Chap. 14: Welder in Ghost of Whose Daughter). Young males might be disturbed for reasons other than those associated with delayed marriages or a too long delay from the wedding to Gauna, and their responses do not in all cases involve ghost illness or possession. Forceful ran away and enlisted in the army, as did Loafer; Hippie ran off after failing his examinations. Tippler went through a number of complex emotional states and various responses when he failed his examinations and was to mate with his first wife: he ran away, had an accident and was hospitalized. Then he murdered his first wife and later became an alcoholic. Young Groom also murdered his first wife. The mental states of Tippler and Young Groom, both Jats, should be classified as abnormal, but no one ever said that after murdering their wives they were possessed by their ghosts (Chaps. 13, 14, 15).

These cases of the Bairagis, Lohars, and Potters again point out the ways in which ghost beliefs, ghost illness, and possession are related to biological, cultural, environmental or ecological, and psychological causes. In the Bairagi case, Watchman's first mate and her infants died during the influenza and plague epidemics and became ghosts. Fearful hurt her knees when she was pilfering fruit and later sprained her wrist, the sort of mischances made more likely because she was upset and distracted by the separation of her joint family. She was possessed by a male and a female ghost, Handsome and Delicate Flower. Jolly, the granddaughter of Fearful and daughter of Family Man and Atheist I, was possessed by the ghost of Tippler's first wife when she attained menarche before first mating. Delicate Flower, an epileptic, whom Fearful sold to an old man, died of "Fever," possibly complicated by the stress of marriage. Fearful's brother, Handsome, was frightened by the ghost of Cat Woman, who appeared in his dream. His death was attributed to this ghost. Fearful's troubled family relations, poverty, and her guilt from bad actions contributed to her possessions. Her daughter-in-law, Atheist I, did not suffer from ghost illness, although she and her husband were very poor. Jolly was possessed, no doubt, as a result of early conditioning by Fearful, living near Tippler, and having seen his first wife when she was a small child, as well as from the stress of adjusting to physiological changes at menarche and marriage (R. Freed and S. Freed, 1985: 164–169).

In the Lohar case, Difficult suffered from the ghost of her husband's first wife. She also had health problems, which contributed to her estrangement from her husband. She reported the cases of her son and daughter who suffered from ghost illness as a result of their dreams of female ghosts and of drowning in a well. She conditioned her children to fear ghosts and ghost illness brought by Fever, which could be fatal. She and Fearful, who had similar problems, told and frequently retold stories about female ghosts who haunted the village, especially the ghosts of first wives who died tortured in childbirth, committed suicide, or were drowned by their husbands in village wells. Difficult herself was haunted by the ghost of Sorrowful's first mate, and she and other villagers believed that the female ghosts of first wives had seized the soul of Urbanite's first wife and second infant son, causing them to die. The question also arose as to whether Difficult's negligence during delivery and seclusion of her daughters-in-law and other relations with them contributed to the death of Urbanite's first wife and second infant and to the death of Clerk's infant son, and whether her belief in ghosts provided an escape from her guilty conscience.

The possessions of the Outsiders' two sons after their weddings but before first mating revealed the same first- and second-wife ghost motif and introduced recent sources of stress, namely, the need to pass examinations and to find modern employment. The Outsiders had serious health problems, notable among them typhoid and malaria during the epidemics and an abscessed ear for one daughter in 1977–78. They were also poor and had more children than Mrs. Outsider could manage. One of their twin daughters died shortly after birth due largely to poverty and Mrs. Outsider's inability to care for twins when she had so many other children, household chores, and had to help her husband to make pottery. This death added to the belief in the inauspiciousness of twins.

These cases also indicate how some curers are selected. Treatment for ghost possessions in 1958 generally was by family, kin, and neighbors, and by Lord of Ghosts. Outsider's brother was fetched from as far away as Bikaner, Rajasthan, because he was a brother and because he had learned exorcism from an esteemed exorcist, given the title of a maharajah. For setting bones and sprains, Fearful went to a wrestler in the City of Delhi. In 1977–78, although Home Trained was most often called for curing within the village, the Outsiders went to a Catholic dispensary in a nearby town for some medical problems and to Illusionist or New Priest to exorcise ghosts.

CHAPTER 21: BREAKUP OF OLD BRAHMAN LANE

The gathering and analysis of ethnographic information is often an odyssey in the exploration of human behavior, as proved to be the case for the Brahmans who lived in Old Brahman Lane. To understand the geographic dispersal and the readjustments of interpersonal relations of the compact group of families resident in Old Brahman Lane in the 1950s required census data, geneologies, drafting kinship charts, a knowledge of the personalities of the chief people who influenced the breakup and the significant events in their lives, changes in village culture from the 1950s to the 1970s, and the great importance of ghosts as motives for the various changes in residence and adjustments of inter- and intrafamily relations. Information from the 1950s was essential for understanding the situation in the 1970s when all the ramifications of the breakup were revealed. The main problems were widow remarriage, adultery, illicit pregnancy, murder, and numerous ghosts.

The Brahmans of Old Brahman Lane claim to be descendants of the first settlers in Shanti Nagar, but the assertion is disputed by the Jats, who seem to have the stronger position (Chap. 4: History of Region). In any case, the ancestors of these Brahmans are the first of their caste to have settled in Shanti Nagar. In 1958, these Brahmans formed three lineages designated: (1) Merchant, Muslim, Priest, (2) Three Brothers and Old Bachelor, and (3) Old Grandfather. Their earliest remembered ancestors date to the end of the 18th century or the beginning of the 19th century. At that time, the earliest departure from Old Brahman Lane took place when the father of Merchant in the Merchant-Muslim-Priest lineage moved to the west side of the village. One possible reason was that his agricultural fields were located there. However, the lineage kept its old house in Old Brahman Lane where Progenitor's father, the second son of Merchant's son, lived. In 1958 and 1978, Progenitor, his second wife, Fertility, and several of their sons still lived there (Append. III: Chart 1.1, Merchant's son, no. 4; father of Progenitor, no. 10; Chart 1.3. Progenitor, no. 21; Append. IV: Map 4, no. 17). The geneology of Three Brothers and Old

Bachelor is given in Chart 10.1; that of Old Grandfather, in Chart 10.2.

Although Progenitor, his second wife, Fertility, and their sons still lived in Old Brahman Lane in the late 1950s, his two sons by his long-dead first wife, Fence Sitter and Cowherd, separated from their father in 1958-59 and moved to the family cattle shed, located on the main Jat lane on the east side of the village. Progenitor had never done much for them, they were not interested in their half brothers, and the move put them at some distance from their old house where the ghost of Progenitor's first wife lurked and haunted Fertility and other family members. In the 1960s, Cowherd, who never married, died without issue and became a ghost. By 1977, this shed had been converted into apartments for Fence Sitter and two of his half brothers (Append. IV: Map 4, Lane II, no. 34; Chap. 12: Merchant's Descendants; The Families of Progenitor and Gentle Soul).

THE JOINT FAMILY OF THE THREE BROTHERS

In 1958, we were alerted to the future breakup of the joint family of the three brothers, Senior, Withdrawn, and Junior, during a census interview with Senior, the eldest brother and head of their joint family. Interviewed in the two-story building which he had recently built for the family, he said that parts of the structure were incomplete because he was waiting to see if the joint family would split. Another indication of the coming breakup was that Senior's eldest son, One Eyed, who had an eighth grade education and was a clerk in a brick factory located at some distance from Shanti Nagar, lived near his job with his wife, Strong Minded, and their children. Senior noted that Strong Minded was the widow of Dead Issue of the Merchant-Muslim-Priest lineage. This situation was not customary at the time and hinted at trouble. When viewed in cultural context, censuses generally provide information far beyond demographic data and may even provide clues as to what might happen. For example, both Senior and Withdrawn were widowers, which suggested the possibility that their wives had become ghosts, which we later learned had happened. Thus, the unsettling effects of family ghosts and the widow's remarriage could be potential causes of the dissolution of a joint family.

The joint family of three brothers had a number of problems. One was the persistent ostracizing of the family because of the marriage of One Eyed to Strong Minded, the widow of Dead Issue, who died about 1947 (Chap. 12: Dead Issue). Therefore, the couple and their children lived away from the village near the brick factory where One Eyed worked. Still part of the joint family, One Eyed kept in touch with his father, but by 1959 he considered separating from the family. The ostracizing affected all the members of this joint family.

The parents of the three brothers died around the time of the influenza epidemic (1918–19) (Append. III: Chart 10.1, Generations III, IV). Senior was born about 1893, Withdrawn in 1903, and Junior in 1908. They had no education. Junior wanted to go to school, but his sister-in-law, Senior's wife, who raised him after his parents died, would not let him. Withdrawn worked for a while in the City of Delhi to provide for the care of his father's younger brother and sister. These two siblings died without issue and became ghosts. By 1958, the three brothers, aged 65, 55, and 50, lived in Shanti Nagar, farmed, and took care of their cattle.

The brothers had married sisters, but the wives of Senior and Withdrawn died in 1943. Senior's wife left two surviving sons, One Eyed born in 1923, and Talkative, in 1928. Withdrawn's wife died of tuberculosis when he was 40 years old. No one in the joint family told us about the tuberculosis until Withdrawn revealed it in 1978. Withdrawn's only child, a newborn son, died before the mother. Withdrawn did not remarry because of his age. The parents of the three brothers, Withdrawn's infant son and wife, and Senior's wife were believed to have become ghosts (Append. III: Chart 10.1, Generations III, IV, V).

Shortly after the death of Dead Issue, One Eyed married Strong Minded. By 1958, they had four children. A number of Brahman women mentioned that he and Strong Minded lived away from the village because Brahmans frowned on widow remarriage, not acknowledging the Hindu Widow Remarriage Act of 1856 (Derrett, 1978: 81, 211). The couple endured persistent stress from caste and lineage disapproval, augmented by the belief that one-eyed individuals are inauspicious. One Eyed's father, Senior, could not arrange a marriage for him because of his defect. The self-arranged marriage saved One Eyed from the lonely life that Withdrawn led after the death of his wife but left a blot on the family as a whole. Dead Issue had a one-eyed brother who never married and died without children about the same time as Dead Issue died. His sorry fate may have contributed to Strong Minded becoming fond of One Eyed and marrying him. Thus, the family's situation was difficult. Further, Strong Minded added two other ghosts to the contingent of ghosts believed to be haunting this family, the ghosts of her first husband and their infant son (Chap. 12: Dead Issue).

After One Eyed's mother and his aunt, the wife of Withdrawn, died in the first half of the 1940s, only one wife remained in the household, the wife of Junior, who in early 1943 was 19 years old and had born her first child, a son, three years earlier. One Eyed was the same age as Junior's wife, and his younger brother, Talkative, was 14 years old. The deaths of the two older women, especially the wife of Senior who had ruled the women in the household, left the burden of women's work on Junior's wife. In the last part of 1958 at the age of 35, she headed the women in the household, but Mrs. Talkative, 28, and Strong Minded, 31, were too close to her age for them to remain subordinate. Their similar ages in time also contributed to the breakup of this joint family. However, One Eyed's marriage to a widow which resulted in ostracism by other Brahman families in Old Brahman Lane, including the part of the Three Brothers and Old Bachelor lineage headed by Old Bachelor, and differences in individual temperaments and life styles were important too. In 1959 One Eyed no longer sent money home because he was considering breaking off from the joint family.

The village fear of the inauspiciousness of a one-eyed man may have been inspired by aversion to persons who are disfigured, lame, or have any defect (Krappe, 1964: 210). In

Hindu belief, physical defects are due to bad actions in past lives, which bring misfortune. The story of Sukra, who tried to prevent Bali from giving land as a charitable act, and, therefore, was blinded in one eye by Vishnu, reinforces the belief. The marriage of Strong Minded and One Eyed not only violated the ban on widow remarriage in Brahman castes but also flouted the belief that marriage to a one-eyed man is best avoided.

A Brahman woman, not a member of the lineages of Old Brahman Lane, gives an apt description of the attitude of Brahmans to widow remarriage in 1958. She said:

In the lane where the oldest Brahman settlers live, a widow, who today has four children, three sons and one daughter, remarried when her first husband died. She had born a son for her first husband; the son also died. There was no living brother of the husband, but marriage to a brother would not have been approved since Brahmans do not take widows as levirate spouses as do the Jats. . . . She made a mistake when she remarried because she lost the property from her husband. It went to the next of male kin. This widow and her first husband lived separately; no other close male relatives were alive. They owned a little over three acres of land and two big houses. All this property went to Raconteur and his brothers, and to Progenitor and Gentle Soul when the widow remarried. She should have lived by herself. Her husband died about 1946 to 1947, and the first child from her second marriage was born eleven years ago.

If any Brahmans enter into a marriage like this, other Brahmans do not offer the hookah to them or eat with them. Among Jat widows, however, the widow may be taken by another man. This widow's second husband had never been married because he is one-eyed. A Brahman widow is not supposed to marry again. If a young girl has been married only five to six days and the husband dies, then the parents can arrange another marriage for her, but this woman had been married a number of years and had born a child who died. Her parents told her that they would try to remarry her

elsewhere; but she said, "No, I want to go to this man."

This informant was bothered by the somewhat contradictory evidence of karma reflected in her own life as compared to the lives of Strong Minded and One Eyed. All four of her children died as infants. She was proud of her good actions, and yet she suffered four tragedies. In contrast, One Eyed and Strong Minded who had four children, including a son, had ignored the ban on widow remarriage and the evidence of bad karma for both of them. One Eyed was inauspicious due to his one-eyedness, a result of bad actions. His wife was inauspicious because she was a widow before she married him. Widowhood was interpreted as due to bad karma too. To make matters totally inexplicable, the inauspicious couple was blessed with children, among them an ardently desired son. Although people who believe in karma and rebirth never know the sum of their own actions in past and present lives, they nonetheless feel that proper current behavior ought to have an appropriate reward in the present. These contradictions disturbed our informant who led a well behaved life and yet her children died.

By 1958, One Eyed's younger brother, Talkative, had been married some years. His wife had borne four sons before 1958, all of whom died in infancy. A fifth son survived and was three-and-one-half years old in 1958. He had been nursed by Mrs. Junior. She was able to nurse the infant because she had not weaned her three-year-old son. When the infant was born, Mrs. Talkative was sent to her parents for a year while Mrs. Junior nursed him (Append. III: Chart 10.1, Generations V and VI).

When several infants die because their mother has difficulty nursing them or because they cannot or will not take her milk, people may blame the mother for different reasons: that a ghost is attached to her and is trying to take the souls of her infants, or that she is evil and wants her children to die (Kakar, 1982: 146–148; Gray, 1982: 220–221, 234–235; R. Freed and S. Freed, 1985: 134, 136–137). Because of the fear about naming a ghost, none of the members of this joint family in 1958 named the ghosts of the wives of Senior and Withdrawn, nor the ghosts of two other Brahman women, Progenitor's and Luck's first wives, who could have been the ghosts who took away the souls of Mrs. Talkative's infants. Neighboring Bairagi and Lohar women identified them indirectly by their family relationships and said why they died and became ghosts (Chap. 12: The Families of Progenitor and Gentle Soul). Within the joint family of the three brothers, information regarding the deaths of Withdrawn's and Senior's wives, the deaths of Mrs. Talkative's children, and details about Mrs. Talkative's inability to nurse her children were hinted at only vaguely. The implication was that Mrs. Talkative had been sent to her parents so that Mrs. Junior could nurse the fifth Talkative infant. It was believed that if Mrs. Talkative nursed her fifth infant son, he too would be seized by one of the ghosts and die because the deaths of the Talkatives' infants were most often blamed on the ghost of Withdrawn's wife. Behind the strategy of sending Mrs. Talkative away was the belief that the ghost would be fooled by her absence and would not know that her infant was being nursed by Junior's wife. In any case, the infant was the first child of the Talkatives to survive.

Among the members of the joint family who in 1958 lived in one household, five were adult males, one of whom has the pseudonym Dr. John, the 19-year-old eldest son of Mr. and Mrs. Junior. He was completing his training as a compounder and his wife was pregnant for the first time. After he became a compounder, the villagers appended Doctor before his name. Only three adult women were household members, Mrs. Junior, Mrs. Talkative, and the young wife of Doctor John. Mrs. Talkative had one surviving son; the Juniors, in addition to Doctor John, had a six-year-old son and a daughter age ten. Two other infants were added to the household when Mrs. Talkative bore her second surviving son, Gabbler, in early 1959, and Mrs. Doctor John bore her first child, a son, in the spring of the same year. Thus, by 1959 the three women took care of five children and five adult men. The two elderly, widowed brothers, Senior and Withdrawn, did not do heavy fieldwork, such as plowing, but Senior supervised the work and Withdrawn tended the cattle. As was customary, the women did the housework, cooking, took care of the children, and worked in the fields gathering fodder and helping with the planting, weeding, and harvesting (Append. III: Chart 10.1, Generations IV, V, VI).

In 1959, tension in the family mounted due to Mrs. Talkative's nursing difficulties with her second living infant, financial problems, and the two older men, who were often underfoot in the house. Withdrawn in particular disturbed the women, for he tormented the first surviving son of Talkative by tickling and hugging him and trying to obtain affection from the child. Teasing and tickling may be a form of play between an elderly man and a small boy, but if the child dislikes and fears the man, the situation becomes difficult. We noticed that Talkative's small son was reluctant to hug Withdrawn, who nevertheless persistently bothered the boy. Because of Withdrawn's behavior and the ostracizing of One Eyed's family, Talkative often spoke of separating from the joint family. Withdrawn worried because he did not know what would happen to him if the family divided. During this period, Withdrawn suffered ghost possessions. Shortly thereafter he was persuaded (or compelled) to move from the main house of the joint family. He then lived by himself in the family's cattle shed, which was located adjacent to the Sweepers' compound at the corner of the crossroads with the entrance on the main lane leading to the grave of the Headless Sweeper.

WITHDRAWN'S POSSESSIONS IN 1959

After Withdrawn was possessed early in 1959 and then isolated in the cattle shed, he had a series of ghost possessions. Two Brahmans, High Strung and Plowman, exorcised the ghost. High Strung, well known for exorcising ghosts among the Brahmans, was said to be sensitive to their presence. The two men obtained a liquid from Sanskritist, the Brahman in a nearby village who exorcised ghosts. The liquid was poured on a fire to produce fumes that would drive out the ghost. Early in our fieldwork, Plowman claimed not to believe in ghosts, so on this occasion he said at first that the smoke drove away bad winds possessing the person. High Strung, in order not to offend Plowman, said, "The winds get disturbed and the man starts talking crazily so people say the ghost has come." Plowman's father's elder brother, Snakebite Curer, disagreed, saying that ghosts do indeed come and possess people and that Withdrawn was possessed by Breadstuff, a Sweeper. Sanskritist, who officiated at weddings and birth ceremonies in Shanti Nagar, came to assist in exorcising the ghost. He related this incident:

In my village three or four years ago the daughter-in-law of a Potter was possessed by the ghost of a Sweeper man who had been killed in the fields outside the village. The daughter-in-law went to the spot unknowingly and ate something sweet so the ghost of the man who had been killed attached himself to her. This possession took place three years ago. The ghost spoke through her. He said he had been murdered and robbed and accused his brother. He also talked through the girl about a number of events which the girl could not possibly have known about because she was a new bride in the village. To exorcise the ghost they called an exorcist from Bowana. He took the ghost away.

After this statement Plowman admitted that Withdrawn had been possessed by a ghost (Chap. 18: Brahmans as Exorcists and Curers).

A series of interviews during the next month revealed various viewpoints and stories about Withdrawn's possessions. Loafer, the husband of Bruised Flower, in a group conversation said, "Withdrawn was possessed by a ghost last night. The ghost has been visiting him for 17 days. High Strung smoked him with incense and helped to drive the ghost away. The ghost was the Headless Sweeper."

The discussion then drifted to comments about ghosts and corpses. A carpenter from out of the village, who was working on a door frame, said, "The soul migrates into another life, so say the Hindu laws, and the body is burnt. Where then do ghosts come from? It is all nonsense." Mrs. High Strung said, "I have seen corpses rise up with life in them." She stood by her statement in the face of mild disclaimers from the men, despite the widely recounted tale of two men of the same name from the Chamar and Jat castes who were

dying at the same time. As related earlier, the Chamar died and his soul went to the far off Himalayas. When his body was about to be cremated, it was found that the Jat was the one whose time had come because the Chamar's big toe wiggled and he rose from his death bed (Chap. 9: Life, Death, Soul).

Two Jats, Nutmeg and Dissembler, denied most vigorously the existence of ghosts. Dissembler claimed that something was wrong with Withdrawn's feet which caused him to have a fever and become delirious. Nutmeg, though in all likelihood ignorant of Freudian theories, loved to gossip about the relationship of the sexes. He claimed that Withdrawn was possessed because he had no wife and asked Mrs. Junior, his sister-in-law, to have sexual relations with him, but she turned him down. Adulteress, a wife in Old Grandfather's lineage who lived near Withdrawn, said, "Withdrawn was possessed by a ghost, but I no longer talk with the women in that house because I was the one who contributed to Illusion's downfall. In fact, I don't talk to anyone anymore." (Chap. 15: Illusion's Death; Append. III: Chart 10.2, Generations IV, V).

Talkative and Junior contributed their opinions. Junior, Withdrawn's younger brother, said, "Withdrawn was ill for a number of days." When he was asked whether the illness was ghost illness, he replied, "I am not sure." He was also asked whether he had heard that a man named Breadstuff was the ghost. Junior answered:

I am not sure although a voice shouting that name came out of Withdrawn. Breadstuff was a Sweeper from another village, who was somewhat out of his mind and who lived in this village for some time; then he died in a neighboring field. But I do not really know whether he possessed my brother. We fetched some medicine from a Brahman in the next village and put it into Withdrawn's nostrils and eyes. Then he was all right.

Talkative, Withdrawn's nephew, said that Withdrawn was definitely possessed by the ghost of a Sweeper from a more distant village. Withdrawn had been eating halva and other sweets when the Sweeper's ghost seized him. Talkative also said that the same illness had overtaken Withdrawn 15 or 20 years previously. Approximately 15 years coincides with the time following the deaths of Withdrawn's and Senior's wives in 1943. Although Talkative did not go into detail about the possessions, he talked obsessively because he had been temporarily laid off and was worried about the permanency of his job. Also, Gabbler, his second son, had been born a month previously, and Talkative and his wife were afraid that the ghost of Withdrawn's dead wife would seize the soul of the infant as had been the fate of four of their earlier sons.

Policeman, the 18-year-old son of Progenitor, who lived with his father near the joint family headed by Senior (Append. IV: Map 4: nos. 17, 18a), asserted that Withdrawn suffered from ghost possessions from time to time ever since an old woman had died in his household because of some dispute. Policeman said, "I was just a child then and do not know the details, not even whether the woman was murdered or committed suicide." This woman was Senior's wife.

High Strung, who was born in 1922 after the death of the Headless Sweeper, contributed the following information based on what he had learned from others and from Withdrawn's possession as to the identity of the ghost possessing Withdrawn:

The Headless Sweeper was moving from place to place when he died. When he came to the village, there was an epidemic. Whoever dies an unnatural death—is run over by a train, struck down with a club or some other way—becomes a ghost. The soul cannot find a home in the next life. Death in an epidemic is unnatural. The ghost of the Headless Sweeper enters many people in this village. Withdrawn has been attacked before by this ghost. Forceful's younger brother, Ill Fated, was also possessed by the Headless Sweeper. More than 20 years ago he died of this possession. However, the Headless Sweeper did not enter anyone after Ill Fated's death until he possessed Withdrawn. The Headless Sweeper was buried on the lane going out on the northeast side of the village. His ghost likes to eat sweet things. Withdrawn ate *khir* [rice pudding] and other sweets and

then went along the lane where the headless ghost was buried so the ghost entered him [Append. IV: Map 4, XX]. Not everybody who has eaten sweets and passes that grave is possessed. Some people are more receptive to ghosts than others. The way to turn the ghost out is to smoke the man with medicine. If this particular medicine is not available, one may also smoke him with pig's excreta. He was inside Withdrawn for ten days. The ghost asked for the Chuhra's hookah. They offered the Brahman hookah, but the ghost would not smoke it. He insisted on the Chuhra hookah; then they knew the ghost of the Headless Sweeper had entered him. The ghost also shouted his name and said he wanted sweet things to eat—brown sugar, rice pudding, and candy. The ghost claimed that Withdrawn ate sweet things but had not given him any. No sweets were offered the ghost, for that would have tempted him to stay permanently. Withdrawn has been treated a number of times. Now the ghost has gone, but we cannot be sure he will not return. [Chap. 16: The Headless Sweeper in a Line of Hereditary Exorcists]

Thus, High Strung and Old Codger perpetuated the belief that Withdrawn and Ill Fated were possessed by the ghost of the Headless Sweeper. As indicated above, the Headless Sweeper's grave was on Lane II beyond the cattle shed in which Withdrawn was isolated. The cattle shed was located at the crossroads, another place where ghosts were believed to gather. The Sweeper's compound was situated on Lane I near Withdrawn's cattle shed. The clustering of these places contributed to the belief that the Headless Sweeper's ghost still haunted the village (Append. IV: Map 4, Lanes I, II, III; CR, XX).

Relatively isolated from his family and community, Withdrawn lived in the vicinity of the Sweeper caste. That two Sweepers, Breadstuff and the Headless Sweeper, were implicated in Withdrawn's possessions is therefore hardly surprising. Family members never named the female ghosts who were former members of Withdrawn's family as causing his possessions. The identification of the ghosts as men rather than women followed the general village position at the time that men were only possessed by the ghosts of men, if they admitted to having been possessed at all, or were so diagnosed by villagers or exorcists. Withdrawn, a Brahman, who was born in 1903 and grew up in a time when the low castes were called Untouchables and when members of his family died from dread diseases, must have been deeply affected by their deaths and was greatly disturbed by his proximity to the Sweeper compound, the crossroads, and the grave of the Headless Sweeper.

The other part of the Three Brothers and Old Bachelor lineage consisted of one family: a Brahman widow, Pure Goddess, and her three sons and two daughters, headed by Old Bachelor, a lifelong celibate and the brother of the widow's dead husband. When her husband died in the 1930s, she had three sons, one of whom had a twin, a sister who died at three years of age. Her father wanted to sell her when she was born because twins, especially brother-sister twins, are considered inauspicious, as in the tales from the Mahabharata and the Markandeya Purana of Yama and Yami, twin brother and sister (Daniélou, 1964: 96, 132—133). To block this plan, Pure Goddess, who usually accompanied her husband in his government capacity as a *zilidar*, took all her children and returned to Shanti Nagar. With this background of celibacy and widowhood, the family strongly opposed the remarriage of Brahman widows and ostracized One Eyed and Strong Minded. In 1958, the Three Brothers and the Old Bachelor families lived just across Old Brahman Lane from each other (Append. IV: Map 4, nos. 16, 18a; Chart 10.1).

THE LINEAGE OF OLD GRANDFATHER

Serious misbehavior in 1958 by some members of the Old Grandfather lineage created problems not only for its members but for all families in Old Brahman Lane and contributed significantly to their dispersal in later years. At the time, the lineage had three families. Old Grandfather, 80 years old, headed a large joint family with his elder son, Householder, and Householder's sons and their families. Old Grandfather's younger son, Justice, had separated from his father. The third family was headed by Indecisive, a cousin of Householder and Justice (Appendix III: Chart 10.2).

Indecisive and Justice were married to sisters. Indecisive's wife fell ill and died. During the illness, her younger sister, age 14, came to Shanti Nagar to help. After her older sister's death, she was immediately married to Indecisive and her first child, a son, was born when she was 15. The seemingly hasty marriage followed soon after by the birth gave a vaguely disreputable air to the proceedings. Nothing was said directly, but the wife of Justice, after the death of her daughter, Illusion, dropped some veiled hints. In any event, the suggestion of impropriety foreshadowed later serious misbehavior (Chap. 15: Illusion's Death).

Indecisive's wife bears the pseudonym Adulteress not simply because of rumors of impropriety but because she was caught in the act. One day early in our fieldwork, we heard shouting from Old Brahman Lane and saw a crowd gathering. We ran to find out what was happening. Just before we arrived at the scene, Actor, a Jat, caught us in the lane in front of his house and invited us to have some hot milk, the token of village hospitality, for he did not want us to learn about something that would damage village prestige. Not wanting to be rude, we sat down. However, the shouting continued; we were dying of curiosity, managed to excuse ourselves, and rushed to where a dispute was raging.

Adulteress had been caught *flagrante delicto* with a Jat, a young handsome man whose face was red either with anger, embarrassment, or both, and who was arguing with several men. Our arrival probably served to calm everyone sooner than would otherwise have happened, for village prestige was at stake. Adultery is not taken lightly, especially if the woman is of a higher caste than the man.

What happened that day was characteristic of Adulteress. A year earlier, she had been beaten by the men of her lineage because of her adultery. That matters had reached such a pass brought discredit to Indecisive. Men are expected to control their households. If they fail to do so for whatever reason, they lose respect. Nonetheless, there were mitigating factors in Indecisive's case. He worked in the city and was seldom at home. He was born posthumously. His mother, who was inauspicious because she was widowed early in life, was thought to cast the evil eye. Moreover, Indecisive suffered from the defect of strabismus, which had a role in shaping his personality. The absence of a father, an inauspicious mother, and a physical defect provided little basis for the development of a strong personality. Indecisive was not a forceful man and generally tried to avoid trouble.

Adulteress was incorrigible. Possibly because of ill will toward Justice or perhaps just from thoughtlessness, she maneuvered her son and Illusion, the daughter of Justice, into an intimate relationship. She allowed him to see Illusion while she was bathing. This impropriety set off a sequence of events that culminated in the murder of the pregnant Illusion by her father, the ostracizing of Indecisive's family, and the haunting of Old Brahman Lane by the ghost of Illusion (Chap. 15: Illusion's Death). By the end of 1958, Strong Minded, One Eyed, Adulteress, and to a lesser extent Indecisive were being ostracized, and the possibility of ghost possessions augmented tense relationships. These factors, general crowding, and changes brought about by increased education and new forms of employment contributed to an exodus from Old Brahman Lane.

RELOCATION OF MEMBERS OF JOINT FAMILY OF SENIOR, WITHDRAWN, AND JUNIOR

From 1960 to 1977, several families or parts of families moved from Old Brahman Lane. First, Withdrawn was isolated in his family's cattle shed located at the crossroads of Lanes I, II, and III. It was not unusual for older men who had no wives to take care of them to live in a family's cattle shed, especially if they presented problems to members of their family. Withdrawn generally lived there alone, but whenever One Eyed visited the village he stayed with him. Senior had a building constructed that incorporated this cattle shed as the ground-floor apartment with its entrance on Lane II, later adding a second story with an entrance on Lane I. Junior and his family took over the second-

story apartment. One Eyed remained a part of the joint family but continued to live near the brick factory where he worked. On retirement in 1973, One Eyed and his family moved into the ground floor apartment of the new two-story building, and Senior joined them. Talkative's family remained in the old brick building that Senior had first built in Old Brahman Lane. At the same time, two cattle sheds had been built at a distance from the new house, one for One Eyed and Withdrawn, in which Withdrawn lived after One Eyed and his family along with Senior moved into the ground-floor apartment of the two-story building. Withdrawn was thus segregated from the household with its many children, and his meals were brought to him by Strong Minded. The other shed belonged to Junior and Dr. John (Append. IV: Map 4, nos. 2, 3, 43, 45). Until Senior died in 1975, he lived with One Eyed but was near his brother Junior and Dr. John. After his death, the land and other property of the joint family were divided.

Talkative with his wife and children remained living separately in the old house at the corner of Old Brahman Lane. When his eldest son married and the couple had children, he built an apartment for them which completed Senior's work on the second story of the building. Talkative worked in the city and did not want to be involved in the village problems. It did not matter to him that Indecisive and his wife, Adulteress, lived near him. Mrs. Talkative had not liked being sent away while Mrs. Junior nursed her first surviving son. She did not want to live in the same household with Mrs. Junior or Strong Minded. Further she did not want her family to be anywhere near Withdrawn. However, their next to eldest son, Gabbler, was lonesome in Old Brahman Lane and spent most of his leisure time with his patrilineal relatives: the sons of One Eyed; Dr. John's younger brother, Student Doctor; and Dr. John's eldest son, age 19, born the same year as Gabbler.

During the exodus of Senior's group to the northeast corner of the village, other families of Old Brahman Lane began moving to New Brahman Lane. The groundwork was laid earlier when cattle sheds were established there. Old Bachelor, Pure Goddess, and her three sons moved from Old Brahman Lane to New Brahman Lane to avoid Adulteress and also members of Senior's joint family because of the widow remarriage. They also needed more room for growing families. However, Story Teller, the youngest son of Pure Goddess, maintained the old building in Old Brahman Lane so that his sons might live there when they married. Therefore, he maintained a small path from New Brahman Lane to Old Brahman Lane to check the condition of the old building and to use it for storage (Append. IV, Map 4, Path 3).

Householder's group of families of the Old Grandfather lineage also moved, including Justice, Householder's brother, who blamed Adulteress for Illusion's pregnancy which ultimately forced him to kill her. Justice nonetheless suffered from having killed his own daughter, who had predictably become a ghost haunting the Brahman community. Eventually only the Talkatives, Progenitor and his family, and Indecisive and Adulteress remained in Old Brahman Lane.

During this period, One Eyed's family was flourishing. In 1977, when taking his family census, we first met him, a very pleasant man, who proved to be truly one-eyed. He was unable to open the lid of one eye and could not see with it. No one ever told us how One Eyed lost the vision of one eye. At the time, One Eyed's joint family numbered 18 people: Withdrawn, One Eyed, Strong Minded, five sons, ages 30, 25, 21, 16 and 12, one daughter, 17, the eldest son's wife with the couple's five children, 3 boys and 2 girls, and the next eldest son's wife and their two daughters. Two of One Eyed's unmarried sons, 21 and 16 years old, were engaged. Their double wedding took place in the late spring of 1978 immediately after the wedding of their 18-year-old sister who had been 17 at the time of the census (Append. III: Chart 10.1, Generations V and VI). Because One Eyed married a widow, arranging marriages for his children had not been easy until he found another large Brahman family with a similar problem. Thereafter, the marriages of the children were arranged between these families.

While we censused One Eyed's household, Strong Minded held her five-month-old granddaughter in her arms. Something

seemed to be wrong with the child's eyes so Strong Minded was asked about it because we wondered if it might be related to an hereditary trait from One Eyed. She replied that the child's eyes were fading. We asked what the family did for medical treatment. The answer was that Doctor John supplied them with medicine from his shop whenever they were ill. The five-month-old infant may have had congenital infantile glaucoma, but the information obtained from her grandmother made this a speculative diagnosis (Berkow, 1982: 2008, 2010).

In the 1977 census interview with Junior, he listed 11 people living in his joint family: Junior and his wife; their two sons, Dr. John, age 39, and Student Doctor (also known as Atheist III), age 25; Dr. John's wife and the couple's six children (4 sons, ages 19, 12, 5, and 3 years, and two daughters, 16 and 14). Doctor John's sister was no longer a member of the household, for she had married, had children, and lived with her in-laws in the City of Delhi. She had been a schoolteacher before her marriage (Append. III: Chart 10.1, Generations IV, V, VI).

Dr. John earned most of the income for his household while his father, Junior, supervised the farming of what little land they owned. The only time Doctor John was seen in the village was late at night. He and Lady Doctor owned a pharmaceutical shop in what had once been a village but had become a town of around 7500 to 8000 people. Student Doctor, Doctor John's 25-year-old brother, worked part-time in the shop as did Lady Doctor and Doctor John. The shop provided both Ayurvedic and Western medicine. In addition, Doctor John worked as a compounder in a government dispensary located in another town. This dispensary provided Ayurvedic treatment, which in recent years had been supplemented with Western medicine. Both places were within commuting distance of the village. Doctor John managed to work long hours because he had a motorcycle for traveling between his home, the shop, and the government job. The location of his apartment was convenient for his comings and goings.

The eldest son of Doctor John had finished higher secondary school and planned to attend Delhi University the following year. The next to eldest son, 12 to 13 years old, was in sixth grade and present during the interview. Junior said that this boy had been ill with Fever the previous night and had vomited so his father, Doctor John, gave him an injection. He was feeling better but was weak at the time of the interview. His illness was not attributed to ghost illness but was said to be due to eating sweet potatoes from the village shop and *singhara*, the thorny fruit of the water chestnut, *Trapaceae bispinosa* (Maheshwari, 1976: 164; Pathak, 1976: l085). The plant grew at the edges of the nearby village pond, which was filled with dirty, stagnant water and could easily have caused the illness. Dr. John's treatment is another instance of a compounder's application of popular pharmaceutical medicine. The pond was where the Brahman girl, Whose Daughter, drowned (Chap. 14: The Ghost of Whose Daughter; Append. IV, Map 4. Lane III, P).

We found that the majority of women, regardless of caste, generally worked hard to keep their houses and outdoor cooking places clean, but some women were poor housekeepers. In 1977–78 the quarters of Junior and One Eyed provided contrasting examples and one explanation for the separation of these families. Both families were extremely friendly and the children of the related families, including Talkative's, were constantly back and forth between the buildings. The quarters of One Eyed and his family were crowded, noisy, filled with flies, and very dirty, but the houses of Junior and Doctor John and of Mr. and Mrs. Talkative, who had remained in the old dwelling in Old Brahman Lane with the upstairs apartment for their married son and daughter-in-law, were clean and tidy.

Talkative earned only a small salary, but he and his family lived comfortably in the old house. In 1978, his eldest son, 23 years old, was married, worked in a factory, and the young couple had a one-year-old daughter. After Talkative's second surviving son, Gabbler, was born in 1959, Mrs. Talkative bore two more surviving children, a son, aged 15 in 1977, and a daughter aged 10. All four children were given as much education as Talkative could afford (Append. III: Chart 10.1, Generations V, VI, VII).

Education was one of the major changes which took place in the village from the beginning of the 20th century. It began slowly and at first involved only high-caste boys, but both educational attainments and the numbers of the educated increased rapidly from the 1950s. Boys and girls of all castes benefited. All children in both One Eyed's and Junior's families attended school. In contrast, Senior and his two brothers never went to school. One Eyed, son of Senior, was the first in his lineage to go to school; he completed eighth grade at a time when Hindi was written in Urdu script. Later he taught himself Devanagari script from his children's text books. Talkative, however, remained nonliterate although his wife learned to read and write in an adult education class held in the village (S. Freed and R. Freed, 1976: 46–51; R. Freed and S. Freed, 1981: 119).

MRS. DOCTOR JOHN, POLIO, AND KARMA

Although Mrs. Doctor John in the following interview (1978) did not mention ghost illness, her account of her son's illness and its cause indicates the importance of the effect of the sum of past actions on one's soul, which may result in ghost illness, among many other consequences. The interview began with Mrs. Doctor John describing the festivals celebrated by the family and naming their chosen deities. She said, "We do not worship Hanuman [the lieutenant of Rama Chandra], because we worship Shiva. In a house where Devi [the goddess Durga, a consort of Shiva] is worshipped, we worship Shiva, not Vishnu." Large lithographs of Shiva and Durga hung on the wall. As she said, where Shiva and Durga are worshipped, people do not worship Vishnu or the avatars of Vishnu, Rama Chandra or Krishna, as their chosen deities. The worship of Shiva in this family provides another example of the deity's association with disease and curing, for Doctor John was a compounder and curer.

During this interview, two of Doctor John's children were present: a daughter, age 14, who had Fever, and a small boy, who was between three and four years old. A third person, the 19-year-old son of Doctor John, wandered in and out (Append. III: Chart 10.1, Generations V, VI). The small boy, who was watching our research assistant, a large, heavy man, suddenly said to his mother, "Get the pen of that fat man who is sitting there." His mother laughed and said, "In the evening this boy tells his father, 'Sister-fucker, why don't you bring me a watch.'"

Mrs. Doctor John then said:

We do not scold this boy because his heart is weak. If we scold him, he turns blue. On Diwali less than two years ago, this child had Fever and was wandering around in water. He had some contact with air [*vayu*] and was paralyzed below the waist. Now he can walk all right. When this happened to him, all the doctors refused to help him so I went by bus to a Nai [a member of the Barber caste] in a village two-and-one-half miles from here. The Nai provided indigenous medicine—leaves to be used in hot packs and also for bathing him and to be put in his drinking water. We carried out this treatment for six months. He was very little then, about two years old. He regularly drank the boiled essence of the leaves, but now he won't. He can't remember what happened to him because he was only two years old. At the time, his neck touched his chest; he could not speak for he had lost his voice. He had something similar to what is called paralysis, but the doctors called it polio, so now we do too. The Nai also massaged his body and said, "Do not move the boy." He could not walk or go outside to urinate or defecate.

This misfortune is not our luck; it is the misfortune of the boy due to the past actions of his soul. He does not like to leave me for long so he goes outside for about an hour and then comes back. He is not in school yet, for they will not admit him until he is five or six, but he reads a small booklet, a primary reader, which we bought in Delhi. It has an alphabet and pictures in it. By looking at the pictures, he can tell everything about the book. Some of the stories are about Ganesh [the elephant-headed deity and son of Shiva's consort, Parvati. Her son served as her guard. Shiva, who had been absent when he was born and for years afterward, did not know who he was and sent his men against the boy. They cut off his head. When Shiva saw Parvati's sor-

row, he severed the head of an elephant and joined it to the boy's body (Daniélou, 1964: 292; Dowson, 1950: 106–108)].

Mrs. Doctor John continued, "I learned many stories about deities from the books my children read. My father told many of them to me so now I tell the children some, and then they tell me some. Doctor John is so busy that he cannot tell them stories because he comes home late at night. However, the children do not go to sleep until he comes home." Mrs. Doctor John's description of her small son's illness, poliomyelitis, was a good description of this disease and its symptoms and the only case of polio that we encountered in Shanti Nagar.

Although poliomyelitis is almost worldwide and probably existed even before the written records or surviving art forms that depict the disease (Paul, 1971: Chap. 2), it was not recognized as a disease in all its forms until relatively late. The disease is most often contracted from persons carrying the virus, although the virus may be found in feces and in water. Since poliomyelitis is caused by an enterovirus, now known as *poliovirus*, it requires a host to multiply. The multiplication takes place in the human host by passing into the throat, tonsils, intestines, cervical, and other lymph nodes, the first line of defense against the disease. The disease may be stopped at this point and thereafter the person has immunity to poliomyelitis. This aspect of the disease has been labeled the *minor illness* of poliomyelitis, which occurs chiefly in young children and does not damage the central nervous system. The Nai Barber's treatment of the boy had some elements similar to biomedical therapy for polio patients (Berkow, 1982: 210–212).

One of many terms formerly used to identify the disease was infantile paralysis because originally the disease was believed to attack only infants and small children. If children do not acquire immunity from the *minor illness* or from vaccines to prevent polio, then they remain susceptible to the *poliovirus*. If the defense line does not fight off the disease, then the virus penetrates the central nervous system and causes lesions. The clinical signs are a stiff neck and back. When the lesions become extensive, weakness of muscles develop which depend for motor nerves on the brain and spinal cord, part of the central nervous system. Thus, the *poliovirus* is most destructive when it reaches the central nervous system, for once the motor nerve cells are destroyed they cannot regenerate. Paralysis is permanent. Because none of this was known before this century and then was discovered only gradually, children who died in infancy may have had polio. Infants who contracted the *minor illness* and recovered were simply considered to have had a slight illness and no one knew that thereafter they were immune (Paul, 1971: 2–9, 98–99, 100; Berkow, 1982: 173–174, Table 12–1, 206–207, 210–212; Append. I: Discoveries—1908–12, 1931, 1950s, Poliomyelitis; Descriptions—Poliomyelitis).

In view of the potential effects of polio and the description Mrs. Doctor John provided of her small son's case, he was very fortunate to have recovered without lasting disability. His case was probably the *minor illness*.

In India, clinical cases of infantile paralysis were reported in 1903 and thereafter. In 1949, an epidemic began in large cities, such as Bombay. As the incidence of reported cases grew, the disease became notifiable by law in various places, first in Bombay and Delhi in 1949. The polio vaccine was first administered in 1961 to children under five years of age in Andra Pradesh (Basu, 1966).

An interesting aspect of Mrs. Doctor John's description of the child's attack of poliomyelitis was that she said some wind (*vayu*), one of the three humors of the *tridosa*s (*vayu*, *kapha*, and *pitt*), attacked him when he had Fever and was wandering around in the water of the nearby pond. Villagers who believe in ghosts link the pond with ghost illness, for it lies between the crossroads and cremation grounds and is a place where people have drowned (Append. IV: Map 4, Lane III, P). The idea of air, *vayu*, causing the disease is Ayurvedic, but villagers may not distinguish between *vayu* (air or wind) and *hawa* (air which may be used for an apparition, as in *upri hawa*) (Pathak, 1976: 981, 1143). From a biological and ecological viewpoint, the nearby pond where children played and cattle were washed may have been a constant source of infectious disease.

From the statement of Mrs. Doctor John,

"We do not scold this boy because his heart is weak, and if we scold him he turns blue," the child may have had congenital heart disease and was what is popularly called a "blue baby." If he was, would he have been able to recover from polio? (Berkow, 1982: 429–434). Perhaps the heart problem was an aftereffect of polio. When Mrs. Doctor John stated that her son's illness was not the misfortune of his parents but the misfortune of the boy because of actions in his soul's past lives, she reflected the belief from which ghost illness stems. At the same time she gave lip service to Ayurveda when she said, "He had some contact with *vayu*," and to Western Biomedicine when she spoke of polio and described her son turning "blue." Thus, the beliefs and knowledge within this household combined the old and the new, but the belief in past actions affecting present lives and causing illness was strong, as will be seen in the following ghost possessions, which took place in the family of Junior and his son, Dr. John, as well as in the family of One Eyed and Withdrawn.

GABBLER AND STUDENT DOCTOR

In early spring of 1978 with the steady rise in temperature, malaria and ghost possessions were troubling the villagers. In One Eyed's house on March 29, we carried on a rambling, general conversation with Gabbler, the son of Talkative, and Student Doctor, the brother of Doctor John. It covered a number of topics in addition to ghosts. Gabbler started by describing his weekly worship of Hanuman, traditionally celebrated on Tuesday, when he fasted and placed *prasad* (an offering) of *churma* (a sweet) and ate some in front of Hanuman's picture in the puja (worship) room in One Eyed's house. The rite indicated that One Eyed's and Talkative's families were followers of Rama Chandra, Vishnu's avatar, for Hanuman is Rama Chandra's lieutenant.

Gabbler was having trouble furthering his education because his father had a small income, so he was considering military service. He bought a book to prepare for the entrance examination and sat twice for the test, having been caught cheating the first time. He did not say what happened the second time. Instead he switched the subject to ghosts and mentioned two recent possessions among the Chamars: Sunny, the daughter of Kin, and Immature, a new bride. He discussed the ghost attacks on Farmer (quoted in Chap. 22), a neighboring Arya-Samaj Jat, concluding with an observation about sweets: "If someone eats sweets and then crosses where four lanes meet, the ghost attacks. If one eats chilies, then the ghosts go away. If you go to the crossroads at one p.m. and eat sweets there, the ghosts will get you."

At the mention of sweets, Student Doctor jumped into the discussion:

I will give you some *ladoo*s [ball-shaped sweetmeats] and go with you and eat sweets there or at the cremation grounds and we will see what happens. Hindus believe in ghosts so you have to pay attention. There is a man in the nearby town whose profession is exorcising ghosts. He [Respected Leader] is a group captain in the air force, but he drives out ghosts. My brother's son [the son of Doctor John] formerly was affected by ghosts and remained unconscious for hours at a stretch. He would say, "I see a woman wearing a red sari who is going to take me with her." The family recognized his description as Vishnu Devi [the consort of Vishnu] so they took offerings to her and then took the boy to the River Yamuna. Then the ghost stopped coming in the boy. This is how people start believing such things. The boy was only four years old at the time [1970].

Young children do not believe such things, but as they grow older they start believing. I do not believe in such things or in Bhagwan because I am training to be a doctor. My only belief is that one should not cause harm to any living thing. That is my god. I come home at midnight and have to pass the cremation grounds. Once a man had died shortly before I arrived there, but I was not afraid and passed on. Another time I came home at 10 p.m. from my brother's shop where I work and heard the jingle of bangles ahead of me. I was a little afraid but carried on. After walking another 100 to 200 yards I saw a dog with two jingling bells on him. If I had not seen the dog, I would have thought that a ghost was there. That is how the ghost belief is cre-

ated. Seeing the dog cured me of believing in ghosts. I think my brother's son instead of being possessed by a ghost may have had some disease. Later the boy had fits [*daura*].

When Student Doctor was asked about a village woman, who had recurrent fits (*daura*), he said he did not know about her but said that his mother's brother's son, who was 17 to 18 years old, regularly had fits. He would make a sound and then fall unconscious. Student Doctor added:

The people who exorcise ghosts declared that a ghost had affected the boy so his family took him to be treated two to three days ago, but the boy has not had any relief. Before that he was shown to doctors, who said they could not help him, but they said he had epilepsy [*mirgi*, the fits associated with epilepsy]. They treated him for a long time but still there was no relief so the family decided a ghost was afflicting him.

Once my father's brother [Withdrawn] went to a wedding where he ate some *ladoo*s. Then he walked through the crossroads and was affected by a ghost. I saw it happen when he was here. He said, "I'm coming, I'm coming," and when red chilies were put in his eyes, he said, "I'm going, I'm going." These states still come to him rarely after two to three years. Then we give him the chili pepper treatment. Formerly, my father's eldest brother [Senior] performed the task; now my father [Junior] takes care of him.

Student Doctor was then asked whether there was any difference between Withdrawn's possessions and epilepsy. Student Doctor said, "Yes. The symptoms of epilepsy are that foam comes out of the mouth, the body stiffens and then falls." Student Doctor then made the following unsolicited statement:

Women have hysteria, which they call ghost possession. Usually this is because the husband does not satisfy the wife. In India sex education cannot be imparted even by a father to a son. A mother may tell her daughter about menstruation, but a father cannot speak to his son about it. In education in India even to the M.A. level students are not told anything about sex except for medical degrees. There are two medical degrees: MBBS and BAMS. The first is Medical Bachelor and Bachelor of Surgery, and it is the equivalent of a British medical degree; the second is Bachelor of Ayurvedic Medicine and Surgery. Ayurvedic degrees are preferred to allopathic because Ayurveda roots out the disease; allopathy only puts it down. The best Ayurvedic training is at the Tibbia College in Delhi. Previously they provided a degree known as BIMS [Bachelor of Intergrade Medicine and Surgery]. The students learned 50/50, Ayurvedic and allopathic medicine. This degree was given formerly because doctors could not practice without the help of allopathic medicine because research in Ayurvedic medicine was not deep enough. Now through research Ayurveda has all kinds of medicines available so the degree has been changed to BAMS.

Recently in Kerala, South India, medical students for the MBBS degree staged their third demonstration against the state government, whose Health Minister is a diploma-holder in Ayurveda because the government decided "to reserve two seats in the Master's degree course (M.S. Surgery) for teachers of indigenous Indian ayurveda stream of medicine and homeopathic medicine. . . ." The students stated: "We are against the prostitution of allopathy by mixing different streams of medicine." They contended that the mixing of homeopathy and Ayurveda would only encourage quacks (India Abroad, 1990, 20(33): 26). These students, contrary to Student Doctor, favored Western medicine (cf. Jeffery, 1988: Chap. 7, for an understanding of the complexities of the Kerala and national situation).

After explaining the difference between the two medical degrees, Student Doctor discussed his premedical training and his work with his brother, Doctor John, while studying for a degree. He seemed well informed about different colleges in the region, but he felt that in the villages children had no proper guidance about how to prepare for professions. Student Doctor believed that because children were not given sex education they went astray and then could not continue studying.

He ended by saying, "The great rishis [saints] in India have said that if one controls the five senses, one can be successful. But nobody pays attention to their teachings any more. People have become liars and cheats."

To some degree Student Doctor's comments were reminiscent of the interview in 1958 with Fence Sitter about types of ghosts (Chap. 10: Fence Sitter's Ambivalence). Student Doctor was also somewhat of a fence-sitter on the subject of ghosts, for although he denied their existence and said he was an atheist, he provided descriptions of the attack on Farmer and the possessions of Withdrawn, one of Dr. John's sons, and the possible possessions and fits of his mother's brother's son. He represented a new generation of young adults, somewhat skeptical of traditional beliefs but still conditioned by them. Based on his disavowal of Bhagwan, his alternate pseudonym is Atheist III.

WITHDRAWN'S INTERVIEW

As a result of Student Doctor's comments about Withdrawn's recurrent possessions, he was interviewed on April 4, 1978 in the cattle shed where he lived alone and spent most of his time. Although we were primarily interested in ghosts, the interview was open-ended as were most of our interviews, and Withdrawn moved from topic to topic. He spoke about the past, how much everything had changed, and dropped a subject or went on to another one when something bothered him. He began, "I have no children. I was married but my wife died 35 years ago. I was then 40 to 45 years old; I am now 75." By our reckoning, his wife died when he was 40. As indicated earlier, Withdrawn had a son who died at birth and became a ghost, shortly before his wife died (Append. III: Chart 10.1).

Apparently to avoid recalling the past, Withdrawn then talked about a variety of subjects: the land consolidation in the early 1970s, planting tobacco in a small plot that he owned, and the coming marriages of two sons and one daughter of One Eyed. To bring him back to his own life, he was asked why he had not remarried when his wife died. He responded:

I was working in the City of Delhi, my parents had died, and I looked after my father's younger brother and father's sister. But nobody took care of my remarriage after my wife died. I did not want to marry again. We had a son but he died; then my wife took sick and died. She had Fever; it was Old Fever. Old Fever is TB. Now there is a lot of TB in the village, but no one else in our joint family had TB when my wife died. Although many people in the village now have TB, no one names them. Some Jats but no Brahmans have it. If I were to name them, they would feel bad and fight with me.

When we asked him whether he believed in ghosts, Withdrawn replied:

Yes, I do. I recognize ghosts but now none are left. Previously there were many in the village. Now people do not recognize them. They used to say that a ghost stays in this place or that place, or this is the place where a sayyid stays, or where the dead reside. The villagers formerly recognized and worshipped at these places, performed holy ceremonies, and went to the Ganges River, but now all this has changed. Brahmans were once worshipped, but now all castes— Jats, Brahmans, Baniyas—mix freely.

Withdrawn continued about various changes until he began to wind down and we asked: "Did you ever see a ghost?" He replied:

No, but people used to talk about ghosts. Now they do not. Ghosts are air which moves around and enters a person, who then starts talking nonsense. People don't recognize them, but they are there. Over 20 years ago, I had a ghost enter me. Then I went to many *siyana*s for treatment. The *siyana*s asked the name of the ghost and scolded the ghost. The ghost damaged many people and cattle here in the village. A *siyana* came here to the low-lying land near the pond and across the road where the cremation grounds lie. With the help of mantras, he took the ghost away. I was possessed two to three different times. First I was attacked about 20 years ago and then again eight years ago. The last time the *siyana* captured the ghost. That *siyana* probably came from a distant village. A Jat brought him here because the *siyana* was

an intelligent man and knew the mantras needed to help the people against the ghost.

The Jat to whom Withdrawn referred was Old Codger, who himself said he brought a mullah from Palam to exorcise the ghost. However, Withdrawn did not mention his still recurrent possessions exorcised by Junior.

Withdrawn was then asked whether the ghost that bothered him was male or female and the ghost's name. He answered, "The ghost was a man, but I do not know his name. The people who heard the ghost speak from me said that he was an outsider, who came here, died here, and was buried. He was a Chuhra Sweeper, a Harijan. He was buried because in olden times Chuhra Sweepers were buried. Now all of them are cremated. I was 15 years old when this Sweeper roamed around here. Then I heard that the Sweeper had died and was buried in a pit. It happened about 50 or 60 years ago."

Withdrawn, born in 1903, was a youngster around the time that the Headless Sweeper died of bubonic plague. When Withdrawn was asked the cause of the Sweeper's death, he replied, "The Sweeper came from some unknown place. He was starving and thirsty and walked around for five to ten days. He might have come here with a disease. Then he died here after five to ten days." It is possible that Withdrawn, whose memory about the past was not accurate due to repression, confused Breadstuff, a Sweeper who was mentioned in his 1959 possessions, with the Headless Sweeper, who was also mentioned. He most probably attributed his possessions to the ghosts that the exorcists said possessed him.

At this point we were interrupted by some boys from One Eyed's family, who were cutting berseem (clover used for fodder). While they were working, they jumped around and played. Withdrawn said that this behavior was the boys' way of playing and being naughty but they did not harm the berseem.

When Withdrawn was asked how he felt when the ghost possessed him, he said, "I was embraced by the ghost. After that I was unconscious. Some people told me that a ghost had entered me and the ghost asked me for brown sugar, milk, and sweets, which I had eaten earlier. I had eaten these sweets and then had gone to a place where I fell ill. Then I became delirious by the time I returned home. The ghost asked me why I had eaten all the sweets and then came to the place where he had been buried without giving him any of the sweets."

When we asked Withdrawn where he lived when he was possessed by the ghost, he replied, "We were all living jointly on the corner of Old Brahman Lane." To a question about the identity of the ghost which possessed him the second time, he said that it was the same ghost as in his first seizure. "The way I know is that the ghost spoke inside of me and then others told me that it was the same ghost. I had taken my food and some milk and gone to the jungle [i.e., to the fields to relieve himself]. When I returned, I was attacked by the ghost who complained, 'This man has been given his food and there was no one to provide for me.' I had gone to the very place where the ghost tarried on the road running out from the crossroads." Then Withdrawn stated, "Now the ghost has left. The *siyana* caught hold of the ghost and took him away, and he has not returned. A Jat brought the *siyana* here because many people were troubled by this ghost. The Jat is Old Codger."

Withdrawn was then questioned about the past separations of his joint family. Withdrawn said, "We separated 15 years ago [ca. 1963]; then two years ago my elder brother [Senior] died." Although Withdrawn did not mention his brother's name, he hesitated before going further and then stopped, so we asked whether he was troubled when they separated. He responded:

No. I was bothered because I was alone and had to stay with one of my brothers so I stayed with my elder brother [Senior] and his family. They separated first, but Talkative and One Eyed stayed joint with me and my elder brother for five to six years. My younger brother [Junior] and his family lived apart. Then a second separation took place. Talkative remained in the old building, and my elder brother and his son, One Eyed, along with me took over one-half of the new building.

The first time I was possessed we all lived together; we were a joint family. My first possession took place when I had taken some cattle to the fields to graze. At that time the jowar [great millet] was ripe. I cooked some food in a pot in the fields, placed it on a leaf with brown sugar and ate it. Then and there I was attacked by the ghost. The field was in the low-lying land near the cremation grounds and pond.

However, Withdrawn did not indicate his possessions in 1943 after his wife's death or the possessions in 1959. The interview with Withdrawn was again interrupted by Strong Minded coming into the shed and reporting on Fever, ghost illness, and possessions in her household. She precipitately exclaimed:

Five people in the house have Fever. Some of them have Fever with chills. Home Trained is giving them medicine, tablets, and injections. Two of them are vomiting and have loose motions [diarrhea]. One of them at first did not have Fever. Suddenly he started vomiting and having loose bowels. My daughter-in-law also started vomiting and having loose motions only today. Both my daughter and daughter-in-law now have Fever, loose motions, and are vomiting. Two of my grandsons and one son have Fever. Another son was attacked by a ghost and he or the ghost has been talking nonsense. When we pulled his hair to frighten the ghost, he claimed that the ghost of a Chamar woman [Hairless] attacked him [Chap. 23: Hairless, Haunted, Immature].

Here Withdrawn interjected, "Some people go around in circles and have a bad day. It even happens to kings." When he was asked whether he thought it was a bad day, he replied, "For some it is good; for others, bad. For one who has Fever it is bad. The ghost of a Chamar woman has attacked him."

Withdrawn was a difficult person to interview, particularly when questions touched on his personality. After the interruptions by the boys and especially Strong Minded, the interview became even more difficult. Withdrawn characteristically avoided discussing ghosts and his relationships with them, but then victims of ghost possession do not remember what happens during their attacks.

Strong Minded, undeterred by Withdrawn's comments, said "The ghost is probably the first wife [Hairless] of Government Worker. After she died, she began attacking. She entered and possessed people." When Strong Minded was asked, "Why, so?," she answered, "Bhagwan makes such things. One cannot say where Bhagwan will send a soul and what the soul will become in the next life. Bhagwan can make an animal or anything. Now my son is doing nothing; he is just lying down. We smoked some incense over him when he was unconscious and talking nonsense. Previously he was not ill. He had gone to the fields to gather berseem and was preparing to go to school, but then at noon he took sick."

Both Gabbler and Student Doctor confirmed on the same day that Strong Minded's 16-year-old son had been possessed. A few days later, One Eyed's eldest grandson, age 10, described the possession of his 16-year-old uncle:

When he was possessed, they put ash on him, caught hold of his hair, and struck him. He was possessed by two ghosts: a male and a female. The male was a Chamar who would not tell his name; the female was also a Chamar and would not give her name. Even Gabbler could not control him [the victim] when he ran away. Gabbler slapped him, and then the ghost ran away. He had eaten some *ladoo*s and the ghost wanted them. He was also suffering from malaria and was sitting on his cot weeping. When they took him aside and gave him milk to drink, two ghosts entered him. I was present at the time. First the ghosts asked him who he was and then they entered his body. When Gabbler struck him, the female ghost left, but the male ghost said, "I won't go." When they hit him again, the male ghost said, "I am going."

This grandson was asked what he thought of the possession. He replied, "I was not scared." Then he said, "A ghost becomes air and enters the body. Now he is all right and will go to school." The main basis for deciding that ghosts possessed his uncle was hearing the ghost speak from him, "talking nonsense," and the victim, supposedly controlled by the male ghost, running away.

Of the five family members that Strong Minded reported as having fallen ill, all had

Fever, the index of ghost illness; in addition, some of them variously had chills, diarrhea, and were vomiting. Fever and chills at that time of the year could be symptoms of malaria. She reported a sixth member of the family, her 16-year-old son, as being possessed and talking nonsense, but the grandson of One Eyed, a nephew of the 16-year-old son, said he also had malaria, thus, a combination of ghost illness and possession. The low-lying location of the family house made it especially susceptible to invasion by mosquitoes. While diarrhea may have many causes, including malaria, it was most often due to bacillary or viral dysentery, which were endemic in the region. The crowded living conditions could have contributed to the spread of infections. Moreover, in preparing for the weddings, soon to take place, the older boys painted the house inside and outside, and the fumes of the paint may have caused diarrhea. In any case, all six people, including the 16-year-old boy who was possessed, could have been suffering from more than one malady.

Strong Minded's 16-year-old son, soon to be married, was the only one of the sick people who was possessed by the ghost of Hairless. His 21-year-old brother and 18-year-old sister, also soon to be married, were not possessed. Although ghost possession commonly afflicts people passing through major changes in their lives, with accompanying stress, by no means are all such persons affected. Susceptibility to ghost possession obviously involves many personality factors, somatic diseases, social and cultural variables, ecological conditions, and their complex interaction.

In 1977 and 1978, the peripheral low-lying parts of the village near ponds had more cases of malaria and ghost possession than the more central area on slightly higher ground. For example, the families of Junior and One Eyed lived near the stagnant, polluted pond, which was ideal for the breeding of mosquitoes as well as being a source of bacteria and viruses. On the western edge of the village where Troubled, the Jat, lived with his family, the field around his house had formerly been a pond and what was left of the pond was low-lying land infested with mosquitoes. Stagnant water was augmented by irrigation water let into the fields from the canal and tube wells and by drainage from the ubiquitous hand pumps. The resistance of mosquitoes to insecticides was a major factor in the comeback of malaria.

NEW BRAHMAN LANE

By 1977 seven families from Old Brahman Lane had buildings on both sides of New Brahman Lane. The heads of three of these households were sons of Pure Goddess and her husband. After the husband's death many years before 1958, Old Bachelor, his brother, took care of his widow, Pure Goddess, and her children. Together Old Bachelor, who died before 1977, and Pure Goddess scrimped in order to provide excellent educations for her three sons. The middle son, Police Inspector, obtained an M.A. and was a police officer in New Delhi where he lived, but he maintained a dwelling in New Brahman Lane where his mother, Pure Goddess, lived. The eldest brother, Trusted Employee, and his family lived next door. Trusted Employee's next to eldest daughter worked as a telephone operator and lived in his city apartment with her husband as did his daughter-in-law, also a telephone operator, with her husband, his eldest son. The youngest son of Pure Goddess, Story Teller, a Sanskrit teacher, had degrees for Sanskrit and political science. At times Story Teller was called upon to exorcise ghosts for the members of his lineage and the Old Grandfather lineage in New Brahman Lane. He did so by reciting mantras and putting ashes on the foreheads of those who were possessed (Append. IV, Map 4, Lane V).

The three families of Householder's four sons (two brothers lived jointly) also moved from Old Brahman Lane as did the family of Justice, Householder's younger brother. Justice smoked incessantly and suffered from lung cancer, for which he had been hospitalized more than once. His wife, the sister of Adulteress, never spoke to her again after the death of her daughter, Illusion (Chap. 15: Illusion's Death). Village Brahmans said Justice was suffering for his actions in his past and present lives, especially for the execution of his daughter, Illusion.

Householder died early in 1977 so the families of his sons were still mourning him. Earnest, Householder's eldest son, maintained the joint household with his widowed mother, Mrs. Householder, his wife, their children, and his city-employed youngest brother with his wife and children. The next-to-eldest son of Householder, who worked in the city, also lived on New Brahman Lane. His daughter, Beauty, had been possessed by the ghost of Illusion. The third family was headed by the next to youngest son. He had served in the air force, married a wealthy girl, become an accountant, and lived in the city but visited the village on weekends to maintain his property. Of Householder's four sons, only the two youngest were educated.

The three village-resident sons of Householder were married to three sisters. It is noteworthy that they had the same *gotra* as their wives. Ordinarily marrying within the same *gotra* is contrary to custom; however, in these cases, husbands and wives represented different *shasan*s of the *gotra* (R. Freed and S. Freed, 1980: 413). There were a few other cases of in-*gotra* marriage among the Brahmans. Pure Goddess came from the same *gotra* as her dead husband but a different *shasan*. In the family line of Teacher (Chap. 14: A Ghost Took My Son), two men had married women from the same *gotra*, but different *shasan*s. They said these marriages took place because it was difficult to find wives because Shanti Nagar was a small hamlet and in any case the other *shasan* had split off long ago. On the other hand, at least one of the men, Plowman, was very troubled about his in-*gotra* marriage, especially since his first wife and two children had died. He felt that this marriage (bad karma because of the violation of custom) affected his second marriage, which was with a woman of a different *gotra*, and caused the death of additional children because the ghost of the first wife took their souls. As a result, that line of Brahmans stopped marrying within the *gotra* even though the *shasan*s had long been separated geographically (Chap. 14: A Ghost Took My Son).

MRS. EARNEST

Mrs. Earnest, age 45, married to the eldest son of Householder, occasionally went into possession-trance. Her 50-year-old husband, an easy-going frank man, provided the following information about the possessions of his wife. He said that she was possessed by the ghost of his younger brother, who died at the age of two-and-one-half or three years. When his ghost entered Mrs. Earnest, he spoke through her. Before the ghost possessed her, Mrs. Earnest would sneeze four or five times; then she would fall unconscious for four to five minutes and at first could not speak. Villagers believe that when a person sneezes a ghost may enter through the nose (Saini, 1975: 84). Anyone in the family who needed advice or was troubled, asked the ghost what to do and the ghost replied, speaking through Mrs. Earnest. The ghost never harmed anyone, gave good advice, and never entered anyone except Mrs. Earnest. When the ghost came, he stayed for 15 to 45 minutes and then left. When Mrs. Earnest regained consciousness, she remembered nothing about what had happened. College Girl, who lived across the way, said that Mrs. Earnest was possessed by the ghosts of a Muslim and a member of the Householder line of descent. Earnest said that College Girl's report about the Muslim was unfounded.

When Mrs. Earnest went into possession-trance, either Illusionist, High Strung, or Story Teller was called to exorcise the ghost, depending on who was readily available. As stated earlier, Story Teller's knowledge of Sanskrit and being a Brahman imbued him with the power to exorcise ghosts, according to the Atharva-Veda. In 1959 Sanskritist, the brother-in-law of Story Teller who also taught Sanskrit, assisted in exorcising the ghost possessing Withdrawn.

Earnest's description of his wife's possessions was a first-hand, accurate report, according to other family members. He indicated that her possessions were not taken seriously, but rather that she had become a family prophet and advisor. Since the possessions did not last long and helped to solve domestic problems, they did not upset the family.

Mrs. Earnest had suffered emotional stress from a number of recent deaths. In 1977, the same year in which her father-in-law, Householder, died, Mrs. Earnest attended the 13th-day commemoration of the death of her third brother. She was particularly angry about the way in which the 13th day after death was traditionally celebrated and after returning to Shanti Nagar, she was angry, sad, and wept inconsolably. A number of people tried to comfort her and subdue her weeping. Her brother's recent death was the last of five that took place within a short time and deeply affected her: first her father, then two other brothers, her father-in-law, and finally her third brother. She proclaimed that something was wrong with Hinduism because at the 13th-day commemoration of the dead, relatives held a feast and ate sweets, to some extent making a joyous occasion of the rite. The 13th day after death is the day on which the soul of the dead, which becomes a ghost upon cremation, is expected to leave the cremation grounds, the village, and its former dwelling to journey to Yama in the Land of the Dead. Despite this general belief, Brahmans and other villagers also believed that the ghosts of members of their family or lineage, who had recently died, might visit the family, lineage, and village during the year of mourning.

Although this rapid series of deaths had not started Mrs. Earnest's possession-trances, for she had experienced them for some time, the stressful deaths may have resulted in specific recurrences. The loss of her own father and brothers also affected her sisters, who were the wives of two of her husband's brothers. With the recent death of her father-in-law, the shifting of family authority was resolving itself, for Earnest now headed the family. Technically, Mrs. Householder headed the women, but Mrs. Earnest appeared to be a person who knew her own mind and may have found it difficult to bend to her mother-in-law's will. Although we found Mrs. Householder to be a likable woman, daughters-in-law and mothers-in-law sometimes have different perspectives. In addition to Householder's death and the reorganization of family authority, a serious and continuing problem was that both Mrs. Earnest's sister and her sister's daughter, who lived in the same household, had speech defects which made communication within the household difficult. Through her possession-trances and her prophesies, Mrs. Earnest was able to restore harmony within the troubled household when it was most needed.

No other possessions were reported in

Shanti Nagar which resembled Mrs. Earnest's possession-trances. That the prophetic ghost was the small son of Mrs. Householder may have been due to her conversations about him with her daughter-in-law. Generally, it was believed that the soul of a child who died before the age of six years, the age of reason, did not remain a lingering ghost (Chap. 11: Becoming A Ghost).

Carstairs and Kapur (1976: 111–112) distinguished between voluntary and involuntary possessions in their study of Kota in Southwestern India (not the Kotas in the Nilgiri Hills). People whose possessions were brought on voluntarily would summon the spirit or ghost, become possessed, and then provide solutions to problems. Some of these people earned their living through their prophecies and advice; others gained in status. Carstairs and Kapur did not report any involuntarily possessed persons who had a spirit speaking from them to prophesy or offer advice. With regard to involuntary possessions, on the other hand, they reported evidence of family disharmony, as in the family of Earnest.

The case of Mrs. Earnest, with its prophetic ghost, raises the question of whether her possessions were voluntary or involuntary. Generally ghost possession in this village is believed to be involuntary. Bourguignon (1979: 245–262) based her useful distinctions between possession, possession-trance, and trance on her distributional study of possession states and used the following definitions: (1) Possession is due to a supernatural being seizing a person; from the point of view of the victim, the possession is involuntary. (2) Possession-trance is due to an individual voluntarily summoning a supernatural being to possess him or her. (3) Trance is also voluntary, but takes place without the participation of a supernatural being.

Although Earnest and other Brahmans spoke of Mrs. Earnest's dissociative states as ghost possession, they are best classified as possession-trance because they took place when family problems arose and she appeared to summon the benevolent ghost by sneezing four or five times. The sneezes alerted family members to Mrs. Earnest's oncoming possession and gave her their attention when the ghost, speaking from her, prophe-

sied and advised. The events preceding and during the possession followed a regular pattern of behavior. The ghost who entered Mrs. Earnest did not enter anyone else, and no one in the family feared the ghost, in contrast to the common malevolent, pathological ghost. Teja et al. (1970: 83–84) mentioned that one or more women in a group of females in Punjab become possessed and offer "solutions to problems." We have no evidence that Mrs. Earnest knew of such groups, but Punjab is within the intermarrying and kin network of Shanti Nagar.

I. M. Lewis (1978: 30–31, 44–46) found that in possession states, including trance, women more often than men were mediums for the dead due to their exclusion from authority and other spheres of life. Mrs. Earnest fits this pattern. Were it not for her mother-in-law, she would have been the senior woman in the household to rule the other women and bring about harmony. Lewis's finding that men are usually possessed by the ghosts of women, and women by male ghosts might fit this case since the ghost was male. However, the cross-sexual tendency described by Lewis seems to be a stereotype, just as was the opposite declaration expressed in Shanti Nagar in 1958–59 that male ghosts possessed males, and female ghosts, females. Despite this village stereotype in the 1950s, we have shown that individuals may be possessed by ghosts of either sex. The stereotype of the 1950s was tied into the social segregation of males and females due to the custom of purdah. However, even in 1958, one recently married young Potter man was possessed by the ghost of The Lady. By the 1970s purdah had been eased, and more possessions by the opposite sex were reported.

BEAUTY

The information about the possessions of Beauty, the daughter of the next to eldest son of Householder, was obtained from her grandmother, Mrs. Householder. Beauty had been wedded when she was ten years old. Because of her youth, she had not gone to her husband for first mating. In the meantime, her husband contracted tuberculosis and entered a tuberculosis hospital not too far from Shanti Nagar. Beauty's mother, therefore, took his meals to him as was often the case for villagers who were hospitalized. Despite the hospitalization, the boy died. After his death when the widowed Beauty was 12 years old, her ghost possessions began. The ghost attacking her was identified as the ghost of Illusion, whose father, Justice, lived next door to Beauty (Append. III: Chart 10.2). Mrs. Householder said:

My granddaughter was about 12 years old when she was first possessed. When she was in school, she would be attacked by the ghost, fall unconscious, and someone would then pick her up and bring her home. When the ghost seized her, we slapped her, had her smell pig droppings, and then had her treated by a pandit who was also a *siyana*. He treated her by reciting mantras. He even gave his own blood to the ghost to drink; he cut his wrist to do so. The ghost troubling my granddaughter was the daughter [Illusion] of my husband's younger brother [Justice]. We found out because the ghost spoke through her and identified herself. The treatment through mantras primarily took place during school holidays and went on for three years. Since that time when she was 15 years old, two years have passed and the ghost has left her. When this happened, we were very happy. My granddaughter was so pleased she even distributed *prasad* [offerings, usually sweets].

Mrs. Householder added that during the three years of Beauty's ghost possessions, the family spent 1500 to 2000 rupees on her cure. The *siyana* charged 250 to 300 rupees a day for treatment. He was considered a specialist in exorcising ghosts and came from the City of Delhi.

The teen-age daughter of Justice who was a friend of Beauty said that at times when the ghost of her dead sister [Illusion] bothered Beauty, Justice would tell the ghost to go away and leave Beauty alone. As Illusion's father, his teen-age daughter believed that he had the authority to make her ghost leave. While Beauty was growing up, she heard about Illusion's adultery, illicit pregnancy, and subsequent execution by Justice from her grandmother and others in the lineage, for Beauty had not yet been born when Illusion died.

The distress which Beauty suffered was due to four fears: the first was the fear of tuberculosis; the second, the fear that she would remain a widow; the third was the possibility that while a widow she too might become pregnant; and the fourth and greatest fear was that Illusion's ghost would take her soul. These four fears were based on the belief in the fruit of her soul's actions. They were reinforced by the traditions of the Householders' lineage, for its members had the reputation of being the most orthodox of the village Brahmans. For example, they still did not allow the husband of a new mother to see her and her child until after Dasuthan, a ceremony performed to purify the mother, child, and household the tenth day after birth. It was this group who most strongly ostracized Strong Minded and One Eyed's family because of the widow's remarriage.

Beauty's ghost possessions had a happy ending, for when she was 17 years old she was married to a fine young man in the spring of 1978. The Brahman priest who conducted the wedding ceremony was a follower of Sanatan Dharma. In 1958, he had been the postman for this and surrounding villages. Professional priests for wedding ceremonies were found through a network of relationships as were exorcists and other curers. These men gradually increased their clientele and the time that they devoted to their respective professions.

COMMENTS

The foregoing cases took place among a group of Brahmans, descendants of the earliest Brahman residents in the village, who settled in Old Brahman Lane. Victims were both males and females, children and adults. Stressful events that contributed to the possessions were the death of a spouse resulting in ghosthood, the heightened anxiety that accompanied marriage, and family problems. Possessions were treated by relatives, neighbors, and village curers. For persistent possessions judged to be serious, villagers consulted exorcists from the City of Delhi or mullahs from Palam.

By 1977, many of these Brahmans had moved away from Old Brahman Lane. One group moved to New Brahman Lane, partly in an attempt to escape the ghost of Illusion

possessions and eventually died from ghost illness about 1924–25. He was treated by Old Priest. Little Boy (described in Chap. 13: Deaths of Little Boy and Scapegoat) suffered ghost illness and died but did not have any ghost possessions. Amiable, the wife of Old Codger, was possessed in 1958 by the ghost of Scapegoat, her friend of many years who committed suicide in the main village well. Thereafter she had ghost illness but recovered (Chap. 13: Old Fever). For all the various cases described in this chapter, curers came from within and beyond the village. The attacks suffered by Farmer and Mrs. Barker warrant special attention, for they not only deal with possible nightmares and poltergeists but also bear some resemblance to the sleep paralysis and fright taxons (Hughes, 1985b; 1985c; Simons, 1985b; 1985c).

WIDOWS, PATRIARCHS, TWINS

Despite many sorrows, the members of this family line were among the pleasantest people in the village. They were members of the main, founding lineage of Jats, whose men tended to be aggressive, but the people in this family line were not. They were friendly with Jats and Brahmans and did not display the competitiveness which often existed between these two castes.

Until 1945 everyone belonged to a single joint family, consisting of three brothers, their mother, wives, and offspring. By 1958 the family had split into three households. The two eldest brothers, Patriarch (born 1908) and Benevolent (born 1918), worked as taxi drivers from 1937 to 1945 for their father's sister's husband, who owned five taxis in the City of Delhi. While working as taxi drivers, they rented quarters in the city and brought their wives and children to live with them instead of leaving them in the village with Matriarch, their widowed mother, and their younger brother, Short Life, and his family. Short Life worked the land, which the three brothers owned jointly. He died at the end of 1944, age 24 (born 1920), leaving his wife, Widow-in-Between, 21 years old (born 1923); a son, Only Heir, two years old (born 1942); and a daughter, Resourceful, three years old (born 1941). The two older brothers, Patriarch and Benevolent, and their families then

returned to the village in 1945 (Append. III: Chart 11).

For a short time the two elder brothers maintained a joint family with their mother and the survivors of their late brother's family, but after having lived in the city, Patriarch's and Benevolent's families did not adjust to living with the two widows, Matriarch and Widow-in-Between, and separated, dividing the house (Append. IV: Map 4, nos. 6, 7). As his family increased in numbers, Patriarch built a separate house on another lane and moved there with his wife and children in 1952. Matriarch headed the family of her widowed daughter-in-law and two children. She arranged to have their share of the land, from which as widows they benefited for life and which was to be the heritage of Only Heir, the son of Short Life, sharecropped on a 50-50 basis. The arrangement reduced their return from the land by half.

RESOURCEFUL, ONLY HEIR, AND MATRIARCH

By 1958, 16-year-old Resourceful had married, lived permanently with her husband, and had borne one son. Her pseudonym denotes her resourcefulness as an adult. Since she was about two-and-a-half years old when her father died, the household was without adult males while she was growing up. She suffered ghost possession twice: first, when she was eight years old, one to two years after the murder of Tippler's first wife; second, at first mating with her husband, around age 14. The ghost possessing her was said to be Tippler's first wife, not surprising since she lived next door to Tippler. In 1977–78, her possessions were still remembered by Jat families in her lineage. Little Goddess, age ten, and Pragmatic, the 13-year-old granddaughter of Patriarch, both of whom were born after her possessions, knew about them.

Although the two widows had economic difficulties, they managed to arrange the marriages of Resourceful and her brother, Only Heir. In due course, Only Heir and his wife had two sons and two daughters. In 1976 at age 33, he was killed by a motor vehicle while working, leaving Widow III. The misfortune of his death was somewhat mitigated by a monthly pension of Rs. 250 paid to his widow. Three months after he died, his widow bore a posthumous daughter. Although father and son, Short Life and Only Heir, qualified for ghosthood, no Jats spoke to that effect (Append. III: Chart 11).

Prior to Only Heir's death, Matriarch died in 1967, when she was said to be 90 years old but she herself never knew her exact age. During the last 20 or more years of her life, Matriarch acted as midwife for women in the largest Jat lineage. For example, she delivered the last child born to Worn Down (Chap. 15: A Maternity Death). Because of her long life, a feast called a Kaj was given to commemorate her death. Matriarch, who was a close friend of Honesty, Manipulator's mother, died about a month after Honesty.

Some years before Only Heir died, his wife asked Resourceful, his sister, if she would send three of her sons to live with them and help with the agricultural work while they also attended school. Resourceful did so. In 1977 a year after Only Heir died, Resourceful's eldest son was 20 years old, had finished high school, and was the oldest male in the household. He worked in an office in New Delhi but continued living with the two widows and contributed to the household expenses. Resourceful's other sons were 18 and 16 years old. The 16-year-old was still in school. The 18-year-old had finished high school and carried out the agricultural work. Thus, the land was no longer sharecropped once the boys came to live with the widows. These boys contributed to household expenses and provided assistance and protection while Only Heir's children were growing up. They were still young: the youngest son was just under ten years old; the eldest son was 12. The three daughters were seven and five years old and the posthumous child, one year old (Append. III: Chart 11).

THE BENEVOLENTS

Benevolent, the middle brother, reported after our census was taken in 1958, that an infant son of his had died of tetanus neonatorum shortly after his birth in 1957, indicating that he did not attribute the infant's death to ghost illness. The Benevolents, both well liked, died in 1976, the wife slightly before her husband. The causes of death were attributed by some informants to tuberculosis, by others, to cancer, but husband and wife were said to have died of the same disease. Because they were in their sixties when they died and had sons, they were not candidates for ghosthood. The Benevolents' two married sons continued to live jointly with their wives, children, and their unmarried younger brother, born in 1960, who was still in school. The Benevolents' three daughters had long been married and lived with their husbands (Append. III: Chart 11).

THE PATRIARCHS

In 1958 Patriarch and Mrs. Patriarch, well liked in the village, had four sons and five daughters. One of the daughters, the eldest child, had already married and lived permanently with her husband; she was then 20 years old and had one son. Some years later after the birth of her second child, another son, she died. The Patriarchs' eldest son was married and about to complete military service when in November 1958 he came home on leave for the birth of his first child, a daughter, Beloved. He was the first village husband to break one of the rules of seclusion during his wife's lying-in by seeing her and the baby the day after delivery. Two of Patriarch's five daughters were identical twins. Their pseudonyms are Morning Star and Evening Star. In 1958 they were 15 years old. Patriarch's youngest daughter was seven years old, and the next to eldest was 17 (Append. III: Chart 11).

Some months after her birth, Beloved fell ill, and Patriarch called a *vaid* from a nearby town. The *vaid*, who was married to Patriarch's sister, arrived on a motorcycle, diagnosed the illness as pneumonia, provided the necessary medicine, and the child recovered. Between 1959 and 1977 the Patriarchs' other sons and daughters married and had children.

Eighteen people lived with the Patriarchs in 1977–78. Mrs. Patriarch said that with so many family members she no longer knew where to go to be alone. Patriarch had replaced his old cattle shed with a brick *baithak*, which had electricity and a hand pump. This building was across Lane II from the dwellings of the joint family of the sons of Benevolent, and the widows of Short Life and

Only Heir. The Patriarchs still lived in the original two-story house completed in 1952. The men's house, formerly used only by men, in 1977-78 was used by men, women, children and occasional guests. The men and women were no longer segregated socially (Append. IV: Map 4, nos. 23, 36).

From 1959 to 1977 three daughters of the Patriarchs died: (1) the eldest after the birth of her second son; (2) the next to eldest from Fever, leaving a son and daughter; (3) and Evening Star at 33 years of age in 1976 in a hospital from pneumonia. Her death probably distressed her twin most. The son and daughter of the Patriarchs' next to eldest dead daughter were raised by the Patriarchs until 1975, at which time the children went to live with their father when he married the Patriarchs' youngest daughter, who had been taking care of the children and grown quite fond of them. When Evening Star died, she left three daughters and one son. In 1977 the youngest daughter, age seven, was staying with the Patriarchs and attending school in Shanti Nagar. Although the early deaths of the Patriarchs' three daughters qualified them for ghosthood, they all had children (Append. III: Chart 11). We never heard that the dead daughters' souls had become ghosts or that ghosts took their souls. The Arya-Samaj disbelief in ghosts, despite some contradictions, should be taken into account where Jats are concerned.

In the fall of 1977 a daughter was born to the Patriarchs' third son, age 25, an electrician who worked in the city. The baby was his first child. Everyone admired the beautiful infant, who had curly black hair. A month later when the child fell ill, Doctor John treated her for pneumonia. She recovered as had Beloved in 1958. At least three people in Patriarch's family fell ill from what was diagnosed as pneumonia: his daughter, Evening Star, and two of his granddaughters, but only Evening Star died of it. Pneumonia was common in the Delhi region (Gazetteer Unit, Delhi Adm., 1976: 859).

We know neither the remedies used to treat Evening Star and the two granddaughters nor the type of pneumonia that they contracted. It has proven difficult to determine the causative agent of the pneumonias, which may be a pneumococcus with different serotypes or a virus. The tests necessary for making precise diagnoses were in practice unavailable to villagers, for whom pneumonia was simply one illness. Dowling (1972) outlined the various treatments for pneumonia before the development of sulfonamides and antibiotic drugs. Bleeding the patient, an old remedy going back to Galen in A.D. 230, continued as one of a number of remedies into the 20th century. The sulfonamides were used from the mid-1930s well into the 1940s. After World War II, penicillin and the sulfonamides overlapped, but penicillin's lack of toxicity favored it. Since then, the antibiotics and sulfonamides were met with such enthusiasm by the medical profession that it still has not found a way to temper their indiscriminate and excessive use (Dowling, 1972: 1344), which in India, as elsewhere, has spilled over into popular pharmaceutical medicine. However, pneumococcal pneumonia can be effectively treated by antibiotics, which are commonly used by practitioners of popular pharmaceutical medicine, such as Dr. John. If the electrician's daughter did indeed have pneumococcal pneumonia, Dr. John's medicine, in all probability an antibiotic, would have been beneficial. In any case, the child recovered (Append. I: Discoveries—1908-1930s, Sulfanilimide; 1921–43, Penicillin; Descriptions—Pneumonia).

BELOVED

When Beloved, the Patriarchs' granddaughter, was in higher secondary school in the 1970s, her parents had her travel there by bus. Otherwise she would have stopped and chatted with boys on the way. Despite this proclivity, she did fairly well in school and was admitted with her girl friend, also a Jat, to a coeducational college a few miles from the village. Both girls were said to have a number of boy friends, unheard of in the 1950s, but then so was higher secondary school and a college education for girls. Once in college, Beloved did not attend classes regularly, went to movies, and enjoyed herself with boys. When her class was planning a picnic, Beloved asked her father for money to go. He refused because he had found out that she had not been attending school regularly and instead went to movies. Although Beloved promised her father that she would not go to the picnic with her girl friend, the boys were willing to pay their expenses so both girls went and did not tell their parents. That night when the girls were supposed to come home from school, they did not return. The boys had booked a room at a hotel where they took the girls, drank a lot, and some were unconscious. The hotel owner called the police, who took the boys and girls to their parents' homes.

According to one informant, Beloved's father was so ashamed of what his daughter had done that for a while he left the village very early in the morning before anyone awoke. To complicate the situation, Beloved was pregnant. Her mother found out after the picnic and sent Beloved to stay in her brother's house for an early abortion before the soul vested in the fetus. Therefore, the fetus could not become a ghost. Shortly thereafter her parents arranged her marriage to a young man studying to be a medical technician. Beloved did not visit her natal home again until the death of Only Heir, her father's patrilineal cousin, in 1976. Beloved's parents loved her and had a more lenient outlook than did Illusion's father who executed her in 1958 when she became illicitly pregnant. The different outcomes illustrate not only the personalities of the two fathers but also the changing times.

MRS. PATRIARCH AND THE HEALTH OPINION SURVEY

In 1978, Mrs. Patriarch talked at some length about her health in answering the Health Opinion Survey (Append. VI). She suffered from persistent headaches, which she attributed to old age. She would not wear the glasses prescribed by her physician because she said, "I have to look up over them to see anybody at a distance." She also felt shy when she wore them. In the 1950s very few villagers wore glasses. By the 1970s, more villagers went to physicians and clinics. Older people sometimes wore glasses and a few had cataract operations.

Mrs. Patriarch's major health problem, according to her and her daughter-in-law, Beloved's mother, was heart trouble. In 1977

Mrs. Patriarch had a heart attack, which she described as follows:

After just coming from the cattle shed, I was sitting still and planned to go to sleep when I had the heart attack. I had no worries at the time. A doctor here in the village, Home Trained [the village Nai, who had learned popular pharmaceutical medicine and Ayurvedic theories from his brother-in-law] helped me immediately. The pain started in my chest with increased feelings of suffocation. Then my hands and feet went limp. When the doctor gave me the injection, it was as if I could see my chest going down. After a number of injections it has never been as serious, but sometimes I feel as though something in my chest has burst. Then sometimes I lie down.

Beloved's mother, who was present during part of the interview, mentioned that when her mother-in-law had the attack she was near death and gasping for breath. Mrs. Patriarch added that on the day of her attack she had not done any hard work, for her daughters-in-law did most of it. Usually she went to the fields and picked tomatoes and sometimes cut fodder, bringing a load back on her head. She claimed she was fond of working because her hands were strong.

In answer to question 4: "Are you bothered by your heart beating loud," Mrs. Patriarch's said:

When lying on my bed, no. My heart beat hard only once. When I had the heart attack, I did not feel it beating, I just felt something had burst, and the thing started climbing upwards when I was given the injections. No one lets me rest; they took me to the fields after my heart attack.

Her daughter-in-law explained that without her mother-in-law's supervision they would be lost and would not know what work should be done. This statement pleased Mrs. Patriarch.

Question 6: "Do you have any trouble getting to sleep or staying asleep?" elicited this reply:

I swear on my mother that I do not go to sleep. I just shift around on my bed. I have not been sleeping for the past two to three months. I do not know why I can't sleep, but there's no use telling anyone. The other women in the family do not know that I cannot sleep because they all sleep in their own beds. All the people in the family sleep here and there, children, and men; they go back and forth. Visitors who come sleep in the men's house, but some sleep here. My daughter [Morning Star], who is visiting, sleeps here.

The eighth question was whether she was bothered, frightened, or upset by bad dreams. She laughed and said, "I have just finished telling you that I do not sleep at night." Then she said she was able to tell whether she had good or bad dreams. Sometimes she dreamt that a buffalo or camel was after her and tried to kill her. Then she ran and hid. In the dream she would climb up to the roof by the stairs and a ladder to escape. This question started a discussion between mother-in-law and daughter-in-law about an incident when a bull attacked Mrs. Patriarch. She could have been killed, and the experience was frightening. They said this bull was in the habit of killing people. When they were in the fields one night, the bull chased them. They ran, but the bull pursued them to the village before turning away. In 1977–78 no camels were owned by villagers, but in 1958–59, Schemer, a neighboring Jat, owned a camel, used for plowing. Village women were afraid of the animal, which may explain Mrs. Patriarch's dream of a camel. Doniger O'Flaherty (1984: 22) indicated that in ancient Sanskritic texts men possessed by goblins might see camels and other animals in their dreams, but this attribution may not apply to Mrs. Patriarch's dreams.

During the course of the interview, Mrs. Patriarch was asked what worried her the most. She answered, "Farming, husband, animals, and children," in that order. Her daughter-in-law, however, said that her mother-in-law worried most about the cattle, especially when they did not give milk. Presently only their zebu cow was lactating, so they prepared tea two times a day for the adults, giving milk only to the young children. When their two buffaloes were lactating, everyone had milk to drink. This way of using milk was common in village families.

In reply to Question 19, as to whether she felt in good spirits, she answered, "Sometimes I am in good spirits, sometimes in bad. This goes on in every household when there is good and bad news or a fight. For example, when my twin daughter died, it was bad news."

People who seemed well adjusted to their way of life usually answered the last question, "Do you sometimes wonder if anything is worthwhile anymore" by saying nothing was worthless or useless. Mrs. Patriarch's reply was along this line, but she added that she liked to take care of the buffaloes.

After the last question, Beloved's mother left for work in the fields. A close friend of Mrs. Patriarch, the recently widowed mother of the girl who had gone to the picnic with Beloved, climbed to the roof where the interview had been taking place. The two women discussed how Matriarch, Mrs. Patriarch's mother-in-law, had acted as a midwife and delivered their children and Mrs. Patriarch's grandchildren. The interview closed with the gossip session about Tippler and Barker and their wives beating them (Chap. 13: Old Codger, Barker, and Mrs. Barker; Chap. 15: Tippler's First Wife).

Mrs. Patriarch's total score on the Health Opinion Survey was 29; Anxiety = 7; Depression = 8. Normal scores range from 20 to 29; scores above 29 are interpreted as indicating excessive mental stress. In view of her recent heart attack, the deaths of her three daughters, Beloved's pregnancy and abortion, the ghost possessions of Morning Star to be described, and all the people living with and visiting the Patriarchs, her score was good (Append. VI: Health Opinion Survey). Mrs. Patriarch and her husband were enduring, hardy people with a generally optimistic outlook. However, her heart attack worried her because someone told her that she would have two more.

PRAGMATIC AND MORNING STAR

Some time around 1974 Pragmatic, the daughter of Morning Star, came to stay with her grandparents both to avoid her mother's ghost possessions and to attend the nearby school (Chap. 10: Jat Children). Morning Star was possessed intermittently beginning in

1973 or 1974, when she was 31 years old, through 1978. During this time, her twin, Evening Star died, which may have contributed to her stress. The accounts of Pragmatic, Mrs. Patriarch, and Morning Star about Morning Star's possessions show differences in detail although they are generally in agreement. The different details are probably due partly to the fact that Pragmatic and Mrs. Patriarch were not present at the first possession; moreover in 1974 Pragmatic was only nine years old. In any case, versions of the same event obtained from different people usually vary.

In her response to the Health Opinion Survey, Pragmatic discussed ghosts:

I am afraid of ghosts and dacoits. I have seen people possessed by ghosts. When a ghost talks through a person, I am afraid. A ghost possesses my mother. The ghost is a man. When the ghost is asked who he is, he says his name. My father and my father's elder brother ask his name. Then they call a man to cure my mother. The man lives elsewhere, but he does not come to the village to cure so they take my mother there. Then that man tells them what is going on in my father's village which causes my mother to be possessed by a ghost. He takes my father's money, but my mother has not had any relief. He is paid from five to twenty rupees. These possessions have been going on for a number of years, but now my mother takes medicine from a *siyana*. The ghost of the man who possesses my mother lived near the house of my grandfather and was related to him. I do not know the exact relationship, but he was the elder brother-in-law of my mother, not a real brother-in-law [but a patrilineal cousin of Morning Star's husband]. He died before my mother was born. Once my mother and father were driving in a buggy over a place where the man died, and these possessions started.

Then Pragmatic mentioned the possession of Little Goddess and that Illusionist cured her. She called Illusionist a bhagat and said that a *siyana* knows everything, but that Illusionist did not and was only a bhagat, not a *siyana*. Despite the tendency for females more often to be possessed by female ghosts, Pragmatic said that women were more often possessed by the ghosts of men. This statement was probably due to the possessions of her mother by a male ghost.

In reponse to the question on dreams, Pragmatic had a dream about nine to ten days earlier and related it. She saw a *bitaura* that had been broken open, an omen that someone will die. A *bitaura* looks like a little hut; it is a pile of dry dung cakes sealed for storage with a covering of dung. Straw is put on top to add protection. Subsequent events often support the interpretation of a broken *bitaura* as an omen of death, for death is frequent in the village. Pragmatic's total Health Opinion Survey score was 22; Anxiety = 6; Depression = 7, well within the normal range, as was expected from her personality suggested by the pseudonym, Pragmatic (Append VI).

One day in April 1978, Mrs. Patriarch overheard us conversing about ghosts in front of her house and spoke about Morning Star's possessions:

Morning Star's possessions are an old subject. The first one took place four to five years ago [ca. 1973–74 when she was 30 to 31 years old], but they have been recurring since that time. We took her to a man in the City of Delhi, who recites mantras. He said that she should stay here with us, her parents, for one and a quarter months. The time is not yet up. The man who Pragmatic said possessed my daughter is not a real elder brother-in-law. He died a long time ago. My daughter was going along the road in a cart, passed over a crossroads, and kicked a brick which was lying there.

In Shanti Nagar, as was customary in the region, a brick located at the crossroads represents the shrine of the Crossroads Mother Goddess (Append. IV: Map. 4, CM; S. Freed and R. Freed, 1976: 19, fig. 1).

The same afternoon, Pragmatic came to our quarters to talk about Sunny, the schoolgirl who had recently been possessed and about Little Goddess, who had again been possessed. She was not sure who had tried to cure Little Goddess by tying a *ganda* around her neck but thought it was Illusionist. Pragmatic said that the ghost who kept possessing Morning Star was very powerful and that her mother went to a *siyana* in Delhi, who gave her some medicine and told her to stay with her parents in Shanti Nagar for one and a quarter months. She could leave the village for a little while now and then. She added that sometimes the ghost came to her mother, Morning Star, here and sometimes in her marital village. Pragmatic recounted:

Sometimes my mother lies on a cot in a terrible condition so that eight or nine men cannot control her. Sometimes she falls off the cot and is hurt. The ghost does not say anything in this village, but he does in my father's village. I start weeping when she is possessed. Once the ghost possessed my mother and asked for my four-year-old brother who was sick from malaria and lying on a cot. The demand scared me. The ghost said to my mother, "There are two ways for you to go. Either jump in a well or lie on the railway tracks." At that point, my mother started walking towards the well. Then I started weeping because my mother would die. This happened during the Dusehra holidays when I was visiting my father. A lot of people grabbed my mother. When my mother came here, again it happened. It was a month ago on a Sunday.

At this point Pragmatic's mother came in with her son who was suffering from malaria. He was a stalwart little Jat, who at times could be seen standing in the lane, switching cattle with a small stick. Pragmatic took her brother home while her mother stayed to talk. Morning Star began by speaking about her son:

He will not take the malaria tablets. There are no injections for malaria so they cannot reduce Fever. I took him to the nearby dispensary where his blood was tested but they gave him no injection even though he has a temperature. I tried mixing his medicine with milk, but even then he would not take it. The doctors told me that unless he takes the tablets, he will keep on having malaria.

Her statements reflect the village viewpoint that injections may drive out Fever. However, she was an exception, for she repeated what the doctors told her, i.e., there were no injections for malaria.

When Morning Star was asked about her own health, she answered that she was all right, but previously she had been sick for

months. Everyone said that it was a ghost because she fell down unconscious. When this happened, five or six men had to hold her because she might fall and break her neck. She was taken to a Muslim, a *siyana*, in Ghaziabad, a town about 18 km east of Delhi. He tied a *ganda* around her neck to protect her for 40 days. The ghost talked in front of the *siyana*. The ghost said, "Why did you pass over me when you were in the bullock cart." Morning Star went on:

One day in the month of Karttik [October-November], my husband's younger brother and I were riding in the bullock cart. He was driving and we crossed over a place where a dead body had been cremated. I did not know this because it was near a tube well and away from the cremation grounds. Immediately the ghost came into me.

For the dead man to have been cremated away from the cremation grounds is an unexplained and puzzling oddity.

When Morning Star was asked why the ghost had not possessed her brother-in-law, she answered, "The ghost said that my brother-in-law had left the cart at the crossroads and only I was in it." On arriving home, Morning Star fell down unconscious so the family had her sniff chili peppers. Then the ghost spoke, "Because the bullock cart passed over me, I will seize you." The identity of the ghost was pursued with these results. Morning Star's husband had three real brothers. The eldest brother died three to four years previously after a long illness. Shortly afterward Morning Star was possessed by his ghost.

When Morning Star was asked about arguments or fights in her husband's family, she said that one took place two months previously and others had occurred prior to that time. The brothers lived jointly and would not separate. Her husband spoke very little so that the fights died out. The fights were mostly among the men, but sometimes the women fought. Her husband always kept quiet because he followed in his father's footsteps. After the eldest brother died, her husband, the next eldest brother, became head of the family. Morning Star said that sometimes she fought with her younger sister-in-law. Her father-in-law was dead, but her mother-in-law who was still alive fought with all her sons.

Morning Star was then asked about fights in her natal family when she was growing up. She said there were none. The suggestion was made that she might be upset by fighting and then be vulnerable to the ghost. She answered, "The fighting does not bother me. What can one do?" and changed the subject to her son's malaria. Because he had become very pale from the malaria, she was afraid that the boy's father would beat her. She added that all the children slept under mosquito nets, but still this child had malaria. However, they had not started using the nets until he came down with malaria. At this point Pragmatic came to call her mother and they left. Morning Star was wedded when she was about 18 years old and had three children by 1978 when she was 35: her daughter, Pragmatic; her four-year-old son; and an older son who was living with his father (Append. III: Chart 11). Sons are important so even a son's seemingly minor illness, and malaria is not minor, would make parents anxious. Under such circumstances, Morning Star would be blamed for any illness, so it is not surprising that her husband beat her.

Although Morning Star's version showed some differences from Pragmatic's and Mrs. Patriarch's versions regarding the identity of the ghost, the number of years of her possessions, and the conveyance in which Morning Star was riding when the ghost entered her, Morning Star's report has been taken as the most accurate because she was the one possessed and knew all her in-laws. According to her, the man riding in the cart with her was her husband's younger brother. Traditionally, the younger brother of a woman's husband has a warm, close relationship with his brother's wife. She may be the woman who provides instructions for him before he first mates with his wife. In olden times and occasionally in the late 1950s, it was reported that an elder sister-in-law provided her husband's younger brother's first sexual experience. Although there was no evidence for this relationship between Morning Star and her younger brother-in-law, they were at least friendly. The relationship may have been the reason for fights between Morning Star and the wife of her younger brother-in-law. More

information about Morning Star's relations with the members of her husband's family was not forthcoming.

Morning Star was a healthy, pleasant woman. She spoke easily and was friendly. However, she feared her husband's displeasure and beatings, which may have been his only outlet for the times he remained quiet during family fights. Morning Star had not been beaten by her father or mother, for members of her natal family were peaceful and harmonious. Her marital family was not, which the *siyana* may have discovered when he recommended that Morning Star stay with her parents.

Morning Star and her daughter, Pragmatic, mentioned that when Morning Star was possessed a number of men had to hold her down so that she did not fall and break her neck. This description is similar to the case of Sita, who for three years was possessed by ghosts; then she began having fits, *daura*. When she did so, a number of men had to hold her so she would not hurt herself or run to a well or railroad to commit suicide (R. Freed and S. Freed, 1985: 202–203). From a psychiatric viewpoint according to DSM-III, Morning Star's possession states could be classified as a Dissociative Disorder. If her ghost possessions became fits, the classification could be a Conversion Somatoform Disorder. More would need to be known about her physical condition, possible causes of stress, and whether her ghost possessions had become fits and were recognized as such (Am. Psych. Assn. DSM-III, 1980: 241–260; R. Freed and S. Freed, 1985: 187–188, 202–205).

POSSIBLE DISEASE FACTORS IN PATRIARCH'S FAMILY

Two of Patriarch's infant grandchildren had pneumonia but recovered, and a 33-year-old daughter died of it. Three cases in one family, which was in comfortable circumstances by village standards, suggests the possibility of enhanced susceptibility. Kolata (1987: 260) indicated that small children with the sickling genetic trait which prevents malaria frequently are not able to fight off streptococcal pneumonia. Moreover, children generally have weaker immunological systems than adults. In fact a child may seem well until six hours before death, which could account for the death from pneumonia of Clerk's son, the Lohar child (Chap. 20: The Lohar Blacksmiths: Sorrowful and Difficult). It is possible that the two infant grandchildren of the Patriarchs may have been especially susceptible to streptococcal pneumonia because the sickling genetic trait is found in the population of this region (Friedman and Trager, 1981: 159; Diamond, 1989: 10, Map 12).

Another of the Patriarchs' children, their third son, whose first child was born in the fall of 1977, died in April 1978 at the age of 25 or 26. Employed as an electrician in Delhi, he came home one day quite ill with stomach pains, vomiting, and diarrhea. The illness came on him suddenly. Because he needed immediate attention, Home Trained was called and gave him injections of antibiotics. When Patriarch's son grew steadily worse, he was rushed to a hospital in the city where he died. The cause of his death was diagnosed as either staphylococcus or salmonella food poisoning. The use of antibiotics for either of these conditions is unwarranted. His mother's medical history suggests that poisoning by salmonella was more likely than by staphylococcus. His mother said that she never had malaria. It is therefore possible that she carried the recessive gene for the sickle-cell trait, a buffer against malaria. Thus, her son may also have carried the gene for the sickling trait. A male with this gene is more susceptible to the deadly effects of salmonella poisoning than is a female (Friedman and Trager, 1981: 159). The disease may be fatal when normal intestinal bacteria are suppressed by antibiotic drugs (Davey and Wilson, 1971: 89–90, 157; Goble and Konopka, 1973; Berkow, 1982: 765).

FARMER

The ghost attacks that plagued Farmer were different from the reported possessions of villagers, except to some extent Mrs. Barker. In the common form of ghost possession, the victim first saw the ghost; then the ghost invaded the victim causing a variety of alternate states with associated forms of behavior. Villagers recognized that the victim was possessed when they heard the ghost speak from the victim. After regaining consciousness, the victim had no memory of what happened. Farmer's attack by a poltergeist differed from possession, for he remembered what happened during visits by the poltergeist, and he did not pass through alternate mental states or attempt suicide while in such states. He reported his experiences after he had been physically disturbed by the poltergeist. The ghost that attacked Farmer was definitely a poltergeist, defined as a noisy and usually mischievous ghost, a spirit capable of making mysterious noises, such as rappings, knockings, tappings, or rattlings (Gove, 1986: 1756). Hess (1989), citing Wedenoja (1978) and others, called attention to poltergeists attacking victims and infesting their households and workplaces rather than possessing the victims. He also noted that traditionally poltergeists are exorcised, and that in several cases they have been linked with frustration and hostility on the part of the victim and members of the family. Further, a poltergeist's attack can startle the victim, who then fears persistent attacks. The poltergeist's attacks on Farmer startled, frightened, and semiparalyzed him when he was asleep. In other words there were elements of the startle response as well as fright and sleep paralysis among the symptoms found in this case history. Mrs. Barker's case showed some of the symptoms found in Farmer's attacks. Because the information about her attack came secondhand from Old Codger, it is not possible to confirm that she was attacked by a poltergeist except that the family problems and symptoms found in Mrs. Barker's case tend to show that she did not have amnesia for the attacks. Furthermore, her attacks were probably triggered by being startled while sleeping and feeling pressure on her chest and other parts of her body. As in Farmer's case, startle, fright, and semiparalysis were present.

The distinction between ghost attacks and possession is best conveyed in village terms— *bhut grasth* (attacked by a ghost) and *bhut lagna* (possessed by a ghost). The distinction sometimes became fuzzy when villagers talked about cases which they had not witnessed.

Farmer belonged to the same lineage as the Patriarchs. Because the lineage embraced Arya-Samaj tenets, reports in 1978 of Farmer's poltergeist attack as well as the possessions of Morning Star, Little Goddess, and Resourceful came as a surprise, as did similar reports in another Jat lineage, Old Fever. Old Codger of the Old Fever lineage had not been present during Mrs. Barker's (his son's wife) attacks or when the ghost or ghosts attacked Farmer, but Gabbler, a young Brahman, was present at a later attack upon Farmer. His account therefore has more details than Old Codger's and is in all likelihood more useful. Gabbler said, "The ghost visited him every day. First the ghost came to him only once or twice, but he's a coward so now the ghost visits him daily. Once he was attacked at his tube well and was very afraid. Some people put smoking incense in front of him to drive the ghost away." Then Gabbler, pointing to ashes lying on a stand in the puja room of One Eyed's house, said some of the members in the house used the ashes (*bhabhut*) to drive the ghost away. Gabbler added that when Farmer was with his daughters at his tube well, three male ghosts disturbed him, probably because he had eaten sweets (Chap. 21: Gabbler and Student Doctor). Gabbler's comment on Farmer being afraid and a coward ties in with the villagers' attitudes when they try to drive a ghost away; they tell victims of ghost possession not to be afraid and to threaten the ghost. Despite Old Codger's and Gabbler's comments, the simplest and most accurate description of Farmer's attacks came from Farmer himself, for he remembered the details of his persistent attacks.

The neighborhood in which Farmer lived had seen many ghost incidences reflecting the persistence of ghost beliefs among Brahmans, Bairagis, Chamars, Chuhras, and Jats. All his life, Farmer lived next door to Matriarch, Widow-in-Between, and Widow III, whose husbands were consanguines of Benevolent and Patriarch and who were members of his own lineage. On the other side of Farmer's house lived a Bairagi family and in another building further north but across Lane I lived the Brahmans: One Eyed and his sons and their families; Junior, the father of Doctor John and Dr. John's family, all of them formerly from Old Brahman Lane. Withdrawn, part of this group of Brahmans, lived in a cattle shed near the cremation grounds and still suffered ghost possessions (Chap. 21:

Withdrawn's Possessions). Little Goddess lived above her father's shop, across the main Jat lane from Farmer; her father was Farmer's father's brother's son. Despite the men of this Jat lineage customarily denying the existence of ghosts, a number of people in the vicinity were known to have been possessed or attacked by ghosts, among them Farmer, Resourceful, Morning Star, and Little Goddess, all Jats, and a Bairagi girl, Jolly, the granddaughter of Fearful (Chap. 20: The Bairagis). During the malaria and ghost epidemics of 1977–78, the ghosts who were most often said to haunt the east side of the village and the Chuhra and Chamar compounds were Tippler's first wife, Little Bride, Hairless, Housewife, Whose Daughter, the Headless Sweeper, and the roster of wives who committed suicide in the main village well. Illusion's ghost haunted the abodes of Brahmans: New Brahman Lane on the south side of the village; the lane where Teacher and Truthful lived; and the cul-de-sac called Old Brahman Lane and Lane VI in mid-village where the first Brahmans settled.

Farmer was a stolid, matter-of-fact, unimaginative man, age 50 in 1978, whose wife was 49 years old. Mrs. Farmer had borne her husband nine children, five daughters and four sons. One son, age 5, and one daughter, age 2, died; seven children survived. The deaths according to Mrs. Farmer's beliefs were due to ghost illness and the ghost taking the children's souls. By 1977, the oldest three daughters lived with their husbands; the youngest daughter, age 7, attended school. The three surviving sons, ages 16, 14, and 11, also went to school and were not yet married. Thus, Farmer had the expenses of dowries, weddings, and gifts for the married daughters, and in the future, the still unmarried daughter. He had not yet arranged the marriages of his three sons and would not receive the dowries and gifts from their wives' parents until the sons were married.

During a conversation with a number of women about ghost illness and possession, Mrs. Farmer mentioned the possessions of Little Goddess and said, "A child of any age can be attacked or possessed by a ghost, even an infant." She added that an exorcist is called to exorcise the ghost bothering the child. Members of the senior generations, including

Farmer, were nonliterate, but the children of the Farmers born after 1958 attended school. Farmer and his sister were the only surviving children of Farmer's parents. His mother died when he was around ten years old. His father did not marry again.

Farmer's grandmother took care of her grandchildren and the house until Farmer married. In 1959 the grandmother was still alive and lived with Farmer, his wife and children, and his father. Her son claimed that she was 80 years old (born ca. 1878) and the oldest woman in the village. She was blind, deaf, and senile and died some years later. Like other older Jat women, she continued to believe in ghosts and passed on her beliefs to the children in the family. Farmer's father, still alive in 1977–78, age 70 (born 1907), was 16 years old when the Arya Samaj with its disbelief in ghosts and multiple supernatural beings was introduced in the village. Therefore, his comments during the following interview with Farmer are not surprising.

Farmer cultivated 17 acres (6.9 hectares) of land. His father was the head of the family and tended to belittle his 50-year-old son. He publicly criticized his son's care of their expensive tube well, stating that his son was not as competent as he was and that he could take much better care of the tube well. Farmer was one of the few cultivators still plowing with bullocks in 1978. The conservative Farmer and his father chose to forego the tractors that were used by most farmers.

When Farmer was interviewed on March 31, 1978, he was putting up a new roof on his house because the old one leaked. The first thing he said was that he and his sons were doing the work themselves because they could not afford to hire anyone. Resourceful's eldest son, who was standing in Farmer's courtyard, said that Farmer was still suffering from ghost attacks and that the ghost was probably a man. Although this young man did not know much about the ghosts of Shanti Nagar, he said that many villagers had recently learned that Farmer had been attacked for some time and that Mr. and Mrs. Farmer had gone to Palam to seek the help of a siyana.

Farmer was very straightforward and honest in discussing his ghost attacks. He put down his hammer and started to talk about them. "For the past four days, I have been all right. One Eyed and his sons gave me some bhabhut [sacred ash from their puja room]. I went to Palam because there is a fair there where thousands of people gather, including siyanas and bhagats. One does not have to pay a fee but just give prasad to the siyana."

Farmer was then asked to describe the attacks. He said that when he was sleeping at night, someone tapped him hard all over his body while he was lying on his cot. Whatever or whoever it was also pressed his legs but did not talk. Even when he was lying on his cot smoking his hookah, the ghost came and tapped his legs and the cot, always at night between 8 p.m. and 4 a.m. This trouble went on for three months (approximately January, February, and March). The first month he did not believe in ghosts so he tried to ignore the ghost, but when it persisted, he obtained some amulets and a ganda for his neck, but they did not help. Next he went to see the siyana at Palam where he worshipped Hanuman (contrary to Arya-Samaj tenets) and offered Rs. 1.25 and sweets worth the same amount to Hanuman. For a while the ghost stopped bothering him, but then started again. Recently, One Eyed and his son gave him bhabhut from their puja room and black pepper to drive out the ghost. Thereafter he took a pinch of black pepper and ash in the morning and evening with water. For five days, including the day of the interview, he had relief from the ghost or ghosts.

On his visit to Palam, the siyana asked him and his wife many questions. Then he gave him some ash and told him to rub the ash on his palms and turn them upward toward the siyana, who carefully looked at them. Farmer thought that the siyana must have seen something in his palms but what it was would be known only to Bhagwan and the siyana. Then the siyana patted him and said that he would be all right. Pugh (1984) too has shown how astrologers use the palm in conjunction with astrological counseling in Benares. Palam, the location of the International Airport, was a center for exorcists who also counseled their clientele by reading palms. Farmer, however, did not derive anything from the reading of his palm except assurance from the siyana that he would be all right.

When pressed to tell more about the ghost or ghosts, Farmer said, "I do not know the identity of the ghost or ghosts; only Bhagwan knows. If the ghost was a man, I might have seen his apparition." When asked whether the ghost was an animal, Farmer replied, "No, but it went over my body like a horse though it was not as big as a horse. When the ghost scratched my side, I would turn over and press on the ghost. I felt that the ghost was breaking my side but I could not catch it. When I crushed it, I could feel the bones. I was very afraid because at times the ghost jumped all over my body a lot. Even when I was not asleep, the ghost came at 8 p.m."

When Farmer was questioned about any illnesses he might have had, he replied, "I have been without illness until now. I never take any medicine." In reply to the question of whether he drank alcoholic beverages, Farmer said, "Drinking liquor is not essential to me. I might drink some country liquor when a guest visits me, perhaps once every six months."

When Farmer was asked whether the ghost could have been a small animal, such as a baby horse, he answered:

I was sleeping alone in the cattle shed, but afterwards some people slept in the same place with me because they wanted to see the ghost or whatever it was and catch it. But it was invisible to them. It would run all over my bed. First it pressed my legs and pulled at my quilt, then it ran all over. Then I thought it was a ghost. It pressed my legs just like a daughter-in-law, but I don't have a daughter-in-law. The first month I could not imagine what was bothering me, but the second month I began to wonder so I tried doing different things to catch whatever it was. I would lie down in the daytime to sleep, but the ghost only came at 8 p.m. even when I was not sleeping. I felt shy telling anyone about ghosts, even members of the family, because ghosts do not attack Jats.

Farmer then showed how his wrists and fingers had grown thinner due to the ghost haunting him. He said that he had lost weight from worry and lack of sleep and had also lost his appetite, indications of stress, recently termed "idioms of distress" (Nichter,

1981; Ullrich, 1987a). At this point Farmer's father interrupted the session and said, "All this about ghosts and eating sweets at the cremation grounds is nonsense. We used to harvest wheat near there and ate there too, but nothing happened." Farmer immediately retorted:

My father does not know. I was the man affected by the ghost. Even when I smoked my hookah through the night, the ghost came. I did not tell anyone at first because people would joke about it and make a fool of me. My tube well is near the bus stop [not far from the cremation grounds]. For a while I stayed there day and night instead of sleeping in the cattle shed, and the ghost came there too. [Append. IV: Map. 4, BS, CG]

When I had been sleeping in the cattle shed, the *siyana* said that three ghosts attacked me. One was at the head of my cot, one at the foot, and one ran around me. The ghosts were two men and one woman. The *siyana* came to the village and hammered a nail into each of the four posts of my cot, but the nails did not stop the ghosts. [Saini (1975: 83) stated that when iron nails are driven into a cot, the iron keeps ghosts away. Kakar (1983: 29) reported a *siyana* blowing on five iron nails and hammering one into each corner and the middle of a room where a ghost might have been.] That was a month ago. All of this took place in the cattle shed. No one except me slept there because the other people in the family were afraid and would not sleep there. I had to stay because all the cattle are there, and I had to watch them.

Cattle thieves have been stealing cattle, but no one knows who they are. Some thieves have also been stealing tube-well motors so a man has to sleep there too. A buffalo can cost 3500 rupees; a tube-well motor of 10 horsepower is worth 4000 rupees. A small motor costs Rs. 100; a motor of 7.5 horsepower costs Rs. 3000. Not only the motors but other parts of the tube well are harmed when a motor is stolen. My father sleeps near the tube well to guard it. I sleep in the cattle shed, and my wife and children sleep inside the house.

During the fieldwork in 1977–78, three

tube-well motors were stolen: two were 7.5 horsepower and one, 10 horsepower. Early in 1978 some cattle were stolen by thieves who came in a large truck at night. These thefts caused considerable anxiety and fear that during the night thieves would try to steal cattle and tube-well motors, as Farmer's interview indicates. The fear was so pervasive in the village that the Brahman, Justice, father of Illusion, brought his cattle inside his living quarters at night. In addition, a young village Nai Barber, who had robbed a post office in the city, had recently been released by the police. Previously he had engaged in petty pilferage, going into village houses and stealing small items when no one was there. His return to the village added to the stress from the recent tube-well and cattle robberies. Other misfortunes affecting most villagers and heightening stress were an excessive monsoon, which damaged the crops of Farmer, followed by a typhoid epidemic in the fall of 1977, and a steady annual increase in the incidence of malaria. A nearby tornado and a hailstorm in the village in March 1978 caused further crop damage.

Shortly after interviewing Farmer, we asked other people about his ghost attacks. Old Codger claimed that the ghost disturbing Farmer was the Headless Sweeper. A month earlier, Old Codger had brought a mullah from Palam to cure Farmer. He claimed that the mullah had taken away the ghost of the Headless Sweeper so that it no longer troubled Farmer. Farmer himself told a different story. He said that the ghost, a bhut and not a jinn, the term Old Codger used for the Headless Sweeper, still was troubling him until five days before our interview and that he had been cured by One Eyed, the Brahman, and his sons, who gave him *bhabhut* and black pepper when he was attacked at his tube well (statement corroborated by Gabbler, above).

Thus, the poltergeist ceased to bother Farmer after treatment by One Eyed and his sons and compliance with their instructions to take pinches of black pepper and *bhabhut* every morning and evening. These simple remedies appear to have allayed Farmer's fears and anxiety and were compatible with the older belief in the curing power of Brahmans and the more recent remedy of taking medicine regularly. Moreover, the threat to

the cattle and tube wells had somewhat subsided, the weather returned to normal, and the typhoid epidemic had abated earlier in the year, all of which lessened the stress on Farmer and other villagers (Sapolsky, 1988).

Two women in Farmer's lineage were interviewed about his attacks, Mrs. Authority and her daughter-in-law. In 1958 and 1959, neither of these women mentioned ghosts to us, for Mr. Authority was a very strict Arya Samaji. By 1978 he had died. When his widow (age 75) and his daughter-in-law (age 55) were asked if they had heard of the ghost possessions of Little Goddess and the ghost attacks on Farmer, they said that they had not heard about Little Goddess, but the daughter-in-law confirmed Farmer's attacks. She said, "I have never seen one [a ghost] but I have heard about them and recently learned that Farmer was disturbed by ghosts who would not let him sleep. The ghosts removed his clothing." The last statement was not heard from anyone else in the village.

A Mahar Potter woman (age ca. 70), who lived across the lane from Mrs. Authority and had joined the session, said, "There are bhuts, *pret*s, and jinns, and they talk to people." The three women were asked what caused a person to become a ghost. They agreed that not everybody became a ghost. The Potter woman said that if everyone became a ghost, then no one would be left in the world, or if a person died at his allotted time, he would not become a ghost. Mrs. Authority added that no one knew when one's time was up, but if a person died before his time, then he became a bhut, *pret*, or jinn.

Another commentator on Farmer's possessions was the Chamar, Buddhist I, who said that Farmer was not attacked by a bhut, but by a jinn. A jinn, according to him, was more ferocious than a bhut or a *pret* and even seized a man while he was sitting with other people. This statement about Muslim ghosts being feared more than Hindu ghosts has been reiterated by Kakar (1983: 63). Buddhist I added that a jinn might come and lie down beside a man, as the jinn did with Farmer, who changed his position in his bed and tried to catch the jinn. It was underneath him, but he could not catch it. Buddhist I claimed that there was no treatment for a jinn except by a very great, intelligent man, a *siyana*.

Actor, a fanatic follower of the Arya Samaj, became livid if anyone tried to prove that there were ghosts. He said, "Farmer never suffered from ghost possessions because no ghosts exist. He has a blood pressure problem. His pressure goes up, and he thinks someone is pressing his body. Uneducated people like Farmer call this a ghost, but it is due to blood pressure. He is very fat. All this about ghosts is nonsense. Great men who are very strong die. If they were to become ghosts, they would be so powerful after death that they would take revenge. But this about ghosts is not so. Fear is a ghost. Whoever is afraid, that is the ghost."

Various reports of Farmer's ghost attacks are somewhat inconsistent with one another and with Farmer's own straightforward description. Old Codger claimed that Farmer was attacked by the Headless Sweeper, a jinn, and had been cured by the mullah from Palam. Although Buddhist I claimed that a jinn attacked Farmer, in another much earlier interview he said that the Headless Sweeper had long ago left the village. Gabbler said that while he was at Farmer's tube well with Farmer and his daughters, Farmer was attacked. This statement was contrary to Farmer's who said One Eyed and his sons were there and used black pepper and *bhabhut* to exorcise the ghost. Further, all but Farmer's youngest daughter lived at a considerable distance with their husbands and were not in the village at that time. Gabbler also said that three male ghosts had attacked Farmer at once, which was not confirmed by Farmer. Mrs. Authority's daughter-in-law said she had heard that the ghost took off Farmer's clothes. Although Farmer used the term bhut for the ghost attacking him, others used jinn. The *siyana* said there were three ghosts, two men and a woman. Actor characteristically claimed that Farmer suffered from high blood pressure. The different reports reflect the personalities involved, the spatial and social distances within the village, how gossip spreads, and changes in the reporting of events.

Farmer's interview and the stress that he was under at the time clearly point to a poltergeist's attack. There was no amnesia. He described the attacks carefully. They always occurred at specific times and places, mainly in the cattle shed at night, but once at the tube well. Farmer worried about thieves coming to rob both places so he slept alone in the cattle shed to guard it while his father and sometimes one of his sons slept in the tube-well shed. Farmer was disturbed but not possessed and could describe the attacks in some detail. The poltergeist haunted him at his cattle shed and once at his tube well, places vitally important to him but currently linked to danger and fear because of thieves. Farmer's state of mind at the time is basic to the analysis of poltergeist attacks. He was worried about crops and thieves and had ongoing family problems with his 70-year-old father, his three unmarried sons and seven-year-old daughter who were still in school, and the lack of any daughters-in-law to help with the family's work.

Although Farmer's attacks did not fit into the full sleep paralysis or fright illness taxons, elements of being startled, frightened, and immobility during sleep were some of the symptoms in his case. Because he slept in the cattle shed to guard the cattle, he was away from his usual more comfortable family environment and had to keep somewhat alert at night. Thus, as he dozed while village dogs barked and his cattle shifted around in the shed at night, he was at first startled and then frightened while half asleep. The stages of sleep may have affected his dreams and cognizance of what was happening because an individual has variant reactions while in the first light slumber stage of sleep, and later in the REM (rapid eye movement) stage, or in light transitional stages (Krueger, 1989: 40–41). Thus, his attacks are related to being startled awake nightly and the attendant fear of attack by thieves. The movement of his quilt, the feeling of someone tapping on his body, and his attempts to crush and catch whatever it was, were probably due to his subconscious attempts to be alert to catch the thieves and at the same time he was tired owing to lack of sleep.

Farmer's attacks can be compared to the startle reflex found among the "Jumpers" of Maine. This folk ethnographic label derives from lumberjacks' experiences in Maine and Canada. The lumberjacks had to take care of stabled horses in addition to their lumberjack work. They were afraid the horses would kick them. A teasing game developed among them.

One lumberjack would try to scare another by coming up behind him and making a neighing sound like a horse. This caused the startle reflex, whose accompanying symptoms were obedience, echolalia, and striking out at people (Rabinovitch, 1965; Kunkle, 1967). While Farmer's experiences with domestic animals differed a good deal from those of the lumberjacks, his reactions while sleeping contained elements of startle reactions, fright, and semiparalysis due to fear. When one is frightened and half asleep, one may feel partially paralyzed and unable to move. When the symptoms persisted, he then believed that he was being attacked by a ghost, was afraid and semiparalyzed.

Sleep paralysis and fright illness have been well documented and show similarities to the Old Hag of Newfoundland, believed by its victims to be a form of supernatural assault whose principal features are a subjective impression of wakefulness, immobility (sleep paralysis), realistic perception of the environment, and fright (Hufford, 1982: 25; Simons, 1985b: 115–116; 1985c: 329–331; Hughes, 1985b: 147–148; 1985d: 488, 495; Ness, 1985: 123–146; Bloom and Gelardin, 1985: 117–122). A feeling of pressure on the chest, the sensation of a supernatural presence, and a supine position when an attack of the Old Hag occurs are common. In Farmer's case, the attacks came when he was lying down and sleeping. He felt pressure on his body, sensed the presence of a ghost, was aware of his surroundings, and was "very afraid." The sleep paralysis and fright taxons have been used here only to point out that the symptoms found in Farmer's case, which were due to anxiety, fear, and disturbed sleep, have elements of the startle reflex, fright, and semisleep paralysis. Farmer's case, like others in this study, is characteristic of our holistic method in ethnographic fieldwork and is similar to Simons's (1988: 528) position that what is needed in describing the syndromes or symptoms in a case are "the causal chains which generate the observed and experienced behaviors" which "include biological, psychological, social, and cultural components which are intertwined in situationally specific ways." (Cf. R. Prince and Tcheng-Laroche, 1987, and Simons, 1987: 15–16, on sorting the symptoms into specific groups for an international classification of diseases.)

With regard to Actor's charge that high blood pressure contributed to Farmer's attacks, Dressler (1984: 265–269, 277, quote on p. 269), basing his statement on Selye's concept of stress, indicated that perceived "stress arises from conflicts, events, and inconsistencies in the social environment," and it is accumulated stress which may or may not cause hypertension. In any case, the stress from crop damage, the typhoid and malaria epidemics, and the cattle and tube-well thieves along with the necessity of sleeping in the cattle shed to keep watch, plus the belittling remarks by his old father, when he himself was a man of 50 who did most of the heavy work, provided enough stress to result in the ghost attacks of a poltergeist. In March after almost three months of restless sleep in the cattle shed, Farmer was attacked at the tube well. When he thought he might relax and not worry about the cattle, the noise of the tube-well motor and the fear of dacoits startled him when he was in a light sleep after smoking his hookah. Thus, the attack by the poltergeist took place in Farmer's workplaces, his cattle and tube-well sheds. Hess's (1989: 33; 1990: 407–408) distinction between ghost possession and infestation of workplaces by a poltergeist fits this case history.

This analysis is further affirmed by Hess (1989: 33), who commented that, in the past, poltergeists have been primarily described by folklorists, who treat their infestations as interesting stories, but that from a cultural and psychoanalytical viewpoint, ghost attack by a poltergeist is an idiom of distress, a position supported by Farmer's case. He further stated that Wedenoja (1978), an anthropologist, has investigated the phenomena in Jamaica and has found that poltergeists appear to be related to intrapsychic and interpersonal family and community conflicts, which sometimes are resolved as a result of the poltergeist. Hess (1989: 34) noted that the traditional treatment is exorcism.

Mrs. Barker's ghostly encounter (Chap. 13: Old Codger, Barker, and Mrs. Barker) has been described as a nightmare with the feeling of something pressing on her chest, a symptom of attack by a poltergeist or of the sleep paralysis taxon. If she talked in her sleep, anyone present might interpret her nightmare as the ghost speaking from her, and therefore a case of ghost possession. However, it seems that she was not amnesiac about what happened because she told people about her experiences, possibly Old Codger or else her daughter-in-law or son who in turn told Old Codger. The absence of amnesia shows that she was attacked but not possessed by a ghost. The repeated attacks with pressure on her chest when she was supine are similar to attacks by the Old Hag and resemble sleep paralysis. They also took place in the same dwelling and persisted off and on over a period of years when Barker was in and out of the hospital and Mrs. Barker was under great stress. The diagnosis of a poltergeist attack is based on the symptoms, on the fact that the attacks always took place in her home, suggesting that a poltergeist frequented the house, and on the disturbed state of the household due to Barker's accident and hospitalization, plus the problems Mrs. Barker faced due to Barker's drunkenness. In his drunkenness over the years, he may often have stumbled over her while she was sleeping and pressed down upon her.

LITTLE GODDESS

In 1977–78, Little Goddess was nine to ten years old and in fifth grade. She lived with her mother and father who was a police officer, two older brothers, 16 and 12 years old, and one younger sister, age seven. She was a fetching sight with her gold earrings gleaming beneath her cropped hair, which had been cut when she had typhoid in the fall of 1977. Females customarily did not have their hair cut except girls who had typhoid.

The family dwelling was a two-story building with a shop on the ground floor and the family's living quarters on the second floor. Another building for their cattle adjoined the house to the north. These buildings were located near the crossroads and the houses of Farmer and One Eyed. Two roads went eastward from the crossroads. One led to the school located not far from the cremation grounds; the other passed the pond where Little Goddess's girl friend, Whose Daughter,

had drowned in 1976. Little Goddess walked back and forth in these areas almost every day (Append. IV: Map 4, Lanes I, II, III; Dwellings nos. 2, 5a, 5b, 38, 39, 40; Codes: CR, P, S, CG).

Little Goddess's ghost possessions started in the fall of 1977 four or five days after she recovered from typhoid. The ghost was said to be Whose Daughter (Chap. 14: The Ghost of Whose Daughter). Little Goddess was reluctant to speak about Whose Daughter's death and was amnesiac for her possessions. However, she recounted trying to lead the buffalo into the pond where she and Whose Daughter were washing the animal and Little Goddess dropped the rope. She would not say more because she did not want to talk about her friend's death and would not mention her name.

Little Goddess said that Illusionist exorcised the ghost when she was possessed but that she never knew what happened because she was unconscious. Her first possession took place upstairs in her home. Someone called Illusionist, who told her parents to bring her outside because Chamars did not usually go into Jats' living quarters. When they did, he placed ashes on her forehead and recited mantras. After Little Goddess recovered, Illusionist prepared an iron amulet with a blue thread inside that she was to wear on her arm. Mrs. Farmer told us about the amulet, a protective device against ghosts. She added that the ghost of Whose Daughter caused Little Goddess to fall ill from typhoid, and after recovery from typhoid, her first ghost possession was brought on when she ate something sweet.

The next time Little Goddess was possessed was when she was looking for her mother. She ran across the lane to Farmer's house calling, "Ma, Ma," entered his courtyard, and fell down unconscious. Illusionist was again called to exorcise Whose Daughter's ghost. He pulled Little Goddess's hair, in effect abusing and threatening the ghost within her, and asked the ghost to identify itself. Then the ghost ran away. Little Charmer related this incident, which had been relayed to him by his brother, a lieutenant in the army, who was in front of the shop and witnessed the possession. Little Charmer said, "After the ghost left, Little Goddess was placed under a fan in her father's shop and was then all right." Pragmatic said that whenever Little Goddess was possessed, she would just lie quietly until Illusionist performed the exorcism and tied a *ganda* around her neck.

Little Goddess's seven-year-old sister reported that the third possession of Little Goddess took place in the family shop. This possession happened during the coincident epidemics of malaria and ghost possession when the weather was becoming quite warm in the first week of April 1978. Illusionist again exorcised the ghost.

That the mother of Little Goddess's father died when he was a child and he had a stepmother accounts for a heightened awareness of ghosts in Little Goddess's family, for her father knew that the ghost of his mother haunted his stepmother. As soon as he obtained employment as a policeman, he separated from his father. The Jat boy, Little Charmer, said that Little Goddess's father sometimes was drunk and acted funny. Responding to the Health Opinion Survey, Little Charmer and Faithful discussed being dizzy and indicated that they were disturbed by people who were drunk (Chap. 10: Jat Children). The drinking of Little Goddess's father probably upset his family, pointing to an element of stress within the family. Moreover, Little Goddess probably felt guilty about the death of her girl friend, Whose Daughter, because she had dropped the rope holding the buffalo. The animal then pushed Whose Daughter deeper into the pond where she drowned. Living close to the crossroads where ghosts linger, walking past the pond where Whose Daughter died, and passing near the cremation grounds on her way to and from school subconsciously must have prodded her memory of Whose Daughter's death and fostered the fear that her ghost was trying to seize her. In addition, Fever, a symptom of typhoid and an index of ghost illness, in all likelihood made her susceptible to ghost possession.

SUMMARY OF JAT CASES

Reports of attack and possession by ghosts show that females were disproportionately afflicted. Among Jats five females and two males suffered. One of the men and four of the women had connections to the individuals whose ghosts attacked or possessed them. Ill Fated suffered a series of possessions by the ghosts of his father and two uncles. He then had ghost illness, was treated by Old Priest, but nonetheless died. Little Boy suffered ghost illness from an unidentified ghost. The women in the family summoned a *siyana*, which infuriated Curmudgeon, the child's grandfather, who then called a *vaid*, after which the boy died (Chap. 13: Deaths of Little Boy and Scapegoat). The poltergeist that attacked Farmer was never identified.

The wife of Old Codger, Amiable, saw the ghost of Scapegoat, was possessed and then fell ill but recovered. Scapegoat, who committed suicide, had been her best friend and was the widow of Unknown and the levirate spouse of Curmudgeon, both brothers of Old Codger. Little Goddess's typhoid was attributed to the ghost of Whose Daughter, who later possessed her; Morning Star was possessed by her husband's elder brother; and Resourceful by Tippler's first wife who had lived near her. Only Mrs. Barker, whose case is different and somewhat resembles that of Farmer, was said by Old Codger to be bothered by the ghost of the Headless Sweeper with whom she had no connection, either through friendship, kinship, or proximity.

Various stresses generally precede ghost attacks and possessions. Ill Fated was under considerable family stress. Farmer had to contend with his father's disparaging attitude, had three unmarried sons and one seven-year-old daughter all in school, three married daughters to whom gifts were sent periodically, crop losses, and worry about men stealing cattle and tube-well motors. For two of the women, the underlying stresses were common, namely, family problems and the stress of marriage, menarche, and first mating. Resourceful's possessions started with the death of her father when she was a small child. She grew up with two widows, her grandmother and mother, who had economic problems. Her later possessions came at the time of menarche and Gauna when young females are vulnerable to ghost possession. Morning Star's possessions were related to her marital family. Little Goddess's circumstances were unusual: the drowning of her friend about whom she had guilt feelings, then ghost illness in the form of typhoid with Fever and delirium. Thereafter she had ghost possessions. Amiable's ghost possession and ghost illness, from which she recovered, was due to her long friendship with Scapegoat and possibly some regret that she had not been able to help her when Curmudgeon abused her about Little Boy's death. Although Honesty and a Nai Barber woman also saw Scapegoat's ghost, they did not fall ill and were not possessed.

Jats used exorcists both from inside and outside the village. Sometimes several curers were used in a specific case. The environs of Delhi, especially Palam, were the main source of Muslim exorcists.

Our sample of Jat cases is relatively small, perhaps due to the influence of the Arya Samaj. By 1977–78 some male Jats had begun to move away from the strong Arya-Samaj position that no ghosts exist. A young Jat male declared that "Nobody is Arya Samaj now," and mentioned that some Jats now worshipped idols (Chap. 10: Jat Viewpoints). Jat women, on the other hand, had retained traditional ghost beliefs through the decades and passed them on to their children who in turn carried them into adulthood, in an attenuated or dormant state by men but more openly acknowledged by women. What is particularly revealing was the willingness and openness of Mrs. Patriarch, Pragmatic, and Morning Star to talk about Morning Star's possessions. Jat boys after age six began to adopt the dominant male position about ghost beliefs, that is, fear is the ghost. Therefore, because they wanted to be like the men, they said that ghosts do not exist.

CHAPTER 23: HAIRLESS, HAUNTED, IMMATURE

IMMATURE'S POSSESSIONS

The morning of March 30, 1978, consisted of interviews with Gabbler and Student Doctor, Brahmans, in and around the domiciles of One Eyed, and of Junior and Dr. John. At that time Gabbler listed a number of persons who had recently been possessed by ghosts, among them the 17- to 18-year-old wife of Constable, a Chamar. We placed her on the list of possible interviews. In the afternoon we set out to learn about her possessions. As we turned into the lane leading toward the Chuhra Sweeper and Chamar quarters and passed One Eyed's house, Gabbler shouted, "The ghost [Hairless] has entered Constable's wife." The hullaballoo arising from the Chamar quarter was considerable so we scurried through the Sweeper quarter. There we met Loyal, a Sweeper woman. She confirmed Gabbler's statement, and a Sweeper girl led us to the house of Security Guard, the father-in-law of Immature, the girl who had just been possessed. Many people were standing around talking and shouting while the girl, covered by a quilt, was lying unconscious on a cot outside the house. Her mother-in-law, Worrier, the wife of Security Guard and mother of Constable, stood in the yard beside her, looking worried, upset, and harassed. She was so distracted that at first she did not respond but then confirmed that her daughter-in-law had just been possessed by a ghost. She added: "It is difficult to drive the ghost away. We fold hands and ask it to go away. Previously the ghost came rarely. Now it comes frequently." When asked Immature's age, Worrier answered: "She is 15 to 16 but has come to stay permanently and somebody has gone to fetch a *siyana*." Further questioning elicited the information that two ghosts were possessing Immature: the first wife (Hairless) of Worrier's husband's elder brother (Government Worker) and a Jat woman (Housewife) (Append. III: Chart 12; Chap. 15: Murder or Suicide).

An older man, one of many people milling about in the lane because of Immature's possession, interrupted to explain: "She has been troubled by the ghost or ghosts for the last three days. The first ghost pulls her toward the fire; the second ghost, toward the well." Then he told Worrier to grind black pepper and put it in Immature's eyes. She said she would. He also said: "Red chillies don't have a permanent effect, but if black pepper is put in the eyes, then the ghost will say, 'You hurt me,' and go away." Another man said, "I can suggest a *siyana* if you want me to."

Worrier added: "The girl doesn't eat anything and just vomits. She came here the day before yesterday. Before that she was in her own [natal] village and the ghost went there and possessed her there. Again she was possessed in her mother's brother's village. This time when the girl first came here, she was possessed by the ghosts. At the time of her wedding, she had not yet mated. Presently her husband is away on duty."

Worrier was then asked: Why do you think the ghost or ghosts do this to your daughter-in-law? She replied: "I don't know. It is God's will. We know when the ghost comes because she runs toward the pond or the well, but we don't let her go out of the house. Many women have to catch hold of her; she's strong and young. When the ghosts come, she becomes very powerful. Now she is weak. Sunny [Kin's daughter] is affected by the same ghost [Hairless], the first wife of Government Worker" (Chap. 17: Illusionist's Patients).

Other women added that ghosts of village wives and the ghosts of two girl friends of Immature also possessed her. One woman said that when Government Worker's first wife fell ill her brain and blood turned to water and she was taken to a hospital where a tube was inserted to take out the water. Still another woman stated that anyone can become a ghost, and Hairless was a good and simple woman. These statements indicated that Hairless died of ghost illness and her soul became a ghost. As a nonsequitur, Worrier chipped in the information that Immature went to fifth grade in school.

During the conversation, Immature was lying on the cot, well covered by a quilt, to recover from the ghost possession. Then she awoke and peeked out at us. Her eyes had deep circles around them. We told her who we were and that we wanted to find out about her ghost possessions. She said that now she was all right, but there was something wrong

with her neck. One woman explained that when the ghost bothers her, she bangs her head on the ground so the back of her neck and head hurt. The ghost puts pressure on her head and tries to bend it. Immature added that when the ghost tries to enter her she is afraid. The ghost talks to her a bit and then completely enters her. The ghost has long teeth, big eyes, and no hair on her head. Another woman stated: "Immature has no sickness except the ghost possessions. Many ghosts possess her and throw her around. The ghost of Government Worker's wife [Hairless] is so strong she can even throw this man [pointing to a large, heavy man]. After her wedding visit, on her second visit to her husband [for Gauna], Immature had her first possession."

Then Immature opened her eyes widely, sat up, and said, "This is my fourth visit. I returned here after nine days at my parents'[house]." She told us her name and that she could hear us while we were talking but had no interest in what we said. She also said: "I can't say the ghosts' names and never saw the women before they died and became ghosts. I have never seen any of the women, not even the woman whose ghost appears before me naked and scares me [Hairless]."

Another woman mentioned the ghost of Housewife, identifying her only by her husband's name (Pawn) and saying that she jumped in a well, was of medium height and color, but she did not know why she jumped because one doesn't know what goes on in another family. She added that she herself was attacked by the ghost of Government Worker's first wife (Hairless), had pain in her body, lay down, and her jaws snapped shut. Her pseudonym is Haunted. Worrier, the sister of Haunted and wife of Security Guard, Government Worker's brother, identified Haunted as the second wife of Government Worker. We asked Immature which ghost was the main ghost bothering her. She replied that she did not know but she thought a woman in her own family was protecting her from the ghost. Haunted then said, "It is just the opposite. Her mother-in-law is protecting her."

We asked Immature: "During this visit was your husband here, have you mated with him, and are you afraid of mating." She answered:

"We mated at earlier visits and I was not afraid of mating. I like my husband because he helps me face my trouble with the ghosts." Asked whether she had ever been possessed before her marriage, her answer was "No, it was only on the second visit when I heard about this ghost [Hairless] for the first time." She volunteered the information that her husband's father's younger brother (whose pseudonym is Parcelman because he worked in the Parcel Department of the railway) and his wife, Go-Between, had gone to fetch the *siyana* from his village, explaining that two of Go-Between's sisters were married to two sons of the *siyana* and therefore she was acting as an intermediary. The *siyana* was expected to come back with them by evening.

Immature's neck again began to pain her. When asked whether she fell down when the ghost entered her, she replied: "Yes. I fell down from the bed to the ground. My whole body pains, but I did not feel anything until after the ghost left." A woman said, "If they don't catch hold of her, she can break her head." Immature said, "One man or one woman cannot control me." The same woman said, "At least two or three strong people are needed."

Immature then said that now she was feeling all right but wanted to go somewhere else, not back to her own village, nor did she want to stay here. When asked if she felt sad, she said, "Yes and angry too because I never had this happen to me before I was married." When we suggested that she let her anger out by hitting her hands together, she disclosed that she shivered whenever the ghost tried to enter her. Then Worrier added, commenting on shivering, "We can't put the quilt on her because she jumps around, but we try to catch hold of her. Then she asks for water but doesn't drink it. The women who help her tell the ghost to go away. The ghost, speaking from the girl, says, 'I'll take this girl with me.' The woman who died [Hairless] had no hair on her head so when they pulled Immature's hair, it had no effect." This lack of effect reflects the fact that when the ghost is within its victim, it displaces the victim's identity; thus, it is not the victim's but the ghost's hair that is pulled to drive it out. Since Hairless had no hair, neither did her ghost, so pulling Immature's hair would not affect the ghost.

At this point Parcelman and his wife, Go-Between, returned from the *siyana*. They reported that the *siyana* could not come until Sunday (three days later). In the meantime, he instructed them to tell the ghost, when it came again, that it had better go away, otherwise the *siyana* would break it in pieces. He also gave the couple two types of ashes for Immature: the first was to put on the body; the second was black pepper mixed in ashes to be eaten by her. The *siyana* promised them that he had hold of the family ghost (Hairless) and that Immature would not be bothered until he came on Sunday.

When Immature was asked if she was feeling better, she replied, "No, but when I eat the ashes, I'll probably feel much better, but not until then. People affected by ghost possessions are used to them, but I am not." Then Immature washed her face with water. We said, "These people are taking good care of you." Immature responded, "Yes, my father-in-law is so worried about me that he does not take his food." She continued: "I am almost 18 years old, which is not very old but because my parents fed me well I look strong. My father is a gardener and works across a bridge near Shanti Vani [the City of Delhi cremation grounds]. My parents live in a village at a distance from the cremation grounds. My father never talks about them."

Here Parcelman said that the *siyana* told him that two ghosts accompanied the main ghost (Hairless), who was his eldest brother's first wife. Because Haunted was standing nearby, we asked whether she was affected by other ghosts. She replied that she was affected only by the ghost of her husband's first wife (Hairless). One woman said that Immature was affected by the ghost of the first wife and two other ghosts. Haunted said that she suffered spells of unconsciousness from the ghost of Hairless but that the same ghost drives Immature to the well. Immature confirmed this statement but added that she did not know she ran to the well until women told her about it after she regained consciousness. When Immature was asked whether she thought the ghost or ghosts were trying to kill her, she replied: "I do not know what will happen to me, but if I die, I'll become a ghost too. Everyone is helping me ward off these ghosts." Then one old woman said, "That is how I've been advising her. She should not be afraid. When the ghost comes and talks to her, she should scold the ghost and tell her that she will not go with her. You have to scare these ghosts."

Another woman volunteered:

When the ghost leaves, Immature worries about it. She worries because now we are here and will help her, but some day she may be alone and the ghost will get her. Once Immature was sitting with me and another woman, and some children were watching her, but at that time Immature's mother-in-law and others in the family had done nothing to protect her. When her ghost possessions continued here, at her parents' house, and her mother's brother's house, she had been eating and then ran to the railway line when the train was due to run through there. She ran there, returned, and then fell down unconscious.

Because of the welter of comments, Immature was asked the order and places of her possessions. She recapitulated: "I was first possessed here in this village the fourth night after first mating with my husband. The first three nights I was all right before and after mating. I do not remember the exact time of the attack, but my husband was with me on the bed where I am now sitting. My husband is not a man who would be afraid because he is a constable in the President's house in New Delhi, where my father-in-law is also employed."

We asked Immature whether she liked being married. She answered: "It is good to be married because unmarried girls roam around and it does not look good." She also told us that she had four living sisters and two living brothers. She was the oldest surviving child in the family but a number of her mother's children died as infants. Because she was the first to survive and the eldest, her parents brought her up in a loving way. Then her husband's younger brother (dewar), said that when the siyana comes, she will get better.

In winding up this session, Worrier reasoned: "A student [Sunny, Kin's daughter, a Chamar] was recently affected by the same ghost [Hairless]. The schoolteacher asked, 'Why doesn't the ghost possess me.' That evening the ghost left the student and pos-

sessed the teacher. In the same way, the ghost may possess anyone tonight" (Chap. 17: Illusionist's Patients).

On April 2, 1978, the siyana came to the village and joined hands with Illusionist to drive out the ghosts haunting the village. We did not hear of this event until after it took place, and all we learned was that they had joined hands and exorcised the ghosts. It was not possible to interview Immature alone after her ghost possession due to the termination of our fieldwork a few weeks later. An in-depth interview could have revealed facts pertinent to her possessions, particularly about the ghosts of her two girl friends who possessed her. They may have been the main ghosts disturbing her, just as the ghost of Sita's cousin was the main one haunting Sita, whose case is described below and compared to Immature's case.

Salient features of Immature's life, her social environment, and her ghost possessions are here summarized.

(1) She saw the ghost before it entered her and the ghost talked to her and frightened her.

(2) She shivered before she was possessed.

(3) Women tried to put a quilt or quilts around her, which was customary when a victim of possession shivered before the ghost entered.

(4) When possessed, she ran toward the pond, well, or railroad. Villagers interpreted this behavior as attempts at suicide. Therefore she had to be watched.

(5) Although she fell and hurt herself during possessions, she did not feel pain until emerging from the alternate mental states experienced during possession.

(6) After recovering from possession, she had amnesia for what happened during the attack, only finding out when she was later told about it.

(7) In her natal family, she was the first surviving child. A number of infants born before her died, so she was well cared for and brought up in a loving way. Although just short of 18 years old when we interviewed her, she said that she looked strong because her parents fed her well.

(8) Both Immature's natal and marital families were strongly affected by ghost beliefs. Her father worked as a gardener at Shanti

Vani and did not like to talk about the cremation grounds, evidently because he feared ghosts. One of the most feared of the village ghosts, Hairless, was the first wife of the eldest brother of Immature's father-in-law. Hairless tried to possess the second wife, Haunted, as well as Immature. Haunted, Worrier, and Go-Between were sisters, and two other sisters were married to two sons of the *siyana*. Thus, familial links existed between these families and the world of ghosts (Append. III: Chart 12). It is no wonder that these ties of descent and marriage and a strong tradition of ghost beliefs among the Chamars made Immature vulnerable to possessions.

(9) Villagers have methods of exorcising a ghost in the absence of an exorcist. Some substances, such as black pepper, chili pepper, and ashes are effective. Methods of intimidation, such as scaring, threatening, and abusing ghosts are almost always employed. Victims are closely watched to prevent suicide.

(10) The times of Immature's possessions are of major significance, especially the first which took place the fourth night after first mating with her husband on her second visit to the village. On her third visit to her husband, Immature brought her four-year-old sister with her, but the child wept and was afraid when Immature was possessed so Immature did not bring her again. She was also possessed at the villages of her parents and her mother's brothers, and on the occasion of her fourth visit to her husband in March 1978, when she knew she was to remain permanently in her marital home.

Although Worrier gave Immature's age as 15 to 16 years old, she was reported as 17 to 18 years old in our 1977 fall census, and she herself said she was almost 18 on March 30, 1978 when this session took place. She seemed to be apologizing for looking older than she was. It was not unusual for a mother-in-law to reduce the age of a new daughter-in-law, possibly because 14 to 15 was generally believed to be the age at which menarche took place and thus the age for first mating. Immature's physical description is also pertinent because dissociative disorders, also known as alternate mental states, may be due to somatic complaints. However, she appeared to be healthy. Her height and weight

were well within the ranges for village women. Her face was not gaunt, but she had dark circles around her eyes, perhaps signs of fatigue and stress.

At the time of first mating in 1978, she had not yet menstruated and did not do so until after the birth of her first child in August 1979. Thus, at the time of her possessions in the spring of 1978, she may have been ovulating but had not yet menstruated. Her second child was born in August 1981, and her third child in January 1983.

According to her husband, the third child was conceived before she had begun to menstruate after the birth of the second, which might indicate some physical problem regarding menstruation. However, had she nursed her second child for at least one-and-a-half years without giving the child supplementary foods, she would not have begun to menstruate. Lactation without supplementary feedings prevents ovulation and menstruation. The belief that menstruation is necessary to conceive is common, but pregnancy is possible for a girl who has begun to have intercourse before she begins to menstruate providing she ovulates (Harrell, 1981: 797–805).

Immature seems to have attained menarche when she was either 18 or 19 years old which is late but not exceptional, for menarche may be reached from age 11 to 18. Age 19, however, is about three years later than average in Shanti Nagar. In 1959, we interviewed 40 women about their age at menarche: the average age was approximately 16 years. In the early years of her marriage when she was experiencing the stress of adjusting to marital life, the lack of menses may have disturbed her and contributed to her ghost possessions along with her fear of the ghosts of Hairless and Housewife, stories about other village ghosts, and the ghosts of her two girl friends. Physical and psychological stress as well as somatic complaints are important in analyzing ghost possessions (Selye, 1956: 47, 216–218; Chaps. 9, 13; Frisch and Revelle, 1970; Frisch and McArthur, 1974; Delora et al., 1980: 61; Sandler et al., 1980: 84–85; Berkow, 1982: 1655–1657, 1658–1660; R. Freed and S. Freed, 1985: 160, fn. 22; 190–191).

When women in Shanti Nagar were asked

how girls found out about menstruation, the consistent answer was that parents did not tell them because they were shy about such matters. Sometimes girl friends told them. Although mothers and daughters did not speak about such things, a brother's wife might tell her younger sister-in-law. Knowing nothing about menstruation, a girl might be working in the fields when her clothing became blood-stained. When she could not understand why, a girl friend told her about menstruation. According to these informants, girls and young women feel that menses are natural, but when they start menstruating, they do not tell their mothers or elder sisters. Often the mothers do not know that their daughters have reached menarche until one or two years after the event, possibly because their daughters are too shy to tell them, or because they want to avoid going to their husbands, relative strangers, for first mating.

Immature showed symptoms of either physical or psychological stress, probably both. Prior to her possessions, she saw the ghost of Hairless who spoke to her, then she shivered, but when the women tried to cover her with quilts, she jumped and ran about. Shivering before possession may be due to chills and change in body temperature. It is one of the first signs of ghost possessions, just as a flushed, hot face and hot body skin are signs of Fever and ghost illness. Seeing the ghost, being frightened, shivering, and being covered with quilts are indices of the beginning of possession. Shivering on March 30, 1978, the day of Immature's possession, would most likely not have been due to the weather because the temperature was about 87°F. Tremors, which may be what the villagers described as shivering, consist of "involuntary movements in one or more parts of the body produced by successive alternate contractions of opposing muscle groups. Tremors often reflect extrapyramidal or cerebellar disturbance. Transient tremors without particular significance may occur normally with hunger, chilling, physical exertion, or excitement" (Berkow, 1982: 1357). The following statement from Berkow, (1982: 1359) may be pertinent to ghost possessions: "Tremors associated with functional disease may simulate those of organic CNS [Central Nervous System] disease and make diagnosis difficult. Psychiatric evaluation is helpful.

Tremor is a fairly common symptom in both chronic and acute anxiety states. . . . Frequently fine and rapid, the tremor may also be a coarse irregular shaking intensified by emotion and voluntary movement." Certainly fear and anxiety states characterized Immature.

The relation of shivering and tremors to possession is discussed here partly because of similarities of possession in Shanti Nagar to the possession-trance of devotees of the Dravidian god Murugan during the Thaipusam festival in Kuala Lumpur, Malaysia (Simons et al., 1988; Ervin et al., 1988). (Cf. Bourguignon, 1979: 247–265 on distinctions between possession, possession-trance, and trance without possession, cited in Chap. 21 of this text: Mrs. Earnest.) While training for the festival, devotees fasted, were sexually continent, and refrained from a variety of social activities, a regime that must have induced stress. Prior to their entry into trance, devotees were frightened in anticipation of pain. Part of the experience of devotees during the festival is the insertion of *vel*s (spears), the symbolic weapon of Murugan, into the devotees. Hooks and needles were also inserted in their tongues. The theory advanced by R. Prince, a participant in the research and an M.D. and Director of Social and Transcultural Psychiatry at McGill University, Montreal, is that the endorphins of the body act as opiates to reduce the pain and allow the devotees to enter into analgesic trance (Ervin et al., 1988: 281). The devotees believe that Murugan possesses the power to prevent suffering. The first visible sign of entering trance is an increase in muscle tension, which often becomes a visible physiological tremor throughout the entire body, and which may be similar to the shivering reported in victims of ghost possession in Shanti Nagar.

R. Prince (1982b: 413–414) suggested that the tremors associated with trance can be explained by Cannon's fight or flight hypothesis, namely that the individual who is possessed sees the ghost, fears it, and then flees. Thus, in Immature's case seeing the ghost before possession and fearing that it would enter her, shivering, and then in her possessed state running to the pond, well, railway, or a fire are physical activities in accord with the flight hypothesis. On the other hand, Immature's "flight" activities could be interpreted as suicide attempts arising from depression. On emerging from her possession, Immature said that she no longer wanted to stay in Shanti Nagar and that she felt "sad." Victims fear ghosts and flee because they believe that if a ghost takes their souls they will die. On the other hand, it is also possible that in a state of possession a victim's subconscious takes over so that the victim tries to commit suicide. Where pain is involved as well as fear, R. Prince (1982b: 414) further suggested that trembling is "a kind of endorphin pump," and by similar reasoning, that the physical activity of flight may generate and maintain the analgesic state due to endorphin effects. This suggestion also applies to Immature running about when possessed. (For further information on endorphins, see Henry, 1982; Saffran, 1982.)

Further to Prince's suggestion, it is worth noting that although Immature had fallen and hurt herself and also banged her head on the ground during possessions, she did not feel pain until after the ghost left her, i.e., when she came out of the alternate mental states, which was also when the level of endorphins no longer worked as opiates. Although the techniques which the villagers use to drive out ghosts include unpleasant substances and physical force, they are directed at the ghost, not the victim. They no doubt have some effect on possessed persons, but due to amnesia victims cannot remember their effect any more than they can recall whatever may have caused pain during possession. Exorcists and villagers use both psychological and physical methods. However, unlike villagers, exorcists are believed to have supernatural powers and can summon their familiars to aid them. They also use soothing and hypnotic techniques. Thus, their methods are designed to reassure victims and their families that they can control ghosts, which therefore should not be feared. Both villagers and exorcists act to provide support for the victims, a sign that practical and perhaps effective measures are being taken.

IMMATURE AND SITA

The case of Immature shows similarities to the possessions of Sita, a Chamar woman. In 1958 at the age of 15 on the fourth night after first mating and for the following three years, Sita suffered a series of ghost possessions. In September 1958, we conducted three lengthy interviews with Sita about her early life, natal family, girl friends and matrilateral cousin, her dreams, and her attitudes toward menses, marriage, mating, and childbearing. After the birth of her first child, her possessions became fits (*daura*). In March 1978, we interviewed members of Sita's marital family and talked with Sita twice. On April 1, 1978, Sita, age 35, recounted her psychomedical history in the course of a four-hour interview. She commented on Immature's possessions, recognizing similarities to her own early ghost possessions. She also knew about City Girl's possessions and others that had taken place in the village (Chap. 19: City Girl's Possessions).

Both Sita and Immature were raised in a more urbanized environment than Shanti Nagar and perhaps had to make a greater adjustment than usual to their marital village. Both girls experienced their first possessions on the fourth night after first mating. Sita was the first born of her mother's children. Four boys and five girls were born after Sita; all died in infancy. They could not digest their mother's milk because of infant hypolactasia due to recessive genes for a lactase deficiency (R. Freed and S. Freed, 1985: 138–142). Then two boys were born who survived infancy, but one died at age 14 from unknown causes. Three more children were born and died as infants. The deaths of Sita's siblings were attributed to ghost illness. Immature was the first child to survive after a number of her mother's infants died, so there were multiple deaths of infant siblings in both cases. The familial and caste traditions of both Sita and Immature shared beliefs in ghosts, ghost illness, and possession with the possibility of death due to the seizure of souls by ghosts. The souls of the victims themselves then became ghosts. In Immature's case, her father's work at Shanti Vani added to the fear of ghosts.

Sita had three girl friends, all of whom died before she herself was married. One girl was raped by a schoolteacher. Blaming her for the assault, her furious father raped her, cut her throat, and threw her in a well. Frightened by the teacher's attack, Sita's parents took her out of school when she had just entered fifth grade. This ended her ambition of becoming a teacher. Immature finished fifth grade. With regard to education, Sita differed from low-caste Chamar and Chuhra girls in Shanti Nagar, of whom none had gone to school in 1958. She had attended school in her natal village. Education in Shanti Nagar only gradually entered village life, first with the upper castes and boys, later for all castes and both sexes. Only the Chamar caste lived in Sita's urbanized, natal village, which meant that there was no repression from the high castes, and both boys and girls attended school (R. Freed and S. Freed, 1981: 138; 1985: 144–146; S. Freed and R. Freed, 1976: 49–50).

Before her marriage but after she had stopped school, Sita and her mother lived for some months in Sita's mother's brother's village. While living there, Sita and her matrilateral cousin flirted with boys. The cousin, her closest girl friend, was intimate with a young man and became pregnant. When her father found out, he sent her to her husband for first mating. The husband's parents, recognizing she was pregnant, returned her to her parents. Her father then implacably told her to commit suicide in a well, and she did (R. Freed and S. Freed, 1985: 143–146).

Sita's third friend died just after being sent to her husband's village for mating. She is reported to have come down with a combination of typhoid and malaria. However, Sita seemed to associate her friend's death with marriage and residence in a strange village, that of her husband. Strangers can cause illness. Sita linked fears about strangers, illness, death, marriage, mating, and birth in a growing anxiety complex about her future marriage (R. Freed and S. Freed, 1985: 146).

The ghosts of Sita's three girl friends possessed her in the early years of her marriage, but the ghost of the cousin who committed suicide was the one Sita saw before her first possession. She not only haunted Sita in the early years of her marriage but possessed her thereafter in the form of fits (daura). When interviewed in 1978, Sita claimed that her cousin's ghost had also possessed her cousin's mother. Sita believed that she was infected by her cousin's ghost through contact with her cousin's mother (R. Freed and S. Freed, 1985: 192). Two of Immature's girl friends were also among the ghosts haunting her, but we did not find out any details about them

or their relation to Immature. Because Immature was possessed both in her parents' village and in her mother's brother's village, it is possible that one friend was from her natal village and the other from the mother's brother's village.

With the birth of Sita's first child, her possessions changed to fits, which took place periodically through the years and were still occurring in the spring of 1978. Before the onslaught of her possessions on her second visit to her husband's village for first mating, which was put off until her third visit because she was afraid, Sita either accidentally or intentionally fell into a well but was saved by two men. Some years later when she had fits, she sometimes ran toward the railroad tracks but was stopped by her husband and his brothers. Immature also ran toward the railroad tracks or the well. Similar suicide attempts or gestures crop up in other ghost possessions. The ghost is believed to make the victim behave in this way to obtain the victim's soul.

Sita feared marriage and mating because of the experiences and deaths of her girl friends and the deaths of the many infants her mother had borne. Immature, who was the first surviving child of her parents, may also have worried due to her late menarche and the general ignorance of brides about mating, the conception of children, the possibility of their own and their infants' deaths, as well as the pervasive fear of ghosts. After her first possession in Shanti Nagar, Immature learned about the ghosts of wives who had been murdered, committed suicide, and died of a dread disease, particularly Hairless and Housewife, and believed that they were trying to seize her soul.

We were able to conduct long interviews with Sita in 1958 and during the spring of 1978 and also at both times with members of her marital family so her medical case history is far more complete than Immature's. A number of exorcists were called for Sita's possessions. When her first possession took place, her in-laws and bystanders applied the usual home remedies. Sita's early possessions ran through the dark fortnight of August–September 1958, during which time four exorcists attempted to rid her of the three ghosts said to possess her. The first exorcism was carried out by a man from a nearby village. The next exorcist was a Dhobi (Washerman) fetched from the City of Delhi by Government Worker who knew him because they worked in the same place. The Dhobi conducted two curing sessions. In the second session he used herbs to induce Sita's possession. When she continued to be possessed, her father was notified and brought two exorcists, one from New Delhi and the other from Mehrauli, a city south of New Delhi. These men conducted an all-night session in their attempt to drive off the ghosts. Sita then went to stay with her father and mother for some time so no further information was gathered from her in 1959 (R. Freed and S. Freed, 1985: 165–173).

In the April 1978 interview, Sita told us that the ghost of her matrilateral cousin was the main cause of her possessions and later fits. To exorcise her cousin's ghost she consulted a number of exorcists. She wore a *tawiz* which she believed helped her control the fits brought on by her cousin's ghost. For her physical complaints she went to doctors and hospitals. Sita detailed her pregnancies, illnesses, and operations during the almost 20 years since we last saw her in 1958. Just prior to her wedding when she was 15 years old, she attained menarche, stained her clothing, and was told about menses by a girl friend, not by her mother. As a result of a genetic trait of adult hypolactasia, she suffered from a calcium deficiency. One of her children had infant hypolactasia, but Sita was instructed about a suitable diet for this condition by a physician at a hospital, where both she and the child were being treated. She was afflicted with endometriosis and persistent premenstrual tension. She had nine pregnancies, her second and fourth ending in miscarriages. After the fourth pregnancy, she had an operation to remove kidney stones. Two of her pregnancies lasted 11 months. In 1972, she had her ninth and last pregnancy aborted and then was sterilized. Thereafter, she suffered from intermittent bleeding. Despite all these problems, in 1978 she had five surviving children: two daughters and three sons (R. Freed and S. Freed, 1985: 186–205).

Anxiety and stress combined with her persistent physical disorders contributed to Sita's possessions and later fits. From a psychiatric viewpoint, her case would be classified as a Conversion Somatoform Disorder under the category of Dissociative Disorders (Am. Psych. Assn., DSM-III, 1980: 253–260; R. Freed and S. Freed, 1985: 114).

Sita was the only village woman to provide a complete description of her fits. She said that her ghost possessions turned into fits after her first child was born in 1961, three years after her wedding. Sita's description of her fits follows:

They start from the head. I feel giddy and drowsy. Then I can't see anything and everything goes dark. My legs, hands, and veins stiffen, then a pain goes to my stomach. I don't know what happens, but I have a pain in my heart, my eyes shut, and my tongue comes out. I shriek so loud that the whole village, even the Brahmans, know I am having a fit. I have a weak heart. Whenever there is a fight in the family or elsewhere, or if I see a dead body, I have fits.

Based on information from Sita and members of her marital family, her fits had the following characteristics:

1. She may fall unconscious from one to four hours.
2. When the fits first take her, she may get up from her bed and then fall unconscious.
3. She becomes violent so that it takes at least four people to hold her; or according to Sita, eight or nine people. At these times she tears her clothes and hits people; she is also very strong.
4. People who hold her down press the veins of her stomach to afford her some relief (Ayurvedic treatment somewhat like cupping) (Kutumbiah, 1969: 162–163; R. Freed and S. Freed, 1979: 330).
5. Since her sterilization, blood and urine come out of her mouth at the time of her fits.
6. A hakim diagnosed her fits as due to an insect's bite and said she had a weak heart, possibly because she said she had pains in her heart at the time of her fits.
7. According to her father-in-law, every 20 days to one month when new blood is made in her body [the reference is to her menses], the fit is most apt to affect her. Climatic conditions such as hailstorms and a

tornado affect her, which he attributed to air touching her body (an Ayurvedic concept).

8. Sita and her brother-in-law attributed her fits to fears, worries, and emotional disturbances. Her brother-in-law said that when she worries she twists her hands and shouts loudly.

9. Unpredictable events, such as storms, injury to crops, family fights, deaths, or fears of deaths, bring on the fits. (Adapted from R. Freed and S. Freed, 1985: 202–203.)

We had far less information about Immature than about Sita because we did not learn about her until our fieldwork was about to end. Also, in 1978 Immature was not quite 18 years old and Sita was 35. Therefore, Immature had fewer life experiences to report but, like Sita, had begun to experience possessions the fourth night after first mating. Another interesting parallel between the two was that they both had to be held down during their possessions, as was also the case with Morning Star, the Jat woman (Chap. 22: Pragmatic and Morning Star). Sita ascribed this need for restraint to her fits. Other women in Shanti Nagar mentioned that their possessions changed to fits, *daura* (R. Freed and S. Freed, 1985: 121). Carstairs and Kapur (1976: 102–111, 163), using the International Classification of Diseases, report "hysterical fits" in South India, which are linked with possessions, last for long periods, and have a history of psychological stress and, sometimes, of somatic complaints.

Toward the very end of the 1977–78 fieldwork, we found that three other women and one man suffered from possessions and later fits, but were unable to obtain long interviews with them. Timid, Lord of Ghosts' daughter-in-law, a Sweeper woman, was one of the three women. The man was Eluded, the youngest brother of Lord of Ghosts, whom we never met as he was living in the City of Delhi in 1958–59 and, when transportation later became more convenient, was commuting to work in 1977–78. He too was possessed for a while and the possessions turned into fits (Chap. 16: Lord of Ghosts). A Brahman woman and the Chhipi Tailor woman, the latter in a 1977 discussion about the death of her daughter and her subsequent possessions and later fits, said they regularly experienced fits, which had been preceded by possessions (Chap. 9: Action, Rebirth, Release). The frequency with which cases of possession turn to fits is worth further research.

HAIRLESS AND HAUNTED

The trials of Hairless, Haunted, Government Worker, and their children are a veritable jeremiad, but Haunted bore her tribulations with surprisingly good nature. In the spring of 1978, Hairless, the first wife of Government Worker, was the most malevolent and feared ghost in the village, particularly in the Chamar compound where she had lived. How and why she became a ghost and whom she haunted are related to the cases of Haunted and Immature. Haunted, the second wife of Government Worker, provided most of the information about the ghost of Hairless.

In 1958, a young woman, age 25, whose soul after death became the ghost of Hairless, was married to Government Worker, age 31. This couple had not attended school, but as an adult Government Worker had gone to school for six months, learned to read and write, knew basic arithmetic, and could read and speak some English. He worked for the Government in the City of Delhi. In 1958, the couple had two daughters, ages 7 and 3. Their nuclear family was part of a large, joint family consisting of Government Worker's father, Government Worker, his next younger brother with his wife and children, and his youngest brother still in school. The mother of these three brothers had died.

In late 1967 or 1968, Government Worker's wife fell ill with an unidentified disease, lost all her head hair, and was taken to a hospital where she died, age 34 to 35. In village lore, she became the ghost of Hairless. She left two sons, ages 7 and 5, and two daughters, ages 16 and 12. While a number of women were talking about the ghost of Hairless after this ghost possessed Immature, one Chamar woman said, "When Government Worker's wife fell ill her brain and blood turned to water and she was taken to a hospital where a tube was inserted to take out the water" (Append. III: Chart 12).

The description of the illness of Hairless suggests that she may have suffered from an infectious illness which damaged her central nervous system, in particular, her brain. Meningitis encephalitis (Berkow, 1982: 1339–1346), prevalent in the region, is a possibility. She became a ghost because she died before her time, tortured by a disease, and lost all her hair, which made her illness far worse than other ghost illnesses.

HAUNTED

After the death of Hairless, the three brothers separated, the father remaining with his eldest son, Government Worker. The brothers claimed that they separated because the two sisters of Haunted who married the two younger brothers always fought, but they themselves pulled on well together, an oft repeated refrain when brothers separated. It is not clear whether the ghost of Hairless and the disease from which she died contributed to the separation of the families, but fear of a ghost can be a factor in the division of a family, as in the case of Little Goddess's father who separated from his own father partly because his mother's ghost was haunting his stepmother.

In 1968, Government Worker, age 41, married again. Shortly thereafter, his second wife, Haunted, age 27, was possessed by Hairless. Perhaps her possession contributed to the separation into three families. Haunted had the care of the household, the first wife's daughters and sons, and her father-in-law. The elderly father of Government Worker died early in 1977 when he was 79 years old. In 1977–78 his sons were observing the year of mourning. His death and the mourning period recalled times past and stimulated persistent ghost beliefs about Government Worker's first wife, Hairless.

At the end of March 1978, Haunted in a long interview said that Hairless possessed her immediately after her first mating with Government Worker. Then she suffered ghost illness in the form of diarrhea and went to her natal home. Later when she returned to her husband, she was possessed by the ghost, and again had ghost illness. Her illness continued. She was all right for two to four days and then she was sick again. She had to lie in bed for a month and a quarter. When the ghost possessed her, she felt pain throughout

her body, had Fever, and her jaws snapped together. Many times she was unconscious and people would pry her jaws open with a pitchfork. After the birth of her first daughter in 1968, she was again possessed by the ghost of Hairless, and family members and curers put various substances in her eyes (chili pepper, black pepper, etc.). Haunted said that the ghost came and said, "I have come to meet my sister in this house." Haunted replied, "I don't want this woman here." In 1978, although Haunted had not been possessed for the past four to five years, she said that her children were still possessed and also had ghost illness. She added that when the ghost of Hairless attacked her, she first saw the ghost and then the ghost fell on her like a great weight so that she could not talk. This description indicated a possession resembling paralysis. In addition to her first child, Haunted had three more children: two sons born in 1970 and 1973, and another daughter born in 1975. All four children were alive in the spring of 1978 (Append. III: Chart 12).

The two daughters of Hairless, ages 26 and 22, were present during this interview. They were on friendly terms with their stepmother, Haunted, and had come for a visit because their father, Government Worker, was home on leave. They stated that they had not been possessed by the ghost of their mother after she died, which is consistent with the belief that the ghost of a first wife does not harm her own children.

When Haunted was asked why she thought Hairless possessed her, she replied:

First the ghost of Hairless said to me, "Why don't you take care of your own children." The ghost would come, then I would be treated by a bhagat or *siyana*, then the ghost would go away. Nowadays when my children have Fever, it is because her ghost attacks them. The ghost speaks through the children and tells me to call a bhagat. The bhagat will then tell me that the ghost is from my own household and ask me to take brown sugar and place it at the shrine of the Crossroads Mata and that will bring relief. The bhagat is my youngest sister's father-in-law. [As indicated earlier, Haunted had four sisters: two were married to Government's Worker's brothers, Security

Guard, the father-in-law of Immature, and Parcelman; the other two were married to the sons of the *siyana*. He was called from his natal village to exorcise the ghost of Hairless and other ghosts when they afflicted Haunted, her children, and Immature. Haunted used the words *siyana* and bhagat interchangeably.]

Today I cooked halva for my stepdaughters, but I did not give any to my own children when they went to school. If I had, they would have eaten the sweet halva on the way toward the bus stop and would immediately have been affected by the ghost as they passed by the cremation grounds and the pond. The ghost roams around there on the road.

Haunted, holding her two-year-old daughter in her arms, said that the child currently was afflicted by Hairless, adding that all four of her children had ghost possessions and ghost illness brought by the ghost of her husband's first wife. Once her eldest stepdaughter and her son paid a visit to express sorrow for the death of Government Worker's younger brother's sons. That night, the boy had Fever. The boy died five days after he and his mother returned home. Haunted attributed the illness and the death of her stepdaughter's son to the ghost of Hairless. Further, her stepdaughter consulted a bhagat who told her that someone in her natal family had become a ghost and had attacked the child. That the ghost of Hairless attacked her own daughter's child is surprising because a ghost is believed to be benevolent toward her own children. This case is the only one told to us by villagers where the ghost of a first wife attacked her own grandchild. Haunted's 15-year-old stepson, who was present during the interview, did not remember anything about the ghost causing illness. Neither did her own seven-year-old son.

Haunted was asked whether she had ever seen a ghost before marrying Government Worker and coming to live in the village. She answered that earlier in life she had never had Fever or known anything about ghosts. Her statement is questionable considering her life history, for she was brought up in a caste with the belief that much illness and death

are caused by ghosts. She had been married before her marriage to Government Worker and bore her first husband five children in quick succession who died as infants, so her husband returned her to her parents. Haunted was very pleasant and liked talking with us, but she was not very accurate about her facts and without a doubt repressed whatever caused her five children with her first husband to die. Further, it is possible that she was older than she said because she was vague about ages and dates. Her eldest stepson supplied the census data in his father's absence and seemed protective and most helpful to Haunted. In any case, given her own beliefs about ghosts, it is probable that the deaths of her five children from her first marriage were attributed to a ghost.

When her father wanted to arrange another marriage for her, at first she refused, but three years later she agreed to marry Government Worker. Her two sisters were married to Security Guard and Parcelman sometime before she married Government Worker. They were living in the village when Hairless died. When Haunted was asked whether she regretted having married Government Worker, she laughed and said, "No, but I am sorry that I have had so many troubles." Then she mentioned the previous day's possession of Immature, the daughter-in-law of her husband's younger brother. She said the same bhagat, the father-in-law of her two sisters, would come to exorcise the ghosts troubling the young bride.

Haunted was asked whether she took her children to any doctors or visited the nearby medical center. She answered that she did when they were ill. The first time her eldest daughter was ill, she took her to the medical center, but the child had no relief. She also went to hospitals in the City of Delhi and to a children's hospital in Narela, but to no effect. At the same time, she had a bhagat exorcise the ghost of Hairless who was causing the childrens' ghost illnesses. Sometimes in the case of Fever and stomach pain, the doctors provided relief, but not when Hairless's ghost seized them. The only relief from the ghost was from a bhagat. Her belief in the effectiveness of trying both modern medicine and exorcism for a given illness was similar to Mrs. Fence Sitter's except that she herself did not exorcise the ghost (Chap. 12: The Families of Progenitor and Gentle Soul).

Haunted once carried her ill infant daughter, born in 1975, to a hospital for treatment. The doctor took her pulse and said that the pulse beat had gone into her arm and that she would be all right. He gave the infant two spoonfuls of medicine, which must have put the child to sleep, for the doctor asked Haunted to wait two hours at the clinic so that he might see how the child responded to the medicine. After two hours the child awoke, and the doctor gave her two more spoonfuls of medicine. He then assured Haunted that the child would be better. Haunted said that her daughter was cured and was better and fatter, but on the occasion of Hoi, a day celebrated for the health and protection of children (Append. V: Calendric Events in month of Karttik), she fed the infant girl some sweet rice and again the ghost attacked the child. Here the motif of eating sweets, thus causing ghost illness, crops up again. Haunted then gave the child some tablets procured from the bhagat and the child was all right. Once for two days continuously, her infant daughter lay without moving, a state similar to Haunted's paralysis, which Haunted attributed to ghost possession although the child also had Fever. Haunted claimed that this state was due to an attack of the *oopra* (the ghost of a wife, i.e., Hairless), similar to her own possession. For two days and nights, she stayed awake and sat with the child. In 1977–78, this daughter was two years old.

During the foregoing interview, Government Worker, Haunted's children, her stepsons, and her two stepdaughters with their own children trooped in and out of the small room and interrupted the flow of responses. Haunted, in spite of these interruptions, was pleasant and apparently wanted to talk about the ghost of her husband's first wife and the ghost illnesses and possessions she brought. Haunted, like many village women, was nonliterate, could not count accurately, and seemed more poorly informed than the average village woman. Her house was dirty and filled with flies, which proliferate in spring. On very hot days, flies dropped dead from the heat.

Haunted's eldest stepson looked quite worried but was very cooperative. He was in the third year of higher secondary school; his younger brother, in the second year. The 17-year-old boy said that his father had recently been transferred from the City of Delhi to Assam and that as a consequence his salary had been reduced from Rs. 400 per month to Rs. 350. Because of an illness, he had medical expenses and did not send any money home. Instead family members had to send him money. Due to these circumstances, this young man had tried unsuccessfully to operate a small shop in the Chamar compound. At the time of the interview he had been rejected by the Navy because no science courses were taught in his school. He was currently trying to obtain employment in the Water Works Department of the Old Secretariat in Delhi. The dates of job applications were advertised in a newspaper, at which time he planned to go there and try his luck for a job as a tap fitter (fixing faucets).

Unless the family had an unknown source of income or some savings, it was difficult to understand how they found money to send to Government Worker and still have enough for themselves. Since many Chamars worked for landowners in their fields, very probably Haunted and her two stepsons did so too. However, the earnings from this work were seasonal and sparse. It seems strange that Government Worker needed his total salary to live. He may, however, have had to pay for his food, housing, and other necessities in addition to his medicine since as a driver, he was a civilian employee, not in military service.

To add to Haunted's worries, Government Worker had poor health. Haunted said that he had been ill ever since he was transferred from his job in Delhi to Assam in the fall of 1977. The water and food did not agree with him. She added that his employment did not cover his medical costs. Before he returned on leave, he had been bitten between two fingers by a flea. The hand had become swollen and turned into a serious infection so he was operated on and four stitches were needed in the hand, which was still bandaged at the time of Haunted's interview. His physician in Assam described his illness, not counting the infected hand, as follows: loss of appetite, worms, stomach disorder, pain in the abdomen, occasional constipation. This description was provided in a letter from the physician, who said that Government Worker should submit the letter to his employer as grounds for a transfer. However, he would have to return to Assam for three months before he could return to Delhi.

Haunted was left much on her own in the absence of her husband and had little or no money and no education. Yet she had to decide what to do when her children were ill. She attributed all family illness to the ghost of Hairless. Even with the poxes ascribed to the matas, she had a bhagat exorcise the ghost causing illness. She did not act immediately when her children first fell ill but waited until they grew worse. Then she had a bhagat exorcise the ghost, made an offering to the Crossroads Mata, and sometimes went to a local clinic or hospital. Thus, when her two-year-old daughter fell ill, she finally took her to the hospital where she died in late 1978 of typhoid (Kanti Mata).

During this visit to the hospital, Haunted found out that she was five months pregnant. Although the government midwife had given her condoms, she did not use them but buried them somewhere in the village because she did not want the children to blow them up as balloons and play with them. Moreover, she then said she was 40 to 41 years old and thought that she might have gone through the menopause. Her claim to be 40–41 in late 1978 is inconsistent with her statement that she was 27 when she married Government Worker in 1968, which would make her 37 in 1978. She tried to abort the pregnancy with a mixture of carrot seeds, gur (brown sugar), and bamboo husks, boiled in water for about an hour, cooled, and then drunk. However, the attempt at abortion was too late. Her son and last child was born four months later in the hospital. After his birth she was sterilized and she and the infant stayed in the hospital because he was suffering from malaria and typhoid. He died there of typhoid in 1979 a month or so after birth.

The decoction used as an abortifacient by Haunted is of considerable interest. It contains carrot seeds. We have previously noted (S. Freed and R. Freed, 1985: 255) that wom-

en of Shanti Nagar use an abortifacient ". . . known as *karha*, a decoction whose basic ingredient was almost always carrot seeds, which are said to be 'very hot' and to burn anything in the womb." Riddle and Estes (1992: 232) pointed out that the seeds of the wild variety of the domestic carrot, known as Queen Anne's lace (*Daucus carota* L.), contain substances with estrogenic activity. Carrot seeds bring on the menses and abort an embryo. A few women in North Carolina in the Appalachian Mountains and women in rural Rajasthan use the seeds of Queen Anne's lace to reduce fertility. Women recognized the effect 2000 years ago, and Hippocrates prescribed the plant in the fifth century B.C. for preventing or aborting pregnancy. Modern researchers have experimented with the seeds. The evidence is conflicting but nonetheless, ". . . the seeds (or their active ingredient, which has not been isolated) have been viewed as a promising post-coital antifertility agent" (Riddle and Estes, 1992: 232). The effect, if any, of the other components of *karha* (variously gur, tea leaves, millet, bamboo, and fenugreek seeds) is unknown.

What was most apparent in interviewing Haunted was that she firmly believed that illness, including the poxes brought by the matas, was caused by ghosts. Villagers often repeated that a first wife who dies becomes a ghost, haunts the second wife, and tries to take her soul and the souls of her children. It is, therefore, not surprising that Haunted believed that the possessions and illnesses of herself and her children were caused by Hairless.

Haunted and Government worker were born into families and a caste with strong beliefs in ghosts. Two of her sisters were married to the brothers of Government Worker and held the same beliefs. Further, two other sisters of Haunted were married to the sons of the *siyana* whom Haunted called for exorcising illness and possession. Thus, cultural conditioning to ghost possession and ghost illness together with somatic disorders and the stressful, relatively impoverished life of Government Worker and Haunted could have caused the ghost illnesses and possessions of Haunted and her children.

DSM-III and DSM-III-R link somatoform disorders to dissociative states, such as ghost possessions. In DSM-III-R (Am. Psych. Assn., DSM-III-R, 1987: 35) the category of "undifferentiated somatoform disorder" has been added. R. Prince (1990a: 35–36) suggested that, instead of an undifferentiated disorder, all the known disorders should be listed under one rubric. As the information about Haunted and her children indicates, the problem is how to identify the disorders and complaints in a village such as Shanti Nagar. Regular medical examinations and medical histories are a part of Western medicine but not of the health culture of Shanti Nagar. However, despite the difficulties of identifying specific diseases with confidence, whatever symptoms and descriptions are available should be useful in research about ghost possession.

CHAPTER 24: GHOST POSSESSIONS IN THE FOUR STAGES OF THE LIFE CYCLE

This chapter breaks down all cases of ghost possession by four stages of the life cycle, roughly, childhood, young adulthood, middle age, and old age. Stress factors that lead to ghost possession and how they differ between women and men are noted. Also the symptoms of ghost possession are summarized, and attacks by poltergeists are briefly defined.

A sequence of specific symptoms characterizes ghost possession. A victim shivers, moans, and then falls down unconscious. Shivering, probably muscle tremors from fear, and moaning are brought on when the victim sees a ghost and fears being possessed. The two symptoms constitute the onset of possession. They are followed by various dissociative states, also referred to as alternate mental states, including complete unconsciousness, jumping and running about— sometimes to a pond, well, railroad, or fire— interpreted as suicide attempts, and talking nonsense, interpreted as a ghost or ghosts speaking through the victim. The ghost may demand something, often sweets, because the victim had eaten some but none was given to the ghost. Villagers accept the ghost's demand and its justification more or less at face value, namely, that the ghost has been slighted and insists on recompense. The rule not to eat sweets before going out or while outside may derive from this frequently enacted episode with a ghost. However, from a psycho-logical viewpoint, the demand may be interpreted as the victim, rather than the ghost, having been deprived of something which someone else in the family had been given, i.e., the possessed person was slighted.

Related to the dissociative states are the neurotransmitters, which are chemical messengers in the endocrine system (Whybrow and Silberfarb, 1974). For example, endorphins are endogenous opiatelike substances, which carry a message to the nerve cells. They have an analgesic effect and may trigger dissociative states. The victim does not remember the possession after recovering from it (R. Prince, ed., 1982; R. Freed and S. Freed, 1985: 112–113).

Some characteristics of possessions are correlated with the sex of the victim. For females, possession may take place during the period of first mating (Gauna), as in the cases of Immature and Sita, possessed on the fourth night of Gauna (Chap. 23: Immature and Sita). A female is also susceptible to possession and later fits after the birth of her first child. In such cases, pain and stress from the introduction to coitus and/or the delivery of a first infant and difficulties of adjustment in her husband's family may set the stage for these states. For males, problems of sexual repression due to village beliefs about masturbation and wasting semen may be related to possession. Delayed first mating because the parents of the bride will not send her for various reasons, such as their failure or delay in paying all of the dowry, their reluctance to let their daughter leave home, and more recently because the groom has not found employment, contribute to such male sexual problems. Equally important, for both males and females, is the underlying anxiety that may accompany first mating.

That the behavior of possessed persons tends to follow similar patterns suggests that a mimetic effect may be present. Conditioning to similar patterns of belief and behavior occurs when children and adults hear repeated stories about ghosts and see frequent examples of possessions which take place publicly. In situations of stress, an individual's subconscious memory may take over and produce similar patterns of behavior. Ghost possessions are well known in Shanti Nagar so when an individual is possessed, the villagers know what steps to take until an exorcist can be summoned. Their actions and techniques are to some extent similar to those of an exorcist. However, the average villager is not believed to possess the supernatural power of an exorcist that supposedly is derived from his familiar.

The steps taken to care for victims of ghost possession consist of wrapping them in quilts when shivering starts, propping them in a sitting position, conversation with the intrusive ghost, guarding against suicide attempts, and a series of shock treatments applied to victims. They consist of hair pulling, slapping, and placing chili peppers and black pepper in the eyes or mouth of victims. Incense, pig excreta, and cow dung may be thrown on a fire so that their fumes drive out the ghost. Their ashes and also *bhabhut* (holy ashes) may be applied to the victim's body. A noteworthy technique, which may serve as a shock treatment, is to abuse and threaten ghosts verbally. Exorcists use these same techniques and additional means, such as calling on their supernatural powers (familiars), hypnotic effects, and drugs to induce dissociative states so that the ghosts can be summoned, confronted, and banished.

Although two cases of poltergeist attacks are presented in the text, they are not possessions, for the ghost does not enter and speak from the victim and the victim remembers the attack (Chap. 13: Old Codger, Barker, and Mrs. Barker; Chap. 22: Farmer). The two

cases are therefore not listed in this chapter. The attack of a poltergeist is recognized by a series of noises and activities which upset the victim and infest the household and/or workplace. Attacks are correlated with stressful conditions in the family and community. Being startled, frightened, and semiparalyzed are among the symptoms found in poltergeist attacks. The main remedy for an attack by a poltergeist is similar to ghost possession, namely, exorcism.

Ghost illness, always indicated by Fever, occurs so often that investigators almost certainly miss many cases because, among other reasons, villagers are reluctant to talk about them for fear that the involved ghost will trouble the person who mentions it (cf. Chap. 3: Fieldwork, Techniques, and Problems). Even though a voice may speak from a victim delirious with Fever, the case is one of ghost illness, not possession (cf. Chap. 12: The Families of Progenitor and Gentle Soul). Cases of ghost illness are not listed in this chapter devoted to possessions. However, it is well to remember that villagers believe that ghosts try to take the souls of their victims whether in possessions, poltergeist attacks, or ghost illness. In each case, the remedy is exorcism.

The cases of ghost possession are described here in ethnographic, familial, and biographical context. For comparison, they are arranged under the following four stages in the life cycle: (1) Survival in Childhood; (2) Coping with Coming of Age; (3) Midlife Crises; and (4) The Wear and Tear of Age. Because their possessions and/or fits continued for many years, three cases overlap two stages and are included in each. Resourceful appears in Stages 1 and 2; Sita, in Stages 2 and 3; and Withdrawn, in Stages 3 and 4. Based on a holistic approach to these cases, various biological, cultural, ecological, economic, and psychological stresses have been identified. Data on age, sex, caste, and, when known, the identification of the ghost or ghosts are given in addition to the chapters where the possessions are described.

STAGE 1: SURVIVAL IN CHILDHOOD

Mrs. Farmer, a Jat, whose niece, Little Goddess, was possessed, commenting on her possession, said, "A child of any age can be possessed by a ghost, even an infant." However, infants cannot speak and, therefore, a ghost does not speak within them, but an infant's ghost illness is recognized by incessant crying, bodily convulsions, and Fever. Our youngest case of ghost possession is a two-year-old girl. The seven individuals (4 females and 3 males) in Stage 1 range in age from two to 10 years. The cases are listed by caste (1 Brahman, 4 Chamars, and 2 Jats).

Brahman:

1. Boy, age 4, son of Dr. John, was possessed by a woman wearing a red sari, identified by the family as Vishnu's consort (Chap. 21: Gabbler and Student Doctor).

Chamar:

2, 3, 4, 5. Haunted said that all four of her children, two girls ages 9 and 2, and two boys, ages 7 and 4 were possessed by the ghost of Hairless at various times before 1978 (Chap. 23: Haunted).

Jat:

6. Resourceful, age 8, daughter of Widow-in-Between, was possessed by the ghost of Tippler's first wife (Chap. 22: Resourceful, Only Heir, and Matriarch).

7. Little Goddess, age 10, had three possessions after recovering from typhoid in 1977. The ghost was Whose Daughter, her Brahman girl friend, who drowned (Chap. 14: The Ghost of Whose Daughter; Chap. 22: Little Goddess).

STAGE 2: COPING WITH COMING OF AGE

The majority of cases in Stage 2 are due to the problems of menarche, puberty, and mating. The 16 individuals (10 females and 6 males) range in age from 12 to 29 years. For females the problems arise from anxiety about mating, pregnancy, death of infants, adjustment to marital families, and separation from natal families. The problems of males have changed through time due to the need for obtaining an education, passing examinations, and finding a job. However, some of their problems hinge on taboos against wasting semen linked with sexual frustration due to their wives' parents not sending their daughters to them for first mating. The cases are listed by caste (1 Bairagi, 6 Brahmans, 4

Chamars, 1 Chuhra, 2 Jats, and 2 Gola Potters).

Bairagi:

1. Jolly, 14 to 15 years old. At time of wedding and first mating, she was possessed by the ghost of Tippler's first wife (Chap. 20: The Bairagis: Fearful, Handsome, and Delicate Flower).

Brahman:

2. Beauty, widowed at age 12, from ages 12 to 15 was possessed by Illusion's ghost (Chap. 21: Beauty).

3. Honesty, age 14. She was possessed by a neighboring Brahman woman who committed suicide (Chap. 19: Honesty and Moneylender).

4. Love Song, age 14 to 15. She was possessed by an unidentified ghost after the wedding of her patrilineal cousin, Young Lawyer (Chap. 12: The Families of Progenitor and Gentle Soul).

5. New Priest, age 21, was possessed by the ghost of Old Priest (Chap. 12: Death of Old Priest).

6. Welder, age 22, unmarried and unemployed, was possessed by Whose Daughter's ghost (Chap. 14: The Ghost of Whose Daughter).

7. One Eyed's son, age 16, was possessed by the ghost of Hairless and also a man during the malaria epidemic and before his wedding in 1978 (Chap. 21: Withdrawn's Interview).

Chamar:

8. Sita, age 15, possessed on fourth night after first mating. Possessions continued until the birth of her first child when the possessions became fits. Evidence of genetic and somatic complaints that contributed to her dissociative states (Chap. 23: Immature and Sita).

9. Immature, age 17 to 18, was first possessed by Hairless on fourth night after first mating in 1977 and thereafter into 1978. She had not yet attained menarche in 1978 (Chap. 23: Immature's Possessions).

10. Sunny, age 14, was possessed by Hairless three times in the spring of 1978 after the wedding of her brother. History of possessions of her mother (Chap. 17: Illusionist's Patients).

11. Haunted, age 27, was possessed after first mating with her second husband, Government Worker. Later she was again pos-

sessed, most recently in 1973–74. The ghost was Hairless, first wife of Government Worker (Chap. 23: Haunted).

Chuhra:

12. Timid, at ages 17 and 19, was possessed after births of her first and second infants. Later her possessions became fits and she became blind in one eye. Daughter of a *siyana* and daughter-in-law of Lord of Ghosts, a bhagat. Part of triangles of jealousy and folie à deux. Ghost unidentified (Chap. 16: Family Jealousies and Sorcery).

Jats:

13. Resourceful, age 14 to 15. First possessed when she was eight years old and again at first mating. The ghost was Tippler's first wife (Chap. 22: Resourceful, Only Heir, and Matriarch).

14. Ill Fated, age 17 to 18, was possessed by the ghosts of his father and two uncles. He had to care for three women and had not yet mated with his wife because her parents would not send her until an older male headed the household. Later he died of ghost illness (Chap. 13: Senior Branch).

Gola Potters:

15. Eldest Son, age 14 to 15, was possessed by The Lady when the parents of his bride would not send her for first mating (Chap. 20: The Potters and the Lady).

16. Younger Son, age 21 to 22, suffered ongoing possessions by The Lady because he had no job and his bride's parents would not send her for first mating (Chap. 20: The Potters and the Lady).

In addition to the foregoing individuals who suffered possessions when faced with the changes and pressures of coming of age, we have described a few cases of young men who were not possessed but sought to avoid problems by flight from the village. An early case is Forceful, a Jat, who in 1916 at age 19, ran away and joined the army. After nine years, he returned home (Chap. 13: Senior Branch). Another man who joined the army was Loafer, a Brahman. He, too, returned later. Perhaps he influenced his nephew, Hippie, who ran away for three years after failing his exams (Chap. 14: The Boy Had to Die). Tippler, a Jat, when he was 17 to 18 years old, ran away from home when he too failed his exams and was faced with mating with his first

wife. When he later returned to the village, he murdered her and her soul became one of the feared, malevolent ghosts. Through the years Tippler escaped from whatever troubled his conscience by becoming an alcoholic. Young Groom also murdered his first wife, Little Bride (Chap. 15: Little Bride). Teenage girls had no such opportunities, for if they ran away, they would have little chance to become anything except prostitutes or beggars.

STAGE 3: MIDLIFE CRISES

The age range for the eight cases of Stage 3 (6 females and 2 males) is 30 through 49. The sources of stress are varied, and more than one can be involved in a specific case. Menopause may be stressful for women and can be a factor in possession. Other sources of stress which contribute to possession are changes in joint families, death of a spouse and chronic grief, accident and hospitalization, a husband's drinking, social isolation, and changes in life style. The cases as listed by caste: 6 Brahman, 1 Chamar, and 1 Jat).

Brahman:

1. City Girl, age 31. After the death in 1967 of her first husband, College Man, she married Tricky, his younger brother, whom she did not like. Her first possessions were by the ghost of College Man in 1977. After living in the city and a suburb of Delhi, she had to learn the village life style and agricultural work. She became the family drudge, had no recreation, and no say about the health and schooling of her children (Chap. 19: City Girl's Possessions).

2. Mrs. Manipulator, age 42, and undergoing menopause, had five daughters and two surviving sons; two sons died. She was twice possessed in 1958–59 by the ghosts of Nondescript and his wife. At the time there were constant family problems and fights (Chap. 19: Mrs. Manipulator's Possessions).

3. Sudden Grief, age 42 to 43, was possessed by the ghost of her murdered husband some 10 years after the event. The principal element in her possessions was chronic grief aggravated by the return of her husband's murderer from prison and his election as pradhan. Her eldest brother-in-law exorcised the ghost (Chap. 15: Jats vs. Brahmans).

4. Mrs. Earnest, age 45, had experienced possession-trance for some time, which she brought on by sneezing. The ghost was the 2½ to 3 year old infant son of Mrs. Householder, her mother-in-law. Mrs. Earnest's possessions brought about harmony in the household due to the prophecies of the ghost (Chap. 21: Mrs. Earnest).

5. Merchant, age 30 to 35. In the 1850s, he had Fever as a result of eating the sweets left at a Muslim's grave, on which he then urinated. Thereafter he had ghost illness and was possessed for six months by Muslim Ghost. He then became an exorcist with Muslim Ghost as his familiar (Chap. 12: The Legend of Merchant and Muslim Ghost; Death of Old Priest).

6. Withdrawn, age 40. He was first possessed after the deaths of his mother, wife, and infant son in 1943. Although the ghost was not identified, she probably was the ghost of his dead wife. In 1958–59, when he was 55 to 56 years old, he was again possessed. The ghost was identified as either Breadstuff or the Headless Sweeper. Withdrawn's possessions continued to 1978 when he was 75 years old. He had a difficult personality, created problems in the joint family from which he was increasingly isolated, was a celibate from age 40 to age 75, and as a Brahman worried because he would die without issue and his soul would become a ghost (Chap. 21: Withdrawn's Possessions).

Chamar:

7. Sita, age 15 to 35, was first possessed in 1958, the fourth night of Gauna. The possessions continued until her first child was born and then became fits. The last recorded incident took place when she was 35 years old in March 1978 (Chap. 23: Immature and Sita).

Jat:

8. Morning Star was 31 years old when first possessed and had on-going possessions from 1973–74 to 1978. They started in her marital village when the cart in which she was riding passed over the crossroads where the bones of her husband's elder brother were buried, thus allegedly arousing his ghost. Because a number of men had to hold her down during her possessions, it is possible that they had become fits (Chap. 22: Pragmatic and Morning Star).

STAGE 4: THE WEAR AND TEAR OF AGE

The five cases (2 females and 3 males) range in age from 50 to 75. A theme that seems to run through the various cases as a source of stress is chronic insecurity rather than the problems of surmounting specific often transitory challenges, such as adaptation to marriage. The cases as listed by caste: 1 Bairagi, 2 Brahmans, 2 Chuhras.

Bairagi:

1. Fearful, age 55, was possessed in 1958 by the ghosts of her brother, Handsome, on whom she had always depended for help, and her daughter, Delicate Flower. She was much younger than her husband and only eight years old when wedded. Because she was too young to come for Gauna, her husband took his twin brother's widow, who was Fearful's sister, as his levirate spouse. Fearful did not go to him for eight years. The levirate wife bore six infants in rapid succession, all of whom died at birth or shortly thereafter. The mother along with the last infant died immediately after delivery. After she died, Fearful came to mate with her husband. As frequently happens in cases of a deceased first spouse, Fearful was at one time possessed by the ghost of the levirate spouse, her sister; later, by the ghosts of Handsome and Delicate Flower. Fearful was an anxious, frightened, insecure woman in a relatively poor family. In 1958 her possessions were brought on by falling while pilfering fruit from the Mali's garden near the cremation grounds, the separation of her eldest son's family from her joint family, perhaps a guilty conscience for having arranged Delicate Flower's marriage to an old man, and possibly by working for us (Chap. 20: The Bairagis: Fearful, Handsome, and Delicate Flower).

Brahman:

2. Affine, age 53, was possessed by the ghost of a Muslim in 1977–78. Later he was reported as having died of asthma by a professed nonbeliever in ghosts. He had retired and was living with his sister and sister's son, Teacher, after spending most of his life in the City of Delhi. Adjustment to village life was difficult (Chap. 14: A Ghost Took My Son).

3. Withdrawn, age 50 to 75. His posses-

sions began when he was 40 years old (1943), as indicated in Stage 3, and still continued in 1978. Villagers identified the ghost either as the Headless Sweeper or as Breadstuff, both Chuhras. From the end of the 1950s to 1978, Withdrawn lived near the Chuhra Sweeper quarter, the crossroads, and the grave of the Headless Sweeper. In 1978 he still lived in that vicinity but by himself in a cattle shed. His meals were brought there by Strong Minded, his nephew's wife. It is therefore not surprising that villagers identified the ghost possessing him as a Sweeper. His difficult personality resulted in his reclusion. His irritating personality, semi-isolation, celibacy, childlessness, fear that he too might become a ghost, and the breakup of his joint family made him vulnerable to possession (Chap. 21: Withdrawn's Possessions; Withdrawn's Interview).

Chuhra Sweepers:

4. Lady of Ghosts, age 50 to 55. Her first possessions were caused by the ghost of her husband's first wife; later she became paranoid, a condition that villagers characterized as madness (*pagalpan*), as a result of the family triangles of jealousy. Lord of Ghosts, her husband, could not cure her or his daughter-in-law, Timid, of their possessions. No ghosts were identified except the first wife of Lord of Ghosts. What was first a folie à deux be-

tween Lady of Ghosts and Timid later enmeshed Lord of Ghosts and expanded to include Timid's father, a *siyana*, and his disciple, both of whom were suspected of sorcery (Chap. 16: Lord of Ghosts).

5. Eluded, age 60, brother of Lord of Ghosts, lived away from the village in 1958–59 and was seldom seen there in 1977–78 when he was identified as suffering possessions which later became fits. The ghost that troubled him was not identified. His case adds another instance of the prevalence of ghost beliefs in the family line of the Headless Sweeper, Eluded's grandfather (Chap. 16: Finale).

The possessions of 33 individuals are described above but because three individuals appear in two stages (Resourceful reported in Stages 1 and 2; Sita, in Stages 2 and 3; and Withdrawn, in Stages 3 and 4), there are 36 numbered items in the list, as follows: 22 females, 14 males; and by caste, 2 Bairagi, 15 Brahman, 9 Chamar, 3 Chuhra, 5 Jat, and 2 Gola Potter. Cases about which we heard but have little information are not included in the above list. The poltergeist attacks suffered by Farmer and Mrs. Barker, although interesting manifestations of ghost beliefs, have not been included here because they are not ghost possessions.

CHAPTER 25: CONCLUSION

This chapter highlights the basic themes of the study, summarizes the findings, and suggests directions for future research. The advantage of a descriptive and comparative case-study treatment of ghost illness and possession is twofold. First, the basic themes that run through many or all cases stand out from the welter of detail that characterizes specific individuals. Second, various forms of the phenomena can be identified. Thus, we have ghost illness, ghost possession, and attacks by poltergeists, all involuntary and involving malevolent ghosts, and the voluntary sum-

moning in possession-trance of a benevolent ghost as family counselor.

Placing the phenomena in as broad a context as possible leads to a much deeper understanding than if the analysis were more narrowly circumscribed, for example, to psychological analysis. The point is not new. Richard Salisbury, for one, pleaded ". . . for studying possession states with an open mind, taking into account the possibility that they may be culturally sanctioned and not assuming that they are symptoms of neurosis or psychosis" (R. Prince, 1990b: 74–75). Few would disagree with this position today. However, our contextual analysis is of broader scope than is common, taking into account social structure, culture, history, ecology, mythology, theories of health and curing, current events, and individual life and family histories. That such diverse data gathered largely for purposes other than the study of ghost beliefs nonetheless proved to be vital for this study is a powerful argument in favor of intensive holistic fieldwork of the kind that has been traditional in ethnography and which remains its distinctive characteristic.

The context in which we view ghost beliefs, ghost illness, and supernatural causes of Fever and disease can be extended not only to psychological theory and to a broad cultural context but also to Europe, where a different explanation of epidemic disease obtained before the advent of scientific medicine. In Europe, epidemics were attributed to the machinations of humans rather than supernaturals. Many Europeans sought scapegoats for pestilence, and massacre was the remedy. In 14th-century Europe in the torment of the Black Death, Jews were accused of causing the disease by poisoning wells. Although the Church and the authorities in most places at first tried to protect the Jews, they succumbed to popular pressure and the temptation of seizing Jewish property. In Basle in 1349, the entire Jewish community of several hundred was burned to death in a specially constructed wooden building. A month later, the Jews of Strasbourg were burned at the stake. Nothing like this took place in India. The supernatural theory of disease preempted the explanatory role and served as a barrier to another possible explanation, scapegoating a whole community, with its murderous consequences (Tuchman, 1979: 112–114; Bishop, 1987: 308–310).

The accusation of witchcraft, as it developed in England from medieval times to the early 18th century, was also a form of scapegoating. On the one hand, it involved individuals and therefore differed from the scapegoating of whole communities that was common during the plague epidemics of Europe; on the other hand, with its supernatural element, it resembled to some extent the Indian theory of the supernatural cause of disease. Before the Reformation, people took ritual precautions to ward off evil spirits and malevolent magic. After the Reformation, such counter-magic was prohibited and had to be clandestine while legal prosecution was approved and supported by civil legislation enacted from 1542 to 1604. In many cases of witchcraft accusation, the charge was a psychological defense mechanism on the part of the accuser who transferred to the alleged witch his/her feelings of guilt for rejecting the witch's request for charity or aid. The process was set in motion by the accuser's individual misfortune, the drama acted out in the context of drastic social change and particular personal animosity. The result was a legal process against an alleged witch, usually an older woman (LeVine, 1973: 256–270).

Witchcraft accusations in India are also a form of scapegoating of individuals. People who suffer misfortune may lay the blame on an elderly woman widely regarded as a witch. Medieval England and contemporary India differ concerning the involved psychological mechanism. Feelings of guilt on the part of the accuser underlay witchcraft accusations in England. In India, the accuser, instead of suffering pangs of guilt, may envy the witch and/or fear her because of disliked personality traits, such as quarrelsomeness. However, the remedies against witchcraft were generally similar in both places. Various measures (charms, spells, offerings) were taken to invoke supernatural aid or the witch might be attacked either physically or through legal means, as in England. Although the evil eye may be an attribute of witches, it may be cast, sometimes unconsciously, by any envious person. Envy can be a motive both of the person who casts the evil eye and also of people who accuse others of witchcraft.

Carstairs (1983: ix, Chap. 2, quote on p. ix) described in detail a case of witchcraft in the village of Sujarupa, Rajasthan where ". . . [a woman] was believed to be a witch and was held responsible for the deaths of several women and children." Through the years, she was threatened, beaten, and finally beaten to death. She was the mother of the wealthiest landlord of the village and was both envied and feared. Woodburne (1992: 56) noted that the evil eye in India is based on envy (or jealously in his usage). An admiring glance directed at children or domestic animals may cloak the evil eye, which is cast mostly by women. Although the villagers of Shanti Nagar never mentioned witches to us, they did believe in the evil eye as described in Chapter 16: Techniques for Curing the Evil Eye and Ghost Possession. Ruth Freed was believed to be suffering from the evil eye, and Lord of Ghosts was summoned to perform a rite of exorcism.

The Hindu beliefs in ghost illness and possession are embedded in a pan-human phenomenon (the belief in souls), a sophisticated system of moral causality (dharma, karma, and rebirth), and an ancient sacred literature and mythology. Combined and distilled for generations, these components are part of the village ideology, the way villagers perceive themselves, their environment, and their relations with the supernatural world. After death and cremation, the eternal soul is released from the body and travels to the Land of the Dead for judgment by Yama or by Bhagwan to determine the time of its rebirth and its allotted life span. Three reasons for a soul to become a lingering ghost are: (1) dying before the allotted time, (2) dying tortured, or (3) behavior contrary to village customs. All three are related to karma, the sum of the soul's actions from its many lives. The sum of good and bad karma may lead to various outcomes, one of which is ghosthood. It is also believed that if the proper funeral rituals are not performed, the soul cannot be released from the cremation grounds for judgment by Yama and will not achieve rebirth or release from the cycle of rebirths. Instead it becomes a ghost and haunts those who neglected the ceremonies. Malevolent ghosts may cause illness and death by seizing the soul of a living individual. In general, a ghost lingers until its allotted time expires although the ghost may be removed temporarily by an exorcist.

The mythological connotations of Fever as a supernatural being are a basic aspect of ghost illness but not possession. Not only do villagers see a close connection between Fever and illness but they also believe that Fever signals ghost illness. These identifications are linked to the belief that Shiva, in his aspect of Hara (Death the Remover) sends his messenger, Fever, to bring disease and death to human beings. Shiva is known also as Lord of Ghosts. Thus, Fever in village belief became an index of ghost illness. While ghost illness is primarily identified by the symptom of Fever, ghost possession has a different set of symptoms. It is more dramatic and may be classified as a Dissociative Disorder with alternate mental states. If a biological cause is involved, ghost possession may be classified as a Somatoform-Conversion Disorder. Among the symptoms of possession are the victim seeing and fearing the ghost, shivering (body tremors from fear), and the passing into alternate mental states with a voice or voices speaking from the victim, such voices identified as intrusive ghosts trying to seize the victim's soul.

The ideology that underlies ghost beliefs is not shared equally by all villagers. Jats, followers of the Arya Samaj, a reform sect of Hinduism, believe only in Bhagwan (God). They disbelieve in multiple deities, thus rejecting ghosts, although most Jat women continue to believe in them. In addition to Jats and a few non-Jat Samajis, some urbanized individuals and college students also profess not to believe in ghosts. Many other villagers follow Sanatan Dharma, the more orthodox variety of village Hinduism, or a simplified Hinduism called Popular Hinduism. They all believe in many deities and other supernatural beings, such as ghosts.

The epidemics, endemic diseases, famines, turbulences and other disruptions in the Delhi region served to nourish ghost beliefs. Disasters of the scope of the smallpox epidemics of the late 19th century, the plague from 1896 to 1921, the cholera pandemic of 1916, the influenza pandemic of 1918–19, and endemic diseases like malaria and diarrhea led to a great many untimely deaths and fostered the belief that the dead become ghosts. Among these disturbances were numerous famines, such as the Great Famine in the Punjab in 1876–78 and the two famines of 1896–97 and 1899–1900 that were equally severe. In the 20th century it is estimated that food shortages have occurred every two years and a major scarcity every 12 years although the development of high-yielding varieties of food grains have in recent years ameliorated this pattern. That an average life expectancy of no more than 30 years persisted well into the 20th century testifies to the uncertainty of life and to the inadequacy of the medical treatment and public health measures then available. The villagers' persistent belief in ghosts is related to untimely deaths and also to basic concepts of Hinduism that are expressed in sacred literature, especially the well-known epics and Puranas. More recently, cinema and television have reinforced the belief in ghosts.

The health culture of Shanti Nagar is an amalgam of various traditions, some quite ancient. The Prevedic Age probably contributed to the belief in mother goddesses, perhaps to a forerunner of Rudra-Shiva, Agni, the word for fire and the God of Fire, as well as to the belief that something, the soul, escapes from the body at death. Shamanism in all likelihood came from this earlier time, combining elements of belief from the Indo-Aryan invasion and the indigenous tribals of the subcontinent of India. Vedic medical theory, which has been dated by various authorities as beginning about 1200 to 900 B.C., affirms that deities and ghosts cause illness owing to a soul's bad karma. The Atharva-Veda consists of rituals and mantras used by Brahman priests to exorcise the supernatural agents causing illness. Ayurveda, a major component of Hindu health culture today, developed from about 600 B.C. to A.D. 200. Early Ayurveda tried to separate the diseases that could be explained by the *tridosa* theory from mental diseases, for which animistic explanations were invoked and supernatural cures were used. However, the separation was incomplete, for the theory holds that imbalance of the humors leads to various mental disturbances. In any event, the worst form of madness in Ayurvedic theory is not due to disturbance of the *tridosa*s but to possession by a ghost or demon. The remedy is appeasement or exorcism of the ghost.

The unique contribution of Islamic medicine (Unani and Unani Prophetic Medicine) to the health culture of Shanti Nagar is pulsing as both diagnosis and treatment. Originally from China, pulsing entered India via Muslim traders and invaders. It is now a prominent feature of village medical practice. Villagers believe that pulsing is essential to diagnosis and cure. Pulsing is related to the *tridosa* system, serving to pinpoint the humor causing an illness, and as such is only loosely connected to ghost illness. The major contribution of Unani Prophetic Medicine is that it reinforced the concept of curing ghost illness by exorcism and employed amulets as protection against both ghosts and the evil eye. Its belief that disease is inflicted by supernatural beings as retribution for sin is compatible with the Hindu concept of karma.

Western medicine and its common form, popular pharmaceutical medicine, are the most recent additions to village health culture and have become as prominent as Ayurveda. Although the villagers have rather slowly accepted Western medical theory and treatment by physicians, they have adopted Western medicine, including injections, quite rapidly. As regards the effectiveness of Western medicine in the treatment of ghost illness and possession, villagers who believe in ghosts consider it to be useless. Only an exorcist can cure ghost illness. On the other hand, Western medicines are used to combat Fever, a symptom of ghost illness. Hence, dual treatment is used by some villagers: medicine for Fever and exorcism to get rid of the ghost that is causing the problem. Villagers receive most Western medicine from local practitioners of popular pharmaceutical medicine.

A common feature of ghost possession, aside from the symptoms that are manifest in nearly all cases, is that individuals become susceptible when in circumstances generally regarded as stressful. Brides, usually teenagers, are especially vulnerable as they try to cope with moving to a strange village, new relatives, required submissive patterns of behavior, sexual adjustment, and the worries of pregnancy and first childbirth. A variant of the vulnerable bride theme is the situation of a second wife who is often attacked by the ghost of her husband's dead first wife. The ghost tries to take the souls of the second wife and especially her infants. Young men sometimes have trouble adjusting to marriage, but for them the postponement of first mating until they have passed school examinations and secured a job is a greater source of stress. The breakup of a joint family produces stress more likely to afflict older family members than children or adolescents. Many individuals who suffer ghost possession are never again possessed once they surmount their difficulties.

Some common motifs of ghost possession

are entirely cultural in the sense that they do not involve psychological stress or difficult family relationships. The belief that ghosts frequent crossroads, the village pond, and cremation grounds, that they are especially malevolent at midnight or high noon in the cremation grounds, and that they have a fondness for sweets are examples of such beliefs, some of which have a distribution beyond India.

Environmental and general social stress can set off an epidemic of ghost possession, as happened in 1977–78 when the government-sponsored sterilization drive, an excessive monsoon which damaged crops and helped to cause a typhoid epidemic, a nearby tornado and two hailstorms, which again damaged crops, a malaria epidemic, and cattle and tube-well thefts affected a substantial number of villagers, 10 of whom (5 females and 5 males) suffered ghost possessions, some more than once. Also during this time, not numbered in the epidemic, are three substantiated cases of recurrent fits: two females and one male, plus the possibility of two more females not clearly substantiated, and the poltergeist attacks on Farmer.

Epidemics of Dissociative Disorders are not rare. For example, Teoh and Tan (1976) report an epidemic of ghost possessions by jinns in a Muslim girls' boarding school in West Malaysia. A series of devastating floods triggered the epidemic. Another factor was mismanagement by a Headmaster. He failed to distribute funds for flood relief, necessary to maintain proper living conditions at the school. Worse still, he made unannounced rounds of the living quarters, and the girls feared that he would appear while they were undressing. Five girls were possessed, either together or separately. Two exorcists were called and eventually the possessions ceased. Moreover, a Headmistress was appointed. In this case, menarche may have been a contributing factor, both because of the accompanying physical and psychological changes and because the Headmaster instructed the girls to throw their soiled sanitary napkins into a disused mining pool to avoid clogging pipes. The girls believed that the mining pool was the abode of jinns and that their possessions were due to the jinns having been disturbed.

A noteworthy characteristic of ghost possession is that it often evolves into fits (daura). Fits are believed to be brought on by ghosts, but a ghostly voice does not speak from the victim. The outstanding symptom of a fit is that victims become exceptionally strong and so violent that several people are needed to restrain them. Kakar, a psychiatrist with an eclectic background, saw such phenomena among rural women possessed by ghosts. He notes their accumulated, repressed rage due to lack of social emancipation. In one case, that of Urmila, her fits of rage, which began immediately after marriage when she complained of body aches and difficulty breathing, were such that it took "two or three strong men to restrain her." She would get so hungry and thirsty that she would eat the food cooked for a whole family and drink a bucket of water. Urmila stated that she had never been angry before marrriage, but "when the bhuta comes, I don't remember what happens to me." Her life history revealed that she had long harbored a violent rage which she suppressed, but after marriage she could no longer control it and then it was discharged in her states of possession (Kakar, 1983: 76–77, 79, quotations p. 77).

In India and other societies, ghosts play an important role in the ideology and activities of the living. Belief in ghosts is reinforced by ancient traditions, often embodied in sacred literature, and specific cases of ghost possession reflect the relations that the living had with the dead. Tradition defines the various types of ghosts, tells how souls become ghosts, and explains their connection to illness and curing practices. Analysis of social structure, interpersonal relations, and stages in the life cycle, such as marriage, reveals the occasions when individuals are subjected to such stress that they become vulnerable to ghost possession. Ghost beliefs permeate village life, affecting the behavior even of people who profess not to believe in them. An aspect of the wonderful complexity of human behavior, ghost beliefs are worthy of scientific attention from the point of view of anthropology, sociology, psychology, and psychiatry. With the discovery of the endorphins, messengers that bind the central nervous system and the neuroendocrine system, phenomena such as ghost possession, fits, and exorcism are seen as a manifestation of an intricate, intimate relationship of the brain and the rest of the human body. Future research on this subject will in all likelihood involve analytical medical techniques (e.g., Simons, et al., 1988; Ervin, et al., 1988) as well as biological, psychological, and psychiatric theories and techniques in combination with ethnography.

REFERENCES

Abrams, R.
1989.   Out of the blue: the rehabilitation of electroconvulsive therapy. The Sciences, Nov.–Dec.: 24–30.
Ackerman, E.
1983.   Medical care in the countryside near Paris, 1800–1914. In J. W. Dauben and V. S. Sexton (eds.), History and philosophy of science: selected papers. Ann. New York Acad. Sci. 412: 1–18.
Aggarwala, O. P.
1956.   The Punjab tenancy act. Delhi, India: Metropolitan Book Co.
Am. Psych. Assoc., DSM-III
1980.   Diagnostic and statistical manual of mental disorders, 3rd ed. Washington, D.C.: Am. Psych. Assoc.
1987.   Diagnostic and statistical manual of mental disorders. 3rd ed. revised. Washington, D.C.: Am. Psych. Assoc.
Anderson, P.
1983.   The reproductive role of the human breast. Curr. Anthrop. 24(1): 25–45.
Anderson, R. M.
1985.   Predisposition in hookworm infection in humans. Science 228(4707): 1537–1539.
Andreasen, N. C.
1985.   The broken brain: the biological revolution in psychiatry. New York: Harper & Row.
1988.   Brain imaging: application in psychiatry. Science 239(4846): 1381–1388.
Angel, R., and P. Thoits
1987.   The impact of culture on the cognitive structure of illness. Cult. Med. Psychiatry. 11(4): 465–494.
Angrosino, M. V.
1989.   The case history of an East Indian Trinidadian alcoholic. Ethos 17(2): 202–225.
Avalon, A. (Pseudonym for Sir J. G. Woodruff)
1913.   Tantra of the great liberation. London: Luzac.
Balasubrahmanyan, V.
1982.   Medicine and the male utopia. Econ. Pol. Weekly 17(43): 1725.

Balfour, E.
1885.   The cyclopaedia of India and of eastern and southern Asia, 3rd ed. Vol. 1–3. London: Bernard Quaritch.
Banerjea, J. N.
1953.   The Hindu concept of god. In K. W. Morgan (ed.), The religion of the Hindus, pp. 48–82. New York: Ronald Press.
Bardhan, P.
1982.   Little girls and death in India. Review of B. D. Miller, The endangered sex: neglect of female children in rural north India. Ithaca and London: Cornell Univ. Press, 1981. Econ. Pol. Weekly 17(36): 1448–1450.
Basak, R.
1953.   The Hindu concept of the natural world. In K. W. Morgan (ed.), The religion of the Hindus, pp. 83–116. New York: Ronald Press.
Bascom, W.
1984.   The forms of folklore: prose narratives. In A. Dundes (ed.), Sacred narratives: readings in the theory of myth, pp. 5–29. Berkeley: Univ. California Press.
Basham, A. L.
1954.   The wonder that was India. New York: Grove Press.
Basu, S. N.
1966.   History of poliomyelitis in India. Indian Pediatr. 3(Feb): 60–61.
Baxi, U.
1982.   The crisis of the Indian legal system. New Delhi: Vikas.
Berkow, R. (ed.)
1982.   The Merck manual of diagnosis and therapy, 14th ed. Rahway, NJ: Merck.
Berland, J. C.
1982.   No five fingers are alike: cognitive amplifiers in social context. Cambridge, MA: Harvard Univ. Press.
Berreman, G. D.
1963.   Hindus of the Himalayas. Berkeley: Univ. California Press.
Beveridge, W. I.
1978.   Influenza: the last great plague, an un-

finished story of discovery. New York: Prodist.

Bhatia, J. C., D. Vir, A. Timmappaya and C. S. Chuttani
1975.   Traditional healers and modern medicine. Soc. Sci. Med. 9: 15–21.

Bhattacharyya, S.
1953.   Religious practices of the Hindu. *In* K. W. Morgan (ed.), The religion of the Hindus, pp. 154–205. New York: Ronald Press.

Bishop, M.
1987.   The Middle Ages. Boston: Houghton Mifflin.

Blackburn, S. H., P. J. Claus, J. B. Flueckiger, and S. S. Wadley (eds.)
1989.   Oral epics in India. Berkeley: Univ. California Press.

Bloom, B. R. and C. J. L. Murray
1992.   Tuberculosis: commentary on a reemergent killer. Science 257: 1055–1064.

Bloom, J. D., and R. D. Gelardin
1985.   Uqamairineq and Uqumanigianiq: Eskimo sleep paralysis. In R. C. Simons and C. C. Hughes (eds.), The culture–bound syndromes: folk illnesses of psychiatric and anthropological interest, pp. 117–122. Dordrecht: D. Reidel.

Blunt, E. A. H.
1931.   The caste system of northern India. London: Oxford Univ. Press.

Bochner, A., G. Veereman, and M. Van Caillie-Bertrand
1988.   Evaluation of near-miss sudden infant death: the importance of investigations to determine etiology. *In* P. J. Schwartz, D. P. Southall, and M. Valdes-Dapena (eds.), The sudden infant death syndrome: cardiac and respiratory mechanisms and interventions. Ann. New York Acad. Sci. 533: 469–470.

Bock, P. K.
1980.   Continuities in psychological anthropology: a historical introduction. San Francisco: W. H. Freeman.

Bordewich, F. M.
1986.   Dowry murders: a bride whose family can't reward the groom may pay with her life. Atlantic Mon. July: 21–27.

Borthwick, M.
1982.   The Bhadramahila and changing conjugal relations in Bengal 1850–1900. *In* M. Allen and S. N. Mukherjee (eds.), Women in India and Nepal. Australian Natl. Univ. Monographs on South Asia 8: 105–135. Canberra, Australia: Australian Natl. Univ. Printing.

Bourguignon, E.
1979.   Psychological anthropology: an introduction to human nature and cultural differences. New York: Holt, Rinehart & Winston.

Bühler, G. (translator)
1969.   The laws of Manu. New York: Dover.

Bürgel, J. C.
1976.   Secular and religious features of medieval Arabic medicine. *In* C. Leslie (ed.), Asian medical systems: a comparative study, pp. 44–62. Berkeley: Univ. California Press.

Carstairs, G. M.
1953.   The case of Thakur Khuman Singh: a culture-conditioned crime. Br. J. Delinquency 4(1): 14–25.
1958.   The twice-born: a study of a community of high-caste Hindus. Bloomington: Indiana Univ. Press.
1969.   Changing perception of neurotic illness. *In* W. Caudill and Tsung-Yi Lin (eds.), Conference on mental health research in Asia and the Pacific, pp. 405–414. Honolulu: East-West Center Press.
1983.   Death of a witch: a village in north India, 1950–1981. London: Hutchinson.

Carstairs, G. M., and R. L. Kapur
1976.   The great universe of Kota: stress, change and mental disorder in an Indian village. Berkeley: Univ. California Press.

Carter, K. C.
1981.   Semmelweiss and his predecessors. Med. Hist. 25: 57–72.

Casagrande, J. B.
1964.   Preface by J. B. Casagrande (ed.), In the company of man: twenty portraits of anthropological informants, pp. ix–xvii. New York: Harper Torchbooks.

Chagnon, N. A.
1977.   Yanomamö: the fierce people, 2nd ed. New York: Holt, Rinehart and Winston.

Chandrasekhar, S.
1959.   Infant mortality in India, 1901–55: a matter of life and death. London: George Allen & Unwin.

Channa, V. C.
1984.   Hinduism: a cultural profile of the gods, goddesses, rituals, romance and fables in today's Hinduism. New Delhi: National.

Chapple, E. D.
1970.   Culture and biological man: explorations in behavioral anthropology. New York: Holt, Rinehart and Winston.

Chatterjee, S. C.
1953.   Hindu religious thought. *In* K. W. Mor-

gan (ed.), The religion of the Hindus, pp. 206–261. New York: Ronald Press.

Cherfas, J.
1990. Malaria vaccines: the failed promise. Science 247: 402–403.

Clark, M.
1970. Health in the Mexican-American culture: a community study. Berkeley: Univ. California Press.

Clayman, C. B. (ed.)
1989. The American Medical Association encyclopedia of medicine. New York: Random House.

Cohen, M. L.
1992. Epidemiology of drug resistance; implications for a post-antimicrobial era. Science 257: 1050–1055.

Cohen, S. P.
1971. The Indian army. Berkeley: Univ. California Press.

Cohn, B. S.
1965. Anthropological notes on disputes and law in India. Am. Anthrop. 67(2): 82–122.

Collier, R.
1964. The great Indian mutiny. New York: E. P. Dutton.

Collins, L., and D. Lapierre
1976. Freedom at midnight. New York: Avon Books.

Colson, E.
1984. The reordering of experience: anthropological involvement with time. J. Anthrop. Res. 40(1): 1–13.

Crane, J. G., and M. V. Angrosino
1974. Field projects in anthropology: a student handbook. Morristown, NJ: General Learning Press.

Crooke, W.
1894. An introduction to the popular religion and folklore of northern India. Allahabad, Gov. Press, North-Western Provinces and Oudh.

1896. The tribes and castes of the north–western provinces and Oudh, Vol. 1–4. Calcutta: Supt. Gov. Printing, India.

1968. The popular religion and folk-lore of northern India. Revised from 2nd ed., 1896, Vols. I, 2. Nai Sarak, Delhi, India: Munshiram Manoharlal.

Crosby, A. W., Jr.
1977. The pandemic of 1918. In J. E. Osborn (ed.), History, science, and politics: influenza in America, 1918–1976, pp. 5–14. New York: Prodist.

Crossette, B.
1991. India's population put at 844 million: census shows growth of 161 million in the last decade. The New York Times, March 16, 1991: A6 L.

Dandekar, R. N.
1953. The role of man in Hinduism. In K. W. Morgan (ed.), The religion of the Hindus, pp. 117–153. New York: Ronald Press.

Daniel, E. V.
1984. The pulse as an icon in Siddha medicine. In E. V. Daniel and J. F. Pugh (eds.), South Asian systems of healing. Contributions to Asian Studies 18: 115–126. Leiden: E. J. Brill.

Daniélou, A.
1964. Hindu polytheism. Bollingen series 73. New York: Pantheon.

Das, V.
1980. The mythological film and its framework of meaning: an analysis of Jai Santoshi Ma. In P. Krishen (ed.), Indian popular cinema: myth, meaning, and metaphor. India Int. Centre Q. 8(1): 43–56.

Datta, V. N.
1988. Sati: A historical, social and philosophical enquiry into the Hindu rite of widow burning. Riverdale, MD: Riverdale.

Davey, T. H., and T. Wilson
1971. Davey and Lightbody's the control of disease in the tropics: a handbook for medical practitioners, 4th ed. revised. London: English Language Book Society and H. K. Lewis.

Debus, A. G. (ed.)
1968. World who's who in science. Chicago: Marquis-Who's Who.

Delora, J. S., C. A. B. Warren, and C. R. Ellison
1980. Understanding human sexuality. Boston: Houghton Mifflin.

Derrett, J. D. M.
1978. The death of a marriage law: epitaph for the Rishis. New Delhi: Vikas.

DeVinne, P. B. (ed.)
1987. Rasputin. American Heritage illustrated encyclopedic dictionary, p. 1395. Boston: Houghton Mifflin.

Diamond, J.
1989. Blood, genes, and malaria. Nat. Hist. (Feb): 8, 10, 12, 14, 16, 18.

Dissanayake, S. A. W., and P. De Silva
1983. Sri Lanka. In L. A. Headley (ed.), Suicide in Asia and the Near East, pp. 167–209. Berkeley: Univ. California Press.

Dobkin de Rios, M.
1973. Curing with ayahuasca in an urban slum. In M. J. Harner (ed.), Hallucinogens and shamanism, pp. 67–85. New York: Oxford Univ. Press.

Doniger O'Flaherty, W.
1980.   The origins of evil in Hindu mythology. [Original edition 1976.] Berkeley: Univ. California Press.
1984.   Dreams, illusion and other realities. Chicago: Univ. Chicago Press.
Douglas, J. D.
1961.   The social meanings of suicide. Princeton, NJ: Princeton Univ. Press.
Dowling, H. F.
1972.   Frustration and foundation: management of pneumonia before antibiotics. JAMA 220(10): 1341–1345.
Dowson, J.
1950.   A classical dictionary of Hindu mythology and religion, geography, history, and literature. [Original edition 1891.] London: Routledge & Kegan Paul.
Dressler, W. W.
1984.   Hypertension and perceived stress: a St. Lucian example. Ethos 12(3): 265–283.
Dube, L.
1983.   Misadventures in amniocentesis. Econ. Pol. Weekly 18(8): 279–280.
Dube, S. C.
1955.   Indian village. Ithaca, NY: Cornell Univ. Press.
Dutt, E.
1992.   New leprosy test omits India. India Abroad Feb. 14: 28.
Edgerton, F. (translator, interpreter)
1965.   The Bhagavad Gita. [Original edition 1944. 3rd printing.] Harvard Oriental Series 38. New York: Harper Torchbooks.
Eliade, M.
1964.   Shamanism: Archaic techniques of ecstasy. [Original edition 1951.] W. R. Trask (translator). Bollingen Series 76. New York: Pantheon Books.
1978.   A history of religious ideas: from the Stone Age to the Eleusinian Mysteries, Vol. 1. [Original edition 1976.] W. R. Trask (translator). Chicago: Univ. Chicago Press.
Embree, A. T.
1972.   The Hindu tradition. New York: Vintage Books.
Encyclopaedia Britannica
1966.   Encyclopaedia Britannica. Chicago: William Benton.
1992.   The New Encyclopaedia Britannica. Chicago: Encyclopaedia Britannica.
Engel. G. L.
1968.   A life setting conducive to illness: the giving-up—given-up complex. Bull. Menninger Clinic 32: 355–365.

Ervin F. R., R. M. Palmour, B. E. P. Murphy, R. Prince, and R. C. Simons
1988.   The psychology of trance II: physiological and endocrine correlates. Transcult. Psychiatr. Res. Rev. 25(4): 267–284.
Farquhar, J. N.
1915.   Modern religious movements in India. New York: MacMillan.
Farwell, B.
1989.   Armies of the Raj: from the Mutiny to Independence, 1858–1947. New York: W. W. Norton.
Fenichel, O.
1945.   The psychoanalytic theory of neurosis. New York: W. W. Norton.
Foster, G.
1984.   The concept of "neutral" in humoral medical systems. Medic. Anthrop. 8(3): 180–194.
Foster, G., T. Scudder, E. Colson, and R. Van Kemper (eds.)
1979.   Long-term field research in social anthropology. New York: Academic Press.
Foulks, E. F., and F. Schwartz
1982.   Self and object: psychoanalytical perspectives in cross cultural fieldwork and interpretation, a review essay. Ethos 10(3): 254–278.
Fox, C. H., and M. Cottler–Fox
1986.   Second sight: the microscope in medicine. Med. Heritage 2(6): 453–460.
Fraser, L.
1911.   India under Curzon & after. New York: Henry Holt.
Freed, R. S.
1971.   The legal process in a village in north India: the case of Maya. Trans. New York Acad. Sci. Ser 2, 33(4): 423–435.
1977.   Space, density, and cultural conditioning. In L. L. Adler (ed.), Issues in cross-cultural research. Ann. New York Acad. Sci. 185: 593–604.
Freed, R. S., and S. A. Freed
1962.   Two mother goddess ceremonies of Delhi state in the great and little traditions. Southwest. J. Anthrop. 18(3): 246–277.
1964.   Calendars, ceremonies and festivals in a north Indian village: necessary calendric information for fieldwork. Ibid., 20(1): 67–90.
1966.   Unity in diversity in the celebration of cattle–curing rites in a north Indian village: a study in the resolution of conflict. Am. Anthrop. 68(3): 673–692.
1979.   Shanti Nagar: the effects of urbanization in a village in north India. 3. Sickness

and health. Anthrop. Pap. Am. Mus. Nat. Hist. 55(2): 285–348.

1980. Rites of passage in Shanti Nagar. Ibid., 56(3): 323–554.

1981. Enculturation and education in Shanti Nagar. Ibid., 57(2): 51–156.

1985. The psychomedical case history of a low–caste woman of north India. Ibid., 60(2): 101–228.

1989. Beliefs and practices resulting in female deaths and fewer females than males in India. Popul. Environ. 10(3): 144–161.

1992. Letter from Ruth and Stan Freed (New York) in response to *Ghost Illness and Pathological Grieving* by R. Prince, M. D. and J. Paris, M. D. in TPRR 28(1991): 303–311. Transcult. Psychiatr. Res. Rev. 29(1): 73–76.

Freed, S. A.
1963a. Fictive kinship in a north Indian village. Ethnology 2(1): 86–103.

1963b. An objective method for determining the collective caste hierarchy of an Indian village. Am. Anthrop. 65(4): 879–891.

1970. Caste ranking and the exchange of food and water in a north Indian village. Anthrop. Q. 43(1): 1–13.

Freed, S. A., and R. S. Freed
1964. Spirit possession as illness in a north Indian village. Ethnology 3(2): 152–171.

1969. Urbanization and family types in a north Indian village. Southwest. J. Anthrop. 25(4): 342–359.

1971. The relationship of fertility and selected social factors in a north Indian village. Man in India 51(4): 274–289.

1972. Some attitudes toward caste in a north Indian village. J. Soc. Res. 15(1): 1–17.

1976. Shanti Nagar: the effects of urbanization in a village in north India. 1. Social organization. Anthrop. Pap. Am. Mus. Nat. Hist. 53(1): 1–254.

1978. Shanti Nagar: the effects of urbanization in a village in north India. 2. Aspects of economy, technology, and ecology. Ibid., 55(1): 1–153.

1980. Swastika: a new symbolic interpretation. *In* C. M. Sakumoto Drake (ed.), The cultural context: essays in honor of Edward Norbeck. Rice Univ. Studies 66(1): 87–105.

1982. Changing family types in India. Ethnology 21(3): 189–202.

1983. The domestic cycle in India: Natural history of a will-o'-the-wisp. Am. Ethnologist 10(4): 312–327.

1985a. Fertility, sterilization, and population growth in Shanti Nagar, India: a longitudinal ethnographic approach. Anthrop. Pap. Am. Mus. Nat. Hist. 60(3): 229–286.

1985b. Two decades of sterilisation, modernisation, and population growth in a rural context. Econ. Pol. Weekly 20(49): 2171–2175.

1987. Uncertain revolution: panchayati raj and democratic elections in a north Indian village. Anthrop. Pap. Am. Mus. Nat. Hist. 64(1): 1–78.

Freeman, J. M.
1979. Untouchable: an Indian life history. Stanford, CA: Stanford Univ. Press.

Freud, S.
1962. A general introduction to psychoanalysis. [J. Riviere (translator).] New York: Washington Square Press.

1965. Three essays on the theory of sexuality. [J. Strachey (translator, ed.).] New York: Avon.

1967. The interpretation of dreams. New York: Avon.

Friedman, M. J., and W. Trager
1981. The biochemistry of resistance to malaria. Sci. Am. March: 154, 155, 158–164.

Frisch, R. E., and J. McArthur
1974. Menstrual cycles: fatness as a determinant of minimum weight and height necessary for their maintenance and onset. Science 185: 949–951.

Frisch, R. E., and R. Revelle
1970. Height and weight at menarche and a hypothesis of body weights and adolescent events. Science 196: 397–399.

Gadd, C. J.
1979. Seals of Ancient Indian style found at Ur. In G. L. Possehl (ed.), Ancient cities of the Indus, pp. 115–122. New Delhi: Vikas.

Gadd, C. J., and S. Smith
1979. The new links between Indian and Babylonian civilization. Ibid., pp. 109–110.

Garrett, J.
1990. A classical dictionary of India. [Original edition 1871.] Delhi: Low Price.

Gazetteer Unit, Delhi Adm.
1976. Delhi Gazetteer. Nasik: Gov. India Press.

Ghosh, S.
1986. Discrimination begins at birth. Indian Pediatr. 23(1): 9–15.

Gillispie, C. C. (ed.)
1970–78. Dictionary of scientific biography. New York: Charles Scribner's.

Goble, F. C., and E. A. Konopka
1973.   Sex as a factor in infectious diseases. Trans. New York Acad. Sci., Series 2, 35(4): 325–346.

Goldstein, M. C.
1987.   When brothers share a wife: among Tibetans, the good life relegates many women to spinsterhood. Nat. Hist. 96(3): 38–39.

Goldwater, L. J.
1972.   Mercury: a history of quicksilver. Baltimore: York Press.

Gole, S.
1983.   India within the Ganges. New Delhi: Jayaprints.

Good, B. J. (ed.)
1987.   Culture bound syndromes featured in this issue of Cult. Med. Psychiatry. 11(1): 1–121.
1988.   Review articles on Simons and Hughes, The culture-bound syndromes: two reviews and a response. Ibid., 12(4): 503–529.

Good, B. J., and A. Kleinman
1985.   Culture and anxiety: cross-cultural evidence for the patterning of anxiety disorders. In A. H. Tuma and J. Maser (eds.), Anxiety and the anxiety disorders, pp. 297–323. Hillside, NJ: Lawrence Erlbaum.

Gordon, J. E., H. Gideon, and J. B. Wyon
1965a.   Midwifery practices in rural Punjab, India. Am. J. Obstet. Gynecol. 93: 734–742.
1965b.   Complications of childbirth and illnesses during the puerperium in 862 Punjab village women: a field study. J. Obstet. Gynecol. (India) 15(2): 159–167.

Gordon, J. E., S. Singh, and J. B. Wyon
1965.   Causes of death at different ages, by sex, and by season, in a rural population of the Punjab, 1957–1959: a field study. Indian J. Med. Res. 53(9): 906–917.

Gothi, G. D.
1982.   Epidemiology of tuberculosis in India. Indian J. Tuberculosis 29(3): 134–148.

Gove, P. B. (ed.)
1986.   Webster's third new international dictionary, unabridged. Springfield, MA: Merriam-Webster.

Goyal, S. S., G. P. Mathur, and S. P. Pamra
1978.   Tuberculosis trends in an urban community. Indian J. Tuberculosis 25(2): 77–82.

Gray, J.
1982.   Chetri women in domestic groups and rituals. In M. Allen and S. N. Mukherjee (eds.), Women in India and Nepal. Aus-tralian Natl. Univ. Monographs on South Asia (8): 211–241. Canberra: Australian Natl. Univ. Printing.

Gulani, K., B. Devaneson, S. Mammen, E. Joseph, and P. Saraf
1977.   MS. Results of a pilot study of the effects of teaching programme for fathers on completion of infant immunization schedule in rural India. On file with Freeds.

Gumperz, J. J., J. Rumery, A.B. Singh, C.M. Naim, R. Moore, and S.M. Jaiswal
1967.   Conversational Hindi-Urdu. Devanagari ed., Vol. 1. Delhi: Radhakrishna Prakashan.

Guz, D.
1989.   Population dynamics of famine in nineteenth century Punjab, 1896–7 and 1899–1900. In T. Dyson (ed.), India's historical demography, studies in famine, disease and society. Collected papers on South Asia 8: 197–221. London: Curzon Press. Riverdale, MD: Riverdale.

Hammond, P.B.
1978.   An introduction to cultural and social anthropology. New York: Macmillan.

Harrell, B. B.
1981.   Lactation and menstruation in cultural perspective. Am. Anthrop. 83(4): 796–823.

Harris, W. H., and J. S. Levey (eds.)
1975.   The new Columbia encyclopedia. New York: Columbia Univ. Press.

Hart, G.
1973.   Social aspects of venereal disease. Br. J. Vener. Dis. 49: 542–547.

Hasselmeyer, E. G., and J. C. Hunter
1988.   A historical perspective on SIDS research. In P. J. Schwartz, D. P. Southall, and M. Valdes-Dapens (eds.), Sudden infant death syndromes: cardiac and respiratory mechanisms and interventions. Ann. New York Acad. Sci. 533: 1–5.

Henry, J. L.
1982.   Possible involvement of endorphins in altered states of consciousness. Ethos 10(4): 394–408.

Hess, D. J.
1989.   Spirit manifestation as an idiom of distress: Intervention strategies and their psychocultural contexts. Transcult. Psychiatr. Res. Rev. 26(1): 33–37.
1990.   Ghosts and domestic politics in Brazil: some parallels between spirit possession and spirit infestation. Ethos 18(4): 407–438.

Hoch, E. M.
1974. Pir, faqir and psychotherapist. The Human Context 6(3): 668–676.

Hochstein, G.
1968. Pica: a study of medical and anthropological explanation. In T. Weaver (ed.), Essays on medical anthropology. Southern Anthrop. Soc. Proc. 1: 88–96. Athens: Univ. Georgia Press.

Hockings, P.
1980. Sex and disease in a mountain community. New Delhi: Vikas.

Hoebel, E. A.
1968. The law of primitive man. New York: Atheneum.

Hoffman, M.
1991. Hepatitis a vaccine shows promise. Science 254: 1581–1582.

Hopkins, D. R.
1983. Princes and peasants: smallpox in history. Chicago: Univ. Chicago Press.

Hrdy, S. B.
1984. When the bough breaks: there may be method in the madness of infanticide. The Sciences Mar.–Apr.: 45–50.

Hufford, D. J.
1982. The terror that comes in the night: an experience-centered study of supernatural assault traditions. Philadelphia: Univ. Pennsylvania Press.

Hughes, C. C.
1985a. Culture-bound or construct bound? the syndromes and DSM-III. In R. C. Simons and C. C. Hughes (eds.), The culture-bound syndromes: folk illnesses of psychiatric and anthropological interest, pp. 3–24. Dordrecht, Holland: D. Reidel.
1985b. The sleep paralysis taxon: commentary. Ibid.: 147–148.
1985c. The fright illness taxon: commentary. Ibid.: 405–407.
1985d. Glossary of "culture–bound" or folk psychiatric syndromes. Ibid.,: 469–505.

Hunter, D. L., and P. Whitten (eds).
1976. Encyclopedia of anthropology. New York: Harper & Row.

Hutton, J. H.
1963. Caste in India: its nature, function, and origins. Bombay: Oxford Univ. Press.

Illich, I.
1976. Medical nemesis: the expropriation of health. New York: Random House.

Imperato, P. J.
1983. "The great leveler." Review of D. E. Hopkins, Princes and peasants: smallpox in history. Chicago: Univ. Chicago Press, 1983. Nat. Hist. (Dec.): 34, 36.

India Abroad (a weekly newspaper)
1987. 17(28): 1, 8 (on feticide).
17(32): 4 (on dowry murder).
17(52): 4 (on Sati).
18(2): 6 (on Sati).
18(4): 40 (on Sati).
18(5): 35 (on Sati).
1988. 18(23): 19 (on feticide).
18(44): 8 (on cholera in Delhi).
19(6): 41 (on dengue fever in New Delhi).
19(10): 39 (on dowry murder).
1990. 20(33): 26 (on furor over Ayurvedic Medicine).

Indian Express, The
1978. Malaria epidemic in worst form this year. April 19, 1978: 3.

Ingalls, D. H. H.
1957. Dharma and moksa. Philos. East West 7: 41–48.
1958. The Brahman tradition. J. Am. Folklore 71(281): 209–215.

Jeffery, P., R. Jeffery, and A. Lyon
1989. Labour pains and labour power: women and childbearing in India. London: Zed Books.

Jeffery, R.
1988. The politics of health in India. Berkeley: Univ. California Press.

Jeffery, R., and P. Jeffery
1983. Female infanticide and amniocentesis. Econ. Pol. Weekly 18(16–17): 654–656.

Jeffery, R., P. Jeffery, and A. Lyon
1984. Female infanticide and amniocentesis. Soc. Sci. Med. 19(11): 1207–1212.

Jilek, W. G.
1982. Altered states of consciousness in North American Indian ceremonials. Ethos 10(4): 326–343.

Johnson, J. D.
1981. The regional and ethnic distribution of lactose malabsorption: adaptive and genetic hypotheses. In D. M. Paige and T. M. Bayless (eds.), Lactose digesting: clinical and nutritional implications, pp. 11–22. Baltimore: Johns Hopkins Univ. Press.

Johnson, J. D., N. Kretchmer, and F. J. Simoons
1974. Lactose malabsorption: its biology and history. In I. Shulman (ed.), Adv. in Pediatr. 21: 197–237. Chicago: Yearbook Medical Publishers.

Jolly, J., (G. G. Kashikar, translator)
1951. Indian medicine. [Original edition, Indische Medizin. Strassburg, 1901.] Poona: Gurjar.

Jones, K. W.
1976. Arya Dharm. New Delhi, India: Manohar.
Jones, S. K.
1976. Limbu spirit possession: a case study. In J. T. Hitchcock and R. L. Jones (eds.), Spirit possession in the Nepal Himalayas, pp. 22–28. New Delhi: Vikas.
Jordens, J. T. F.
1978. Dayananda Sarasvati: his life and ideas. Delhi: Oxford Univ. Press.
Juergensmeyer, M.
1982. Religion as social vision: the movement against untouchability in twentieth-century Punjab. Berkeley: Univ. California Press.
Kakar, S.
1982. The inner world: a psychoanalytic study of childhood and society in India. [Original edition 1978.] Delhi: Oxford Univ. Press.
1983. Shamans, mystics and doctors: a psychological inquiry into India and its healing traditions. [Original edition 1982.] Boston: Beacon Press.
Kales, A., C. R. Soldatos, A. B. Caldwell, D. S. Charney, J. D. Kales, D. Markel, and R. Cadieux
1980. Nightmares: clinical characteristics and personality patterns. Am. J. Psychiatry. 137: 1197–1201.
Kerry, F.
1985. Doctors demand immediate action to abolish rabies. India Abroad, Oct. 25: 22.
Klayman, D. L.
1989. Weeding out malaria. Nat. Hist. (Oct.): 18–27.
Kleinman, A.
1981. Patients and healers in the context of culture. Berkeley: Univ. California Press.
Kleinman, C. S.
1987. Turnabout: a physician's battle with Hodgkin's disease. The Sciences (Nov.–Dec.): 20–29.
Klerman, G. L.
1983. The significance of DSM-III in American psychiatry. In R. L. Spitzer, J. B. W. Williams, and A. E. Skodol (eds.), International perspectives on DSM-III, Chap. 1. Washington, D.C.: Am. Psychiatric Press.
Kolata, G.
1984. The search for a malaria vaccine. Science 226(4675): 679–682.
1987. Panel urges newborn sickle cell screening. Science 236(4799): 259–260.

Konner, M.
1987a. False idylls. The Sciences (Sept.–Oct.): 8–10.
1987b. The gender option. The Sciences (Nov.–Dec.): 2–4.
1987c. The many faces of madness. The Sciences (July–Aug.): 6–8.
1989. Art of darkness. The Sciences (Nov.–Dec.): 3–5.
Krappe, A. H.
1964. The science of folklore. [Original edition 1930.] New York: W. W. Norton.
Krueger, J. M.
1989. No simple slumber: exploring the enigma of sleep. The Sciences (May–June): 36–41.
Kulkarni, S. N.
1990. Famines droughts and scarcities in India. Allahabad: Chugh.
Kumar, B., A.P.S. Narang, A. Koshy, S.C. Sharma, and S. Kaur
1982. In vivo and in vitro drug metabolism in patients with leprosy. Leprosy India 54(1): 75–81.
Kumar, D.
1983a. Male utopias or nightmares? Econ. Pol. Weekly 18(3): 61–64.
1983b. Amniocentesis again. Ibid. 18(24): 1075–1076.
Kunkle, E. C.
1967. The "Jumpers" of Maine: a reappraisal. Arch. Intern. Med. 119: 355–358.
Kurtz, S.
1984. MS. Correspondence & misc. papers on Santoshi Mata. On file with Freeds.
Kutumbiah, P.
1969. Ancient Indian medicine. Bombay: Orient Longmans.
Lamb, B. P.
1975. India: a world in transition. New York: Praeger.
Landy, D.
1977. Conceptions of healing statuses and roles. In D. Landy (ed.), Culture, disease, and healing: studies in medical anthropology, pp. 415–418. New York: Macmillan.
Langer, W. I.
1974. Infanticide: a historical survey. Historical Children's Q.: 1(3): 353–365.
Langness, L. L.
1965. The life history in anthropological science. New York: Holt, Rinehart and Winston.
Leasor, J.
1957. The Red Fort: the story of the Indian Mutiny, 1857. New York: Reynal & Cox.

Levine, N. E.
1987. Differential child care in three Tibetan communities: beyond son preference. Popul. Dev. Rev. 13(2): 281–304.

LeVine, R. A.
1973. Culture, behavior, and personality. Chicago: Aldine.

Lewis, I. M.
1978. Ecstatic religion: an anthropological study of spirit possession and shamanism. [Original edition 1971.] New York: Penguin.

Lewis, O.
1958. Village life in northern India. Urbana: Univ. Illinois Press.

Lindholm, C.
1982. Generosity and jealousy. New York: Columbia Univ. Press.

Lloyd, G.
1962. Right and left in Greek philosophy. J. Helenic Stud. 82: 56–66.

Lomax, E.
1977. Heredity or acquired disease? early nineteenth century debates on the cause of infantile scrofula and tuberculosis. J. Hist. Med. 32: 356–374.

Lowie, R. H.
1948. Primitive religion. [Original edition 1934.] New York: Liveright.

Lucas, C. (ed.)
1926. The empire at war, Vol. 5. London: Oxford Univ. Press.

Ludwig, A. M.
1966. Altered states of consciousness. Arch. Gen. Psychiatry. 15: 225–234.

Luthra, S. K.
1961. A socio–economic study of village Jhatikra. Census of India, Delhi: 19, Pt. 6(8). Delhi: Supt. Census Operations.

Lyght, C. E. (ed.)
1956. The Merck medical manual of diagnosis and therapy, 9th ed. Rahway, NJ: Merck.

Lynch, O.
1972. Dr. B. R. Ambedkar—myth and charisma. In J. M. Mahar (ed.), The untouchables in contemporary India, pp. 97–112. Tucson: Univ. Arizona Press.

Mackay, E. J. H.
1979. Further links between ancient Sind, Sumer and elsewhere. In G. L. Possehl (ed.), Ancient cities of the Indus, pp. 123–129. New Delhi: Vikas.

Maheshwari, J. K.
1976. The flora of Delhi. INSDOC, New Delhi.

Maine, H. S.
1963. Ancient law. [Original edition 1861.] Boston: Beacon Press.

Majumdar, D. N.
1958. Caste and communication in an Indian village. Bombay: Asia Publishing House.

Malinowski, B.
1984. The role of myth in life. [Original edition 1926.] In A. Dundes (ed.), Sacred narrative: readings and theory of myth, pp. 193–206. Berkeley: Univ. California Press.

Mandelbaum, D. G.
1964. A reformer of his people. In J. B. Casagrande (ed.), In the company of man, pp. 273–308. New York: Harper & Row.
1970. Society in India: Continuity and change, Vol. 1. Berkeley: Univ. California Press.
1972. Society in India: Continuity and change, Vol. 2. Berkeley: Univ. California Press.
1973. The study of life history: Gandhi. Curr. Anthrop. 14(3): 177–206.
1974. Human fertility in India: social components and policy perspectives. Berkeley: Univ. California Press.
1988. Women's seclusion and men's honor: sex roles in north India, Bangladesh, and Pakistan. Tucson: Univ. Arizona Press.

Mani, A., E. B. Crowell, Jr., and M. Mathew
1982. Epidemiologic features of Hodgkin's disease in Punjab. Indian J. Cancer 19: 183–188.

Mani, M. Z., and M. Mathew
1981. Leprosy in Punjab: an analysis of 4 years of O.P.D. data. Leprosy in India 53(3): 395–405.

Marshall, E.
1990. Malaria research—what next? Science 247: 399–402.

Massie, R. K.
1985. Nicholas and Alexandra. New York: Dell.

Mathur, K. S.
1964. Caste and ritual in a Malwa village. New York: Asia Publishing House.

Mayo, K.
1932. Mother India. [Original edition 1927.] New York: Blue Ribbon.

McCracken, R. D.
1971. Lactase deficiency: an example of dietary evolution. Curr. Anthrop. 12(4–5): 479–517.

McCreary, C. B.
1968. Tuberculosis control in India. Dis. Chest 53: 699.

McNeill, W. H.
1976. Plagues and peoples. Garden City, NY: Anchor Books.

Millar, J. D., and J. E. Osborn
1977. Precursors of the scientific decision-making process leading to the 1976 na-

tional immunization campaign. *In* J. E. Osborn (ed.), History, science, and politics: influenza in America, 1918–1976, pp. 15–27. New York: Prodist.

Minturn, L., and J. T. Hitchcock
1966. The Rajputs of Khalapur, India. Six Culture series: 3. New York: Wiley.

Moreland, W. H., and A. C. Chatterjee
1957. A short history of India. [Original edition 1936.] London: Longmans, Green.

Morgan, K. W. (ed.)
1953. The religion of the Hindus. New York: Ronald Press.

Morris, W. (ed.)
1969. The American heritage dictionary of the English language. Boston: American Heritage Publishing and Houghton Mifflin.

Mukherjee, S. N.
1982. Raja Rammohun Roy and the debate on the status of women in Bengal. *In* M. Allen and S. N. Mukherjee (eds.), Women in India and Nepal. Australian Natl. Univ. Monographs on South Asia 8: 155–178. Canberra: Australian Natl. Univ. Printing.

Müller, M. (ed.)
1898. The sacred books of the east described and examined, AV: 1–68. London: Christian Literature Society for India.

Mutiah, A.
1982. Comments on A. Ramanamma and U. Bambawale, The mania for sons: an analysis of social values in south Asia. Soc. Sci. Med. 16: 875.

Myers, J. A.
1977. Captain of all these men of death. St. Louis, MO: W. H. Green.

Nandi, D. N.
1979. Psychoanalysis in India. *In* M. Kapur, V. N. Murthy, K. Sathyavathi, R. L. Kapur (eds.), Psychotherapeutic processes: proceedings of the seminar held at Nimhans in October 1978, pp. 21–32. Bangalore: Bhandare.

Nautiyal, K. C.
1961. Mandi: socio-economic study of rural folk. *In* B. Raj, Supt. Census Operations (ed.), Census of India 19(6): No. 9.

Neelan, P. N., S. K. Noordeen, and N. Sivaprasad
1983. Chemoprophylaxis against leprosy with acedapsone. Indian J. Med. Res. 78: 307–313.

Neki, J. S.
1979. Psychotherapy in India: traditions and trends. *In* M. Kapur, V. N. Murthy, K. Sathyavathi, and R. L. Kapur (eds.), Psychotherapeutic processes: proceed-

ings of seminar at Nimhans, Oct. 1978, pp. 113–134. Bangalore: Bhandare.

Ness, R. C.
1985. The Old Hag phenomenon as sleep paralysis: a biocultural interpretation. *In* R. C. Simons and C. C. Hughes (eds.), The culture-bound syndromes: folk illnesses of psychiatric and anthropological interest, pp. 23–145. Dordrecht: D. Reidel.

Nichter, M.
1981. Idioms of distress: alternatives in the expression of psychosocial distress: a case study from South India. Cult. Med. Psychiatry 5: 379–408.

Nilsson, M.
1964. A history of Greek religion. F. J. Fielden (translator). New York: W. W. Norton.

Ober, W. B.
1977. Hodgkin's disease: historical notes. New York State J. Med. 77(1): 126–133.

O'Dwyer, M.
1925. India as I knew it: 1885–1925. London: Constable.

O'Malley, L. S. S.
1935. Popular Hinduism: the religion of the masses. London: Cambridge Univ. Press.

Oman, J. C.
1906. The great Indian epics: the stories of the Ramayana and the Mahabharata. London: George Bell.

Opler, M. E.
1958. Spirit possession in a rural area of north India. *In* W. A. Lessa and E. Z. Vogt (eds.), Reader in comparative religion, pp. 553–566. White Plains, NY: Row, Peterson.
1963. The cultural definition of illness in village India. Human Org. 22(1): 32–35.

Otten, C. M.
1985. Genetic effects on male and female development and on the sex ratio. *In* R. Hall (ed.), Male-female differences: a bio-cultural perspective, pp. 155–217. New York: Praeger.

Padmanabha, P.
1982. Mortality in India: a note on trends and implications. Econ. Pol. Weekly 17(32): 1285–1290.

Pakrasi, K. B.
1972. On the antecedents of infanticide act of 1870 in India. Bull. Cult. Inst. Calcutta 9(1–2): 20–30.

Pakrasi, K. B., and B. Sasmal
1971. Infanticide and variation of sex-ratio in a caste population of India. Acta Medica Auxologica, Italy 3(3): 217–218.

Paris, J.
1992. Dhat: the semen loss anxiety syndrome. Transcult. Psychiatr. Res. Rev. 29: 109–118.

Parkin, R.
1988. Reincarnation and alternate generation equivalence in middle India. J. Anthrop. Res. 44(1): 1–20.

Parrott, T. M.
1938. Shakespeare: twenty-three plays and sonnets. New York: Scribner's.

Pathak, R. C. (ed.)
1976. Bhargava's standard illustrated dictionary of the Hindi language, Hindi-English ed. Varanasi: Bhargava Bhushan Press.

Pattanayak, S., and R. G. Roy
1980. Malaria in India and the modified plan of operations for its control. J. Commun. Dis. 12(1): 1–13.

Paul, J. R.
1971. A history of poliomyelitis. New Haven and London: Yale Univ. Press.

Pearson, G.
1982. The female intelligentsia in segregated society: early twentieth century Bombay. In M. Allen and S. N. Mukherjee (eds.), Women in India and Nepal. Australian Natl. Univ. Monographs on South Asia 8: 136–154. Canberra: Australian Natl. Univ.

Peters, L. G.
1981. Ecstacy and healing in Nepal: an ethnopsychiatric study of Tamang shamanism. Malibu, CA: Udena.

Peters, W.
1975. Guest editorial. J. Tropic. Med. Hyg. 78(8): 167–170.

Petros, H.R.H. Prince of Greece and Denmark
1963. A study of polyandry. The Hague: Mouton.

Pinnas, J. L., and P. A. Bunn
1971. Salmonella infections in Osler's day and ours. New York State J. Med. 71: 654–656.

Pizza, M., A. Covacci, A. Bartolini, M. Perugini, L. Nencioni, M. T. DeMagistris, L. Villa, D. Nucci, R. Manetti, M. Bugnoli, F. Giovannoni, R. Olivieri, J. T. Barbieri, H. Sato, and R. Ruppuoli
1989. Mutants of pertussis toxin suitable for vaccine development. Science 240(4929): 497–500.

Planalp, J. M.
1971. Heat stress and culture in north India. Natick, MA: U.S. Army Res. Inst. Envir. Med., U.S. Army Med. Res. and Develop. Command.

Porkert, M.
1976. The intellectual and social impulses behind the evolution of traditional Chinese medicine. In C. Leslie (ed.), Asian medical systems, a comparative study, pp. 63–76. Berkeley: Univ. California Press.

Pospisil, L.
1971. Anthropology of law: a comparative theory. New York: Harper & Row.

Prince, I.
1989. Pica and geophagia in cross-cultural perspective. Transcult. Psych. Res. Rev. 26(3): 167–197.

Prince, R.
1982a. The endorphins: a review for psychological anthropologists. Ethos 10(4): 303–316.
1982b. Shamans and endorphins: hypotheses for a synthesis. Ethos 10(4): 409–423.
1990a. Somatic complaint syndromes and depression: the problem of cultural effects on symptomatology. Abstract & review of manuscript presented at spring convention of the Korean Neuropsychiatric Assoc., May 1989, Seoul, Korea. Transcult. Psychiatr. Res. Rev. 27(1): 31–36.
1990b. Obituary: Richard Frank Salisbury (1916–1989). Transcult. Psychiatr. Res. Rev., 27(1): 73–75.

Prince, R. (ed.)
1982. Issue devoted to shamans and endorphins. Ethos 10(4).

Prince, R., and J. Paris
1991. Ghost illness and pathological grieving. Transcult. Psychiatric. Res. Rev. 28: 303–312.

Prince, R., and F. Tcheng-Laroche
1987. Culture-bound syndromes and international disease classifications. Culture, Med. Psychiatry 11(1): 3–19.

Pugh, J. F.
1983. Astrology and fate: the Hindu and Muslim experiences. In C. F. Keyes, and E. V. Daniel (eds.), Karma: an anthropological inquiry, pp. 131–146. Berkeley: Univ. California Press.
1984. Concepts of person and situation in north Indian counseling: the case of astrology. In E. V. Daniel and J. F. Pugh (eds.), South Asian systems of healing. Contrib. to Asian Studies 18: 85–105. Leiden: E. J. Brill.

Rabinovitch, R.
1965. An exaggerated startle reflex resembling a kicking horse. Can. Med. Assoc. J. 93: 130.

Raghavan, V.
  1953.   Introduction to the Hindu scriptures. *In*
          K. W. Morgan (ed.), The religion of the
          Hindus, pp. 265–398. New York: Ron-
          ald Press.
Rai, L.
  1967.   A history of the Arya Samaj. [Original
          edition 1914.] Revised, expanded and
          edited by R. Sharma. Bombay: Orient
          Longmans.
Ramanamma, A., and U. Bambawale
  1980.   The mania for sons: an analysis of social
          values in south Asia. Soc. Sci. Med. 14B:
          107–110.
Rao, A. V.
  1978.   Some aspects of psychiatry in India.
          Transcult. Psychiatr. Res. Rev. 15: 7–
          27.
  1983.   India. *In* L. A. Headley (ed.), Suicide in
          Asia and the Near East, pp. 210–237.
          Berkeley: Univ. California Press.
Rao, K. B.
  1952.   Obstetrics in ancient India. J. Indian
          Med. Assoc. 21: 210–213.
Rao, P. S. S., et al. [Names of et al. authors not
given.]
  1982.   A study of leprosy among urban and
          rural school children of Andhra Pra-
          desh. Leprosy India 54(1): 100–109.
Rao, S. R.
  1979.   Contacts between Lothal and Susa. *In*
          G. L. Possehl (ed.), Ancient cities of the
          Indus, pp. 174–175. New Delhi: Vikas.
Rawlinson, H. G.
  1965.   India: a short cultural history. [Original
          edition 1937.] New York: Praeger.
Ray, S.
  1989.   India is criticized on population growth.
          India Abroad April 7: 27.
Redfield, R.
  1967.   Primitive law. *In* P. Bohannan (ed.), Law
          and warfare, pp. 3–24. Garden City, NY:
          Natural History Press.
Redman, C. L.
  1978.   The rise of civilization: from early farm-
          ers to urban society in the ancient Near
          East. San Francisco: W. H. Freeman.
Res. and Ref. Div. Ministry of Inform. and Broadcasting, Gov. of India
  1978.   India: a reference annual, 1977 & 1978.
          Faridabad: Gov. of India Press.
Riddle, J. M. and J. W. Estes
  1992.   Oral contraceptives in ancient and me-
          dieval times. Am. Sci. 80: 226–233.
Rivers, W. H. R.
  1971.   The genealogical method. [Original edi-
          tion 1910.] In N. Graburn (ed.), Read-
          ings in kinship and social structure, pp.
          52–59. New York: Harper & Row.

Romanucci-Ross, L.
  1977.   The hierarchy of resort in curative prac-
          tices: the Admiralty Islands, Melanesia.
          In D. Landy (ed.), Culture, disease, and
          healing: studies in medical anthropol-
          ogy, pp. 481–487. New York: Macmil-
          lan.
  1983.   On madness, deviance, and culture. *In*
          L. Romanucci-Ross, D. E. Moerman,
          and L. R. Tancredi (eds.), The anthro-
          pology of medicine: from culture to
          method, pp. 267–283. New York: Prae-
          ger.
Rosin, R. T.
  1983.   Notes on dread and the supernatural in
          Indian society. Man India 63(2): 115–
          140.
Roth, E. A.
  1985.   Population structure and sex differ-
          ences. In R. Hall (ed.), Male-female dif-
          ferences: a bio-cultural perspective, pp.
          219–298. New York: Praeger.
Rubel, A. J.
  1977.   The epidemiology of a folk illness: susto
          in Hispanic America. [Original edition
          1964.] In D. Landy (ed.), Culture, dis-
          ease, and healing: studies in medical an-
          thropology, pp. 119–128. New York:
          Macmillan.
Rubel, A. J., C. W. O'Nell, and R. Collado
  1985.   The folk illness called susto. *In* R. C.
          Simons and C. C. Hughes (eds.), The
          culture-bound syndromes: folk illnesses
          of psychiatric and anthropological in-
          terest, pp. 333–350 Dordrecht: B. Rei-
          del.
Sabom, M.
  1982.   Recollections of death: a medical in-
          vestigation. New York: Harper & Row.
Saffran, M.
  1982.   The amino acid alphabet in the brain.
          Ethos 10(4): 317–325.
Sahi, T.
  1978.   Progress report: dietary lactose and the
          aetiology of human small-intestinal hy-
          polactasia. Gut 19: 1074–1086.
Saini, B. S.
  1975.   The social & economic history of the
          Punjab, 1901–1939 (including Haryana
          & Himachal Pradesh) Delhi: Ess Ess.
Sandler, J., M. Myerson, and B. N. Kinder.
  1980.   Human sexuality: current perspectives.
          Tampa, FL: Mariner.
Sapolsky, R. M.
  1988.   Lessons of the Serengeti: why some of
          us are more susceptible to stress. The
          Sciences 28(3): 38–42.
Saraswati, D.
  1956.   The light of truth. [G. P. Upadhyaya

(translator); Original edition, Lunar half: Samvat 1939.] Allahabad: Kala Press.

Sarkad, U.
1975. Malaria rides again. J. Indian Med. Assoc. 65(6): 185–186.

Sarma, D. S.
1953. The nature and history of Hinduism. *In* K. W. Morgan (ed.), The religion of the Hindus, pp. 3–47. New York: Ronald Press.

Sayce, A. H.
1979. Remarkable discoveries in India. [Original edition 1924.] In G. L. Possehl (ed.), Ancient cities of the Indus, p. 108. New Delhi: Vikas.

Sehgal, H., S. P. Gupta, and K. K. Sidhu
1980. Tetanus neonatorum as seen in Kalawati Saran Children's Hospital, New Delhi in the year 1965 and a decade later. Indian J. Public Health 24(2): 88–91.

Selye, H.
1956. The stress of life. New York: McGraw–Hill.

Sewell, R., and S. B. Dikshit
1896. The Indian calendar. Tables of eclipses by R. Schram. London: Swan Sonnenschein.

Shryock, R. H.
1969. The development of modern medicine: an interpretation of the social and scientific factors involved. [Facsimile of 1947 edition, original edition 1936.] New York: Hafner.

Sigurdsson, H., and S. Carey
1988. The far reach of Tambora. Nat. Hist. 97(6): 67–72.

Silverman, P. H.
1977. Malaria vaccines. Science 196(4295): 1156.

Simon, B.
1980. Mind and madness in ancient Greece: the classical roots of modern psychiatry. Ithaca, NY: Cornell Univ. Press.

Simons, R. C.
1985a. Sorting the culture-bound syndromes. *In* R. C. Simons and C. C. Hughes (eds.), The culture-bound syndromes: folk illnesses of psychiatric and anthropological interest, pp. 25–38. Dordrecht: D. Reidel.

1985b. Introduction: The sleep paralysis taxon. Ibid., pp. 115–116.

1985c. Introduction: The fright illness taxon. Ibid., pp. 329–331.

1987. A feasible and timely enterprise: commentary on "Culture-bound syndromes and international disease classifications" by R. Prince and F. Tcheng-Lar-

oche. Cult., Med. Psychiatry. 11(1): 21–28.

1988. III: Round three. Cult., Med. Psychiatry. 12(4): 525–529.

Simons, R. C., and C. C. Hughes (eds.)
1985. The culture-bound syndromes: folk illnesses of psychiatric and anthropological interest. Dordrecht: D. Reidel.

Simons, R. C., F. R. Ervin, and R. Prince
1988. The psychobiology of trance: I: training for Thaipusam. Transcult. Psychiatr. Res. Rev. 25(4): 249–266.

Singh, K.
1956. Train to Pakistan. New York: Grove Press.

Singh, K., N. R. Jain, and B. M. Khullar
1971. A study of suicide in Delhi state. J. Indian Med. Assoc. 57(11): 412–419.

Skinner, G. W.
1984. Asian studies and the disciplines. Assoc. Asian Stud. Newsl., April: 7–8.

Skinsnes, O. K.
1973. Notes from the history of leprosy. Int. J. Leprosy 41: 220–244.

Slater, P. E.
1971. The glory of Hera: Greek mythology and the Greek family. Boston: Beacon Press.

Sleeman, W. H.
1858. A journey through the kingdom of Oude, in 1849–1850. Vols 1, 2. London: Richard Bentley.

1915. Rambles and recollections of an Indian official. [Original edition 1844.] Revised annotated edition by V. A. Smith. London: Oxford Univ. Press.

Smith, V. A.
1958. The Oxford history of India. 3rd ed., P. Spear (ed.). Oxford: Clarendon Press.

Spate, O. H. K.
1954. India and Pakistan: a general and regional geography. New York: E. P. Dutton.

Spiro, M. E.
1967. Burmese supernaturalism: a study in the explanation and reduction of suffering. Englewood Cliffs, NJ: Prentice-Hall.

1977. The exorcist in Burma. *In* D. Landy (ed.), Culture, disease, and healing: studies in medical anthropology, pp. 419–427. New York: Macmillan.

1984. Review of C. F. Keyes and E. V. Daniel (eds.), Karma: an anthropological inquiry. Berkeley: Univ. California Press, 1983. Am. Anthrop. 86(4): 1002–1004.

Spitzer, R. L., J. B. W. Williams, and A. E. Skodol (eds.)
1983. International Perspectives on DSM-III. Washington, DC: American Psychiatric Press.

Stedman, T. L.
1976.   Stedman's medical dictionary, illustrated. Baltimore: Williams & Wilkins.
Steel, F. A.
1929.   The garden of fidelity: the autobiography of Flora Annie Steel, 1847–1929. London: Macmillan.
Sternbach, L.
1951.   Law. In W. N. Brown (ed.), India, Pakistan, Ceylon, Chap. 10. Ithaca, NY: Cornell Univ. Press.
Stevenson, M. S.
1971.   The rites of the twice-born. [Original edition 1920.] New Delhi: Oriental.
Stutchbury, E. L.
1982.   Blood, fire and mediation: human sacrifice and widow burning in nineteenth century India. In M. Allen and S. N. Mukherjee (eds.), Women in India and Nepal. Australian Natl. Univ. Monographs on South Asia 8: 21–75. Canberra: Australian Natl. Univ. Printing.
Stutley, M. and J. Stutley
1977.   Harper's dictionary of Hinduism, its mythology, folklore, philosophy, and history. New York: Harper & Row.
Surya, N. C.
1969.   Ego structure in the Hindu joint family. In W. Caudill and Tsung-Yi Lin (eds.), Conference on mental health research in Asia and the Pacific, pp. 381–382. Honolulu: East-West Center Press.
Swan, H. T.
1990.   The antibiotic record. Science 247: 1387–1388.
Tandon, P.
1968.   Punjabi century, 1857–1947. Berkeley: Univ. California Press.
Tart, C. T.
1979.   Putting the pieces together: a conceptual framework for understanding discrete states of consciousness. In N. E. Zinberg (ed.), Alternate states of consciousness: multiple perspectives on the study of consciousness, pp. 158–219. New York: Free Press.
Tawney, R. H.
1947.   Religion and the rise of capitalism. [Original edition 1926.] New York: Penguin.
Taylor, C. E.
1976.   The place of indigenous medical practitioners in the modernization of health services. In C. Leslie (ed.), Asian medical systems: a comparative study, pp. 285–299. Berkeley: Univ. California Press.

Teja, J. S., B. S. Khanna, and T. B. Subhramanyam
1970.   Possession states in Indian patients. Indian J. Psychiatry. 12: 71–87.
Temple, R. C.
1883.   A dissertation on the proper names of Panjabis, with special reference to the proper names of villagers in the Eastern Panjab. Bombay: Educ. Soc. Press, and London: Trübner.
1884.   The legends of the Punjab, Vol. 1. Bombay: Educ. Soc. Press, and London: Trübner.
1885.   Ibid, Vol. 2.
1900.   Ibid, Vol. 3. London: Kegan Paul, Trench, Trübner.
Temple, R. C. (ed.)
1883–87.   Punjab notes & queries. 1: 1883–1884; 2: 1884–1885; 3: 1885–1886; 4: 1886–1887. Allahabad, India: Pioneer Press.
Teoh, J.-I., and E.-S. Tan
1976.   An outbreak of epidemic hysteria in West Malaysia. In W. P. Lebra (ed.), Culture-bound syndromes, ethnopsychiatry, and alternate therapies. Mental Health Res. Asia Pacific 4: 32–43.
Thapar, R.
1976.   A history of India, Vol. 1. [Original edition 1966.] Harmondsworth, Middlesex, England: Penguin.
Thompson, S.
1946.   The folktale. New York: Dryden Press.
Thorner, D., and A. Thorner
1950.   India and Pakistan. In R. Linton (ed.), Most of the world: the peoples of Africa, Latin America, and the East today, pp. 548–653. New York: Columbia Univ. Press.
Times of India
1978.   Getting married. Feb. 14, 1978.
Tinker, H.
1966.   South Asia: a short history. New York: Praeger.
Titiev, M.
1946.   A Dasehra celebration in Delhi. Am. Anthrop. 48: 676–680.
Tod, J.
1920.   Annals and antiquities of Rajasthan or the central and western Rajput states of India. [Original edition 1829.] Revised edition, W. Crooke (ed.), Vol. 2. London: Oxford Univ. Press.
Trager, W.
1984.   Malaria research. Science 226(4681): 342.
Trostle, J. A., W. A. Hauser, and I. S. Susser
1983.   The logic of noncompliance: management of epilepsy from the patient's point

of view. Cult., Med. Psychiatry 7: 35–56.

Tuchman, B. W.
1979. A distant mirror, the calamitous 14th century. New York: Ballantine.
1988. The first salute, a view of the American Revolution. New York: Ballantine.

Tylor, E. B.
1958. Religion in primitive culture. [Original edition 1871.] New York: Harper Torchbooks.

Ullrich, H. E.
1987a. A study of change and depression among Havik Brahmin women in a south Indian village. Cult., Med. Psychiatry 11(3): 261–287.
1987b. Marriage patterns among Havik Brahmins: a 20-year study of change. Sex Roles 16(11/12): 615–635.

Underhill, M. M.
1921. The Hindu religious year. London: Oxford Univ. Press.

Usborne, C. F.
1905. Panjabi lyrics and proverbs: translations in verse and prose. Lahore: Civil and Military Gazetteer Press.

van Buitenen, J. A. B. (translator, ed.)
1980. The Mahabharata, 1. The book of the beginning. [Original edition 1973.] Chicago: Univ. Chicago Press.

van den Dungen, P. H. M.
1972. The Punjab tradition: influence and authority in nineteenth century India. London: George Allen & Unwin.

van Gennep, A.
1961. The rites of passage. [Original edition (French) 1908.] M. B. Vizedom and G. L. Caffee (translators). Chicago: Univ. Chicago Press.

Verbrugge, L. M.
1982. Sex differentials in health. Pub. Health Rep. 97(5): 417–437.

Visaria, P., and L. Visaria
1981. Indian population scene after 1981 census: a perspective. Econ. Pol. Weekly 16(44–46): 1717–1780.

Vishwanath, L. S.
1983. Misadventures in amniocentesis. Econ. Pol. Weekly 18(11): 406–407.

Vohra, H. R.
1985. India may receive malaria vaccine. India Abroad, June 14: 5.

Wadley, S. S.
1983. Vrats: transformers of destiny. In C. F. Keyes and E. V. Daniel (eds.), Karma: an anthropological inquiry, pp. 147–161. Berkeley: Univ. California Press.

Waldron, I.
1983. Sex differences in human mortality: the role of genetic factors. Soc. Sci. Med. 17(6): 321–333.

Walsh, (Sir) C.
1977. Indian village crimes with an introduction on police investigation and confessions. New Delhi: Asian Publication Services.

Warner, R.
1980. Deception and self-deception in shamanism and psychiatry. Int. J. Soc. Psychiatry 26(1): 41–52.

Weber, M.
1958. The protestant ethic and the spirit of capitalism. [Original edition (German) 1904–1905.] T. Parsons (translator) New York: Scribner's.

Wedenoja, W.
1978. Religion and adaptation in rural Jamaica. Ph.D. diss. San Diego: Univ. California at San Diego, Dept. Anthropology.

Weiss, G.
1973. Shamanism and priesthood in the light of the Campa ayahuasca ceremony. In M. J. Harner (ed.), Hallucinogens and shamanism, pp. 40–47. London: Oxford Univ. Press.

Weiss, R.
1992. On the track of "Killer" TB. Science 255(5041): 148–150.

West, L. J.
1975. A clinical and theoretical overview of hallucinatory phenomena. In R. K. Siegel and L. J. West (eds.), Hallucinations: behavior, experience, and theory, pp. 287–311. New York: Wiley.

Westermeyer, J.
1989. Overview: psychiatric epidemiology across cultures: current issues and trends. Transcult. Psychiatr. Res. Rev. 26(1): 5–25.

Whybrow, P. C., and P. M. Silberfarb
1974. Neuroendocrine mediating mechanisms: from the symbolic stimulus to the physiological response. Int. J. Psychiatr. Med. 5(4): 531–539.

Wig, N. N.
1983. DSM-III: a perspective from the Third World. In R. L. Spitzer, J. B. W. Williams, and A. E. Skodol (eds.), International perspectives on DSM-III, pp. 79–89. Washington, DC: American Psychiatric Press.

Wilkey, I. S.
  1973.   Chloroquine suicide. Med. J. Australia 1: 396–397.
Williams, C. D., and D. B. Jelliffe
  1972.   Mother and child health: delivering the services. London: Oxford Univ. Press.
Williamson, L.
  1978.   Infanticide: an anthropological analysis. *In* M. Kohl (ed.), Infanticide and the value of life, pp. 61–75. Buffalo, NY: Prometheus.
Wingard, D. L.
  1984.   The sex differential in morbidity, mortality and lifestyle. Ann. Rev. Pub. Health 5: 433–458.
Wingate, P.
  1972.   The penguin medical encyclopedia. Aylesbury, Bucks: Penguin.
Wiser, C. V. and W. H. Wiser
  1930.   Behind mud walls. New York: Richard R. Smith.

Wood, C. S.
  1979.   Human sickness and health: a biocultural view. Palo Alto: Mayfield.
Wood, O., and R. Maconachie
  1882.   Final report on the settlement of land revenue in the Delhi district. Lahore: Victoria Press.
Woodburne, A. S.
  1992.   The evil eye in South Indian folklore. *In* A. Dundes, (ed.), The evil eye, a casebook. Madison: Univ. Wisconsin Press, pp. 55–65.
World Health Organization
  1992.   World health statistics annual, 1991. Geneva: World Health Organization.
Wyon, J. B., and J. E. Gordon
  1971.   The Khanna study: population problems in the rural Punjab. Cambridge, MA: Harvard Univ. Press.

APPENDIX I: DISEASE

INTRODUCTION

Appendix I documents the epidemics and endemic infectious and parasitic diseases that were rampant in North India for centuries. Prior to the mid-20th century, they were the principal causes of death. The high mortality rate that they produced, especially among infants and young people, reinforced the Hindu belief in ghost illness.

Disease is covered in two sections. The first section, Discoveries, lists the scientists who discovered the causes of major diseases and/or the vaccines, inoculations, and other means for their prevention, control, and cure, with the dates. The second section, Descriptions, consists of an alphabetized descriptive list of diseases, almost all of which are referred to in the preceding case histories. Discoveries and Descriptions have a dual historical component: (1) the history of medicine worldwide, and (2) the history of epidemics and disease in India.

This information is relevant to the present study because it shows that scientific medicine became available relatively recently even in the West, and in Indian villages, only very recently, if at all. Moreover, it is convenient

for the reader to have brief descriptions of important diseases readily at hand. Much of the scientific medicine that Westerners today take for granted dates only to the 20th century although there were significant developments in the 18th and 19th centuries. Most modern medicine and bioscience were developed in the West, and diffusion to rural areas in distant countries took time. Even in the West, change was gradual, for example, in France as described by Ackerman (1983: 1–18).

Much of the information about descriptions of diseases and discoveries was taken from easily available, frequently consulted standard sources, namely, Berkow, 1982; Clayman, 1989; Davey and Wilson, 1971; Debus, 1968; Encyclopaedia Britannica, 1966, 1992; Gillispie, 1970–78; Harris and Levey, 1975; Shryock, 1969, and Stedman, 1976. Trivial discrepancies among sources, such as differences of one year in dates and different spellings of names, are ignored. The selection of medical and scientific developments judged to be "significant" follows to a great extent Shryock's (1969) history of medicine, modified in terms of the health culture of Shanti Nagar.

HISTORY

The past history of disease in India has been horrendous. The principal epidemics—plague, influenza, cholera, and smallpox—have attracted the most attention, but malaria, dysentery, and puerperal fever are also major killers along with famine which exacerbates the effects of disease. Victims are numbered in the tens of millions. It should be born in mind that the mortality figures given here are estimates which may vary from one source to another.

The death toll from the plague epidemic, which reached India in 1896 and lasted until 1921, was about 10 million. Plague was reported to have selectively stricken young adults and thus to have affected the Indian birth rate. The causal microorganism of plague, *Pasteurella pestis*, is spread by fleas, parasites of black rats. The rats themselves suffer and die from the disease. The rats have spread far from their original ecological niches by traveling mostly by ship, for they are skilled climbers and board ships by ascending mooring ropes. The plague was probably endemic in borderlands between China and India and in the Eurasian steppe from Manchuria to the Ukraine. In the early 19th century, the upper Salween River was the boundary between infected and uninfected regions. When a military revolt broke out in Yunnan in 1855, soldiers were sent across the Salween, contracted the disease and brought it back to the rest of China. In 1894, the disease reached Canton and Hong Kong and began to spread to other parts of the world. In India, Bombay Presidency, the Punjab, and the United Provinces were especially affected (Wyon and Gordon, 1971: 174; McNeill, 1976: 123–126, 152–153).

Mortality from the influenza pandemic of 1918–19 exceeded even that of the plague epidemic. Some 12 to 13 million Indians died during the first three to four months (Wyon and Gordon, 1971: 175). Cholera took a terrible toll over the first half of the 20th century, the number of victims reaching the figure posted for the plague. Between 1910 and 1954, 10.2 million people died of cholera in India, and since 1947, there were nearly 200,000 additional deaths from cholera in Pakistan, formerly part of India (McNeill, 1976: 352, note 49). As late as the summer of 1988, a cholera epidemic was reported in a poor settlement in the City of Delhi (*India Abroad*, 1988, 18(44): 8).

Malaria declined after World War II due to effective insecticides, until the mosquitoes developed resistance. It was also found that some insecticides, especially DDT, had dangerous side effects and could no longer be used so that malaria again became epidemic and endemic throughout India beginning in 1965. In 1988, epidemics of encephalitis, malaria, and kala azar (spread by sandflies) took place in Uttar Pradesh and Bihar, and dengue fever was present in New Delhi (*India Abroad*, 1988, 19(6): 41).

Mental illness sometimes accompanies infectious disease, as in the case of syphilis, and some chromosomal anomalies have deleterious mental effects, for example, Down's syndrome, which is due to chromosomal disorders in older mothers. However, ghost illness and ghost possession are much more complicated phenomena. As illustrated and discussed throughout this monograph, they have intricate social, cultural, and psychological concomitants.

From the late 19th into the 20th century, four men contributed to theories of mental illness which later developed into the psychoanalytic and neurologic treatment of mental illness. Emil Kraepelin described, identified, and classified major mental illnesses. Jean Martin Charcot influenced Sigmund Freud regarding the nature of hysteria. Carl Gustav Jung at first worked with Freud concerning psychoanalysis but later disagreed with him. However, both Jung and Freud contributed to the psychoanalytic treatment of mental illness.

In the 1960s and 1970s, psychoanalysis was criticized on the grounds that diagnoses regarding various mental states were unreliable and that labeling had negative effects. Moreover, psychologists and psychiatrists in non-Western countries and anthropologists with experience in such countries questioned whether the categories of mental illness derived from Western European culture and in terms of which diagnoses were made are necessarily relevant cross-culturally (Klerman, 1983: 10–11; R. Freed and S. Freed, 1985: 107–125, for a summary of the literature).

Such criticisms resulted in the development in the USA of DSM-III, a diagnostic and statistical manual of mental disorders (Am. Psych. Assn., 1980), which in turn led to International Perspectives on DSM-III (Spitzer et al., 1983).

Psychoanalysis has now been diminished and/or complimented by new treatment based on greater knowledge of the brain due to brain imaging and by the use of drugs for specific mental illnesses. Kraepelin laid the ground for the recent biological revolution in the treatment of mental illness.

Andreasen (1985: 191) stated that "'Wonder Drugs' are now available to diminish the symptoms of three out of four of the major categories of mental illness: affective disorders, schizophrenia, and anxiety disorders." Such advanced measures were used in the case of Troubled (Chap. 13) who was diagnosed by brain imaging as suffering from an affective disorder known as the bipolar syndrome. He was hospitalized and treated with lithium carbonate, neuroleptics, and electroconvulsive therapy (cf. Andreasen, 1985: 36, 157–158, 164–165, 200–201). Epilepsy, due to brain damage, is also treated with drugs (see the case of Pawn, an epileptic, described in Chap. 15: Murder or Suicide). Schizophrenia appears to be related to possible damage of the frontal lobes, which may suggest how the patient should be treated. Experiments with chlorpromazine (Thorazine) by two French psychiatrists, Jean Delay and Pierre Deniker, have made it the standard treatment for schizophrenia. Since then, additional drugs have been used (Andreasen, 1985: 120–121, 192–193, 209–212).

An important development of the late 1970s and 80s was the discovery of the endorphins, the opiatelike messengers found in the brain and throughout the nervous system. The endorphins highlight the intricate relationship of the brain and the rest of the body and have brought a new perspective to the analysis of alternate mental states (also known as dissociative disorders), such as ghost possession (R. Prince, ed., 1982; R. Prince, 1982a; 1982b; Klerman, 1983; Encyclopaedia Britannica, 1992, 4: 491).

Indian psychiatrists are aware of the special cultural and social characteristics of mental illness in India. Kakar (1983: 1–5), a Jungian psychiatrist, born in India and practicing there today, conducted a three-year study of various forms of curing for mental disorders in India. He noted the wide range of practitioners or curers and the relationship of cures and curers to concepts of "soul health," karma, and ghosts or spirits, as he dubs them, in addition to the living members of family and lineage who contribute to problems of "soul health." The link between soul, karma, family members, and ghosts must be understood in the treatment of mental distress, especially ghost possession.

Nandi (1979: 21–29) pointed out that some 70 years after psychoanalysis was introduced in India and the Indian Psychoanalytical Society was founded in Calcutta in 1922, psychoanalysis has still not caught on too well. It is a long drawn-out process, costly, not especially popular even in the cities, and extremely rare in the rural areas. Villagers have yet to comprehend the value of paying for talking with a psychoanalyst over a long period of time to probe mental illness. These problems are brought out specifically in the cases of Troubled (Chap. 13) and Withdrawn (Chap. 21), as well as in the comparative analysis of ghost possessions found in Chapter 24. Despite the reliance of the vast majority of people on exorcists for the treatment of ghost possession and their disinterest in and ignorance of psychiatry and psychoanalysis, there is nonetheless provision in the City of Delhi for psychiatric treatment and rehabilitation from mental illness at the Shahdara Hospital (Gaz. Unit, Delhi Adm., 1976: 885).

DISCOVERIES

. . . before the eighteenth century the demographic impact of the profession of medicine remained negligible . . . Only with the eighteenth century did the situation begin to change; and it was not really until after 1850 or so that the practice of medicine and the organization of medical services began to make large-scale differences in human survival rates and population [McNeill, 1976: 239–240]

. . . . the modern concepts of diseases and nosology did not emerge in Western Europe until the 18th century. . . . Two discoveries were particularly noteworthy: 1. The correlation of clinical syndromes and structural changes noted in autopsy, by either gross morbid anatomy or histopathology. . . . 2. The discovery of microorganisms by Pasteur, Koch, and others resulted in delineation of many clinical disorders associated with specific bacteria or other microorganisms [Klerman, 1983: 9].

The following list of scientific and medical discoveries by years has been selected chiefly in terms of the infectious and parasitic diseases that have afflicted villagers in the Union Territory of Delhi and Punjab. It shows that the identification of the organisms causing such diseases and the development of methods and/or drugs to curb and cure them have taken place almost entirely within the 19th and 20th centuries. After a paragraph about the principal instrument of microbiological research, the microscope, this selective, historical compilation of dates and findings begins with Jenner's vaccination for smallpox in 1796 and continues through the first half of the 20th century. Although the tally reaches back to 1796, the pace of discovery and invention has steadily increased, which means that most of the developments have taken place in the last half of the period in question. Excluded from the list are the degenerative diseases of old age, the various cancers and cardiovascular diseases that are major killers in the advanced industrialized countries. The expectation of life at birth in India did not exceed 40 years until after 1950. Even in the decade 1961–70, it was only about 45.5 years (Visaria and Visaria, 1981: 1749).

1590-1930s, Microscope: The study of microorganisms, the causal agents of most of the diseases that have ravaged India until recent times, has gone hand-in-hand with the development of the microscope. The first compound microscope, introduced in 1590 by Zacharias Janssen gave only small magnification. The simple microscope developed in the latter 17th century by Antonie van Leeuwenhoek was an improvement and widely used until the early 19th century. Various technical problems solved by Joseph J. Lister in 1829 led to rapid progress in microscopy. By the end of the 19th century, optical microscopy had achieved its maxi-

mum resolution and both lenses and stands were excellent. Various specialized microscopes were developed in the 20th century. Light microscopy permitted the observation of protozoa and bacteria. Viruses could not be seen until the electron microscope was introduced in the 1930s (Encyclopaedia Britannica, 1966, 2: 1010, 15: 385, 396–397; 1992, 14: 995, 998; Gillispie, 1973, 8: 126, 414).

1796, Smallpox vaccine: Edward Jenner's vaccination to prevent smallpox derived from the Near Eastern practice of inoculating against the possibility of a severe case of the disease by using crusts from lesions of very mild cases, a procedure known as variolation. The inoculated smallpox virus provided protection against smallpox acquired in the normal way, for it commonly resulted in only a sparse eruption of pocks and its fatality rate was much lower than that of normally acquired smallpox. This oriental practice of using an attenuated microorganism (i.e., one whose virulence has been reduced) to induce active immunity was brought from Constantinople to London by Lady Mary Wortley Montague and others. The practice carried with it the idea of infection by a contagious disease. It was one of the factors, along with the popular observation of the antagonism of cowpox and smallpox, that led to Jenner's experiments and the discovery that vaccination with cowpox would provide immunity against smallpox. Jenner's vaccination laid the foundation for the science of modern immunology. By 1980, smallpox had been eradicated from the earth (Encyclopaedia Britannica, 1966, 12: 998, 22: 922–923; 1992, 6: 530; Shryock, 1969: 75; Gillispie, 1973, 7: 96–97; Harris and Levey, 1975: 1409, 2540; Berkow, 1982: 188; Hopkins, 1983: 310).

1832, Hodgkin's disease: Thomas Hodgkin published his article describing the disease which has been named after him (Ober, 1977: 126).

1847, Puerperal fever: About 1847, Ignaz P. Semmelweis showed that puerperal fever (childbed fever) was contagious and insisted that attendants at a confinement first wash their hands in a solution of chlorinated lime, an antiseptic. He published this account in 1861, but his views were not accepted until the later work of Joseph Lister and Louis

Pasteur. Antiseptic measures at confinement were not used in Shanti Nagar until over a century after the discoveries of Semmelweis, and then not routinely at all confinements (Encyclopaedia Britannica, 1966, 20: 318; Wingate, 1972: 372–373; Gillispie, 1975, 7: 294–297; Carter, 1981; Fox and Cottler–Fox, 1986).

1856-65, 1900, Genetics: Gregor Mendel experimented with sweet peas. He discovered dominant and recessive characteristics and developed the principle of factorial inheritance by which paired elementary units of heredity sort themselves and recombine in successive generations while maintaining their identity. His work, reported in 1865 and published in 1866, was the beginning of genetics. Mendel's research was unnoticed until 1900 when three investigators (Hugo de Vries, Carl Correns, and Erich von Tschermak), working independently, confirmed his results. Each one acknowledged Mendel's work (Debus, 1968: 1160; Gillispie, 1974, 9: 277, 281; Harris and Levey, 1975: 1057).

1863-82, Anthrax bacillus and vaccine: The study of anthrax, especially by Louis Pasteur and Robert Koch, has played a prominent role in bacteriology and immunology. Anthrax was the first disease of animals and humans shown to be caused by a specific microorganism, first by C. J. Davaine in 1863 although he did not succeed in isolating the bacillus. In 1876, Koch isolated the anthrax bacillus and obtained a pure culture, produced the disease by inoculating a healthy animal, and recovered the same organism from the blood of the newly infected animal, thus proving the causal connection of the organism and the disease. Pasteur developed a vaccine against anthrax in 1881 (Encyclopaedia Britannica, 1966, 2: 34–35, 17: 439–440; Debus, 1968: 951; Shryock, 1969: 295; Gillispie, 1974, 10: 395–398; Clayman, 1989: 114).

1864, Antiseptic surgery: Joseph Lister instituted the practice of using chemicals to prevent surgical infections by microorganisms. Antiseptic agents were used to disinfect the hands, surgical instruments, and wounds. He later abandoned the use of a phenol spray in the operating theater in favor of asepsis, scrupulous cleanliness based mainly on sterilization. Some women in Shanti Nagar sterilized implements to be used in a confinement by immersing them in boiling water or in warm or hot water containing a disinfectant. No one mentioned such measures during the fieldwork of 1958–59, but trained midwives began to practice at that time and very probably introduced the use of a sterilized knife or scissors. They were noted in our 1977–78 fieldwork, which suggests that they were first used in Shanti Nagar at least a century after the time of Lister (Encyclopaedia Britannica, 1966, 14: 101–102; Shryock, 1969: 281; Gillispie, 1973, 8: 403–405).

1870s, Bacteria: Ferdinand J. Cohn worked out the fundamental biology of bacteria (Encyclopaedia Britannica, 1966, 6: 32; Shryock, 1969: 281; Gillispie, 1971, 3: 338).

1872, Relapsing fever: Otto H. F. Obermeier discovered *Borrelia recurrentis* (*Spirillum recurrentis*), the spirochete that is the causative agent of European louse-borne relapsing fever (Debus, 1968: 1272; Shryock, 1969: 281).

1873, Leprosy: Gerhard H. A. Hansen discovered *Mycobacterium leprae*, the organism causing leprosy. The disease is also known as Hansen's disease in honor of his discovery (Debus, 1968: 749; Gillispie, 1972, 6: 101; Skinsnes, 1973: 225).

1875, Dysentery: Friedrich Lösch discovered the causative agent of amoebic dysentery, *Entamoeba histolytica*, and thus distinguished it from all other forms of dysentery (Debus, 1968: 1068; Shryock, 1969: 281).

1879, Gonorrhea: Albert L. S. Neisser discovered the bacillus causing gonorrhea, named it gonococcus in 1882 and proved its specific nature (Debus, 1968: 1244; Shryock, 1969: 286).

1877-1901, Malaria: Alphonse Laveran working in Algeria from 1878 to 1880 was the first person to describe the malarial parasite and to recognize it as the cause of the disease, November 6, 1880. Sir Patrick Manson showed the causal relationship of filaria worms to filariasis and their transmission by mosquitoes. Manson provided the first proof of the necessary involvement of an arthropod vector in the life cycle of a parasite, 1877–78. In 1895, Sir Ronald Ross was sent to India to investigate the hypothesis of a connection of mosquitoes and malaria. In 1898, Ross proved that bird malaria is transmitted by *Culex* mosquitoes. In November 1898, Giovanni B. Grassi with the help of Amico Bignami and Giuseppe Bastianelli first experimentally transmitted human malaria by the bite of female anopheline mosquitoes (males do not bite), described the full development of the parasite in humans, and in 1901 described the complete life cycle of the parasite. The effectiveness of quinine against malaria was known long before the disease was understood. In recent years, the parasites have increasingly developed resistance to drugs, and the mosquitoes, to insecticides (Encyclopaedia Britannica, 1966, 14: 669; Shryock, 1969: 288; Gillispie, 1972, 5: 503; Harris and Levey, 1975: 1541; Marshall, 1990).

1880-84, Typhoid: Karl J. Eberth discovered the typhoid bacillus in 1880. It was first isolated in pure culture and cultivated by Georg Gaffky in 1884 (Encyclopaedia Britannica, 1966, 22: 646; Shryock, 1969: 286; Gillispie, 1971, 4: 276).

1884, Rabies: L. Pasteur produced a vaccine for rabies. In 1884, he successfully inoculated dogs and in 1885, he demonstrated that prompt use of the vaccine prevented the development of the disease in humans when he successfully treated a boy who had been bitten by a rabid dog (Encyclopaedia Britannica, 1966, 18: 983–984; Shryock, 1969: 296; Gillispie, 1974, 10: 400–406; Harris and Levey, 1975: 2263).

1882-1921, Tuberculosis: R. Koch identified the tubercle bacillus in 1882. In 1890, he announced the preparation of tuberculin from dead tubercle bacilli. Tuberculin raised hopes, never realized, that Koch had discovered a cure. However, tuberculin was useful, for when injected into animals or humans previously infected by TB it caused an inflammatory reaction but not in uninfected persons. A positive reaction also shows infection with the bacillus but not necessarily an active case. In 1895, Wilhelm Konrad Röntgen discovered x-rays, now well-known as a diagnostic agent for tuberculosis (Myers, 1977: 60). Diagnosis today combines chest x-rays with other procedures, such as the tuberculin test and an analysis of sputum.

In 1888, George Cornet stated the inhalation theory of contagion, namely, that sputum from TB patients after drying may become part of the dust and cause infection. Result: anti-spitting campaigns in various parts of the world (Myers, 1977: 46). Before effective medication, control of TB depended on aggressively educating the public about contagion and the relationship of unsanitary conditions and practices with disease (Encyclopaedia Britannica, 1966, 13: 437, 22: 531, 533; Gillispie, 1973, 7: 423–430; Myers, 1977: 46, 60, 85).

Albert Calmette introduced the theory that a mild natural infection or one introduced artificially with attenuated tubercle bacilli should take place as soon after birth as possible. In 1921, Albert Calmette and Camille Guérin introduced in France a preventive inoculation against TB known as the BCG vaccine (Bacillus Calmette-Guérin). It is not a *virus fixe*; mutations occasionally occur and its virulence has changed. Various cultures began to produce lesions at the sites of administration and elsewhere. Although its effectiveness has been called into question and its use is regarded by some public health specialists as inimical to an effective compaign against TB, it is currently the most widely used vaccine in the world. For a time, the "Lübeck disaster" proved to be a reverse in efforts to spread the use of the BCG. In 1930, 249 infants were vaccinated with BCG in Lübeck, Germany; by autumn, 73 had died. The vaccine was contaminated. This episode recalls a similar case in the Punjab where plague vaccine contaminated by tetanus killed 19 villagers. After that, people refused to be vaccinated (Chap. 5). (Encyclopaedia Britannica, 1966, 22: 532, 535; 1992, 23: 785; Gillispie, 1971 (3): 22; Myers, 1977:113–114, 151–156; Bloom and Murray, 1992: 1056.)

1883-84, Diphtheria: Edwin Klebs found the causative bacillus of diphtheria in 1883; in 1884 it was cultivated and isolated by Friedrich Löffler (Encyclopaedia Britannica, 1966, 7: 471; Shryock, 1969: 286; Gillispie, 1973, 8: 448–449).

1883-84, Cholera: In 1883, R. Koch with Georg Gaffky and Bernhard Fischer went to Egypt where a cholera epidemic was raging. They reported finding a comma bacillus, which was always associated with cholera. On a trip to India the following year, Koch found the same bacillus in cholera victims and asserted that it was the specific cause of cholera.

subject to periodic major shifts in antigenic composition, and so the vaccines have to be modified accordingly (Encyclopaedia Britannica, 1966, 12: 242–243; 1992, 4: 928, 6: 311, 29: 502; Debus, 1968: 50—51; Paul, 1971: 414).

1944-51, Antituberculosis drugs (streptomycin, PAS, and isoniazid): In 1944, S. A. Waksman, A. Schatz, and E. Bugie discovered streptomycin, produced from the mold *Streptomyces griseus* (*Actinomyces griseus*). Experiments with guinea pigs in 1944 and clinical trials on people with TB in 1946 showed that streptomycin had a suppressive effect on the course of the disease. Streptomycin, the first successful drug for the treatment of human tuberculosis, remains important. It is now used in conjunction with the other first-line antituberculosis drugs, namely, PAS (para-aminosalicylic acid) and isoniazid. After these first-line drugs became available, other antituberculosis drugs were developed, some of which proved so effective that they achieved first-line status. Tubercle bacilli can acquire resistance to most antituberculosis drugs. Treatment consists of skillfully combining drugs. Drug-resistant TB has recently become a grave public health problem (Encyclopaedia Britannica, 1966, 21: 468, 22: 535; 1992, 12: 457–458, 23: 785, 26: 750; Myers, 1977: 174–177).

DESCRIPTIONS

Anthrax (splenic fever, malignant pustule, woolsorters disease, coal, charcoal): a serious febrile bacterial infection of livestock that occasionally infects people, anthrax occurs worldwide. Epizootics have occurred. The causal agent, *Bacillus anthracis*, spreads to people from handling materials from infected animals, the bacteria entering the body via a scratch or sore, from inhaling spores of the bacillus, or from eating infected meat. Livestock become infected by grazing on land contaminated by the spores. Symptoms vary somewhat depending on the mode and/or site of infection. The most common type occurs as a localized infection of the skin in the form of a carbuncle beginning with a raised itchy area that develops into a large vesicle with a black necrotic center. The intestinal form (caused by ingestion of contaminated meat)

shows the symptoms of severe gastroenteritis with fever, diarrhea, and vomiting. If spores are inhaled (woolsorter's disease), anthrax takes the form of severe pneumonia, which is usually quickly fatal.

Villagers in Shanti Nagar were aware of the possibility of catching disease from cattle. Describing one such process, which to some extent recalls anthrax although no specific term was used, a woman said, "The smell of the urine of cattle can cause fever, TB, and cough, etc. The smell enters the brain and is very harmful to the brain. At the place where cattle urinate, germs are born, which enter the body. The germs are very small and cannot be seen with the naked eye. These germs enter the body and cause fever."

Anthrax can be prevented by vaccinating cattle, a measure used in the Union Territory of Delhi and in Shanti Nagar, but epidemics of cattle disease occur nonetheless. One such took place at the end of the monsoon period, September 1958, when we were resident. We did not identify the disease, but it was serious; many animals fell sick and five or six died within a few days. The village-wide rite, known as Akhta, was held to exorcise the disease (cf. Chap. 13). Villagers feared that the disease could pass from infected cattle to people, and the men who performed the rite of exorcism and therefore came near the village cattle took the precaution during the rite of not talking in order to prevent the transfer. At the time, we interpreted this precaution as reflecting the belief in intrusive spirit forces, but it is also possible that keeping the mouth closed could minimize the possibility of infection from inhaling spores (R. Freed and S. Freed, 1966: 683, 687). We were aware of no human cases of anthrax during the time we lived in Shanti Nagar. However, the ubiquitous practitioners of popular pharmaceutical medicine routinely use penicillin for a variety of ill-defined febrile diseases, and penicillin is the treatment of choice for anthrax (Encyclopaedia Britannica, 1966, 2: 34–35; Berkow, 1982: 93; Clayman, 1989: 114).

Cholera (Asiatic, Indian, or epidemic cholera): an acute often fatal infection caused by *Vibrio cholerae*. The vibrio does not emit an extracellular toxin but is itself toxic so that when it disintegrates the endotoxin is liberated in the intestinal tract and causes a profuse watery diarrhea, extreme loss of fluid and electrolytes, falling blood pressure, and collapse. Infection is usually from contaminated food and water. Various diseases designated as cholera can be subclinical, a mild uncomplicated episode of diarrhea which is self-limited, with recovery in about three to six days. These diseases are of diverse etiology. True cholera (Asiatic or Indian cholera), caused by the cholera vibrio, is highly fatal, with a death rate in untreated cases of about 40 to 60 percent. Epidemics are common in India and many pandemics have occurred. There are two endemic areas, one in India, the other, in China. Cholera vaccine gives partial protection in endemic areas but booster injections are required every six months. Some doctors consider the vaccine to be useless. Cholera is readily controlled by protecting sources of water and modern methods of sewage disposal, neither of which is ordinarily available in rural India (Encyclopaedia Britannica, 1966, 5: 674–677; Stedman, 1976: 269; Berkow, 1982: 106–107; Clayman, 1989: 274).

Diphtheria: an acute contagious disease of the upper respiratory tract, caused by *Corynebacterium diphtheriae*, that is associated with the formation of a characteristic false membrane, which can suffocate a victim, and a highly potent toxin. The toxin produces an inflammation of the mucous membrane of the throat, nose, and sometimes the tracheobronchial tree as well as degeneration in the peripheral nerves and heart muscle. Symptoms are fever, sore throat, weakness, vomiting, rapid fall of the pulse, and paralysis. The disease is spread mainly by exposure to discharge from the nose or throat of infected persons or of carriers, who may never have suffered from the disease. Infection can also take place through milk. Epidemics occur. Immunization is by an antitoxin. The triple vaccine, known as DPT (diphtheria, pertussis, and tetanus) should routinely be given to children in the first year of life (Encyclopaedia Britannica, 1966, 7: 470–472; Berkow, 1982: 93–95; Clayman, 1989: 362).

Dysentery, bacillary: an infectious disease of the bowels marked by the sudden onset of frequent watery stools, often with blood and mucus, and accompanied by pain, tenesmus, fever, vomiting, and dehydration. It is caused by any of four bacilli of the genus *Shigella*. The disease is spread by contaminated food and water. Although unpleasant, most cases are mild and patients recover without serious aftereffects. However, there is an acute form which can be fatal. Children are especially vulnerable. Death takes place from toxemia and dehydration. It is a common disease in Shanti Nagar to judge from our occasional observations of children passing semiliquid stools in the lanes and the complaints heard occasionally from adults whose diarrhea kept them in the fields "the whole night" (Encyclopaedia Britannica, 1966, 7: 828–831; Berkow, 1982: 104).

Dysentery, amoebic: a parasitic infection which may be confused with bacillary dysentery and other diseases, for it is difficult to diagnose. It is an ulcerative inflammation of the colon that is caused by *Entamoeba histolytica* or other amoebae and results in diarrhea. Infection takes place through contaminated water. We do not know if anyone in Shanti Nagar suffered from the disease, for diarrhea is a common symptom and the appropriate diagnoses are not made. Since the water supply is not treated or protected, water-borne disease is always a possibility (Encyclopaedia Britannica, 1966, 7: 828–831; Berkow, 1982: 230–236).

Gonorrhea: an acute infectious inflammation of the genital mucous membrane caused by the gonoccocus *Neisseria gonorrhoeae*, usually spread by sexual contact. The infection takes place in the epithelium of the urethra, cervix, and rectum. Treatment is with antibiotics (Stedman, 1976: 598; Berkow, 1982: 1612–1614).

Helminths, parasitic infections caused by various species of worms: Hookworm is a parasitic infection caused by *Ancylostoma duodenale* or *Necator americanus*. The worms live in the small intestine where they suck blood, and eggs are passed in the feces. Infection occurs when a host contacts infective larvae in the soil which then penetrate the skin, the more common method of transmission. Such larvae can also be swallowed. A scourge in tropical countries, hookworm disease results in inflammation of the bowel, anemia, and a wide range of symptoms, among them abdominal tenderness, the alternation of diarrhea and constipation, fatigue, apathy, and an appetite for unusual substances, for example, clay (Encyclopaedia Britannica, 1966, 11: 671–672; Berkow, 1982: 248).

Two filarial worms transmitted to humans by mosquitoes are important in India. *Wuchereria bancrofti* and *Brugia malayi* (formerly *Wuchereria malayi*) both inhabit the lymphatic glands and vessels. Their presence often causes local inflammation, dilation, and rupture of lymphatics, hyperplasia and fibrosis which may cause lymphatic obstruction leading to elephantiasis and other clinical lesions. The vectors for these two worms are many species of mosquitoes. Although generally similar in their effects, *W. bancrofti* involves the genital region and lower extremities more than *B. malayi* which produces a greater incidence of disease in the upper extremities (Encyclopaedia Britannica, 1966, 9: 264; Davey and Wilson, 1971: 194, 195, Table on Filarial Worms Infecting Man, pp. 196–200; Stedman, 1976: 199).

Hepatitis: Acute viral hepatitis is a diffuse inflammatory disease of the liver, with a worldwide distribution, caused by at least three different viral agents. The principal symptoms are enlargement of the liver and sometimes the spleen, jaundice, fatigue, nausea and vomiting, anorexia, headache, and fever and chills. Virus A spreads primarily by fecal-oral contact although blood and possibly secretions are also infectious. Virus B is mainly transmitted parenterally, formerly through blood transfusions, today chiefly through sexual contact or by contact with infected blood, as through the sharing of needles by drug abusers. Hepatitis C is transmitted largely through blood transfusions. Vaccines have been developed against hepatitis B. Gamma-globulin has been used against hepatitis A but it is only 80 to 90 percent effective and protection has to be renewed after six months. A new vaccine has just been developed against hepatitis A that is claimed to be 100 percent effective and provides protection for as long as seven years. Occasional outbreaks of hepatitis occur in the City of Delhi, especially when raw sewage gets into the water supply. The disease is a constant threat in the rural areas where sewage is untreated (Berkow, 1982: 837–843;

Clayman, 1989: 532–534; Hoffman, 1991: 1581–1582).

Hodgkin's disease: a chronic disease of unknown cause characterized by progressive inflammation and enlargement of the lymph nodes. Diagnosis depends on finding Dorothy Reed cells (sometimes called Reed-Sternberg cells) in lymph nodes or other sites. Generally the symptoms are intense itching, fever, night sweats, weight loss, and involvement of the liver and bone marrow. Treatment and outlook depend on the stage of the disease. In an early stage, radiation therapy is usually curative; in a later stage when many organs are involved, anticancer drugs are recommended, sometimes in conjunction with radiation. Most people who receive treatment at an early stage are cured; 70 to 80 percent of patients who are treated survive at least five years. In the USA, the disease has a bimodal incidence with one peak at ages 15 to 34 and another after age 54. Mani et al. (1982) indicated a trimodal incidence for Hodgkin's disease in Punjab: young people in the second decade of life, young adults ages 20 to 34, and after age 50 with a high preponderance of males in the latter group. The disease is rare—only three new cases per 100,000 people annually in the USA.

We mention the disease only because we knew of two cases in Shanti Nagar: College Man, who died at 28, and Unfortunate's first wife, who died at the age of 22 or 23 years. Ober (1977) provided a history of the disease and theories as to its cause, most recent among them a virus which may reside in the female birth canal, exposing the newborn at the time of birth and gaining access via the oral and respiratory passages (Encyclopaedia Britannica, 1966, 11: 571–572; Berkow, 1982: 1146, 1148–1149; Clayman, 1989: 543–544).

Influenza (also grippe, grip, or flu): an acute, viral, respiratory disease caused by myxoviruses, classified as Types A, B, and C. Type A is further subdivided. The types are unrelated antigenically. The disease is spread by virus-infected droplets coughed or sneezed into the air. Influenza is characterized by fever, muscular aches, cough, headache, malaise, and inflamed respiratory mucous membranes. In the form of types A and B, the disease commonly occurs in epidemics which develop quickly, spread rapidly, and infect up to 40 percent of a population. Epidemics of type A occur in cycles of two to three years; of type B, four to five years. Mortality is usually low with the exception of the great pandemic of 1918–19 which in a few months killed 20 million worldwide of whom 12.5 million were Indians. Type C occurs in an endemic form (Encyclopaedia Britannica, 1966, 12: 242–245; 1992, 6: 311–312; Millar and Osborn, 1977; Berkow, 1982: 172, 191–192; Clayman, 1989: 588).

Kala azar (black disease) or visceral leishmaniasis: an often fatal infectious endemic or epidemic disease caused by the protozoan parasite *Leishmania donovani*, which is transmitted by various species of sandflies of the genus *Phlebotomus*. Chiefly a disease of young adults, it is characterized by fever of long duration, enlargement of the spleen and liver, anemia, and progressive emaciation. Symptoms gradually worsen. Death occurs one to two years after infection in 95 percent of untreated cases, often as a result of a secondary infection. This disease is most prevalent in Eastern India, particularly in the plain and delta of the Ganges and along the Brahmaputra Valley into Assam (Encyclopaedia Britannica, 1966, 13: 189, 926; Davey and Wilson, 1971: 207–208; Table on Main Types of Leishmanial Infections, 208; Stedman, 1976: 769).

Leprosy (Hansen's Disease): a bacterial disease caused by *Mycobacterium leprae*. The disease takes two main forms, lepromatous (the more serious form) and tuberculoid. Leprosy has a long incubation period, about three to five years, and progresses slowly. Transmission may take place via skin-to-skin contact, infected nasal discharges, and possibly by fomites and arthropods. Of the 3.2 million currently known or registered cases in the world, 2 million live in India (Dutt, 1992: 28). However, other estimates place the number of afflicted persons in recent decades worldwide at from 9 to 20 million. In all types of leprosy, lesions of the skin and peripheral nerves stand out in the early clinical findings. As the disease progresses, peripheral nerves swell and become tender. Hands, feet, and facial skin become numb, and muscles, paralyzed. Cartilage and bone

are eroded. Blindness and disfigurement follow. The disease is greatly feared and its victims, shunned and segregated. Many sufferers hide their condition to avoid incarceration. There was some leprosy in the City of Delhi, but probably none in Shanti Nagar (cf. Chap. 14: The Ghost of Whose Daughter [case of Wrestler]) (Encyclopaedia Britannica 1966, 13: 980–982; Skinsnes, 1973; Mani and Mathew, 1981; Berkow, 1982: 140, 142 ff.; Kumar et al., 1982; P. S. S. Rao, 1982; Neelan et al., 1983; Clayman, 1989: 634–635).

Malaria: an infection caused by any of four protozoan parasites of the red blood cells: *Plasmodium vivax*, *P. falciparum* (the most pathogenic parasite), *P. malariae*, and *P. ovale*. The infection is transmitted by the bite of an infected female anopheles mosquito, blood transfusion from an infected donor, or use of a common syringe by drug addicts. *P. falciparum* infects red blood cells of all ages whereas the three other varieties attack only young and old cells. *P. falciparum* is therefore more dangerous. It features prolonged irregular fever with chills and sweating at irregular intervals and can be fatal within a few hours of the first symptoms. The other three varieties of malaria exhibit the classic malarial ague: regular, often cyclical, attacks every other day or every third day of chills and fever followed by a sweating stage. Hyperendemic malarious areas are in the tropics. Worldwide, malaria afflicts some 300 million people every year, and it is a major killer of children under five years of age. The disease is common in the Delhi region. Treatment is by chemotherapy, originally by quinine, more recently by chloroquine, but now *P. falciparum* is not affected by chloroquine. Mefloquine is now the drug of choice of some specialists in tropical medicine, but there are already signs in Asia and Africa that *P. falciparum* is resistant to it as well (Encyclopaedia Britannica, 1966, 14: 668–672; Wood, 1979: Chap. 7; Berkow, 1982: 118; Clayman, 1989: 659–660; Cherfas, 1990: 402–403; Marshall, 1990: 399–400).

Measles: (1) Rubeola (morbilli; nine-day measles) is a highly contagious, worldwide viral disease. It is spread primarily by airborne droplets of nasal secretions. In developing countries, measles accounts for one

million deaths per year, especially of mal-
nourished children. The World Health Organization (1992: 23) reported that worldwide deaths of children less than five years
due to measles, either alone or in combination with other diseases, declined from an
estimated 2 million in 1985 to 880,000 in
1990. Measles is characterized by fever,
cough, congestion of the mucous membranes
of the nose and throat, sore eyes, eruption
(Koplik's spots) on the buccal or labial mu-
cosa, and a spreading skin rash. Normally a
mild childhood illness, it can lead to serious
complications of the brain (encephalitis) and
lungs (bronchopneumonia). It can be prevented by vaccines. (2) Rubella (German
measles, three-day measles) is a viral disease
of mild course, formerly epidemic and endemic, unless vaccinated. Symptoms are
malaise, fever, headache, rhinitis, and enlargement of the lymph glands in the neck
and back of the ears. Congenital rubella results from primary maternal infection. Infection during the first trimester of pregnancy
or immediately before conception may cause
abortion, stillbirth, and congenital defects
(Encyclopaedia Britannica, 1966, 15: 25–26;
Berkow, 1982: 171, 174, 178, 180, 182; Clayman, 1989: 668–669, 876–877).

Pertussis (whooping cough): an acute, communicable bacterial disease that leads to inflammation of the entire respiratory tract and
is characterized by a spasmodic cough that
usually ends in high-pitched, crowing inspi-
ration (the whoop). Infected persons spread
the disease by coughing out airborne droplets. The causal agent is *Bordetella pertussis*.
Attacks of whooping cough caused by a closely related organism, *B. parapertussis*, resemble those of *B. pertussis* but are milder and
less often fatal. Pertussis is endemic throughout the world and among the most important
acute infections of children. Worldwide, an
estimated one million children, 90 percent
under five years old, die annually of whooping cough. The World Health Organization
(1992: 24) reported that the figure for children less than five years had been reduced
from 600,000 in 1985 to 360,000 by 1990.
Pertussis is prevented by vaccination during
childhood, preferably at two, four, and six
months of age, with DPT (diphtheria, pertussis, tetanus vaccine). However, the per-

tussis component of the vaccine causes a high
number of complications so it is not used in
many parts of the world (Encyclopaedia Britannica, 1966, 23: 587–588; Berkow, 1982:
110; Clayman, 1989: 787; Pizza et al., 1989:
497–500).

**Plague (also called Bubonic Plague, Pestis,
and Black Death):** a severe infectious fever
caused by the bacillus *Yersinia pestis* (*Pasteurella pestis*). Plague occurs mainly in wild
rodents but is transferred from rodents to
humans by the bite of an infected flea. It has
three clinical forms in people: the bubonic
form characterized by swelling of the lymph
nodes (buboes), the pneumonic form that involves the lungs, and the septicemic form
when a strong invasion of the bloodstream
leads to rapid death. A typical case may involve fever, shivering, severe headache,
vomiting, and delirium, but the distinctive
sign is the appearance of buboes. When there
are no distinctive clinical signs, bacteriologic
examination is essential to identify the disease. Plague may also be spread from person
to person by inhalation of droplet nuclei
ejected by coughing patients with bubonic or
septicemic plague who have developed pulmonary lesions. Epidemics of plague have
ravaged Europe and taken a huge toll in India.
The best-documented epidemic of plague in
India began in Bombay in 1896 and lasted
until about 1921. After that year people continued to die from the plague but their numbers declined substantially. The worst year
was 1907 when about 1.3 million people died
(cf. Chap. 16; Encyclopaedia Britannica, 1966,
17: 1150–1156; Clayman, 1989: 799).

Pneumonia: an inflammation of the lungs
caused by a variety of bacteria and viruses.
It may also be induced by physical or chemical injury to the lungs. Symptoms include
fever, chills, shortness of breath, and coughing that produces rusty sputum and sometimes blood. The disease can cause a number
of infections in various parts of the body. It
is most useful to refer to pneumonia as bacterial or nonbacterial, or according to its specific etiological agent, if known. If the exact
cause of the disease can be identified, pneumonia can often be treated effectively. The
necessary analyses are ordinarily not available to the people of Shanti Nagar or would
not be sought in Delhi before the disease had

passed through the most critical period. Practitioners of popular pharmaceutical medicine, who are near at hand and quickly available, can be useful in the case of pneumococcal pneumonia, which can be treated with antibiotics, widely dispensed by such curers. The mortality rate is 30 percent in untreated cases and about 5 percent in patients who receive antibiotics (Encyclopaedia Britannica, 1966, 18: 80–82; Berkow, 1982: 89–90, 120, 651–666, 1764; Clayman, 1989: 803–804).

Poliomyelitis (polio, infantile paralysis, acute anterior poliomyelitis): an acute viral infection of the central nervous system with a wide range of manifestations, including nonspecific minor illness, aseptic meningitis (nonparalytic poliomyelitis), and flaccid weakness and paralysis of various muscle groups (paralytic poliomyelitis) followed by atrophy. Among early symptoms are headache, fever, sore throat, nausea, and diarrhea. Epidemics occur. In much of the relatively nonindustrialized world where low standards of public sanitation may be common, most children become infected and develop immunity at an early age when polio rarely causes serious illness. The incidence of polio has been greatly reduced with the use of vaccines beginning in the mid 1950s (Encyclopaedia Britannica, 1966, 18: 157–159; Paul, 1971; Berkow, 1982: 173, 210–212; Clayman, 1989: 806).

Puerperal fever (childbed fever): Puerperal infection of some part of a woman's reproductive tract is presumed when her temperature rises to 38°C (l00.4°F) or above on any two successive days during a 10-day period after the first 24 hours postpartum, and other causes are not apparent. A variety of bacteria may cause puerperal fever, infection taking place through lacerations of any part of the genital tract. The most deadly of all the organisms is the hemolytic streptococcus, normally not present in the vagina but conveyed to patients from the respiratory tract of attendants. Prolonged labor, traumatic deliveries, retention of placental fragments within the uterus, and postpartum hemorrhage dispose both normal vaginal bacteria and introduced bacteria to become pathologic in the puerperium (the period from the termination of labor to the complete involution of the uterus, usually 42 days). Puerperal fever was

common in Shanti Nagar because of unsanitary lying-in conditions (Encyclopaedia Britannica, 1966, 18: 846–847; Berkow, 1982: 1721–1722).

Rabies (hydrophobia): an acute, usually fatal, infectious viral disease of the central nervous system of mammals, especially carnivores. The virus, which is often present in the saliva of rabid animals, spreads among wild carnivores (such as coyotes, skunks, and mongooses), domestic dogs, and from them to people by the bite of an infected animal. Although rabies can be controlled in domestic dogs, wild animals are a reservoir that can reinfect an area. Animal rabies is characterized by irritation of the central nervous system as shown by such early symptoms as irritability, aggressiveness, and viciousness without apparent cause, followed by paralysis and death. Initial symptoms of human rabies are a low-grade fever, headache, loss of appetite, restlessness, hyperactivity, and seizures, then depression of the central nervous system and paralysis. Death may occur during the excitation phase from a convulsive seizure. The hydrophobic symptom consists of painful contractions of the throat in attempting to swallow, which may be elicited by the sight of water. The incubation period varies but averages from 30 to 50 days. Although villagers learn to recognize rabid animals, especially dogs, such animals may appear healthy and seem friendly but still be in the early stages of rabies and bite at the slightest provocation. The problem of rabid animals, especially dogs, biting humans exists throughout the Union Territory of Delhi. Very effective and safe anti-rabies vaccines are available. Villagers generally use them when bitten by a clearly rabid dog (Chap. 13: Troubled). Folk remedies are used in the case of other bites (Encyclopaedia Britannica, 1966, 18: 983–984; Davey and Wilson, 1971: 277; Berkow, 1982: 214–215, 217; Clayman, 1989: 843).

Relapsing fever (tick, recurrent, famine fever): caused by several species of *Borrelia* spirochetes and transmitted from person to person by lice of the genus *Pediculus* and from animals to people by ticks of the genus *Ornithodoros*. Neither the bite nor the excreta is infectious. Human infection takes place when the louse is crushed against the skin while scratching. Although the louse-borne and tick-borne forms show some differences, their symptoms are generally similar. The disease is characterized by sudden onset and violent febrile symptoms, which may persist up to a week. Then there is a period of recovery followed by a return of the fever. We were not aware of any cases in Shanti Nagar. The disease is mentioned here chiefly because we saw people who had head lice, which suggested that lice were perhaps rather common. Hence the potential for disease transmitted by lice was present. Second, relapsing fever may be confused with such common fevers as malaria, dengue, typhus, influenza, and the enteric fevers which would tend to reduce the possibility that it would be specifically identified. Antibiotics like those dispensed by practitioners of popular pharmaceutical medicine are effective therapeutic agents (Encyclopaedia Britannica, 1966, 19: 95; Berkow, 1982: 144).

Salmonella infections: Based on clinical presentations caused by the organisms, the 1400-odd salmonellae can be classified into three groups: (l) enteric fever, caused by *Salmonella typhi*; (2) localized diseases, by *Salmonella choleraesuis*; and (3) gastroenteritis, which includes the many other salmonellae. Except for typhoid fever, salmonella infections (especially gastroenteritis) are an increasing public health problem. Salmonellae are often implicated in outbreaks of food poisoning. Typical symptoms are nausea, vomiting, abdominal pain, and diarrhea. In Shanti Nagar, salmonella infection might be inferred, but the symptoms are rather general. Because convalescence is rapid, the villagers would not ordinarily consult the kind of medical practitioner who would use a diagnostic test. However, one case of fatal food poisoning, probably due to salmonella, did come to our attention. The third son of the Patriarchs became suddenly ill with stomach pain, nausea, and diarrhea. When he grew worse, Home Trained gave him an antibiotic injection. He was rushed to a hospital where he died. The diagnosis was food poisoning (Chap. 22). (Encyclopaedia Britannica, 1966, 9: 534–535; Pinnas and Bunn, 197l; Berkow, 1982: 99–104.)

Smallpox (variola): an acute highly contagious viral disease, whose initial symptoms are high fever, chills, backache, and headache. It is characterized, about two days later, by a progressive cutaneous eruption that often results in permanent pits and scars on healing. The progression is from pimple to blister to pustule to scab to scar. Complications include blindness, pneumonia, and kidney damage. Smallpox is spread by contact, direct or indirect, with a preceding case, presumably by inhalation of particles bearing the virus. There is a naturally occurring mild variety (variola minor) and a severe strain (variola major). Smallpox was lethal in India and greatly dreaded. It had a worldwide distribution and, before it was declared eradicated by the World Health Organization in 1980, all ages, sexes, and races were susceptible (Encyclopaedia Britannica, 1966, 20: 816–818; Stedman, 1976: 1294; Berkow, 1982: 188; Clayman, 1989: 918).

Syphilis: an infectious disease caused by a microbe, takes two forms. The venereally transmitted form is due to *Treponema pallidum*. Hours after the spirochete enters the body, it begins to spread by way of the bloodstream throughout the body. The disease passes through several stages and shows such a variety of symptoms that it has been called the "great imitator." The most dreaded symptoms are those that accompany the widespread destruction of the brain. Syphilis in pregnancy increases the probability of stillbirth and infantile death, and many surviving children suffer from congenital syphilis. Venereal syphilis is a problem in the Delhi region, but if there were any cases in Shanti Nagar, they were kept secret. Some villagers said that syphilis was a problem in the cities but not in places like Shanti Nagar.

The other form is known as endemic syphilis. Although nonvenereal, it is spread by body contact. The spirochete that causes endemic syphilis is morphologically and serologically indistinguishable from the treponemes of venereal syphilis and from those of yaws and pinta. Endemic syphilis, yaws, and pinta have limited geographical distributions and most probably do not occur in Shanti Nagar. However, we suspected that Wrestler might have had some form of *Treponema* because some villagers blamed his condition on mercury poisoning; mercury at one time was used as a remedy. But all villagers whom we questioned denied that syphilis was a possibility (Chap. 14: The Ghost of Whose Daughter). Soldier and his two wives were more likely candidates for syphilis (Chap. 13, Curmudgeon, Cattleman, Soldier, and Families; Encyclopaedia Britannica, 1966, 23: 41–45, 880; Wood, 1979: 215–217, 219–220, 222, 224, 226–229, 231–234, 240; Berkow, 1982: 144, 1616 ff.).

Tetanus (lockjaw): a serious, sometimes fatal infectious disease of the central nervous system characterized by convulsions and painful tonic spasms of voluntary muscles. There may also be a fast pulse, slight fever, and profuse sweating. Asphyxia is a danger. The disease is caused by the exotoxin, tetanospasmin of the bacillus *Clostridium tetani*, whose spores are widely distributed in the soil. Fecal contamination from animals and humans increases soil pollution. Entry into the body is through a wound, even a trivial one. Spasm of the masseters accounts for the name "lockjaw." Tetanus neonatorum is a form of tetanus that affects newborns, usually through the open end of the severed umbilical cord. Hence, a sterilized or new instrument should be used to sever the umbilical cord, a precaution that was not taken in Shanti Nagar until relatively recently. Tetanus neonatorum was a serious danger in Shanti Nagar. Tetanus may also occur in the postpartum uterus. Clinical disease does not confer immunity. In Shanti Nagar, some children and infants were immunized against tetanus with DTP (diphtheria-tetanus-pertussis), a threefold vaccine used in the Union Territory of Delhi (Encyclopaedia Britannica, 1966, 21: 969–971; Gaz. Unit, Delhi Adm., 1976: 870; Berkow, 1982: 60–61, 113; Clayman, 1989: 975).

Tuberculosis (phthisis or consumption, often called TB): an acute or chronic infection caused by *Mycobacterium tuberculosis*. Of the infectious diseases, TB is the leading cause of death in the world, a yearly death toll of 2.9 million. The fatality rate everywhere for untreated TB is between 40 and 60 percent. Most commonly attacking the lungs, it may affect almost any tissue or organ. Infection is passed from person to person by airborne droplets expelled by coughing or sneezing. It can also be acquired from cow's milk contaminated by *Mycobacterium bovis*. Tubercle

bacilli are ingested by phagocytes and carried in lymph vessels to the bloodstream and on to the heart, then to the lungs, and from there they enter the systemic circulation and are lodged in extrathoracic organs including kidneys, brain, bones and joints (cf. The case of Barker, Chap. 13: Old Codger, Barker, and Mrs. Barker). Cases where the lungs are not primarily affected but rather other organs are especially common in bovine TB. Bovine TB has almost disappeared in developed countries where milk is pasteurized but perhaps may still occur in Shanti Nagar. Although villagers boil their milk, such home treatment is not always carefully monitored and may sometimes be ineffective. Because TB usually affects the lungs, its main symptoms are coughing (sometimes with blood), chest pain, fever, night sweats, shortness of breath, poor appetite, and weight loss. Diagnosis can be made from x-rays, examination of sputum, and a skin test (cf. Chap. 13).

Vaccination with the attenuated Bacillus Calmette-Guérin (BCG) is still used in India (including Delhi Union Territory) and other parts of the world and in groups and populations where the incidence of TB is high, but it is not used in the USA. Modern drugs in combination are very effective against most TB, although drug-resistant strains are an increasing problem. A recent one-month survey in New York City found that 19 percent of TB patients have a strain of the disease that is resistant to the two main drugs (*The New York Times*, April 26, 1992, p. 18E).

Perinatal TB may be acquired by infants by transplacental spread through the umbilical vein to the fetal liver, by aspiration or ingestion of infected amniotic fluid, or by exposure to active TB in close contact. That about 50 percent of children born to mothers with active pulmonary TB will develop the disease during the first year of life if treatment is not given supports the villagers' belief that TB is an inherited disease through the mother. TB is a serious disease in Shanti Nagar and Delhi Union Territory, the more so because drug-resistant strains are now appearing (Chap. 13: Old Fever; Encyclopaedia Britannica, 1966, 22: 531–535; Gazetteer Unit, Delhi Adm., 1976: 865; Myers, 1977: 73–75, 78–79, 116–117, 142 ff., 159–162; Berkow, 1982: 127–139, 1810 ff.; Clayman, 1989:

1013–1014; Weiss, 1992; Bloom and Murray, 1992: 1055–1057).

Typhoid (typhoid fever): a serious contagious disease in regions where standards of public hygiene are low. It is caused by a bacterium, *Salmonella typhosa*, which enters the body through the mouth. The bacteria spread from the small intestine to the spleen and liver where they multiply, accumulate in the gallbladder, and are released in enormous numbers into the intestine. Symptoms appear after 10 to 14 days. Severe headache is followed by persistent fever, loss of appetite, general aches, lassitude, restlessness, and constipation which soon gives way to diarrhea. During the second week of fever, a rash of small rose-colored spots appears on the trunk. It is this rash that is the diagnostic symptom in Shanti Nagar; the other symptoms may accompany one or another disease, and recourse to diagnostic laboratory tests is rare. Typhoid leads to many complications, among them intestinal bleeding, renal failure, heart failure, encephalitis, peritonitis, mental confusion and delirium. By the end of the third week, the patient is prostrate and emaciated. Recovery begins at the start of the fourth week. Untreated cases are fatal 25 percent of the time. Antibiotics are effective, and there is a vaccine that gives partial protection but requires a booster after two to three years. Naturally acquired typhoid confers lifelong immunity so that in endemic areas the disease is more common among adolescents and young adults than among older people. Typhoid appears to be milder in children younger than five years. Paratyphoid, caused by a group of organisms related to the typhoid bacillus, especially, *S. paratyphi*, is a disease almost identical to typhoid but less severe (Chap. 22: Little Goddess).

An outbreak of typhoid took place in Shanti Nagar during our residence in 1977–78. The disease is spread by contaminated feces and urine. The fields around Shanti Nagar are used as latrines so that feces are exposed to flies, which carry the disease to food. The water supply is unprotected and easily contaminated, especially during the rainy season. There is always a reservoir of the disease, as 5 percent of recovered cases become long-term carriers, shedding the bacteria for years, and 30 percent are transient carriers, excreting the bacilli in feces and urine for weeks or months. Prevention depends on proper sewage treatment and the filtration and clorination of water (Encyclopaedia Britannica, 1966, 22: 646–647; 1992, 12: 88; Davey and Wilson, 1971: 39–46; Clayman, 1989: 772, 1017).

Typhus: any of a group of closely related acute infectious diseases caused by different species of *Rickettsia* and transmitted by arthropods. The most important type is epidemic typhus (jail fever, war fever, camp fever, European, classic, or louse-borne typhus) spread by the human body louse. The causative agent is *Rickettsia prowazekii*. Lice are infected by feeding on a person sick with the disease. Lice then deposit their feces on the skin of an uninfected person, and the causative agent infects the new host through abrasions from scratching. The disease is associated with human misery and characteristically occurs after war or natural disaster has disrupted normal life and led to crowded unsanitary living conditions. Its symptoms are the sudden onset of intractable headache, chills, fever, general pains, and constipation followed in three to five days by a rash like that of measles, prostration, and, often, delirium. Mortality rates range from 5 to 25 percent with the death rate among the elderly many times that of children. Although at one time typhus was prevalent worldwide, it has largely disappeared from countries with hygienic living conditions. However, in the second half of the 20th century it still occurred in North India. Typhus is treated by antibiotics and measures to relieve symptoms. Preventive measures involve delousing, and there is a vaccine.

Endemic (murine) typhus, whose causative agent is *R. mooseri*, is a disease of rats that can be spread to humans through the feces of infected fleas. Its symptoms are indistinguishable from those of epidemic typhus but the disease is milder. Murine typhus occurs in India as does another variety, scrub (mite-borne) typhus. The agent is *R. tsutsugamushi* spread by the larvae of two closely related mites. The larvae live in the upper layers of the soil and can crawl on vegetation. Therefore, farmers and others who work in fields are endangered in infected areas (Encyclopaedia Britannica, 1966, 22: 648–650; 1992, 12: 88–89; Stedman, 1976: 1504; Berkow, 1982: 168; Clayman, 1989: 1017).

APPENDIX II: SACRED HINDU TEXTS

The sacred literature of Hinduism is a living force in village belief and practice. The gift that the village council presented to us at our departure well illustrated this point: eight small paperback books, each one on an aspect of Hindu beliefs. The earliest Hindu prayers and hymns, which for some time were transmitted orally, are over 3000 years old. For centuries, the sacred literature has been elaborated in epics, tales, moral writings, and philosophical discourses. The pinnacles of Hindu sacred writings, such as the Bhagavad Gita, are masterpieces of world literature. Since various sacred Hindu works have been mentioned throughout this text, this outline of Hindu sacred literature is presented as a basic guide. This appendix is roughly chronological rather than alphabetical in order to show the development of Hindu texts and related beliefs.

The content of the Vedas and their language, which is the oldest form of Sanskrit, known as Vedic Sanskrit, shows that they are very ancient. Sanskrit is the ancestral language of the widespread Indo-Aryan language family. Before writing, the Vedas were transmitted orally, as was the Mahabharata, the tales of which were recited by bards. Although the Vedas and epics (Mahabharata and Ramayana) are known to be old, authorities can date them only to broad time periods. Dates gradually became more precise after writing was introduced in India ca. 800 B.C., but even then it was many centuries before dates began to show much precision. Panini's grammar, which stabilized classical Sanskrit (later then Vedic Sanskrit), was written centuries after the introduction of writing, yet it cannot be dated more precisely than sometime in the 4th century B.C. The writing materials that are common today, especially paper made from pulp which was invented in China ca. A.D. 105, arrived in India long after a literate tradition was well established. Early writing materials in India were birch bark in the north and palm leaves in the south. They were succeeded by papyrus, introduced in Egypt and used throughout the ancient world; then by parchment, first used in Pergamum, Asia Minor, in the 2nd century A.D. The Turks brought paper and the practice of writing chronicles to Northwest India in the 11th and 12th centuries. Printing came much later (Balfour, 1885, 3: 122–123; Basham, 1954: 388–389; Moreland and Chatterjee, 1957: 10, 38–39, 143–144; Encyclopaedia Britannica, 1966, 17: 280, 297, 338; Harris and Levey, 1975: 2062–2063, 2219, 2419–2420).

Veda (literally, "knowledge"): refers to the "supreme sacred knowledge" contained in the four books that are basic to Hinduism: the Rig-Veda, Yajur-Veda, Sama-Veda, and Atharva-Veda, the Brahmanas appended to them, and the Aranyakas and Upanishads added to the Brahmanas. The Vedas range in descending order of age from the Rig-Veda to the Atharva-Veda. The Rig-Veda is the original work. The Yajur-Veda and the Sama-Veda are merely different arrangements of its hymns for special purposes. The Atharva-Veda differs from the others. The first three Vedas approach the deities with awe, to be sure, but also with love and confidence. In contrast, the divinities of the Atharva-Veda are regarded with a kind of cringing fear.

Each Veda is divided into three parts: Samhita or Mantra, Brahmana, and Sutra. The first part, Samhita, consists of mantras or hymns. The term "Samhita" may also refer to a collection of compositions of a similar character, such as the four Vedas. The Brahmanas, written in prose rather than metrical form, contain explanations and applications of the hymns, which are illustrated by numerous legends. The Aranyakas and Upanishads are mystical and philosophical treatises. The Sutras are aphorisms. The Vedas are said to have been revealed orally to the Rishis, inspired poets or sages, under whose names they stand. Thus, the Vedas are collectively known as Sruti, "what was heard." All other texts are referred to as Smriti, "what was remembered" (Dowson, 1950: 345; Sarma, 1953: 7).

Opinions vary about the age of the Vedas. Doniger O'Flaherty (1980: 11) dated the Rig-Veda to about 1200 B.C. and the other three, from 1000 to 900 B.C. Basham (1954: 31, 38) favored dates for the Rig-Veda from 1500 to 1000 B.C., and for the other three, from 1000 to 900 B.C. Dowson (1950: 345) believed that the Vedas were composed between 1500 and 1000 B.C. However, the Atharva-Veda is much later than the rest (Balfour, 1885, 3: 998), and Dowson believed that it is of comparatively modern origin. Balfour offered the view that the Samhitas (hymns) were composed about the 17th or 15th centuries B.C. but not committed to writing and therefore not collected before the 8th century B.C. He reported a calculation of the age of the Vedas based on the precession of the equinoxes, the slow retrograde movement of the equinoctial points along the ecliptic at the rate of one degree every 72 years. During the Vedic epoch, the summer solstice is alleged to have been in the middle of the ninth lunar mansion (Aslesha), which meant that Regulus (a bright star in the constellation Leo) was 15°40' east of the summer solstice. The longitude of Regulus on Jan. 1, 1859, showed that the summer solstice had retrograded through 42°2'8" since that time, which translates into a date of 1181 B.C. for the Vedas.

Rig-Veda: The Samhita of the Rig-Veda comprises songs that the ancient Aryans addressed to deities who personified the powers of nature. The Vedic poets asked them for prosperity, extolled their prowess in the struggle between light and darkness, praised them for preservation in battle, and thanked them for the fruits of the earth. Chief among these nature deities were Agni (fire), Indra (god of the firmament), and Surya (sun). Other important deities were Rudra, who ruled the tempest, and Yama, god of death and judge of souls. Finally, and by no means least, was the mysterious Soma, personification of the fermented juice of the soma plant, a creeper once thought to be either the *Sarcostemma viminale* or *Asclepias acida* or possibly the fly agaric mushroom (*Amanita muscaria*). Oblations were made either with ghee or fermented soma juice. Many of the important deities of modern Hinduism, such as Shiva, Krishna, Rama, Kali, and Durga, are not mentioned in the Vedas. However, Rudra is the Vedic equivalent of Shiva, a word that meant "auspicious" in the Vedas (Balfour, 1885, 3: 998–999; Dowson, 1950: 346–347; Daniélou, 1964: 188, fn.1, 65; Stutley and Stutley, 1977: 283.)

Yajur-Veda: is composed almost entirely of hymns from the Rig-Veda, somewhat modified. The hymns are arranged to serve as a book of office for priests. In contrast to the other Vedas, the Yajur-Veda has two Samhitas, known as the Black and the White Yajur-Veda. The verses of both Samhitas relate to the soma offering. The Black Yajur is the older of the two, dating to the 3rd century B.C., and includes sacrificial prose formulae, while the White Yajur is a collection of pure verse-mantras (Balfour, 1885, 3: 998; Dowson, 1950: 347–348; Raghavan, 1953: 267; Stutley and Stutley, 1977: 344–345).

Sama-Veda: Almost all the verses of the Sama-Veda Samhita have been traced to the Rig-Veda. The verses have been arranged to be chanted at offerings of the Soma. Invocations are addressed to Soma, Agni, and Indra. The Sama-Veda is the oldest form of Indian music and the source of later musical tradition, which holds that music is an aid to meditation and salvation (Dowson, 1950: 349; Raghavan, 1953: 267).

Atharva-Veda: The chief characteristic of the Atharva-Veda is its multitude of incantations designed to ward off harm from a host of malevolent supernaturals, designated commonly as Rakshasas. However, the commonest and most dreaded disease was "Fever." Incantations could be pronounced either by the suppliants or more often by sorcerers on their behalf. When sorcerers offered incantations as a cure for illness, they might also give suppliants an amulet, such as a necklace, or medicine with supernatural power. The Atharva-Veda is also called the Brahman Veda, for it is the Veda of the chief sacrificial priest, the Brahman. The Atharva-Veda is recognized as the basis of Hindu medicine. Its connection to some aspects of the modern health culture of Shanti Nagar is remarkably clear as shown in this monograph (Dowson, 1950: 350–351; Stutley and Stutley, 1977: 30).

Brahmanas (belonging to Brahmans): Ritualistic, liturgical, and abounding with illustrative legends, these works are intended for the guidance of Brahmans in using the hymns of the Vedas and in conducting the sacrifice. They were written after the Mantra part of the Vedas but are nonetheless considered Sruti. Each Veda has at least one Brahmana (Balfour, 1885, 1: 436; Dowson, 1950: 60–61; Sarma, 1953: 7).

Aranyakas (Forest Books): Forming the latter part of the Brahmanas and closely connected to the Upanishads, the Aranyakas are Hindu texts intended to be used by Brahmans, who have renounced the secular world, as sources of meditation in the forests. There are four Aranyakas (Dowson, 1950: 20–21; Raghavan, 1953: 268).

Upanishads (sitting near a teacher to learn esoteric doctrine): Composed later than the Samhitas and the Brahmanas, the Upanishads, like the Aranyakas, were subsequently attached to particular Brahmanas, which in turn were attached to particular Vedas. The Upanishads mark the end of the Vedic period. Of the 150 to 200 or so Upanishads, only 13 or 14 contain esoteric teaching. Most of the Aranyakas and Upanishads represent a reaction to Brahmanical fundamentalism and exclusiveness. The Upanishads deal with such questions as the origin of the universe, the nature of the deity and the soul, and the connection of mind and matter. The Upanishads posit a unity of deities and adopt the view that, despite the manifold appearances of the phenomenal world, the entire universe is essentially one. The universe is pervaded by Brahman (neuter), the supreme soul and divine essence of the universe, which is incorporeal, uncreated, invisible, and without either beginning or end (Balfour, 1885, 3: 974; Dowson, 1950: 56, 325–326; Raghavan, 1953: 268; Stutley and Stutley, 1977: 312; Sarma, 1953: 7–8).

Mahabharata: Of the two great epics of the Hindus, the Ramayana being the other, the Mahabharata is the longer, containing about 220,000 lines divided into 18 books. It is the world's longest epic. The events depicted probably date to the ninth or eighth century B.C. The epic was written probably between 300 B.C. and A.D. 300. The Mahabharata is a collection of ancient stories of different dates, the principal one describing a war between the Pandavas and their cousins, the Kauravas, for control of the kingdom of the Kurus ruled by Dhritarashtra. The ruins of his capital, Hastinapura, have been found about 57 miles northeast of Delhi on an old bed of the Ganges River. Dhritarashtra was father of the Kauravas and uncle of the Pandavas. The two sets of brothers were rivals. When Dhritarashtra named the eldest of the Pandava brothers rather than his own eldest son as heir-apparent, the rivalry grew into

bitter hatred on the part of the Kauravas, and Dhritarashtra had to exile the Pandavas. Thought for a time to be dead, the Pandavas reappeared at a contest in which they won Draupadi, daughter of Drupada, king of Panchala, as their joint wife. Dhritarashtra then recalled them and divided his kingdom between his sons and nephews, the Kauravas keeping Hastinapura and the Pandavas being given Indraprastha, situated on the Yamuna River close to Delhi. The two sides continued to plot, especially the Kauravas, who succeeded in forcing the Pandavas into 13 years of exile where they had many adventures. The Pandavas were determined to recover their kingdom. Finally, the issue was settled in a great 18-day battle on the plain of Kurukshetra, near Delhi. Although the Pandavas won and their eldest brother was crowned at Hastinapura, the war was a disaster for them as well as for the vanquished Kauravas. The Mahabharata retains a powerful hold on Hindus; a recent serial dramatization of the epic on television fascinated India for many weeks (Balfour, 1885, 2: 771–773; Dowson, 1950: 183–192; Raghavan, 1953: 353–362; Basham, 1954: 407–408; van Buitenen, 1980, Book 1: xlix).

Bhagavad Gita (Song of the Blessed One): The Gita, part of the Mahabharata and a late addition to it, is a long discussion in verse between Krishna, an avatar of Vishnu, and Arjuna, one of the five Pandava brothers. It takes place on the plain of Kurukshetra just before the climatic battle. Arjuna is dismayed by the prospect of killing his relatives and friends. At this fateful moment, Krishna teaches Arjuna that the dharma (duty) of caste requires him to fight even at the expense of friends and kin. The Gita inculcates the doctrine of bhakti (faith, devotion) and deals with many philosophical issues, such as the soul and body of human beings, karma, rebirth, and release from the round of rebirths. The poem summarizes the teachings of the Vedas and Upanishads (Dowson, 1950: 43–44; Sarma, 1953: 8; Edgerton, 1965: Chap. XII).

Ramayana (story of Rama): Among the several versions of the story of Rama, the two that are best known are the Valmiki Ramayana and the Tulsidas Ramayana. Valmiki wrote his Ramayana in Sanskrit. Tulsi Das wrote his version in Hindi. The Ramayana of Tulsi Das is not a translation of the Sanskrit version. Tulsi Das made important changes in emphasis and content. His Ramayana exhibits a high moral and didactic tone and exemplifies proper conduct for today's Hindu population of northern India. It also emphasizes love and bhakti (devotion). Channa (1984: 68) commented ". . . [T]he Tulsidas Ramayana gives peace of mind and helps devotion, whereas the Valmiki Ramayana leaves a painful impact on the mind." The people of northern Indian are intimately familiar with the Ramayana not only from the written versions but also because of yearly public performances in North Indian cities of the 11-day religious play known as the Ram Lila (drama of Rama). Accounts of the Ram Lila performances describe huge enthusiastic crowds (Oman, 1906: 75–86; Titiev, 1946; Channa, 1984: 60–70).

The story concerns the life of Rama, an avatar of Vishnu, who was born to the king of the city state of Ayodhya. The heart of the story is the war between Rama and Ravana, king of the Rakshasas (demons), who lived in Lanka (modern Sri Lanka). Rama is exiled from his father's kingdom, Ravana kidnaps Rama's wife, Sita, Rama kills Ravana and rescues Sita with the help of Hanuman, the monkey god, who is Rama's lieutenant, and Rama returns to his father's kingdom. His father had died, and Rama's younger brother relinquishes the kingdom to Rama, who becomes king. The tale continues with the trials of Sita. Although chaste, she had been in the power of the demon Ravana, which sowed the seeds of doubt. The versions of Valmiki and Tulsi Das differ concerning the relations of Sita and Rama after he rescues her. In the Valmiki Ramayana, Rama and Sita are estranged over the issue of her chastity. The Tulsidas Ramayana defuses this issue and has a happier ending. The Ramayana is very popular in North India, and in the 1980s it was shown as a serial on national television (Dowson, 1950: 261–262, 264–265; Basham, 1954: 412–415).

Doniger O'Flaherty (1980: 11) dated the epic from 200 B.C. to A.D. 200. Stutley and Stutley (1954: 247) noted that there is no general agreement about dates for the Ramayana. Opinions about the date of the core

story vary from 500 to 300 B.C.; the additions, from 300 B.C. to A.D. 200. Dowson (1950: 190, 261–263) dated the Ramayana to about the 5th century B.C., and its present form a century or two later. Basham (1954: 39, 412) did not commit himself to specific dates but indicated the time was around the same period as the Mahabharata.

Puranas (old): The 18 major and 18 minor Puranas, collections of ancient legends written in Sanskritic verse, were composed at various times, generally after the epics. The Puranas are written in the form of a dialogue between an exponent and an inquirer. They should expound five subjects; the creation of the universe, its destruction and renovation, the genealogy of gods and patriarchs, the reigns of the Manus (mythological ancestors), and the history of the Solar and Lunar races of kings. All except the Vishnu Purana deviate from this ideal scheme.

All the Puranas are sectarian, advocating faith in some one deity, chiefly either Shiva or Vishnu. The major Puranas are classified according to which of the three gunas (qualities) are most prominent in them. Puranas relating to Vishnu are called *sattvika*, with guna sattva (purity) prevailing; those concerning Shiva are designated *tamasa*, with guna tamas (gloom, ignorance) dominant; and Puranas relating to Brahma are called *rajasa*, with guna rajas (passion) predominating. Although some of the *Rajasa* Puranas extol Brahma, they advocate mainly the worship of Vishnu or Shiva. The Bhagavata Purana, glorifying Vishnu and the childhood of his avatar, Krishna, is said to be the most popular (Sarma, 1953: 8). The Vishnu Purana is also well known. The Puranas foster discussions in Shanti Nagar and thus transmit Vedic teachings to everyday people and disseminate the pantheistic pre-eminence of some one deity or one of his manifestations (cf. Chap. 10 on the gunas; Balfour, 1885, 3: 313–315; Dowson, 1950: 245–247; Stutley and Stutley, 1977: 236–237).

Doniger O'Flaherty (1980: 11) divided the Puranas into three periods: Early, 300 B.C. to A.D. 500; Middle 500 to 1000: Late, 1000 to 1500. Basham (1954: 58) dated the Puranas from the beginning of the first Gupta dynasty, ca. A.D. 300.

Tantras: a class of Hindu texts from the middle ages going back to about the 7th century, which established a new form of ceremony practiced by sects that worshipped female deities. Both sexes participated in the rituals. Prominence was given to female energy, personified in Shiva by his consort, Shakti. Shiva's consorts are Shakti, energy; Parvati, peacefulness; Kali, destruction; and Sati, the faithful wife and daughter of Daksha, who threw herself on the ritual fire. Since Tantric rites emphasize the participation of women along with men, the female deities and consorts of the male gods are important in the rites. For example, the object of veneration for worshippers of Vishnu is his consort, Radha. The Tantric texts advocate breaking some Hindu tabus. Devotees indulge in the 5Ms: *madya* (alcohol), *mamsa* (meat), *matsya* (fish), *mudra* (symbolic hand gestures), and *maithuna* (sexual intercourse). Worshippers believe that by correctly pronouncing the right formula (mantra) or by drawing the correct magical symbol (yantra), they might force the gods to bestow magical power on them and lead them to the highest bliss. In back of these thoughts is the belief that the power which the male god receives from his consort, especially Shiva from Shakti, may be passed on to the worshipper. Devotion to Shakti as Shiva's consort implies the special energy of sexual intercourse and magical powers, and devotion to Shakti promotes sexual freedom and excessive behavior. The sects are variously identified as Tantric (from their scriptures), Shaktic (from worshipping Shakti), or left-hand from the fact that the Goddess sits on the left side of her Lord. Uma, Parvati, and Gauri are gentle forms of Shiva's Shakti; Durga and Kali are fierce forms. Shakti is worshipped especially in her fierce forms. In the late 1950s, we attended a ceremony for Durga worship which took place in a temple in a middle-class suburb of Old Delhi. Men, women, and children participated, with symbolic dancing by women and children. Seating arrangments were not segregated by gender. Participants neither ate, drank, nor participated in sex (Dowson, 1950: 86–88, 317–318; Basham, 1954: 213, 280, 337; R. Freed and S. Freed, 1962: 255, 274–275; Garrett, 1990: 633–635).

Dharmashastras (Instructions in the Sacred Law): These texts deal with Hindu law, especially moral law. The Dharmashastras follow the Dharmasutras, manuals of brief aphorisms, which are sources of early Hindu law. The Dharmashastras are the prose Sutras expanded and put in verse. The Dharmashastras and Dharmasutras together are Smriti (remembered) as distinct from earlier Vedic literature, which is Sruti (heard). The Dharmashastras are generally in three parts: rules of conduct and practice, judicature, and penance. Sages, variously enumerated from 18 to 42, are the authors. The three principal texts considered Dharmashastras are (1) The Code of Manu, compiled sometime between 200 B.C. and A.D. 100; (2) The Code of Yajnavalkya, written between A.D. 100 and 300; and (3) The Code of Narada, composed between 100 B.C. and A.D. 400. Manu is concerned with general human conduct, but the works of his successors more and more take the form of legal textbooks. Many later jurists wrote commentaries on Smriti literature. The Mitakshara, composed in the 11th century is the leading commentary on The Code of Yajnavalkya. With regard to succession and inheritance, two schools of thought exist, based on the Mitakshara and the Dayabhaga. The latter was written between the 13th and 15th centuries and is a digest of the laws of inheritance (Balfour, 1885, 1: 934, 2: 961–962; Dowson, 1950: 89, 209; Sternbach, 1951: 117–120; Basham, 1954: 112–113).

Mantras: Sanskritic verbal formulas of a syllable, word, or group of words, which possess supernatural or divine power. Mantras pervade Hinduism. They serve a host of specific purposes but in general are used to ensure success and avoid disaster. Mantras from the Atharva-Veda are invoked to exorcise the supernaturals that cause Fever and disease. Mantras are of infinite diversity but can be classed in four categories according to their effects: (1) sure mantras (*Siddha*), which bring results within a specific time; (2) helpful mantras (*Sadyha*), which bring results when used with rosaries and offerings; (3) accomplished mantras (*Susiddha*), which bring results immediately; and (4) enemy mantras (*Ari*), which destroy those who utter them. Mantras that involve curing deal with acquisition of superhuman powers, communication with ghosts and other spirits, avoidance of evil, cure of disease, and control of minor deities and ghosts (Daniélou, 1964: 337–338; Stutley and Stutley, 1977: 180–181).

Gayatri Mantra: The most sacred verse of the Rig-Veda, the Gayatri is the best known mantra in Shanti Nagar. It is an invocation to the Sun as Savitri, the supreme generative force, to be kind to worshippers and to bless their undertakings. It has twice twelve syllables and hence is a solar mantra. Personified as a goddess, Savitri is the wife of Brahma, mother of the four Vedas and of the twice-born castes. Males of twice-born castes should recite it during periods of meditation in the morning, at midday, and at sunset. It should not be spoken by women or by men of low caste. Translations and interpretations vary, but the Gayatri basically is an appeal to the Sun to shed a benign influence. One translation reads: "AUM. O terrestrial sphere. O sphere of space. O celestial sphere. Let us

contemplate the splendor of the solar spirit, the Divine Creator. May he guide our minds. AUM." (Daniélou, 1964: 345.) AUM is a sacred syllable that some regard as the basis of all mantras, the eternal syllable that encompasses the past, present, future, and all else. The letters *a*, *u*, and *m* are said to represent the Hindu triad, Brahma (*a*), Vishnu (*u*), and Shiva (*m*) (Dowson, 1950: 111–112, 224; Daniélou, 1964: 339–341; Stutley and Stutley, 1977: 97, 213).

Brahma Gayatri: This form of the Gayatri may be uttered by all: "May we know the Immense Being. Let us contemplate the transcendent Reality. And may that Being guide us" (Daniélou, 1964: 345–346).

Shiva Mantra: This mantra consists of five letters and is used by all Hindus: "AUM. To Shiva I bow." The mantra "represent[s] the symbols of the fivefold aspects of all the forms of the world of life, beginning with the five elements" (Daniélou, 1964: 348).

APPENDIX III: KINSHIP CHARTS

INTRODUCTION

Each chart in this appendix diagrams the relationships of the personnel involved in one of the cases or family histories presented in the preceding text. Most of the personages in a specific case are related, and the reciprocal roles of kin are often of major importance in the unfolding of events. Unless the structure of the kinship network is made clear, it is difficult to understand what happens and why. A kinship chart is by far the most effective way to present a pattern of relationships.

The charts are not meant to show all the people who are or have been members of a lineage. In most cases, the genealogies are truncated. Genealogical information was collected in the field using the standard method first described by Rivers (1971: 52–59), modified according to circumstances and augmented by data obtained from general interviews in the 1950s and 1970s. The notation "identified by name" which appears several times in Chart I relates to Rivers' genealog-

ical method, that is, the use of names in the collection of kinship terminology and genealogical information.

Some features of the charts, especially the ages of individuals in early generations, involve reckoning backward from relatively firm contemporary data. This task starts with our censuses of families when we asked the age of each individual, which could then be converted into an approximate date of birth. Working backward from these dates and taking into account such factors as average life expectancies, the prime reproductive years, and differences in the ages of husbands and wives where known, it was possible to estimate the year of birth of deceased persons and, as a corollary, the intervals between generations. Average life expectancies prior to about 1900 are based on all-India figures; for the 20th century, specific data from the Delhi region and Punjab are used.

This procedure must be used with caution. Distortion is likely from the application of an all-India figure, or even regional figures, to a single village. Moreover, trends in life expectancy are not necessarily smooth but subject to noteworthy short-term changes owing to epidemics, war, famine, and turbulence, as for example, the influenza pandemic of 1918–19, the more than two-decade epidemic of plague that began in 1896, and the major famines of the 1890s. The effects of such calamities can be somewhat different even over relatively small areas.

We used the procedure first with the largest and deepest genealogies, those of Merchant, Muslim, Priest (Chap. 12) and Old Fever (Chap. 13). Neither genealogy could be handled in a single diagram as could all the other cases except that of the Breakup of Old Brahman Lane. Merchant, Muslim, Priest required four charts (nos. 1.1–1.4) and Old Fever, three (nos. 2.1–2.3). Generation I, the oldest that could be recalled by informants, dates to about the beginning of the 19th century. Generation VII is the most recent. All the charts give approximate years of birth and death when known, gender, the number and sequence of spouses, deceased individuals significant in a particular case study, and sometimes the number of miscarriages, again when such information seems pertinent. The same pseudonyms are used as in the text.

In general, the genealogies tend to overrepresent males in the early generations, for North India is patrilineal. Men are better remembered because lineage affiliation and inheritance are traced through them and residence after marriage is virilocal and usually patrilocal. For later generations, data about women were routinely collected in our census interviews.

The genealogies suggest a massive population increase since the early 19th century. To a large extent, this impression is an artifact of the diagrams. The genealogies begin with a single person or couple and trace all or most descendants. The result is a pyramid with a large base. Moreover, informants selectively forget. They remember much more easily their own children than the siblings of great grandparents. However, there has been population increase, even if not to the extent indicated by the kinship charts, based chiefly on the control of epidemics and famine since the 1920s. Once influenza and plague had run their course and the threat of famine was greatly reduced, conditions were favorable for population increase. Somewhat later, smallpox and cholera ceased to be menaces, and vaccines could control measles and pertussis.

Such public health advances are part of the reason that population increase is one of the major contemporary problems of India. Despite the introduction of family planning and fertility control in the 1960s, India's annual rate of population increase is still over 2 percent (Ray, 1989: 27). From the late 1950s to the late 1970s, the population of Shanti Nagar grew by 65 percent.

CODING

The charts use conventions which are generally standard. Triangles denote males, circles represent females, and squares are used for persons of unidentified gender. Vertical and horizontal lines indicate consanguineal relationships between and within generations, respectively. A set of siblings of the same gender is diagrammed in descending order of age, the eldest at the left. Generations are identified by a roman numeral at the right of the chart. An X between a male and a female symbolizes marriage or a union with a levirate spouse.

Numbers beneath symbols identify individuals. Numbers are used in sequence from 1 to n, proceeding from left to right and from top to bottom of each chart. A single symbol may represent more than one individual, in which case a number inside the symbol gives the total. For example, a circle with a "three" inside means three females. Sequential numbers under the symbol continue to be used in such cases.

The letter "L" inside a circle indicates a levirate spouse. She is numbered sequentially with her first husband and the same number is given her as a levirate wife. That is, she appears twice in a chart, once with each husband, but only a single number is used to denote her. A triangle followed by an X and a circle and then another X and another circle indicates that a man took a second wife when his first wife died. An "E" between a male and female denotes an engagement. "M" inside a symbol is used for a miscarriage. A notation such as (1860–?) means that the individual was born in 1860 and has died, but the date of death is unknown. The absence of information in the captions concerning any individual diagrammed in the charts indicates that we lack additional data.

The abbreviation MG means "married, gone to husband(s)." The standard abbreviations, b. meaning "born," d. meaning "died" and c meaning "about" are used with dates.

CONNECTED CHARTS FOR MERCHANT, MUSLIM, PRIEST

This genealogy covers seven generations and 140 individuals. It requires four charts to diagram this many people. The charts are numbered and titled as follows:

Chart 1.1: Merchant, Muslim, Priest: Ancestral Generations.
Chart 1.2: Merchant, Muslim, Priest: Raconteur, His Brothers, Their Families, and Descendants.
Chart 1.3: Merchant, Muslim, Priest: Progenitor, Gentle Soul, Their Families, and Descendants.
Chart 1.4: Merchant, Muslim, Priest: Dead Issue, End of a Line of Descent.

Although four separate charts are used, the numbering system is continuous in order to show that the four charts are integrated into a single master chart. The basic connecting links among the charts are the males numbered 9, 10, and 11 in Chart 1.1. The people in Chart 1.2 are descended from no. 9, therefore that man carries the same number both in charts 1.1 and 1.2. The individuals in Chart 1.3 are descended from no. 10, and that man is identified by no. 10 in both 1.1 and 1.4. A similar situation obtains for the man marked no. 11. The numbering for Generation V is continous across charts 1.2, 1.3, and 1.4. The last number in Generation IV of Chart 1.1 is 13. Thus, the first number of Generation V, Chart 1.2 is 14 and the last number is 20. The first number of Generation V in 1.3 is 21 and the last number is 25. The first number of Generation V, Chart 1.4, is 26. The numbering system for generations VI and VII is similar. For example, the last number in Generation V is 45 (Chart 1.4); this means that the first number of Generation VI (Chart 1.2) is 46.

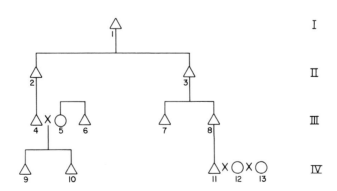

Chart 1.1. Merchant, Muslim, Priest: Ancestral Generations (cf. Chap. 12: Merchant, Muslim, Priest).
Generation I: (1) first known ancestor.
Generation II: (2) Merchant, b. c1815–1820, died some years before 1876, (3) identified by name.
Generation III: (4) husband of Old Priest's sister (1858–?), (5) sister of Old Priest (1860–?), (6) Old Priest (1866–1962), (7) died without issue, (8) identified by name.
Generation IV: (9) died before 1958, (10) died before 1958, (11) identified by name, (12, 13) no information.

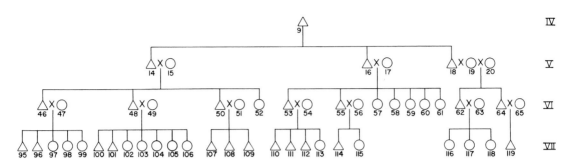

Chart 1.2. Merchant, Muslim, Priest: Raconteur, His Brothers, Their Families, and Descendants (cf. Chap. 12: Merchant, Muslim, Priest).

Generation IV: (**9**) the same man as no. 9 on Chart 1.1, **NB**, nos. 10–13 are on Chart 1.1.

Generation V: (**14**) Raconteur, b. 1898, (**15**) (1903–64), (**16**) Lieutenant, b. 1912, (**17**) Mrs. Lieutenant, b. 1923, (**18**) Security Officer, b. 1921, (**19**) (c1923–?), died without issue, (**20**) (1924–48), **NB**, nos. 21–25 are on Chart 1.3; nos. 26–45 are on Chart 1.4.

Generation VI: (**46**) Guard, b. 1928, (**47**) b. 1933, (**48**) Conductor, b. 1937, (**49**) b. 1941, (**50**) b. 1940, with wife (**51**) and children 107–109 in South India, 1977–78, (**52**) b. 1953, MG, (**53**) New Priest, b. 1941, (**54**) b. 1942, (**55**) b. 1943, (**56**) b. 1949, (**57**) b. 1933, MG, (**58**) b. 1938, MG, (**59**) b. 1946, MG, (**60**) b. 1949, MG, (**61**) b. 1952, MG, (**62**) Physician, b. 1945, (**63**) Nurse, b. 1949, (**64**) Young Lawyer, b. 1948, (**65**) Mrs. Young Lawyer, b. 1953, **NB**, nos. 66–93 are on Chart 1.3; no. 94 is on Chart 1.4.

Generation VII: (**95**) b. 1962, (**96**) b. 1966, (**97**) b. 1952, MG, (**98**) b. 1955, married but not gone to husband, (**99**) b. 1958, (**100**) (1970–78), (**101**) b. 1972, (**102**) b. 1962, (**103**) (1963–63), infant death, (**104**) b. 1968, (**105**) (1966–74), (**106**) b. 1968, (**107-109**) in South India with parents, nos. 50, 51, (**110**) b. 1962, (**111**) b. 1970, (**112**) b. 1976, (**113**) b. 1965, (**114**) b. 1976, (**115**) b. 1974, (**116, 117**) b. 1970 are twins, (**118**) b. 1976, (**119**) b. 1976.

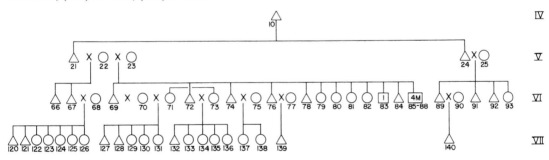

Chart 1.3. Merchant, Muslim, Priest: Progenitor, Gentle Soul, Their Families, and Descendants (cf. Chap. 12: Merchant, Muslim, Priest).

Generation IV: (**10**) the same man as no. 10 in Chart 1.1, **NB**, nos. 11–13 are on Chart 1.4; nos. 14–20 are on Chart 1.2.

Generation V: (**21**) Progenitor, b. 1906, (**22**) (1909–33 or 1934) committed suicide in main village well because of infant's death, (**23**) Fertility, b. 1917, (**24**) Gentle Soul, b. 1913, (**25**) b. 1923, **NB**, nos. 26–45 are on Chart 1.4; nos. 46–65 are on Chart 1.2.

Generation VI: (**66**) Cowherd (1927–lst half of 1960s), (**67**) Fence Sitter, b. 1932, (**68**) Mrs. Fence Sitter, b. 1936, (**69**) Luck, b. 1937, (**70**) committed suicide in main village well, (**71**) b. 1937, sister of no. 73, (**72**) Policeman, b. 1940, (**73**) b. 1945, (**74**) b. 1951, (**75**) b. 1952, (**76**) b. 1952, out of country 1978, (**77**) b. 1957, (**78**) b. 1955, (**79**) b. 1939, MG, (**80**) b. 1941, MG, (**81**) b. 1944, MG, (**82**) (1948–73), (**83**) infant death, (**84**) infant death, age 2, (**85-88**) 4 miscarriages, (**89**) b. 1947, (**90**) b. 1952, (**91**) b. 1951, (**92**) b. 1958, (**93**) Love Song, b. 1954, **NB**, no. 94 is on Chart 1.4; nos. 95–119 are on Chart 1.2.

Generation VII: (**120**) b. 1960, (**121**) b. 1963, (**122**) b. 1953, MG, (**123**) b. 1955, MG, (**124**) (1959–59) infant death, (**125**) b. 1966, (**126**) b. 1969, (**127**) b. 1960, (**128**) b. 1969, (**129**) b. 1963, (**130**) b. 1960, (**131**) b. 1971, (**132**) b. 1962, (**133**) b. 1966, (**134**) b. 1970, (**135**) b. 1972, (**136**) b. 1978, (**137**) b. 1973, (**138**) b. 1975, (**139**) b. 1976, (**140**) b. 1975.

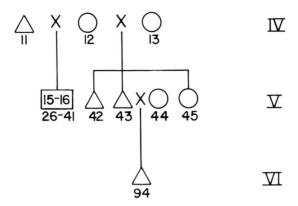

Chart 1.4.   Merchant, Muslim, Priest: Dead Issue, End of a Line of Descent (cf. Chap. 12: Merchant, Muslim, Priest).

Generation IV: (**11, 12, and 13**) the same people as nos. 11, 12, and 13 in Chart 1.1, **NB**, nos. 14–20 are in Chart 1.2; nos. 21–25 are in Chart 1.3.

Generation V: (**26-41**) died as infants, (**42**) d. 1940s, never married because one-eyed, (**43**) Dead Issue, he and infant son (no. 94) died in 1947 to end the line of descent, (**44**) Strong Minded, b. 1927, widow of no. 43, remarried to One Eyed, (Chart 10.1; Chap. 21), (**45**) MG, **NB**, nos. 46–65 are in Chart 1.2; nos. 66–93 are in Chart 1.3.

Generation VI: (**94**) d. 1947.

CONNECTED CHARTS
FOR OLD FEVER

This genealogy covers seven generations and 109 individuals. Three separate but related charts are needed to handle this many people. The charts are numbered and titled as follows:

Chart 2.1: Old Fever: Ancestral Generations.

Chart 2.2: Old Fever: Senior Branch of Lineage.

Chart 2.3: Old Fever: Junior Branch of Lineage.

As in the case of Merchant, Muslim, Priest, the numbering system is continuous in order to show that the three charts are integrated into a single master chart. The connecting links among the charts are the males numbered 8 and 12 in Chart 2.1. The people in Chart 2.2 are descended from no. 8, therefore that man carries the same number both in charts 2.1 and 2.2. The individuals in Chart 2.3 are descended from no. 12, and that man is identified by no. 12 in both 2.1 and 2.3. The numbering for Generation IV is continuous across charts 2.2, and 2.3. The last number in Generation III of Chart 2.1 is 12. Thus, the first number of Generation IV, Chart 2.2 is 13 and the last number is 20. The first number of Generation IV in 2.3 is 21 and the last number is 28. The numbering system for generations V and VI is similar. For example, the last number in Generation IV is 28 (Chart 2.3); this means that the first number of Generation V (Chart 2.2) is 29. Note that Old Fever, a Jat lineage, has three levirate marriages. The wives appear twice on the charts but retain a single identification number, the one that they were assigned on the basis of their first husband. Thus, the woman labeled 22 in Chart 2.3 appears at both the left and far right of Generation VI.

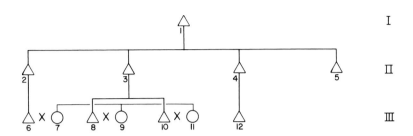

Chart 2.1.   Old Fever: Ancestral Generations (cf. Chap. 13: Old Fever).

Generation I: (**1**) first known ancestor.

Generation II: (**2, 3, 4**) no further information, (**5**) died without issue.

Generation III: (**6**) Old Groom (1884–1924), died without issue, (**7**) Dancer (1903–late 1960s or early 1970s), died without issue, (**8**) Capable (1877–1918), (**9**) Sparrow (1880–1925 to 1930), (**10**) Fateful (1883 to 1st decade of 20th century), (**11**) Long Lived (1887–1978), died without issue, (7,9,11) sisters, (**12**) no further information.

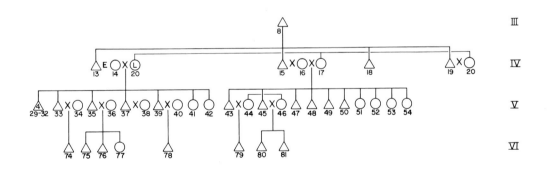

Chart 2.2.   Old Fever: Senior Branch of Lineage (cf. Chap. 13: Old Fever).

Generation III: (**8**) the same man as no. 8 in Chart 2.1, **NB**, nos. 9–12 are on Chart 2.1.

Generation IV: (**13**) Forceful, b. 1897, (**14**) died as child, (**15**) Taciturn, b. 1903, (**16**) died without issue, (**17**) Timely, b. 1927, sister of no. 20, (**18**) died in childhood, (**19**) Ill Fated (1907–25), died without issue, (**20**) Felicity, b. 1912, sister of no. 17, after death of no. 19 became levirate spouse of no. 13, never mated with no. 19, **NB**, nos. 21–28 are on Chart 2.3.

Generation V: (**29–32**) four infant deaths, (**33**) Politico, b. 1938, (**34**) Mrs. Politico, b. 1938, (**35**) b. 1945, in Army 1977–78, (**36**) b. 1952, (**37**) b. 1954, (**38**) b. 1960, (**39**) b. 1957, (**40**) b. 1956, (**41**) b. 1945, MG, (**42**) b. 1955, MG, (**43**) Troubled, b. 1949, (**44**) Mrs. Troubled, b. 1952, (**45**) Friendly, b. 1951, (**46**) Mrs. Friendly, b. 1954, (**47**) Athlete, b. 1953, (**48**) b. 1959, (**49**) b. 1967, (**50**) b. 1969, (**51**) (1947–78) MG, died of TB, (**52**) b. 1956, MG, (**53**) b. 1962, (**54**) b. 1965, **NB**, nos. 55–73 are on Chart 2.3.

Generation VI: (**74**) b. 1965, (**75**) b. 1971, (**76**) b. 1977, (**77**) b. 1974, (**78**) b. 1977, (**79**) b. 1971, (**80**) b. 1974, (**81**) b. 1977.

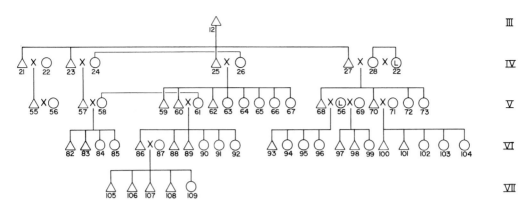

Chart 2.3.   Old Fever: Junior Branch of Lineage (cf. Chap. 13: Old Fever).

Generation III: **(12)** the same man as no. 12 in Chart 2.1, **NB**, nos. 13–20 are on Chart 2.2.

Generation IV: **(21)** Unknown (1889–1934), **(22)** Scapegoat (1898–1958), who after death of no. 21 became levirate spouse of no. 27 whose wife **(28)** was her sister, committed suicide in main village well after her son **(55)** died, **(23)** Jabberer (1892–1932), **(24)** (1903–74), **(25)** Old Codger, b. 1898, **(26)** Amiable (1898–1974), **(27)** Curmudgeon, b. 1900, **(28)** (1904–1960s or early 1970s, **NB**, nos. 29–54 are on Chart 2.2.

Generation V: **(55)** (1925–46), died without issue, **(56)** Misfortune, b. 1928, after death of no. 55 became levirate spouse of Soldier **(68)**, **(57)** Reformer, b. 1932, posthumous son of no. 23, **(58)** Mrs. Reformer, b. 1933, **(59)** died age 5 before 1956, **(60)** Barker, b. 1927, **(61)** Mrs. Barker, b. 1931, **(62)** died age 3, **(63)** (1918–76), **(64)** b. 1921, MG, **(65)** b. 1932, MG, **(66)** b. 1935, MG, **(67)** b. 1938, MG, **(68)** Soldier (1933–79), **(69)** Concubine, 2nd mate or wife of no. 68, **(70)** Cattleman, b. 1942, **(71)** b. 1947, **(72)** b. 1923, MG, **(73)** b. 1929, MG, **NB**, nos. 74–81 are on Chart 2.2.

Generation VI: **(82)** b. 1958, **(83)** b. 1966, **(84)** b. 1955, MG, **(85)** b. 1962, **(86)** b. 1951, **(87)** b. 1953, **(88)** b. 1953, **(89)** b. 1961, **(90)** b. 1948, MG, **(91)** (1959–59), infant death, **(92)** infant death, **(93)** Little Boy (1955–58), **(94)** b. 1953, MG, **(95)** b. 1957, MG, **(96)** b. 1963, **(97)** b. 1970, **(98)** b. 1971, **(99)** b. 1973, **(100)** b. 1969, **(101)** b. 1976, **(102)** b. 1962, **(103)** b. 1965, **(104)** b. 1973.

Generation VII: **(105)** b. 1971, **(106)** (1973–73) died premature birth, **(107)** (1974–74) died premature birth, **(108)** b. 1977, **(109)** (1972–72) died premature birth.

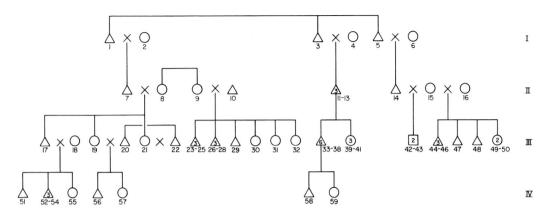

Chart 3.   A Ghost Took My Son (cf. Chap. 14: Death of Children).

Generation I: (1) grandfather of Teacher, elder brother of nos. 3 and 5, (2) widow of no. 1, died after 1959, (3) Snakebite Curer, b. 1898, senile in 1977–78, (4) d. 1939, (5, 6) died before 1958.

Generation II: (7) d. 1945, 7 months before birth of Teacher, (8) b. 1918, (9) b. 1923, (10) Affine, (1924–80), (11–13) sons of Snakebite Curer, (14) Plowman, b. 1913, parents died when he was a small child, raised by Snakebite Curer, (15) died young, became a ghost, same *gotra* as Plowman but different *shasan*, (16) b. 1928.

Generation III: (17) Teacher, b. posthumously 1945. (18) Truthful, b. 1949, her first child, a son (no. 51), taken by a ghost, (19) MG, (21) MG, (23) (1943–45), (24) (1946–47), (25) (1948–48), (26) b. 1955, (27) b. 1958, (28) b. 1960, [nos. 26–28 living in Delhi in 1977–78], (29) b. 1949, living on father's land in Uttar Pradesh, (30) (1946–47), (31) b. 1949, MG, (32) b. 1965, living with teacher in 1978, (42–43) died as infants, (44–46) died at birth, (48) died at birth.

Generation IV: (51) (1967–67), taken by ghost 15–16 days after birth, (56) b. 1960, lives with Teacher and Truthful, (57) b. 1966, lives with Teacher and Truthful, (58, 59) children of one of six men, nos. 33–38.

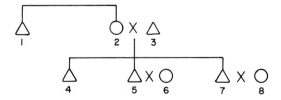

Chart 4.   The Newcomers (cf. Chap. 15: Death of Adults, An Attempted Murder or Suicide). (1) member of Gola Potters' lineage in Shanti Nagar, deceased, (2) deceased, (3) a widower, (5) Newcomer and his brothers (nos. 4 and 7) alleged to have tried to murder no. 8, (6) Mrs. Newcomer, (8) alleged victim of failed murder plot or suicide attempt or accident.

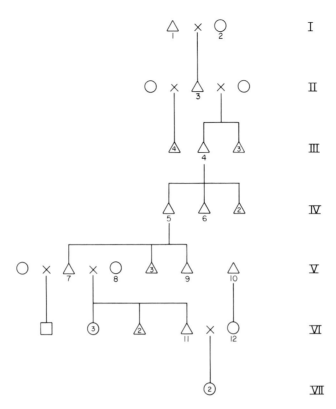

Chart 5.   The Headless Sweeper in a Line of Hereditary Exorcists (cf. Chap. 16: The Headless Sweeper in a Line of Hereditary Exorcists).

Generation 1: (1) Banjara, never lived in the village but took a Sweeper wife (2).

Generation II: (3) Founder.

Generation III: (4) Headless Sweeper, died during plague epidemic.

Generation IV: (5) Absent Son, (6) Old Survivor (c1878–after 1959).

Generation V: (7) Lord of Ghosts (1898–1974), (8) Lady of Ghosts, b. 1903–08, died before 1974, (9) Eluded, b. 1917, (10) Siyana.

Generation VI: (11) Good Natured, b. 1934, (12) Timid, b. 1935.

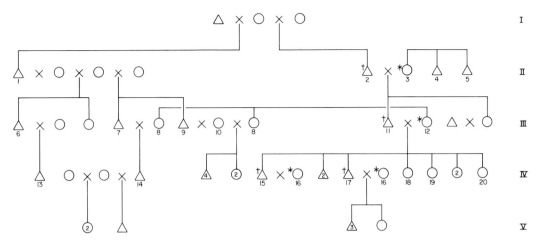

Chart 6. Three Wives and Four Husbands. The three wives are identified by asterisks; the four husbands by daggers (cf. Chap. 19: Three Wives and Four Husbands).

Generation II: (1) Bad Temper (1887–1945), (2) Moneylender (1893–1945), (3) Honesty (1895–1967), (4) Lambardar (before 1880–1946 or 1947), (5) Old Soldier (1882–1966).

Generation III: (6) Nondescript, died late 1940s, (7) Driven Mad, b. 1923, (8) Fomenter, b. c1923, sister of no. 12, wife of no. 7, later mate of no. 9, (9) Close Mouth, b. 1925, (10) first wife of no. 9, became a ghost, (11) Manipulator, b. 1915, (12) Mrs. Manipulator, b. 1915.

Generation IV: (13) No Trouble, b. 1933, (14) Unfortunate (1942–78), (15) College Man (1939–67), first husband of no. 16, (16) City Girl, b. 1946, wife of no. 15 and then of no. 17, (17) Tricky, b. 1946, 2nd husband of no. 16, (18) Forthright, b. 1936, (19) Bright, b. 1947, (20) Baby, b. 1956.

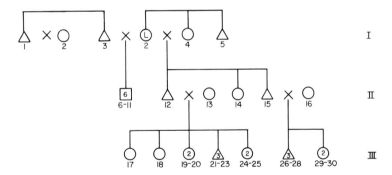

Chart 7. The Bairagis: Watchman, Fearful, Handsome, and Delicate Flower (cf. Chap. 20: First and Second Wives).

Generation I: (1) 1893–1911 or 1912, twin brother of no. 3, died without issue, became a ghost, (2) d. 1919, sister of no. 4, widow of no. 1, then levirate spouse of no. 3 for whom she bore 6 infants who died [she and her 6 infants became ghosts], (3) Watchman, b. 1893, twin of no. 1, (4) Fearful, b. 1903, sister of no. 2, (5) Handsome, d. 1956, became a ghost.

Generation II: (6–11) b. and d. 1911–19, became ghosts, (12) Family Man, b. 1926, (13) Atheist I, b. 1933, (14) Delicate Flower (1937–51) epileptic, died without issue, became a ghost, (15) b. 1941, youngest son of Fearful and Watchman, married after 1959.

Generation III: (17) Pink Flower, b. 1945, wedded in 1959, (18) Jolly, b. 1949, wedded in 1959, (19–20) both born after 1958, (21–30) all 10 persons born after 1959.

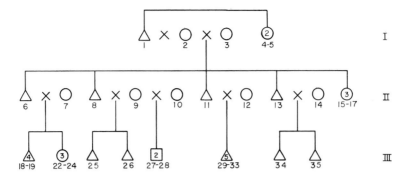

Chart 8.   The Lohar Blacksmiths: Sorrowful and Difficult (cf. Chap. 20: First and Second Wives).

Generation I: (1) Sorrowful, b. c1908, (2) first wife of Sorrowful (1913–25), committed suicide in main well, became a ghost, (3) Difficult, b. c1908, 2nd wife of Sorrowful, (4–5) probably died in childhood.

Generation II: (6) b. 1934–35, village blacksmith, (7) b. 1941–42, (8) Urbanite, b. 1936, had ghost illness and recovered; after 1958 he and nuclear family lived in city, (9) first wife of Urbanite, d. 1956 after birth of second infant, became a ghost, (10) b. 1936, 2nd wife of Urbanite, (11) b. 1944, in 1977 commuted to work in city, separated from parents, (12) b. 1946, (13) Clerk, b. 1950, (14) Mrs. Clerk, b. 1955–56, (15–17) all MG, the youngest, b. 1946, had ghost lllness and recovered.

Generation III: (18–24) no information, (25) Sprightly, b. 1954, (26) (1956–56) died when mother died, (27–28) both childhood deaths, (29–33) no information, (34) (c1975–78), (35) b. 1977.

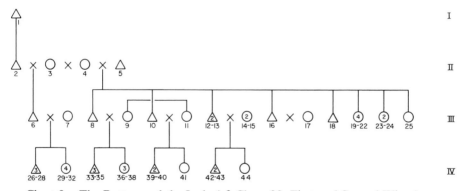

Chart 9.   The Potters and the Lady (cf. Chap. 20: First and Second Wives).

Generation I: (1) first known ancestor of the Insiders, the patrilineage from no. 1 through nos. 2 and 6 to nos. 26–28 with wives and daughters.

Generation II: (2) died after marriage to 2nd wife, no. 4, (3) first wife of no 2, died of dread disease, became ghost known as The Lady, (4) b. c1917, 2nd wife of no. 2, stepmother of no. 6 [when no. 2 died, she married Outsider, no. 5, and became Mrs. Outsider; her stepson was raised by his grandfather], (5) Outsider, b. c1912, 2nd husband of no. 4.

Generation III: (6) Insider, b. 1931 or 1932, (8) Eldest Son, b. c1944, possessed by The Lady in 1958 after his wedding but before first mating, (9) b. c1947, (10) b. 1946, wedded at same time as no. 8, (11) b. 1950, (12) b. 1950, (13) b. 1952, (14) b. 1953, (15) b. 1957, (16) Younger Son, b. 1956, possessed in 1977–78 by The Lady, (17) b. 1960, (18) b. 1964, (19–22) all born before 1959 and MG, (23, 24) twins b. 1958, one died, the other MG, (25) b. 1964. For the many children of Generation IV, no further information given here.

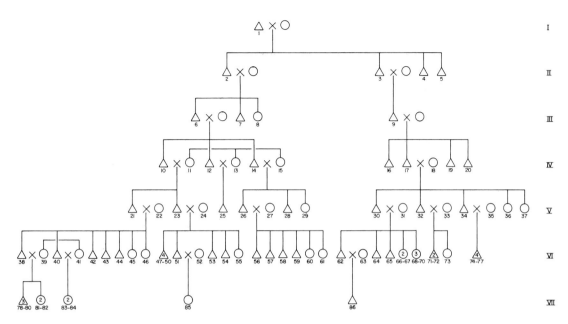

Chart 10.1. Breakup of Old Brahman Lane: Lineage of the Three Brothers and Old Bachelor (cf. Chap. 21: Breakup of Old Brahman Lane.)

Generation I: (**1**) first named ancestor.

Generation II: (**4, 5**) both died without issue, became ghosts.

Generation III: (**6**) eldest son of no. 2, (**7**) died without issue, became a ghost, (**8**) taken care of by no. 12 in city after no. 7, her brother, died, then died without issue and became a ghost.

Generation IV: (**10**) Senior (1893–1975), (**11**) Mrs. Senior, d. 1943, became a ghost, (**12**) Withdrawn, b. 1903, possessions in 1940s–70s, (**13**) d. 1943 of TB after death of her infant son, no. 25, and became a ghost, (**14**) Junior, b. 1908, (**15**) Mrs. Junior, b. 1923, (**16**) died without issue, (**17**) Zilidar, d. 1930s, (**18**) Pure Goddess, b. c1899, widow of no. 17, (**19**) died without issue, became a ghost, (**20**) Old Bachelor, b. 1908–10, d. 1976–77, a lifelong celibate, took care of Pure Goddess and children after his brother's death.

Generation V: (**21**) One Eyed, b. 1923, 2nd husband of Strong Minded, (**22**) Strong Minded, b. 1927, widow of Dead Issue of Merchant-Muslim-Priest lineage, (**23**) Talkative, b. 1928, (**24**) Mrs. Talkative, b. c1930, (**25**) died at birth, (**26**) Dr. John, b. 1938–39, (**27**) Mrs. Dr. John, b. 1940–41, (**28**) Student Doctor also called Atheist III, b. 1952, (**29**) married with 2 children, lived with in-laws in city in 1977–78, (**30**) Trusted Employee, b. 1925, (**31**) b. 1929, (**32**) Police Inspector, b. 1935; in China, 1977–78, (**33**) b. 1937, (**34**) Story Teller, b. 1934, (**35**) Mrs. Story Teller, b. 1941, (**36**) (1934–37) twin sister of no. 34, (**37**) MG, her 13-year-old son lived with Pure Goddess and attended school.

Generation VI: (**38**) b. 1947, (**39**) b. 1949, (**40**) b. 1952, (**41**) b. 1951–52, sister of no. 39, (**42**) b. 1956, married in 1978 to a sister of nos. 39 and 41, (**43**) b. 1961, ghost possession before marriage in 1978, (**44**) b. 1965, (**45**) alive in 1958, died sometime before 1977, (**46**) b. 1960, wedded in 1978, (**47–50**) all four died shortly after birth, (**51**) b. 1954, (**52**) b. 1956, (**53**) Gabbler, b. 1959, (**54**) b. 1962, (**55**) b. 1967, (**56**) b. 1959, (**57**) b. 1965, at age 4 possessed by Vishnu Devi, (**58**) b. 1972, going to Catholic nursery school, (**59**) b. 1974, had polio, (**60**) b. 1961, wedded in 1978, (**61**) b. 1968, (**62**) b. 1952, lawyer living in Trusted Employee's apartment in city, (**63**) telephone operator [a sister of no. 62 also works as a telephone operator and lives with nos. 62 and 63 in Trusted Employee's city apartment], (**64**) b. 1957, (**65**) b. 1964, (**66**) b. 1953, MG, (**67**) b. 1955, telephone operator, MG, (**68**) College Girl, b. 1959, (**69**) b. 1961, (**70**) b. 1965, (**71**) b. 1958, (**72**) b. 1961, (**73**) b. 1955, MG, (**74–77**) b. 1961, 1963, 1965, 1969.

Generation VII: (**78–80**) b. 1967, 1972, 1974, (**81–82**) b. 1969, 1977, (**83–84**) b. 1974, 1977, (**85**) b. 1976, (**86**) b. 1974.

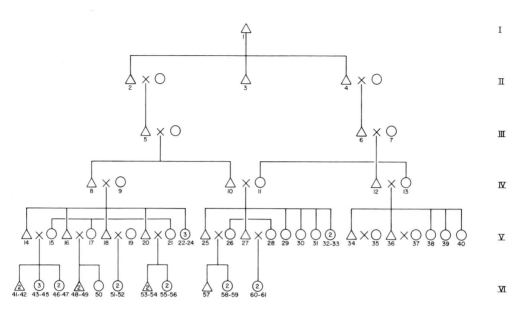

Chart 10.2.   Breakup of Old Brahman Lane: Lineage of Old Grandfather (cf. Chap. 21: Breakup of Old Brahman Lane).

Generation I: (**1**) first named ancestor.

Generation II: (**2**) grandfather of Householder, (**3**) died without issue, became a ghost, (**4**) grandfather of Indecisive.

Generation III: (**5**) Old Grandfather (of the lineage) (1878–before 1977), (**6**) d. 1917–18 before birth of Indecisive, no. 12, (**7**) Inauspicious (1888–before 1977), widow of no. 6.

Generation IV: (**8**) Householder (1907–77), (**9**) Mrs. Householder, b. 1907, living with sons nos. 14 and 20, (**10**) Justice, b. 1917, (**11**) b. 1922, sister of no. 13, (**12**) Indecisive, b. posthumously 1917–18, defective vision in one eye, retired railway employee in 1977, (**13**) Adulteress, b. 1924.

Generation V: (**14**) Earnest, b. 1927, (**15**) Mrs. Earnest, b. 1932, went into possession-trance and prophesied, (**16**) b. 1931, worked in city, (**18**) b. 1939, tax accountant in city where he lived, (**20**) b. 1949–50, lived jointly with Earnest, no. 14, worked as an electrician in city, commuted, (**21**) b. 1951–52, nos. 15, 17 and 21 are sisters, (**22–24**) MG, (**25**) b. 1945, military service, 1977–78, (**26**) b. c1952, (**27**) b. 1948, served in air force, (**28**) b. 1954, sister of no. 26, (**29**) Illusion (1943–58), killed by Justice, became a ghost, haunted village in 1977–78, (**30**) b. 1961, wedded but not yet mated in 1978, (**31**) b. 1963, wedded but not mated, (**32–33**) MG, (**34**) b. 1941, impregnated Illusion, no. 29, which led to her death, then married a city girl and left village permanently, (**36**) b. c1956, trained as pipe fitter but no job in 1977–78 so farmed family land, (**37**) b. c1957–1958, (**38**) MG, (**39**) b. 1957, (**40**) b. c1959, wedded but not mated in 1978.

Generation VI: (**43–45**) MG, (**50**) Beauty, b. 1961 [at age 12 she was possessed by ghost of husband who died of TB when he was 12, possessions for 3 years, remarried 1978].

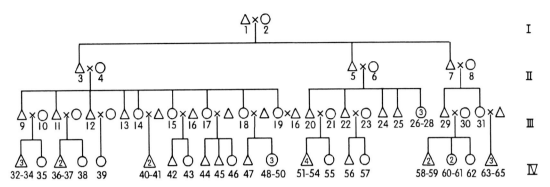

Chart 11.   Widows, Patriarchs, Twins (cf. Chap. 22: Ghost Attacks and Possessions of Jats).
Generation I: (1) died before 1944, (2) Matriarch (c1888–1967).
Generation II: (3) Patriarch, b. 1907, former taxi driver, then farmer, (4) Mrs. Patriarch, b. 1917, (5) Benevolent (1918–76), (6) Mrs. Benevolent (1918–76), (7) Short Life (1920–44), (8) Widow-in-Between, b. 1923.
Generation III: (9) b. 1936, military service ending in 1958; clerk in Delhi, 1977, (10) b. 1947, (11) b. 1947, clerk in Govt. Press, 1977, (12) (1952–78), electrician, worked in city, died of food poisoning, (13) b. 1955, B.A. in physical training, unemployed, 1977, (14) (1938–?) MG, died in childbirth, (15) (1941–?) MG, died of Fever, (16) after death of no. 15, married Patriarch's youngest daughter, no. 19, (17) Morning Star, b. 1943, twin of Evening Star, no. 18, MG [ghost possessions 1974–78, in 1977–78, she, her daughter, and her youngest son stayed with the Patriarchs while she was being treated for ghost possessions, her daughter, Pragmatic, lived with the Patriarchs because of her mother's possessions], (18) Evening Star (1943–76), MG, died of pneumonia, twin of Morning Star [her 7-year-old daughter lived with the Patriarchs, her son and two other daughters lived with their father], (19) b. 1951, took care of the children of nos. 15 and 16 when their mother died, then married their widowed father, (20) b. 1941, head of family after Benevolent's death, clerk in Delhi post office in 1977, (21) b. 1943, (22) b. 1945, (23) b. 1943, (24) (1958–58) died of tetanus neonatorum, (25) b. 1960, (26) b. 1943, MG, (27) b. 1950, MG, (28) b. 1961, MG, (29) Only Heir (1943–76), killed in accident one month before death of Evening Star, (30) Widow III, b. 1947, (31) Resourceful, b. 1942, ghost possessions at age 8 and at *Gauna*.
Generation IV: (32) b. 1960, (33) b. 1963, (34) b. 1965, (35) Beloved, b. 1958, (36) b. 1973, (37) b. 1977, (38) b. 1972, (39) b. 1977, (44) living with father in 1977–78, (45) b. 1973, living with mother and Patriarchs in 1977–78, (46) Pragmatic, b. 1964, lived with Patriarchs since 1974 when her mother's possessions began, (47) living with father, mother dead, (48–50) one daughter with the Patriarchs, the other two with father, (51) b. 1960, (52) b. 1962, (53) b. 1967, (54) b. 1971, (55) b. 1964, (56) b. 1971, (57) b. 1968, (58) b. 1965, (59) b. 1967, (60) b. 1970, (61) b. 1972, (62) born posthumously 1976 to Widow III, (63–65) 3 sons of Resourceful, no. 31, lived with Widow III, no. 30.

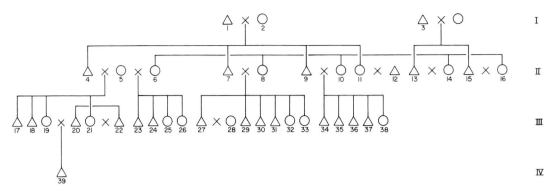

Chart 12. Hairless, Haunted, Immature (cf. Chap. 23: Hairless, Haunted, Immature).

Generation I: (1) (1898–1977), (2) died before 1958, (3) Siyana, father of sons nos. 13 and 15 [married to sisters nos. 14 and 16, who are also sisters of nos. 6, 8, 10], with sons, daughters-in-law, etc., he did not live in Shanti Nagar.

Generation II: (4) Government Worker, b. 1927, (5) Hairless (1940–67), ghost of first wife of no. 4, (6) Haunted, b. 1941, 2nd wife of no. 4 [afflicted by ghost of first wife, Hairless, in previous marriage Haunted's infants died shortly after birth], (7) Security Guard, b. 1937, (8) Worrier, (9) Parcelman, b. 1942, (10) Go-Between, (11) MG.

Generation III: (17) b. 1960, (18) b. 1962, (19) b. 1951, MG, (21) b. 1955, MG, (23) b. 1970, (24) b. 1973 [a third son was born to nos. 5 and 6 and died in a hospital in 1979], (25) b. 1968, (26) (1976–78), died of typhoid, (27) Constable, b. 1954, (28) Immature, b. 1960, ghost possessions, (29) b. 1960, (30) b. 1969, (31) b. 1971, (32) b. 1966, (33) b. 1975, (34) b. 1962, (35) b. 1965, (36) b. 1968, (37) b. 1973, (38) b. 1970.

Generation IV: (39) died about age 4 to 5, fell ill with Fever (ergo ghost illness) while mother was visiting her natal village; boy died after returning to father's village.

APPENDIX IV: MAPS

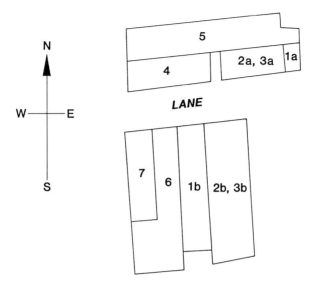

Map 1.   Properties of the Two Lineages in 1958–59: Old Fever and Merchant, Muslim, Priest (cf. Chap. 12: Merchant, Muslim, Priest and Chap. 13: Old Fever).

Coding: Family properties are designated by numbers that refer to the pseudonyms of family heads. The small *a* and *b* that follow some numbers denote *ghar*s and *gher*s, respectively. The *ghar* is where the women live. A family's *gher*, which shelters cattle and serves as a storage shed, may also be combined with a *baithak*, rooms for men. In some cases, a family has only a single building which then serves as *ghar*, *gher*, and *baithak*.

Old Fever lineage. 1a, 1b: Curmudgeon; 2a, 2b: Old Codger; 3a, 3b: Reformer; 4: Taciturn; 5: Forceful.

Merchant, Muslim, Priest lineage. 6: Raconteur; 7: Gentle Soul.

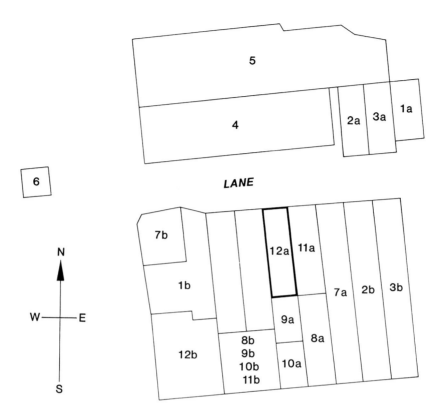

Map 2.   Properties of the Two Lineages in 1977–78: Old Fever and Merchant, Muslim, Priest (cf. Chap. 12: Merchant, Muslim, Priest and Chap. 13: Old Fever).

Coding: same as in Map. 1.

Old Fever lineage. **1a**, **1b**: Curmudgeon and Cattleman; **2a**, **2b**: Old Codger and Barker; **3a**, **3b**: Reformer; **4**: Taciturn; **5**: Forceful; **6**: Troubled; **7a**, **7b**: Soldier, son of Curmudgeon.

Merchant, Muslim, Priest lineage: **8a**, **8b**: Raconteur and Conductor; **9a**, **9b**: New Priest, son of Lieutenant; **10a**, **10b**: youngest son of Lieutenant; **11a**, **11b**: Young Lawyer, son of Security Officer; **12a**, **12b**: Gentle Soul.

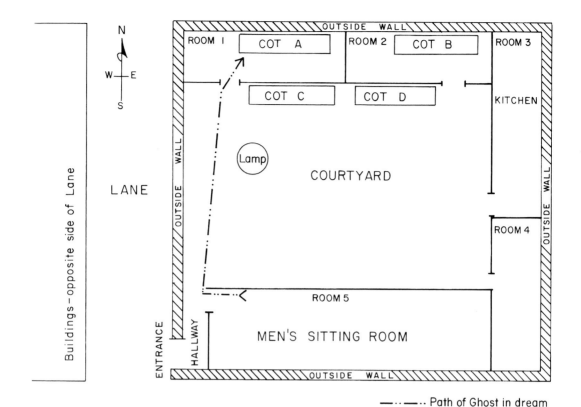

— ·· — ·· Path of Ghost in dream

Map 3. Dwelling of Truthful and Teacher Described in "A Ghost Took My Son" (cf. Chap. 14). Room 1: where Truthful slept with her infant son on Cot A; Room 2: where one of Truthful's sisters-in-law slept on Cot B; Room 3: kitchen; Room 4: room of Truthful's mother-in-law; Room 5: *baithak*, men's sitting room where Affine slept; Hallway: entrance from lane to *baithak* (Room 5) and courtyard; Courtyard: oil lamp, which ghost put out by waving his arm; Cot C where Truthful's mother-in-law slept; Cot D where another sister-in-law slept.

Lane outside dwelling: mainly inhabited by Brahmans.

Dotted Line from Room 5 to Hallway and across courtyard to Room 1 where Truthful and infant slept indicates the ghost's path. In 1978, Truthful and others were interviewed in the courtyard.

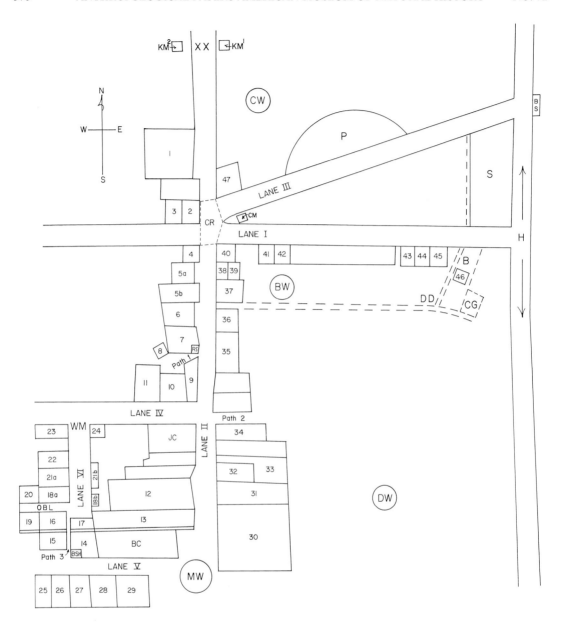

Map 4:   Crossroads, Pond, Cremation Grounds, Buildings, and Other Places Associated with Ghosts.
    To understand better the history of the village layout and its association with ghosts, some details are added to the locations to help the reader recall the associations. The village is outlined and divided by the highway (H) on the east, by major lanes, and by paths. The map is highlighted by places associated with ghosts, which are identified by letter codes. Buildings are numbered sequentially with information about their owners. Reference is frequently made to chapters in the text.

Lanes in Map 4

Lane I: An east-west lane running from the highway (H) westward to the crossroads (CR) and then through the compounds of the Chuhras, Chamars, and Gola Potters. Buildings east of the crossroads are the properties of the Jats, Bairagis, Lohars, Brahmans, and Malis.
Lane II: North-south main village lane on east side of the village, originally occupied by the first Jat settlers; most buildings still belong to Jats.

Lane III: a mostly uninhabited diagonal lane from the highway (H) and bus stop (BS) passing by the school (S) and pond (P) and forming the crossroads (CR) with lanes I and II.

Lane IV: An east-west lane from Lane II through the high-caste side of the village to the western edge of the village habitation site.

Lane V: Recent east-west lane, also called New Brahman Lane, inhabited by Brahmans.

Lane VI: short lane running south from Lane IV to a dead end at building no. 17. Inhabited by Brahmans and Jats.

Old Brahman Lane (OBL): a short, very old lane from Lane VI to a dead end at buildings 19 and 20, inhabited by descendants of the first Brahman settlers (Chap. 15: Illusion's Death).

Paths in Map 4

Three small paths were used by villagers as shortcuts.

Path 1: connects Lane II with the Chuhra Sweeper and Chamar Leatherworker compounds.

Path 2: provides easy access from Lanes II and IV to the fields lying east of the village.

Path 3: a very narrow path connecting Old Brahman Lane and New Brahman Lane (Lane V), used by Story Teller in 1977–78 as a shortcut to the then empty building (no. 16), formerly occupied by Old Bachelor's joint family (Chap. 21: Breakup of Old Brahman Lane).

Places in Map 4

The list of places is arranged geographically from east to west, starting with the locations lying near the highway (H), then sites in the vicinity of the crossroads (CR), followed by outlying sites south and north, and then the places west of Lane II and south of the Ration Shop and Path I.

H: Highway, runs north-south on eastern edge of village.

BS: Bus stop, located at the intersection of Lane III and the highway (H), used by most villagers.

S: School located on west side of the highway (H) between Lanes I and III.

B: Mali's *bagh* (garden) where the Malis also had their house, located just west of the intersection of Lane I and the highway (H).

CG: Cremation grounds, located near the intersection of Lane I and the highway (H), adjacent to the Malis' *bagh*. The cremation grounds and the Malis' garden were places where ghosts danced at night (Chap. 10: Jat Children).

DD: Drainage ditch where Fearful fell when trying to jump across it to pilfer fruit from the Mali's garden (B) (Chap. 20: The Bairagis: Fearful, Handsome, and Delicate Flower). The dotted lines mark the ditch which parallels Lane I from Lane II almost to the highway (H) with a branch northward to Lane 1.

P: Pond, located on Lane III, where Whose Daughter drowned (Chap. 14: The Ghost of Whose Daughter, and Chap. 22: Little Goddess).

CR: Crossroads formed by lanes I, II, and III, and indicated by dotted lines. A place where ghosts were believed to linger (Chap. 10: Jat Children; Chap. 11: Ghosthood).

CM: Shrine of Crossroads Mother Goddess, a small square at the vertex of the angle formed by Lane I and Lane III where they meet at the crossroads (CR). At the site, the shrine is marked by a brick.

BW: Bairagi well, where Little Bride's body was deposited by Chamar servants after she was killed by Young Groom and Passion Flower. Located in fields between the intersection of Lane I and Lane II and the drainage ditch (DD) (Chap. 15: Little Bride).

CW: Chamar well in field between the pond (P) and Lane II where Tippler drowned his first wife (Chap. 15: Tippler's First Wife).

DW: Dissembler's well, where the daughter of Dissembler, found Housewife's body. Located in Dissembler's fields between his house (31) and the highway (H) (Chap. 15: Murder or Suicide).

KM1: Shrine of Kanti Mata, Goddess of Typhoid. Located just east of Lane II at the northern edge of the village.

KM2: Shrine of Kali Mata, Goddess of Death and Destruction. Located just west of Lane II at the northern edge of the village.

XX: Grave of the Headless Sweeper, located north of the village buildings on Lane II between KM1 and KM2 (Chap. 16: The Headless Sweeper in a Line of Hereditary Exorcists).

RS: Ration shop, located in building no. 7 at intersection of Lane II and Path 1.

JC: Jat *chopal* (caste meeting house) used for panchayats and to house wedding guests. It served as the village school in the 1950s. Located at the intersection of Lane II and Lane IV.

BC: Brahman *chopal* used principally for panchayats, some nuptial ceremonies, and to house wedding guests, located at the intersection of Lane II and Lane V.

MW: Main well where high-caste women drew water and a number committed suicide. Located at intersection of Lane II and Lane V (Chap. 15: Death of Adults).

BSh: Bhumiya shrine for the founding ancestor of the village. Maintained by Brahmans, it was visited at weddings, and offerings were left there at births of humans and cattle. The shrine was located in a very small area at the intersection of Lane V and Path 3.

WM: Where Woodsman was killed at intersection of Lanes IV and VI (Chap. 15: Brother vs. Brother).

Buildings and Properties in Map 4

Sequential numbering begins with the northernmost building on the west side of Lane II, runs down the west side of Lane II to Lane V and the Brahman *chopal*, turns west to Path 3 and then northward along Path 3 and Lane VI to Lane IV (no. 24). The numbering then jumps back to the southwesternmost property on Lane V (no. 25), next east to Lane II and the main village well, north on the east side of Lane II to Lane I (no. 40), east to the highway (H) and no. 46, and then jumps back westward to no. 47 at the corner of Lane II and Lane III.

1. House of Woodsman (Chap. 15: Brother vs. Brother).
2. *Ghar* of One Eyed and family from Old Brahman Lane (Chap. 21).
3. *Ghar* of Junior, Dr. John, and family, from Old Brahman Lane. Second story above no. 2 (Chap. 21).
4. House of Sad Memories' grandson and family (Chap. 14).
5a, 5b. *Ghar* and *gher* respectively of Farmer, father, and family (Chap. 22).
6. House of three Jat widows (Chap. 22).
7. *Ghar* of the Benevolents' sons (Chap. 22).
8. *Ghar* of Eluded (Chap. 16).
9. *Gher* of Tippler and Rival's widow.
10. Tippler's *ghar*.
11. Rival's widow's *ghar* (for nos. 9, 10, and 11, see Chap. 15: Tippler's First Wife).
12. House of Young Groom, his second wife and children (Chap. 15: Little Bride).
13. Mahar Potter's *ghar* (Chap. 15: Suicides and Questionable Deaths).
14. *Ghar* of Police Inspector where his mother, Pure Goddess, lived (Chap. 21: New Brahman Lane).
15. *Ghar* of Trusted Employee (Chap. 21: New Brahman Lane).
16. Story Teller's building, empty in 1977–78; in 1958–59 inhabited by joint family of Old Bachelor (Chap. 21).
17. Progenitor's *ghar* (Chap. 12).
18a, 18b. Talkative's *ghar* and *gher*. In 1958–59 joint family of Senior, Withdrawn, and Junior lived in 18a whose entrance was on Lane VI. In 1977–78, only Talkative lived there and his *gher* (18b) was opposite 18a on east side of Lane VI (Chap. 21).
19, 20. *Ghar* and *gher* of Indecisive, Adulteress, and their children (Chaps. 15: Illusion's Death; 21: Beauty).
21a, 21b. *Ghar* and *gher* of Schemer in 1958–59. By 1977–78, property divided between Favorite and Marketeer, Schemer's eldest and youngest sons (Chap. 15: Brother vs. Brother).
22. *Ghar* of Actor.
23. Patriarchs' *ghar*, entrance on Lane IV (Chap. 22).
24. *Ghar* of family of Faithful and Shy (Chap. 10. Jat Children).
25. *Ghar* of Justice (Chaps. 15: Illusion's Death; 21: Beauty).
26. *Ghar* of Beauty's father (Chap. 21: Beauty).
27. *Ghar* of Mrs. Householder, Earnest and Mrs. Earnest, et al. (Chap. 21: Mrs. Earnest).
28. *Ghar* of next to youngest son of the Householders (Chap. 21).
29. House of Story Teller (Chaps. 18: Brahmans as Exorcists and Curers; 21: New Brahman Lane).
30. This large building of the Authorities was divided into separate apartments, *ghars*, *ghers*, and *baithak* (Chap. 15: Rule of Authority).
31. *Ghar*, *gher*, and *baithak* of Dissembler (Chap. 15).
32. *Ghar* of Devious (Chap. 15: Little Bride).
33. *Gher* of Army Officer (Chap. 15: Little Bride).
34. Building divided into separate apartments for sons of Progenitor: Fence Sitter, Luck, Policeman (Chap. 12).
35. *Ghar* of Politician (Chap. 15: Brother vs. Brother).
36. *Baithak* and *gher* of Patriarch (Chap. 22).
37. *Baithak* and *gher* of Politician (Chap. 15).

38. Shop of Little Goddess's father (for nos. 38, 39, and 40, cf. Chaps. 14: The Ghost of Whose Daughter; 22: Little Goddess).

39. *Ghar* of Little Goddess's Family, upper story.

40. *Gher* of father and grandfather of Little Goddess.

41. Former *ghar* of Mali Gardeners, used by them in 1977–78 as a potting shed and storehouse.

42. House where Fearful and her youngest son's family lived in 1958–59 and 1977–78. No. 42 and a row of buildings represented by the long blank rectangle eastward up to no. 43 was where most of the Bairagis and Lohars lived in 1977–78 (Chap. 20: The Bairagis).

43. *Gher* of Junior and Dr. John (Chap. 21).

44. *Gher* of Talkative, who lived on Lane VI (18a) and had another *gher* (18b) on the east side of Lane VI (Chap. 21).

45. *Gher* of One-Eyed and Withdrawn in 1978 (Chap. 21: Withdrawn's Interview).

46. House of Malis in their garden (B) (Chap. 10: Jat Children).

47. *Ghar* of Army Officer, where his wife, Passion Flower, lived in 1977–78 (Chap. 15: Little Bride).

APPENDIX V: CALENDRIC EVENTS

The dates of most of the calendric events listed below in table 3 are set by the Hindu lunisolar calendar that is used in Shanti Nagar for ceremonial purposes. The dates of a few holidays follow the Gregorian calendar and the Indian National Calendar, adopted in 1957; both are solar and used for civil purposes. The ancient lunisolar calendar, adopted about 1181 B.C., uses two modes of computing the length of the year. One is the sidereal year of about 365 days, measured with respect to fixed stars. It is the time taken by the sun to pass through the 12 signs of the zodiac. The other is the lunar year of about 354 days, consisting of 12 lunar months (the synodic period of the moon) of roughly 29.5 solar days. The month is divided into fortnights of approximately 15 days. The first fortnight begins with the dark (*badi*) half of the month when the moon is waning and therefore ends with the dark night of the moon (new moon), Amavas. The second fortnight is the bright (*sudi*) fortnight when the moon is waxing. It therefore ends with the full moon, Purinmashi. Dates of the lunisolar ceremonial calendar are designated by month, fortnight, and day. For example, Chaitra *badi* 1 is the first day of the first fortnight of the month of Chaitra. In the next fortnight, the bright fortnight, the first day is designated as Chaitra *sudi* 1.

The new moon (Amavas) and the full moon (Purinmashi) are observed ceremonially every month. Amavas is considered inauspicious so on the day following the dark night men and bullocks rest. Widows and widowers, sometimes accompanied by family members, go to the Yamuna River to take a dip. On Purinmashi people may fast all day and offer grain and water to the moon when it rises. Three other days may be observed ceremonially in every month in Shanti Nagar, observance usually depending on caste and on an individual's chosen deity (*ishta devata*). All three are in the bright fortnight. Ashtami (eighth) is for Rama, Krishna, or Durga, and Ekadashi (eleventh) is Vishnu's day. Mangalvar (Tuesday), named after the planet Mars, is observed on any Tuesday of a bright fortnight for Rama's lieutenant, Hanuman, the monkey god. Mangalvar is noted in table 3 only the first time that it occurs, in Chaitra. For the few who worship Shiva, his birthday is celebrated in the dark fortnight, Phalgun *badi* 14.

Although a month begins with the *badi* fortnight and ends with the *sudi* fortnight, the lunisolar year ends with the last day of the *badi* fortnight of Chaitra. The new year then begins with Chaitra *sudi* 1, the first day of the second fortnight of Chaitra. Thus, table 3 that lists dates and ceremonial events begins with

Chaitra *sudi* 1 and ends with Chaitra Amavas, the 15th day of the dark fortnight.

A complexity in the lunisolar calendar derives from the difference between the lunar year of 354 days and the solar year of 365 days and the need to correlate them. The difference must be adjusted periodically, which is done chiefly by adding and deleting months. Such an adjustment takes place every two-and-a-half to three years. When we were in Shanti Nagar in 1958–59, an additional month of Shrawan was inserted between the fortnights of Shrawan. The inserted month was called *adhika* (added) Shrawan and the other Shrawan was called *nija* (true) Shrawan. Table 3 is based chiefly on our work in Shanti Nagar in 1958–59, hence the added month is shown in the table. For more information, consult Sewell and Dikshit (1896), Underhill (1921), and R. Freed and S. Freed (1964).

TABLE 3

YEARLY CYCLE OF CALENDRIC EVENTS

Date	Calendric Event
Chaitra (March–April)	
sudi 1	New year.
sudi 8	Devi ki Karahi (The Cooking Pot of the Goddess), also known as Durga Ashtami. In Shanti Nagar only Kumhars worship Durga on every bright eighth.
sudi 11	Ekadashi (an eleventh), a monthly fast day observed by Brahmans for Vishnu.
Purinmashi	Full moon, a monthly all-day fast. Water and grains are offered to the moon when it rises.
	Mangalvar (Tuesday). This weekday of every bright fortnight is for Hanuman, the monkey god. One may fast, feed monkeys, and light a lamp for worship.
Baisakh (April–May)	
badi 9	Baisakhi (Spring Festival), a civil holiday which occurred on Chaitra 23 of the Indian National Calendar in 1958.
Amavas	The day following the night of the new moon is a day of rest for men and bullocks. Widows and wid-

owers may bathe in the Yamuna River.

Purinmashi	Full moon.
Jyesth (May–June)	
badi 10	Jyesth ka Dusehra (the tenth of Jyesth), which occurs after the wheat harvest when one may go to the Ganges River or Yamuna River to bathe in honor of the rivers.
Amavas	New moon.
sudi 11	Nirjala Ekadashi (Waterless Eleventh), a special eleventh when Brahmans fast and do not drink water. They may eat melons in the afternoon and give presents of fruits and fans.
Purinmashi	Full moon.
Asharh (June–July)	
badi 1–15	Many marriages occur in this fortnight.
Amavas	New moon.
sudi 11	The gods go to sleep before the rains start, when muddy roads make travel difficult, and no marriages should occur until the gods awake in Karttik. This is a major eleventh but the only observance is the usual fast. Because improved roads have made travel easier, not everyone today observes the tabu on marriages until the gods awake.
Purinmashi	Full moon.
Shrawan (July–August)	
Nija badi 1	Swings are hung from trees prior to celebrating Tijo.
Amavas	New moon.
Adhika sudi 3	Tijo (Third), festival of swings. Young girls and women dress in their best clothes and swing and sing. Presents are sent to daughters and daughters-in-law. In some areas this festival is associated with Radha and Krishna.
Adhika badi Nija sudi Purinmashi	Rakhi Bandhan (Charm Tying), also known as Salono for the nymph of the month of Shrawan. Sisters tie charms on their brothers' wrists; Brahman priests tie them on the wrists of their clients, and employees tie them on the wrists of their employers.

Bhadrapad (August–September)

badi 8
Janamashtami (Birth Eighth), celebration of the birth of Krishna, avatar of Vishnu.

badi 9
Guga Naumi (Guga's Ninth), for birth of Guga Pir, who may have lived in the tenth century A.D., and was said to have miraculous power over snakes. He was a Hindu but after his death became a popular Muslim saint because he had converted to Islam and buried himself alive.

Amavas
New moon.

sudi 2
Budh ki Duj (Old Man's Second), a minor festival in honor of a local hermit who achieved some renown as a holy man. A minor regional celebration.

Purinmashi
See Ashvin *badi* 1 below.

Ashvin (September–October)

badi 1
Akhta, a cattle curing festival, which began in the evening of Bhadrapad *sudi* 14 and continued for the next two days, Purinmashi and Ashvin *badi* 1. It is held from sundown on a Friday to noon of the following Sunday only when an epidemic of cattle disease occurs (cf. R. Freed and S. Freed, 1966).

badi 1–*sudi* 1
Shraddha (Ancestor Worship). Also known as Kanagat. Commemorates ancestors. The first 15 days are celebrated by Brahmans; the 16th day is celebrated by Shudras and is used to commemorate any ancestor omitted in the first 15 days.

Amavas
New moon

sudi 1–*sudi* 9
Sanjhi, the name of the festival, is the name of a young married woman. The festival is also known as Navratra, Nine Nights, for it is celebrated for nine nights preceding Dusehra and the Ram Lila. There is some ambiguity regarding Sanjhi, but probably she is associated with the goddess, Durga, who in the Ramayana helped Rama defeat Ravan. The festival reflects the practice of a young married woman visiting her parents and after nine nights returning to her husband and in-laws. Figures of Sanjhi and a small child, probably her sister, are displayed on a wall. A third figure,

added later, represents her brother who will accompany her to her husband. The figures are removed on *sudi* 8–9 and, except for Sanjhi's face, thrown into the village pond. In the evening, all the faces are placed in pots with lighted candles and floated on the village pond.

sudi 10
Dusehra (The Tenth) marks the victorious return of Rama from Lanka (now Sri Lanka) (cf. Ramayana, Append. II).

Purinmashi
Full moon.

Karttik (October–November)

badi 1
From the first to end of this month, girls rise early in the morning and go singing to the well where they bathe. By the late 1970s when girls had more freedom, they went to the Yamuna River for a dip.

badi 3
Karva Cauth (Pitcher Fourth). Although the name of the festival suggests that it is observed on the fourth, it is celebrated on the third because the fourth is inauspicious. Women observe a day of fasting to prevent widowhood. Celebrated only by women of twice-born castes in Shanti Nagar.

badi 7
Hoi (a mother goddess) worshipped for the welfare and protection of children.

badi 13
Dhan Teras (Wealth Thirteenth), one of the days preceding the celebration of Diwali. One may buy new dishes in preparation for Diwali.

badi 14
Giri or Giriri, the day preceding Diwali when one cleans and whitewashes the house.

Amavas
Diwali (The Festival of Lights). In the evening candles or lamps are lit inside and outside the house. Brahmans and Baniyas close their accounts and worship Lakshmi, Goddess of Fortune, and then they feast. In 1977, some electric lights were lit.

sudi 1
Gobardhan (Cowdung Wealth), celebrated by everyone in the village. A figure of a man is made of cowdung, and the male members in a family worship him. This festival derives from Krishna worship.

sudi 2
Bhai Duj (Brother Second). On this

day a sister places a barley sheaf behind her brother's ear and cooks food for him. He gives her money. The day formerly commemorated the relationship between the fraternal twin deities, Yama and Yami, who later became the river Yamuna.

sudi 11   Dev Uthani Gyas (Gods Awakening Eleventh). A major eleventh when there is feasting and weddings again take place.

Purinmashi   Ganga Nahan (Bathing in the Ganges), a time of pilgrimage to the Ganges.

Margashirsh (November–December)

No Hindu events are observed except Amavas and Purinmashi, but The Big Days, the Christmas holidays, are civil holidays for government workers. Dates set by Gregorian Calendar.

Paush (December–January)

Makara Sankranti, the winter solstice. It may fall in Paush or Margashirsh. Daughters-in-law give presents to their in-laws. Amavas and Purinmashi are observed as usual.

Magh (January–February)

Republic Day, date determined by the Indian National Calendar on Magh 6; on January 16 of the Gregorian Calendar. Amavas and Purinmashi, as usual.

Phalgun (February–March)

badi 14   Shivaratri (Shiva's Night), commemorating Shiva's birthday.

Amavas   Pre-Holi skits begin and continue nightly until Holi.

sudi 11   Amla Sinchan Gyas (Amla Watering Eleventh), an *ekadashi* celebrated by women of the Brahman, Baniya, Bairagi, Lohar, and Jhinvar castes. The Amla plant commemorates Parasurama, an avatar of Vishnu.

Purinmashi   Holi (a saturnalia). A bonfire is lit with the rising of the moon at night. Holi is linked with the story of Prahlad and his father's sister, Holikah. Prahlad was a devotee of Vishnu.

Chaitra (March–April)

badi 1   Dulhendi (second day of Holi celebration). Colored water is sprayed on everyone; people play pranks (called playing Holi) and beat each other with sticks.

badi 7   Sili Sat (Cold Seventh). This day is also known as Sitala ki Saptami (Sitala's Seventh) and Basora (Stale Bread Festival). Sitala is the goddess of smallpox. With the decline of smallpox, this day now celebrates all the mother goddesses who bring poxes. They are worshipped for the welfare of children.

Amavas   New moon and mid-month of Chaitra, the last day of the luni-solar year.

APPENDIX VI: THE HEALTH OPINION SURVEY (HOS)

The Health Opinion Survey (HOS), devised by Allister Macmillan and developed by Alexander Leighton and associates, consists of 20 questions about physiological responses of the body to stress. It was first applied in Leighton's study of Stirling County in the United States. The responses to each question are scored from 3 (high stress) to 1 (low stress), and the total score across the 20 questions measures an individual's stress. Subscores can be derived to measure anxiety and depression from the following 12 questions. Questions 2, 3, 4, 8, 9, and 17 probe anxiety. Depression is measured by the subscore for questions 5, 13, 16, 18, 19, and 20. Total scores of 20 to 29 are within normal limits of stress; scores of 30 to 34 indicate borderline stress; scores of 35 and above indicate too much stress. However, a total score of 35 is close to a score of 34 and should be so considered (Crane and Angrosino, 1974: 135–142).

For use cross-culturally, the test must be translated into the local language. Although tests can be scored by someone who is unfamiliar with the respondents, one must know something of their lives and their culture in order to understand the reasons for a test score showing, say, excessive stress. Some individuals tolerate stress better than others; nonetheless certain common situations (illness, new relationships after a change of status) are stressful and usually produce physiological responses that are reflected in the scores.

The initial Hindi translation of the HOS that was worked out with our research assistants was tested with a few people before it was used in our survey. Reformer (cf. Old Fever, Chap. 13) was chosen as one of the key villagers to test how well the questions would be understood because he was highly intelligent, had lived in the village all his life, was completely familiar with village idiom, had a good idea of what we were trying to accomplish, and was sympathetic with our study.

A sample of 66 individuals responded to the HOS. The sample was not randomly chosen, for we planned no statistical analysis for which such a sample would be needed. Instead, we selected individuals from our 1977–78 village census, taking into account age, gender, and caste. We wanted an equal number of males and females representing a wide range of ages and most of the village castes in rough proportion to their populations. Ages ranged from 19 to 70 years, with the exception of three Jat children, two girls (ages 10 and 13) and one boy (age 8). We distributed our respondents, other than the three children, by age in terms of three groups: 19–30, 31–49, and 50–70. Caste representation ranged from 18 Jats, the largest village caste with 385 members, to one Carpenter, the next to smallest caste with only three members resident in the village.

Because the HOS survey was planned and carried out before the epidemics of ghost possessions and malaria in 1978, the project was not influenced by the ghost research. However, the following individuals, identified by pseudonyms, who participated in the HOS survey also have been discussed in this study of ghosts. They are therefore listed in Table 4, by caste, with their scores.

QUESTIONNAIRE

1. Do you have any physical or health problems at the present?
   3. Yes   1. No

2. Do your hands tremble enough to bother you?
   3. Often   2. Sometimes   1. Never

3. Are you troubled by your hands or feet sweating so that they feel damp and clammy?
   3. Often   2. Sometimes   1. Never

4. Are you bothered by your heart beating hard?
   3. Often   2. Sometimes   1. Never

5. Do you tend to feel tired in the morning?
   3. Often   2. Sometimes   1. Never

6. Do you have any trouble getting to sleep or staying asleep?
   3. Often   2. Sometimes   1. Never

7. How often are you bothered by having an upset stomach?
   3. Often   2. Sometimes   1. Never

8. Are you bothered by nightmares (dreams that frighten or upset you)?
   3. Often   2. Sometimes   1. Never

9. Are you troubled by "cold sweats"?
   3. Often   2. Sometimes   1. Never

10. Do you feel that you are bothered by all sorts (different kinds) of ailments in different parts of your body?
    3. Often   2. Sometimes   1. Never

11. Do you smoke?
    3. Often   2. Sometimes   1. Never

12. Do you have loss of appetite?
    3. Often   2. Sometimes   1. Never

13. Does ill health affect the amount of work (or housework) that you do?
    3. Often   2. Sometimes   1. Never

14. Do you feel weak all over?
    3. Often   2. Sometimes   1. Never

15. Do you have spells of dizziness?
    3. Often   2. Sometimes   1. Never

16. Do you tend to lose weight when you worry?
    3. Often   2. Sometimes   1. Never

17. Are you bothered by shortness of breath when you are not exerting yourself?
    3. Often   2. Sometimes   1. Never

18. Do you feel healthy enough to carry out the things that you would like to do?
    1. Often   2. Sometimes   3. Never

19. Do you feel in good spirits?
    1. Often   2. Sometimes   3. Never

20. Do you sometimes wonder if anything is worthwhile anymore?
    3. Often   2. Sometimes   1. Never

TABLE 4
Health Opinion Survey (HOS) Selected Scores

Individual[a]	Age	Anxiety	Depression	Total
Brahman				
1) Bruised Flower (f)	ca. 55	16	13	51
2) City Girl (f)	31	7	11	30
3) Conductor (m)	40	6	10	26
Chhipi Dyer				
4) Wife of Chhipi Tailor (f)	52	8	11	34
Gola Potter				
5) Mother of baby girl killed by mother-in-law or son (f)	29–30	10	12	38
Jat				
6) Felicity (f)	64–65	8	8	33
7) Little Charmer (m)	8	10	8	32
8) Faithful (f)	10	10	8	32
9) Pragmatic (f)	13	8	6	24
10) Mrs. Patriarch (f)	60	7	8	29
11) Second Wife of Young Groom (f)	34	10	8	32
Nai Barber				
12) Home Trained (m)	27	6	7	22

The "Score" header spans the Anxiety, Depression, and Total columns.

[a] Caste, pseudonym, and sex (m = male, f = female) are given.

APPENDIX VII: DAILY TEMPERATURES, MARCH–APRIL 1978

The temperatures used here were those reported for Delhi in the newspapers. Shanti Nagar is close to Delhi and the terrain between city and village is flat with little difference in elevation. The reading for Delhi would closely approximate temperatures in Shanti Nagar.

Date	Temperatures		Date	Temperatures	
	°C	°F		°C	°F
3/3	26	78.8	4/7	34	93.2
3/14	Temperature not obtained		4/10	37	98.6
	but cooler than usual.		4/11	37.8	100
3/15	29	84.2	4/12	38.3	100.9
3/16	27	80.6	4/13	38.7	101.7
3/17	29	84.2	4/14	40.2	104.4
3/21	27.7	81.8	4/16	37	98.6
3/22	28.2	82.5	4/18	35.3	95.5†
3/23	27.4	81.3	4/19	35	95
3/28	32.5	90.5	4/20	35.1	95.3
3/29	30.5	86.9	4/21	37	98.6
3/31	30.5	86.9	4/25	34.8	94.6
4/3	28.3	82.9*	4/26	38.3	100.9
4/4	31.5	88.7	4/27	39.6	103.3
4/5	30.1	86.2	4/28	40	104
4//6	32.1	89.8			

* Weather cooler due to storm.
† Lightning and shower in evening.

INDEX AND GLOSSARY

NOTE: Asian words, mainly Hindi and Sanskrit, contained in *Webster's Third New International Dictionary, Unabridged*, are not italicized in the index. Unitalicized words also include ceremonies, deities, and commonly used terms, such as lambardar. Brief definitions are given for all Asian words. Fuller definitions can be found in the text. Pseudonyms are listed in this index with gender (M = male; F = female) and caste indicated for each.

aan (obligation), 201, 205
abortion, 127
  amniocentesis-cum-abortion, 41–42
  carrot seeds, use of, 304
  Government promulgation of, 51
  induced, 126
  spontaneous, 126, 127, 132
Absent Son (M, Chuhra), 181, 183
action, rebirth, and release cycle, 63–69, 71
Actor (M, Jat), 41, 163–164, 168, 173, 197, 257, 287
Adulteress (F, Brahman), 160, 161–162, 257–258, 272
Advocate (M, Jat), 169
afara (indigestion; wind in the stomach), 119
Affine (M, Brahman), 134, 135, 137, 139–140, 141
affines, rules regarding, 140
agni (fire), 34
Agni (God of Fire), 34, 194–195
Agnivesa, 47
Ajit Singh, ruler of Mewar, 35
Akbar, emperor, 35, 197
akhta (a tree), 72
Akhta (cattle-curing ceremony), 39, 56, 114, 204, 207
Alam II, Shah, 23
alcoholic beverages, 153, 155
alienation, 188
All-India Act of 1870, 39, 40
All India Medical Institute, 76
Amavas (new moon), 68, 106, 373, 374–376
Ambedkar, B. R., 57
Amiable (F, Jat), 113, 115, 125, 274, 291
amrta (beverage-of-immortality), 34
amulet, 51, 65, 102, 208, 210–211
ancestral ghosts, 106, 127. *See also* pitri (semi-divine ancestor)
Angrezi (English) medicine, 51–53, 118
anna (1/16th of a rupee), 193
anxiety, 231–232, 244
  tremors in state of, 296
Aranyakas (forest books), 347, 348–349
Ari (enemy mantra), 351
Arjuna (character from Mahabharata), 71, 81, 349
Army Officer (M, Jat), 158
Arya Samaj (reform sect of Hinduism), 9, 22, 49, 55–56, 57, 62, 74, 77, 273, 291
  denial of ghost beliefs, 107

interviews with followers of, 58–60
  multiple deities, disbelief in, 312
  worshipping or commemorating the dead, beliefs regarding, 106
ashes used to cure ghost illness, 272, 283, 284, 286, 295, 306
ashram (religious retreat), 52, 87, 109, 112, 204, 206
Ashtami (Eighth), 373
Aslesha (a lunar mansion), 348
astrology, 70–71
asura (genie), 217
atelectasis, 138
Atharva-Veda, 46, 56, 312, 348
Atheist I (F, Bairagi), 60–61, 237, 240, 250
Atheist II, also called Mrs. Illusionist (F, Chamar), 61
Atheist III, also known as Student Doctor (M, Brahman), 61
Athlete (M, Jat), 108
atman (soul), 15, 17
  as ghost, 17
Aurangzeb, emperor, 35
Authority, Mrs. (F, Jat), 63, 168, 169, 173, 185, 286
Authority (M, Jat), 168–170
avatar (incarnation), 58, 65, 154, 210, 350
average life expectancy, 24
ayah (wet nurse), 55
Ayurveda (system of medicine based on Ayurvedic Samhitas (texts)), 9, 44–45, 46–49
  diseases peculiar to children, theory as to cause of, 49
  food classification, 47, 110
  gunas (qualities) theory, 47–48
  hereditary diseases, 49, 104
  Laws of Manu and hereditary diseases, 49
  madness and possession, categories of, 48–49
  mental diseases, classification of, 48
Ayurvedic Samhitas, 44, 47

babaji (respected elder), 185, 215
Baby (F, Brahman), 224, 227, 230, 232, 233
Bachchal, Queen (character in Guga Pir story), 178–179
bad actions, 18, 168
  child's death attributed to actions in past lives, 126

past actions, ghosthood attributed to, 161
soul and, 175
youth as excuse for, 158
badi (dark fortnight), 373, 374–376
Bad Seed, Mrs. (F, chamar), 191
Bad Seed (M, Chamar), 191
Bad Temper (M, Brahman), 213, 214, 218, 233
bagh (garden), 371
Bairagi Mendicant Priests, 235
baithak (men's sitting room), 76, 77, 122, 146, 151, 367, 372
bajra *kicheri* (food consisting of cooked lentils and bulrush (pearl) millet), 110
Balfour, E., 25, 35
Bali (king of genii), 217, 253
Bangle Wearer (F, Jat), 162–163, 164
Banjaras, 180, 181
banyan (a tree, *Fiscus bengalensis*), 90
Barker, Mrs. (F, Jat), 113, 115, 116–118, 245, 274, 282
    poltergeist attacks, 116–117, 118, 125, 288–289
Barker (M, Jat), 113, 114, 115, 117, 118, 119, 122–123, 123, 124, 125
    bone deterioration, 116
    disease and moral character, view on connection between, 124
    hygiene or cleanliness, discussion on, 124
basa (a tree), 72
Basak Nag (chief of snakes, character in Guga Pir story), 179
Basham, A. L., 21
batasha (a sweet), 193, 239
Baxi, U., 36, 148
BCG (Bacillus Calmette-Guérin), 123, 194
Beauty (F, Brahman), 206, 268, 270–271
    ghost possession, 271
behavior or conduct. *See* dharma (proper conduct, duty)
beheading
    Guga Pir, legend of, 178–179
    Headless Sweeper, 176–180
    in Hindu mythology, 179
    Kabandha, the Beheaded, 178
    legends associated with, 176–180
Beloved (F, Jat), 276–277
Bemata (goddess), 100–101
Benares, 8
Benevolent, Mrs. (F, Jat), 275
Benevolent (M, Jat), 172, 274, 275
benevolent ghost, 166
Bengal, Sati practice in, 35
benjamin, 100
benzoin (*Loban*), use of to cure ghost illness, 100
ber (jujuba, a fruit), 236
Berkow, R., 188, 296
Berreman, G. D., 81
berseem (Egyptian clover), 265, 267
bhabhut (holy ashes), 205, 209, 283, 284, 286, 306

bhagat (exorcist), 66, 78, 115, 119, 126, 133, 137. *See also* exorcist
    Chamars as bhagats and users of bhagats, 207–208
    types of, 183
Bhagavad Gita, 47, 61, 70, 71, 80–81, 347, 349
Bhagavata Purana, 137, 350
Bhagvan-Shiva. *See* Shiva
Bhagvan-Vishnu. *See* Vishnu
Bhagwan (God), 41, 55, 57, 58, 62, 67, 71, 72, 84, 125, 126, 136
bhagya (luck, fortune, fate), 57
Bhairava (First Physician). *See* Shiva
bhakti (devotion), 61, 70, 349, 350
bhakti-yoga (salvation through devotion), 71, 203
bhang (decoction of cannabis), 99, 153, 272
bhawishya kal (future time), 122
Bhima (character from Mahabharata), 71
bhopa (exorcist), 81. *See also* exorcist
Bhumiya (male godling), 68
bhuta (element), 48, 123
Bhutesvara (Lord of Ghosts). *See* Shiva
bhut (ghost), 20, 76–77, 80, 84, 103, 122, 125, 286
bhut *grasth* (ghost-possessed), 17, 282
bhut *kal* (past time), 122
bhut *lagna* (attacked by ghost), 17, 282
bhutonmada (ghost madness), 49
bigha (measure of land; .21 acres; .08 ha), 89, 105, 150
bin (flute), 183
biomedical differences between genders, effect on longevity, 33–34
bipolar disorders, 111, 112, 332
    treatment for, 112
biradari (brotherhood of locally resident caste mates), 148
births, 127–128
    delivery room, substances placed in, 142
    economic consequences, 131
    midwife, delivery by. *See* midwife
    multiple, 129–130, 133–134
    premature. *See* premature births
    registration of, 24–25
    stillbirths. *See* stillbirths
bitaura (stack of stored dung cakes), 279
black pepper, use of to cure ghost illness, 100, 286, 287, 292, 295, 306
Bock, P. K., 172
Bordewich, F. M., 43
Bourguignon, E., 270
Brahma, 16, 350, 352
Brahma Gayatri, 352
Brahman (the Universal Absolute), 62
Brahmanas, 348
Brahmans, 55, 56, 57, 58, 125
    alcoholic beverages as tabu, 153
    Brahman-Jat settlement, 22–23
    as exorcists and curers, 125, 204–206

Gaur Brahmans, 22
  widow, traditional role of, 160
Brahmo Samaj (reform sect of Hinduism), 35,
    56, 57
Breadstuff (M, Chuhra), ghost of, 255, 256, 265
Breakdown (M, Jat), 170
bridal suicide, 43
Bright (F, Brahman), 223–224, 226–227, 232
Bright Light (M, Chamar), 61, 200
Brihaspat (Thursday, Jupiter), 196
Brown, Dr. , 142
Bruised Flower (F, Brahman), 145, 146–147
bubonic plague, 177, 178, 336, 342
Buddhism, 57
Buddhist I (M, Chamar), 57, 66–67, 176, 287
Buddhist II (M, Chamar), 72–76, 183
  disbelief in ghosts, 192
burials of infants, 67–68
Burma, exorcists in, 201, 203
Burmese Supernaturalism (Spiro), 57
Business Man (M, Jat), 169

calendric events, 373–376
Calmette, A., 123
Capable (M, Jat), 104–105, 106, 125
  shrine of, 106, 125
Carstairs, G. M., 73–74, 81, 82, 91, 153, 186, 249,
    260, 300, 314
caste, 22–23, 55, 56, 58, 64
  exorcists, of, 46
  See also specific headings, e.g., Brahmans;
    Chuhra; Jats
cattle, dispute over trespass by, 164–165
cattle disease, 119–120
  ceremony to cure. *See Akhta* (cattle-curing cer-
    emony)
Cattleman (M, Jat), 114, 120
Cat Woman (F, Chamar), ghost of, 131–132, 236,
    242, 250
causes of death, 21, 24–31
  decline in population, 24
  disease. *See* disease as cause of death
  famine. *See* famine as cause of death
  Fever, attributed to. *See* Fever
  grief, 166
  massacres, 26
  smallpox, 29, 331
  untimely deaths, 24
  war as a cause, 25–26
Celsius, 104
cerebral malaria, 113
Chamars, 57, 63, 64, 74–76, 190, 232
  as bhagats and users of bhagats, 207–208
  hookah worship, 192
Chandrasekhar, S., 24
chapati (bread), 212
Charaka, 47, 48, 127
Charaka Samhita, 47, 48

Chhathi (Mother Sixth), 100–101
Chhipi Dyer caste, woman of, 63–64
childbearing, frequent, 108
Child Marriage Restraint Act, 212
children
  See also infants
  Ayurvedic theory as to cause of diseases in chil-
    dren, 49
  cremation of, 67–68
  death of. *See* children, death of; infants, death of
  female infanticide. *See* infanticide, female
  funeral rituals for, 144
  ghost of child, 19
  ghost possessions, 307
  inoculations, 128, 129
  Jat children, interviews with, 76–79
  souls of, 85, 126–127
  supernatural cures for illnesses, 114–115
  tuberculosis, contracting, 101
children, death of, 126–147
  age at time of death, relevance of, 126
  causes of, 128–129, 130–131
  economic consequences, 131
  tragic deaths, 133
chili peppers
  dog bites, use in treating, 111
  ghost illness, use of to cure, 100, 273, 280, 292,
    295, 306
chloroquine tablets used to treat malaria, 110–
    111, 113, 118
cholera epidemics, 28, 29, 331, 335–336, 338–339
chopal (men's meeting house), 371, 372
Chuchi Dhona (nipple-washing ceremony), 136
Chuhra Sweepers, 50–51, 58, 64, 125, 178
  founding of caste, 180, 181
churail (low-caste female ghost), 81, 82
churel (ghost of a woman who died while preg-
    nant), 83
churma (a sweet), 262
Citra-Gupta (Yama's assistant), 62
City Girl (F, Brahman), 205, 227, 228–232, 234,
    235
  ghost possessions, 229–232, 233–234
  Health Opinion Survey and, 230–231
  remarriage of, 228
  sterilization of, 229
Clark, M., 204
Clerk, Mrs. (F, Lohar), 245
Clerk (M, Lohar), 245
Close Mouth (M, Brahman), 214, 219, 220–222,
    234
College Girl (F, Brahman), 201
College Man (M, Brahman), 158, 218, 219, 224.
    227–230, 234
  ghost of, 229–230
  Hodgkin's disease, affliction with, 227
  marriage of, 227
Collins, L., 26

colonization projects, 153
coming of age, ghost possession related to, 307–308
compounders, 109, 147
Concubine (F, Jat?), 120, 121
Conductor (M, Brahman), 91, 95
Constable (M, Chamar), 200
Constitution of India, 57
cow dung, smoke of burning; use in exorcism, 209, 306
Cowherd (M, Brahman), 92, 98, 99, 100, 102, 251
Cowife I (F, Brahman), 141–142
Cowife II (F, Brahman), 142
cremation grounds, 77, 80
cremation of children, 67–68
Crooke, W., 38
Crossroads Mother Goddess, 195
cultural values, 12
Culture-Bound Syndrome, 244–245, 249
Culture-Bound Syndromes, The (Simons and Hughes), 245
Cunningham, Sir Henry, 28
curers, 51, 52, 105, 108. See also exorcists
Curmudgeon (M, Jat), 113, 114–115, 120, 122, 290
Curzon, Lord, 30

Daksha (Ritual Skill), 16, 34, 178
danava (antigod, demon), 178
Dancer (F, Jat), 104, 105, 125
Daniel, E. V., 34, 50
Daniélou, A., 80, 198
danishwari (wise, learned), 87
darshan (blessing received from viewing an eminent person), 10
daru (a liquor), 153
Dasuthan (a birth ceremony), 271
daughter-in-law vs. mother-in-law, 133–134
daura (fit associated with ghost possession), 65, 197, 263, 281, 297, 298, 299–300, 314
  hysterical fits, 300
Davey, T. H., 108, 110, 120
Dead Issue (M, Brahman), 91, 92–93, 102, 252
Deaf Woman (F, Jat), 168–169
death(s)
  antibiotics, attributed to use of, 53
  biomedical differences between genders, effect on longevity, 33–34
  Births and Deaths Act, Registration of, 24
  causes of. See causes of death
  disease as a cause. See disease as a cause of death
  dowry murders, 43
  by drowning, 148
  by falling, 148
  famine as a cause of death. See famine as a cause of death
  females, 34–44, 101
  feticide, female, 41–43

homicide. See homicide
  infanticide, female, 35, 37–41, 42
  life, death, and soul cycle, belief in, 62–63
  of male members, economic effects, 131
  maternal, 43–44, 101
  maternity death, 172–173
  puerperal fever as cause, 101
  questionable, 168–170
  reporting, 24–25
  suicide. See suicide
  tortured deaths, 84, 148, 165
  unnatural deaths, 82
  untimely death, 82
  Yamuna associated with, 129
Delhi Land Reforms Act (1954), 149, 160
Delhi region, historical background of, 21–23
  battle for Delhi, 23, 25
  Christianity, influence of, 22
  demography, 24
  Islamic influence, 21, 22
  location, 23
  origin of name Delhi, 21
Delicate Flower (F, Bairagi), 236, 238, 239, 250
  epileptic fits, 238–239
depression, 231–232
depressive disorders, 112
Derrett, J. D. M., 36, 93
desi (indigenous), 118
Devanagari (Hindi alphabet), 91
devata (godling), 20, 83, 84, 153, 230, 234
dev-gun (godlike), 73, 81
Devious (M, Jat), 157, 159
dewar (husband's younger brother), 113, 294
dhar (political party), 148
dharma (proper conduct, duty), 12, 18, 54, 59, 69, 71–72, 85, 88, 102, 349
Dharmashastras (books of Hindu sacred law), 49, 87, 351
Dharmasutras (early Hindu scriptures on law), 351
dharmsala (shelter for travelers), 167
Dharti Mata (Mother Earth), 65
dhat (bad habit, seminal weakness), 249
Dhobi (caste of washermen), 299
dhoti (loincloth), 91
Dhritarashtra, 21, 349
diarrhea, 119, 267
Dickens, Charles, 160
Difficult (F, Lohar), 241–245, 250
  fear of ghosts, 243–244
  ghost possessions, 242–246
  illness of, 242
diphtheria, 99, 128–129, 335, 338
discipline, 71
disease, 330–346
  Ayurvedic theory as to cause of diseases in children, 49
  descriptions, 338–346
  diphtheria. See diphtheria

discoveries, scientific and medical, 332–338
hereditary diseases, Laws of Manu and, 49, 125
historical background, 331–332
supernatural forces as cause, 82
tuberculosis. *See* tuberculosis
disease as cause of death, 28–31, 33
cholera, 28, 29, 331
diphtheria, 128
edema, 95
hyaline-membrane disease, 138
imbalance of bile, 28
influenza, 31, 104, 125, 331
leishmanial infections, 96
malaria. *See* malaria
plague epidemics. *See* plague epidemics
smallpox. *See* smallpox
spleen, disease of the, 28, 95
tetanus neonatorum. *See* tetanus neonatorum
tuberculosis. *See* tuberculosis
typhoid. *See* typhoid
Dissembler (M, Jat), 60, 74, 171–172, 173, 255
Dissociative Disorder, ghost possession classified
    as, 17, 189, 281, 295, 314
dissociative states, 304, 305, 331
Diwali (Festival of Lights), 90, 137, 192
Doctor John, Mrs. (F, Brahman), 207, 254, 260–
    262
children of, 260
festivals celebrated by family, description of,
    260
son's affliction with polio, description of, 261
Doctor John (M, Brahman), 61, 109, 202, 205,
    254, 258, 259–260, 272
dog bites, 111
Doniger O'Flaherty, W., 16, 21, 179, 278
Douglas, J. D., 172
Dowling, H. F., 276
dowry, 32, 43, 131, 148, 157
anti-dowry laws, 43, 149
Dowry Prohibition Act of 1961, 43, 149
murders, 43, 159, 175
Draupadi (character from Mahabharata), 349
Drdhabala, 47
dreams of ghost, significance of, 137
Dressler, W. W., 288
Driven Mad (M, Brahman), 214, 220–222
Driver (M, Chamar), 232–233
dropsy, 125
drunken behavior compared to ghost posses-
    sion, 79
Drupada (charater from Mahabharata), 349
Dry Stick (M, Brahman), 88
DTP (diphtheria, tetanus, pertussis), 194
Dube, L., 38, 42, 43
Dube, S. C., 82
dupatta (headcloth), 238
durbar (formal reception of Indian dignitaries
    hosted by the British Government in India),
    23, 40, 216

Dusehra (The Tenth, victorious return of Rama
    Chandra from Sri Lanka), 90, 280
Dutiful (M, chamar), 191

Earnest, Mrs. (F, Brahman), 268–270, 272
ghost possessions, 269–270
Earnest (M, Brahman), 269, 270
eclectic system of beliefs, 54, 59, 71, 72
economic trends, 12
edema, 95
education, 106–107, 125, 151, 260, 263–264
children of non-literate parents, 107
health education, 128
science education in schools, 53, 124
Ekadashi (Eleventh), 373
Eldest Son (M, Gola Potter), 247, 248
Eliade, M., 202
Eluded (M, Chuhra), 189, 300
Emergency Period (1975–1977), 12, 229
endorphins of body acting as opiates, 296, 297
epilepsy, 238–239, 263, 332
ethnography, 11
Evening Star (F, Jat), 276
evil eye, 114–115, 311–312
evil spirit, 117
exogamy, 160
exorcists, 46, 51, 52, 95, 114–115, 116, 118–119,
    125
characteristics of, 201–203
health network of. *See* health network of exor-
    cists and other curers
Illusionist (M, Chamar), 190–203
Lord of Ghosts (M, Chuhra), 182–189
Old Survivor (M, Chuhra), 180–182
shamans distinguished from, 202
sorcery practice, 185

Faithful (F, Jat), 76–79, 290
faithfulness. *See* Sati
fakir (Muslim ascetic, curer), 51, 93, 94, 184
alienated role of, 188
Family Man (M, Bairagi), 237, 240
Family Planning Programme, 51
famine as cause of death, 26–28, 28, 219, 312
Ballad of Famine (folk ballad of Punjab), 28
Great Famine of 1876–1878, 26
Punjab, 26
Tamboro volcano, eruption of; effects, 26
Farmer, Mrs. (F, Jat), 283, 306–307
Farmer (M, Jat), 116, 117, 208, 245, 274, 282–
    289
poltergeist attack, 282–283, 287
fate, karma interpreted as, 70
Fateful (M, Jat), 104, 105, 125
favored status of males. *See* males, favored sta-
    tus of
Favorite (M, Jat), 162–164, 173
Fearful (F, Bairagi), 60, 132, 235–239, 243, 249–
    250

ghost possessions, 236–240, 245–246
Felicity (F, Jat), 105, 106
female ghost, 135. *See also oopra* (female ghost)
Fence Sitter, Mrs. (F, Brahman), 96, 99–101, 129
    son's ghost illness, 100
Fence Sitter (M, Brahman), 61, 72–74, 92, 98, 99, 251
    regular worship at Merchant's shrine, description of, 90
Fertility (F, Brahman), 92, 98–99, 100, 101, 102, 251
feticide, female, 41–43
    amniocentesis-cum-abortion, 41–42
    amniocentesis tests and, 41–42
fetus
    age at time of death, relevance of, 126
    stillbirth, classification as, 127
    vesting of soul and death of, 85, 126–127
Fever, 9, 15, 16–17, 28, 46, 53, 78, 95, 99, 100, 110, 114, 145, 227, 312
    as Hara-Shiva's messenger, 16
    infant deaths and, 126, 129
    Khanna study, reference in, 128
    post-famine deaths attributed to, 27
fever
    disease identified as, 16
    puerperal fever. *See* puerperal fever
fieldwork, generally, 9–10, 18–20
    behavior, evaluating, 18
    family history, obtaining, 19–20
    pseudonyms, use of, 8, 58
    techniques used, 18–19
fight or flight hypothesis, 296–297
fire ceremonies, 55, 56, 88
first wives
    death of, 98, 125
    haunting second wives; case histories, 235–250
Folie à deux (shared paranoid disorder), 188
Folk Illness of Psychiatric Interest, 244
Fomenter (F, Brahman), 219, 220–222
Forceful (M, Jat), 104, 105, 106, 125, 249, 308
fornication, 85, 148
Forthright (F, Brahman), 84, 219, 225, 226, 235
    annulment, 226
    marriage of, 222–223
Founder (M, Chuhra), 180–181
Fraser, L., 29–30, 30
fraternal polyandry, 38, 42–43, 150–151, 153–154, 172
Freed, R., 182, 239
Freed, S., 196
Freud, S., 99, 172
Friendly, Mrs. (F, Jat), 107, 108
Friendly (M, Jat), 107–109
fright illnesses, 244, 288
fright taxon, 244
fruit of action, 70
funeral ceremonies, 67–68, 84, 85, 106, 114, 198
    for children, 144

Gabbler (M, Brahman), 254, 256, 258, 262–263, 267, 283, 291
Galen, 50, 104
ganda (paper with mantra on it), 114–115, 201, 210, 280
Gandhi, Indira, 12
Ganesh (elephant-headed deity, son of Shiva), 262
Ganga (Goddess of River Ganges), 68
Ganges, 137, 140
ganja (cannabis), 99
Gauna (ceremony at time of first mating), 37, 91, 151, 213–214, 218, 290, 305
Gaur Brahmans, 22, 87
Gautama Buddha, 57
Gayatri Mantra, 72, 352
gender differences, effect on longevity, 33–34
Gentle Soul (M, Brahman), 91, 92, 93, 97, 102
    family of, 102–103
George V, King of England, 23, 216
ghal (mischief; destruction; ruin), 123
ghar (house), 367, 372–373
ghee (clarified butter), 39, 89, 109, 120, 348
gher (cattle shed), 367, 372–373
Ghori, Muhammad, 21
ghosthood, 80, 286
    ancient traditions, 80
    becoming a ghost, 84–86
    causes for, 80, 28, 81
    diseases and calamities caused by supernatural forces and, 82
    ghost defined, 80
    malevolent ghost, 159
    pan-Indic traditions, 81–82
    past actions, attributed to, 161
    suicide and, 82
    three classes of ghosts, 81–82
    unnatural deaths and, 82
    untimely death and, 82
    village terms for ghosts, 82–84
ghost illness defined, 17
    symptoms, 46
ghost possession defined, 17, 273
    poltergeist attack distinguished, 17, 273
    symptoms, 46
Go-Between (F, Chamar), 293
Gola Potters, 58, 126, 246
Goldstein, M. C., 38
Goldwater, L. J., 143
Good, B. J., 244
good actions, 18
    soul and, 175
Good Natured (M, Chuhra), 182, 185–186, 188, 189
Goody (F, Brahman), 102, 144
Goraknath, Guru (founder of a Hindu sect and character in Guga Pir story), 179
Gordon, J. E., 29, 31
Gothi, G. D., 124
gotra (clan), 39, 85, 87, 138–139, 180, 268

Government Worker (M, Chamar), 108, 200, 201, 300–304
*graha*s (nine heavenly bodies), 49, 178, 197
Granth Sahib (Sikh holy text), 196
Grassi, G., 95
Greek humoral medicine
    phthisis viewed as hereditary disease, 104
    Unani (Islamic medical system), incorporation in, 50
grief
    as cause of death, 166
    as element in ghost possession, 165–166
Grief Stricken (F, Brahman), 144–146, 147
    bad dreams of, description of, 145–146
Guard (M, Brahman), 91, 96
Guérin, C., 123
gugal (incense), 204
Guga Naumi (festival for Guga Pir), 56, 61, 98, 178
Guga Pir, 56, 98, 178–179
    snakes, power over, 179
Gulani, K., 128
guna (qualities; strings), 47–48, 71, 80, 81
guna rajas (passion, forceful), 47, 81, 350
guna sattva (virtue, wisdom), 47, 81, 350
guna tamas (dullness, stupid), 47–48, 81
Gupta, S. P., 128
gur (brown sugar), 181, 304
gurdwara (Sikh temple), 186
guru (religious teacher, spiritual guide), 195, 202, 205, 208
Guruvar (Thursday), 196
Guz, D., 27

Hairless (F, Chamar), ghost of, 200, 267, 291–293, 300–304
hakim (Muslim physician), 51
haldi (tumeric), 197
halva (a cooked sweet), 223
Hammond, P. B., 54
Handsome (M, Bairagi), ghost of, 236, 238, 249, 250
Hanuman (monkey god), 136, 210, 262, 350, 373
Harappan Culture, 45
Hara-Shiva. *See* Shiva
Harijan (low-caste person), 56, 64, 68
Harischandra (character from Markandeya Purana), 160
Haunted (F, Chamar), 292, 293, 300–305
    Hairless, ghost possession by, 301–304
havan (fire ceremony), 200, 209
havan kund (pit for fire (ceremony) sacrifice), 200
havildar (sergeant), 215
hawa (air), 83, 123, 262
Head Clerk (M, Jat), 169
Headless Sweeper (M, Chuhra), ghost of, 116, 122, 125, 256
    death of, account by Old Codger, 176–180

as malevolent ghost, 176
    traditional attributes of ghost, exhibiting, 177
health culture, 9, 44–53
    Ayurveda, 44–45, 46–49
    homeopathy, 51, 52
    Islamic medicine and practices, 49–51
    popular pharmaceutical medicine, practice of, 52, 53, 146, 276
    Prevedic Age, of, 45–46
    Vedic Age, practices from, 44, 46–49
    Western influence, 45, 51–53
health network of exorcists and other curers, 203–211
    becoming a curer, 203
    Brahmans, 204–206
    Chamars as bhagats and users of bhagats, 207–208
    hierarchy of resort in seeking curer, 204
    Jat *vaid* (Ayurvedic physician), 206
    mullahs (Muslims) from Palam, 208
    traits of exorcists and curers, 203
    villagers as exorcists and exorcism, 208–211
Health Opinion Survey (HOS), 19, 76, 78, 122, 145, 146, 290, 377
    City Girl, 230–231
    Patriarch, Mrs., 277–278
    Pragmatic, 279
heat stroke, 110
heaven, belief in, 62
hell, belief in, 62
helminths, infection by, 95–96, 339–340
Helpful (M, Jat), 122, 123, 163, 197
hereditary diseases
    dropsy, 125
    Laws of Manu and, 49, 125
    tuberculosis viewed as, 103–104, 107–109
Hess, D. J., 288
High Strung, Mrs. (F, Brahman), 255
High Strung (M, Brahman)
    on identity of ghost possessing Withdrawn, 256
Hinduism, 54–55, 58, 62
    Arya Samaj. *See* Arya Samaj (reform sect of Hinduism)
    Sanatan Dharma. *See* Sanatan Dharma (orthodox Hinduism)
Hindu Succession Act of 1956, 24, 149
Hindu Widows' Remarriage Act (1856), 36, 252
Hindu Women's Rights to Property Act (1937), 93, 149
Hippie (M, Brahman), 145, 147, 249, 308
Hippocrates, 50, 103, 304
Hir and Ranjha (star-crossed lovers), 38
Hitchcock, J. T., 40, 79
Hoch, E. M., 83, 94, 152–153, 184, 188, 203
Hockings, P., 82
Hodgkin's disease, 227–228, 333, 340
Hoi (a festival), 303
Holi (a saturnalia), 90, 94, 114, 137, 155, 190, 192

holistic ethnography, 11
homeopathy, 51, 52
Home Trained (M, Nai), 108, 121, 135, 146, 207, 250
homicide, 148–168
  adultery as motive, 148
  brother vs. brother, 162–164
  case histories, 149–166
  Chamar vs. Chamar, 166
  family honor as motive, 148, 160, 166
  Illusion's death, 159–162
  inheritance of land as motive, 162–164
  Jats vs. Brahmans, 164–166
  justifiable, 148
  Little Bride's death, 156–159
  manslaughter, 148, 164–166
  motives, 173–174
  murders, 148–165, 166, 169, 170–172, 173–174, 175
  premarital chastity as motive, 166
  Tippler's first wife, 151–152, 154, 156
  trespass by cattle, dispute over, 164–165
  underreporting, 172, 175
Honesty (F, Brahman), 62, 114–115, 159, 182, 212–215, 217, 220, 222, 223, 225, 235
  death of, 228
  first mating, description of preparation for, 212–213
  ghost possession, 233
hookah smoking, 108
hookah worship, 192
horoscopes, use of, 70–71
HOS. See Health Opinion Survey (HOS)
Host (M, Chamar), 74–75, 76, 166
Householder, Mrs. (F, Brahman), 68–69, 70, 269, 271
Householder (M, Brahman), 160, 268
Housewife (F, Jat), 167, 170–172, 173, 200
Hughes, C. C., 244–245
hypertension, symptoms of, 242
hysterical fits, 300

ideological interviews, 58–69
  Atheist I (F, Bairagi), 60–61
  Atheist II, also called Mrs. Illusionist (F, Chamar), 61
  Atheist III, also known as Student Doctor (M, Brahman), 61
  Authority, Mrs. (F, Jat), 63
  Buddhist I (M, Chamar), 66–67
  Chamar baithak (men's sitting room), discussion in, 74–76
  Chhipi woman, 65
  Dissembler (M, Jat), 60, 74
  Doctor John (M, Brahman), 61
  Faithful (F, Jat), 76–79
  Fence Sitter (M, Brahman), 61, 72–74
  Honesty (F, Brahman), 62

Householder, Mrs. (F, Brahman), 68–69, 70
identifications, 58
Illusionist, Mrs., also called Atheist II (F, Chamar), 61
Jat children, 76–79
Jat viewpoints, 74
Jhinvar Watercarrier man, 65–66
Little Charmer (M, Jat), 76–79
Little Goddess (F, Jat), 76–79
Mahar Potter family, member of, 66
Mali Gardener family, head of, 66
Nutmeg (M, Jat), 63–64
Old Bachelor (M, Brahman), 59–60
old Chamar woman, 66
Old Priest (M, Brahman), 59
Plowman (M, Brahman), 64
Pragmatic (F, Jat), 76–79
problems encountered, 18–19
pseudonyms, use of, 8–9, 58
Raconteur (M, Brahman), 59, 60
Shy (F, Jat), 76–79
Snakebite Curer (M, Brahman), 63
Widow-in-Between (F, Jat), 67–68, 69, 72
ideology concept, 54–86
  action, rebirth, and release cycle, 63–69, 71
  Arya Samaj. See Arya Samaj (reform sect of Hinduism)
  believers in ghosts versus nonbelievers, 72–79
  discipline, 71
  Fence Sitter (M, Brahman), 61, 72–74
  fruit of action, 70
  ghosthood, 80–86
  karma (ethical sum of good and bad actions), 61, 64, 70–71
  life, death, and soul cycle, belief in, 62–63
  nonbelievers in ghosts versus believers, 72–79
  Sanatan Dharma. See Sanatan Dharma (orthodox Hinduism)
Ill Fated (M, Jat), 104–106, 107, 110, 125, 177, 273–274
  death of, 105
  ghost possession, 105, 256
Illusion (F, Brahman), death of, 159–162, 258, 277, 283
Illusionist, Mrs., also called Atheist II (F, Chamar), 61, 191, 192–194, 196, 207
Illusionist (M, Chamar), 61, 75, 76, 78, 118, 121, 183, 190–203, 250
  background, 190–194
  curing and interviewing techniques, 196–199
  as exorcist, 201–203
  hookah worship, description of, 192
  learning to be exorcist, 194–196
  patients of, 199–201
Immature (F, Chamar), 263
  ghost possessions, 291–297
  similarities to possessions of Sita, 297–300
  social environment, 294–295

inauspicious
  crippled person considered as, 135
  maimed person considered as, 135
  one-eyedness, inauspiciousness of. *See* one-eyedness, inauspiciousness of
  signs, 129, 223, 224
  sterility considered as, 175
  twins considered as. *See* twins, inauspiciousness of
  widow as, 36, 93
Inauspicious (F, Brahman), 159–160
incest, 160
Indecisive (M, Brahman), 159–160, 161, 162, 257–258
India Abroad (a newspaper), 37
Indian Express, The (a newspaper), 12
Indo-Aryan invasion, 45
Indra (God of Firmament), 77, 348
Indraprastha, 21
infant hypolactasia, 191, 299
infanticide, female, 35, 37–41, 42, 44, 114
  anti-infanticide acts, 40
  ban on sex determination tests, 43
  chorionic-villus test and, 42
  factors contributing to, 37
  Jats, practice among, 38, 150, 151
  mudar (shrub used in infanticide), 39
  Rajputs, practice among, 39
  Sikhs, practice among, 40
  suffocation, by, 40
infanticide, male, 118
infanticide, passive, 129
infantile scrofula, 101
infants
  burials of, 67–68
  death of. *See* infants, death of
  ghost of child or infant, 19–20
  infanticide, female. *See* infanticide, female
  infanticide, male, 118
  male, 44, 101
  Medical Childbirth Survey, 117
  soul of, ghost taking, 101
infants, death of, 126–134, 136–140
  age at time of death, relevance of, 126
  atelectasis as cause of, 138
  causes of, 128–129, 130–131
  Fever as cause, 129
  inauspicious sign, children born under, 129
  infanticide, passive, 129
  Khanna study, 128
  male infants, 44, 101
  mortality, 43–44, 51, 101, 127, 128, 129
  on Mother Sixth, 132
  neonatal, 127
  perinatal, 127
  postneonatal, 127, 138
  premature infant, 126
  SIDS (Sudden Infant Death Syndrome), 138

  tetanus neonatorum as cause of, 44, 101, 127–128, 194
  vesting of soul, 126–127
influenza, 31, 104, 125, 176, 178, 331, 337–338, 340–341
  miasmas as cause of epidemic, 177
  poisonous gas as cause of epidemic, 177
Ingalls, D. H. H., 71, 72, 81
inherited diseases. *See* hereditary diseases
inoculations, 128, 129, 230
  plague, against, 129
  smallpox, against, 29, 51
insecurity, ghost possession related to, 308–309
Insider (M, Gola Potter), 246–247, 249
interviews, ideological. *See* ideological interviews
involuntary versus voluntary possessions, 270
Iradat Khan, Moghul ruler, 22
ishta devata (one's own chosen deity), 373
Islamic medicine and practices, 22, 49–51
isoniazid, 108, 338
izzat (honor or prestige), 142, 171

Jabberer (M, Jat), 113
Jahar (Muslim-Hindu saint), 61
jaman, *jamun* (a tree, java plum), 217
Janamashtami (Krishna's birthday), 205
janeu (sacred thread), 88, 195
Jatav (subcaste of Chamars), 57
jati (subcaste), 149
Jats, 55, 58, 64, 74, 148
  drinking among, 153, 155
  early history of, 22–23
  female infanticide practice, 38, 150, 151
  as followers of Arya Samaj, 55, 56, 103, 125, 273
  fraternal polyandry practice, 37, 42–43
  ghost attacks and possessions of; case histories, 273–291
  Old Fever lineage. *See* Old Fever lineage
  polyandry, practice of, 150–151
jaundice. *See piliya* (jaundice)
Jeffery, P., 42
Jeffery, R., 42
Jewar, Raja (character in Guga Pir story), 178–179
Jews, 311
jhara (form of exorcism), 78, 182
jinn (Islamic spirit or ghost), 50, 81, 84, 89, 123, 286, 314
  defined, 176
jirjan (seminal weakness), 249
jiva (life, soul), 66
jivanmukti (living release), 99, 203
jnana-yoga (spiritual knowledge), 71, 203
Jolly, J., 48
Jolly (F, Bairagi), 240, 250
Jordens, J. T. F., 55
jot (wick, light as an offering), 93, 94

jowar (great millet), 266
Junior, Mrs. (F, Brahman), 253–254
Junior (M, Brahman), 251–252
    relocation of family members, 258–260
Justice (M, Brahman), 159, 160–161, 257, 259,
    271, 286

kabaddi (a game), 108
Kabandha, the Beheaded, 178
kachcha (crude, raw), 88, 91
Kachchal (character in Guga Pir story), 179
Kaj (funerary feast), 275
Kakar, S., 94, 105, 180, 286, 314
Kali Mata (Goddess of Death and Destruction),
    193
Kalkaji (Goddess of Cremation Grounds), 61, 185
kamiz (shirt), 181
Kanagat (rite to commemorate ancestors), 59
Kanti Mata (typhoid), 129, 192
Kanyadan (gift of bride, gifts to bride's father), 39
kapha (phlegm), 262
Kapur, R. L., 188, 260, 300
karha (an abortifacient), 304
karma (ethical sum of good and bad actions), 9,
    15, 46, 50, 61, 64, 70–71, 85, 91, 102, 103,
    124, 312
    murder, association with bad karma, 159, 169
karma-yoga (the way to release through selfless
    action), 71
Karna (character from Mahabharata), 60
karva (pitcher), 137
Kashi, 8, 87, 88
katha (story), 62, 71
Kauravas, 21, 349
Kerala, South India, 264
Ketu (descending node of the moon), 178
khadira (acacia tree), 81
khaj (eczema), 120
Khanna, B. S., 127, 128
kharisa (headless ghost), 82
khil (popped rice), 144
khir (rice pudding), 256
Kin (M, Chamar), 74, 191, 199
kins (a tree), 72
kinship charts, 352–366
    coding, 353–354
kismet (fate), 56
Kitasato, S., 30
Kleinman, A., 244
Kolata, G., 281
Konner, M., 18
Kota, 188
Krishna, 58, 80–81, 137, 154, 260, 349, 373
Kshatriya (second Hindu (military and governing)
    varna), 55, 56, 64
kundalini (latent energy coiled at base of spine;
    serpent energy), 99

Kunwar, Roop, 37
Kutumbiah, P., 29, 48, 49, 127

lactation without supplementary feedings, 295
ladoo (a sweet coconut ball), 263
Lady Doctor (F, caste unknown), 145, 147
Lady of Ghosts (F, Chuhra), 182, 184, 185–187,
    188–189
    hallucinations, 188–189
Lagan (prenuptial letter, also ceremony at which
    letter is presented to bridegroom's family), 88
Lakshmi (Goddess of Fortune), 57
Lal, R., 57
lambardar (village revenue official), 22, 150, 212,
    214
land mutations, 154
Landy, D., 201, 203
Lapierre, D., 26
Leasor, J., 25
legal system, 148
legislation
    All-India Act of 1870, 39, 40
    anti-dowry laws, 43, 149
    Births and Deaths Act, Registration of, 24
    Child Marriage Restraint Act, 212
    Delhi Land Reforms Act (1954), 149, 160
    Dowry Prohibition Act of 1961, 43, 149
    Hindu Succession Act of 1956, 24, 149
    Hindu Widows' Remarriage Act (1856), 36, 252
    Hindu Women's Rights to Property Act (1937),
        93, 149
    on property, 148
    Sarda Act, 212
leishmanial infections, 96
leukorrhea, 119, 146
levirate arrangements, 113, 114, 120, 148, 157,
    162, 170, 239, 252
Lewis, I. M., 270
Lewis, O., 209
Libidinous (M, Jat), 173
Lieutenant, Mrs. (F, Brahman), 91, 97
Lieutenant (M, Brahman), 91, 95, 96–97
life, death, and soul cycle, belief in, 62–63
life cycle
    ghost possession in four stages of, comparative
        review of, 305–310
    rites of passage, 56
life expectancy, average, 24
"Life in the Desert" (Punjabi poem), 11
Light of Truth, The (Saraswati), 49, 56
lineage histories, 86–126
    Merchant-Muslim-Priest lineage, 86–103, 125–
        126, 129, 251, 354–356
    Old Fever lineage, 93–94, 103–126, 356–357
lineages, 353–354
    Old Brahman Lane, breakup of, 251–273
    Old Grandfather lineage, 257–258
    Three Brothers and Old Bachelor, 251–257

lingam (phallic symbol; emblem of Shiva), 99
Little Boy (M, Jat), 114–115, 125
Little Bride (F, Jat), death of, 156–159, 173, 174, 200
Little Charmer (M, Jat), 76–79, 199–200, 289–290
Little Goddess (F, Jat), 76–79, 143, 274, 279, 283, 289–291
liturgical recitations of names of ancestors, 20
Loafer (M, Brahman), 146–147, 249, 255, 308
Loban (benzoin, incense), use of to cure ghost illness, 100, 209
Lohar, 65, 241
Lok Sabha (Parliament), 212
Long Lived (F, Jat), 104, 105, 108, 110, 125
loo (hot wind), 11, 110
loo lagna (to be affected by the *loo*), 110
Lord of Ghosts (M, Chuhra), 67, 176, 182–189, 190, 202
   evil eye, techniques for curing, 182–184
   family history, 182
   ghost possession, techniques for curing, 182–184
   jealousies in family, 184–188
   Timid, attempt to exorcise ghost possessing, 185
Love Song (F, Brahman), 102, 103
Lowie, R. H., 54
Loyal (F, Chuhra), 200–201
Luck (M, Brahman), 98, 99, 101, 125
   first wife, ghost of, 242–243
Luthra, S. K., 82

Macbeth (Shakespeare), 117
Maconachie, R., 26, 28
mada (intoxication, excitation), 49
madya (alcohol), 351
Mahabharata, 16, 21, 34, 44, 46, 49, 60, 71, 129, 257, 347, 349
Mahmud, Sultan, 25
Mahmud of Ghazni, 178
mahua (a kind of tree), 153
Maine, H. S., 20, 161
maithuna (sexual intercourse), 351
Majumdar, D. N., 82
mala (rosary), 196
malaria, 9, 11–12, 27, 28, 108, 109, 110–111, 331, 334–335, 341
   cause of, 95
   cerebral malaria, 113
   chloroquine tablets used to treat, 110–111, 113, 118
   jaundice caused by, 110
   mefloquine, use of, 111
   Plasmodium falciparum, 111, 113
   quinine treatment, 111
males, favored status of, 32–34, 37, 44
   dowry, 32
   economic reasons, 32
   patrilineal descent, custom of, 32
   ratio of females to males, 32

malevolent ghost, 159, 166, 172, 312
Malinowski, B., 89
Mama (tall ghost), 81
mamsa (meat), 351
Mandelbaum, D. G., 38
mandir (Hindu temple), 140
Mangalvar (Tuesday), 373
manic-depressive disorders, 111, 112
Manipulator, Mrs. (F, Brahman), 219, 220, 222–226, 229, 232–233, 235
   children of, 223–229
   ghost possessions, 225–226, 233
   personality and character, 220
Manipulator (M, Brahman), 41, 48, 51, 60, 70, 95, 140, 154, 155, 159, 163, 170, 171, 214, 215, 217–220, 226–228, 229, 232–235
   daughters of, 226–227
   on death of his son, 223
   and family, 217–220
   murder attempts on, 218
manslaughter. *See* homicide
Mantarwadi (curer), 188
mantra (sacred verbal formula), 72, 105, 114–115, 195, 351–352
Manu, 49, 351
maps, 367–373
Markandeya Purana, 129–130, 160, 257
Marketeer (M, Jat), 162
marriage
   average age at, 212
   early, 108
married women, ghost of, 19
masan (a kind of ghost, cremation ground), 184
Ma-Sati, Mother-Sati, 35
masturbation, 249
masurika (smallpox), 29
maternal deaths, 43–44, 101
maternity death, 172–173
Matriarch (F, Jat), 67, 173, 274–275
matsya (fish), 351
maund (measure of weight, 37.3 kg, 82.28 lbs.), 88
maya (illusion), 161
Mead, Margaret, 18
Medical Childbirth Survey, 117, 132, 133
meditation, 71
mefloquine, 111
menstruation, 119, 142, 160, 290, 295–296
   pregnancy before, 295
Merchant (M, Brahman), 72, 86, 87, 94, 103, 126
   descendants of, 91–93
   legend of Merchant and Muslim Ghost, 89–91, 99, 126
   shrine of, 90, 103, 125
   transformation into an exorcist, 95
mercury, 142–143
   syphilis, used to treat, 143
midlife crises, ghost possession related to, 308–309
midwife

government, 51, 114, 119, 127, 132, 133, 171, 194
  village, 117, 127, 132, 133
Military Man (M, Jat), 168–169
milk, 105, 109, 136
  infant hypolactasia, 191, 299
  pasteurization, 120
  tuberculosis, transmission of, 108, 120
Minturn, L., 40, 82
mirgi (fits associated with epilepsy), 238, 263
miscarriages, 126, 127, 132
Misfortune (F, Jat), 113, 114, 120, 121
moksha, mukti (release from rebirth), 71–72
Moneylender (M, Brahman), 212, 214–215, 218
Morning Star (F, Jat), 278–281, 291
mother goddesses
  belief in, 45–46
  list of, 46
  Sili Sat festival to honor, 29, 46
mother-in-law vs. daughter-in-law, 133–134
Mother Sixth (Chhathi), 100–101, 127
  death on, 132
motifs of ghost possession, 303, 313–314
  sneezing. *See* sneezing as motif of ghost possession
  sweets, eating. *See* sweets as motif of ghost possession, eating
mudar (shrub used in infanticide), 39
mudra (symbolic hand gesture), 351
mukti, moksha (release from rebirth), 71–72
mullah (Muslim prayer leader), 93, 116, 208
Mul Nakshatra (a lunar mansion), 223, 224, 234
Mulshankar (Saraswati), 55
murders. *See* homicide
Murugan (Dravidian god), 296
Muslim Ghost (M, caste unknown), 72, 86, 89–91, 94–95, 103
  legend of Muslim Ghost and Merchant, 89–91, 99, 125, 126
Mutiny in 1857, 25, 57
Mycobacterium tuberculosis, 120

Nai Barbers, 58, 65, 134, 206–207
  popular pharmaceutical medicine and, 206–207
naik (corporal), 215
names of ancestors, liturgical recitations of, 20
naming of ghost, link with ghost possession, 19, 136, 253
Narada, 351
naraka (hell), 62
Narayan, Naryana. *See* Vishnu
Narayan or Naryana (a deity, commonly identified with Vishnu), 137
nazar (evil eye), 114–115
neem (margosa tree), 179, 200
  significance of leaves, 142
Nehru, Jawaharlal, 216
Neki, J. S., 50
neurotransmitters, 305

New Brahman Lane, 268, 271–272
Newcomer, Mrs. (F, Potter), 172
Newcomer (M, Potter), 172
New Delhi, 21
New Priest (M, Brahman), 91, 94, 97, 111, 125, 204, 250
Nicotiana persica (tobacco suitable for the hookah), 183
nightmares, 116–117, 145–146
Nondescript, Mrs. (F, Brahman), 225
Nondescript (M, Brahman), 217, 221, 225
No Trouble, Mrs. (F, Brahman), 221
No Trouble (M, Brahman), 221
Nutmeg (M, Jat), 63–64, 156, 157, 169, 182, 255

occupations, principal, 14
O'Dwyer, M., 25, 40
ojha (exorcist), 182
Old Bachelor (M, Brahman), 59–60, 259, 268
Old Brahman Lane, breakup of, 251–273
  Merchant-Muslim-Priest lineage, 251
  Old Grandfather lineage, 257–258
  three brothers, joint family of, 251–254, 258–260
Old Codger (M, Jat), 113, 115–116, 117, 122, 123, 125, 208, 256, 286
  Headless Sweeper, account of death of, 176–177
Old Fever lineage, 93–94, 103–126
  Junior Branch, 104, 113–122, 125
  Senior Branch, 104–113, 125, 126
  tuberculosis, family history of, 107–109, 116, 121
Old Grandfather (M, Brahman), 160, 257
Old Groom (M, Jat), 104, 105, 125
Old Hag, attack of, 288
Old Priest (M, Brahman), 59, 86–89, 91, 102, 103, 105, 111, 125, 177, 204, 272
  death of, 93–95
  shrine for, 125
  training to professional priest, recollection of, 88-89
Old Soldier (M, Brahman), 161, 215–218, 272
  recounting changes seen in Delhi, 216
Old Survivor (M, Chuhra), 180–182, 183
  on curing and curing techniques, 181
O'Malley, L. S. S., 58
One Eyed (M, Brahman), 93, 221, 251, 252–253, 258, 259, 260, 267, 272, 286
one-eyedness, inauspiciousness of, 91, 135, 217, 252–253
Only Heir (M, Jat), 67, 274–275
oopra (female ghost), 77, 81, 82, 83, 85, 101, 123, 140
opium, 121
Opler, M. E., 50, 81
orhna (headcloth), 113, 114
Outsider, Mrs. (F, Gola Potter), 247, 250
Outsider (M, Gola Potter), 246–249, 250
Outspoken (F, Jat), 163, 164

pagalpan (madness), 48, 182
Pakistan, 219
Pakrasi, A. B., 39
Palam, 284
    mullahs (Muslims) from, 208
panchama (Harijan), 64
panchayat (village council), 148, 161
Pandavas, 21, 349
pandit (wise or learned man, Brahman), 52, 87
Pandora's Box (Greek myth), 52–53
Panini, 347
pap, papa, evil, sin, 18
Papua, New Guinea, 113
paralysis, 116
Parameshwara (supreme ruler, Vishnu), 68
Paranoia, 188–189
Parcelman (M, Chamar), 293
Paris, J., 165
Parkin, R., 127
Parmeshwara. *See* Vishnu
partition of India, 23
Passion Flower (F, Jat), 157, 159
Pathak, R. C., 123
Patri (curer), 188
patria potestas, theory of, 161
Patriarch, Mrs. (F, Jat), 116, 275–276, 279
    Health Opinion Survey and, 277–278
Patriarch (M, Jat), 274, 275–276
    disease factors in family, possible, 281–282
Pawn (M, Jat), 171
Petros, H.R.H. Prince of Greece and Denmark,
    150–151, 172
phthisis, 103–104, 123
Physician (M, Brahman), 97, 126, 204
pica, 96
pigeon excreta used as internal medicine, ground,
    121
pig excreta, smoke of burning; use in exorcism,
    209, 306
piliya (jaundice)
    malaria, caused by, 110
pinda (balls of cooked flour used as offerings), 137
Pink Flower (F, Bairagi), 237, 240
pipal (a tree, *Ficus religiosa*), 68
pir (Muslim saint), 56, 94, 184
    alienated role of, 188
pitri (semidivine ancestor), 20, 80, 81, 83, 84, 89,
    103, 125, 153, 230, 234
pitt, pitta (bile), 28
plague epidemics, 29–31, 104, 125, 331, 342. *See
    also* bubonic plague
Planalp, J. M., 47
Plasmodium falciparum, 111, 113
Plowman (M, Brahman), 64, 136, 138–139, 141,
    176, 234, 254–255, 268
pneumonia, treatments for, 276
Policeman (M, Brahman), 98. 99, 256, 268
    Little Flower's death, discussion on, 158
poliomyelitis, 261–262, 336, 343

Politician (M, Jat), 164–165, 176
Politico (M, Jat), 106–107, 122, 123, 124, 126,
    173
    murder conviction, 165
poltergeist attack defined, 17
    ghost possession distinguished, 17, 273
polyandry. *See* fraternal polyandry
polygyny, 148
popular pharmaceutical medicine, practice of, 52,
    53, 146, 276
    Nai Barbers, 206–207
population
    of India, 24, 32
    of Shanti Nagar, 13–14
possession-trance, 270, 296
Postman (M, Jat), 162
Potter and The Lady, case of, 246–249
pradhan (village headman), 107, 110, 118
Pragmatic (F, Jat), 76–79, 274, 278–281
    Health Opinion Survey and, 279
prasad (offering), 195, 262, 271, 284
pregnancy, 126–127, 128
    before menstruation, 295
    refrain from sexual intercourse during, 163
premarital chastity, 166
premature births, 117, 127
pret, preta (ghost, body of dead person), 76–77,
    80, 83, 123, 286
Prevedic Age, 45–46, 312
    animistic beliefs, 45
    mother-goddess cults of, 45
Prince, I., 96, 165
Prince, R., 296–297, 305
Prithvi Raj, 21, 22
Progenitor (M, Brahman), 91, 92, 93, 102, 125,
    251
    family of, 98–102
Prophet Muhammad, 50, 51, 94
pseudonyms, use of, 8–9, 58
Ptolemy, 21
public, ghost possession in, 208–209
puerperal fever, 101, 132, 331, 333–334, 343
Pugh, J. F., 70
puja (worship), 66, 262, 284
pukka (cooked, ripe, brick), 88
pulmonary tuberculosis, 103, 123
pulsing, 50, 313
pun, punya (good, pure, holy, auspicious), 18
Punjab, 8, 23, 26, 57
    Muslim population, 178
Puranas (ancient legends and tales), 16, 46, 50, 62,
    350
purdah (seclusion of women), 233, 270
Pure Goddess (F, Brahman), 130, 140, 167–168,
    257, 258–259, 268
Purinmashi (full moon), 106, 373, 374–376
purohit (family priest), 55, 56, 60
Putana, 137
pyschotherapist, alienated role of, 188

quinine treatment, 111

rabies, 112, 335, 343
Raconteur (M, Brahman), 59, 60, 86, 89, 91, 93, 95, 97, 103, 125, 126, 176, 204, 208
   recounting death of Old Priest, 93–94
Rahu (ascending node of the moon), 178
rajas, as a guna (passion, energy), 47, 81
rajasa (having quality of rajas), 71, 81, 350
Rajasthan, 82
rajoguna (quality of rajas, person of power), 47
rakshas-gun (demonlike), 73, 81
Rama Chandra, 58, 68, 136, 178, 235, 241, 260, 350, 373
Ramayana, 71, 136, 347, 349–350
Ram Lila (drama of Rama), 350
Ranjha and Hir (star-crossed lovers), 38
Rao, A. V., 175
rasa (taste), 48
rashi (sign of the zodiac), 49
Rasputin, 188
ration cards, 25
Ravana, 178, 350
rebirth
   action, rebirth and release cycle, 63–69, 71
   of soul, 127
Redfield, R., 148
Reformer (M, Jat), 113–114, 115, 118–120
   cattle disease, discussion on, 119–120
   contagious disease in general, discussion on, 120
release cycle, action, rebirth and, 63–69, 71
remarriage of widows, 36, 92–93, 140, 212, 228, 252–253
Resourceful (F, Jat), 67, 78, 274–275, 290
Respected Leader (M, Brahman), 144
Retired Inspector (M, Jat), 169
Rig-Veda, 46, 56, 129, 347, 348
rishis (saints who "see" the truth, divine law, authors of vedic hymns), 264, 347
Rival (M, Jat), 150, 151, 152, 153–154, 154, 173
   death of, 154
Romanucci-Ross, L., 79, 204
Ross, R., 95
roti (unleavened bread), 144, 200
Roy, Ram Mohan, 35
Rubel, A. J., 244
Rudra (Vedic god), 16, 45, 80, 348
rupee (basic Indian monetary unit), 24, 68, 190, 192, 216

sacred Hindu texts, 347–352
sacred thread ceremony, 55, 88
sadhu (Hindu mendicant ascetic), 52
Sadhya (helpful mantra), 351
Sad Memories (F, Bairagi), 131
Saini, B. S., 81
Salisbury, Richard, 310
salmonella poisoning, 282, 344

samadhi (tomb of eminent person; intense contemplation), 153
Sama-Veda, 347, 348
Samhita (part of each Veda), 29, 47, 347
   Ayurvedic Samhitas, 44, 47
   Charaka Samhita, 47
   Susruta Samhita, 29, 47
Sanatan Dharma (orthodox Hinduism), 22, 55, 56, 57, 58, 62, 71, 72, 125
   interviews with followers of, 58–60
   Universal Absolute, belief in, 58, 59, 62
Sanskrit, 57
Sanskritist (M, Brahman), 52, 205, 255
Santoshi Mata (a goddess), 61, 70, 74, 77
Santoshi Mata (film), 61
Sapolsky, R. M., 211
Saraswati, Swami Dayananda, 49, 55, 56, 57, 60, 70, 71, 125, 204
   bhuta, definition of, 123
   early life of, 55
   on heaven and hell, 62
   moksha (release from rebirths views on), 62, 72
   preta, definition of, 123
   release of soul, views on, 62
Sarda Act, 212
sarsam (delirium), 238
Sati (faithfulness, wife of Shiva, widow burning), 16, 34–37, 351
   attempts to abolish practice, 35
   Bengal, Sati practice in, 35
   Ma-Sati, Mother-Sati, 35
   Muslim emperors against practice of, 35
   Roop Kunwar case, 37
   stones, 34–35
sattoguna (quality of satva, truthful person), 47
sattva or sattvam, as a guna (goodness, purity, wisdom), 47, 81
sattvika (having quality of sattva, truthful person), 71, 350
sayyid (eminent Muslim), 94, 125
Scapegoat (F, Jat), 113, 114, 115, 125, 168, 225, 290
   ghost of, 115, 125
   suicide by, 114, 115, 156, 166
scapegoating, 311
Schemer (M, Jat), 60, 156, 158, 162–163, 164, 237, 241
scrofula, 101, 103
second wives, first wives haunting; case histories, 235–250
Secretary (M, Jat), 168–169, 170, 173
Security Guard (M, Chamar), 301–302
Security Officer (M, Brahman), 91, 95, 96, 97, 125
seer (measure of weight, 1/40th of a maund, .93 kg), 68, 193, 199
Sehgal, H., 128
Senior (M, Brahman), 251–252
   relocation of family members, 258–260
sepoy (Indian soldier), 57

seven as auspicious number, 196
Seyle, Hans, 211, 288
Shahab-ud-Din, 25
Shahjahan, emperor, 21
shaiad (ghost of Muslim), 81
Shakespeare, William, 117
Shakti (wife of Shiva, power), 351
shamans, 202–203
   distinguished from exorcists, 202
Shared Paranoid Disorder, 188–189
shasan (geographical division of a *gotra*), 139, 268
Shastras. *See* Dharmashastras
Shiva, 16, 58, 77, 80, 153, 178, 198, 201–202,
      260, 312, 350, 373
   names for, 16
   snake as emblem of, 99
   wife of. *See* Sati
Shiva Mantra, 352
shivering and tremors, relationship to possession,
      296
Short Life (M, Jat), 67, 274, 275
Shraddha (rite to commemorate ancestors), 59
Shudra (fourth Hindu varna, menial workers), 56,
      58, 64
Shy (F, Jat), 76–79
Siddha medicine, pulsing in, 50
Siddha (sure mantra, system of medicine), 351
Sidhu, K. K., 128
Sili Sat festival, 29, 46, 207
silwar (baggy trousers worn by women), 181
Simons, R. C., 244, 245, 288
Singh, K. et al, 174
Singh, Kushwant, 219
singhara (water chestnut), 260
sirkata (headless ghost), 180
Sita (F, Chamar), 8, 208, 294
   exorcism, 299
   fits (*daura*), description of her, 299–300
   ghost possessions, 297–300
Sita (Rama's wife), 350
Sitala Mata (goddess of smallpox), 29, 46
siyana (curer, wise man), 89, 91, 114, 115, 125,
      135, 136–137, 184–185, 187, 265, 271, 279,
      280, 284, 285, 293, 294
Slater, P. E., 53
Sleeman, W. H., 35–36, 39, 90
sleep disturbances, 116–117
sleep paralysis, 288
smallpox, 29, 128, 331, 344
   inoculation against, 29, 51, 333
Snakebite Curer (M, Brahman), 63, 138, 139, 141,
      205
snakes, 98–99
   Basak Nag (chief of snakes, character in Guga
      Pir story), 179
   black snake, 99, 164
   Guga Pir's power over, 179
   symbols represented by, 99
   Tatig Nag (snake, character in Guga Pir story),
      179

sneezing as motif of ghost possession, 81, 269, 270,
      309
social trends, 12
Soldier (M, Jat), 114, 120–122
   death of, 121
Soma (a deity), 34, 348
soma (ancient intoxicating beverage as offering to
      gods), 34, 348
Somatoform-Conversion Dissociative Disorders,
      17, 189, 281, 299, 312
Sorrowful (M, Lohar), 241–242, 245
soul, 126–127, 175
   See also atman (soul)
   of children, 126–127
   cycle of life, death and, 62–63
   of fetus, 85, 126–127
   of infants, 101
   lingering ghost, becoming, 312
   of murdered person, 159
   rebirth of, 127
Sparrow (F, Jat), 104, 105, 107
Spiro, M. E., 57, 70, 201, 202, 203, 205
Sprightly (M, Lohar), 242, 243, 245
Sri Lanka, 174
stages in life cycle, comparative review of ghost
      possessions by four, 305–310
Steady (M, Brahman), 142, 144
Steel, F., 22, 28, 40
sterility
   inauspiciousness, 175
   suicide, as motive for, 170, 174, 175
sterilization, 118, 126, 132, 170
   Government promulgation of, 12, 51
Stevenson, M. S., 81–82
stillbirths, 126, 127
Story Teller (M, Brahman), 130, 205, 259, 269
streptomycin, 108, 338
stress
   nightmares, relationship of, 117
   relationship to ghost possession, 10, 11–12, 271,
      288, 290, 306, 308–309, 313–314
Stress of Life, The (Seyle), 211
Strong Minded (F, Brahman), 92–93, 221, 251,
      252–253, 259, 266–267, 272
Student Doctor (M, Brahman), 258, 262–264
   alternate pseudonym as Atheist III, 264
   medical degrees, on differences between, 263–
      264
   sweets, discussion on, 263
Sudden Grief (F, Brahman), 145, 165–166
sudi (bright fortnight), 373–376
suicide, 114, 148, 149–150, 156–157, 167–172,
      174–175
   bridal suicide, 43
   chloroquine tablets, overdose of, 113
   classification of death as, 172
   first wife, by, 98
   ghosthood and, 82
   grief and, 115

isolation as motive, 175
kin-based unhappiness as motive, 174
loneliness as motive, 175
male, 174, 175
motives for, 174, 175
rate of, 174
sterility as motive, 170, 174, 175
study of, 174–175
trains, in front of, 175
underreporting, 172, 175
wells, by jumping or falling into, 156, 167–168, 170–171
Sunny (F, chamar), 200, 263, 279
supernatural beings, villagers' attitudes toward, 180
supernatural powers, strangers viewed as having, 178
superstition, 54
Susiddha (accomplished mantra), 351
Suspicious (F, Jat), 168–169
Susruta, 47, 48, 127
Susruta Samhita, 29, 47
suttee. *See* Sati (faithfulness, wife of Shiva, widow burning)
Svaha (offering, daughter of Daksha, Ritual Skill), 194
svarga (heaven), 62
swami (Hindu religious teacher), 52, 109, 112
swastika (auspicious symbol), 201
sweets as motif of ghost possession, eating, 77, 95, 100, 144, 199, 200, 209–211, 248, 255–256, 260, 265–267, 283, 285, 302–303, 305
  black pepper as remedy, 100, 286
  chili peppers as remedy, 100, 273
  salt solution mouthwash as remedy, 77, 144
syphilis, 121–122, 143, 336

tabes dorsalis (locomotor ataxia), 121
Taciturn (M, Jat), 104, 106, 107, 108, 109, 125, 164
tahsil (revenue subdivision), 23
Talkative, Mrs. (F, Brahman), 253–254, 258, 260
Talkative (M, Brahman), 252, 255–256, 258, 260
tamas, as a guna (darkness, dullness, inertia), 47–48, 81
tamasa (having quality of tamas), 71, 350
tamoguna (people predominantly devils, quality of tamas), 48
Tan, E.-S., 314
Tantras, 351
Tapei, China, 244
Taraka (F, Chamar), 8, 208
Tatig Nag (snake, character in Guga Pir story), 179
tawiz (locket), 102, 114–115, 136, 137, 195, 198, 210, 299
Taylor, C. E., 52
TB. *See* tuberculosis
Teacher (M, Brahman), 134–135, 136, 137, 138, 139–140
Temple, R. C., 178
Teoh, J.-I., 314

tetanus, 345
  cause attributed to ghost, 129
  neonatorum, 44, 101, 127–128, 194
Teva (writing the Lagan), 88
than (shrine for ancestors), 84, 89, 94, 106
The Lady (F, Gola Potter), 246, 248, 249
three wives and four husbands, case of, 209–235
Timely (F, Jat), 106, 107, 108
Times of India (a newspaper), 212
Timid (F, Chuhra), 185–187, 188, 189, 300
Timur, 25
Tippler (M, Jat), 9, 111, 112, 116, 150–156, 158, 159, 249, 308
  cinema, effect of, 152
  drinking problem, 153, 154, 155–156
  first wife of, death of, 151–152, 154, 156
  Little Flower's death, discussion on, 157–158
  second marriage, 152
  violent behavior of, 152, 154
Tod, James, 35, 38, 39
tornado, 12
"Traditional Healer and Modern Medicine" (study), 52
Train to Pakistan (Singh), 219
trance, 270, 296
  tremors associated with, 296
transportation provisions, 13
tremors, 296
Tricky (M, Brahman), 206, 223–224, 225, 227, 228, 232, 233, 234
*tridosa*s (three humors (bile, phlegm, wind)), 47, 48, 262, 313
Troubled (M, Jat), 107, 108, 109–113, 206
  electroshock treatments given to, 109, 111, 112
  fits of madness, description of his, 112
Trusted Employee (M, Brahman), 201, 268
Truthful (F, Brahman), 134, 140–141
tuberculosis, 101, 119, 123–124, 129, 335, 345–346
  BCG, use of, 123
  bone deterioration caused by, 116
  bovine, 120
  drugs prescribed for, 108
  hereditary disease, viewed as, 103–104, 107–109, 123
  infection rates, 124
  Mycobacterium tuberculosis, 120
  "Old Fever" as euphemism for, 104
  phthisis, 103–104, 123
  pulmonary, 103, 123
  raw milk, transmission through, 108, 120
  scrofula, 101, 103
  terms used for, 103–104
  transmission of, list of factors, 108
  United States, 124
Tuchman, B. W., 16
Tughlak, Mahmud, 25
Tulsi Das, 349–350
twins, inauspiciousness of, 129, 239, 250, 257
typhoid epidemics, 9, 11, 28, 219, 335, 346

Unani (Islamic medical system), 22, 49–51
   Greek humoral theory, incorporation of, 50
   pulsing, incorporation of, 50, 313
Unani Prophetic medicine, 49–50, 50–51
undifferentiated somatoform disorder, 305
Unfortunate (M, Brahman), 110, 220, 234
Union Territory of Delhi, 8, 21, 22
Universal Absolute, belief in, 58–59, 62
Unknown (M, Jat), 113
unmada (madness), 48
Upanayan (rite of bestowing sacred thread), 195
Upanishads (ancient philosophical and mystical
   texts of Hinduism), 62, 347, 349
upri hawa (ghost), 83, 262
Urbanite (M, Lohar), 242, 243, 245
Usborne, C. F., 28, 30
uterus, wandering, 50

vaid (Ayurvedic physician), 47, 52, 115, 121, 173,
   206, 275
Vaidya-natha (Lord of Physicians, name of Shiva),
   202
Vaishya (third Hindu (agricultural or commercial)
   varna), 55, 56, 64
Va¹miki, 349–350
van Buitenen, J. A. B., 21
van Gennep, A., 178
varnas (four ancient Hindu classes of castes), 56
vart kal (present time), 122
vayu (air, wind), 261
Vector (M, Jat), 164
Vedas (ancient Hindu scriptures), 16, 34, 46, 57,
   72, 347–348
Vedic Age, 44, 46–49
vel (Spear), 296
venereal diseases, 121–122, 143
Victim (M, Brahman), 145, 165, 166, 173
Victoria, Queen of England, 23
village setting, 12–14
violence, 107, 112, 116
Vishnu, 58, 62, 64, 65, 68, 101, 217, 260, 350
Vishwanath, L. S., 38, 42
voluntary versus involuntary possessions, 270
vrat (vow), 70

Wadley, S. S., 70
Walsh, C., 150
war as cause of death, 25–26
   Delhi, battle for, 25
   Mutiny in 1857, 25, 57
   World War I, 25
Warner, R., 202
Wastrel (M, Jat), 170
Watchman (M, Bairagi), 237–238, 245, 249
   twin brother of, 239
Wealthy Landowner (M, Brahman), 134, 141–142,
   144
   death of, 141
   wives of, 141–142

Wedenoja, W., 288
Welder (M, Brahman), 102, 144, 205
Well Worship (a birth ceremony), 92
Western medicine, influence of, 45, 51–53, 313
   homeopathy, 51, 52
Whose Daughter (F, Brahman), ghost of, 102, 134,
   141, 143–144, 290
Whose Son (M, Jat), 154, 156
WHO (World Health Organization), 109, 122
widow
   burning. *See* Sati
   inauspicious, 36, 93
   as levirate spouse. *See* levirate arrangements
   remarriage of, 36, 92–93, 140, 212, 228, 252–
      253
   traditional role of Brahman, 160
   Yamuna associated with widowhood, 129
Widow III (F, Jat), 274–275, 283
Widow-in-Between (F, Jat), 67–68, 69, 72, 144,
   274
wife beating, 238
Wig, N. N., 48
Wilson, T., 108, 111, 120
Wiser, C. V., 70
Wiser, W. R., 70
witchcraft accusations, 311
Withdrawn (M, Brahman), 116, 176, 177, 205,
   208, 251–252, 254
   celibacy, 272
   ghost possessions, 254–257, 265–266, 272
   interview with, 264–268
   relocation of family members, 258–260
Womanizer (M, Jat), 60
Woodsman (M, Jat), 162
World Health Organization (WHO), 109, 122
Worn Down (F, Jat), 171, 173
Worrier (F, Chamar), 291–292
Wrestler, Mrs. (F, Brahman), 141
Wrestler (M, Brahman), 141–144
   skin disease, 141, 142–143
Wyon, J. B., 29, 31

Yajnavalkya, 351
Yajur-Veda, 347, 348
yaksha (male genie), 80
yakshini (female genie), 80, 81
Yama and Yami, mythology of, 129, 239, 257
Yama (God of Death), 59, 62, 64, 71, 80, 84, 85,
   126, 312, 348
Yamuna, 129
yantra (magical symbol, drawing), 351
Yersinin, A., 30
yoga, yoke (disciplined activity), 71
Younger Son (M, Gola Potter), 248
Young Groom (M, Jat), 156–159, 174, 249
Young Lawyer, Mrs. (F, Brahman), 97, 102–103
Young Lawyer (M, Brahman), 95, 97, 102, 126
Yudhisthira (character from Mahabharata), 71

zilidar (a government official), 257